IN ATHENA'S CAMP

PREPARING FOR CONFLICT IN THE INFORMATION AGE

John Arquilla and
David Ronfeldt, e

Foreword by
Alvin and Heidi Toffler

Prepared for the
Office of the Secretary of Defense

National Defense Research Institute

RAND

To the memory of Barry Horton

We have been posing our ideas about conflict in the information age for some years now, beginning in 1991 with our original ruminations about cyberwar, then about netwar, and lately about "information strategy." With each step, we have kept returning to a favorite set of themes—organization is as crucial as technology in understanding the information revolution; this revolution is giving rise to network forms of organization; and the rise of networks will continue to accrue power to nonstate actors, more than to states, until states adapt by learning to remold their hierarchies into hybrids that incorporate network design elements. Meanwhile, we have kept our eyes on emerging trends in conflict—from the end of the Persian Gulf War, through recent developments in places like Chechnya and Chiapas— to further our understanding that the context and conduct of conflict is changing from one end of the spectrum to the other.

New modes of war, terrorism, crime, and even radical activism—are all these emerging from similar information-age dynamics? If so, what is the best preparation for responding to such modes? When the subject is warfare, for example, it is common wisdom that militaries tend to prepare for the last war, and there is much historical evidence to support this notion. Today, however, it is clear that defense establishments around the world—and especially in the United States—are thinking about how war will change, how the "revolution in military affairs" (RMA) will unfold, and how the next war may well be quite different from the last. Whether the focus is warfare, terrorism, crime, or social conflict, we have striven to anticipate what the spectrum of future wars and other types of conflicts will look like. If our approach proves correct, then perhaps this volume can help defense planners prepare for the next war instead of the last.

We hope that our own and our contributors' views are largely correct, and that our collective insights will prove useful to those, both civilians and military personnel, who are entrusted with developing and implementing national security strategy. We also hope that the studies in this volume are clear and compelling enough to attract a broad, general readership, since, without greater public understanding and support, all efforts to prepare effectively for conflict in the information age could go astray.

The preparation of this volume has been supported by RAND and by the Office of the Assistant Secretary of Defense (Command, Control, Communications, and Intelligence) and was carried out in the Acquisition and Technology Policy Center of RAND's National Defense Research Institute, a federally funded research and development center sponsored by the Office of the Secretary of Defense, the Joint Staff, and the defense agencies.

CONTENTS

ACKNOWLEDGMENTS

We owe many debts to our colleagues, sponsors, and contributors who, over the years, have helped immeasurably to advance the state of knowledge in a field that is both complex and still emerging. This volume benefits, and attempts to distill, from the many sharp—but almost always civil—debates that have unfolded among those of us who spend our time thinking about the future of conflict. RAND colleagues to whom we are especially grateful for their intellectual stimulation and comments along the way include Robert Anderson and Carl Builder. Additionally, we thank David Gompert, Gene Gritton, Richard Hundley, Greg Treverton, and Robert Nurick, who provided both encouragement and funding for this volume. RAND's Publications Department did a timely, efficient job of production.

At the Office of the Assistant Secretary of Defense (Command, Control, Communications, and Intelligence), Captain Richard O'Neill (U.S. Navy) has been our constant intellectual companion—often our mentor—and always our good friend. Finally, we acknowledge our enduring gratitude to the late Barry Horton—to whose memory this volume is dedicated—who encouraged us to explore our ideas, to whatever frontiers of thought they might lead. We hope readers will agree that we have found and explored some important new paths in strategic thought.

FOREWORD: THE NEW INTANGIBLES

*Alvin and Heidi Toffler**

The way any society engages in conflict reflects the way it does a lot of other things—especially the way its economy is organized. And just as the industrial revolution industrialized warfare, and mass production led to mass destruction, with Clausewitz as the theoretical genius of the era, so today the entire society is going beyond the industrial age—and taking the military with it. This turns out to be a revolutionary moment in the fullest meaning of that much overworked word.

A true revolution occurs when the entire structure of a society changes, not just when the palace and the local television station are captured by "coup plotters." In a real revolution, civil institutions fall into crisis. Family and role structures change. Other changes shake the culture and the value system. Technological breakthroughs (or breakdowns) create an economic upheaval. Taken together, all these produce something far more profound than "revolution" in the customarily narrow sense of the word. And this revolution in the larger sense causes a revolution in military affairs as well.

---

*Alvin and Heidi Toffler are partners in the strategic advisory firm Toffler Associates and the co-authors of *Future Shock* (New York: Random House, 1970); *The Third Wave* (New York: William Morrow and Co., 1980); *Powershift: Knowledge, Wealth, and Violence at the Edge of the 2lst Century* (New York: Bantam Books, 1990); *War and Anti-War: Survival at the Dawn of the Twenty-First Century* (New York: Little, Brown and Company, 1993); and other works translated into some 30 languages around the world. This foreword is condensed from an interview at RAND, Santa Monica, August 14, 1997.

Today's Third Wave transformation is as deep in its way as the Neolithic and industrial revolutions that, respectively, launched the great First and Second Waves of change in history. Moreover, it is faster and more global in character.

INTANGIBLE ASSETS

At its heart lies a shift in the relationship between tangible and intangible methods of production and destruction alike. Knowledge, in its broadest sense, has always been a factor in the economy. Today, however, it has moved from a peripheral to a central position, where ideas, innovation, values, imagination, symbols, and imagery, not just computer data, play more and more important roles.

The same shift toward intangibility is evident in military affairs. In the past, intangibility in military matters usually referred to morale, leadership quality, courage, and strategic insight. Today all of these remain important, but intangible assets also include what is inside our data banks as well as the skulls of our soldiers. They include the power of software, the ability to blindside an opponent's information technology, the superiority of information collection and dissemination, the compatibility of information-enhancing tools, and much more.

Just as each previous "wave" changed the nature of warfare, so, once more, a revolution is transforming the military in parallel with the economy. What is known as the Revolution in Military Affairs or RMA, therefore, is extremely important, but it is, nevertheless, just one facet of the larger civilizational shift, and it needs to be understood in that context. Seen in this light, it is likely that as the entire economy moves from the tangible to the intangible, the RMA, too, will inevitably place increasing emphasis on the value of intangible assets to the military.

None of this is to suggest that tangible, material resources and technologies are going to vanish in a puff of dematerialization. Obviously, things matter, and weapons matter more than most things. Software still needs hardware. Soldiers cannot eat data. Nonetheless, the fundamental relations between the tangible and what might be called the "new intangibles" are increasingly crucial to military effectiveness, in both waging war and trying to prevent it.

As is true in the case of the economy, the military's transition from Second Wave massy tangibility to Third Wave demassification and intangibility is incomplete. America is the source of the most stunning knowledge-enhancing technologies, and most of its workforce is engaged in one or another form of knowledge work. More Americans are employed in making computers, software, and related goods and services than in manufacturing cars. Nevertheless, the United States still has a residual sector of the economy based on low-skill muscle-work. And the U.S. military reflects a similar duality.

This is not unreasonable, given the stage of transition the United States is in, and the threats it may face in the future. But it explains why many in the military place an enormous overemphasis on large-scale, heavy weapons systems as distinct from their harder-to-define, harder-to-quantify, and harder-to-understand intangible counterparts.

The truth is that in both the economy and the military we still do not know how to organize, enhance, protect, and deploy the new intangibles for maximum benefit. Most businesses have not yet learned that to get the most out of information technology requires substantial reconceptualization and reorganization of the work to be done—that Third Wave tools applied to a Second Wave organization deliver only a fraction of their potential. The military has barely begun to recognize this as an issue.

The business community is troubled by the ambiguities of terms like "knowledge management" and "intellectual capital." The defense community is correspondingly troubled by the imprecision of even fuzzier concepts surrounding the new intangibles. We have not even arrived as yet at broadly acceptable definitions of concepts like "information warfare" or "knowledge strategy," "cyberwar" or "netwar," and "information dominance" or "information superiority."

It would be foolish, in the interests of analytic convenience, to define the role of the new intangibles too narrowly. Nor should the early lack of clarity and quantifiability lead anyone to underestimate the revolutionary importance of what we cannot fully understand and what we cannot measure. That would be like the drunk who justifies searching under a street lamp for a key lost miles away, because "here is where the light is."

In Athena's Camp is a vital antidote to such thinking. The distinguished authors in its pages may differ on much; but they largely agree that winning the conflicts of tomorrow, both large and small—or better yet, preventing, limiting, or mitigating them—will increasingly depend on how the new intangibles, including everything from satellite-based tactical intelligence to strategic perception management at the geopolitical levels, are exploited—whether we agree on definitions and precise measurements or not. As the Third Wave further transforms the economy, society, and global power relations, the importance of the new intangibles to the military will only grow.

So will the significance of intangibles that are not under the control of armed forces, or even of governments, for that matter. In the era of intangible weaponry, some of the biggest guns of all are deployed by the media.

BLURRY BOUNDARIES

The United States currently has some very big "media howitzers" that nobody else has. It has Hollywood. It has CNN. In short, the most powerfully pervasive media in the whole world. But while paranoids around the world regard these media as witting ideological agents of the U.S. government, Washington not only does not control their output, it does not even have a sophisticated grasp of how the media impact global affairs.

Arab organizations recently charged the Disney company, for example, with promoting anti-Arab violence in a movie called *GI Jane*, in which Arabs are "massacred" by the protagonists. Similarly, China has protested against a Disney film about Tibet, charging that it promotes support for separatists. Arabs and Chinese are hardly alone in supposing that because the media in their own countries are heavily influenced or controlled by government, the same must be true of the U.S. media.

Americans are no less cynical about governments, but by and large they know that Disney, like most corporations, is more driven by profit considerations than by the wishes of the White House, the CIA, or Foggy Bottom. Disney has no Assistant Secretary for Asia, no desk staffed by old Middle East hands. The films of Disney and other Hollywood studios reflect the currently fashionable views of Hollywood stars, screenwriters, and producers far more than U.S. foreign policy, which is at best so vacillating and contradictory that it is often hard to know if it exists at all.

Indeed, it may be that companies like Disney or CNN, with their powerful influence on public perceptions, indirectly influence the U.S. government's output of foreign policy more than the government influences their output of images.

Moreover, America's near-monopoly of powerful Second Wave media will not last. The "howitzers of the mass media," for example, will not long remain the property of the United States or, for that matter, the West. There are going to be Asian Rupert Murdochs and Muslim Ted Turners as the skies fill with private satellites and channels of communication continue to multiply.

Nor will the mass media dominate forever. While the Second Wave mass media are still spreading into previously unfilled markets like Eastern Europe, Russia, and parts of Asia, the new media of the Third Wave include powerful new technologies that "de-massify" audiences and permit one-to-one customized communication. They also put cheap diffusion power in the hands of anyone with access to the Internet. Marshall McLuhan once said that the photocopying machine made everyone his or her own publisher. That was true on a tiny scale. The Internet makes everyone a potential media producer on a global scale.

Thus any idea that the U.S. government or its military should attempt to rationalize or to impose broad controls on the U.S. media in the interest of a coherent information warfare doctrine is anachronistic and counterproductive. The further a country advances toward Third Wave economic and social systems, the less likely central censorship or control will work. Third Wave economies thrive on open ideas and information systems, the irrepressible Internet being the most obvious example. The attempt by the Soviets to micromanage opinion through monopoly control of the media, and their efforts to quarantine the population against news and opinion from the outside world, stifled the spirit of innovation—and hence the very technical and economic progress that they needed to survive. The Soviets, in fact, waged information warfare against their own people and shot themselves in the brain.

This having been said, however, the line between the military and civilian sectors in the United States is blurring, raising prickly new questions about who exactly is responsible for what.

The strength of the United States depends as much on its civilian communications and information infrastructure as it does on its purely military capability. Without this infrastructure, its economy would stutter to a halt very quickly. But the civilian economy's near-total dependence on computers, telecom systems, and electronics creates strange new vulnerabilities as well. If an adversary state were to launch a missile attack on, say, Los Angeles—a possibility one brash Chinese official alluded to during the 1996 crisis in the Taiwan Straits—it would without question be regarded as an act of war requiring a military response.

But what if some adversary—state or nonstate—employed intangible means to damage or destroy that city's computer networks, including those needed by its police, airport authorities, electrical systems, banks, and the like? Even assuming the source of the attack could be identified and verified, would the situation call for a military response? Whose responsibility would it be to retaliate and how? And what if, at the same time, riots were provoked in the city by televised scenes broadcast from pirate transmitters in Mexico or Mexican airspace, showing false but convincingly gruesome police or military brutality against Latinos in L.A.? If someone were engaging in information warfare against the United States from both inside and outside the United States, would retaliation be the responsibility of the FBI—many of whose computers and systems are outworn relics—or would some of the responsibility fall to the military?

The biggest boundary blur of all is that between "foreign" and "domestic," so that a new term has been invented: "intermestic." As the informationalization of the economy proceeds at an ever-accelerating pace, military thinkers, strategists, and planners will need to broaden their focus beyond what have been conventionally regarded as "military matters." That means worrying more than some U.S. military leaders do at present about the civilian economy's new intangible vulnerabilities and especially its links to the fast-changing global economy.

DEEP COALITION

The distribution of power and the alignment of states and nonstate actors is already changing dramatically as a result not simply of the end of the Cold War, but of the impact of the Third Wave. Today's changes foreshadow conflicts involving complex coalitions. To reflect this new reality, we recently introduced the concept of what we call "deep coalition."

Deep coalition stands in contrast to the Gulf War alliance, which was the last Second Wave (i.e., industrial age) nation-state coalition. The emergent global system is populated by nonstate actors of increasing importance, both in numbers and diversity. In testimony before the U.S. Senate Foreign Relations Committee in 1975, we pointed out that there were then already over 3,000 international nongovernmental organizations or NGOs in every field, from ceramics and metallurgy to religion and sports. Today there are over 25,000.

Nonstate actors are not only increasingly important, but may sometimes even take over or mutate into states. A de facto deep coalition—instead of being limited to nation-states as in the Gulf War alliance—might consist, for example, of three nation-states, fourteen civil society organizations, a *narcotraficante* here or there, a couple of private corporations with their own self-interests at stake, an individual speculator, and who knows what other components. The deep coalition involves players at many levels of the system. It is multidimensional, with all of these groups operating all the time, in continuous flow—multiplying, fissioning, then fusing into others, and so on. It is part of a nonequilibrial order in which there may be instability at one level and temporary stability at another. Unlike the nation-state system that emerged in the wake of the Treaty of Westphalia of 1648, the new system is based less on "balance of power" relations among major nations than on the ability to configure the right combination of players at every level. More important than the balance of power is the "power of balance"—the ability of a major state to keep its senses in the midst of this turbulence, and to match its economic and military capabilities with high-level knowledge resources.

The world, thus, is entering into a global order—or disorder, as the case may be—that is post-Westphalian, and post-Clausewitzian. It is something new. In a dialectical sense, it bears some resemblance to the pre-Westphalian order of diverse kinds of polities, but it involves a much higher order of complexity among actors, and, above all, it changes at hyper-speed.

That is why the traditional, nation-state concept of coalition warfare must be rethought—something the Pentagon, the National Security Council, and the White House all seem unable to do so far.

Driven by the shift in the role of knowledge in the new wealth creation system, these changes, however, are only part of a larger historical reconfiguration of the global power system that can be understood only within a theoretical framework.

A THEORY OF CONFLICT

Any theory of social or political change unaccompanied by a corresponding theory of conflict is not worth the paper or digital storage expended on it. In *War and Anti-War*, we outlined a "wave theory of conflict," which, we believe, can help us better understand many of today's conflicts, and to anticipate others that may lie ahead. Much of what appears in the pages of *In Athena's Camp* is, we believe, compatible with that theory.

No significant socioeconomic change takes place without conflict, especially large-scale, high-speed economic change. For the most part, the conflict takes cultural, religious, social, or political forms, but under some circumstances the result is violence.

When a new system for wealth creation arrives, its spread is obstructed by the traditions, codes, laws, tax regulations, administrative roles, family structures, and moral attitudes of the preexistent system. The elites of the old system—facing a loss of authority, prestige, and economic and political power—typically cling to the old system as long as possible. At some point, as the new system develops and spreads, new elites associated with it demand and fight for change.

That fight may take the form of demands for free trade or protection, for changes in taxation, labor law, or immigration policy. It may take cultural forms in literary, musical, and artistic disputes between modernists and traditionalists. It may take political forms with struggles over nationalism and centralization versus localism and decentralism. It may even wear the garb of religious or ethnic conflict.

What makes wave conflict so far-reaching and often so passionate is that a new system for creating wealth touches on all these. It is not just a matter of who gets rich and who does not, although that is surely a key part of it. Wave conflict is a struggle over an entire way of life—a civilization.

For example, when the industrialization process or Second Wave reached a certain point in Britain, the country saw a prolonged political battle between First Wave agrarian elites and the rising Second Wave urban-industrial elites. In Britain this conflict was contained within the framework of politics and culture. By contrast, in the United States, First Wave/Second Wave conflict exploded into the Civil War, with a rising urban-industrial North fighting a South ruled by elites devoted to the preservation of an agrarian, slave-based way of life. The victory of the North committed America for the first time to full-speed industrialization. In Japan the Meiji Revolution also posed industrializers and modernizers (whose troops carried rifles) against feudal elites (many of whose troops still wore Samurai swords).

On a larger, global scale, the colonial wars of the 19th and early 20th century pitted machine guns against lances as Second Wave industrial powers in Europe, North America, and Japan fought and conquered First Wave agrarian countries in Africa, Asia, and elsewhere.

In fact, this collision of civilizations is much larger and more encompassing than the so-called "clash of civilizations" set forth by Samuel Huntington, whose view, in our judgment, posits more or less static and unchanging civilizations (mainly synonymous with religions) and radically underestimates the impact of economics and the technological revolution. We, too, believe we face a "clash of civilizations" but that Huntington's civilizations are actually religions or cultures and, as such, form only a subset of what we call a civilization. Thus, like the agrarian civilization before it, industrial or Second Wave civilization had not only a Christian or Judeo-Christian variant, but Confucian, Hindu, Muslim, and other variants as well.

The conflict of civilizations defined in this much larger and more inclusive sense is a "super-struggle" or "master conflict" that triggers many tributary disputes that appear to be based on religion, ethnicity, or "thousand-year-old hatreds," but often derive from the larger economic and civilizational collision.

Thus the former mayor of Belgrade explained the battle over Sarajevo as a war of "the mountain people against the city people." In Afghanistan one saw the Taliban forces attempting to impose a constricted village-based morality on the urban population of Kabul. We believe that a close look at many other contemporary conflicts would reveal an underlying split between rural and urban—First Wave and Second Wave—people and interests.

The potentials for conflict are even more complicated in some parts of the world because the theory of conflict includes the concept of concurrence—the fact that a society may be undergoing more than one wave of change at a time.

Brazilians are killing Amazonian Indians to seize land for further agriculturalization as the First Wave completes itself on the planet. Elsewhere in Brazil, massive Second Wave industrialization proceeds—with its assembly lines, smokestacks, traffic jams, and pollution. In recent years, the Third Wave of informationalization has surged across parts of Brazil, producing its own set of economic needs and opportunities, a computer culture among the middle-class young, and other challenges to the values and political power of the country's First and Second Wave interests.

In China, close to a billion peasants still live under First Wave conditions, while Second Wave industrialization proliferates low-tech, low-wage factories and swells the urban-industrial population. Concurrently, a small but growing group of Third Wave entrepreneurs, software designers, programmers, network integrators, cell phone system operators, and their employees form a new culture that has more in common with Singapore, Taiwan, Bangalore, Vancouver, and Silicon Valley than with other Chinese. Their Third Wave interests are not the same as those of agrarian

China or, for that matter, of traditional, industrial, urban China either.

TRISECTION

Concurrent internal waves of change, each bearing its own potential for conflict, are mirrored on a macro scale at the global level. Thus, at the global level we are moving away from a bisected model of power toward a trisected one. Whereas power was once split between agrarian states on the bottom and industrial states on top, the Third Wave knowledge-based system of wealth creation, as it wedges its way into the world, brings a new third tier of power to the globe.

In the emergent "trisected" power structure, those states whose Third Wave sector is most developed command the heights, industrial smokestack states are camped in the middle, and agrarian states remain on the bottom. So clear is this trisection by now that we find everyone scrambling competitively to move up to "higher value added" economic production based on information-intensive technologies. This includes agrarian states seeking, as they put it, "to skip a stage."

One of the most fundamental of "grand strategy" questions, therefore, is how these three classes or groups of societies should relate to one another.

A question frequently asked us as we travel through what is still patronizingly termed the "developing world" is whether this trisection brings with it a permanent "neo-neo-colonialism"—in which the states furthest along in the Third Wave transition will necessarily dominate the rest of the world.

We regard that as an unlikely, or at most, a transient condition. During the 19th century, the European imperial powers were able to exploit their dominance for long periods. The British imported cotton from India and Egypt (at prices negotiated with soldiers or gunboats nearby); manufactured clothing in Birmingham, Manchester, and Leeds; and sold it back to the colonists (at prices set with the same soldiers or gunboats in view). The raw materials came from the colonies, but the factories stayed in Britain.

The difference now is that in Third Wave economies, factories often count for less than the knowledge needed to run them. And while it is easy to keep a factory in, say, Leeds, it is much harder to keep knowledge there.

Knowledge, despite intellectual property treaties, has a way of seeping out, or, worse yet, becoming obsolete. That, moreover, includes not merely economic knowledge, but military knowledge as well. How the overarching question about neo-neo-colonialism in a trisected world is answered will have much to do with whether the world disorder will remain within "tolerable" bounds.

This, then, is the larger historical and geopolitical context in which this volume appears. David Ronfeldt and John Arquilla not only make profound contributions to current worldwide debates about information war, war in the information age, Third Wave war, or netwar and cyberwar (their own preferred terms). They bring together some of the most acute and brilliant analysts of future conflict. *In Athena's Camp* makes possible a significant leap forward in our understanding of the strange and sometimes dangerous new world we inhabit.

Chapter One

A NEW EPOCH—AND SPECTRUM—OF CONFLICT
John Arquilla and David Ronfeldt

Look around. No "good old-fashioned war" is in sight. There are a few possibilities—for example, on the Korean peninsula; or between China and Taiwan; or India and Pakistan; and, as usual, in the Middle East—but these do not seem imminent. Moreover, the most recent war, the Gulf War of 1990–1991, reflected the advent of the "revolution in military affairs" among U.S. forces and thus was more new- than old-fashioned—perhaps enough to discourage would-be conventional warmakers elsewhere from supposing they could win anytime soon against the newest generation of U.S. military forces. If another conventional war involving the United States occurs, it is likely to be radically different—as different from the Gulf War as it was from what had gone before, and largely for the same reason: the deepening impact of the information revolution on military affairs. And once a new war occurs, it may then be observed that the 1990s were not simply the post–Cold War period but also a new interwar period, one filled with radical change in which the contours of future conflicts were being shaped.

In this regard, the 1990s resemble the 1920s—the period after World War I. It was assumed by most political and military leaders then that major war was no longer likely. However, others worried about the possible return of major war. The worriers proved right. They were indeed living in an interwar period. It was also a time of major technological changes—with improvements in tanks, planes, and electronic warfare—leading to new doctrines that would optimize their use (e.g., *blitzkrieg*). Those who recognized that this was an interwar period thought through the conceptual problems of the day

1

and achieved striking successes in the opening phases of World War II—most notably, the Germans, who, in their victory in the Battle of France in 1940, achieved success in four weeks on the same ground where victory had eluded them for four years during the previous war. That is why analysts today would be well advised to be worried anew about the possibility that the present time indeed does not spell the end of major war.

When a new-fashioned war breaks out, what will it look like? On land, there may be no fronts, because fighting may occur almost anywhere anytime in a theater. The modal size of operational units of maneuver will become quite small—perhaps below the size of the typical 700-man battalion. At sea, the need for aircraft-carrier battle groups is sure to end. They will be replaced by smaller, faster, and equally capable fighting formations. The same is likely to hold for aerial warfare, which is already moving away from traditional formations, long carefully specialized in air wings of bombers and fighters. Today, the blending of the various types of aircraft in composite wings is occurring; and through stealth technology and improvements in the "information packages" of air-launched missiles, the air forces of the future will be able to do much more—with less.

Information, in all its dimensions, will enhance both the destructive and the disruptive capabilities of small units for all the services; in an information-age "battlespace," massed forces will simply form juicy targets for small, smart attackers. In the new epoch, decisive duels for the control of information flows will take the place of drawn-out battles of attrition or annihilation; the requirement to destroy will recede as the ability to disrupt is enhanced.

Despite the absence today (summer 1997) of a sizable conventional war, it takes only about one every decade or so to keep the notion high in people's minds that this is what war is really all about—the kind of war that matters most. However, for most of the world, the daily reality remains otherwise. Irregular conflicts abound; they pepper the conflict spectrum. Bands of Chechen ethnonationalists, organized more like clans than corps, have repelled the clanking, Cold War–era Russian army in bitter, murderous fighting. Hamas terrorists, disdainful of Palestine Liberation Organization (PLO) leaders, continue to hit Israeli targets. In Mexico, the Zapatista National Liberation Army (EZLN), with minimal fighting but strong protective support from human-rights and other nongovernmental organizations (NGOs), has used novel "information operations" to put the government on the defensive, both politically and militarily. On the frontiers of violent crime, drug traffickers from Colombia and elsewhere have built huge transnational enterprises protected by paramilitary forces. Far away, high-seas pirates threaten oil-tankers and other lucrative targets, even as they expand and diversify their trade as smugglers in waters off China.

Everywhere, speculations about the kinds of conflicts that may prevail in the future emphasize these and other kinds of messy irregular conflicts that revolve around the rise of highly networked nonstate combatants and criminals, whose principal targets may, in many cases, be states. As terrorist organizations move away from traditional "great man" leadership structures (as exemplified by the PLO's Yasser Arafat) and develop diffuse, dispersed, network structures (as in the cases of Hamas and Hezbollah), they will be better able to deny culpability and may become increasingly disposed to more violent behavior. Criminal networks may become the covert arms of states aiming to pursue "strategic crime" and "criminal mercantilism," all the while denying their involvement, as some believe is likely in the case of China's involvement with the East Asian sea pirate networks.

In short, and for myriad reasons, the world is entering—indeed, it has already entered—a new epoch of conflict (and crime). This epoch will be defined not so much by whether there is more or less conflict than before, but by new dynamics and attributes of conflict. Qualitative changes will be as strong, if not stronger, than quantitative changes. The outlines of these changes have already emerged, as can be seen in the cases previously noted. These changes will involve high-tech sensors and weapons that can enable both distant stand-off and close-in swarming attacks. The protagonists, and their attacks, will be more widely dispersed and more decentralized than ever before—and more surreptitious. Offense and defense will be blended. The temporal and spatial dimensions of conflict will at times be compressed, and at other times elongated. Disruption may often be the intended strategic aim rather than destruction. Nonstate actors, many of them transnational, will play roles as crucial as nation-state actors. Odd alliances may occur, notably between political and criminal and between state and nonstate actors. Often it will not be clear who is aiding whom or fronting for whom. Traditional hierarchical actors will lose many battles as well as entire wars to newly networked actors. Notwithstanding the roles of high-tech weapons, sensors, and information and communications systems in this new epoch, less advanced technology will continue to play a role. Curious combinations of premodern and postmodern elements will appear in antagonists' ideologies, objectives, doctrines, and organizational designs.

These are just a few of the trends that are anticipated. What underlies many of them—the crucial causal and contextual dynamic—is the information revolution. How theorists and practitioners comprehend that dynamic and its effects on military affairs will guide how they seek to prepare for what may lie ahead.

RETHINKING THE DYNAMICS OF CONFLICT: CYBERWAR AND NETWAR

This book of essays about conflict in the information age shows how the information revolution is altering the nature of conflict, and why it is bringing new modes of warfare, terrorism, and crime to the fore, requiring analysts, advisers, policymakers, and folks on the front lines to rethink organization, doctrine, and strategy. While the book is admittedly a vehicle for disseminating our own writings to a broad public audience—in particular our ideas about "cyberwar" and "netwar"—the book also provides a balanced selection of some of the most insightful, instructive writings we encountered as we pondered our own notions. Indeed, many of the pieces included here were on a list of key readings about information-age conflict that circulated at high levels of the Pentagon during the end of 1996 and the beginning of 1997.

Several thematic threads run through the essays, which have been selected in part because they speak to these themes. We believe that a consensus is emerging around them (but we also know that they are not yet widely accepted and still arouse resistance in some quarters, a point to which we return in the concluding chapter).

The most basic theme is that conflicts will increasingly depend on, and revolve around, information and communications—"cyber" matters—broadly defined to include the related technological, organizational, and ideational structures of a society. Indeed, information-age modes of conflict (and crime) will be largely about "knowledge"—about who knows what, when, where, and why, and about how secure a society, military, or other actor feels about its knowledge of itself and its adversaries.

A second theme is that the information revolution is not solely or mainly about technology; it is an organizational as well as a technological revolution. Thus, the emphasis in this volume is less on the advance of technology than on the challenges for organization—and on the interactions between technological and organizational changes that have implications for doctrine and strategy.

A third theme, which is closely related to the second, is that the information revolution favors and strengthens network forms of organization, while making life difficult for hierarchical forms. The rise of network forms of organization—particularly "all-channel networks," in which every node can communicate with every other node—is one of the single most important effects of the information revolution for all realms: political, economic, social, and military. It means that power is migrating to small, nonstate actors who can organize into sprawling networks more readily than can traditionally hierarchical nation-state actors. It means that conflicts will increasingly be waged by "networks," rather than by "hierarchies." It means that whoever masters the network form stands to gain major advantages in the new epoch. Some actors, such as various terrorists and criminals, may have little difficulty forming highly networked, largely nonhierarchical organizations; but for other actors, such as professional militaries that must continue to uphold hierarchies at their core, the challenge will be to discover how to combine hierarchical and networked designs to increase their agility and flexibility for field operations.

A fourth cross-cutting theme—reflective of the preceding three—is that the conflict spectrum is being remolded from end to end. Major alterations are looming in the nature of adversaries, in the threats they may pose, and thus in the defenses and other responses required to counter them. Information-age threats are likely to be more diffuse, dispersed, nonlinear, and multidimensional than were industrial-age threats. This will place U.S. military (and police) forces under growing pressures to formulate new concepts for organization, doctrine, strategy, and tactics.

The fifth theme—one we impose on the volume, and that may not be fully shared by all of our colleagues here—is that two new modes of conflict in particular are going to define the information-age conflict spectrum: what we term "cyberwar" and "netwar." Both terms refer to *comprehensive* approaches to conflict based on the centrality of information—comprehensive in that they combine organizational, doctrinal, strategic, tactical, and technological innovations, for both offense and defense. Each term refers to a different end of the conflict spectrum.

Cyberwar—a comprehensive information-oriented approach to battle that may be to the information age what *blitzkrieg* was to the industrial age—will, in our view, be an ever-more-important entry at the military end of the spectrum, where the language is normally about high-intensity conflicts (HICs) and major regional conflicts (MRCs).[1] [See the end of each chapter for notes.] *Netwar*—a comprehensive information-oriented approach to social conflict—will figure increasingly at the societal end of the spectrum, where the language is normally about low-intensity conflict (LIC), operations-other-than-war (OOTW), and other, mostly nonmilitary, modes of conflict and crime. Whereas cyberwar will usually feature formal military forces pitted against each other, netwar will often involve nonstate, paramilitary, and irregular forces. Cyberwars and netwars may even be mounted at the same time, in mixes that pose uncomfortable societal dilemmas. Both concepts are consistent with the views of analysts like Van Creveld (1991) who believe that a transformation of war is under way that will lead to its increasing "irregularization." In this sense, the coming epoch of conflict will be more about Van Creveld than Von Clausewitz.[2]

At present, the U.S. military is the world's leader in thinking, planning, and preparing for the advent of cyberwar, both offensively and defensively. The United States is the only country with the array of advanced technologies (e.g., for command and control, surveillance, stealth, etc.) as well as the organizational and doctrinal flexibility to make cyberwar an attractive and feasible option. But its potential adversaries, especially nonstate adversaries, may have the lead in regard to netwar. Here, the U.S. emphasis may have to be on defensive measures. This would continue a long trend in which the United States has prepared for waging major wars, while its adversaries may instead wage guerrilla war, terrorism, and other irregular modes of conflict. This may be partly the result of displacement—some adversaries, seeing that they should avoid or could not win at regular warfare, have opted for irregular modes, which the U.S. military may then try to treat as "lesser-included cases." Such displacement may occur again with netwar and other new, LIC-like modes of conflict and crime. But, we hope, netwar will not be perceived as a lesser-included case of information-age conflict—for it is not.

Instead of using terms like cyberwar or netwar, many analysts have treated such points under the rubric of the "revolution in military affairs" (RMA). Yet, the meat of this concept is the information revolution and its effects and implications. Early exponents viewed technological innovation as the key dynamic of the RMA. But other, recent exponents now accept that the RMA is equally, if not mainly, about organizational and doctrinal innovation—a view we have preferred since beginning our own efforts to conceptualize cyberwar and netwar. Even so, discussions about the RMA tend to focus on HICs and MRCs that revolve around regular, albeit much-modified, military forces. Exponents of the RMA have generally had less to say about the LIC (or netwar) end of the spectrum.

All these themes lead to a sixth theme that surfaces only occasionally in this book: Conflict in the information age will *not* consist primarily of "infowar" or "strategic information warfare" (SIW) or "Internetwar." In these types of conflicts, the threat is thought to reduce, one way or another, to attacks on, or by way of, computerized infrastructures for information, communications, and other crucial services. That kind of threat must be taken seriously. However, from the broad perspective of preparing comprehensively for conflict in the information age, two caveats are needed. First, while the information technology revolution is facilitating the rise of technological modes of conflict, the newest technologies may not be the only crucial factors for a cyberwar or netwar actor. Older means of communication, like human couriers and ham radios, and other mixes of old and new systems may, in some situations, do the job for the protagonist. Second, modes of conflict like cyberwar and netwar can be facilitated by, but do not necessarily depend on, "the Net" (i.e., the Internet); nor do they occur only in "cyberspace" or the "infosphere."

Some key *battles* may take place there, but a *war's* overall conduct and outcome may depend mostly on what happens in the "real world"—it will continue to be, even in the information age, generally more important than what happens in cyberspace or the infosphere. In our view, information-age modes of conflict may, or may not, involve SIW—and they may involve a lot more than SIW, especially when the protagonists are more interested in keeping the Net up than taking it down, so they can use it to mobilize their forces, disseminate their views, and try to affect the beliefs and opinions of other people.

Not everybody represented in this volume agrees entirely with our concepts of cyberwar and netwar. Some authors are not comfortable with any of the *nouveau* terms, while others would prefer different terms or phrases, like the "revolution in military affairs," or the "new way of war." Or they might define cyberwar or netwar differently from the way we do—after all, these concepts are in flux, serving the purpose of helping focus attention on the new dynamics of conflict, but are still far from being settled as to their precise definition and implications. Nonetheless, the first four themes resonate in most of the selections and help bring the authors together in what we call "Athena's camp."

NEW METAPHORS: ATHENA AND *GO*

Epochal shifts call for new metaphors. Metaphors and analogies help convey new concepts by providing simplified images that encapsulate complex points. We recommend the two following metaphors or analogies for better understanding the phenomenon of conflict in the information age.

The first is a mythological metaphor that speaks to the title of this book. Information has been associated with power, war, and the state since at least the time of the Greek gods. One ordinarily thinks of Ares, or the Roman refinement Mars, as the classical god of war. But Ares was a rather narrow, undisciplined, middle-ranking god who did not think much about what he was doing—he just stood there and fought, often rather impulsively. This is not an appropriate analogy for an epoch in which, increasingly, knowledge is fused to power. Athena, the warrior goddess of wisdom who sprung fully armed from Zeus's head and became the benevolent, ethical, patriotic protectress and occasionally wrathful huntress who exemplified reverence for the state, is the Greek god of war best attuned to the information age. Where warfare is about information, she is the superior deity.[3]

Athena is the only member of the Pantheon typically depicted with both sword and shield, symbols of her capabilities for both offense and defense. She could be wrathful, but unlike Ares, she took no pleasure in war and preferred to see conflicts settled peacefully, according to laws and with a sense of mercy. She was careful about bearing arms in times of peace, but when needed, she had ready access to Zeus's aegis (a unique, impenetrable body shielding) and to his devastating thunderbolt. While the owl and the olive tree were her chief symbols, she also attached to her hand-held shield the frightening head of the Gorgon Medusa, whose live gaze could turn a viewer to stone. Athena had previously instructed man in the art of confronting such terrors as the Gorgon, showing Perseus how to decapitate Medusa by using his shield as a mirror so that he could approach and combat her without making direct eye contact. Finally, one of Athena's best skills was weaving—a metaphor for network-building?

She stood for expanding the boundaries of civilization and defending them against ignorant barbarians, and, within a civilization, for pursuing intellectual enlightenment as much as material gain. One myth is particularly evocative for accepting her metaphorical relevance to the information age. According to Virgil, Troy would be powerful enough to withstand all its enemies so long as it possessed and honored the Palladium, a sacred statue of Athena provided by Zeus or Athena herself to city-states that worshipped her. Knowing this, the Greeks arranged to steal the Trojans' Palladium, spiritually denying them their access to the goddess of wisdom and war. As a result, she sided with the Greeks in the Trojan War, where she bested Ares in battle and conceived the idea, communicated to Odysseus, of the wooden "gift horse" secretly loaded with Greek soldiers. The Trojans made the epic misjudgment of hauling it inside their fortress, over the protestations of the priest Laocöon and the seer Cassandra. The rest is history, and legend.

Ever since, examining the relationship between information and power has attracted all manner of political and military theorists. In our view, to be in "Athena's camp" is to understand that conflict—not to mention the "revolution in military affairs"—is about far more than technology; it is also about utilizing the highest levels of information—knowledge and wisdom—and about the importance of willpower and idealism in all worthy endeavors. Indeed, viewing Athena, not Mars, as the emblematic god (or goddess) of war in the information age is consistent with Clausewitz's dictum that knowledge must become capability.

More to the point, Athena corresponds, by way of her association with her namesake city-state, Athens, to the defense of democracy. To be in her camp is to uphold democracy, by viewing information (or knowledge and wisdom) as a vital dimension of a democratic society that must be protected lest it be fouled and used to weaken that society—a point to which we will return in a later discussion of "guarded openness" as a U.S. information strategy.

The second metaphor is about strategic games. In America and Europe, chess is often viewed as a metaphor for war. But, for the information age, the Oriental game of *Go* more accurately reflects the nature of conflict than does chess—Western proclivity for the game aside.

In chess, each side has a king and five other types of specialized pieces. Each piece, including the king, has a different "value" and a different ability to move. Each side lines up its pieces in assigned positions on opposite sides of the game board. Thus the two sides start by facing off along fronts separated by a "no man's land." Then, each side maneuvers in ways that are generally designed to fight for control of the board's center, to shield valuable pieces from capture, to use combinations of pieces to threaten and capture the opponent's pieces, and ultimately to achieve checkmate (decapitation) of the one-and-only king. Conventional warfare before World War II was often like this, and it has generally retained this linear flavor up through the Persian Gulf War.

The game of *Go* provides a better analogy for conflict in the information age, especially for irregular warfare and for networked types of conflict and crime at the low-intensity end of the spectrum. Whereas chess starts with all pieces on the board, *Go* begins with an empty board. It resembles a vast, grid-like chessboard with lots of tiny squares. Each side takes turns placing pieces called "stones" anywhere on the board, one by one. But the stones are placed not in the squares as in chess, but on the points where the grid lines intersect. All stones are alike—there is no king to decapitate, and no queen or other specialization.

Once placed, a piece cannot move; it can only be removed, if surrounded and captured according to the rules. But in this game, taking pieces has secondary importance. The goal is to control more of the battlespace than one's opponent does. Once emplaced, a piece exerts a presence in that part of the board, making it easier for the player to place additional pieces on nearby points in the process of surrounding territory. As a result, there is almost never a front line, and action may take place almost anywhere on the board at any time. The key battles are less for control of the center than of the corners and sides (since they are easier to box off). And whereas in chess no piece is ever totally secure, in *Go* a piece of territory can be made totally secure if it is surrounded in a particular way (in *Go* parlance, when the occupying pieces have two "eyes").

Thus *Go*, in contrast to chess, is more about distributing one's pieces than about massing them. It is more about proactive insertion and presence than about maneuver. It is more about deciding where to stand than whether to advance or retreat. It is more about developing web-like links among nearby stationary pieces than about moving specialized pieces in combined operations. It is more about creating networks of pieces than about protecting hierarchies of pieces. It is more about fighting to create secure territories than about fighting to the death of one's pieces. Further, there is often a blurring of offense and defense—a single move may both attack and defend simultaneously. Finally, the use of massed concentrations is to be avoided, especially in the early phases of a game, as they may represent a misuse of time and later be susceptible to implosive attacks. This is quite different from chess, which is generally linear, and in which offense and defense are usually easily distinguished, and massing is a virtue. Future conflicts will likely resemble the game of *Go* more than the game of chess.

INTRODUCTION TO THE SELECTIONS

Most of the authors represented here work on U.S. government and military contracts; they have careers that depend on their ability to conduct policy-oriented research and analysis. Working in that world often involves a challenging tension. On the one hand, researchers are asked to help a particular office resolve a particular issue at a particular time—that is, to write for someone's "in-box." On the other hand, they also strive to produce studies that will engage a broad audience and have some enduring value—that is, to write with a long "shelf-life" in mind. The pieces we have selected by our contributors have each achieved such a shelf-life. They should be read by all who seek to understand the emerging nature of conflict in the information age. And they are being read by theorists and practitioners who aim to fill the next bookshelf full of studies, which will no doubt focus on preparing for conflict in the information age.

We have distributed our chapters into four parts. The first addresses the nature of the revolution in military affairs which, as our contributors note, is mostly an information-driven revolution, though one driven by more than just advanced technology. The second part builds on this theme, examining in some detail the phenomenon of "information warfare" as it may be waged in cyberspace and beyond. The third set of readings considers the societal-level implications of the information revolution, giving special attention to the rise of networked, nonstate actors. The last part provides selections that delineate the emergent paradigms that may come to displace current thinking about the context and the conduct of all forms of conflict. It concludes with a brief "look ahead," which relates our latest suggestions about how to develop an integrated view that will help to prepare conceptually, organizationally, doctrinally, and strategically for meeting and coping with all types of conflict that may emerge in the information age. However, despite these divisions, many chapters are interconnected.

Part I opens with our vision of the future spectrum of conflict, in which we propose the concepts of "cyberwar" and "netwar" and advance an argument about the imminence of radical change. The selections by Stephen Blank and Norman Davis offer careful analyses of the RMA, upholding the view that it is largely information-based and is driven as much by organizational and doctrinal change as by technological advances. Next, Jeff Cooper urges a strategic perspective on the RMA, arguing that the new technologies, doctrines, and organizational designs must be melded together into an operating system that allows for a new way of war. Finally, we excerpt the first half of a study in which we analyze different views of information, relate them to different views of power, and draw implications for the RMA.

The present RMA is but the latest in a string of RMAs since ancient times. Historians Geoffrey Parker (1988) and Jeremy Black (1994)—who focus on the 16th and 17th centuries, respectively—elucidate the point that, RMAs evolve out of particular technological breakthroughs and organizational redesigns that, in turn, have radical effects on doctrine and strategy. There is no single cause of any RMA; all have been complex and ofttimes halting undertakings that required many years to unfold, as multiple forces played around and upon them. Most RMAs were resisted by military old-liners until the innovations proved worthwhile in battle, turning the tide against presumed odds. Some RMAs were fulfilled not by the dominant power of the period, but by rising contenders who had the motivation and the industry to try to become the next dominant power. All the selections in Part I are mainly about the future, but they reflect this historical background; and the need to proceed warily but energetically.

Indeed, if we had enlarged this volume, we would have included selections that show what theorists and strategists in other nations are thinking about information-age conflict, particularly in Russia and China, where some sharp contrasts to the American, technology-oriented approach are taking shape. Both the Russians and the Chinese are focusing on information-based concepts of strategy, doctrine, and organization—putting these at least on a par with technology, while avoiding a single-minded intent on it. In this regard, Americans may have much to learn from both the Russians and the Chinese—about concepts of nonlinearity, about military networks, and about notions that the more technologically advanced an opponent is, the more he may be vulnerable to disruptive attack. Tim Thomas (1996) points out that the Russians are well aware of their organizational and technological limitations—this is one of the reasons that their declaratory strategic policy seeks to deter information attack by threatening the possibility of Russian nuclear retaliation. In the case of China, however, John Arquilla and Solomon Karmel (1997) point out that the Chinese have a sanguine view of the People's Liberation Army's ability to confront even the most sophisticated opponent—so long as the conflict takes place within or near the Chinese sphere of interest. Indeed, it may be that, as far as doctrines are concerned, Mao's view of "People's War" has more relevance to the information age than the U.S. Army's plans for "AirLand Battle."

With the preeminence of information in mind, the selections that form Part II examine the concept of "Information Warfare" (IW). Bruce Berkowitz provides a broad definition of IW, sketching its contours, and then focusing on important enabling factors to identify intelligence requirements for waging IW. Martin Libicki argues the case for moving away from large units of maneuver and toward a vision of "the small and the many." In addition, with a keen skeptical eye, John Rothrock asks—and answers—some key questions about the nature and attributes of IW. The authors in this part concur with the view that IW is not so much about tactical measures to disrupt an opponent's hardware, as it is about the use of information to impose one's will upon an adversary—often via cyberspace, but more often by traditional means (e.g., public diplomacy, propaganda, psychological operations, and perception management). Each author makes a number of concrete recommendations regarding the actions that need to be taken to prepare for IW, broadly defined.

But even though much of IW takes place outside of cyberspace, some IW will occur in the electronic realm. In many ways, IW in the coming years may resemble the early phases of aerial bombardment. In the 1920s and 1930s, it was noted that aircraft provided a capability to attack an enemy's home front directly—without first having to defeat his forces in the field. So, too, IW may enable a combatant to strike electronically at the information, communications, economic, and other crucial infrastructure of a society, without ever having to engage, much less defeat, its armed forces. Richard Hundley and Robert Anderson provide an insightful analysis of the types of "bad actors" that may populate this part of the conflict spectrum in the information age.[4] Hundley and Anderson also raise key questions about the desirability and feasibility of cooperation between the private sector and the government in the area of cyberspace security and safety. Part II concludes with an excerpt from a study by Robert

Anderson and Anthony Hearn in which they derive practical ideas for improving cyberspace security by drawing on their experiences with an "information wargame" based on the "Day After . . ." methodology developed at RAND by Roger Molander (see Molander, Wilson, and Riddile, *Strategic Information Warfare*, 1996).

Part III focuses on the rise of various sorts of nonstate actors, who are expected to play increasing roles in future conflicts. Criminals, terrorists, radical global activists, and others are newly enlivened by the information revolution. In our view, they are uniquely well-suited to exploit the advantages of the network form of organization. We open Part III with our assessment of how these networks may fight "netwars"—against states, sometimes in alliance with states, and finally, in some cases, simply using states as arenas for their wars with each other.

In the next selection, Brian Nichiporuk and Carl Builder ruminate about the effects of the information revolution upon society in general. They emphasize the point that improvements in computing power and interconnectivity tend to empower individuals and small groups, as opposed to nation-states, which may raise the possibility of a new form of supranational civil society—but also may pose the risk of growth in the capabilities of some very "uncivil" actors. Phil Williams explores this latter theme, noting that, in the information age, transnational criminal organizations (TCOs) are likely to exercise very significant influence in international affairs. He notes that criminal enterprises have long employed networked organizational structures, and that the information revolution may now give them the opportunity to actualize their ultimate potential. One need only consider the manner in which criminals have held Colombia hostage—using that troubled country as a hub for their transnational activities—to see that Williams's vision of the future is already being realized.

Much as the information revolution has empowered criminal networks so too will it reinvigorate terrorism, according to Bruce Hoffman. His paper presents the view that terrorists will find in advanced technology both a new set of targets and a means of controlling their own networks of dispersed actors, many of whom may or may not be acting under direct control from the professional cadres. The bombing of the World Trade Center is an example of this "amateurization" of terror; and the rise of the Hezbollah terror network, which has no central leader, heralds the shift away from hierarchical "great man" organizations such as Yasser Arafat's PLO. Hoffman also considers the possibility that terrorists may target key nodes of their enemies' information infrastructures, with either old-style explosives or newfangled cyberspace technologies. This last point may indicate a shift to bloodless information attacks that may provoke less outrage among the target state's public, and a lower likelihood that the perpetrators will be alienated within the terrorist organization itself.

Our own concept of netwar illuminates how networked actors engage in conflict and how social netwars may take on a primarily nonviolent character. This has been the case with the war waged in Mexico since 1994 by activist NGOs to keep the government from a bloody repression of the EZLN. In Chiapas, two weeks of open fighting were followed by more than two years of negotiation and "information operations." Some of this is described in the excerpt from the article on the EZLN by David Ronfeldt and Armando Martinez. However, an ethnonationalist netwar, such as the one waged by the Chechens against Russia, may have a principally violent nature. In the Chechen case, the networking was of bands of fighters, linked by ham radios and runners, who fought and defeated the hierarchical, linear-thinking Russian Army. Thus, as we posit in the opening selection of Part III, traditional organizations have a very hard time coping with networked actors. Indeed, it will likely take networks to fight networks, much as, in an earlier era, it took tanks to fight tanks.

Lastly, Part IV focuses on some paradigms for thinking about the coming era of conflict that intend to spur specific defense planning preparations and processes. First, Richard Szafranski elucidates his concept of "neocortical warfare"—which views information-age conflict as moving extremely slowly, and as being more about fighting over knowledge than over territory or other resources. Szafranski describes the purest essence of war in the information age, suggesting that preparation may depend as much upon developing a mental discipline as on building new technological structures or engaging in the institutional redesign of hierarchical organizations. Next, we present the second half of our paper on new views of information and power, in which we exposit how these new concepts may necessitate reconfiguring American grand strategy in favor of an approach we call "guarded openness." Finally, we conclude this section, and the book, with a "look ahead" at some requirements for achieving an integrated vision of how best to prepare for conflict.

While the selections in this volume cover the six themes discussed earlier, it is not the only volume that should be perused for either introductory or advanced purposes. Two earlier insightful volumes about the future of conflict—Martin Van Creveld's *The Transformation of War* (1991) and Alvin and Heidi Toffler's *War and Anti-War* (1993)—remain timely. Valuable readings can be found in two volumes based on recent conferences at the Center for Strategic and International Studies (CSIS): *The Information Revolution and National Security*, edited by Stuart Schwartzstein (1996), and *The Information Revolution and International Security* (forthcoming from CSIS). For a military bent, see the book of readings edited by Alan Campen, Douglas Dearth, and R.T. Goodden, titled *Cyberwar* (1996) after the term we coined and James F. Dunnigan's *Digital Soldiers* (1996). In addition, the periodic journals *Comparative Strategy* and *Strategic Review* should be watched for essays on information-age conflict. Finally, an interesting array of World Wide Web pages have appeared over the last several years that provide access to a menu of readings, from official documents to critical rants—for example, take a look at these two sites and their links: http://www.stl.nps.navy.mil/c4i/ and http://www.teleport.com/~jwehling/OtherNetwars.html/

Over the past two decades, discussions and debates about the information revolution have gone through cycles of alternating enthusiasm and skepticism. Partly because of overblown expectations in recent years, more critical views are now in vogue—though not in this volume. Nonetheless, we hope that our readers will look beyond these cyclical trends in the debate. The bottom line for us and our contributors has little to do with enthusiasm or skepticism. Rather, it involves exploring these new frontiers of knowledge, trying to find out where the cutting edge is, or should be, and contributing to shaping it.

A GLIMPSE OF THINGS TO COME

If the themes that this volume emphasizes are correct, then we will be looking forward not only to new modes of conflict—and a new spectrum of conflict—but also to new ways of preparing for and dealing with them. Some of these ways were noted in the speculations introducing this chapter: moving to smaller but highly capable units of maneuver; developing vast sensor arrays for real-time intelligence, surveillance, and target-acquisition; building capabilities for distant stand-off as well as close-in swarming attacks; etc. Perhaps the key factor—a result of the information revolution—is the increasing destructive and disruptive power of the small group or unit across the conflict spectrum. It is imperative to adapt to and innovate around this factor.

If the United States does not adjust to smaller units of maneuver, our large field armies, air wings, and naval battlegroups will be vulnerable to the attacks of nimbler foes. But if we can learn to rebuild around smaller (but stronger) military formations, the benefits may include providing for national security and military readiness at significantly reduced costs. Moreover, in light of the possibility that disruption may become more important than destruction, the potential of these small units implies that conflict in the information age may have less need of bloody battle than did warfare in previous eras. Indeed, just as the Oriental game of *Go* is replacing Western chess as the preferred game metaphor for conflict, so Sun Tzu's notions of victory with minimal violence may displace Clausewitz's emphasis on the deadly clash of armies amid fog and friction.

But it will be no easy task to accomplish such adaptation and innovation. The best that we may be able to do, at present, is to identify the key endeavors that must be undertaken to prepare for information-age conflict. As some of the selections in this volume suggest, and as we will elucidate in our concluding chapter, these preparations are bound to entail the following:

- Articulating a better understanding than we currently have of "information"—in a comprehensive sense, what it is, and is not.

- Realizing organizational and institutional redesigns along networked lines, by skillfully blending hierarchies and networks.

- Developing a new doctrine of conflict based on "swarming" that looks beyond AirLand Battle and can be applied across the full spectrum of conflict, from high to low intensity.

- Formulating an overarching strategy of "guarded openness" that will guide the wise use of economic, political, and military capabilities and resources.

These are the key challenges facing the denizens of Athena's camp.

REFERENCES

Arquilla, John, and Solomon Karmel, "Welcome to the Revolution . . . in Chinese Military Affairs," *Defense Analysis*, Fall 1997, forthcoming.

Black, Jeremy, *European Warfare, 1660–1815*, New Haven: Yale University Press, 1994.

Campen, Alan, Douglas Dearth, and R.T. Goodden (eds.), *Cyberwar: Security, Strategy and Conflict in the Information Age*, Fairfax, Va.: AFCEA International Press, 1996.

Dunn Mascetti, Manuela, *Athena: Goddess of War and Wisdom*, San Francisco: Chronicle Books, Little Wisdom Library, 1996.

Dunnigan, James F., *Digital Soldiers: The Evolution of High-Tech Weaponry and Tomorrow's Brave New Battlefield*, New York: St. Martin's Press, 1996.

Fleming, William, *Arts and Ideas*, Third Edition, New York: Holt, Rinehart, and Winston, 1968.

Graves, Robert, *The Greek Myths*, Baltimore, Md.: Penguin Books, 1960.

Hall, Lee, *Athena: A Biography*, Reading, Mass.: Addison-Wesley, 1997.

Hamilton, Edith, *Mythology*, Boston, Mass.: Little, Brown, and Company, 1969.

Molander, Roger, Peter Wilson, and Andrew Riddile, *Strategic Information Warfare*, Santa Monica: RAND, 1996.

Parker, Geoffrey, *The Military Revolution: Military Innovation and the Rise of the West,* Cambridge: Cambridge University Press, 1988.

Power, Richard, *Information Warfare,* San Francisco: Computer Security Institute, 1995.

Schwartzstein, Stuart D., ed., *The Information Revolution and National Security: Dimensions and Directions,* Washington, D.C.: Center for International and Strategic Studies, 1996.

Thomas, Tim, *Russian Views on Information-Based Warfare,* Fort Leavenworth, Kan.: Foreign Military Studies Office, 1996, http://leav-www.army.mil/fmso/

Toffler, Alvin, and Heidi Toffler, *War and Anti-War: Survival at the Dawn of the Twenty-first Century,* Boston: Little, Brown and Company, 1993.

Van Creveld, Martin, *The Transformation of War,* New York: Free Press, 1991.

NOTES

[1] MRC is also sometimes used to refer to middle-range contingencies.

[2] The 19th century Prussian philosopher of war who, in his classic *On War,* distilled the lessons of the Napoleonic Wars, forming the basis for much of modern strategic thought.

[3] Standard sources on Greek and Roman mythology include Graves (1960) and Hamilton (1969). We also drew on Dunn Mascetti (1996) and Fleming (1968). For a darker view of Athena as being coopted by the male attraction to conflict, see Hall (1997). While Ares was refined by the Romans into Mars, Athena became Minerva. But given the Romans' penchant for specializing their gods, Minerva is mainly a goddess of wisdom, stripped of the warrior element. Thus she does not fit our purposes here.

[4] Another excellent selection about this subject is Richard Power's (1995) survey of advanced societies' many cyberspace vulnerabilities. Power also discusses the robustness against attack of these societies' infrastructures.

Part I

THE REVOLUTION IN MILITARY AFFAIRS

Chapter Two

CYBERWAR IS COMING!*

John Arquilla and David Ronfeldt

"Knowledge must become capability."
—Carl von Clausewitz, *On War*

EMERGENT MODES OF CONFLICT

Suppose that war looked like this: Small numbers of your light, highly mobile forces defeat and compel the surrender of large masses of heavily armed, dug-in enemy forces, with little loss of life on either side. Your forces can do this because they are well prepared, make room for maneuver, concentrate their firepower rapidly in unexpected places, and have superior command, control, and information systems that are decentralized to allow tactical initiatives, yet provide the central commanders with unparalleled intelligence and "topsight" for strategic purposes.

For your forces, warfare is no longer primarily a function of who puts the most capital, labor and technology on the battlefield, but of who has the best information about the battlefield. What distinguishes the victors is their grasp of information—not only from the mundane standpoint of knowing how to find the enemy while keeping it in the dark, but also in doctrinal and organizational terms. The analogy is rather like a chess game where you see the entire board, but your op-

*John Arquilla and David Ronfeldt, "Cyberwar is Coming!" *Comparative Strategy*, Vol 12, No. 2, Spring 1993, pp. 141–165. Copyright 1993 Taylor & Francis, Inc. Used by permission.

ponent sees only its own pieces—you can win even if he is allowed to start with additional powerful pieces.

We might appear to be extrapolating from the U.S. victory in the Gulf War against Iraq. But our vision is inspired more by the example of the Mongols of the 13th Century. Their "hordes" were almost always outnumbered by their opponents. Yet they conquered, and held for over a century, the largest continental empire ever seen. The key to Mongol success was their absolute dominance of battlefield information. They struck when and where they deemed appropriate; and their "Arrow Riders" kept field commanders, often separated by hundreds of miles, in daily communication. Even the Great Khan, sometimes thousands of miles away, was aware of developments in the field within days of their occurrence.

Absent the galvanizing threat that used to be posed by the Soviet Union, domestic political pressures will encourage the United States to make do with a smaller military in the future. The type of warfighting capability that we envision, which is inspired by the Mongol example but drawn mainly from our analysis of the information revolution, may allow America to protect itself and its far-flung friends and interests, regardless of the size and strength of our potential future adversaries.

The Advance of Technology and Know-How

Throughout history, military doctrine, organization, and strategy have continually undergone profound changes due in part to technological breakthroughs. The Greek phalanx, the combination of gun and sail, the *levee en masse*, the *blitzkrieg*, the Strategic Air Command—history is filled with examples in which new weapon, propulsion, communication, and transportation technologies provide a basis for advantageous shifts in doctrine, organization, and strategy that enable the innovator to avoid exhausting attritional battles and pursue instead a form of "decisive" warfare.[1]

Today, a variety of new technologies are once again taking hold, and further innovations are on the way. The most enticing include non-nuclear high-explosives; precision-guided munitions; stealth designs for aircraft, tanks, and ships; radio-electronic combat (REC) systems; new electronics for intelligence-gathering, interference, and deception; new information and communications systems that improve Command, Control, Communications and Intelligence (C³I) functions; and futuristic designs for space-based weapons and for automated and robotic warfare. In addition, virtual reality systems are being developed for simulation and training. Many of these advances enter into a current notion of a Military Technology Revolution (MTR).[2]

The future of war—specifically the U.S. ability to anticipate and wage war—will be shaped in part by how these technological advances are assessed and adopted. Yet, as military historians frequently warn, technology permeates war but does not govern it. It is not technology *per se*, but rather the organization of technology, broadly defined, that is important. Russell Weigley describes the situation this way:

> . . . the technology of war does not consist only of instruments intended primarily for the waging of war. A society's ability to wage war depends on every facet of its technology: its roads, its transport vehicles, its agriculture, its industry, and its methods of organizing its technology. As Van Creveld puts it, "behind military hardware there is hardware in general, and behind that there is technology as a certain kind of know-how, as a way of looking at the world and coping with its problems."[3]

In our view, the technological shift that matches this broad view is the information revolution. This is what will bring the next major shift in the nature of conflict and warfare.

Effects of the Information Revolution

The information revolution reflects the advance of computerized information and communications technologies and related innovations in organization and management theory. Sea changes are occurring in how information is collected, stored, processed, communicated and presented, and in how organizations are designed to take advantage of increased information.[4] Information is becoming a strategic resource that may prove as valuable and influential in the post-industrial era as capital and labor have been in the industrial age.

Advanced information and communications systems, properly applied, can improve the efficiency of many kinds of activities. But improved efficiency is not the only or even the best possible effect. The new technology is also having a transforming effect, for it disrupts old ways of thinking and operating, provides capabilities to do things differently, and suggests how some things may be done better, if done differently:

> The consequences of new technology can be usefully thought of as first-level, or efficiency, effects and second-level, or social system, effects. The history of previous technologies demonstrates that early in the life of a new technology, people are likely to emphasize the efficiency effects and underestimate or overlook potential social system effects. Advances in networking technologies now make it possible to think of people, as well as databases and processors, as resources on a network.

> Many organizations today are installing electronic networks for first-level efficiency reasons. Executives now beginning to deploy electronic mail and other network applications can realize efficiency gains such as reduced elapsed time for transactions. If we look beyond efficiency at behavioral and organizational changes, we'll see where the second-level leverage is likely to be. These technologies can change how people spend their time and what and who they know and care about. The full range of payoffs, and the dilemmas, will come from how the technologies affect how people can think and work together—the second-level effects (Sproull and Kiesler, 1991: 15–16).

The information revolution, in both its technological and non-technological aspects, sets in motion forces that challenge the design of many institutions. It disrupts and erodes the hierarchies around which institutions are normally designed. It diffuses and redistributes power, often to the benefit of what may be considered weaker, smaller actors. It crosses borders and redraws the boundaries of offices and responsibilities. It expands the spatial and temporal horizons that actors should take into account. And thus it generally compels closed systems to open up. But while this may make life difficult especially for large, bureaucratic, aging institutions, the institutional form *per se* is not becoming obsolete. Institutions of all types remain essential to the organization of society. The responsive, capable ones will adapt their structures and processes to the information age. Many will evolve from traditional hierarchical to new, flexible, network-like models of organization. Success will depend on learning to interlace hierarchical and network principles.[5]

Meanwhile, the very changes that trouble institutions—the erosion of hierarchy, etc.—favor the rise of multi-organizational networks. Indeed, the information revolution is strengthening the importance of all forms of networks—social networks, communications networks, etc. The network form is very different from the institutional form. While institutions (large ones in particular) are traditionally built around hierarchies and aim to act on their own, multi-organizational networks consist of (often small) organizations or parts of institutions that have linked together to act jointly. The information revolution favors the growth of such networks by making it possible for diverse, dispersed actors to communicate, consult, coordinate, and operate together across greater distances and on the basis of more and better information than ever before.[6]

These points bear directly on the future of the military, and of conflict and warfare more generally.

Both Netwar and Cyberwar Are Likely

The thesis of this think piece is that the information revolution will cause shifts both in how societies may come into conflict, and how their armed forces may wage war. We offer a distinction between what we call "netwar"—societal-level ideational conflicts waged in part through internetted modes of communication—and "cyberwar" at the military level. These terms are admittedly novel, and better ones may yet be devised.[7] But for now they help illuminate a useful distinction and identify the breadth of ways in which the information revolution may alter the nature of conflict short of war, as well as the context and the conduct of warfare.[8]

While both netwar and cyberwar revolve around information and communications matters, at a deeper level they are forms of war about "knowledge"—about who knows what, when, where, and why, and about how secure a society or a military is regarding its knowledge of itself and its adversaries.[9]

Explaining Netwar. Netwar refers to information-related conflict at a grand level between nations or societies. It means trying to disrupt, damage, or modify what a target population "knows" or thinks it knows about itself and the world around it. A netwar may focus on public or elite opinion, or both. It may involve public diplomacy measures, propaganda and psychological campaigns, political and cultural subversion, deception of or interference with local media, infiltration of computer networks and databases, and efforts to promote a dissident or opposition movements across computer networks. Thus designing a strategy for netwar may mean grouping together from a new perspective a number of measures that have been used before but were viewed separately.

In other words, netwar represents a new entry on the spectrum of conflict that spans economic, political, and social as well as military forms of "war." In contrast to economic wars that target the production and distribution of goods, and political wars that aim at the leadership and institutions of a government, netwars would be distinguished by their targeting of information and communications. Like other forms on this spectrum, netwars would be largely nonmilitary, but they could have dimensions that overlap into military war. For example, an economic war may involve trade restrictions, the dumping of goods, the illicit penetration and subversion of businesses and markets in a target country, and the theft of technology— none of which need involve the armed forces. Yet an economic war may also come to include an armed blockade or strategic bombing of economic assets, meaning it has also become a military war. In like manner, a netwar that leads to targeting an enemy's military C^3I capabilities turns, at least in part, into what we mean by cyberwar.

Netwar will take various forms, depending on the actors. Some may occur between the governments of rival nation-states. In some respects, the U.S. and Cuban governments are already engaged in a netwar. This is manifested in the activities of Radio and TV Martí on the U.S. side, and on Castro's side by the activities of pro-Cuban support networks around the world.

Other kinds of netwar may arise between governments and non-state actors. For example, these may be waged by governments against illicit groups and organizations involved in terrorism, proliferation of weapons of mass destruction, or drug smuggling. Or, to the contrary, they may be waged against the policies of specific governments by advocacy groups and movements—e.g., regarding environmental, human-rights, or religious issues. The non-state actors may or may not be associated with nations, and in some cases they may be organized into vast transnational networks and coalitions.

Another kind of netwar may occur between rival non-state actors, with governments maneuvering on the sidelines to prevent collateral damage to national interests and perhaps to support one side or another. This is the most speculative kind of netwar, but the elements for it have already appeared, especially among advocacy movements around the world. Some movements are increasingly organizing into cross-border networks and coalitions, identifying more with the development of civil society (even global civil society) than with nation-states, and using advanced information and communications technologies to strengthen their activities. This may well turn out to be the next great frontier for ideological conflict, and netwar may be a prime characteristic.

Most netwars will probably be non-violent, but in the worst of cases one could combine the possibilities into some mean low-intensity conflict scenarios. Van Creveld (1991: 197) does this when he worries that "In the future war, war will not be waged by armies but by groups whom today we call terrorists, guerrillas, bandits and robbers, but who will undoubtedly hit on more formal titles to describe themselves." In his view, war between states will diminish, and the state may become obsolete as a major form of societal organization. Our views coincide with many of Van Creveld's, though we do not believe that the state is even potentially obsolete. Rather, it will be transformed by these developments.

Some netwars will involve military issues. Candidate issue areas include nuclear proliferation, drug smuggling, and anti-terrorism because of the potential threats they pose to international order and national security interests. Moreover, broader societal trends—e.g., the redefinition of security concepts, the new roles of advocacy groups, the blurring of the traditional boundaries between what is military and what non-military, between what is public and what private, and between what pertains to the state and what to society—may engage the interests of at least some military offices in some netwar-related activities.

Netwars are not real wars, traditionally defined. But netwar might be developed into an instrument for trying, early on, to prevent a real war from arising. Deterrence in a chaotic world may become as much a function of one's "cyber" posture and presence as of one's force posture and presence.

Explaining Cyberwar. Cyberwar refers to conducting, and preparing to conduct, military operations according to information-related principles. It means disrupting if not destroying the information and communications systems, broadly defined to include even military culture, on which an adversary relies in order to "know" itself: who it is, where it is, what it can do when, why it is fighting, which threats to counter first, etc. It means trying to know all about an adversary while keeping it from knowing much about oneself. It means turning the "balance of information and knowledge" in one's favor, especially if the balance of forces is not. It means using knowledge so that less capital and labor may have to be expended.

This form of warfare may involve diverse technologies—notably for C^3I; for intelligence collection, processing, and distribution; for tactical communications, positioning, and identification-friend-or-foe (IFF); and for "smart" weapons systems—to give but a few examples. It may also involve electronically blinding, jamming, deceiving, overloading, and intruding into an adversary's information and communications circuits. Yet cyberwar is not simply a set of measures based on technology. And it should not be confused with past meanings of computerized, automated, robotic, or electronic warfare.

Cyberwar may have broad ramifications for military organization and doctrine. As noted, the literature on the information revolution calls for organizational innovations so that different parts of an institution function like interconnected networks rather than separate hierarchies. Thus cyberwar may imply some institutional redesign for a military in both intra- and inter-service areas. Moving to networked structures may require some decentralization of command and control, which may well be resisted in light of earlier views that the new technology would provide greater central control of military operations. But decentralization is only part of the picture; the new technology may also provide greater "topsight"—a central understanding of the big picture that enhances the management of complexity.[10] Many treatments of organizational redesign laud decentralization; yet decentralization alone is not the key issue. The pairing of decentralization with topsight brings the real gains.

Cyberwar may also imply developing new doctrines about what kinds of forces are needed, where and how to deploy them, and what and how to strike on the enemy's side. How and where to position what kinds of computers and related sensors, networks, databases, etc. may become as important as the question used to be for the deployment of bombers and their support functions. Cyberwar may also have implications for the integration of the political and psychological with the military aspects of warfare.

In sum, cyberwar may raise broad issues of military organization and doctrine, as well as strategy, tactics, and weapons design. It may be applicable in low- and high-intensity conflicts, in conventional and non-conventional environments, and for defensive or offensive purposes.

As an innovation in warfare, we anticipate that cyberwar may be to the 21st century what *blitzkrieg* was to the 20th century. Yet for now, we also believe that the concept is too speculative for precise definition. At a minimum, it represents an extension of the traditional importance of obtaining information in war—of having superior C^3I, and of trying to locate, read, surprise, and deceive the enemy before he does the same to you. That remains important no matter what overall strategy is pursued. In this sense, the concept means that information-related factors are more important than ever due to new technologies, but it does not spell a break with tradition. Indeed, it resembles Thomas Rona's (1976: 2) concept of an "information war" that is "intertwined with, and superimposed on, other military operations." Our concept is broader than Rona's, which focused on countermeasures to degrade an enemy's weapons systems while protecting one's own; yet we believe that this approach to defining cyberwar will ultimately prove too limiting.

In a deeper sense, cyberwar signifies a transformation in the nature of war. This, we believe, will prove to be the better approach to defining cyberwar. Our position is at odds with a view (see Arnett, 1992) that uses the terms "hyperwar" and "cyberwar" (!?) to lay claims that the key implication of the MTR is the automated battlefield; that future wars will be fought mainly by "brilliant" weapons, robots, and autonomous computers; that man will be subordinate to the machine; and that combat will be unusually fast and laden with stand-off attacks. This view errs in its understanding of the effects of the information revolution, and our own view differs on every point. Cyberwar is about organization as much as technology. It implies new man-machine interfaces that amplify man's capabilities, not a separation of man and machine. In some situations, combat may be waged fast and from afar, but in many other situations, it may be slow and close-in; and new combinations of far and close and fast and slow may be the norm, not one extreme or the other.

The post-modern battlefield stands to be fundamentally altered by the information technology revolution, at both the strategic and the tactical levels. The increasing breadth and depth of this battlefield and the ever-improving accuracy and destructiveness of even conventional munitions have heightened the importance of C^3I matters to the point where dominance in this aspect alone may now yield the able practitioner consistent war-winning advantages. Yet cyberwar is a much broader idea than attacking an enemy's C^3I systems while improving and defending one's own. In Clausewitz's sense, it is characterized by the effort to turn knowledge into capability.

Indeed, even though its full design and implementation requires advanced technology, cyberwar is not reliant upon advanced technology per se. The continued development of advanced information and communications technologies is crucial for U.S. military capabilities. But cyberwar, whether waged by the United States or other actors, does not necessarily require the presence of advanced technology. The organizational and psychological dimensions may be as important as the technical. Cyberwar may actually be waged with low technology under some circumstances.

INFORMATION-RELATED FACTORS IN MILITARY HISTORY

Our contention is that netwar and cyberwar represent new (and related) modes of conflict that will be increasingly important in the future. The information revolution implies—indeed, it assures—that a sea change is occurring in the nature of conflict and warfare. Yet both new modes have many historical antecedents; efforts have been made in the direction of conducting warfare from cyber-like perspectives in the past. Information, communications, and control are enduring concerns of warfighters; there is much historical evidence, tactical and strategic, that attempting to pierce the "fog of war" and envelop one's foe in it has played a continuing role.[11]

In an ancient example from the Second Punic War of the 3d Century B.C., Carthaginian forces under the command of Hannibal routinely stationed observers with mirrors on hilltops, keeping their leader apprised of Roman movements while the latter remained ignorant of his. Better communications contributed significantly to the ability of Hannibal's forces to win a string of victories over a period of sixteen years. In the most dramatic example of the use of superior information, Hannibal's relatively small forces were able to rise literally from the fog of war at Lake Trasimene to destroy a Roman army more than twice its size.[12]

In another famous, more recent, example, during the Napoleonic Wars, the British Royal Navy's undisputed command of the Mediterranean Sea, sealed at the Battle of the Nile in 1798, cut the strategic sea communications of Bonaparte's expeditionary force in North Africa, leading to its disastrous defeat. The invaders were stranded in Egypt without supplies, or their commander, after Napoleon's flight, where they remained in place until the British came to take them prisoner.

A few years later, in this same conflict, Lord Cochrane's lone British frigate was able to put French forces into total confusion along virtually the entire Mediterranean coast of occupied Spain and much of France. The French relied for their communications on a semaphore system to alert their troops to trouble, and to tell coastal vessels when they could safely sail. Cochrane would raid these signaling stations, then strike spectacularly, often in conjunction with Spanish guerrilla forces, while French communications were disrupted.[13]

Story upon story could be drawn from military history to illuminate the significance of information and communications factors. But this is meant to be only a brief paper to posit the concept of cyberwar. Better we turn directly to an early example, a virtual model, of this upcoming mode of warfare.

An Early Example of Cyberwar: The Mongols

Efforts to strike at the enemy's communications and ensure the safety of one's own are found, to varying degrees, throughout history. Yet the Mongol way of warfare, which reached its zenith in the 12th and 13th centuries, may be the closest that anyone has come to waging pure cyberwar (or netwar, for that matter). Examining Mongol military praxis should, therefore, be instructive in developing the foundations for waging war in a like manner in the post-modern world. Use of this example also reinforces the point that cyberwar does not depend on high technology, but rather on how one thinks about conflict and strategic interaction.

At the military level, the Mongols relied for success almost entirely on learning exactly where their enemies were, while keeping their own whereabouts a secret until they attacked. This enabled them, despite a chronic inferiority in numbers, to overthrow the finest, largest armies of Imperial China, Islam and Christendom. The simplest way to illustrate their advantage is to suggest an analogy with chess: war against the Mongols resembled playing against an opponent who could hide the dispositions of his pieces, but who could see the placement of both his and one's own. Indeed, under such conditions, the player with knowledge of both sides' deployments could be expected to triumph with many fewer pieces. Moreover, the addition of even significant forces to the semi-blinded side would generate no requirement for a similar increase on the "sighted" side. (Thus the similarity is not so much to chess as to its cousin, *kriegsspiel*, in which both players start "blind" to their opponent's position; in our analogy, one player can see through the barrier that is normally placed between the boards of the players.)

So it was with the Mongols. In one of their greatest campaigns, against the mighty Muslim empire of Khwarizm (located approximately on the territory of today's Iran, Iraq and portions of the Central Asian republics of the former Soviet Union), a Mongol army of some 125,000 toppled a foe whose standing armies amounted to nearly half a million troops, with a similar number of reserves. How could this happen? The answer is that the Mongols identified the linear, forward dispositions of their foes and avoided them. Instead, they worked around the defenders, making a point of waylaying messengers moving between the capital and the "front."

Muhammad Ali Shah, the ruler of Khwarizm, took the silence from the front as a good sign, until one day a messenger, having narrowly escaped a Mongol patrol, made his way into the capital, Samarkand. Muhammad, inquiring about the news from his army, was told that the frontier was holding. The messenger went on to add, however, that he had observed a large Mongol army but a day's march from the capital. The shah fled. His capital fell swiftly. This news, when given to the frontier armies, led to a general capitulation. Muhammad ended his days in hiding on the island of Abeshkum in the Caspian Sea, where he contracted and died from pleurisy.

The campaign against Khwarizm is typical of the Mongol strategic approach of first blinding an opponent, then striking at his heart (i.e., going for checkmate). Battles were infrequently fought, as they were often unnecessary for achieving war aims. However, there were times when confrontations could not be avoided. When this happened, the Mongols relied heavily on coordinated operations designed to break down the plans and controls of their opponents. Against the Polish-Prussian coalition forces at the battle of Liegnitz, for example, the Mongols engaged an army some four times their size, and defeated it in detail. Their success was based on keeping a clear picture of the defending coalition's order of battle, while confusing the opponents as to their own whereabouts. Thus, portions of the Western army chased after small detachments that were simple lures, and ended up in the clutches of the Mongol main force. The Poles and Prussians were defeated piecemeal. Indeed, the Mongols were so sure of their information that they repeatedly used a river crossing during the battle in the intervals *between* its being used by the Poles and Prussians.[14]

What about Mongol advantages in mobility and firepower? Certainly, the Mongols' ability to move a division some eighty miles per day was superior to other armies, and their horn bows did outrange those of their enemies by 50–100 yards, on average. But neither of these factors could offset their foes' advantages in fortification technology; and the body armor of Western forces gave them distinct advantages over the Mongols in close combat. Thus, Mongol tactical operations were often significantly stymied by defended cities,[15] and close engagements were exceedingly hard fought, with the Mongols suffering heavily. Indeed, the ferocity and effectiveness of the Prusso-Polish forces at Liegnitz, especially their cavalry, may have deterred the Mongols from continuing their invasion of Europe.[16] At the battle of Hims, the Mamelukes showed that the forces of Islam could also defeat the Mongols tactically. What neither Islam nor Christendom could do consistently, however, was outwit the Mongols strategically.

Clearly, the key to Mongol success was superior command, control, communication, and intelligence. Scouts and messengers always took along three or four extra horses, tethered, so that they could switch mounts and keep riding when one grew tired. This gave the horsemen, in relative terms, something approximating an ability to provide real-time intelligence, almost as if from a satellite, on the enemy's order of battle and intentions. At the same time, this steppe-version of the "Pony Express" (the Khan called them "Arrow Riders") enabled field generals to keep the high command, often thousands of miles from the theater of war, informed as to all developments within four or five days of their occurrence. For communication between field forces, the Mongols also employed a sophisticated semaphore system that allowed for swift tactical shifts as circumstances demanded. Organizationally, the Mongols emphasized decentralized command in the field, unlike their foes who were generally required to wait for orders from their capitals. Yet by developing a communication system that kept their leadership apprised at all times, the Mongols enjoyed topsight as well as decentralization. The Khan "advanced his armies on a wide front, controlling them with a highly developed system of communication"—that was the secret of his success (Chambers 1985:43).

In strategic terms, the Mongols aimed first to disrupt an enemy's communications, then to strike at his heart. Unlike Clausewitz, they put little store in the need to destroy enemy forces before advancing. Also, Mongol campaigns were in no way "linear." They struck where they wished, when circumstances were deemed favorable. That their Christian and Muslim foes seldom emulated the Mongols' organizational and communication techniques is to their great discredit. When, finally, the Mamelukes defeated the Mongols' attempted invasion of Egypt, it was because they kept track of Mongol movements and were led in the field by their king, Kilawan, who exercised rapid, effective control of his forces in the fluid battle situations that ensued. Also, the Mamelukes, employing carrier pigeons, had developed faster strategic communications than even the Mongols' Arrow Riders, allowing them to mass in time to defend effectively.[17]

As much as they form a paradigm for cyberwar, the Mongols were also adept at netwar. Early in their campaigns, they used terror tactics to weaken resistance. At the outset of any invasion, they broadcast that any city that resisted would be razed, its inhabitants slaughtered. Surrender, on the other hand, would result simply in coming under Mongol suzerainty; this entailed some initial rape and pillage but thereafter settled into a distracted sort of occupation. As a result, peaceful surrenders were plentiful. In later campaigns, when the Mongols learned that both Christians and Muslims saw them as the dark forces of Gog and Magog, heralding the "end of times," they deliberately cultivated this image. They renamed themselves Tartars, as though they were the minions of "tartarum," the biblical nether world. Later, when it was clear that the world was not ending, the Mongols willingly adopted both Christianity and Islam, whichever eased the burden of captivity for particular peoples. This utilitarian approach to religion impeded the formation of opposing coalitions.

Some analysts have argued that the Mongols represent an early experiment with *blitzkrieg*.[18] But in our view the differences between cyberwar and *blitzkrieg* are significant, and the Mongols reflect the former more than the latter.

Blitzkrieg, People's War, and Beyond

The relative importance of war against an enemy's command, control, and communications jumped with the advent of mechanized warfare. In World War II, the German *blitzkrieg* doctrine—in some ways a forerunner of cyberwar—made the disruption of enemy communications and control an explicit goal at both the tactical and strategic levels. For example, having radios in all of their tanks provided German armor with a tactical force multiplier in its long war with the Soviet Union, whose tanks, though more numerous and better built, provided radios only for commanders.[19]

At the strategic level, destroying the Soviets' central communications and control site by capturing Moscow was a key element of the planning for Operation Barbarossa. But when an opportunity arose during the campaign to win large material gains in the Ukraine, Hitler diverted General Guderian's panzers away from their approach to Moscow, and it was never taken. There would be no "lightning" victory for the Germans, who soon found themselves on the weaker side of a massive attritional struggle, doomed to defeat.[20]

Following WWII, information and communication technologies improved by leaps and bounds in the major industrialized nations. But the important wars with lessons for cyberwar were between these nations and the underdeveloped ones of the Third World. A comparison of two key conflicts—the one a people's war waged by North Vietnam and the Viet Cong in the 1960s and 1970s, the other the recent, more conventional conflict between the American-led coalition and Iraq—illuminates the growing importance and applicability of cyberwar principles.

Both wars represent turning points. In the case of Vietnam, the enemy may have applied cyber principles more effectively than did the United States—not only in military areas, but also where cyberwar cuts into the political and societal dimensions of conflict. In the case of the war against Iraq, the United States did superior work applying cyberwar principles—they were not called that at the time, of course—against an enemy whose organization, doctrine, strategy, and tactics were from a different era.

In the Vietnam war, the United States appeared to have advantages up and down the chain of command and control, from the construction of quantitative indicators and computerized models and databases for analyzing the course of the war in Washington, through field radios for calling in prompt air strikes, reinforcements, and rescue operations. But the thrall of computerization and quantitative techniques led analysts to overlook the softer, subtler aspects of the war where the enemy was winning. The excellence of U.S. communications capabilities encouraged inappropriate intrusion from above into battles and campaigns best planned and waged within the theater.

While U.S. forces had superior tactical communications, the guerrillas' strategic communications were largely unaffected. Meanwhile, the North Vietnamese and Viet Cong operated on Mao Zedong's doctrine that "command must be centralized for strategical purposes and decentralized for tactical purposes" (Mao 1961: 114)[21]—a classic combination of topsight and decentralization. The United States, on the other hand, appears to have allowed the timely availability of vast quantities of information at high levels to seduce leadership into maintaining central tactical as well as strategic control, and into believing that they had topsight when they did not.

The Vietnam example illustrates our point that good communications, though they provide necessary conditions, are insufficient to enable one to fight a cyberwar. For this endeavor, a doctrinal view of the overarching importance and value of maintaining one's own communications while disabling the adversary's is requisite. This entails the development of tactics and operational strategies that discard the basic tenets of both set-piece and even traditional maneuver warfighting theories. Neither the grinding attritional approach of Grant nor the explosive thrusts of Guderian will suffice. Instead, radically different models must be considered that focus upon the objective of systemically disorganizing the enemy.

To some extent, the recent American experience in the Gulf War suggests that an increasing sensitivity to cyber principles is taking hold. First, it was made quite clear by President Bush that he had no intention of micro-managing tactical or even operationally strategic actions. This is, in itself, a stark contrast to the classic image of President Johnson poring over maps of North Vietnam, selecting each of the targets to be hit by Operation Rolling Thunder.

The military operations brought significant cyber elements into play, often utilizing them as "force multipliers" (Powell 1992). The Apache helicopter strike against Iraqi air defense controls at the war's outset is but one, albeit very important, example. Also, the Allied coalition had good knowledge of Iraqi dispositions, while the latter were forced to fight virtually blind. Along these lines, a further example of the force multiplying effect of command of information is provided by the ability of a relatively small (less than 20,000 troops) Marine force afloat to draw away from the landward front and tie down roughly 125,000 Iraqi defenders.

A significant effort was made to employ netwar principles as well in this war. The construction of an international consensus against the Iraqi aggression, backed by the deployment of large, mechanized forces, was intended to persuade Saddam to retreat. His intransigent behavior suggests that his vision of war was of a prior generation.

An Implication: Institutions Versus Networks

A military, from a traditional standpoint, is an institution that fields armed forces. The form that all institutions normally take is the hierarchy. Militaries in particular depend heavily on hierarchy.

Yet the information revolution is bound to erode hierarchies and redraw the boundaries around which institutions and their offices are normally built. Moreover, this revolution favors organizational network designs. These points were made in the first section of this paper.

This second section leads to some related insights based on a quick review of history.   The classic example of an ancient force that fought according to cyberwar principles, the Mongols, was organized more like a network than a hierarchy.   A relatively minor military power, the combined forces of North Vietnam and the Viet Cong, that fought to defeat a great modern power operated in many respects more like a network than an institution; these forces even extended political support networks abroad. In both cases, the Mongolian and the Vietnamese, their defeated opponents amounted to large institutions whose forces were designed to fight set-piece attritional battles.

To this may be added a further set of observations drawn from current events. Most adversaries that the United States and its allies face in the realms of low-intensity conflict—international terrorists, guerrilla insurgents, drug smuggling cartels, ethnic factions, as well as racial and tribal gangs—are all organized like networks (although their leadership may be quite hierarchical). Perhaps a reason that military (and police) institutions keep having difficulty engaging in low-intensity conflicts is because they are not meant to be fought by institutions.

The lesson: Institutions can be defeated by networks. It may take networks to counter networks. The future may belong to whoever masters the network form.

ISSUES FOR THE FUTURE

The implications of a revolutionary technology are often not widely perceived at first. That was true of the tank, the machine gun and the telephone. For example, with their newly developed, rapid firing *mitrailleuse*, the French enjoyed a tremendous potential firepower advantage over the Prussians in 1870. Unfortunately, this early version of the machine gun looked more like a field piece instead of a rifle, and it was deployed behind the front with the artillery. Thus, the weapon that would dominate World War I a generation later had almost no effect on the Franco-Prussian conflict. People try to fit the new technology into established ways of doing things; it is expected to prove itself in terms of existing standards of efficiency and effectiveness.

It may take time to realize that inserting the new technology into old ways may create some new inefficiencies, even as some activities become more efficient. It may take still more time to realize that the activity itself—in both its operational and organizational dimensions—should be restructured, even transformed, in order to realize the full potential of the technology.[22] This pattern is documented in the early histories of the telephone and the electric motor, and is being repeated with computer applications in the business world.

Why should anything different be expected for cyberwar? New information technology applications have begun to transform the business world both operationally and organizationally. The government world is, for the most part, moving slowly in adopting the information technology revolution. One might expect the military world to lag behind both the business and government worlds, partly because of its greater dependence on hierarchical traditions. But in fact parts of the U.S. military are showing a keen interest in applying the information revolution. As this unfolds, a constant but often halting, contentious interplay between operational and organizational innovations should be expected.

Growing Awareness of the Information Revolution

An awareness is spreading in some U.S. military circles that the information revolution may transform the nature of warfare. One hears that the MTR implies a period of reevaluation and experimentation not unlike the one in the 1920s and 1930s that resulted in Germany's breakthrough formulation of the *blitzkrieg* doctrine. New questions are being asked about how to apply the new technology in innovative ways. For example, one set of arguments holds that the MTR may increasingly enable armed forces to stand off and destroy enemy targets with high precision weapons fired from great distances, including from outer space. But another set holds that the information revolution may drive conflict and warfare toward the low-intensity end of the scale, giving rise to new forms of close-in combat. Clearly, military analysts and strategists are just beginning to identify the questions and call for the required thinking.

The military, like much of the business world, remains in a stage of installing pieces of the new technology to make specific operations more effective. Indeed, techniques that we presume would be essential to cyberwar may be used to improve the cost-effectiveness of many military operations, no matter what overall strategy is being pursued (even if cyberwar remains unformulated). For example, improved surveillance and intelligence-gathering capabilities that help identify timely opportunities for surprise—to some extent, a purpose of the new Joint Targeting Network (JTN)—can be of service to a traditional attritional warfare strategy. Also, new capabilities for informing the members of a unit in real time where their comrades are located and what each is doing—as in recent experiments with intervehicular information systems (IVIS)—may improve the ability to concentrate force as a unit, and maintain that concentration throughout an operation. The list of new techniques that could be mentioned is long and growing.

We favor inquiring methodically into how the information revolution may provide specific new technical capabilities for warfare, regardless of the doctrine and strategy used. We also favor analyzing what kinds of operational and organizational innovations should be considered in light of such capabilities. And we recognize that it is quite another thing to try to leap ahead and propose that "cyberwar" may be a major part of the answer. But this think piece is not meant to be so methodical; it is meant to be speculative and suggestive, in order to call attention to the possibility of cyberwar as a topic that merits further discussion and research.

Indications and Aspects of Cyberwar

New theoretical ground needs to be broken regarding the information and communications dimensions of war, and the role of "knowledge" in conflict environments. Cyberwar is not merely a new set of operational techniques. It is emerging, in our view, as a new mode of warfare that will call for new approaches to plans and strategies, and new forms of doctrine and organization.

What would a cyberwar look like? Are there different types? What may be the distinctive attributes of cyberwar as a doctrine? Where does cyberwar fit in the history of warfare—and why would it represent a radical shift? What are the requirements and options for preparing for and conducting a cyberwar? Will it enable power to be projected in new ways? What are the roles of organizational and technological factors—and what other factors (e.g., psychological) should be considered? How could the concept enable one to think better, or at least differently in a useful way, about factors—e.g., C^3I, REC, psywar—that are important but not ordinarily considered together? What measures of effectiveness (MOE) should be used? These kinds of questions—some of them touched on in this paper—call for examination.

Paradigm Shift. We anticipate that cyberwar, like war in Clausewitz's view, may be a "chameleon." It will be adaptable to varying contexts; it will not represent or impose a single, structured approach. Cyberwar may be fought offensively and defensively, at the strategic or tactical levels. It will span the gamut of intensity—from conflicts waged by heavy mechanized forces across wide theaters, to counterinsurgencies where "the mobility of the boot" may be the prime means of maneuver.

Consider briefly the context of *blitzkrieg*. This doctrine for offensive operations, based on the close coordination of mobile armored forces and air power, was designed for relatively open terrain and good weather. Its primary asset was speed; swift breakthroughs were sought, and swift follow-ups required to prevent effective defensive ripostes.

> The blitzkrieg is predicated upon the assumption that the opponent's army is a large and complex machine that is geared to fighting along a well-established defensive line. In the machine's

rear lies a vulnerable network, which comprises numerous lines of communication, along which supplies as well as information move, and key nodal points at which the various lines intersect. Destruction of this central nervous system is tantamount to destruction of the army. The principal aim of a blitzkrieg is therefore to effect a strategic penetration. The attacker attempts to pierce the defender's front and then to drive deep into the defender's rear, severing his lines of communication and destroying key junctures in the network.[23]

By comparison, cyberwar takes a different view of what constitutes the "battlefield." Cyberwar depends less on the geographic terrain than on the nature of the electronic "cyberspace,"[24] which should be open to domination through advanced technology applications. Cyberwar benefits from an open radio-electronic spectrum and good atmospheric and other conditions for utilizing that spectrum. Cyberwar may require speedy flows of information and communications, but not necessarily a speedy or heavily armed offense like *blitzkrieg*. If the opponent is blinded, it can do little against even a slow-moving adversary. How, when and where to position battlefield computers and related sensors, communications networks, databases, and REC devices may become as important in future wars as the same questions were for tanks or bomber fleets and their supporting equipment in the Second World War.

Cyberwar may imply a new view not only of what constitutes "attack" but also of "defeat." Throughout the era of modern nation-states, beginning in about the 16th century, attrition has been the main mode of warfare. An enemy's armed forces had to be defeated before objectives could be taken. This lasted for centuries until the grotesque, massive slaughters of World War I led to a search for relief from wars of exhaustion. This in turn led to the development of *blitzkrieg*, which circumvented the more brutish aspects of attritional war. Yet this maneuver-oriented doctrine still required the destruction of the enemy's forces as the prerequisite to achieving war aims; attritional war had simply been "put on wheels."

Cyberwar may also imply—although we are not sure at this point—that victory can be attained without the need to destroy an opposing force. The Mongol defeat of Khwarizm is the best example of the almost total circumvention and "virtual" dismemberment of an enemy's forces. It is possible to see in cyberwar an approach to conflict that allows for decisive campaigning without a succession of bloody battles. Cyberwar may thus be developed as a post-industrial doctrine that differs from the industrial-age traditions of attritional warfare. It may even seek to avoid attritional conflict.[25] In the best circumstances, wars may be won by striking at the strategic heart of an opponent's cyber structures—his systems of knowledge, information, and communications.

It is hard to think of any kind of warfare as humane, but a fully articulated cyberwar doctrine might allow the development of a capability to use force not only in ways that minimize the costs to oneself, but which also allow victory to be achieved without the need to maximize the destruction of the enemy. If for no other reason, this potential of cyberwar to lessen war's cruelty demands its careful study and elaboration.

Organizational and Related Strategic Considerations. At the strategic level, cyberwar may imply Mao's military ideal of combining strategic centralization and tactical decentralization. The interplay between these effects is one of the more complex facets of the information revolution. Our preliminary view is that the benefits of decentralization may be enhanced if, to balance the possible loss of centralization, the high command gains "topsight"—the term mentioned earlier that we currently favor to describe the view of the overall conflict. This term carries with it an implication that the temptation to micromanage will be resisted.

The new technology tends to produce a deluge of information that must be taken in, filtered, and integrated in real time. Informational overload and bottlenecking has long been a vulnerability of centralized, hierarchical structures for command and control.[26] Waging cyberwar may require major innovations in organizational design, in particular a shift from hierarchies to networks. The traditional reliance on hierarchical designs may have to be adapted to network-oriented models to allow greater flexibility, lateral connectivity, and teamwork across institutional boundaries. The traditional emphasis on command and control, a key strength of hierarchy, may have to give way to an emphasis on consultation and coordination, the crucial building blocks of network designs. This may raise transitional concerns about how to maintain institutional traditions as various parts become networked with other parts (if not with other, outside

institutions) in ways that may go "against the grain" of existing hierarchies.

The information revolution has already raised issues for inter- and
intra-service linkages, and in the case of coalition warfare, for inter-
military linkages. Cyberwar doctrine may require such linkages. It
may call for particularly close communication, consultation, and coordination between the officers in charge of strategy, plans, and operations, and those in charge of C^{3}I, not to mention units in the field.

Operational and tactical command in cyberwar may be exceptionally
demanding. There may be little of the traditional chain of command
to evaluate every move and issue each new order. Commanders,
from corps to company levels, may be required to operate with great
latitude. But if they are allowed to act more autonomously than ever,
they may also have to act more as a part of integrated joint operations. Topsight may have to be distributed to facilitate this. Also, the
types and composition of units may undergo striking changes. Instead of divisions, brigades and battalions, cyberwar may require the
creation of combined-arms task forces from each of the services,
something akin to the current Marine Air-Ground Task Force.

There are many historical examples of innovative tinkering with
units during wartime, going back to the creation of the Roman man-
iple as a counter to the phalanx. In modern times, World War II
brought the rise of many types of units never before seen. For example, the U.S. Army began using combat commands or teams composed of artillery-armor-infantry mixes. The German equivalent was
the *Kampfgruppe*. These kinds of units could often fulfill missions
for which larger bodies, even corps, had previously failed. The U.S.
Navy was also an innovator in this area, creating the task force as its
basic operating unit in the Pacific War. Our point here is that what
have often been viewed as makeshift wartime organizational adjust-
ments should now be viewed as a peacetime goal of our standing
forces, to be achieved *before* the onset of the next war.

Force Size Considerations. A cyberwar doctrine and accompanying
organizational and operational changes may allow for reductions in
the overall size of the U.S. armed forces. But if the history of earlier
sea changes in the nature of warfighting is any guide, long-term
prospects for significant reductions are problematic. All revolutions

in warfare have created advantages that became subject to fairly rapid "wasting" because successful innovations were quickly copied.[27]

If both sides in a future conflict possess substantial cyberwar capabilities, the intensity and complexity of that war may well require more rather than fewer forces. The better trained, more skillful practitioner may prevail, but it is likely that having "big battalions" will still be necessary, especially as the relative cyberwar-fighting proficiency of combatants nears parity. In any case, whether future U.S. forces are larger or smaller, they will surely be configured quite differently.

Operational and Tactical Considerations. Cyberwar may also have radical implications at the operational and tactical levels. Tradition-ally, military operations have been divisible into categories of "holding and hitting." Part of a force is used to tie down an oppo-nent, freeing other assets for flank and other forms of maneuvering attacks.[28] Tactically, two key aspects of warfighting have been "fire and movement." Covering fire allows maneuver, with maneuver units then firing to allow fellow units to move. Fire creates maneuver potential. Tactical advance is viewed as a sort of leapfrogging affair.

Cyberwar may give rise to different, if not opposite, principles. Supe-rior knowledge and control of information are likely to allow for "hitting without holding," strategically, and for tactical maneuvers that create optimal conditions for subsequent "fire."

Nuclear Considerations. What of nuclear weapons and cyberwar? Future wars that may involve the United States will probably be non-nuclear, for two reasons. First, the dismantling of the Soviet Union is likely to persist, with further arms reductions making nuclear war highly unlikely. Second, the United States is ill-advised to make nu-clear threats against non-nuclear powers.

Besides the lack of central threat and the normative inhibitions against using nuclear forces for coercive purposes, there is also a practical reason for eschewing them in this context: Bullying could drive an opponent into the arms of a nuclear protector, or spur pro-liferation by the threatened party. However, even a successful prolif-erator will prefer to keep conflicts conventional, since the United States will continue to maintain overwhelming counterforce and countervalue advantages over all nascent nuclear adversaries. Therefore, the likelihood that future wars, even major ones, will be non-nuclear adds all the more reason to make an effort to optimize our capabilities for conventional and unconventional wars by developing a cyberwar doctrine.

In the body of strategic and operational thought surrounding war with weapons of mass destruction, an antecedent of cyberwar is provided. Nuclear counterforce strategies were very much interested in destroying the key communications centers of the opponent, thereby making it impossible for him to command and control far-flung nuclear weapons. The "decapitation" of an opponent's leadership was an inherently cyber principle. All said, though, the dilemmas of mutual deterrence forced this insight into warfighting to remain in a suspended state for some decades.

Before leaving nuclear issues, we would note an exception in the case of naval warfare. Because the United States enjoys an overwhelming maritime preeminence, it is logical that our potential adversaries may seek ways to diminish or extinguish it. Nuclear weapons may thus grow attractive to opponents whose navies are small if the pursuit of their aims requires nullifying our sealift capabilities. A century ago, the French *Jeune Ecole,* by developing swift vessels capable of launching a brand new weapon, the torpedo, sought to counter the Royal Navy's power in international affairs. Today, latter-day navalists of continental or minor powers may be driven to seek their own new weapons.[29]

Fortunately, the U.S. Navy has been following a path that elevates the information and communication dimensions of war to high importance. For, at sea, to be located is to become immediately vulnerable to destruction. In fact, naval war may already be arriving at a doctrine that looks a lot like cyberwar. There may be deep historical reasons for this, in that our naval examples, even from the Napoleonic period, have a strong cyber character.

Suggested Next Steps for Research

Our ideas here are preliminary and tentative, and leave many issues to be sorted out for analysis. Yet we are convinced that these are exciting times for rethinking the theory and practice of warfare—and that cyberwar should be one of the subjects of that rethinking. This is based on our assumption that technological and related organizational innovations will continue moving in revolutionary directions.

We suggest case studies to clarify what ought to be taken into account in developing a cyberwar perspective. As noted earlier, these case studies should include the Vietnam and Gulf conflicts. Combined with other materials—e.g., literature reviews, interviews—about the potential effects of the information revolution, such studies may help to identify the theoretical and operational principles for developing a framework that serves not only for analysis, but potentially also for the formulation of a doctrine that may apply from strategic to tactical levels, and to high- and low-intensity levels of conflict. Such studies may also help distinguish between the technological and the non-technological underpinnings of cyberwar.

We suggest analytical exercises to identify what cyberwar—indeed, the different modalities of cyberwar—may look like in the early 21st century, when the new technologies should be more advanced, reliable, and internetted than at present. These exercises should consider opponents that the United States may face in high- and low-intensity conflicts. The list might include armed forces of the former Soviet Union, North Korea, Iraq, Iran, and Cuba. Cyberwar against a country's command structure may have a special potency when the country is headed by a dictator whose base of national support is narrow.[30] Non-state actors should also be considered as opponents, including some millennialist, terrorist, and criminal (e.g., drug smuggling) organizations that cut across national boundaries. We expect that both cyberwar and netwar may be uniquely suited to fighting non-state actors.

Moreover, we suggest that the exercises consider some potentially unusual opponents and countermeasures. The revolutionary forces of the future may consist increasingly of widespread multi-organizational networks that have no particular national identity, claim to arise from civil society, and include some aggressive groups and individuals who are keenly adept at using advanced technology, for communications as well as munitions. How will we deal with that? Can cyberwar (not to mention netwar) be developed as an appropriate, effective response? Do formal institutions have so much difficulty combating informal networks—as noted earlier—that the

United States may want to design new kinds of military units and capabilities for engaging in network warfare?

All of the foregoing may lead to requirements for new kinds of net assessments regarding U.S. cyberwar capabilities relative to those of our potential opponents. How much of an advantage does the U.S. have at present? How long will the advantage persist? Such assessments should compare not only the capabilities of all parties to wage and/or withstand a cyberwar, but also their abilities to learn, identify and work around an opponent's vulnerabilities.

Finally, despite the inherently futuristic tone of this think piece, two dangers are developing in the world that may be countered through the skillful application of netwar and cyberwar techniques. The first comes from the proliferation of weapons of mass destruction. While the specifics of acquisition and timetables for development of credible, secure arsenals are open to debate, American opposition to proliferation is unquestioned; effective action must be taken now to forestall or prevent it.

The prospects for proliferation in the post–Cold War era create a highly appropriate issue area for the application of netwar techniques, since suasion will be much preferred to the use of preventive force[31] in dealing with most nation-state actors (including Germany and Japan, should either ever desire its own nuclear weapons). A netwar designed to dissuade potential proliferators from acquiring such weapons might consist of a "full court press" along the many networks of communication that link us to them (including diplomatic, academic, commercial, journalistic and private avenues of interconnection). The ideational aspect of the netwar would concentrate on convincing potential proliferators that they have no need for such weapons. Obtaining them would create new enemies and new risks to their survival, while the benefits would be minuscule and fleeting.

The second danger likely to arise in the post–Cold War world is to regional security. American defense spending is likely to continue decreasing for at least the next decade. U.S. forces will be drawn down, and overseas deployments curtailed. The number of air wings and carrier battle groups will decrease. Each of these developments spells a lessened American capability to effect successful deterrence against conventional aggression. From South Korea to the South Asian subcontinent, from the Persian Gulf to the Balkans and across the territory of the former Soviet satellites to the Baltic Sea, American forward presence will vary between modest and nonexistent. Indeed, when we consider the likely rise of age-old ideological, religious, ethnic and territorial rivalries, we see a world in which regional deterrence is going to be a problematic practice.

If regional wars are likely, and if American forces will be fewer and farther away from most regions than in the past, then a cyberwar doctrine may help to compensate for problems of distance and small force size. If we are correct about the implications of cyberwar—that traditional force requirements against opponents varying in size and strength no longer hold—then the United States ought to be able to hurl back aggressors, when it chooses, even with relatively small forces. General Colin Powell summarizes the essence of this notion succinctly, based on his analysis of the Gulf War:

> A downsized force and a shrinking defense budget result in an increased reliance on technology, which must provide the force multiplier required to ensure a viable military deterrent.... Battlefield information systems became the ally of the warrior. They did much more than provide a service. Personal computers were force multipliers (Powell, 1992).

While a cyberwar doctrine should provide us with robust warfighting capabilities against the largest regional aggressors, we must recognize that the small size and (perhaps) unusual look of our forces may have less of an "intimidation effect" on our future adversaries, thereby vitiating crisis and deterrence stability. There are two ways to mitigate this emergent dilemma. First, applying netwar techniques in regions that bear upon our interests may provide early warning signals, and an opportunity to dissuade a potential aggressor as soon as we become aware of his intentions. The second means of shoring up regional deterrence consists of signaling our resolve tacitly. This may involve the deployment or "show" of military force quite early in a crisis, and could even include the exemplary use of our military capabilities.[32] Indeed, if this sort of signaling were aimed at targets suggested by cyberwar doctrine, such as critical communication nodes, the aggressor's capabilities for offensive action might come close to being nil from the outset.

What might a cyberwar against a regional aggressor look like? In broad terms, it would follow a "Pusan-Inchon" pattern.[33] First, the aggressor's "knockout blow" would have to be blunted. Then, American forces would counterattack. The burden of preventing a complete overrun at the outset of a war would surely fall heavily upon the U.S. Air Force and its ability to knock out the attacker's communications and logistics. The details will vary across regions, because some attackers may be more vulnerable to strategic paralysis than others. For example, future Iraqi aggression against the Arabian peninsula would depend on its ability to use a few roads and two bridges across the Tigris River. On the other hand, North Korea has many avenues of advance to the South.

The forces needed to roll back aggression would likely be modest in size. Since the invader will have been blinded by the time U.S. ground forces arrive, the latter will be able to strike where and when they wish. On the Arabian peninsula, for example, even an invading army of a million men would not be able to hold out against an American cyberwar, particularly if a defensive lodgement had been maintained. The attacker, not knowing where the Americans might strike, would have to disperse his forces over a theater measured in many hundreds of kilometers in each direction. American air power would blind him and destroy his forces attempting to maneuver. Then, counterattacking forces would strike where least expected, destroying the invader's very ability to fight as a cohesive force. As the Mongols defeated an army some ten times their size in the campaign against Khwarizm, so modern cyberwarriors should be able routinely to defeat much larger forces in the field. Of course, details will vary by region. Again, the Korean example would be a bit more complicated, although the lack of strategic depth on that peninsula is more than offset by robust South Korean defensive capabilities.

It seems clear that a cyberwar doctrine will give its able practitioner the capability to defeat conventional regional aggression between nation-states decisively, at low cost in blood and treasure. Will it fare as well against unconventional adversaries? This is a crucial question, as many, notably Van Creveld (1991), have argued that war is being transformed by non-state actors, and by smaller states that must ever think of new ways to fight and defeat their betters. Thus, crises will likely be characterized by large, well-armed irregular forces, taking maximum advantage of familiar terrain, motivated by religious, ethnic or tribal zeal. Finally, these forces may move easily within and between the "membranes" of fractionated states.

Cyberwar may not provide a panacea for all conflicts of this type, but it does create a new, useful framework for coping with them. For example, in the former Yugoslavia, where all of the above factors have manifested themselves, the U.S. Army's AirLand Battle, or even Operation Desert Storm, should not be used as models for analysis. These frames of reference lead to thinking that an entire field army (400,000–500,000 troops) is the appropriate tool for decisive warfighting in this environment. Instead, an intervention could easily follow cyberwar's "Pusan-Inchon" approach to regional conflict. For example, indigenous defenders in Bosnia and other areas of the former Yugoslavia could be armed so that they could prevent any sort of overrun (the campaign's "Pusan"). Next, a small combined arms American task force, including no more than a division of ground troops,[34] might strike opportunistically where and when it chooses (the "Inchon"). Enemy forces would be easily locatable from the air, from radio intercepts, and by unmanned ground sensors, especially if they try to move or fight. The fact that the aggressors are dispersed makes them easier to defeat in detail. If they concentrate, they fall prey to tremendous American firepower.

The Balkan crisis may prove to be a framing event for future unconventional conflicts. It may also provide an important case for developing cyberwar doctrine in this sort of setting. We note, however, that our assessment does not imply support for intervention in this case.

While the advent of cyberwar enables us to feel more comfortable about the prospects for maintaining regional security in an era likely to be characterized by American force drawdowns and withdrawals, there is another concern associated with this sort of warfighting capability. Should the United States seek out coalition partners when it fights future regional wars? It seems obvious that we should, since both international and domestic political problems are mitigated by the vision of a group of nations marching arm in arm, if not in step, against an aggressor. However, we should be concerned about trying to incorporate other nations' armed forces into a cyberwar campaign. Aside from difficulties with integration, the United States should not be in any hurry to share a new approach, particularly with allies who may have been recruited on an ad hoc basis. It's one thing to take a long-standing ally like Britain into our confidence. Syria is quite another matter. Perhaps this new tension can be resolved by having our allies defend the lodgements, the "Pusans," while we engage in the "Inchons." It is ironic that our ability to fight and win wars in accordance with the principles of the information revolution may require us to withhold our new-found insights, even from our friends and allies.

BIBLIOGRAPHY

Arnett, Eric H., *Gunboat Diplomacy and the Bomb: Nuclear Proliferation and the U.S. Navy*, New York: Praeger, 1989.

———, "Welcome to Hyperwar," *The Bulletin of the Atomic Scientists*, Vol. 48, No. 7, September 1992, pp. 14–21.

Arquilla, John, "Nuclear Proliferation: Implications for Conventional Deterrence." In Arquilla and Preston Niblack, eds., *American Grand Strategy in the Post–Cold War World*, Santa Monica: RAND, 1992a.

———, "Louder Than Words: Tacit Communication in International Crises," *Political Communication*, Vol. 9, pp. 155–172, 1992b.

Bankes, Steve, and Carl Builder, *The Etiology of European Change*, Santa Monica: RAND, 1990.

———, "Seizing the Moment: Harnessing the Information Technologies," *The Information Society*, Vol. 8, No. 1, 1992, pp. 1–59.

Bell, Daniel, "The Social Framework of the Information Society," in Tom Forester (ed.), *The Micro Electronics Revolution: The Complete Guide to the New Technology and Its Impact on Society*, The MIT Press, Cambridge, Mass., 1980, pp. 500–549.

Bellamy, Chris, *The Future of Land Warfare*, London: Helm, 1987.

Benedikt, Michael, ed., *Cyberspace: First Steps*, Cambridge: MIT Press, 1991.

Beniger, James, *The Control Revolution*, Cambridge, MA: Harvard University Press, 1986.

Bracken, Paul, "Electronics, Sensors, and Command and Control in the Developing World: An Overview of the Issues," draft prepared for discussion at the AAAS Workshop on Advanced Weaponry in the Developing World, Westfields Conference Center, Virginia, June 1992.

Brodie, Bernard, *A Guide to Naval Strategy*, Princeton: Princeton University Press, 1944.

Caven, Brian, *The Punic Wars*, New York: St. Martin's Press, 1980.

Chambers, James, *The Devil's Horsemen*, New York: Atheneum, 1985.

Clausewitz, Carl von, *On War*, Ed. and trans. by Michael Howard and Peter Paret, Princeton: Princeton University Press, 1976.

Curtin, Jeremiah, *The Mongols*, Boston: Little, Brown, 1908.

De Landa, Manuel, *War in the Age of the Intelligent Machines*, New York: Zone Books, 1991.

Delbruck, Hans, *History of the Art of War*, 3 vols. Westport, CT: Greenwood Press, 1985 edn.

Drucker, Peter F., *The New Realities: In Government and Politics, In Economics and Business, In Society and World View*, New York: Harper and Row, Publishers, 1989.

———, "The Coming of the New Organization," *Harvard Business Review*, January–February 1988, reprinted in the unauthored book *Revolution in Real Time: Managing Information Technology in the 1990s*, A Harvard Business Review Book, 1990.

Gelernter, David, *Mirror Worlds, or the Day Software Puts the Universe in a Shoebox . . . How It Will Happen and What It Will Mean*, New York: Oxford University Press, 1991.

Gibson, William, *Neuromancer*, New York: Ace Books, 1984.

Grier, Peter, "The Data Weapon," *Government Executive*, June 1992, pp. 20–23.

Grimble, Ian, *The Sea Wolf: The Life of Admiral Cochrane*, London: Blond & Briggs, 1978.

Guderian, Heinz, *Panzer Leader*, New York: Ballantine Books, Inc., 1972 edn.

Kenney, George, and Michael J. Dugan, "Operation Balkan Storm: Here's a Plan," *The New York Times*, November 29, 1992.

Lamb, Harold, *Genghis Khan*, New York: Macmillan, 1927.

Lawrence, Thomas E., *Seven Pillars of Wisdom*, New York: Double-day, 1938 edn.

Liddell Hart, Sir Basil H., *Great Captains Unveiled*, New York: Put-nam's, 1931.

————, *History of the Second World War*, New York: Putnam's, 1970.

Malone, Thomas W., and John F. Rockart, "Computers, Networks and the Corporation, *Scientific American*, September 1991, pp. 128–136.

Mao Zedong, trans. by Samuel Griffith, *On Guerrilla Warfare*, New York: Praeger Books, 1961 edn.

Mellenthin, F. W. von, *Panzer Battles*, New York: Ballantine Books, Inc., 1976 edn.

Miles, Milton E., *A Different Kind of War*, New York: Doubleday, 1968.

Posen, Barry R., *The Sources of Military Doctrine*, Ithaca: Cornell University Press, 1984.

Powell, Colin L., "Information-Age Warriors," *Byte*, July 1992, p. 370.

Rona, Thomas P., *Weapon Systems and Information War*, Seattle: Boeing Aerospace Co., July 1976.

Ronfeldt, David, *Cyberocracy, Cyberspace, and Cyberology: Political Effects of the Information Revolution*, Santa Monica: RAND, 1991.

————, "Cyberocracy Is Coming," *The Information Society*, Vol. 8, #4, 1992.

Sproull, Lee, and Sara Kiesler, *Connections: New Ways of Working in the Networked Organization*, Cambridge: MIT Press, 1991.

————, "Computers, Networks and Work," *Scientific American*, September 1991, pp. 116–123.

Stolfi, R.H.S., *Hitler's Panzers East: World War II Reinterpreted*, Tulsa: University of Oklahoma Press, 1992.

Toffler, Alvin, *Powershift: Knowledge, Wealth, and Violence at the Edge of the 21st Century*, New York: Bantam Books, 1990.

Van Creveld, Martin, *Command in War*, Cambridge: Harvard Press, 1985.

————, *Technology and War: From 2000 B.C. to the Present*, New York: The Free Press, 1989.

————, *The Transformation of War*, New York: Free Press, 1991.

Waltz, Kenneth N., *Theory of International Politics*, New York: Random House, 1979.

Weigley, Russell F., "War and the Paradox of Technology" (review of Van Creveld, 1989), *International Security*, Fall 1989, pp. 192–202.

NOTES

[1]Delbruck (1985 edn.) describes warfare as a dual phenomenon: it may be waged with either "exhaustion" or "annihilation" in mind.

[2]This notion borrows from an earlier Soviet notion of a Scientific Technology Revolution (STR).

[3]Weigley (1989: 196), quoting Van Creveld (1989: 1).

[4]See Bell (1980), Beniger (1986), and Toffler (1990).

[5]The literature on these points is vast. Recent additions include: Bankes and Builder (1991), Malone and Rockart (September 1991), Ronfeldt (1991), Sproull and Keisler (1991, and September 1991), and Toffler (1990).

[6]Ronfeldt, "Institutions, Markets, and Networks," in preparation.

[7]Terms with "cyber-" as the prefix—e.g., cyberspace—are currently in vogue among some visionaries and technologists who are seeking names for new concepts related to the information revolution. The prefix is from the Greek root *kybernan*, meaning to steer or govern, and a related word *kybernetes*, meaning pilot, governor, or helmsman. The prefix was introduced by Norbert Wiener in the 1940s in his classic works creating the field of "cybernetics" (which is related to *cybernétique*, an older French word meaning the art of government). Some readers may object to our additions to the lexicon, but we prefer them to alternative terms like "information warfare," which has been used in some circles to refer to warfare that focuses on C^{3}I capabilities. In our view, a case exists for using the prefix in that it bridges the fields of information and governance better than does any other available prefix or term. Indeed, *kybernan*, the

root of "cyber-," is also the root of the word "govern" and its extensions. Perhaps rendering the term in German would help. A likely term would be *Leitenkrieg*, which translates loosely as "control warfare" (our thanks to Denise Quigley for suggesting this term).

[8]We are indebted to Carl Builder for observing that the information revolution may have as much impact on the "context" as on the "conduct" of warfare, and that an analyst ought to identify how the context may change before he or she declares how a military's conduct should change.

[9]The difficult term is "information"—defining it remains a key problem of the information revolution. While no current definition is satisfactory, as a rule many analysts subscribe to a hierarchy with data at the bottom, information in the middle, and knowledge at the top (some would add wisdom above that). Like many analysts, we often use the term "information" (or "information-related") to refer collectively to the hierarchy, but sometimes we use the term to mean something more than data but less than knowledge. Finally, one spreading view holds that new information amounts to "any difference that makes a difference."

[10]The importance of topsight is identified by Gelernter (1991: 52), who observes: "If you're a software designer and you can't master and subdue monumental complexity, you're dead: your machines don't work. They run for a while and then sputter to a halt, or they never run at all. Hence, 'managing complexity' must be your goal. Or, we can describe exactly the same goal in a more positive light. We can call it *the pursuit of topsight*. Topsight—an understanding of the big picture—is an essential goal of every software builder. It's also the most precious intellectual commodity known to man."

[11]Van Creveld (1985:264) puts it this way: "From Plato to NATO, the history of command in war consists essentially of an endless quest for certainty . . . ."

[12]See Caven (1980).

[13]Brodie (1944) and Grimble (1978) describe Cochrane's methods in some detail.

[14]Chambers (1985) is the principal reference to Mongol military doctrine for this paper. Curtin (1908) translated the original Mongol sagas, rendering them with eloquence and coherence. Lamb (1927) remains an important exposition of Genghis Khan's approach to strategy.

[15]Perhaps this is why the Mongols slaughtered besieged forces (and civilian supporters) who resisted their attacks. As word of this brutality spread, fewer cities resisted (a gruesome example of netwar).

[16]Domestic political strife within the Mongol empire also played a part in halting operations.

[17]Kilawan also showed sensitivity to the importance of command and control at the tactical level. At the outset of the battle of Hims, for example, he sent one of his officers, feigning desertion, over to the Mongol commander, Mangku-Temur. When close enough, the Mameluke officer struck Temur in the face with his sword. At the same moment the Mamelukes attacked. The Mongol staff officers, tending to Temur, were thus distracted during the crucial, opening phase of the battle, which contributed to their defeat. See Chambers (1985: 160-162).

[18]See Liddell Hart (1931), wherein his early formulation of armored maneuver warfare mentions the Mongols as a possible model for *blitzkrieg*.

[19]The memoirs of Guderian (1972) and Mellenthin (1976) are replete with examples of how radio communication allowed German armor to concentrate fire until a target was destroyed, then shift to a new target. In particular, fire would be initially concentrated on enemy tanks flying command pennants, as the Germans were aware of the radio deficiencies of their foes. Though the Russians were heavily victimized by communication inferiority, even France, with its superior numbers of heavier armed tanks, suffered in 1940 because, while all armor had radios, only command vehicles could transmit. The French also suffered because they deployed their tanks evenly along the front instead of counterconcentrating them. Finally, it is interesting to note that Guderian began his career as a communications officer.

[20]Stolfi (1992) contends that the German "right turn" into the Ukraine fatally compromised Hitler's only chance of winning a war with the Soviet Union by striking at the heart of its strategic communications. Liddell Hart (1970:157–170) refers to the debate over whether to attack Moscow directly, or to destroy Soviet field armies, as the "battle of the theories," which was won by the "proponents of military orthodoxy."

[21]Mao (1961) bases his theoretical point about guerrilla warfare on his experience in fighting the Japanese who, as the Americans would in Vietnam, focused primarily on the disruption of tactical communications. Miles (1968) echoes Mao's point in his analysis of the same conflict. Lawrence's (1938) analysis of the Desert Revolt is also confirmatory.

[22]See the earlier quotation from Sproull and Kiesler (1991).

[23]Posen (1984: 36).

[24]This is another new term that some visionaries and practitioners have begun using. For example, see Benedikt (1991). It comes from the seminal "cyberpunk" science-fiction novel by Gibson (1984). It is the most encompassing of the terms being tried out for naming the new realm of electronic knowledge, information, and communications—parts of which exist in the hardware and software at specific sites, other parts in the transmissions flowing through cables or through air and space. General Powell (1992) nods in this direction by referring to "battlespace" as including an "infosphere."

[25]Bellamy (1987) grapples with some of these issues in his analysis of future land warfare.

[26]Note that the acclaimed U.S. intelligence in Desert Storm rarely got to the division commanders; for them, every major encounter with the enemy's forces reportedly was a surprise. See Grier (1992).

[27]Waltz (1979) considers this phenomenon of "imitation" a major factor in the process of "internal balancing" with which all nations are continually occupied. If a new military innovation is thought to work, all will soon follow the innovator. A good example of this is the abrupt and complete shift of the world's navies from wooden to metal hulls in the wake of the naval experience with ironclads in the American Civil War.

[28]A classic example is the 1944 battle for Normandy. Field Marshal Montgomery's forces tied down the German Seventh Army, allowing General Patton's Third Army to engage in a broad end run of the German defenses.

[29]The authors are grateful to Gordon McCormick for his insights on this topic. Also on this point, see Arnett (1989).

[30]This last point is inspired by the thinking of RAND colleague Ken Watman.

[31]There is a class of proliferator toward which our reluctance to employ forceful measures will be diminished. Iraq, Iran, North Korea, Libya and Cuba are some of the nations whose threatened acquisition of weapons of mass destruction may justify intervention. The notion that the United States should adopt a doctrine of "selective preventive force" against "outlaw" states is discussed in Arquilla (1992a).

[32]Arquilla (1992b) discusses this issue in detail.

[33]This notion is drawn from the Korean War, where U.S. forces began their involvement by preventing the overrun of the Korean peninsula in the opening months of the war. The Pusan perimeter held a portion of South Korea free, serving as a magnet for North Korean forces. The amphibious counterattack at Inchon, far from the battle fronts, threw the invaders into complete disarray.

[34]Kenney and Dugan (1992) call for a "Balkan Storm" without employing *any* American ground forces. We disagree with this approach, rooted as it is in theories of "limited liability" and "air power exceptionalism." Nonetheless, they do identify many of the key types of aerial cyberwar tactics that might be employed, even if their omission of an American ground component would seriously dilute any gains achieved.

Chapter Three

PREPARING FOR THE NEXT WAR: REFLECTIONS ON THE REVOLUTION IN MILITARY AFFAIRS*

Stephen J. Blank

All strategizing occurs under duress, e.g., in the context of the burden of defeat, permanently perceived threats, or simply the eternal scarcity of resources needed to materialize a vision of future war. Reality always constrains strategists' vision and nations' capabilities.

Commanders recognize that the actual clash of arms takes belligerents, as chessplayers say, "out of the books" into *terra incognita* or the fog of war. Since no plan survives actual combat, and the art of forecasting is imperfect, efforts to predict with certainty the future of today's revolution in military affairs (RMA) must inevitably fail. Any view of the RMA will necessarily be only a partial one. Indeed, despite the acceptance of the reality of the RMA, there is still a great deal of argument about its nature, extent, implications, and utility for all kinds of armed conflict.[1]

Nevertheless we must ponder those visible aspects of the revolution in military affairs if we hope to prevail in future wars. Obviously we cannot mechanically assume a linear progression from Operation Desert Storm to the next war. Indeed, some analysts believe that war on that scale is doomed to extinction.[2] If so, the militaries of the U.S. and most other major states face either wrenching and cataclysmic transformations, or future irrelevance as they become grossly mal-

*Stephen J. Blank, "Preparing for the Next War," *Strategic Review*, Vol. 24, No. 2, Spring 1996, pp. 17–25. U.S. Strategic Institute. Used by permission.

adapted to future small wars. Still, many analysts believe that Operation Desert Storm established the technological paradigm for future warfare in which information technologies, and electronic fire strikes are critical. According to that view, electronic operations will be decisive in their own right, and aero-space systems incorporating electronic and information technologies will take warfare into a third dimension.[3]

The costs of maximizing technology's potential impose serious socio-economic burdens as a consequence of the arduous effort necessary to keep abreast of an accelerating rate of change. During times of economic stringency such as our own, leaders concentrate on the immediate future, not on distant strategic horizons and unglamorous issues of economic preparedness and mobilization. But if we are to fight high-tech wars in the future, we must raise those issues now. Only then can we manufacture and procure technologies, systems, and forces that will allow us to perform credibly in future wars.

THE REVOLUTION IN MILITARY AFFAIRS

The impact of this revolution and its policy requirements are widely debated, not only in the U.S. but worldwide. For instance, it is not certain that the United States can maintain its technological superiority without substantial allied contributions. War games conducted by the Pentagon's Office of Net Assessment prominently featured advanced technology and systems in pitting China against the United States in the year 2020. Reportedly, the outcome of the game was unfavorable for the United States.[4]

Technology alone cannot guarantee victory. Future military success does not only mean obtaining high-tech platforms, but also effectively optimizing and organizing forces to supply, use, and command them. What strategies developed under the duress of technological competition will permit the United States to conduct future high-tech wars? What synergies and social changes are needed to stay ahead of the curve in this revolution?

Paul Bracken notes that to master military revolutions, an army or state must successfully move from a coherent, well-developed vision of future war to viable operational concepts that the armed forces can use in war. But those operational concepts are realizable only when practical, substantive organizational transformations or adaptations that optimize the armed forces' ability to realize those concepts occur.[5] States seeking strategic superiority via technological superiority must undergo substantive organizational transformation that enhances adaptability. Today, states move from technological to strategic superiority by achieving organizational superiority. Organizational transformations translate superior technology into superior strategic performance because organization is itself a form of technology. Moreover, the importance of organizational change grows during periods of technological innovation.

> The U.S. can no longer rely on technological advantages to sustain economic and military leadership . . . . The competition in both areas will focus on adaptations of new technologies in organizational structures that are flexible enough to continuously reinvent themselves and that can exploit the connections made possible by the information technology revolution. . . . the real constraints will increasingly shift, however, from access to advanced technology or physical networks to the ability to develop new organizations capable of exploiting precision, flexibility, and integration. The incentives to absorb the inevitable transition costs will come from dynamic, adaptive global organizational networks. The key will not be to protect U.S. institutions from today's competitors, but to nurture patterns of innovation that will exploit new opportunities.[6]

This becomes particularly difficult when trends in defense industry are forcing all defense firms to compete and diffuse their civilian and defense know-how and products globally to survive. Since much new defense technology is dual-use and stems from civilian innovations, techniques, and applications which are difficult to protect, production techniques and even innovation itself are undergoing constant global diffusion. Brisk global competition forces firms into constant struggles to innovate and maximize their organizational capabilities.

> This reality calls into question the viability of defense industrial sectors which fail to develop adequate links to global technology markets. The ability to achieve competence in civilian production and defense-industrial applications is becoming increasingly intertwined. At the same time, market access in the developing world (e.g. in East Asia) increasingly requires technology sharing as an instrument of commercial competition.[7]

Defense industries that cannot adapt, fail or are consolidated into fewer ones.[8] Technology approaches its potential only where a comparable organizational response exists.

Desert Storm illustrates the point that technological innovation alone does not answer strategists' and commanders' prayers. Despite the talk of Desert Storm's air war as a high-tech template validating Douhet's goal of an exclusively aerial strategic operation, most allied platforms dated from the 1960s and 1970s.[9] What was new was the ability to combine them effectively in a new operational plan using new concepts to optimize their strategic potential. The real innovations were organizational adaptation and new operational concepts. Those changes then let commanders think in new ways about using air power, space, and electronic warfare to achieve decisive results. Study of that war indicates that continuing organizational transformation to enhance individual and unit performance, C^2, and new operational concepts is essential to maintain our edge.

Hence organizational imperatives allow field commanders to optimize current and projected technological trends. A recent study of the Air Operations Center ties this organizational and operational response to a new vision or template of warfare.

> The 1991 war in the Middle East offered a new template for modern conflict—strategic conventional war. "Strategic," because many of the targets struck by the air were unrelated to immediate battlefield outcomes, and "conventional," since these targets were attacked with high explosive (and in some cases, non lethal) weapons. Since the advent of atomic weapons, most Air Force doctrine did not even include strategic attack as a mission for the conventional bomber force. In short, there was "no such animal" as strategic conventional war. Yet, six weeks of air war in the Gulf, followed by a short, conclusive ground campaign, energized Air Force proponents of a strategic *conventional* attack against the sources of enemy military capability.[10]

While these observations suggest the sterility of an Air Force strategic doctrine that, despite all the wars since 1945, denied the possibility of strategic conventional war, they also validate Bracken's insights. Only when forced "out of the books" did the Air Force formulate a new template of war and novel operational concepts. Those concepts were available and feasible because of prior innovations in aviation, space, and electronic weaponry, even though doctrine denied their utility and feasibility in warfare. Now the changes wrought by the air campaign over Iraq must be buttressed and institutionalized by organizational changes.

TECHNOLOGY AND ORGANIZATION: LESSONS FROM SOVIET RUSSIA

It is not unprecedented for great strategic visionaries who forge profoundly innovative operational concepts to be unable to implement the policies and organizational adaptations needed to realize their vision in the defense, economic, social-organizational, and/or operational spheres. This happened twice in the Soviet Union: the first failure almost led to the country's demise in World War II; the second failure was instrumental in its ultimate collapse.

In the first instance of Soviet strategic failure, the military could not defend the strategic vision and operational concepts that it had created. Stalin's purges and suppression of independent thinking among commanders precluded viable organizational adaptation of the national command authority. Thus the farseeing ideas of the post-1917 generation, Triandafillov, Tukhachevsky, Svechin, Lapchinsky, etc., were suppressed or discarded. Although it was accepted that the coming war would be a mass war of machines intensely utilizing automotive, aviation, and tank technologies, the effects of the purges, the misapplication of the operational concepts developed during the Spanish Civil War, the belated, incomplete study of German successes in 1939–1940, and the complete incoherence of the command system in 1939–1941 greatly contributed to the Soviet disasters in 1941–1943.[11]

The miserable performance in Finland in 1939–1940 and during 1941–1943 were largely attributable to Stalin's refusal to delegate authority and power to a strategic command system that could enforce the changes needed to adapt to the current wars. Similarly, the economy, while organized for war, was territorially structured. Thus, it was vulnerable to immediate attack. Nor could the forces of 1939–1941 master contemporary high-technology.[12] Accordingly the Soviet military could not devise necessary modern tactics. The result was an appalling failure.

POLITICAL-STRATEGIC IMPLICATIONS

One may also argue that the brilliant commanders who were purged or died before 1941, indeed Stalin himself, failed to thoroughly understand the political-strategic implications of their vision of future war. Evaluation is a necessary and constant feature of a well-oiled organizational system with a well-conceived vision of future war. In postulating mass, mechanized war, and the theory of the deep strike, Tukhachevsky et al. also postulated a revolutionary offensive, i.e. total war.[13] If Russia went to war with another country, it had to be a total war because the outcome of a Soviet victory was the revolution from above and outside of the defeated country. But these thinkers failed to realize that such a theory put the USSR itself at grave risk, because if the offensive failed, the destruction of the Soviet or Stalinist system then might ensue. Any Soviet posture that presumed total war isolated the USSR from potential allies in the West, making it vulnerable to attack, as in 1941, placing its own system at risk. This brilliant Soviet strategic and operational vision promoted only one kind of war: all-or-nothing conflict for both sides.

Opponents of so extreme an offensive vision, such as A.A. Svechin, preached the acceptance of an initial defensive posture during which full mobilization could transpire, i.e., when the Soviet state could fully adapt to total war.[14] Then and only then, could the enemy be annihilated by offensive action. Stalin's preference for avoiding intervention until all of Europe had exhausted itself perhaps owed something to his intuition that the entire system would be placed at risk by the Soviet vision of war.[15]

The failures that attended the war against Finland in 1939–1940 called even Soviet capacity in a war against weak states into question. The unchecked strategic and operational vision of Stalin and his commanders and theorists led to two intolerable scenarios that risked everything. Because nobody could or would articulate the purely organizational and policy innovations needed for the strategic vision to succeed, the USSR in 1941 was caught between incompatible deployments and strategies.[16]

A POLICY-STRATEGY MISMATCH

The second, more recent Soviet failure is equally useful as a caution for forecasters. Only after fifty years could Soviet armed forces execute the operational concepts pioneered by Tukhachevsky et al. The expected Soviet offensive in Europe aimed to reach the Channel within days by means of coordinated deep strikes against NATO using a joint arms approach and even tactical nuclear strikes.[17] As formulated by Chief of Staff Nikolai Ogarkov (1917–1994), this offensive plan entailed a prior sweeping reorganization of command and force structures—with greatly expanded roles for airborne, air assault, naval infantry, and Spetsnaz forces and a greatly transformed relationship between air and ground forces—and Soviet defense industry.

Ogarkov's central point was that the world had entered a new, third revolution in military affairs. Conventional weapons could replace nuclear ones in their effects, while technologies of electronic components, information systems, third-generation nuclear weapons, and aero-space travel must be optimized to provide Soviet forces the means to defeat NATO. Ogarkov and his subordinates knew NATO was embracing those systems: new Soviet operational-strategies, e.g., the Maritime Strategy, Follow-on Forces Attack (FOFA), and Air-Land battle.[18] Indeed the last Soviet Chief of Staff, General Mikhail Moiseev confirmed this author's view that in Operation Desert Storm, the allies successfully executed an ideal version of the Soviet conventional theater offensive.[19]

Once again a brilliant forecast of warfare's future nature and of its associated operational concepts foundered on the shoals of organizational and political response. To realize Ogarkov's vision, Soviet defense industry and the armed forces had to be fundamentally overhauled by massive investments of capital and political will. Yet the regime could not afford the necessary expenses and lacked either the will or vision to transform defense industry. Additionally, other commanders obstructed Ogarkov's programs.[20] Moreover, most political leaders perceived the strategic implications of Ogarkov's script as entailing a vastly more dangerous strategic rivalry with the West.

Accordingly, only the most halting and ill-conceived organizational adaptations were undertaken, and they helped undermine the entire system. The strategic implications of Ogarkov's scenarios for Europe and Asia also arrayed the USSR against the entire world: NATO, the United States, China, Japan, South Korea, Israel, etc. The regime could not sustain the resulting arms race, militarily, economically, or industrially. Consequently Gorbachev was forced into one strategic retreat after another to reduce the burden of a defense industry suited for World War II. Meanwhile, in Afghanistan, the Soviet army showed that in its internal organization, it still could not adapt tactically, strategically, or organizationally to the wars it had to fight. Strategically, the most notable failure of strategic leadership and command was the fact that the USSR began this war apparently against its best professional military advice.

Once again a brilliant strategic forecast of future war and related operational concepts ran aground. The system could not respond to the requirements of a military revolution and make the necessary adaptations. Because there was no scope for organizational innovation, visions of future war could not be materialized nor could anyone show where they ran unwarranted risks or where reality contradicted them. Absent the necessary flexibility, the vision of future war increasingly diverged from the practical means available to implement them. And Russia's invasion of Chechnya, in December 1994 showed a far more advanced state of organizational decomposition and disarray than previously realized.

LESSONS FOR CONSIDERATION

Forecasters of future war and implementers of necessary organizational changes and institutional reforms must ponder these lessons to ensure that we fight our wars and not someone else's. These lessons translate into propositions that are simply stated but difficult to carry out.

First, *the acid test of any vision of future war is the capacity of a state's political leadership and elites to restructure its defense industry, strategic leadership, policy process, and related organizations to realize that vision. That restructuring process, in turn, must clarify what aspects of the new vision and associated operational concepts are too strategically risky or beyond a state's foreseeable capacity.*

Second, *even under conditions of technological superiority, failure to undertake organizational and social innovations or restructuring guarantees that this superiority's impact will be blunted if not negated. In other words, no technology can make up for basic errors in making or implementing strategy.*

States with such superiority have lost wars in which they could not formulate a strategy appropriate to reality. Their organizational and tactical innovations were either misconceived or only partly successful. Vietnam and Bosnia, each in their own way, testify to the result. The ubiquity of such experiences suggests how truly difficult and rare it is to marry vision and a purposeful policy of institutional changes when confronted by a new strategic vision.

BUDGETS AND THE RMA

This returns us to our opening point. Everywhere states are grappling with the RMA's impact when their means of doing so are increasingly circumscribed and their military budgets declining. The U.S. only faces the duress of declining budgets. Others, like Russia, face not only budgetary decline but also the burden of defeat and a pervasive sense of threat. Russia still cannot forge a usable military force.[21] While the United States is sacrificing future systems to current readiness and peace operations, other states may be forging new doctrines, force packages, and economic transformations to maximize their potential. In developing states,

> One of the factors revealed by this perspective on technological diffusion is the importance of organizational and institutional factors to successful defense production and innovation. In particular, domestic systems-integration capabilities are extremely valuable in increasing the technical absorption capabilities of a defense industrial sector. Import substitution in systems integration is thus an important factor in rendering weapons program development efforts robust in the face of foreign technology denial efforts. Not surprisingly, emerging defense industrializers have set the goal of increasing synergies from horizontal technology borrowing and integration within their own defense sectors. This helps foster cooperation and innovation at home, and helps a country to develop indigenous modifications to weapons and related technologies which may in turn create exportable products or processes in the future.

Co-production and co-development in North-South arms transfer agreements intensify the potential for such gains.[22]

The foregoing observations suggest a third lesson; *organization, in and of itself, should also be viewed as a form of applied technology for warfighting purposes.* Only if effective military, political, and defense industrial structures are built can states obtain the force multipliers inherent in new technologies.

The next lesson flows logically from the third one. *Technological superiority, i.e., superior platforms and weapons, mean little without organizational superiority. And organizational superiority alone probably is worth more than superior platforms and weapons. It, not weapons' superiority, is the contemporary equivalent, at least to some degree, of the commander's operational art. Without this, superior weapons have only a tactical significance.*

TECHNOLOGY AND SOCIAL ORGANIZATION

These insights may seem unoriginal, even banal. Such a perception makes them no less useful or fruitful. Modernity's continuous and profound technological changes are inseparable from the parallel revolution in social organization. This is a central seminal insight of pioneers of modern social thought, such as Durkheim and Weber. And the primacy of organizational factors of masses of men and materiel in modern warfare links so disparate a group of "great captains" as Mao Zedong, Lenin and Trotsky, Ho Chi Minh and Vo Nguyen Giap, and Ulysses S. Grant as successful practitioners of far-reaching transformations, if not revolutions in modern warfare. Each in his own way successfully optimized the resources available to them as nobody before them had done.

Current events also validate this insight. In October 1994, anxious to intimidate the allies and the UN into lifting sanctions on Iraq. Saddam Hussein mobilized his forces on Kuwait's border. Within 72 hours thousands of U.S. troops, ships, planes, missiles, etc. were either in the theater or on the way, leading Iraq to retreat. This episode shows the importance of flexible organization. Although U.S. forces are undoubtedly technologically superior and forward deployed against just this possibility, their ability to deploy as a combined force on land, sea, and air within 72–96 hours sufficed to deter Iraq.

Our ability to organize a cohesive, joint, combined arms force that is more than the sum of its parts was crucial. This episode also suggests that organizational flexibility is a greater deterrent than an arsenal of smart bombs and high tech-assets. What counts is usable military power.[23]

Because revolutions transform our understanding of what constitutes usable military power and how it may best be deployed, we cannot simply rely on the information revolution or the digitized battlefield, etc. Technological change increases the importance of strategic vision and operational art (or their functional equivalents) because the boundaries between tactical, operational, and strategic operations or levels are steadily disappearing. In Desert Storm there was only a "first strike," not a campaign.

The October 1994 episode also suggests the dangers lurking in the necessary but risky impending defense cuts. If future developments are to be cut to maintain readiness, we might retain our organizational and technological superiority only to forfeit them in future conflicts. Worse, we may saddle ourselves, not with a hollow force, but rather with one maladapted to many future contingencies.[24] Of course, there is no easy answer to or consensus around the question of how to avoid either danger.

THE UTILITY OF TECHNOLOGICAL SUPERIORITY

Technological superiority as an end in itself has dubious utility and probably is beyond even our means. If not combined with an organizational framework (or frameworks) to optimize the synergies obtained from new technologies and organizations, superior technology possesses only tactical significance. Its initial deployment in war, like the use of mustard gas in 1915, achieves only a tactical local superiority that is not translatable into broader operational or strategic superiority. As with nuclear arms, what ensues is a race to achieve ever more deterrents to the other side's capabilities, few, if any, of which can be safely used.

This is not only a nuclear phenomenon. It happened with the German Navy before World War I, provoking British arms-racing and hostility to Germany. Yet, once war was joined, the German Navy was never used with any strategic effectiveness lest it be lost in battle.

Analogously in 1940, German tanks were neither numerically nor qualitatively superior to Franco-British tanks, but were organized much more effectively at the strategic and operational level. Here organizational superiority based on innovative views of modern war and associated operational concepts was a telling, if not decisive, factor.

Indeed, if the demands of keeping pace with an ever costlier technological revolution outpace a state's organizational and material means for doing so, that state may keep apace with its rivals in perceived military power only to fall further behind in actually usable military power. This was Russia's fate under both Tsarist and Soviet rule: Russia faced an intolerable military burden and its forces became progressively unsustainable. Its military leadership could not accept the requirement to scale back military plans and strategies.

> Meanwhile the Russian army expanded—even during a period of financial stringency—to meet what St. Petersburg perceived as a threat of the first magnitude on the Empire's western borders. Problems of western defense also resurrected the expensive issue of border fortifications. In addition, as the Russians expanded their influence in the Balkans, their boundaries in Central Asia, and their sphere of influence in the Far East, the requirements for military security seemed to grow exponentially. Unfortunately for the Russians, neither the army nor the treasury could keep pace with the combined growth of boundaries, influence, and interest, and once again a dangerous gap opened between state policy and military capability. Rapid technological change contributed to the increasing political, financial, and military complexities of the situation.[25]

Despite repeated lessons, Tsarist leaders rejected the need to choose priorities and cut losses. Thus they triggered a catastrophe that has not yet been overcome. Sadly, this quotation could be written for today with nothing changed, signifying thereby Russia's intractable strategic dilemmas. Indeed, the Soviet leadership had fallen into the same trap by the 1980s.[26]

LESSONS FOR THE U.S.

Our point is not to gloat over Russia's miseries but to encourage constructive thinking about our own intractable dilemmas. We too have spiraling domestic commitments that must be met to maintain the organizational, human, and technological bases of our superiority. And they cannot be met along with multiple peace operations for present contingencies unless the future is sacrificed. To say this is not just a critique of the policy of the current administration. To begin with, some valuable organizational initiatives in procurement are already underway.[27] Nor are all peace operations inherently counterproductive. Rather we recognize an accepted fact that already influences policy. We too must strategize under duress, set priorities, cut losses, etc. Business as usual and preserving obsolete or unsustainable military plant as allegedly still happens, will not save us.

Recent writers have broadened the definition of security to include its economic, ecological, and human bases. In an age of technological explosion and global interdependence, this is probably the appropriate way to treat the question of security. But it offers precious little in the way of an answer. Where warfare has already become five dimensional—land, sea, air, space, electronic (and one could make submarines into a separate dimension)—not only might the volume of information duly obtained overwhelm commanders' ability to exercise command and control or give strategic guidance, ultimately it might prove impossible to organize armed forces to execute a unified strategic vision. Similarly, absent any consensus on the wars and contingencies we might expect, how can we build organizations flexible enough to respond to any threat to national or vital interests?

No definitive answer is possible before actual operations. The Air Force's example strongly confirms this.[28] This is one reason for maneuvers, exercises, etc., as well as for testing operational concepts and organizational adaptations that really do validate new visions of warfare. Undoubtedly there are experiments underway to create new force packages to meet unique contingencies such as in Haiti in 1994.[29] Their relevance to the Persian Gulf or Yugoslavia resides in the creative thinking about tailoring forces to contingencies and to create flexible means of organizing, delivering, and projecting timely military power. Our preexisting superiorities help commanders devise creative replies to unique or unforeseen tactical and strategic challenges. As former Chief of Staff of the Army General Gordon Sullivan wrote, the Army's success in organizing relief efforts for Rwanda's crisis in 1994 represented a triumph of improvisation and flexible organization, not doctrinal foresight or strategic vision about such conflicts.[30]

Accordingly, one cannot stress enough the need for continued, flexible, organizational adaptiveness under current stringent conditions. By striving for technological superiority, we have committed ourselves to achieving a technological surprise on the battlefield, which itself is being revolutionized. But in an age of the globalization of science and of ever higher costs of technology and weapons systems, it seems unlikely that technological surprise will be strategically decisive in the future as it was, e.g., in 1945 with the advent of the atomic bomb.

ORGANIZATIONAL TRANSFORMATION

The United States' progressive inability to fund the cost of protracted theater war, present peace operations, and new platforms has become clear since 1990. Today we rely increasingly on others to supply us with the finances and technologies, or the forward bases and logistical infrastructure needed for military operations. Our quest for qualitative superiority is an ever elusive one whose pursuit entails costs whose implications are only dimly perceived. Thus we have also bound ourselves over to a process that demands continuous organizational transformation, if not revolution, if we are to stay ahead technically. To master the necessary organizational transformations requires much more fidelity to coalition warfare; new, more flexible force packages; dependence on foreign suppliers, organization and coordination of multidimensional warfare; information gathering and dissemination; constant readiness to project power, etc. This in turn requires the constant transformation of our military and political structure, defense industrial base, and overall economy and society.

We have willingly given ourselves over to a revolution whose end is inconceivable, whose nature is under acute debate, whose parameters are also a matter of argument, and whose challenges are perhaps more formidable than ever before. Henceforth, we do not have the luxury of being able to think about these problems before they come. Given the time necessary for weapons development and the other processes involved, we must start serious planning for the years 2015–2020 now. We need to master both the technological and organizational challenges that can already be glimpsed in order to be capable of a viable strategic response to the threats of the future, be they small, protracted theater, and even nuclear wars. Despite our present technological superiority, it is not clear that we fully grasp all the implications of our chosen course.

NOTES

[1] Jeffrey R. Cooper, *Another View of the Revolution in Military Affairs* (Carlisle Barracks, PA: Strategic Studies Institute, U.S. Army War College, 1994), pp. 1–2.

[2] For example Martin van Creveld, *The Transformation of War* (New York: The Free Press, 1991); and *Nuclear Proliferation and the Future of Conflict* (New York: The Free Press, 1994).

[3] Raoul Henri Alcala, "Guiding Principles for Revolution, Evolution, and Continuity in Military Affairs," in Paul Bracken and Raoul Henri Alcala, *Whither the RMA: Two Perspectives on Tomorrow's Army* (Carlisle Barracks, PA: Strategic Studies Institute, U.S. Army War College, 1994), pp. 27–29. As for foreign armed forces, see Jacob W. Kipp, "The General Staff Looks at 'Dessert Storm': Through the Prism of Contemporary Politics," Stephen J. Blank and Jacob W. Kipp, eds., *The Soviet Military and the Future* (Westport, CT: Greenwood Publishing Group, 1992), pp. 115–144. See also Mary C. Fitzgerald, "The Russian Image of Future War" *Comparative Strategy*, XIII, No. 2, Spring, 1994, pp. 167–180.

[4] Thomas E. Ricks, "How Wars Are Fought Will Change Radically, Pentagon Planner Says," *Wall Street Journal*, July 15, 1994, p. 1; and "Top Pentagon Thinker Sees Dramatic Changes for Warfighting Strategy," *Inside the Navy*, August 22, 1994, p. 1.

[5] Paul Bracken, "Future Directions for the Army," in Bracken and Alcala, pp. 1–14. This formulation was taken, however, from his presentation to the U.S. Army War College V Conference on Strategy, April 25–27, 1994. Cooper, pp. 16–26, also emphasizes the importance of organizational adaptation. Andrew Latham, "Military-Technical Revolution: Implications for the Defense Industry," *Canadian Defense Quarterly*, XXIV, No. 4, Summer, 1995, p. 18, conceptualizes these elements as technology, technique (or doctrine), and organization. Eliot Cohen, "The Mystique of U.S. Air Power," *Foreign Affairs*, LXXIII, No. 1, January–February 1994, pp. 116–118, shows the importance in practice of organizational adaptability in Operation Desert Storm.

[6] James R. Golden, *Economics and National Strategy in the Information Age: Global Networks, Technology Policy, and Cooperative competition* (Westport CT: Praeger Publishing Co., 1994) p. 266.

[7] David Mussington, *Arms Unbound: The Globalization of Defense Production* (Cambridge, MA and Washington D.C.: Brassey's 1994), Center for Science and International Affairs, John F. Kennedy School of Government, Harvard University, CSIA Studies in International Security No. 4, pp. 47–48.

[8] This was already apparent in 1992. See Debra Polsky, "Asia States Challenging U.S. Firms," *Defense News*, March 2, 1992, pp. 1,10.

[9] Cohen, p. 112.

[10] Lt. Col. J. Taylor Sink, USAF, *Rethinking the Air Operations Center: Air Force Command and Control in Conventional War*, Thesis Presented to the School of Advanced Airpower Studies, Maxwell AFB, Alabama, September 1994. Sink concludes

by stressing that his suggested remedies are answers to doctrinal and organizational problems. Sink, p. 52 (Italics in original).

[11]Jacob W. Kipp, "Barbarossa, Soviet Covering Forces and the Initial Period War: Military History and Airland Battle," Soviet Army Studies Office, Ft. Leavenworth, KS, 1987.

[12]Ibid.

[13]Mikhail Tukhachevsky, "A Collection of Articles by the Red Army's Leading Military Theoretician," Art of War Colloquium, U.S. Army War College May 1983, pp. 52–58.

[14]Alexander A. Svechin, *Strategy*, ed. and trans. by Kent D. Lee, with Introductory Essays by Andrei A. Kokoshin, Valentin V. Larionov, Vladimir N. Lobov, Jacob W. Kipp (Minneapolis MN: East View Publications, 1992).

[15]In his famous speech of February 9, 1946, Stalin claimed that the imperialists thought the whole system was a "house of cards." Given his penchant for projecting his fears onto others, this may have reflected his deepest concern.

[16]Kipp, "Barbarossa," pp. 23–31.

[17]Lothar Ruehl, "Offensive Defense in the Warsaw Pact," *Survival*, XXXIII, No. 4, September–October 1991, pp. 442–450; Michael Boll, "The Evolution in Soviet Military Doctrine, 1984–1994," in LTC James F. Holcomb and Michael M. Boll, *Russia's New Doctrine: Two Views* (Carlisle Barracks, PA: Strategic Studies Institute, U.S. Army War College, 1994), pp. 18–19; and Beatrice Heuser, "Warsaw Pact Military Doctrine in the 1970's and 1980's: Findings in the East German Archives, "*Comparative Strategy*, XII No. 4, October–December 1993, p. 451.

[18]This is precisely the way Cooper too understands Ogarkov. See Cooper, p. 27; and Dale Herspring, *The Soviet High Command 1967–1989: Personalities and Politics* (Princeton, NJ: Princeton University Press, 1990); Rose Gottemoeller, "Intramilitary Conflict in the Soviet Armed Forces," Bruce Parrot, Ed., *The Dynamics of Soviet Defense Policy* (Washington, DC: Wilson Center Press, 1990), pp. 79–118.

[19]Stephen J. Blank, *The Soviet Military Views Operation Desert Storm: A Preliminary Assessment* (Carlisle Barracks, PA: Strategic Studies Institute, U.S. Army War College, 1991), pp. 31–33. Moiseev's reaction was related by Dr. Tyrus Cobb, then of the Center for Naval Analyses.

[20]Herspring, passim; Gottemoeller, pp. 79–118; Stephen J. Blank, "New Strategists Who Demand the Old System," *Orbis*, XXXVI, No. 3, Summer 1992, pp. 365–378.

[21]This is still the case, as Russia's crisis in military spending shows. Stephen J. Blank, *Reform and the Revolution in Russia's Defense Economics* (Carlisle Barracks, PA: Strategic Studies Institute, U.S. Army War College, 1995), pp. 24–28.

[22]Mussington, p. 62.

[23]Bradley Graham, "Rapid Deployment Plans in the Crucible," *Washington Post*, October 11, 1994, p. A12.

[24]Dov Zakheim, "Haiti Deployment Has Many Costs," *Defense News*, October 10–16, 1994, pp. 23–24.

[25]Bruce W. Menning, *Bayonets Before Bullets, The Imperial Russian Army*, 1861–1914 (Bloomington, IN: Indiana University Press, 1992), p. 92.

[26]Blank, "New Strategists," pp. 365–378. Victor Glukhikh, Chairman of the Russian State Committee for the Defense Industry, recently stated that if Russia cannot sell arms abroad, it could not afford to develop new weapons with which to defend itself. See Foreign Broadcast Information Service, *Central Eurasia*, September 26, 1994, p. 23.

[27]Kenneth Allard, "It's Not Very Flashy, But the Payoff Is Real," *Washington Post Weekly*, October 10–16, 1994, p. 41.

[28]Sink, pp. 47–48.

[29]John F. Harris, "Military's Rapid Switch in Haiti a Tactical Win for Joint-force Planner," *Washington Post*, September 28, 1994, p. A21,

[30]General Gordon R. Sullivan and Lt. Anthony M. Coroalles, *Seeing the Elephant: Leading America's Army into the Twenty-First Century* (Carlisle Barracks, PA: Strategic Studies Institute, U.S. Army War College, 1995), pp. 42–43.

Chapter Four

AN INFORMATION-BASED REVOLUTION IN MILITARY AFFAIRS*

Norman C. Davis

The world is on the cusp of an epochal shift from an industrial- to an information-based society. History demonstrates that changes of this magnitude do not occur without being accompanied by fundamental change in the way war is conducted.[1] This "Information Revolution" is a product of advances in computerized information and telecommunications technologies and related innovations in management and organizational theory.

Today, rapid and far-reaching changes are occurring in how information is collected, stored, processed, and disseminated, and in how organizations are designed to take advantage of this increased availability of information.[2] The Information Revolution is setting in motion forces that challenge the design of many institutions. It disrupts the hierarchies around which modern institutions—particularly military institutions—traditionally have been designed. It diffuses and redistributes power, often to the benefit of those that once may have been considered lesser actors. These changes will inevitably have a profound impact on the means and ends of armed conflict.[3]

*Norman Davis, "An Information-Based Revolution in Military Affairs," *Strategic Review*, Vol. 24, No. 1, Winter 1996, pp. 43–53. U.S. Strategic Institute. Used by permission.

HISTORICAL CONTEXT

Following the Persian Gulf War, many authors focused on the impressive array of high-technology weapons that allowed the U.S.-led coalition to overwhelm the world's fourth largest army in a remarkably short time. They used this conflict as evidence that a Military-Technical Revolution (MTR) had occurred.[4] Unfortunately, use of the term MTR denotes an inordinate emphasis on the importance of technology at the expense of other elements of revolutionary change.[5] For this reason, revolution in military affairs (RMA) is the preferable term as it places the focus on the *revolution*, and implicitly assigns *technology* a supporting role.

CHARACTERISTICS OF RMAs

There are, by definition, significant differences between evolutionary and revolutionary change. In the security context, these differences can be described as follows:

> Evolution is the logical progression of an existing system or framework, while revolution connotes a fundamental break with precedent.... Performance improvements which signal tactical revolutions very rarely justify revolution at the operational or strategic level. A truly revolutionary strategic development alters perceptions of the relationship of means to ends and, most importantly, dictates a reformulation of warfighting doctrine—the codified precepts that govern [military] operations.[6]

Accordingly, revolutions are not merely more clever technological (or organizational) breakthroughs than ordinary evolutionary innovations; these revolutions are more profound in both their sources and implications.[7] They involve fundamental discontinuities, i.e., dramatic breaks with the existing status quo. It is important to recognize that a revolution is not simply an existential condition—i.e., created simply by the appearance of new technological capabilities. Without recognition and exploitation, both requiring positive action, there can be no revolution. Creating a revolution is, therefore, more than pushing the limits of military technology; it is an active process that requires effective adaptation by individuals and organizations for successful exploitation to occur.[8]

Implications of a revolutionary new technology are often not widely recognized at first. Frequently, organizations try to fit the innovative technology into established ways of doing things, and these innovations are expected to prove themselves in terms of existing measures of effectiveness.[9] It may take time to realize that inserting new technology into old systems and organizations may create new inefficiencies, even as some current activities become more efficient or effective. It may take even more time to realize that the activity itself—in both its operational and organizational dimensions—should be restructured, even transformed, to realize the full potential of the new technology.[10]

Truly revolutionary developments often do not merely enhance the ability to fulfill existing missions, but rather are best suited to perform new functions or meet previously unidentified requirements. Unless, however, these new functions are captured in the accepted methods of assessment, innovative developments may not *appear* to offer significant operational enhancements. Thus, as the environment is changed by revolutionary innovation, the old measures of effectiveness may no longer be appropriate to measure the new modes of operation, and may no longer be relevant to altered objectives.[11] With revolutionary military innovation, fundamental change to the existing warfighting paradigm is guaranteed.

PREVIOUS REVOLUTIONS

While the notion of periodic and fundamental change in the conduct of war is not a new one, the systematic study of technology's impact on war is a relatively recent phenomenon. Perhaps the definitive work on the subject is Martin van Creveld's *Technology and War: From 2000 B.C. to the Present.* In this book, van Creveld divides military history into four eras: the "Age of Tools," the "Age of the Machine," the "Age of Systems," and the "Age of Automation."[12] This is not to suggest that there have not been significant changes in the conduct of war *within* these eras—these certainly have occurred—but rather is intended to provide a conceptual framework for exploration of the subject.

During the "Age of Tools," which lasted until approximately 1500 A.D., most technology was driven primarily by energy from the muscles of men and animals. Following the appearance of a few basic inventions (e.g., bronze and iron weapons, the stirrup, and wheeled vehicles), for the two millennia up to c. 1500 A.D. technological change had remarkably little impact on how wars were fought.

The overarching trend during the "Age of the Machine" was toward the requirement for progressively greater professional skills which led to a growing demand for harnessing military potential in an increasingly organized, even institutionalized, manner. The art of war in the "Age of the Machine" was perfected by Napoleon's France, which harnessed, for the first time, the vast resources of a newly industrializing nation to equip and support a mass army. This revolution coincided with three other significant upheavals: a political revolution that led to the rise of the republican nation-state; a socioeconomic upheaval resulting from the Agricultural Revolution; and economic changes produced by the spread of the Industrial Revolution to France. The "nation in arms"—the *levée en masse*—enabled the conduct of military operations across vast distances and marked the start of a continuing trend toward the substitution of firepower mass for manpower mass in warfare.[13]

In the "Age of Systems," the emphasis shifted to the integration of technology into complex networks, with the individual elements of technology becoming integrated with the other elements, first by the railway, then the telegraph, and then through other increasingly complex technologies. This era culminated in World War II with the innovative application of mechanization, aviation, and communications technology to military use in the *Blitzkrieg*, which enabled the German army to re-introduce the strategic and operational mobility, maneuver, and initiative that were conspicuously absent from the Western Front during World War I.[14]

The importance of systems has taken a further leap forward since 1945. According to van Creveld, the unifying theme of this era is not nuclear technology, as one might expect, but rather the "Age of Automation." The real story of the post–World War II era is that ". . . the cardinal result of the invention of invention, and the accelerated pace of technological innovation, was a vast increase in the amount of information needed to 'run' any military unit, make any decision, carry out any mission, conduct any operation, campaign, or war."[15] The increase in the amount of information that must be digested for these purposes has become so overwhelming that only the automation, usually the computerization, of the information gathering and distributing process has permitted military headquarters to keep pace with the expanded volume of data.

In each of these cases, revolutionary change in the conduct of war required the introduction or maturation of new military technologies (e.g., the internal combustion engine and armor), their integration into new military systems (e.g., the tank and the intercontinental ballistic missile), the adoption of appropriate operational concepts (e.g., the armored breakthrough and strategic bombing), and, finally, the requisite organizational adaptation (e.g., the Panzer division and the Strategic Rocket Forces). Technology alone is not sufficient to produce a military revolution; how military organizations adapt and shape new technology, military systems, and operational concepts is much more important.

THE INFORMATION REVOLUTION

The Information Revolution is based primarily on significant technological advances that have increased our ability to collect vast quantities of precise data; to convert that data into intelligible information by removing extraneous "noise"; to rapidly and accurately transmit this large quantity of information; to convert this information through responsive, flexible processing into near-complete situational awareness; and, at the limit, to allow accurate predictions of the implications of decision that may be made or actions that may be taken.[16] This revolution, and the change to a post-industrial world,[17] also seems to imply significant changes not only for the means of warfare, but for its objectives as well.

The Information Revolution is also having an impact on organizations of all kinds as traditional hierarchies are increasingly being replaced by amorphous networks. While institutions are traditionally built around hierarchies and seek to act autonomously, multi-organizational networks consist of often small organizations, sub-elements of existing institutions, and even individuals that have been linked together—often on an *ad hoc* basis. The Information Revolution favors the growth of such networks by making it possible for diverse, dispersed actors to communicate, coordinate, and operate together across greater distances and on the basis of more timely and higher quality information than ever before possible.[18]

ROOTS OF THIS RMA

The desire to substitute firepower for manpower, or what General Van Fleet during the Korean War termed the desire "to expend fire and steel, not men,"[19] has been a focus of U.S. defense policy for many decades. This basic American value led ultimately to an effort to develop a new way of waging war that depended less and less on quantitative material superiority and attrition to ensure victory. Conceived in the 1970s, this approach was part of what former Secretary of Defense Harold Brown called the "offset strategy," which was based on the need to counter the overwhelming quantitative superiority of Soviet and Warsaw Pact forces in Europe. The aim was not simply to field better weapons than the Soviet Union; rather, the offset strategy was intended to give American weapons a systems advantage by supporting them on the battlefield in a manner that greatly multiplied their combat effectiveness.[20]

The Soviets recognized and appreciated the potential impact of these technological developments and the resultant change in American strategy. This appreciation was developed in concepts first put forward in the late 1970s and early 1980s in the series of papers by Soviet Marshal Nikolai V. Ogarkov, including his seminal 1982 paper.[21] Ogarkov worried about how to conduct decisive operations in the European theater, a theater that was dense with heavily-armored mechanized forces and supported by tactical and theater nuclear force on both sides. His concern was that, by the early 1980s, the U.S. may have solved its strategic problem by synthesizing new technologies, evolving military systems, operational innovation, and organizational adaptation into a *whole* that was more powerful than the parts.

The Soviet argument for a dawning RMA focused less on military hardware than on technological advances making possible qualitative transformations in conventional, non-nuclear warfare. Soviet strategists maintained that in the near future, "reconnaissance-strike complexes" would enable commanders to detect targets, then rapidly and effectively attack them at long ranges. These combinations of sensors and weapons would blur the traditional distinctions between the offense and defense and allow the conduct of war over much greater distances than ever before.[22] Ogarkov believed that, in modernizing military theory and practice, "stagnation and a delayed 'perestroika' of views . . . are fraught with the most severe consequences." Throughout the 1970s and 1980s, he lobbied persistently for a timely incorporation of these new non-nuclear technologies into the Soviet conventional military force structure.[23]

The 1991 Persian Gulf War was the prototype of this future kind of war. It was characterized by the widespread availability of precision, deep-strike delivery systems on land and aboard ships and aircraft, together with a large inventory of extremely lethal conventional munitions directed by sophisticated target-acquisition systems to designated targets under near-continuous surveillance. Soviet experts, for example, stressed repeatedly that the coalition won so quickly, and with minimal losses, because of its "overwhelming superiority in contemporary methods of warfare: in aviation, advanced conventional munitions, and means for reconnaissance, command and control, and electronic warfare."[24]

Desert Storm demonstrated that an important advantage of U.S. forces was their ability to execute complex, orchestrated, high-tempo, simultaneous, parallel operations that overwhelmed the enemy's ability to respond. This advantage was built not only on advanced sensors and advanced conventional munitions, but perhaps more importantly on forces supported by modern command, control, communications, and intelligence (C^3I) systems and technologies that allowed the U.S.-led coalition to collapse previous spatial and temporal constraints on simultaneous operations.

ELEMENTS OF THIS REVOLUTION

Advanced conventional munitions have made spectacular advances in lethality by linking near-real-time information to precision-guided weapons controlled by digital command and control systems.[25] Bombing has become so precise that weapon systems can routinely attack not just the building or the room, but "the *corner* of the room that will bring everything down—even the vent shaft that will put the bomb *inside* the shelter."[26] This may enable us to view the venerable military principle of mass from an entirely different perspective and alter the traditional relationship between the offense and the defense. A defender, equipped with these sophisticated munitions, can now inflict unacceptable casualties on an attacker before the latter can close for battle, while a similarly equipped attacker can likewise reciprocate.[27]

The sensor revolution, which was enabled by the computerization of individual platforms and weapon systems, complements these advances in weapons lethality. An individual platform—manned or autonomous—can now detect and track individual vehicles, ships, or aircraft well beyond visual range, and provide targeting information on a near-real-time basis to long-range offensive attack systems. Additionally, these sensors are becoming fully integrated with traditional command and control systems to achieve synergies never before possible. The Airborne Warning and Control System (AWACS) and the new E-8A Joint Surveillance and Target Attack Radar System (JSTARS) aircraft, which couple high-technology sensors and communications with command personnel, are but two examples of this kind of C³I.

In the past, military commanders have not had the C³I capabilities to manage military forces to the limit of their potential effectiveness.[28] They have had to rely on increases in the individual components of combat power—i.e., mass, mobility, reach, and firepower—or the exploitation of an opponent's failings, to make up for these inadequacies. The associated costs were high not only in resources, but also in organizational distortions and operational constraints. What was often referred to as the "fog of war" is in reality disorder—the inability to maintain unity of action due to shortcomings in the C³I systems.[29]

The post-modern battlefield stands to be fundamentally altered by the Information Revolution at the strategic, operational, and tactical levels (if these distinctions even remain valid). The increasing breadth and depth of the battlefield and the inexorably improving accuracy and destructiveness—and therefore lethality—of even conventional munitions have heightened the importance of C³I to the point where dominance in this domain alone may, if exploited properly, yield consistent war-winning advantages.[30]

THE CHANGING SECURITY ENVIRONMENT

While the structural foundations of the post–World War II international system remain in place, there have been profound changes in how this system actually functions. In addition to the dramatic increase in the number of nation-states, there has been a significant change in character of the participants in the international arena. Nation-states remain the primary actors, but increasingly international organizations such as the United Nations, the European Community, the Organization of American States, and a wide variety of other non-governmental organizations, such as Doctors without Borders, are making their presence felt on the international scene. In addition, transnational actors including the media, religious movements, terrorist groups, drug cartels, and countless others exert considerable influence in international relations. In essence, the world is organizing itself in a series of interconnected networks that, while in contact with each other, are not controlled by any traditional hierarchy. Nation-states find themselves pulled simultaneously in fundamentally opposite directions—toward *integration* by international security, trade, and social organizations and *disintegration* by subnational movements that seek to splinter the state.

Furthermore, modern (mostly Western) nations are developing post-industrial, "third wave" economies that are built on information as the fourth critical factor endowment (the others being land, labor, and capital). This trend carries at least three significant implications for the future international security environment.[31]

- This new factor endowment is dependent neither on unchangeable physical resources nor on large, fixed-capital investments that have long depreciation and pay-back periods. As a result, economic power built on this foundation can be developed far more quickly.

- This source of strength is also far more agile and adaptable, and can respond with shorter time constants to changes in the environment; it may well be capable of greater surprises.

- This factor is also more mobile and potentially more transferable; and power growing from it may be subject to greater diffusion.

. Unless Mexico or Canada are suddenly transformed into aggressive regional powers, the U.S. will not, in the foreseeable future, be the direct object of aggression. Therefore, we can expect to fight in conflicts at extended distances, and, with the exception of a regional power that develops weapons of mass destruction coupled with intercontinental delivery systems, without a direct threat to our national survival. Additionally, the collapse of the Soviet Union means that it is unlikely, in the immediate future, that we will face a new security threat of that magnitude.

It is possible that, in the future, few rational opponents will be likely to challenge, or will even be capable of challenging, the U.S. in a contest with large, multi-dimensional military forces. It is certainly conceivable, however, that a future challenger might choose to strike directly against the developing international networks that support the increasing internationalization of trade, culture, and politics. Such an adversary would seek to destroy not the military power, but rather the underlying fabric of the international system and its core values, especially if these values are fundamentally at odds with deeply held cultural, religious, or ideological beliefs.[32]

A LOOK AT THE FUTURE

Although we cannot definitively predict the precise course a future conflict might take, we can almost certainly expect a significant broadening of the extent of the battlefield with the operational tempo increasing by yet another order of magnitude to the point that the levels of war—the strategic, operational, and tactical—essentially merge. Lethal, precision-guided munitions will be able to be launched at ever-increasing ranges, often well beyond the visual range of the enemy. Smaller, combined-arms combat formations with advanced indirect- and direct-fire weapons will be able to dominate even larger areas than in the past.[33] Furthermore, surprise may become *the* decisive factor in determining both the "course and outcome" of a war; in fact, these may now be described as "a single phenomenon." As a result, the initial period may now be in effect the *only* period in future warfare.[34] Operational campaigning under these circumstances must be viewed as an integrated, seamless process in which the time constants of the individual elements are critical to the effectiveness of the overall plan.

Indeed, the analogy between this campaign paradigm to "just-in-time" operations and the older campaign model, with its pre-planning, clearly delineated phases, and reliance on reserves, to an inventory-based manufacturing process is noteworthy.[35] Inventory-based management and production systems, which are the industrial counterparts to existing military command and control architectures, reflected the high likelihood of both information and control failures in the subsidiary production systems. To deal with these imperfections, industrial manufacturing systems use[d] time and excess resources, i.e., inventories, as the "slack variables." Not only did this require carrying large stocks of parts and in-process work, but this method of operations also often resulted in the production and maintenance of large inventories of finished products for which there was no longer a demand.[36]

The traditional military reliance on reserves and redundancy often has been the only method of hedging against operational failures—of overcoming the "fog of war"—by also using time and excess resources as the slack variables. Command and control imperfections increased reliance on pre-planning, thus forfeiting the benefits of the local situational awareness and responsiveness of subordinate commanders to unfolding developments on the battlefield. Under the old limitations on synchronization capabilities, there was no choice but to create hierarchical organizations and processes to enforce centralized direction. Even with pre-planned actions, shortcomings in the supporting information systems did not allow commanders at the top to know, much less fully understand, what was happening. This made it virtually impossible to exercise effective command and control of ongoing operations.[37]

Thus, synchronization efforts have been constrained by the availability of what has been, at best, partial information; and shortcomings tended to keep commanders below the level of "understanding." Modern C^3I systems now offer the opportunity to alter the existing command paradigm. The locus of the decisionmaking can be shifted down the command chain to those who must actually execute the overall plan. These subordinate commanders can now share in the global situational awareness provided by worldwide, near-real-time, integrated C^3I systems while at the same time retaining the benefits of local situational awareness.[38] This promises a significant advantage on the battlefield to the side that can best accomplish it.

EXPLOITING THE RMA

It is certain that careful implementation of the RMA will be needed since revolutions are, by nature of their potential for dramatic operational and organizational changes, antithetical to the cultural norms of existing bureaucratic structures. Detailed theories of innovation relating specifically to military organizations have only recently emerged, but it has long been the conventional wisdom that only catastrophic military defeat can move a military organization to embrace innovation.[39] No one experienced in dealing with military bureaucracies could possibly doubt that innovation in the military sphere is extremely difficult; however, there are many instances where military innovation was preceded by victory, not defeat. The interwar period is a case in point.[40]

Despite this, the historical tendency of military organizations has been to use new capabilities to support existing missions, and to oppose new capabilities that threaten existing missions.[41] For real innovation to occur, the doctrinal and operational implications of new capabilities must be translated by senior officers into new critical military tasks and missions for the entire organization.[42] This takes time, typically a generation or more, to effect.

ENABLING TECHNOLOGIES

The renowned British strategist, J.F.C. Fuller, argued that with each change in weapons, organizations and tactics must also change. Then a determination must be made as to the most dominant weapon around which to arrange the employment of other weapons. It is important to note that it is not necessary for the "master weapon" to be *the* decisive weapon on the battlefield. Its qualifications for mastery are found in its ability to immobilize or upset the enemy's tactics and so enable other weapons to be decisively used. In short, it sets the tactical pace.[43] The key to exploiting this revolution in military affairs will be correctly identifying what system constitutes the "master weapon" in this new era.

In future warfare, the struggle for information will play a central role, taking the place, perhaps, of the struggle for geographical position held in previous conflicts. Information superiority is emerging as a newly recognized, and more intense, area of competition. In response to these developments, C³I systems must be designed to provide commanders at all levels the information and communications needed to direct the dispersion or concentration of their forces and, more importantly, weapons' effects at the decisive point in time and space.

It may now be time to design the command and control system first, based on the full range of technological possibilities, and then select individual weapons systems for acquisition based upon our ability most effectively to integrate them into this C³I system. This is not as far-fetched as it might at first seem. Throughout history, successful military organizations have based their organization and battlefield formations on existing command and control technologies. In a sense, it is the soldiers of the modern age who are out of step with history, acquiring weapons systems and platforms based principally on their mechanical capabilities, then improvising a command and control system that barely meets battlefield requirements.[44]

The ability of the U.S. to construct and amortize a global information network as the foundation of such a command and control system is the principal source of long-term advantage over potential adversaries.[45] While constructing this system will be expensive, the U.S. has already made much of the necessary research and development investment to lay the foundation for these future capabilities. Moreover, many of the important components of such a future system (e.g., the Global Positioning System, worldwide communications, surveillance and reconnaissance platforms, etc.) are already in place. It is this global C³I system that will be the master weapon of the twenty-first century.

C³I systems by themselves, however, do not fight and win wars. The weapons of tomorrow must be designed to take advantage of the possibilities offered by this global system. In fact, the era of precision-strike weapons systems that require both absolute (i.e., latitude and longitude) and relative (i.e., bearing, range, course, and speed) positioning information has already arrived.[46]

An important feature of this RMA is that the supporting technologies are the same as those being rapidly developed in the commercial world. Thus, this revolution can be based on technologies that are also critical for our success and comparative advantage in the global economy. A sound national security investment strategy would focus resources not only on the acquisition of a small number of large-scale, global systems or networks to provide surveillance and targeting information, but also on inexpensive weapons that can be directed by this system. These investments would provide both a significant operational advantage during the short-term, and a flexible foundation on which to build for longer-term, but uncertain security challenges.[47]

HUMAN FACTORS

The primary impact of the Information Revolution is to push the envelope of the decision-making speed-limit, i.e., the speed of thought. The result of these technological advances is that the time required to take action on the battlefield is becoming increasingly limited by the speed at which the human in the loop can make a tactical decision.[48]

In the past, decisions were made at a given command level because only that level had the requisite information to make the appropriate decision. But now, everyone in the chain of command can have access to the same information at essentially the same time. This has important consequences, for both good and ill. Now the President can select bombing targets in North Vietnam and direct helicopters in Iran from the White House, or he may sleep through the night while Libya is bombed. A commander now has to know when to give an order and when to hang up the telephone and let the organization execute the plan he has devised.[49] For action-oriented people, as senior military officers often are, the decision to do nothing is often the hardest to make.

IMPACT ON ORGANIZATIONS

The future shape of military organizations was glimpsed in the 1991 Persian Gulf War. The dependence of modern military organizations on tremendous amounts of information, and the relative ease with which communications technology can disseminate that information, meant that supporting authority would inevitably diffuse out of theater of operations. Now, commanders can tap the expertise of large staffs and other organizations thousands of miles away to formulate plans for actions to be taken during the next several hours. Central Command's formal organizational scheme did not explicitly acknowledge this, but the command system rapidly became dependent on informal, *ad hoc* arrangements.[50] This was not an aberration, but is representative of a trend that will only accelerate in the future.

This trend should not be resisted, but rather embraced and leveraged to our advantage. Implementing this information-based RMA will require that capabilities for the command and control of simultaneous, continuous operations be increased and that the current distinctions between these types of operations be eliminated. Moreover, shortening the time-constants for decision and action will require the decentralization of command authority, and a concomitant relaxation of control downward from top of the command pyramid. Many of the innovations portended by the Information Revolution are already reflected in changes in the organizational structures and decision processes found in the commercial sector, including changes in the role of management and the locus of decision-making in commercial organizations. These changes are intended to dramatically improve the speed of both decision and execution, which are increasingly viewed as the key elements of competitive advantage.[51]

Waging war in the post-modern era will require major innovations in organizational design, in particular a shift from hierarchical to network structures. The traditional reliance on hierarchical designs must be replaced with network-oriented models to allow greater flexibility, lateral connectivity, and teamwork across institutional boundaries.[52] In light of both the reduced costs of information gathering and distribution and the resultant increase in the capability to disseminate real-time information to dispersed consumers, we must rethink the current organizational structures designed under the old span-of-control and information processing constraints. Organizational concepts for increasing combat power that demanded massing and concentration of forces will have to be examined in light of the new opportunities to combine and synchronize disparate elements at low frictional costs; the commercial sector concept of the "virtual corporation" has obvious parallels for this military restructuring.[53]

Beyond these command and control issues, the rapidly expanding operational capabilities of military forces are also challenging the traditional division of labor—the "roles and missions"—of the military services. The further that surveillance and reconnaissance systems can see and weapons systems can shoot, the greater the zone of influence—and interest—of the commanders that control them. The result is that service-specific "battlespaces" increasingly intersect with each other, and will eventually merge.[54] The coming changes cannot help but have a significant impact on the current organizational paradigm.

CONCLUSION

Previous revolutions in military affairs have primarily served to enhance the combat power of military forces by improving the effectiveness of its constituent elements, i.e., mass, mobility, reach, and firepower. Although today's Information Revolution is not a revolution in military affairs, *per se*, it is the foundation on which one can be built. The current RMA results not from the quantity or even quality of information in and of itself, but rather from a combined revolution in higher order cognitive processes and command and control capabilities. As Desert Storm so vividly demonstrated, this revolution promises (or threatens, depending on your point of view) to restore the capacity to achieve decisive results on the battlefield, the Clausewitzian *coup de main*, and to do so in a remarkably short period time.

Fortunately, the U.S. is well-positioned to take advantage of this revolution; its constituent elements are our greatest comparative strengths. As noted earlier, the U.S. is the only nation with the ability to construct and amortize a truly global information network. Such a network can provide the foundation for a significant comparative advantage over potential adversaries for many years to come. To reiterate J.F.C. Fuller's observation, it is around this "master weapon" that we should "arrange for the cooperation of all other weapons." This is not to suggest that traditional elements of military power are now obsolete. We must continue to be prepared to deal with lower-technology challenges of the variety that have historically given us the greatest difficulty.[55]

The coming changes mirror those taking place in the commercial sector as the economic paradigm shifts from the traditional, hierarchical corporation to amorphous networks of cooperative workgroups and even individuals. The blurring of distinctions between management and labor, "physical" and "intellectual" capital, and foreign and domestic markets in the economic sphere parallels the blurring of distinctions between offense and defense and the collapsing of the strategic, operational and tactical levels in the military sphere. Profound changes are taking place that will significantly alter the way we prepare for and wage war. We would be well advised to anticipate these changes and leverage them to our advantage to preserve our security in a dangerous, unpredictable world.

NOTES

[1] As Secretary of Defense William Perry noted on May 5, 1994: "We live in an age that is driven by information. It's an age which Alvin Toffler has called the Third Wave. The ability to acquire and communicate huge volumes of information in real time, the computing power to analyze this information quickly, and the control systems to pass this analysis to multiple users simultaneously—these are the technological breakthroughs that are changing the face of war and how we prepare for war." Quoted in "Information Warfare," Office of the Assistant Secretary of Defense (C^3I) (Washington, DC, July 1994), p. 4A.

[2] "Information is becoming a strategic resource that may prove as valuable and influential in the post-industrial era as capital and labor have been in the preceding industrial age." John Arquilla and David Ronfeldt, "Cyberwar is Coming" (Santa Monica, CA: RAND 1992), p. 2. This article also appeared in the April–June 1993 issue of *Comparative Strategy*.

[3] Particularly with regard to the "exceptional lethality gained by linking real-time information to precision-guided weapons and controlling them with digital command and control." Lt. Col. Thomas X. Hammes, USMC, "The Evolution of War: The Fourth Generation," *Marine Corps Gazette*, September 1994, p. 35.

[4] See, for example, Michael J. Mazarr, et al., *The Military Technical Revolution: A Structural Framework* (Washington, DC: Center for Strategic and International Studies, 1993).

[5] RMAs are intrinsically complex phenomena, i.e., more than just new technology. One view holds that they are made up of four component elements: "operational innovation, organizational adaptation, evolving military systems, as well as emerging technologies." Jeffrey R. Cooper, "Another View of the Revolution in Military Affairs" (Arlington, VA: SRS Technologies, June 1993), p. 21. Unpublished manuscript; cited with permission of the author.

[6] Lt. Leo S. Mackay, Jr., USN, "Naval Aviation, Information, and the Future," *Naval War College Review*, Spring 1992, p. 7.

[7] This adaptation and exploitation is particularly difficult for large, bureaucratic institutions since revolutions are, by nature of the extensive organizational and opera-

tional changes involved, antithetical to existing cultural norms and bureaucratic structures. Cooper, "Another View of the Revolution in Military Affairs," p. 23.

[8]Ibid., p. 23.

[9]Arquilla and Ronfeldt, "Cyberwar is Coming," p. 18.

[10]"Changes in tactics have not only taken place after changes in weapons . . . but the interval between such changes has been unduly long. It can be remedied only by a candid recognition of each change. . . . History shows that it is vain to hope that military men generally will be at pains to do this, but that the one who does will go into battle with a great advantage—a lesson in itself of no mean value." Alfred Thayer Mahan, *The Influence of Sea Power Upon History, 1660–1783* (New York: Hill and Wang, 1957), p. 8.

[11]"For example, if an RMA involves a fundamental shift from an attrition paradigm to one in which speed of execution is as important, then it should follow that the dimension of measurement should shift as well from questions of 'how many killed' to 'how quickly'." Cooper, "Another View of the Revolution in Military Affairs," p. 24.

[12]Martin van Creveld, *Technology and War: From 2000 B.C. to the Present* (New York: Free Press, 1989). This is by no means the only conceptual framework that has been proposed. See, e.g., William S. Lind et al., "The Changing Face of War: Into the Fourth Generation," *Military Review*, October 1989; and Robert J. Bunker, "The Transition to Fourth Epoch War," *Marine Corps Gazette*, September 1994.

[13]The ultimate result of this military revolution was no less important; it provided not just the ability to "conquer a *neighbor*, but to seize a *continent*—or in more modern terms, the means to wage a *theater-wide* campaign." Cooper, "Another View of the Revolution in Military Affairs," pp. 15–16. Emphasis in original.

[14]While the French and British calculated the speed of a combined-arms unit by that of its slowest element, the Germans measured it by that of the fastest—the tank—and insisted that their Panzer divisions move as rapidly as possible. Lt. Col. Douglas A. MacGregor, USA, "Future Battle: The Merging Levels of War," *Parameters*, Winter 1992–93, p. 36.

[15]Van Creveld, *Technology and War*, pp. 235–236.

[16]Jeffrey R. Cooper, "The Coherent Battlefield—Removing the 'Fog of War': A Framework for Understanding an MTR of the Information Age" (Arlington, VA: SRS Technologies, June 1993), p. 23. Unpublished manuscript; cited with permission of the author.

[17]See, for example, Alvin and Heidi Toffler, *The Third Wave* (New York: Morrow Press, 1980).

[18]Arquilla and Ronfeldt, "Cyberwar is Coming," pp. 3–4.

[19]General James A. Van Fleet, USA, quoted in Bernard Brodie, *War and Politics* (New York: MacMillan Press, 1973), p. 91.

[20]William J. Perry, "Desert Storm and Deterrence," *Foreign Affairs*, Fall 1991, pp. 68–69.

[21]Marshal Nikolai V. Ogarkov, "Always in Readiness for the Defense of the Fatherland," *Voyenizdat*, 1982.

[22]Thomas A. Keaney and Eliot A. Cohen, *Gulf War Air Power Survey Summary Report* (Washington, DC: 1993), p. 237.

[23]Mary C. FitzGerald, "The Soviet Military and the New 'Technological Operation' in the Gulf," *Naval War College Review,* Autumn 1991, p. 17.

[24]Ibid., p. 15.

[25]In fact, some have speculated that those capable of producing such weapons will dominate warfare to a degree not seen since Western Europeans conquered and colonized most of the known world. Hammes, "The Evolution of War," p. 35.

[26]Lt. Col. Edward Mann, USAF, "One Target, One Bomb: Is the Principle of Mass Dead?" *Military Review,* September 1993, p. 37. Emphasis in original.

[27]Lt. Col. Lester W. Grau, USA, "In the Wake of Revolution, Continuity and Change: A Soviet General Staff View of Future Theater War," *Military Review,* December 1991, p. 11.

[28]"From Plato to NATO, the history of command in war essentially consists of an endless quest for certainty . . . ." Martin van Creveld, *Command in War* (Cambridge, MA: Harvard Press, 1985), p. 264.

[29]Cooper, "The Coherent Battlefield," pp. 1–2.

[30]Arquilla and Ronfeldt, "Cyberwar is Coming," p. 7.

[31]Cooper, "Another View of the Revolution in Military Affairs," p. 19.

[32]Ibid., pp. 13–14. The Bosnian Serbs appear to be following such a strategy.

[33]Chris Bellamy, *The Future of Land Warfare* (New York: St. Martin's Press, 1987), pp. 298–299.

[34]FitzGerald, "The Soviet Military," p. 38.

[35]Cooper, "Another View of the Revolution in Military Affairs," p. 38.

[36]"The old-style Soviet central planning with huge stocks of unwanted merchandise was the ultimate example of this paradigm." Cooper, "The Coherent Battlefield" p. 26.

[37]Ibid., p. 19.

[38]Ibid., p. 19.

[39]"Armies are more often ruined by dogmas springing from their former successes than by the skill of their opponents." J.F.C. Fuller, "The Tactics of Penetration," *The Journal of the Royal United Service Institution,* November 1914, p. 389. Quoted in Maj. Anthony M. Coroalles, USA, "The Master Weapon: The Tactical Thought of J.F.C. Fuller Applied to Future War," *Military Review,* January 1991.

[40]The Marine Corps' development of amphibious doctrine and techniques in the interwar years, despite the example of Gallipoli during World War I, is one such example.

[41]See Bruce Gudmundsson, "The Multiple Launch Rocket System: On Time and Under Budget," Kennedy School Case Program C16-87-773.0, Harvard University, 1987, for an excellent example of this phenomenon.

[42]Stephen Peter Rosen, "New Ways of War: Understanding Military Innovation," *International Security,* Summer 1988, p. 136.

[43]J.F.C. Fuller, "A Study of Mobility in the American Civil War," *Army Quarterly,* January 1935, p. 271. Quoted in Coroalles, "The Master Weapon."

[44]The Romans, for example, made exactly this sort of decision when they chose to rely primarily on highly disciplined infantry forces instead of uncontrollable masses of cavalry. A millennium later, the hugely successful Mongols designed their cavalry

formations specifically to facilitate control in battle. Maj. Ralph Peters, USA, "The Movable Fortress: Warfare in the 21st Century," *Military Review*, June 1993, p. 66.

[45]Cooper, "The Coherent Battlefield," pp. 33–34.

[46]"In Desert Storm, the effective employment of precision systems such as the F-117/GBU-27 combination required correspondingly precise target information, whereas the areas in which the strategic portion of the air campaign was least effective were precisely those in which fundamental gaps in Coalition understanding of entire target systems existed." Keaney and Cohen, *Gulf War Air Power Survey*, p. 248.

[47]Cooper, "The Coherent Battlefield," pp. 40–41.

[48]As both the *U.S.S. Stark* and *Vincennes* incidents demonstrated, in the age of "information overload" the slowest component in the tactical chain of command is often the human making the decision of whether or not to shoot.

[49]"In a sense, General Norman Schwarzkopf's brilliance in Desert Storm was in knowing when to be quiet." Captain John W. Bodnar, USNR, "The Military Technical Revolution: From Hardware to Information," *Naval War College Review*, Summer 1993, p. 19.

[50]Officers in the basement of the Pentagon helped pick targets and plan attacks; staffs at Langley Air Force Base in Virginia managed CENTAF's spare parts accounts; Space Command provided warning of missile attacks against Israel and Saudi Arabia; and meteorologists processed weather information for use within the theater. Keaney and Cohen, *Gulf War Air Power Survey*, p. 248.

[51]Cooper, "Another View of the Revolution in Military Affairs," p. 36.

[52]"Most adversaries that the United States and its allies face in the realms of low-intensity conflict—international terrorists, guerrilla insurgents, drug cartels, ethnic factions, etc.—are all organized like networks (although their leadership may be quite hierarchical). Perhaps a reason that military (and police) institutions keep having difficulty engaging in low-intensity conflicts is because they are not meant to be fought by institutions." Arquilla and Ronfeldt, "Cyberwar is Coming," pp. 17 and 23.

[53]Cooper, "The Coherent Battlefield," pp. 34–35.

[54]To cite just a few examples, Navy, Marine Corps, and Air Force aircraft now use the same Air Tasking Order; data collected by Air Force surveillance aircraft guides the movement of Army formations; long-range Army missiles strike deep targets while Air Force aircraft engage enemy vehicles in contact with friendly forces; and national sensors alert anti-tactical ballistic missile forces of missile launches. Martin C. Lybicki and CDR James A. Hazlett, USN, "Do We Need an Information Corps?" *Joint Forces Quarterly*, Autumn 1993, p. 89.

[55]"While games can be nice while they last, in our age too there is a real danger that they will be upset by barbarians who, refusing to abide by the rules, pick up the playing-board and use it to smash the opponent's head." Van Creveld, *Technology and War*, p. 296.

ANOTHER VIEW OF THE REVOLUTION IN MILITARY AFFAIRS[1]

Jeffrey R. Cooper

INTRODUCTION

Since the subject was raised within the American defense community[2] [see the end of this chapter for notes], the Revolution in Military Affairs (RMA) has been the subject of at least three summer studies, many conferences, numerous papers and briefings, and a host of war-gaming exercises. As a result of these efforts, DoD is now investigating an RMA initiative. But while the community seems to agree on a number of important issues, concord on other critical points is lacking.

First, almost all participants in the debate now accept that RMAs are more than just new military technologies or systems and involve complex operational and organizational issues; but few agree on the priority among these four elements and identity of *the* key driver (if only one exists). *Second,* while there is agreement that this RMA is but the latest in a historical series of RMAs, little attention has been paid to the broad strategic implications that placing this RMA in its long-term historical context suggests for future changes in the conduct of warfare. *Third,* while the community largely agrees that there

---

[1]Jeffrey R. Cooper, "Another View of the Revolution in Military Affairs," *Conference Proceedings of the Fifth Annual Conference on Strategy,* April 1994. Strategic Studies Institute, U.S. Army War College. Used by permission.

is an RMA to be pursued, whether it is already in progress, is about to start, or is mature and about to end all have adherents. *Fourth,* more problematically, there is no agreement concerning the character of this RMA—i.e., a specific definition of this RMA, not merely identification of constituent technical elements; and, therefore, there is no substantive roadmap for proceeding. Indeed, reviewing the current literature and debates, it appears that there may be several different RMAs that are being discussed (not unlike the parable of the blind men and the elephant). *Fifth,* agreement does exist that a focus on careful implementation will be needed since RMAs are, by nature of the potential operational and organizational changes, antithetical to existing cultural norms and bureaucratic structures. However, few agree on an overall approach to implementation, much less on the initiative's critical next steps needed for successful exploitation of the RMA—i.e., on the procedural roadmap.

Unfortunately, even less agreement exists on two other important, higher-level questions; and these questions carry divergent implications for those issues on which seeming agreement is in hand. The first of these concerns the relevance of the RMA to the evolving U.S. national security problem, and as specific aspects of this question:

- The relevance of the RMA to a broad spectrum of conflict types and intensities that the United States may face;

- The military benefits, at both the operational and tactical levels, across this spectrum of conflict;

- An assessment of whether the RMA is the most appropriate instrument for addressing these evolving problems;

- The strategic implications and consequences (both intended and unintended) of pursuing this initiative; and finally,

- A determination as to whether this RMA is in our long-term national interest.

The second question concerns the role and utility of the RMA as a potential organizing principle for future defense policy, programs and bureaucratic relationships. In particular, what are potential implications of the RMA, with its probable stress on greater force integration and joint command of operations, for future roles and missions of the Services, and what are the divergent implications for each of the Services?

By clearly identifying the key issues for resolution, it is hoped that DoD can (1) define the strategic purpose of the RMA initiative; (2) refine what is expected from the RMA is terms of strategic, operational, and tactical objectives; and (3) assess what is the most appropriate content of this RMA to meet this spectrum of military need. Only with the purpose and content of the RMA accurately characterized can understanding the phenomenology of previous RMAs then assist in determining the most effective means for implementation and exploitation of this revolution. Thus, the two most critical questions that must be answered before agreement can be reached to pursue an RMA (and the concomitant issue of *how best* to do so) are the *purpose* and the *nature* of the RMA to be pursued—what are the character and the core elements of *this* revolution. This monograph is not intended to provide definitive answers to these important questions, a treatment worthy of volumes; but it does propose hypotheses for these important RMA-related issues that can serve to frame the debate for decision makers.

CHOICES FOR THE DECISION MAKER

The RMA is a complex subject, and there are multiple ways that decision makers may choose both to view the RMA and to pursue an RMA initiative, all with potentially divergent implications. Explicit identification and proper assessment of the options for proceeding appear essential for real progress. Defining the objectives for an RMA initiative involves two related but really distinct sets of issues: one related to how the RMA is perceived by decision makers, and the second related to what the RMA really is. This section will discuss the choices that arise from the multiple ways top-level decision makers may perceive the RMA; the question of what the RMA is will be discussed later. From the decision makers' standpoint, these different perspectives on the RMA include: a teleological focus that can be either external or internal;[3] focus on specific challenges or types of threats versus focus on the RMA as a process to adapt to broader and continuing environmental changes; employing the RMA as an instrument for organizational development versus using the RMA as a filter for new technologies; and, finally, the choice of whether to pursue an RMA versus what RMA to pursue.

Depending on their perspective of external or internal objectives for the RMA, decision makers can be separated into two broad groups (that are not, however, necessarily mutually exclusive). The external perspective focuses on the potential role of the RMA as a means of attaining strategic objectives in the evolving geostrategic environment, one in which the United States is likely to face a new set of security challenges. The internal perspective, on the other hand, sees the potential utility of the RMA as an organizing principle for DoD that can assist in determining future policy, programs, and bureaucratic relationships—in essence, as a tool to shape the department, if not the larger community, to the evolving strategic realities, including long-term fiscal pressures and reduced priority accorded to national security by decision makers and the American public. But while both are valid, how the RMA is used to achieve internally-directed objectives appears to depend critically on the choices the decision makers take with respect to the external objectives for the RMA. To assure strategic relevance, moreover, the RMA must address the basic national security challenges at hand— how best to deal with the diverse types of competitors that may emerge over the longer term. These challenges may include old problems posed by new competitors, new problems posed by old competitors, and new problems from emerging competitors (that we may not yet be able to even articulate, much less specifically characterize).[4]

The second perspective, focused on the internal objectives, involves how the DoD leadership intends to use the RMA initiative to shape the future direction of the department once it understands the external purposes for the initiative. These internal choices include whether the RMA can provide a conceptual basis for future strategy; for prioritizing R&D efforts and acquisition programs; a legitimization of change as a way of life (i.e., a way to institutionalize a "permanent revolution"); a rationale for altering roles and missions; a framework for reorganizing bureaucratic structures; or merely an additional filter (as with strategic competitiveness) in the policy process. Indeed, much of the interest in the RMA seems to stem from the potential role an RMA could serve as an organizing principle (or rationale) for the wealth of technology opportunities now appearing, even amid the poverty of budgetary resources for defense needs. Overall, is the RMA as process a generally applicable tool or suited only to specific issues? For many of these purposes, the *idea* of an RMA may be just as important as detailed content since its primary use is as a motivating instrument. Pursuit of an RMA initiative will have significant implications for doctrinal development, operational requirements, force posture, and R&D strategy; and these will create opportunities for major institutional and bureaucratic changes.

The ability of an RMA to address potential disparate security challenges turns on whether it is an idiosyncratic event or a process. If the RMA is a *specific* event that synthesizes particular technologies, military systems, operational innovations, and organizational adaptations to address effectively existing challenges, can it also meet emerging problems? Given the apparent agreement that there is an RMA and that this RMA is but one in a historical series, there are two potential answers to this issue. One, that an RMA is a specific solution to a particular strategic problem, in which case it may not be relevant to emerging challenges. Or two, that RMAs are organic to the broad geostrategic milieu, arising from the general nature of the stage of socioeconomic development and technologies, in which case this RMA will retain its relevance as long as new challenges will also arise from that same general milieu.

If, on the other hand, the RMA is a process for synthesizing strategically appropriate responses, then it can play a longer-term role even if the strategic environment changes dramatically, presenting fundamentally new types of military problems. In this latter case, however, the important question must focus on the broad character of RMAs—not on the mission-specific tasks nor the collection of advanced technologies and military systems supporting them in a particular RMA—since these elements can only usefully be defined as the future circumstances unfold. Analysis of these issues can provide the answers to whether an RMA initiative (or a strategy based on the RMA) can serve as an overall approach to potential competitors; whether an RMA will be consistent with long-term U.S. security interests; and whether an RMA will offer benefits in nontraditional missions such as drug interdiction and peacekeeping.

A final but related analytical issue concerns choice; not only what objectives decision makers may select, but whether or not there is a choice in pursuing the RMA. Should we pursue the RMA for its own sake? Because it can be done? Because it promises substantial advantages in addressing our evolving security challenges? Or finally, because we may have no choice since potential competitors may decide to pursue the RMA regardless of our course? The obverse point is equally important, are we currently good enough to answer potential challenges without the RMA; and if so, why should we disturb this present situation? In this regard, the example of the impact of the *Dreadnought* on the naval balance and subsequent competition before World War I may provide a cautionary note to proceeding before we understand both the purpose and implications of the RMA. By essentially starting the competition from scratch, *Dreadnought* obviated the utility of the large British investment in previous battleship and heavy cruiser fleets.

ISSUES OF STRATEGIC PURPOSE

In order to address the issue of *purpose*, it is essential to understand the range of potential situations in which the RMA might need to be relevant. These issues, therefore, must be addressed in the context of *what* wars may be fought and *how* they will be fought, not only the more usual question of *who* our principal adversary will be. In the new geostrategic environment, what will U.S. strategic objectives be: will the United States employ force only in response to specific acts of aggression or in defense of particular interests, or will it use its military power more generally—to shape the strategic environment, to defend liberty and promulgate values? Will the United States be strategically defensive or strategically offensive during this period? Indeed, in this new international structure three questions emerge. First, who defines the rules of conflict? Second, will the United States be able to define the nature and level of conflict? And third, what constraints can be applied to the conduct of warfare?[5] These questions strike at the heart of whether the United States will have the choice of selecting the types of conflict in which we engage and at how competitors may decide to contest our power or determination—and, therefore, the purpose, role, and utility of an RMA.

The controlling factors may be not only the nature of the evolving competitions but also the very real constraints of size, budgetary pressures, and economic linkages reshaping U.S. military posture and the issue of what impacts these will have on [on] key competitors. With the collapse of the Soviet Union, it is unlikely in the immediate future that the United States will face a new challenger of that caliber. Rather it will have to deal with significantly smaller opponents either singly or in concert. Moreover, in the wake of both the Soviet collapse and the Gulf War, it is also especially important to recognize that the previous U.S. concern for the adverse asymmetry in force size no longer pertains and that U.S. technical advantages need no longer be considered to be merely a necessary qualitative offset to the quantitative advantages possessed by probable opponents. While several nations like China and India continue to possess large conventional force structures, it is likely that in future regional conflicts forces in coalition with the United States will be as large (and almost certainly better equipped and trained) as those of any regional adversary. Furthermore, and often not explicitly recognized, the collapse of the Soviet threat to Western Europe also implies that regional adversaries (the old "half-war" contingencies) must now be prepared to face a United States unconstrained by the need to retain the most formidable parts of U.S. force structure for the European (the classic "one war") contingency that previously dominated our thinking. Even while we may plan on a "two-war" capability, any opponent must be prepared to face the full weight of whatever U.S. military power exists.

Three other, perhaps more subtle, factors are also at work in shaping the strategic environment. First, the collapse of the Soviet Union also removes the only major power capable both of sponsoring regional opponents at distances from their borders (and threatening the United States with strategic forces) and of supplying them with the most advanced conventional weapons and technical assistance on concessionary terms.[6] Second, in a major regional contingency, the United States can apply a range of nonmilitary strictures (such as embargoes and boycotts) against the opponent to further constrain his war effort without fear of opposing superpower intervention to undercut these actions. Coupled with the clear technological, doctrinal, and tactical superiority that was demonstrated during the Gulf War, these factors taken in combination suggest that the United States will possess demonstrable military dominance over regional contenders for the foreseeable future. Third, the likelihood that the United States will fight in future conflicts as part of coalitions not only increases the array of forces an opponent will confront, but also opens significant new vulnerabilities for the United States. The implications of coalition warfare, including political sensitivities, allied casualties, and concern for collateral damage, will have substantial impacts on how these campaigns are conducted. Indeed, these "softer" factors may be as important in planning coalition warfare as the more obvious issues of force integration, standardization and interoperability, and allocation of roles and missions.

These factors suggest that very few rational opponents are likely to wish to challenge (or be capable of challenging) us in a contest with mass theater-wide, multidimensional forces—given the very credible demonstration of U.S. capabilities displayed in DESERT STORM. Therefore, new opponents may decide, if they are determined to challenge us, to pose different problems, challenges that an RMA narrowly focused on the DESERT STORM scenario and based on technologies demonstrated in that conflict may be less capable of addressing successfully. For example, our next opponent could pose the problem of how to respond quickly despite his actively contesting our force deployment, while he may possess nuclear or other weapons of mass destruction (WMD) and long-range delivery systems capable of threatening not only U.S. forces, but allies, and third countries who control essential transit and staging facilities. Moreover, even if an opponent holds the same strategic objectives, he may be able to pursue them through different strategic concepts. Thus, overt cross-border invasion is not the only way of seizing neighboring territory; coups, destabilization, insurgencies, fifth columns, and blackmail are also among the traditional bag of tricks for aggressors.[7] And in these cases, the United States could find itself on the operational offensive against nonmechanized forces already deployed in very difficult tactical environments.

Alternatively, an enemy may also decide to pursue a different set of strategic objectives—damage, disruption to civil society, or interference with key global links, and use different strategic concepts— long-range attack, clandestine forces, urban warfare (as currently in Bosnia and formerly in Beirut), terrorism, or subornation and blackmail of civilian populations, using modern communications to bypass the government itself.[8] While there may be concern that "we don't do windows" (jungles, mountains, cities), even in those mission areas that we do, the next opponent may force us to do things so differently that we don't accomplish these missions very well either—for example, by employing large numbers of light forces, using mines densely on the battlefield, or contesting operations in littoral waters with mines, small but lethal fast attack boats, or conventional submarines. Current national strategy and defense planning largely ignore these potential problems in their narrow focus on heavily armed, largely mechanized, and quite technically sophisticated regional hegemons. Before the United States commits itself to an RMA initiative, it is essential to decide on which parts of the conflict map to focus our exploitation efforts.

The Evolving Conflict Map

Unless either Mexico or Canada unexpectedly transforms itself into an aggressive regional threat, by definition the United States will not in the near-term be the direct object of aggression by a regional power, such as Iran, Iraq, and North Korea. Therefore, we will fight conflicts with them at extended distances, and, with the exception of regional threats that acquire intercontinental strike systems, without direct threat to our national survival.[9] As we did in the Persian Gulf, we will have to transport and support our combat forces; however, unlike in that conflict, we may not have the luxury of six months of force buildup. Our opponent may actively contest our deployment and force buildup, directly or by applying pressure on allies and neutrals that control critical transit and staging facilities. Indeed, it is highly likely that with the lesson of that war in mind, the next regional aggressor may choose to strike quickly, before we can bring major forces to bear; and he may choose a strategic concept that allows him to do so. In addition, he may choose: forces that create lower signatures during his mobilization and buildup phases than armored and mechanized divisions; forces that can move to strike quickly at the target's strategic centers of gravity; or forces that are more difficult to target as he consolidates his position. Given the current strategic focus on a narrow set of regional contingencies, likely to be conducted in unprepared theaters, often without the benefit of in-place heavy infrastructure, logistics support and predeployed forces, the real challenge for U.S. military strategy may not be decisively defeating an opponent once we engage, but projecting power in a timely and responsive manner. Therefore, a key operational challenge will be the need to enhance our ability to move to the theater quickly while improving our capability to wage intense, short-duration combat to destroy enemy forces. The significant change from pre-deployed forward forces to a force projection military waging expeditionary campaigns requires that we alter our entire campaign paradigm, and it should focus our near-term attention on the problems of designing a force capable of rapidly deploying real combat power to a contingency theater against active opposition.

Unfortunately, not all lesser opponents are Iraq, as we had already discovered in Vietnam. Some opponents may be less susceptible to damage and pain, against either their military forces or civil societies (as we discovered during the Korean and Vietnam conflicts).[10] For many regional opponents, however, their military forces may be among the most modern and highest value assets (both in terms of equipment and human capital) they possess. Like the armies of the Italian city-states, they may be too valuable to risk in actual combat. Thus, some opponents may choose strategic concepts and means of execution that are explicitly limited and stylized, to which the large-scale and intense violence of a DESERT STORM-type clash may appear to be neither proportional nor appropriate either to their limited strategic objectives or to their constrained means of combat. And while the United States may currently be transfixed on the problem of stopping rapid cross-border acts of aggression, potential regional opponents may have other objectives that can be better served by alternative strategic concepts, particularly in light of their own vulnerabilities to the type of warfare demonstrated in the war against Iraq.

Furthermore, the canonical set of threats (focused on regional hegemons) represents a very small portion of the potential conflict map that may evolve. And on its face, these threats also appear to be those for which the current operational and organizational posture of the American military is best suited. Unless we believe that no more serious and challenging threats will emerge over the next several decades, we do need to recognize that we will face a major, even if not a "global" opponent, during this future.[11] How or whether a peer competitor emerges is likely to be related both to the evolution of the role of war in interstate relations during this period and to the ability of dominant U.S. military power to deter the emergence of a challenger. However, potential peer competitors do have choices about how they challenge us. While they could seek to do so with the tools of this RMA (the parallel approach), they might attempt to challenge us with mass and older technologies. In either case, the RMA would appear to be germane to these potential contests.

However, the very length of time it may take for a new peer competitor to emerge suggests that the utility of an RMA exploited today with a very narrow focus may no longer be evident at the time a challenge does emerge.[12] The new competitors could attempt to identify the *next* RMA and confront the United States with a whole new set of operational and technical challenges. And it is not clear that if they choose foreign ground (a different strategic concept, a different purpose, a different set of tools), how an RMA narrowly focused on DESERT STORM will necessarily be relevant. Especially since a peer competitor will almost certainly be a major economic power and tightly integrated into the global economy, his inherent degree of societal vulnerability may lead him to pursue his strategic objectives through means that are clearly limited,[13] using the implicit "rules of the game" in an attempt to protect himself from U.S. escalation to more violent forms of conflict.

As one speculative look into the far future, a potential future challenger to the system might decide not to engage the United States or other coalition members militarily, but to strike directly against the diverse network of international linkages that support the increasing globalization (and therefore homogenization) of commerce, culture, and politics. This opponent would be interested in destroying not the military power but the very fabric of the international system and striking at its core values, especially if these values are fundamentally hostile to deep cultural, religious, or ideological principles. Thus, such a challenger might choose to go directly against the linkages that bind major trading partners and regions. As an historical example of this path, it is worth recalling post-Napoleonic France's challenge to British naval mastery. Having determined after the costly loss at Trafalgar that British naval supremacy could not profitably be challenged directly, the French looked at waging a guerre de course against what they perceived to be the glue of the British Empire and of British economic superiority—worldwide trade. The obverse was that trade links of an island nation forced to import food and most raw materials, and also dependent, in return, on earnings from its manufactured exports, were perhaps *the* critical source of vulnerability—as was to be demonstrated during both World Wars. It is interesting to contemplate what an attack today against commerce, both sea- and air-borne, might look like (and how effective it might be) if waged with modern technologies and innovative operational concepts.

While the United States built forces to maintain sea control against a traditional naval opponent such as the Soviet Union, this mission area is now seen as very low priority with the turn in attention to "littoral warfare" and force projection from the sea. But even if the United States were to maintain the force capabilities and effective operational concepts in the interim, how relevant would they be for maintaining sea control against covert forces, perhaps operating large numbers of diverse types of modern commerce raiders? Similarly, could the United States protect the critical routes of commerce against an opponent intent on waging war against international aviation or telecommunications?

In addition to classic challenges, there may be other types of threats emerging in this evolving strategic environment. Indeed, these conflicts seem more probable than larger-scale, more traditional types of wars. At the other end of the conflict spectrum, there are likely to be a series of low-intensity, but not necessarily low-technology, conflicts resulting from the continuing diffusion of power and disintegration of existing states. These conflicts may involve both state and nonstate challengers. Moreover, nonstate challengers, like those in Somalia and Bosnia, may appear with fundamentally different objectives as well as strategic concepts of execution. Rather than attacking a neighbor for territorial aggrandizement, nonstate opponents might be tempted merely to inflict pain, and thereby destabilization, on opposing societies. If the object is pain, not publicity, we may find it difficult to identify the proper target for our response. Alternatively, the opponent may choose to strike from a posture that makes it impossible to avoid large-scale collateral damage to innocent populations in preemptive or retaliatory strikes.[14] These types of challenges may well call for a different focus from an emerging RMA. A shift in focus for near-term operations to the lower end of the conflict spectrum, the increasing importance of peacekeeping/peacemaking operations, the complications of multinational coalition operations, and the "CNN effect,"[15] are likely to produce pressures for limited U.S. casualties and requirements for constraining collateral damage as well. Can the RMA also provide useful capabilities against this more diverse array of possible challenges? Finding a successful path through the thicket of conflicting budgetary and policy pressures may be extremely difficult, but it also has the potential to be a key benefit if the RMA is properly conceived.

Changes in the Conduct of Warfare

Periodic fundamental changes in the nature of war and the conduct of warfare appear to date back far into history.[16] Examples of previous RMAs can help place this RMA in historical context. While there may be even earlier examples, such as development of the Macedonian phalanx and Roman legion, modern examples begin with the Napoleonic RMA (the "nation in arms")—utilizing for the first time in modern history the vast resources of a newly industrializing nation to equip and support a mass army. This RMA was contemporaneous with three other key upheavals: a political revolution that spawned democracy and the rise of the republican nation-state; a socioeconomic convulsion stemming from the Agricultural Revolution; and an economic sea change resulting from the spread of the Industrial Revolution to France. The result of the Napoleonic RMA was no less vast: not just the ability to conquer a *neighbor*, but to seize a continent—or in more modern terms, the means to wage a *theater-wide* campaign.

Since the Napoleonic RMA, many observers believe that, prior to the one now under discussion, there have been four other significant military revolutions. The first of these (encompassing both the American Civil and the Franco-Prussian Wars) built on the railroad and telegraph to extend, at the strategic level, the reach, mobility, communications, and logistics support consistent with the new continental scope of military operations. It also built on the second stage of the Industrial Revolution (such as "the American system of manufactures," i.e., interchangeable parts) to introduce more effective and lethal weapons, including the Minié-ball, breech-loaded artillery, and the "needle gun." The World War I RMA incorporated mass production technologies to equip multimillion man armies to increase mechanization for support logistics, and to employ factory products like the machine gun and barbed wire. This RMA turned the operationally mobile warfare of the previous revolution into fixed, positional, and relatively static, attrition warfare. The art of generalship was lost, replaced by the capacity of manpower rich states to supply soldiers and the means to destroy the other side's soldiers.

The third of these post-Napoleonic RMAs was the dual revolution in the inter-war period based on efficient internal combustion engines, tactical and strategic aircraft capabilities, and the radio to reintroduce strategic and operational mobility, maneuver, and initiative. On the one hand, these factors allowed the Germans to develop *Blitzkrieg*, directed at an operational solution to the problem of waging a rapid campaign to avoid getting bogged down in a two-front war in Europe, as happened in World War I. On the other hand, this same technical foundation supported an RMA by the U.S. Navy that combined carrier aviation, amphibious assault, and long-range submarine operations (supported by strategic bombing from seized forward island bases) to bring about the strangulation of our island opponent. U.S. strategic for the Pacific conflict recognized that the American strategic problem was to employ our vast industrial resources to bring about the decisive defeat of Japan on its home territory. Finally, the last of these four was the nuclear/long-range strike RMA based on atomic weapons and intercontinental strike capabilities that focused on the ability to destroy the economic, political, and social fabric of the modern nation-state, along with the enemy's military.

Few RMAs cause the kind of deep changes that the Napoleonic RMA did in both the nature of war and the conduct of warfare. That was a revolution set in train by a combination of fundamental economic, political, and social forces. It altered the scale of forces by the employment of the mass army (up to 500,000 by 1812) and, at the same time, it shifted the conduct of warfare by changing the scope to continental operations. But more importantly, changes in the underlying conditions set in train by the three contemporaneous upheavals made military forces relatively cheap; and despite the improvements in firepower enabled by industrialization, modern nation-states were able to field and support more forces than any opponent could kill— thus leading to attrition warfare since Clausewitzian-style strategically decisive victories were rarely obtainable through *coups de main*.[17] This 150-year period marked an era of military expansion with the shift to mass armies, continental or global scope of operations, and dependence on attrition warfare due to the difficulty in staging strategically decisive battles.

This era may now have come to a close. It was ended both by the nuclear/long-range strike RMA and by the lethally effective conventional operations that are now emerging from the nascent RMA. This next long-term cycle derives from not only a new era of expensive military forces, but also from a period in which the relative cost of killing is falling rapidly. The combination of rapidly escalating costs of major military systems, together with the enhanced lethality, will culminate in smaller, more valuable forces, along with a recovered ability to effect decisive victories. The result of this combination of factors fundamentally alters the underlying terms for military forces; and this has dramatic implications for the future of warfare as well as the scale and scope of conflicts. This next RMA appears to possess many of the properties of a Napoleonic RMA. It may mark the closing of that era in warfare dominated by large military forces and equally large scopes of military operations. This RMA may usher in a new period of military contraction and a return to wars fought for limited objectives by valuable forces too precious to waste in mass, attrition-style warfare.

These cyclic changes in the scale of military forces and operations appear to have a cousin in similarly cyclical changes at the strategic/political level. It is essential that strategy at both the grand and military levels be appropriate to the environmental circumstances, as much including the socio-cultural and economic dimensions as the political.[18] The same underlying forces—of nationalism, agricultural revolution, and industrial revolution—that allowed Napoleon to create his RMA also altered the objectives, and thus both the nature of war and the conduct of warfare. Napoleon moved modern warfare from "limited wars" fought by absolute monarchs, usually ended with contractual agreements of only modest gains and losses, to wars fought for unlimited ends, such as the destruction of the opposing state or regime, under the rubric of "unconditional surrender."[19] While subsequent RMAs have further raised the scale, broadened the scope, increased the intensity, and heightened the tempo of tactical operations, they have stayed within this fundamental politico-strategic framework. Thus, to the extent that this century has been dominated by conflicts not only between nation-states but between ideological systems, it has been a period of "total war." The circumstance of ideological conflict implied that "absolute ends" were proper and "total means" legitimate.[20] The Soviet notion of exploiting the vulnerability of the rear mirrored Douhet's earlier concept for attacking the enemy's will through strategic bombing. Under these conditions of "total war," there was no functional distinction between attacking the enemy's forces on the battlefield and attacking the enemy's forces by destroying the industrial base (and by extension, the entire political, economic, and social base) that supported them—*nor was there a difference in legitimacy.*

The "Information Revolution" and the change to post-industrial economies also seemed to presage significant changes not only for the means of warfare, but also for the objectives of war. Increasing globalization of commerce, decreasing economic returns to scale, near-real-time global telecommunications, the rise of centrifugal forces within the nation-state, among other trends, all raise questions as to the future objectives of interstate conflict, the appropriate strategies for pursuing national objectives under these conditions, and the operational means for conducting war. The old Clausewitzian objectives for military operations (destroy military forces, capture the territory, seize the leadership) largely mirror the key factors that underwrote the sources of strength of the newly industrializing economies. And these factors, what economists call the classic factor endowments of land, labor, and capital, also happened to be contemporaneous and coterminous with the sources of power of the classic 19th century nation-state. With the increasing integration of the industrial economies and their financial systems (and, at the same time, the decreasing importance of most traditional physical resources and raw materials), many of the classical notions of the objectives for conflict and the means to pursue them may be in the process of changing. Particularly in the absence of deeply-seated ideological conflict, one may speculate that rather than "total war," more limited objectives will be the norm.

Post-industrial (or information-based) economies build on information or knowledge as the fourth critical factor endowment. This carries at least three other significant implications for assessing the future security environment. First, this new factor endowment is not dependent on unchangeable physical resources nor on large, fixed capital investments that have long depreciation and pay-back periods. As a result, economic power built on this foundation can be developed far more quickly. Second, this source of strength is also far more agile and adaptable, and can respond with shorter time constants to changes in the environment; it may well be capable of greater surprises. Third, this factor is also more mobile and potentially more transferable; and power growing from it may be subject to greater diffusion.

IMPLICATIONS FOR THE RMA

To formulate appropriate new strategy and operational concepts informed by the RMA, we must address the nature of war as it may evolve under these circumstances. The concept of "limited war"[21] arose during the cold war in order to differentiate regional conflicts to be fought both for limited aims and with limited means, from the conflict that involved a central challenge to the existence of the two superpowers, which ran the risk of attendant escalation. The twilight of the cold war may have produced with the Gulf War the first "unlimited war" in Osgood's terms—a regional conflict in which a superpower was unconcerned by the potential for escalation to central conflict with the other superpower. In this case, while the objectives (on our side) were limited, the United States employed almost unlimited means against Iraq (with the exception of nuclear weapons). This combination of essentially unlimited means for achieving limited ends, with the acquiescence of the losing side, may make lessons from that war dangerously idiosyncratic.

It is likely that future conflicts, especially those involving multinational coalitions, will demand a closer linkage and greater proportionality between objectives and means in order both to limit the probability of escalation by the losing side and to maintain the political cohesion of multinational arrangements.[22] The move away from an era of total war will limit both means and ends. These limitations may once again raise the traditional distinction between enemy forces on the battlefield and the civil/industrial base. Thus, at the strategic level, whether an RMA that is perceived by a variety of audiences to bring to bear essentially unlimited military power is appropriate under an environment dominated by limitations on objectives is not clear.

Another difficult problem that the United States must confront is one of the complexity of the future conflict map. Multiple potential future threats make it necessary to maintain a range of capabilities to address challenges by potential and as yet unidentified peers at the highest end of the warfare spectrum, while staying prepared for conflicts with less technically capable opponents. The United States must also maintain the mid-term capabilities needed to decisively defeat regional hegemons, including ones that may possess nuclear capabilities. Even if we accept that this RMA can create the conditions for decisive victory in a dense, mechanized theater of war, can it produce the same results in a less dense, non-mechanized, low-intensity, localized conflict? Furthermore, if these revolutions derive from the integration and *synergy* of the four component elements, can "piece parts" be pulled out and applied effectively on a discrete basis, and still be a "revolution"? If the RMA cannot be applied as discrete pieces, should we not define the broader challenges within the focus of this RMA? Whether we can build off a common base of strategic needs and technical tools to appropriately tune the RMA in the exploitation phase to address these dissimilar challenges may, in the new security environment impacted centrally by fiscal constraints, ultimately define the military utility of the RMA as well as the strategic benefits for the decision maker.

To frame the issue most starkly, if the current RMA is nascent (and, based on historical evidence, it will probably take nearly 20 years to completely implement), should it be narrowly focused on a current problem (defeating mechanized regional hegemons) that may no longer be relevant when it comes to fruition or should it be broader and address threats that may evolve in the future? This question is crucial, especially if these Revolutions are not existential (they define themselves and only require recognition) but instead are purposeful creations of human guidance that can be directed towards particular strategic objectives and operational implementations.

UNDERSTANDING MILITARY TECHNICAL REVOLUTIONS

Sophisticated observers recognize the complexity of an RMA—that it is more than just clever new technology. They identify four component elements: operational innovation, organization adaptation, evolving military systems, as well as emerging technologies.[23] Fundamental issues for decision makers are to understand what constitutes a real revolution in military affairs, to recognize the implications of an RMA occurring, and to determine a standard by which they will measure an RMA, either to discern whether it exists or to know how well it has succeeded.

Types of RMAs

Reviewing previous revolutions in military affairs suggests that the issue is complex because there may be three distinct models for these types of fundamental military innovation, thereby complicating both definition and recognition. The first type of RMA is impelled by new, purely military technology, driven by fundamental scientific or technological inventions or developments. This is the type of RMA that has tended to dominate most people's understanding and led to the common perception of RMAs as technology-driven phenomena. It may also be the least frequent kind of RMA, with perhaps the recurved bow and the gunpowder revolution the only other examples of this type. This RMA was well-exemplified by the nuclear/long-range strike revolution created from the synthesis of nuclear weapons and intercontinental strike capabilities.

However, these revolutions present choices as to *what* strategic purpose and *how* to apply these new technologies. The choice of how to apply the clearly revolutionary technological innovation is whether as evolutionary improvements for executing existing missions or to create revolutionary change in the conduct of warfare. But historically, most technical innovations, especially the truly revolutionary ones, have been initially applied enhancing performance in the service of old objectives, without altering the fundamental conduct of warfare. For example, one could well argue that nuclear weapons merely allowed the fulfillment of Douhet's concepts for strategic air warfare. Spectacular technical breakthroughs, such as those that offer "order of magnitude" improvements in effectiveness or efficiency of existing missions, may well mask the need for more fundamental and far-reaching changes, in the same way that too many or too cheap resources are a breeding ground for economic inefficiency.

The second type of RMA, driven by operational and organizational innovation to redress a strategic problem, is well illustrated by the German *Blitzkrieg* developed in the inter-war period. While this type of RMA may not involve change in basic strategic objectives, it clearly involves fundamental change in the conduct of warfare, emphasizing not technological but more usually organizational and operational innovations. Because this type of RMA tends not to be resource-intensive, historically it has often been created by the defeated in the previous conflict. And importantly from today's perspective, because it is less hostage to long development and costly acquisition cycles, it may offer the best opportunity to address our near- and mid-term problems.

The third type, of which the Napoleonic RMA is the classic example, is driven by fundamental economic, political, and social changes outside the immediate military domain. These forces enable deep-seated and fundamental transformation of both the nature and the conduct of warfare. However, because these changes begin outside the military domain, they may be the most difficult to recognize and the most complex to adapt to military purposes.[24]

Revolutions (whether political, economic, socio-cultural, scientific, or military), by definition, imply discontinuity and change. In the case of an RMA, it is the discontinuous increase in military capability and effectiveness that sets an RMA apart from the normal evolutionary accretion of military capabilities, whether from technology insertion or operational innovation. A revolution is not merely an existential condition. Without recognition and exploitation, both necessitating human action, there is no technological revolution. Creating a revolution is more, therefore, than pushing the frontiers of science or the boundaries of military systems; it must be a positivist process that requires adaptation by the organism (or organization) for exploitation to occur. Thus, arguing that the introduction of new technology itself creates an RMA seems to be a misreading of the phenomenology of revolutions. Revolutions, moreover, possess an internal dynamic different from evolutionary development. Revolutions are a recognition that conditions have changed and represent a legitimation of innovation and change, and a call to push at the boundaries. Separate from the process of institutionalizing the revolution, the idea *itself* of a revolution creates new conditions, including threats to existing structures (and bureaucracies).

In addition to an agreed objective function that flows from purpose, determination of a standard to assessing RMAs requires criteria by which to make the measurement. Here an interesting epistemological question arises that affects both purpose and measurement: Is it sufficient to measure against the old norms, or does dealing with a revolution itself require defining new norms in order to capture the *essence* of the revolution?[25] Evolutionary innovations, even extremely clever ones, can be measured effectively with existing measures of effectiveness (MOEs) since the paradigm or model has not been altered. Evolutionary innovations, no matter how clever, merely applique new methods and means while revolutionary innovations create new paradigms. Truly innovative developments often do not only enhance the ability to execute existing tasks, but also attempt to perform new functions or meet new needs. Unless these new functions are captured in the assessment, innovative developments often do not appear to offer significant operational enhancements.[26] As the context is altered by revolutionary innovation, however, the old MOEs are clearly not appropriate in measuring the new model of operations. Perhaps they are no longer even relevant to altered objectives.

If the latter is true, then it follows that the entire analytical construct must also be altered to correspond to the new paradigm, affecting objective function, criteria, measures of effectiveness, as well as modeling and simulation tools. Thus, the nature of the RMA is not only a critical definitional problem, but an analytical one as well; and, therefore, widespread interest in a new revolution in military affairs strongly suggests the immediacy of the need for new analytical tools.

The Process of Revolution

Successful military innovation is a *process* that involves far more than just conceiving or developing new technologies and operational concepts.[27] Not only must the new capabilities be physically developed and their superiority demonstrated, but successful implementation of the innovations requires that they be integrated into the military force structure and operational concepts. Adoption of innovation demands more than just the ability to equip a force or military service with innovative weapons. Organizations, operational patterns, and decision processes must also be modified to implement the innovation as an integral element of the service's ethos.

Considered as a process, a revolution consists of five steps. First the conditions must be right for a revolution to occur. For a military technological revolution this probably implies not only the existence of new technologies that could be exploited, but also altered objective conditions in the geostrategic situation that make the world ripe for change.[28] An RMA involves a new appreciation of both "strategic needs" and "strategic opportunities." The combination of these two conditions presents the opportunity for new problems to be solved, whether or not they have previously even been recognized as problems, what might be called "latent demand." For example, when IBM developed the first personal computer (PC) in the early 1980s, no one forecast the exponential explosion of personal computer use that has occurred—and most importantly, no one understood or predicted the uses to which the PC would be turned or the changes these would produce.[29] But clearly, in retrospect, there was a large unrecognized (i.e., *latent*) demand for the capabilities that were then about to be made available. The second step in the process, then, is the *recognition* of a revolution in the making. The understanding that the appearance of new technical potentials and objective conditions defines new boundaries allows new problems to be identified that can only then be addressed.

The third step is acceptance or *validation* that a revolution is in progress: that the problems which were formerly beyond the horizon are now within our grasp and, therefore, worth addressing. The role of decision makers here may be key. Their acceptance can serve to validate the fact of the revolution, but their inattention can, on the other hand, delay the acceptance and, therefore, slow exploitation of the fruits of the revolution.[30] It is only after this step that adoption and adaptation can begin to occur; it is with this step that Kuhn's paradigm shift begins. Again, drawing on the PC example, it is at this step that the spreadsheet is invented and defines an entire range of problems that can now be solved. It is not that the fundamental problems themselves did not exist before; but because they were beyond the bounds of easy solution, they existed outside the cognitive framework. Now with both the tool and the need identified, these problems can be tackled by anyone with a few thousand dollars, even if they didn't have the technical skills or mathematical expertise previously required to model complex financial situations. The fourth step involves the careful specification of the new problem (or problems) that will be addressed (even if not solved) and the initial understanding of the implications that resolving these issues will have;[31] it is this stage that starts the *institutionalization* of the revolution. Finally, the fifth stage involves the active *exploitation* of the revolution and the widespread understanding of its consequences.

This view of the process of revolution suggests that these five steps should be separated into two phases: first, a phase of "strategic synthesis" that redefines the world and the problems that can be addressed; and second, an exploitation phase, an "operational/tactical syntheses" that defines how the problems will be addressed. This exploitation phase is probably best carried out not as a sequential series of activities (operational innovation, organizational adaptation, and military systems evolution), but concurrently. It needs to integrate these elements in order both to reduce the time cycle and to best obtain synergy among the complex interrelationships of these elements—a process similar to the "concurrent engineering" now in vogue in the commercial sector. The strategic syntheses, however, must precede the exploitation synthesis for the process to be properly tied to national strategy—for it should be only at this point that the decision makers can determine the strategic choices available and the overall directions and priorities to be taken in order to address key strategic problems.

It is important to note that a strategic synthesis can occur even in the absence of technical capabilities to drive or exploit it; and this would appear to confirm the existence of two distinct, sequential phases in the RMA process. Examples from previous Soviet practices would tend to reinforce this point. Changes to organizational structures in response to changing perceptions of the strategic problem, such as the creation of the Strategic Rocket Forces (SRF), the *Protivovoz-dushnaya Oborona* (PVO), and the *Protivokosmicheskaya Oborona* (PKO), each occurred prior to Soviet capability to satisfy the technical requirements for executing the missions assigned to these new organizations. However, the organizational adaptation to the altered strategic perception (the strategic synthesis) in each case led to the creation of a doctrinal foundation which, in turn, led to the creation of system requirements, i.e., the *idea* defined the technical demands.

A review of the elements of the inter-war aviation revolution also illustrates the point. The technical capabilities for (or "core competencies" in): improved aircraft engines aluminum structures, and monoplane designs did not tell decision makers whether to build pursuit aircraft, strategic bombers, long-range escorts, or carrier-based torpedo or dive bombers. "Core competencies" by themselves represent what we *can* do; but without strategy and a campaign plan, we can't determine whether they are what we *should* do.[32] Moreover, even having identified the specific instrument to be built, is it to be applied within the present strategic context or used to overturn that context and create a new strategic approach?[33] This also suggests that any attempt to identify "core competencies" for the U.S. military before the strategic synthesis is completed is doomed to failure. Indeed, the search for core competencies can only occur as part of the exploitation phase since it is only with a strategy that one can determine whether our capabilities are relevant.

The technical invention step may not be very different, whether a particular military innovation is evolutionary or revolutionary. However, the complete process for implementing innovation (and especially the *exploitation* step) has striking differences in these two cases, especially in those measures that are required for getting the organization to *adopt* the innovation. Evolutionary innovations, which offer improved means of accomplishing existing objectives, can be appliqued onto the existing model of warfare,[34] thereby minimizing dislocation and disruption to the organization, as well as to its sponsors and constituencies. This is, in fact, how the British and French actually applied the superior armored capabilities they developed during the inter-war period. In this case, since the calculus can clearly demonstrate either increases in effectiveness or reductions in cost for accomplishing the existing set of tasks, and the costs of disruption are minor,[35] the organization itself often becomes the strongest proponent for adoption of the evolutionary innovation.

In the case, however, in which revolutionary innovations are introduced, the situation becomes more complex and the path to adoption more difficult exactly because of the procedural and organizational implications of revolutionary innovations. *Blitzkrieg* represented this type of challenge to successful implementation.[36] Fundamentally, *Blitzkrieg* did not introduce any new critical technologies; rather it integrated armored forces, tactical aviation, and the radio into a new matrix provided by innovative operational concepts and organizational structures. With revolutionary innovation, fundamental change to the existing paradigm is guaranteed; and, therefore, (unlike the case of a Pareto optimum) while the overall benefits may be extremely large, there will be entities within the organization, and sponsors and constituencies external but linked to the organization, that will pay the price of these disruptions and dislocations. Thus, resistance to profound change is likely to be increased the more profound and discontinuous is the change. In particular, the potential effects of RMAs on the conduct of warfare and operational concepts for future campaigns suggest that attention also needs to be paid to how the services may differentially use these innovations for organizational advantage; not just for increased resources, but for a larger allocation of future roles and missions.

THE CHARACTER OF THIS REVOLUTION IN MILITARY AFFAIRS

While there appears to be general agreement in the community of the character of previous RMAs, there seems to be substantially less agreement either on the character of this RMA or on its role in future U.S. strategy; these differences are critical to the choices decision makers face.

The Roots of This RMA

Whatever the specific character of this RMA now under consideration, it builds heavily on concepts first put forward in the late 1970s and early 1980s in the series of papers by Marshal N. V. Ogarkov, including his seminal 1982 paper.[37] Ogarkov worried about how to conduct *decisive* operations in the European Theater of War (TVD), a theater that was exceptionally dense with heavily-armored mechanized forces, and overwatched by theater nuclear forces on both sides. Operational concepts such as the Independent Air Operation, the Operational Maneuver Group (OMG), and the high intensity battalion flowed directly from his strategic appreciation that tempo and striking power were essential for solution of the problem.[38] He and his colleagues identified many of the critical operational/tactical elements now being discussed for the new RMA; but perhaps most importantly, he correctly understood that a revolution was in the making. In the Soviet case, the *idea* for the RMA clearly preceded the technical capabilities to implement and exploit the concept. This example reinforces the important understanding that a revolution should start with the strategic problem, not the technologies or military instruments—a classically Marxist deterministic approach in which doctrine is derived from the geopolitical conditions.

Ogarkov's real concern, however, was that, by the early 1980s, the United States may have solved his strategic problem by synthesizing the four constituent elements of an RMA that have been previously noted (technologies, evolving military systems, operational innovation, and organizational adaption) into a *whole* that was more powerful than the parts.[39] In particular, he pointed to future U.S. technical capabilities to exploit the revolution as well as the limitations on the Soviets' own technical capabilities.[40] In Ogarkov's terms, the most impressive capability demonstrated by the United States during the Gulf War was probably the ability to conduct tightly synchronized, highly integrated joint operations *across the extent and throughout the depth of the theater*, striking both the enemy's strategic centers of gravity and the enemy's operational forces, in order to produce decisive results[41]—the very capability he had feared that the United States would be able to turn against the Soviets in the European TVD.

Some Current Views of This RMA

A useful place to begin examining current American views might start with what constitutes the most prevalent perception of this new RMA. Many observers see this RMA defined by the technologies demonstrated during the Gulf War: stealth, precision weapons, advanced sensors, C[4]I, and use of real-time (or near-real-time) space systems. They believe that these technical capabilities will allow the United States to dominate large-scale, high-intensity conventional battlefields contested by opponents possessing sizable armored and mechanized forces. In general, those who hold this view of the RMA believe that this type of combat, baselined in the Bottom-Up Review scenarios focused on Iran, Iraq, and North Korea, will be the dominant challenge for the United States for the foreseeable future. Those who take this technologically-driven approach also, in general, view this RMA as ready for implementation, but with significant life left to run from enhanced technology developments. Indeed, those who hold this view also believe that with minor tweaking, the core technologies can also address the other potential problems, such as low-intensity conflict or special operations.

Other observers take a broader, more functionally-oriented view, focused on generalized capabilities flowing from the "Information Revolution": the integration of advanced sensors, C⁴I, brilliant weapons, and simulation—i.e., the fusion of long-range fires and information as the core of this RMA. Many view these new technical capabilities as allowing the United States to move towards a "cybernetic" approach or to implement the Reconnaissance-Strike Complex (RSC) concept (first conceived by Ogarkov), or its newer incarnation, the Reconnaissance-Strike-Defense Complex (RSDC).[42] In their view, this would allow the United States to destroy almost any target on the battlefield instantly (as long as it yields a usable signature). Some others have focused more on sensors and communications capabilities and defined this RMA as "Information Dominance"; and the terms "Information Warfare" or "Information-Based Warfare" are being widely used. All these views take a bottom-up perspective, flowing from either the key technology components or their integration into complex systems; and they lead perhaps to too narrow an assessment of this RMA either as merely bits and pieces or as only clever technology evolution. These views, moreover, fail to capture the essence of revolutionary impacts, and almost certainly misstate the historical lessons of RMAs in general, and for this RMA in particular (discussed below).

Furthermore, these characterizations of the RMA are input-oriented, rather than measuring outputs—they do not characterize the RMA in terms of dramatically increased capabilities. This, therefore, raises the question of how to distinguish an RMA from clever military innovation: by the newness of its constituent elements or by the discontinuous "revolutionary" leap in capabilities? And how are the new capabilities produced by an RMA to be differentiated from simply "good execution"? If, in fact, an RMA is identified by the ability to solve a critical strategic problem through substantially increased effectiveness from new operational capabilities, then it must follow that a focus on the "piece parts" fails to capture the essence of the revolution.

Towards an Output-Based Definition

DESERT STORM demonstrated that a key advantage of U.S. forces was the ability to execute complex, orchestrated, high-tempo, simultaneous, parallel operations that overwhelmed the enemy's ability to respond. This advantage was built not only on advanced sensors and smart weapons, but perhaps more importantly on forces supported by modern C^{4}I systems and technologies that allowed the United States to collapse previous spacial and temporal constraints on simultaneous operations, whether combined arms or joint. These new capabilities will represent a fundamental advantage for the United States compared with any potential opponent and, therefore, should be a central focus in future resource and planning decisions. DESERT STORM may be but a foretaste of true *coherent operations*, but impressive nonetheless in the demonstration of the power of coherence and simultaneity.[43] At the operational level, the impact of these *coherent operations* is to overwhelm the opponent's ability to command and control his forces, denying him the ability to respond to our campaign plan and operations, and forcing him at the limit to execute only uncoordinated preplanned actions. The number and tempo of these simultaneous parallel operations by themselves produce saturation effects that simply overload the enemy's command system and provide American forces with ample exploitation opportunities.[44]

Therefore, at the operational level perhaps a good working definition of this RMA would be as follows: a (massively) parallel series of synchronized integrated operations conducted at high-tempo, with high lethality and high mobility, throughout the depth and extent of the theater, intended to force the rapid collapse of both the enemy's military power and the enemy's will. The power of this RMA would allow the United States the operational-level flexibility to allocate forces and fires in real-time between holding, breakthrough, and exploitation operations; and this allows concentration of effort to defeat enemy forces in detail at our choosing. However, due to the simultaneous parallel operations, the high mobility, the high lethality, and the capability for sustained high tempos of operation, so many enemy units can be defeated in detail simultaneously that the operation may resemble a more classic *coup de main* executed in a single main-force engagement.[45]

At the tactical level, the combination of high lethality and real-time information produces a deadly increase in unit effectiveness due to the short time constants of action by individual units (similar to Colonel John Boyd's concept for air combat of acting inside the enemy's observation/orientation/decision/action cycle). While "information dominance" is increasingly discussed, perhaps a deeper understanding would focus on "cycle-time dominance" on the operational level. Altering the time constants of decision and action to permit increased simultaneity and enhanced coherence will require collapsing the traditional distinctions between strategic, operational, and tactical as well as the command pyramid.

The "Information Revolution" enables this RMA by facilitating the shift to this type of seamless, high tempo parallel operational doctrine; it is an enabler in the same way that the Agricultural and Industrial Revolutions enabled the Napoleonic RMA. It provides two critical capabilities: first, the ability to ascend a *cognitive hierarchy* that starts with data, then provides *information* by correlating data, then *knowledge* based on situational awareness, and finally *understanding* built on the capability to predict and project forward consequences—and thereby improve decision making; and second, the ability to communicate those decisions in real-time with a high degree of assurance that the integrity of the message will be maintained—thus enhancing the action part of the cycle.[46] *Coherent operations*, enabled by the new ability to ascend the cognitive hierarchy, will allow, for the first time, turning C^3I from a supporting coordination function to a capability for real-time orchestration of combat power focused on the decisive point. It will provide the tools to reinforce the traditional role of the commander in exercising command during the battle.[47] And moreover, the impact of this RMA may also alter the advantages traditionally held by the initiator of conflict over the responder, and thus the historic balance between the offense and defense.

Implications for Utility

The very success of the Gulf War (following six months of preparation allowed us by Iraq) may mask the changing phenomenology of our evolving security problems, and, therefore, the utility of this RMA in those circumstances: not massive, theater-level combat between two large, well-equipped *in-place* forces, but prompt response to regional contingencies in which we will not have the benefit of a substantial forward force presence. Is the current goal in exploiting this RMA, therefore, still overly burdened by a cold war mindset formed by guarding the Inner-German Border (IGB) for 40 years or is it truly consistent with the evolving strategic conditions?

The RMA, once correctly defined, can serve the decision makers in a number of ways: as a filter for choosing new technology and programmatic initiatives; as a new organizing principle for force posture and roles and missions decisions; as a lever for bureaucratic change and control; or even as a means for institutionalizing change through a "process of permanent revolution." However, the maturity of the RMA is an important consideration for decision makers attempting to determine both how to use the RMA and how to implement it. What are the different implications if this RMA is in its formative stages, and therefore has considerable life yet to run, or if this is a mature revolution, even if it is relevant to near-term problems? Understanding this factor is critical for judging our competitive position and assessing the ability of potential competitors to engage us with these tools (or to assess their interest in doing so). If, as many observers appear to agree, this is a revolution in its early stages, with much headroom left for improvement in the individual constituent elements, then a relevant question is the degree to which improvements at this level would enhance the overall effectiveness of the RMA—how much edge is necessary to maintain strategic dominance in intense mechanized warfare?

An alternative view is that a DESERT STORM-type RMA is a relatively mature revolution whose relevance and advantages may both be receding. If we follow the logic of Marshal Ogarkov, this is a revolution that has been proceeding for nearly 20 years, but has only reached fruition now as the technical tools to implement it have become available. Will adoption of a mature revolution lock us into a set of old technologies with limited potential for further dramatic improvements? (And moreover, it is a revolution aimed at a specific context that may now be disappearing just as we are able to address it.) A mature revolution would pose several potential implications: first, that the asymmetric capabilities we now hold are likely to be transitory since the sources of technical advantage may already be diffused and beyond our control; second, that challengers are in a position to absorb the operational innovations that the United States has made rather than having to invent them afresh; third, some may also be able to mimic U.S. organizational adaptations (which are open to inspection) if they can overcome their own cultural and bureaucratic impediments;[48] and fourth, that future challengers may choose, rather than countermeasures to this RMA (parallel development, direct counters, passive counters, or asymmetric counters), to alter their overall strategic concept and come at us in ways that limit the relevance and utility of this RMA.[49] Of course, it may be that even if it is mature, it will remain relevant and the United States will be able to maintain a substantial and useful margin of advantage; but this issue requires analysis, not assertion.

IMPLICATIONS OF THIS RMA

The potent increases in operational effectiveness from this RMA can only be obtained by adopting substantial changes in operational concepts and organizational structures that will allow coherence to be maintained across spatial and temporal dimensions, as well as among forces of different types. Existing organizational structures, which are themselves the product of adjusting to the gross imperfections of previous C^3I capabilities, reinforce the tight linkage between *command* and *control*; and moreover, these structures are built around and reinforce the classic distinctions between strategic, operational, and tactical operations.[50] The existing hierarchy of operational levels and the corresponding levels of command will need to be reexamined, rethought, and redefined as part of creating a new warfare paradigm. Critical among these modifications will be changing the nature and location of the decision-making processes that result from the exercise of command and control of military forces in combat.

The existing warfare paradigm: (1) distinguishes among discrete *strategic, operational,* and *tactical* levels of operation; (2) is based heavily on preplanning; and (3) separates the overall operation into discrete phases. Implementing *coherent operations* will require that capabilities for command of simultaneous operations be increased and that the current spatial and temporal distinctions among these types of operations be removed. Moreover, shortening the critical time-constants for decision and action will require decentralization of command authority and a concomitant relaxation of control from the higher levels. But these alterations to the existing distinctions between strategic, operational, and tactical operations will require that the traditional focus, functions, and roles of the commanders in the existing hierarchical (and authoritarian) structure also be modified so that the nature and character of the decisions and actions correspond to the new paradigm.

Thus, it may be worthwhile to benefit from the experience already in the commercial sector on the impacts of these types of changes. Many of the critical enhancements portended by *coherent operations* are already reflected in changes in the organizational structures and decision and operations processes found in the commercial sector, including changes in the role of management and the locus of decision making in organizations. They are designed to improve dramatically the speed of both decision and execution; the key elements in competitive advantage. These changes affect the character of and requirements for *command* and *control* at each level of the organizational hierarchy. Military organizations, operational patterns, and decision processes will have to be similarly modified in order for the U.S. military to capture the potential for enhancing combat effectiveness offered by *coherent operations.*

Relieved of the classic span-of-control constraints by new technologies, organizational structures are being flattened and managers are being refocused to improve rather than impede flows of critical information. Low-value-added activities are being discarded and new foci for decisions at each level in the corporate hierarchy are being developed. "Delayering" and flattening of existing hierarchies are designed to move the locus of decision making closer to those who execute the critical decisions in order to speed up the ability of the institution to respond to unexpected conditions and opportunities. These changes have been upsetting to commercial organizations and to the people affected; and it has taken far longer than anticipated for the benefits from infusing modern "information technologies" to show up in the form of increased productivity and organizational effectiveness. Recent research suggests that the transformation has been so lengthy exactly because these organizations initially attempted to use the new technology to increase efficiency in performing the old tasks, rather than "re-engineering" the entire process based on the new capabilities.

Finally, perhaps the most fundamental change required to exploit the new RMA is the alteration in perspective from improving the individual elements of combat power (and measuring those enhancements) to integrating and focusing the power of the "whole." Integration of the whole rather than enhancement of the parts is the central pillar of this RMA; then the campaign plan and joint operations become the defining level for measuring effectiveness. Assessing the full impact of *coherent operations* on a force projection military in future contingency operations cannot be accomplished by retaining the present emphasis on "stovepipe" operations, or "piece-parts" analyses, of forces executing an old-fashioned campaign model first invented by General John J. Pershing.

These changes suggest many of the restructuring activities that will be required if the U.S. military is to seize the opportunities presented by the RMA. Therefore, the services must be prepared to go beyond the DESERT STORM model to investigate and to exercise new operational as well as organizational concepts. These will include a complete redesign of the traditional campaign paradigm, so that it can define the direction and character of the RMA initiative and understand the potential implications of an RMA that will fundamentally alter doctrine and organizational concepts as well as future system requirements.

In implementing the RMA and transforming the "conduct of warfare," perhaps the real innovation will be found at the level of the campaign plan. The transformation will be in determining in which elements, in what sequence mission tasks are combined, and in how rapidly they are executed, rather than in the individual concepts for these mission tasks (what the military calls tactics, techniques, and procedures). This type of campaign needs to be viewed as an integrated, seamless process in which time constants of the individual pieces are critical to the effectiveness of the overall plan. Indeed, the analogy between this campaign paradigm to "just-in-time production" or "agile manufacturing" and the older campaign model, with its pre-planning, clearly delineated phases, and reliance on reserves, to an inventory-based manufacturing process is striking.[51]

CONCLUSIONS

Despite the difficult definitional issues in characterizing this RMA, the most important determinations that must be made concerning the RMA initiative are not analytical (epistemology), but of purpose (teleology). Decision makers have three problems, all of which involve crucial choices. First is the strategic purpose of the RMA, which depends on the perception of the nature of the future strategic environment. Second is its role in U.S. defense planning, which flows from that prior determination of purpose. Third is to ask what is the best way to exploit our particular implementation of this RMA?

First, while it appears that an RMA based on DESERT STORM would fulfill Ogarkov's search for an operationally decisive instrument for TVD-level planning and operations over the IGB contested by NATO and Warsaw Pact forces, it is not apparent that this strategic problem remains relevant. What is not answered is whether that RMA also would be an appropriate and effective instrument for achieving strategic objectives other than the military dominance of a theater of war, for operations at levels below a theater of war, or for conflicts with nonmechanized, non-Soviet-style opponents. A new strategic synthesis is needed to translate the relevance of the RMA beyond our traditional cold war problem. Consistency of means and ends is important. A revolution in military effectiveness may succeed, and may even be dominant at the tactical and operational levels, but may not produce strategically decisive results unless it is exactly and appropriately related to strategic purpose. While the German *Blitzkrieg* was an appropriate operational solution to the problem of waging a rapid campaign in Europe to avoid getting bogged down in a two-front war as in World War I, it would not have been a relevant response to either the Japanese or U.S. strategic problems in the Pacific theater. More importantly, *Blitzkrieg* may well have been an appropriate operational concept in service of an inappropriate strategy. The real German strategic problem, however, may have been the *prospect* of a two-front war, an event they themselves guaranteed by their attack on the Soviet Union. Completing the new strategic synthesis is essential if the RMA is to be appropriately linked to the strategic purposes relevant to the evolving geostrategic environment.

Second, as an internal instrument, the RMA can serve many different roles. Among them are: a screen for budgetary control, a process for institutionalizing change, a tool for assuring that the Department of Defense is structured to fight *future* wars, and a lever for changes in roles and missions. However, these key roles depend less on the specific internal details of the RMA (deciding between technologies, systems, innovations, and organizational changes) than on correctly capturing the *Gestalt* of this RMA.

In addition to the changing nature of the strategic problems that the United States will face, design of U.S. forces must also address operational and tactical level problems that will certainly change in scale, if not in intensity and duration. While the advanced technologies coupled to largely existing operational concepts and organizational structures were used with great success in DESERT STORM, the Gulf War displayed many idiosyncratic features; and it may well represent the final act of the old strategic environment in which massed, armor-heavy forces represented the critical component of the threat. Although DESERT STORM focused on a major regional challenge, the fact that Iraqi forces were equipped and largely trained along classic Soviet lines, as well as the extended period in which the United States was able to put in place an extensive infrastructure, stockpile huge amounts of logistics, and deploy a diverse array of extremely large combat forces, made this campaign perhaps resemble more traditional cold war contingencies than potential uncertain regional contingencies occurring on short notice into largely unprepared theaters of operations.

If part of the overall effectiveness of this RMA depends on the impact of overloading the enemy's command system, will these advantages still pertain as the operational venue is reduced in scope and scale?[52] Another facet of this issue is whether effective operations at lower echelons employing the constituent tools of the RMA remain a military technical revolution. Finally, a third facet is how much of the impact of this RMA will be due to effective execution which is, in turn, highly dependent on realistic training and exercises. This latter question is exceptionally important for resource allocation decisions between force size, quality, and readiness; and it is also important to our understanding of how to preserve our present competitive advantage.

Finally, in light of the real costs of fundamental organizational change needed to accommodate new operational concepts, the third critical problem is to define an implementation concept that allows this fundamental alteration to both the existing warfare as well as the command and control paradigms; this course must maximize the likelihood of the change being adopted and internalized by the military institutionally, not simply grafted onto old stock. Perhaps more importantly, coupled with the very real fiscal pressures, the success itself of DESERT STORM may accelerate demands to reshape and restructure the American military; and real questions arise whether the potential of an RMA can be seized simply by appliquéing new technologies and systems onto existing structures and concepts or can even be understood and appreciated with the analytical tools developed for the previous environment.

It may be that a dual focus and, therefore, a two phase RMA is required, one that addresses both near-term and far-term strategic problems. Accepting that an RMA is composed not only of technologies and evolving military systems, but also of operational innovation and organizational adaptation, it may be that the major focus for this RMA in the near- to mid-term should lie in these two latter areas so that a common base of technologies and military systems may be able to serve the needs of both the high and low ends of the conflict spectrum—without draining already stressed budgets. And in light of three issues identified in this monograph—relevance to future U.S. strategic problems, the likely challenges to be presented by future opponents, and maturity of this RMA—a case can be made that a major focus of an RMA initiative should be not only to exploit fully the current technical capabilities by creating an appropriate operational and organizational matrix with the *next* RMA. To identify and allocate sufficient resources to forging an RMA *beyond* that is more appropriate to the evolving set of challenges only now dimly perceived on the strategic horizon.

Given the increased globalization of technology resources, it is probably self-evident that over the longer-term (but more debatable in the near-term) the United States will lose the asymmetric advantages we now hold in the underlying technologies needed for this RMA. Improved intelligence collection and analysis in these areas (especially against allies and potential suppliers of the critical technologies) should yield significantly better understanding of these rates of change to allow us to better gauge our relative competitive position. The possibility that challengers may develop totally new operational concepts is clearly speculative, but "gray design bureau" and "plan orange" type games may be extremely useful to explore the possibilities.[53] The degree to which challengers may absorb, or develop on their own, the critical operational innovations and organizational adaptations that are key to the RMA may be the most difficult questions to resolve since they will require both an exceptionally good understanding of the dynamics of an RMA (which is not yet in evidence) and careful analysis of the complex relationships between an RMA and the socio-cultural and economic factors of a wide range of potential competitors. Recent history suggests that these questions will seriously stress our intelligence and analytical communities.

How the operational and tactical levels of warfare are conducted (disregarding politics for the moment) determines roles and missions, the traditional focus of the military services; and an RMA would undoubtedly bring about substantial changes in the current alignment of roles and missions among the services. However, without the benefit of a completed strategic synthesis, current attempts to redefine roles and missions appear too early to have useful impact; these changes appear to be elements that should occur only in the second phase of the revolution—when the operational approach has been determined and the path for exploitation has been clarified.

In summation, using an RMA initiative, intentionally or unintentionally, primarily to define a "technical legacy" makes three crucial errors. First, it misdirects effort toward a probably fruitless search for "silver bullet" technology on which to build the RMA. Second, it misdirects attention away from the critical issues of, and relationships among: purpose, strategy, doctrine, operational innovation, and organizational adaptation that are the essential issues for an RMA. Third, in committing the first two errors, it compounds the problem by being astrategic since it risks wasting very scarce defense resources on new programs that may be irrelevant to future security challenges. This course would be particularly unfortunate since it would squander the rare opportunity presented by the changes in technological conditions to enable an RMA that could appropriately forge America's military for the evolving geostrategic environment; one that is also being reshaped by fundamental changes in the underlying political, economic, and socio-cultural conditions.

NOTES

[1]When exploration of this subject by the American defense community first began, the term commonly employed was the "Military Technical Revolution" (MTR). Unfortunately, MTR denotes too great an emphasis on *technology*. Therefore, much of the interested community now uses the term Revolution in Military Affairs, which focuses on *revolution*, and clearly places *technology* in a supporting role.

[2]The U.S. defense community owes a debt of gratitude to Mr. Andrew Marshall, the Director of Net Assessment, OSD, for identifying this important subject and pressing efforts to have the community begin an RMA initiative.

[3]An external perspective focuses on outer-directed *strategic* objectives while an internal perspective focuses on inner-directed issues such as adapting the organization and overcoming structural barriers to innovation.

[4]It may also be that one objective held by some analysts for the RMA is not to address specific challenges from the diverse array of potential competitors, but to attempt to use the RMA to maintain the aura of unchallengeable, overall U.S. military and technical dominance by shaping perceptions, by "casting long shadows," whether the RMA is an appropriate solution to the specific challenges or not.

[5]Does the nature of conflict result from natural laws (the technical and environmental conditions that Karl Marx called the "sub-structural forces") or from the interplay of sociopolitical and economic factors (the evolving geostrategic interests)? Is the conduct of warfare affected by the stage of social development of the participants or can it be imposed by a key actor?

[6]While Russia and other former Warsaw Pact nations may be prepared to sell advanced weapons at prices that are very low by Western standards, it is less likely that they will, or can, make those sales as "loss leaders" for political or ideological influence.

[7]For example, Hitler's "peaceful" annexation or "reunification" of Austria, the *Ansckluss* [sic], in 1938.

[8]Carl Builder of RAND has written and discussed the latter concept.

[9]This issue, however, has a more complex, and darker side for U.S. planning. While the Gulf War, and similar future conflicts, may represent only limited threats to interests, and therefore limited stakes, for the United States (or potential coalition partners), the regional aggressor may perceive his "strategic interests" or even his very survival (national or regime) at risk once the United States engages with unconstrained military power, even in pursuit of "limited" objectives. In light of the conventional military capabilities demonstrated by the United States in that war, and especially the damage inflicted by the "strategic" air campaign, we should not be surprised if our opponents contemplate the use of their "strategic" weapons—whatever they may be. Therefore, it is likely that we may be forced to employ more limited means in achieving limited ends by the consequences of not doing so.

[10]It is an interesting question to explore this relationship between vulnerability and stage of socioeconomic development; it may well be that nations like Iraq are the most vulnerable, having grafted a thin veneer of modernity onto fundamentally less-developed societies, and thereby creating an exceptionally fragile infrastructure that does not respond well to stress.

[11]And despite the relative optimism expressed earlier, a major threat could emerge sooner. After all, it was only 10 years between the height of the Weimar Republic and the invasion of the Soviet Union in 1941. See Jeffrey R. Cooper, *Implications of a "Long Peace,"* Center for National Security Studies, Los Alamos National Laboratory, December 1991, for a discussion of other historical analogues for the period we have now entered.

[12]This same problem bedevils the concept of "prototyping." While there is certainly utility in proving a new technology or piece of equipment, there is probably little sense in putting it "on the shelf" to await a future conflict since it is likely to be obsolescent at that time. Thus, in this context, both prototyping and the MTR are better viewed as

processes, not products—explicitly designed to maintain ferment in their particular areas.

[13]As Dr. Daniel Gouré, Deputy Director for Politico-Military Affairs, CSIS, has aptly phrased it, "Nintendo Warfare."

[14]This concept is not new. In fact, some had explored this notion in earlier years by suggesting that Pershings be deployed in German town squares in order to force the ugly choice of large-scale civilian deaths in a Soviet preemptive attack.

[15]The "CNN effect" refers to the global, real-time news coverage that is becoming increasingly available and makes conduct of most military operations a matter of immediate public scrutiny.

[16]For the purposes of this monograph, the term *nature of war* will be defined by the entities that engage in the conflict and the objectives over which they fight while *conduct of warfare* will refer to the modalities of the conflict, that is, how the war is fought. Thus, during the past century and a half, the nature of war has been defined by the fact that it has been fought by nation-states for political objectives; warfare has been conducted primarily by mass armies equipped with weapons provided by modern industrial technology. I do recognize that others use *nature of war* to refer to the immutable characteristics such as combat, leadership, valor, and blood.

[17]I am indebted to COL Gary Griffin, USA, TRADOC, for this important insight. Dr. John Hanley has also touched upon this point in "Implications of the Changing Nature of Conflict for the Submarine Force," *Naval War College Review*, Autumn 1993.

[18]The Soviet stress on the political dimension of war and the correspondence of military power with the "stages of socio-cultural development" recognized that strategy exists within a complex web of nontechnical factors.

[19]See, for example, J.F.C. Fuller, *The Conduct of War: 1789–1961*, 1961 (republication by the DaCapo Press, New York, 1992), pp. 15–25, for an excellent discussion of these changes.

[20]See Fuller; the Peace of Westphalia in 1648 ended the Thirty Years War which was a religious conflict of absolute ends and total means, and opened a period of limited conflict objectives. Prior to *raison d' état* of the modern civil state, war in Europe was often fought for absolutist (if not Manichean) religious reasons resembling ideological conflict.

[21]See Robert E. Osgood, *Limited War*, Chicago: The University of Chicago Press, 1957. As Fuller, p. 20, noted, this actually harkened back to pre-Napoleonic objectives of the "absolute" monarchs.

[22]See, for example, Robert W. Tucker, "A Just War?," *National Interest*, Fall 1991. Indeed, domestic reaction fueled by the "CNN effect" to scenes of destruction on the "Highway of Death" was clearly one factor in curtailing coalition combat operations and probably can't be ignored in the future. The new Army FM 100-5 explicitly notes this factor in planning and conducting future operations.

[23]See Dr. Andrew Krepinevich's original 1992 study on the MTR prepared while he was in OSD/NA.

[24]This would be consistent with the literature on technology innovation, transfer, and adoption by firms and industries. Directed, dedicated research, while the most costly, tends to be the easiest and quickest to apply. "Not invented here" developments often find internal sponsorship and adaptation difficult, even once their relevance and implications are recognized.

[25]For example, if an RMA involves a fundamental shift from an attrition paradigm to one in which speed of execution is as important, then it should follow that the dimension of measurement should shift as well from questions of "how many killed" to "how quickly."

[26]GPS is an extremely recent and relevant example of the problem. An older example was the Army's attempt until the 1930s to treat the machine gun as an artillery weapon.

[27]There is an extensive literature on both military and civilian innovation that explores the phenomenology of the entire process, including the complex problems attendant on organizational adoption of the innovation, not just the step of technical invention.

[28]The phenomenology of this cognitive dissonance is the same whether it is in the context of Kuhn's "paradigm shift" or the Marxist-Leninist formulation of "internal contradictions."

[29]A classic problem in the literature on inventions and innovation is the inability to predict the impact a new development may have not in meeting existing needs but in creating entirely new markets. Not only IBM and the "PC" in the early 1980s, but IBM and the mainframe computer in the 1950s, and the Air Force and GPS in the 1970s, are all good examples of unpredictable "latent demands" that could not be forecast in the existing framework. Without understanding of the type and magnitude of the change the invention would introduce, analysis in the existing context was irrelevant.

[30]What is not clear, however, is whether their opposition can stop a revolution; historical analysis could answer this important question.

[31]Given the peculiarly American approach to analysis (decomposition, assessment in detail, only then synthesis, and finally understanding of the whole), the process attendant on revolutionary innovation poses a difficult procedural reversal demanding a "holistic" or *Gestalt* approach *ab initio*.

[32]The concept of "core competencies," developed at Harvard Business School, is currently in use by organizational consultants attempting to reform or restructure private-sector companies; it attempts to identify those particular areas in which an organization is exceptionally proficient as the focus of its energies.

[33]As Dr. Gouré has pointed out, the British invented the tank and employed it piecemeal in the Battle of Cambrai, within that existing strategic context, to support the breakthrough of infantry against machine guns and fortified trench systems. The Germans, on the other hand, organized the tank into armored formations and integrated them with close air support to develop the *Blitzkrieg*, which created a new strategic context. This problem may affect the existing seven DDR&E "thrust areas"; without a stronger link to strategy appropriate to the new security context, pursuit of these areas will not necessarily provide important tools for strategic exploitation.

[34]This paradigm or model includes division of roles and missions among the services, as well as campaign plans at the joint level, and force structure and doctrine within each service.

[35]Thereby creating a Pareto optimum in which no party is made worse.

[36]And adoption of *Blitzkrieg* was strongly resisted by the German Army hierarchy.

[37]Marshal N. V. Ogarkov, *Always in Readiness to Defend the Homeland*, March 25, 1982, is the key paper usually cited. Other shorter papers by Ogarkov date back to fall 1979; and a later important work was his 1984 May Day article.

[38]"Battalions in Military Operations," *Military Herald*, 1985, for example, is a conceptual precursor to the high leverage brigade concept now being discussed by USCENT-COM.

[39]See, for example, the 1982 FM 100-5, *Airland Battle*, and the Follow on Forces Attack (FOFA) concept, both based on the innovative ideas of Generals DePugh, Starry, and others; these could certainly have fueled Ogarkov's concern. These doctrinal changes indicate that the United States also had an intuitive understanding of the revolution that was about to occur; but like Moliere's character, the Army had been speaking prose (the RMA) but didn't know it.

[40]Ogarkov, *History Teaches Vigilance*, April 1985. This appreciation, in turn, led to the support by much of the Soviet military for *perestroika* in order to create the internal preconditions for competing with the United States in this new technical era. Having watched the United States validate the RMA, many in the former Soviet military are likely to be convinced that the correctness of pursuing the path of "denuclearization" by political means and *perestroika* internally has been confirmed. Marshal Grachev, Yeltsin's Defense Minister, for example, has been an outspoken proponent of both elements.

[41]For example, this was highlighted in the *Desert Storm* "Lessons Learned" Study conducted by the Center for National Security Studies, Los Alamos National Laboratory.

[42]All these concepts owe much to Soviet work in "control theory" and automated processes.

[43]See Jeffrey R. Cooper, *The Coherent Battlefield*, SRS White Paper, Arlington, VA, June 1993, for a more complete discussion of *Coherent Operations*.

[44]These effects, in fact, resemble the conditions intended to be produced by Soviet-style "Radio Electronic Combat."

[45]Another benefit of the intense but rapid execution is the likely reduction in American casualties compared with a more drawn out, sequential attrition style operation.

[46]Many commentators have returned to John Boyd's concept of the Observation/Orientation/Decision/Action (OODA) Loop in discussing the impact of the "Information Revolution." Almost uniformly, however, they have focused on the decision side of the cycle (observation/orientation/decision) and neglected the very important implications of significantly enhanced "information technology" for the action element. Real-time, dependable communications have analogous effects to Boyd's key technical requirement for the pilot/aircraft combination, 3000 psi hydraulics, to link more rapid decisions by the commander to responsive actions by his unit.

[47]The new C^4I technologies could also be used to create a new class of remote commanders, not unlike the British and French "Chateau Generals" in World War I, displaced physically but linked to the front by the telegraph. The wide band width and real-time processing capabilities may well tempt the military to this Faustian bargain.

[48]An intriguing and important sociological issue is the relationship of an RMA to the society which fosters it—must it be organic to and consistent with the socio-cultural foundation—or can it be grafted onto alien stock?

[49]As noted earlier, an opposing proposition suggests that much of the U.S. advantage lies beyond the four constituent elements in the ability to execute, which is built on training, exercises, simulation, and supporting elements such as logistics and maintenance—these factors may be even more difficult to replicate and have traditionally been neglected by most militaries outside the developed world.

[50]See, for example, Colonel James G. Burton, "Pushing Them Out the Back Door," *U.S. Naval Institute Proceedings*, June 1993, and subsequent correspondence for views on the confusion in roles and command levels engendered by these changes in our understanding of the command functions at the strategic and operational levels of war. My own view is that the operational level is expanding as the capabilities to engage in Clausewitzian decisive combat are being recovered. As time replaces space as the critical factor, the concurrency and compression of future campaigns may provide opportunities for "tactical" engagements to become decisive.

[51]Once this analogy is drawn, it is interesting to contemplate the disastrous experience of General Motors in automating and robotizing key production lines ("innovative operational concepts") rather than in "re-engineering" the entire production process itself and better integrating existing manual subprocesses.

[52]A useful study would be to analyze the relationships between combat tempo, scope, and parallelism on the one hand, and the number and pace of command decisions on the other; while this smacks of previous Soviet interest in command norms and cybernetic control theory, they may well have intuitively understood this element as an important component of the emerging RMA.

[53]It should be noted that the Japanese attack on Pearl Harbor was not an example of technological surprise, but of both operational and tactical surprise. The tactical surprise was that they could effectively deliver air-dropped torpedoes in shallow, contained waters.

Chapter Six

INFORMATION, POWER, AND GRAND STRATEGY: IN ATHENA'S CAMP—SECTION 1[*]

John Arquilla and David Ronfeldt

Information has been associated with power, war, and the state since at least the time of the Greek gods. One normally thinks of Ares, or the Roman refinement Mars, as the god of war. But where warfare is about information, the superior deity is Athena—the Greek goddess of wisdom who sprang fully armed from Zeus's head and went on to become the benevolent, ethical, patriotic protectress and occasional wrathful huntress who exemplified reverence for the state. According to Virgil, for example, Troy would be powerful enough to withstand all its enemies so long as it possessed and honored the Palladium, a sacred statue of Athena provided by Zeus or Athena herself. Understanding this, the Greeks arranged its theft, symbolically denying the Trojans the benefits granted by access to the goddess of wisdom. So Athena sided with the Greeks in the Trojan War, where she bested Ares on the battlefield and conceived the idea of the wooden "gift horse" secretly loaded with Greek soldiers. The Trojans made the monumental misjudgment of hauling it inside their fortress walls, over the protestations of the priest Laocöon and the seer Cassandra. The rest is history, and legend.

[*]Originally published as "Information, Power, and Grand Strategy: In Athena's Camp," in *The Information Revolution and National Security: Dimensions and Directions,* edited by Stuart J. D. Schwartzstein, Washington, D.C.: CSIS, 1996. Copyright 1996 by the Center for Strategic and International Studies. Reprinted by permission. This section and Section 2 (which appears as Chapter Eighteen of this volume) have been copy edited since the initial publishing.

Ever since, examining the relationship between information and power has attracted all manner of political and military theorists, as indicated by this sampling:

- Sun Tzu observed over 2,500 years ago: "Know thy enemy, know yourself; your victory will never be endangered."

- Francis Bacon considered information the key to Elizabethan England's development as a great power: "For the conduct of war . . . in the youth of a state, arms do flourish; in the middle age of a state, learning; and then both of them together."

- Clausewitz regarded the role of knowledge in warfare as "a factor more vital than any other."

- Michel Foucault, who viewed knowledge and power as inextricably intertwined, considered mapmaking as an example of "knowing" that conveyed juridical, military, and political power: "Once knowledge can be analyzed in terms of region . . . one is able to capture the process by which knowledge functions as a form of power."[1]

What does it mean to believe such statements? Conventionally, it means that something viewed as immaterial and abstract—like a specific piece of information or knowledge—can be put to hard, practical use to strengthen one party over another. The exercise of an actor's power may turn on the possession of such information; it becomes an instrument of power. But that conventional view barely begins to probe the depths of meaning embedded in statements that "information is power."

In this essay, we offer some observations about the relationship between information and power. Our theme is that information, generally thought to be immaterial, is increasingly seen to be an essential part of all matter. In contrast, power, long thought to be based mainly on material resources, is increasingly seen to be fundamentally immaterial, even metaphysical in nature. As information becomes more material, and power more immaterial, the two concepts become more deeply intertwined than ever. These trends may generate some interesting implications for the theory and practice of warfare and for grand strategy in the times ahead.

The assumption that military power and grand strategy will still matter implies that states will still matter, and that the international system will remain state-centric in the emerging information age. We believe this to be the case, and differ from those who argue that the diffusion of information and the attendant erosion of hierarchy will inexorably weaken states, and that a "global village" of nonstate actors may someday even supplant the state system. The information age will surely transform the nature of states in many ways and will probably limit their range of action in many areas unless they cooperate with nonstate actors. But the state will remain vibrant, effective, and desirable as a time-tested form of administrative and political organization for societies, both for those that are still in search of self-determination and sovereignty, and those, presumably like the United States, that are highly advanced and on the verge of developing additional information-age structures. [2]

The endurance of the state and the state system in the information age will affect the tenets underlying both major schools of international political theory: the realist and the interdependence schools. The state-centric realist school will have to continue recognizing that non-state actors are multiplying and gaining power, constraining the roles of states in some issue areas. The interdependence school, which has emphasized the rise of non-state actors, will have to accept that states are going to have significant new political and other instruments at their disposal as a result of the information revolution. A similar conclusion is reached by Eugene Skolnikoff in his recent assessment of how today's scientific and technological revolutions may affect international politics. In his view, these revolutions will require the realist and interdependence schools of international political theory to rethink some propositions, but he finds little reason to doubt that "states remain the dominant structural element in the international system." Indeed,

> it would not be difficult to construct a scenario in which the emergence of major challenges to the planet or to a large part of human society led to much greater centralization of authority in the hands of a few states in the international system.[3]

In our view, the "softening" of power and the increasing "tangibility" of information may usher in a new golden age for states. What may be coming to an end, if anything, is not the state or the state system, but rather the empire and imperialism in their classic forms. Indeed, it is not so much the state but rather the empire that dominated the international system after feudalism ended five hundred years ago. Empires, because of their size and resources, often survived even gross blunders. Witness the resilience evident during the long periods of imperial decline suffered by Rome, Byzantium, Spain, France, Britain, and Russia. However, in the 20th century, nationalism and other factors, including inherent incompetencies, have dealt a series of sledgehammer blows against empires, the last of which collapsed just a few years ago.[4] The state—in both its nascent and advanced varieties—is the key organization to venture into the vacuums created by the end of the classic empire. There is no orderly alternative.

At the same time, a new model of the state may emerge, probably one that is leaner, yet draws new strength from enhanced abilities to coordinate and act in concert with non-state actors. In this vein, Peter Drucker, after arguing that the classic nation-state metamorphosed into the unwieldy "megastate" in the 20th century by taking on excessive social, economic, and military duties, concludes that success in the post-capitalist age will require a different model.[5] Other thinkers are also starting to propose that what lies ahead is not the demise but the transformation of the state.[6]

By implication, the skillful exercise of military power and grand strategy may grow in importance in the information age. States are more compact than empires but have smaller margins for error. To do well in the times ahead, they must strive to understand that the nature of information and power, and the interaction between them, may be changing radically.

THREE VIEWS OF "INFORMATION"

Most people think they know "information" when they see it, and any dictionary can provide a working definition. But like any concept that grows in importance, it has begun to acquire new meanings and imply new possibilities. It deserves closer scrutiny.

Three general views of "information" appear in discussions about the information revolution and its implications.[7] Each view approaches the concept differently; each harbors a different perspective of what is important. Two views are widespread: The first considers information in terms of the inherent *message*, the second in terms of the *medium* of production, storage, transmission, and reception. The emerging third view transcends the former two; it speculates that information may be a *physical property*—as physical as mass and energy, and inherent in all matter.

Information As Message

The first view is the most ancient, classic, and ordinary; indeed, it is the view found in the dictionary. Reduced to bare essentials, it regards information as an immaterial message or signal that contains meaningful (or at least recognizable) content and that can be transmitted from a sender to a receiver. Such information usually comes in the form of "reports, instructions, and programs."[8]

This results in what many analysts call the "information pyramid."[9] (See Figure 6.1.) The pyramid has a broad base of disorganized raw "data" and "facts," atop which sits a stratum of organized "information." The next, still narrower stratum corresponds to information refined into "knowledge." Atop that, at the peak, sits the most distilled stratum, "wisdom"—the highest level of information. A cognitive version would place "awareness" at the base, "knowledge" above, and "understanding" at the peak.[10]

"Information," then, corresponds to part or all of this pyramid, but the term is usually employed in the latter, expansive sense these days. This carries some risk of misunderstanding. The pyramid implies that the higher levels rest on the lower, but that is true only to a degree. Each layer has some independence—thus, more data do not necessarily mean more knowledge. Moreover, critics object sensibly that "information" should not be mistaken for "ideas."[11]

Whatever the merits of these terminological debates, the expansive view of information continues to gain ground and stimulate new insights. In this vein, ethologist Richard Dawkins argues that information comes in varieties: from discardable old news items to

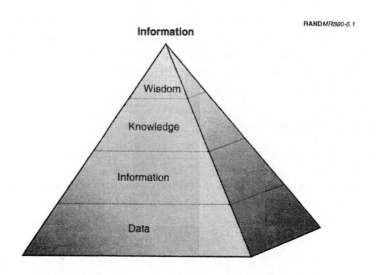

RANDMR880-6.1

Figure 6.1—The "Information Pyramid"

types of information that are so powerful, so laden with vitality, that they may be deemed "alive." Thus the most meaningful information "doesn't merely *embody* order; it advances order and maintains it."[12] This includes not only the biological information in the genetic replicator DNA, but also cultural information (e.g., ideas, fashions) that gets communicated gene-like in "memes"—a term Dawkins coined to convey that cultural as well as biological bodies are based on units of "self-replicating patterns of information":[13]

> Just as genes propagate themselves in the gene pool by leaping from body to body via sperm or eggs, so memes propagate themselves in the meme pool by leaping from brain to brain via a process which, in the broad sense, can be called imitation.[14]

Information As Medium

The second view observes that information relates not just to the message, but more broadly to the system whereby a sender transmits a message to a receiver. So, this view directs the eye to the medium—in contemporary parlance, the conduit—of transmission and reception. The key concern is the ability of a communications system to move signals clearly and precisely—that is, with low noise, low "entropy," and often with high redundancy. In this view, the actual content is irrelevant; what matters are the encodability and the transmittability of a message, regardless of its content.[15] This view is more about communications than knowledge.

This second view gained influence in the 1940s and 1950s under the rubric of information theory, communication engineering, and statistical mechanics. It was elucidated initially by Claude Shannon, and then by Norbert Wiener, who developed "cybernetics" based on principles of control through feedback. This view then also filtered into the social sciences, helping to stimulate Marshall McLuhan's insight that "the medium is the message."[16] Cybernetics influenced the social and related engineering sciences particularly with regard to theorizing about decision-making,[17] artificial intelligence, and the design of computers.

Here are two alluring, widely praised definitions of information that aptly summarize this second view. The first is by Norbert Wiener, the second by anthropologist-cyberneticist Gregory Bateson:

> Just as the amount of information in a system is a measure of its degree of organization, so the entropy of a system is a measure of its degree of disorganization; and the one is simply the negative of the other.[18]

> The technical term "information" may be succinctly defined as any difference which makes a difference in some later event. This definition is fundamental for all analysis of cybernetic systems and organizations. The definition links such analysis to the rest of science, where the causes of events are commonly not differences but forces, impacts, and the like. The link is classically exemplified by the heat engine, where available energy (i.e., negative entropy) is a function of a difference between two temperatures. In this classical instance, "information" and "negative entropy" overlap.[19]

In these and related writings,[20] we see a trend among theorists to equate information with "organization," "order," and "structure"—to argue that embedded information is what makes an object have an orderly structure. As this trend has developed, its emphasis has shifted. At first, in the 1940s and 1950s, information theorists emphasized the concept of "entropy"—and were thus concerned with exploiting feedback to improve "control." Now, the emphasis has shifted to the concept of "complexity"—and this has led to a new concern with the "coordination" of complex systems.[21] Control and coordination are different, sometimes contrary processes; indeed, the exertion of excessive control in order to avoid entropy may inhibit the looser, decentralized types of coordination that often characterize advanced forms of complex systems.[22] What James Beniger called the "control revolution"[23] is now turning into what might be better termed a "coordination revolution."

Entropy and complexity look like opposing sides of the same coin of order. About the worst that can happen to embedded information is that it gives way to entropy, i.e., the tendency to become disorganized. The best is that it enables an object to grow in efficiency, versatility, and adaptability.

Information and Physical Matter

In the first and second views, information remains basically immaterial in nature. But a third view is emerging that has challenging implications. In this view, information is about much more than message and medium (or content and conduit). It is said that information is as basic to physical reality as are matter and energy—all material objects are said to embody not only matter and energy, but also "information." The spectrum for this view runs from modestly regarding information as an output from the behavior of matter and energy; to regarding information as equal in importance to matter and energy in the composition of reality; to regarding information as even more fundamental than matter and energy.[24] Information, then, is an embedded *physical* property of all objects that exhibit organization and structure. This applies to dirt clods as well as DNA strands. New academic fields of study—e.g., "information physics" and "computational physics"—are emerging around such ideas (while also drawing on the older ideas about information).

One proponent, Tom Stonier, amid a highly speculative, abstruse discourse, sums up the basic idea quite clearly:

> Its main thesis is that "information" is not merely a product of the human mind—a mental construct to help us understand the world

we inhabit—rather, information is a [physical] property of the universe, as real as are matter and energy.[25]

A physicist identified with such thinking, Edward Fredkin, reaches farther to say that the entire universe is tantamount to a giant computer.

> What I'm saying is that, at the most basic level of complexity, an information process runs what we think of as physics. At the much higher level of complexity, life, DNA—you know, the biochemical functions—are controlled by a digital information process. Then, at another level, our thought processes are basically information processing.[26]

The views of information as message and medium persist, but are embedded in a view that all matter and energy in the universe are not only based on information but are designed to process and convey it. Information is the prime mover. Both order and "chaos" depend on it.

This line of thinking is not confined to physics. Social theorist Kenneth Boulding remarked that matter and energy "are mostly significant as encoders and transmitters of information."[27] In other words, the organization and the complexity of all objects, including social objects, reflect and depend upon their informational content and processing capabilities.

This third view remains odd and unclear, but quite intriguing. If it proves a cutting-edge rather than a fringe view, it may yet lead to analytic paradigms of as much explanatory power as the first two views. This essay assumes it has some validity, so that we can point out some remarkable implications for military doctrine and strategy, as discussed later.

PARALLEL VIEWS OF POWER

Volumes have been written about the concept of power—far more than about the concept of information. Yet, despite those volumes, power is never easy to define—as is the case with information. We do not attempt a definition.[28] Rather, what is notable here is that three views of power can be discerned that parallel the three views of information—but with a reverse twist.

Our characterization is reminiscent of Kenneth Boulding's analysis of the triune nature of power, which he classified respectively into its destructive, productive and integrative dimensions.[29] The three views we discern, respectively, treat power as being material, organizational (or systemic), and finally immaterial in nature. Our characterization applies whatever strategic realm one is analyzing: political, economic, or military, all of which have material, organizational, and immaterial ideational bases.

Power As Resources

The most basic view regards power in terms of the possession of resources and capabilities that can be used to coerce or otherwise control or influence a nation or some other actor. These are typically tangible material resources and capabilities like petroleum, weaponry, industrial capacity, or manpower. But they may also be less tangible, as in the possession of liquid financial assets, or of an office or instrument endowed with legitimate authority. In many respects, this is a natural, even instinctive, view of power and may be the most ancient of the three views.

This view undergirds most geopolitical analyses. As Inis Claude observed, the power of the nation-state consists of "essentially military capability—the elements which contribute directly or indirectly to the capacity to coerce, kill, and destroy."[30] In more formal academic terms, this view has found expression in the widely used "composite capabilities index," which consists of military, industrial and demographic factors grouped around the size of armed forces and military budgets, steel production and industrial fuel consumption, and total population, particularly the urban portion.[31]

Power As Organization

A second view looks at power in terms of how it is "mediated"—how a people, a nation, or other actor or system is organized to use the resources and capabilities at its disposal. This view emphasizes that power is a function or a reflection of the design and performance of a social system, whatever its resource base. Thus even a nation that lacks many physical resources, like Japan, may still become very powerful, as proved by its rise to the first rank of nations in the early 20th century.

This view has classical roots,[32] but its proponents are mainly contemporary. The pathbreaking studies of administrative behavior in the 1950s illuminated the fact that power depends on organization.[33] (Some of these studies led the way in showing how organizational designs are basically about how communications channels and information flows are structured.) More recent theorists have repeatedly observed that power does not exist in the absence of relationships; "power is a relation among people, not an attribute or possession."[34] Resources matter in this view, but just how depends on the identity, reputation, location, and other relational attributes of the actor or system that has (or lacks) those resources.

The importance of organization for power is noticeable throughout history. Consider the evolution centuries ago from tribes to states— i.e., from kinship to hierarchy as the dominant form of societal organization. States, molded around centralized institutions like monarchies and armies, emerged far more powerful than tribes which, in their classic form, could barely conduct collective agriculture, much less administer conquered tribes.[35] By the 18th century, state institutions proved less capable than competitive market actors for processing complex commercial transactions and energizing industrial development. Today, a fourth major form of organization is on the rise: information-age multi-organizational networks. They are proving "powerful"—more so than the tribal, hierarchical, and market forms—for dispersed civil-society actors, like human-rights groups, who want to share information, coordinate strategies, and act jointly.[36]

In addition, consider whether democratic or authoritarian (or totalitarian) systems are better designed for asserting power. The debates about this question are increasingly resolved in favor of democratic systems over the long run.[37]

Overall, this view implies that power, much like information, is mediated; power's significance (i.e., its meaning) is affected by the medium of expression, by the system of generation and transmission. Moreover, this view implies that power, again like information, is the antithesis of entropy, but potentially subject to it.

Power As Immaterial

The third view moves even farther from the resources view. It looks at power as depending on deep psychological, cultural, and ideational structures; it makes "the power of power" virtually metaphysical. Power becomes more like a message embedded in the air than a raw material raised from the ground. Exactly what power embraces under this third view is often unclear, especially in the more abstract, speculative versions. But in the more grounded versions, it is not entirely separable from the first and second views.

In some respects, this too is a classical view of power. It is well recognized that nationalism and ideology may be sources of power. More to the point, aerial bombing campaigns—a maximalist assertion of material power—have often failed (e.g., in Britain, Germany, Vietnam) to break a resolute people's willpower. Among scholarly theorists and strategists, Hans Morgenthau's expansive definition of national capabilities included ideological and morale factors.[38] For Joseph Nye, the current era is one of the "reduced tangibility" of power, and the rise in importance of its "softer" side.[39]

This view of power receives some of its deepest articulations in modernist philosophizing. From a Marxist perspective, Antonio Gramsci's views regarding "hegemonic" ideologies and media fall into this category.[40] From a different perspective, Friedrich Nietzsche built the body of his philosophy on the notion that power was created as an act of will, and that this "will to power" lay at the root of prevailing ethical-legal systems.[41] Michel Foucault, as noted earlier, was a major exponent of the notion that ideas convey power, making him in some ways a direct heir of Hegel's notions to similar effect.[42]

The appeal of the immaterialist view of power appears to be spreading among speculative thinkers of the information age. Indeed, in many respects, it is a view attuned to the information age.[43]

A Summing Up

These three views of power, rotated against the three views of information, lead to a matrix of possible combinations, as depicted in Figure 6.2. Three cells are notable for this essay. The one where power and information are viewed in their most traditional senses— where power depends on material capabilities, and information is but a useful adjunct—pertains to Mars, the Roman god of war. We identify Athena, the Greek goddess of warrior wisdom, with the far cell where power and information are viewed in post-modern, information-age senses—where information becomes physical and power immaterial, and the two dynamics merge. In between, on the diagonal, is a cell where sociosystemic views of both information and power coincide; this may well be where many people stand today

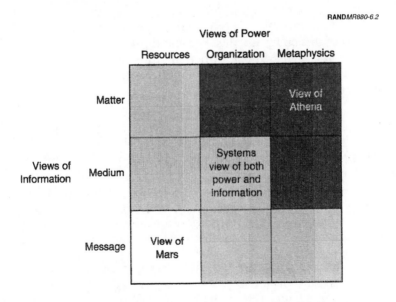

RAND*MR880-6.2*

Figure 6.2—Views of Information and Power Combined

who are trying to think about information and power together—and who may not be aware yet of the Athena cell.

A military force whose doctrine is built around an Athenan view should be able to defeat one built around a systems concept; and it in turn should be able to defeat one built around a Mars view. While we have not discussed each cell in the matrix, in general, a cell should represent a stronger approach than any cell beneath and/or to the left of it. This is roughly indicated by the shading—the darker the shading, the more potent the cell. This depiction parallels Martin Van Creveld's view of military history, wherein he traces the evolution of war in terms of its being based first on the tools and materials of war, second on systems of warfare, and thirdly on information-based technologies like the computer.[44]

Which views or blends of information and power one prefers affects how one proceeds to think about the implications for warfare. In the remainder of this essay, we presume that thinking about information and power is moving in the "Athenan" direction, where Fredkin's views may meet with Foucault's. Our intent is to tease out the implications for doctrine and strategy.

IMPLICATIONS FOR MILITARY DOCTRINE AND STRATEGY

The U.S. military is in the early decades of its own "information revolution," and "information warfare" has become the cutting edge of a "revolution in military affairs" (RMA). Yet, what "information" means for military theory and practice is much in debate. The evolution in thinking about information and power discussed above matches the evolution that is under way in military circles:

- From a traditional Mars-like view that says information has always been important for particular aspects of warfare—e.g., signals, intelligence, C3I, psychological warfare—and sees that those aspects are becoming more salient;

- Toward a new Athena-like view that says information is a bigger, deeper concept than traditionally presumed, and should be treated as a basic, underlying and overarching dynamic of all theory and practice about warfare in the information-age.

This is a dramatic, contentious shift. The quest for new concepts has created new analytical problems and new bureaucratic and budgetary tangles—and opportunities.   Many leading intellectuals grappling with information-age issues affecting the military—e.g., C. Kenneth Allard, Carl Builder, Jeffrey Cooper, Martin Libicki, Thomas Rona, George Stein, Col. Richard Szafranski, Alvin and Heidi Toffler—have one or both feet planted in the newer, broad view. They are all in Athena's camp.[45]   But many operators and practitioners remain firmly rooted in the older, narrow view.

Which view prevails may make a difference bureaucratically as well as militarily. In some versions of the narrow view, there is a tendency to make "information warfare" (IW) mean little more than computer warfare, and to treat it as more an intelligence than a military activity. This in turn reduces the scope of issues to little more than security and safety in cyberspace. This is an important topic, to be sure, but an overemphasis on it could engage the notion that one should improve the U.S. government's ability to control society at large, even if this means making society more closed than open under some scenarios. We share a concern raised by John Rothrock that some interpretations of information warfare could

> require fundamental changes in how we understand conflict and the appropriate responses of our society to it . . . . Does our society want to be the sort that is adept at the degree and types of control of information that some of the more enthusiastic advocates of Information Warfare seem to presume?[46]

The Athenan view of information and power implies that it is advisable to develop a broad vision of "information warfare." This is so partly because this kind of warfare is inherently multidimensional. Additionally, a broad vision should prove less susceptible to authoritarian tendencies.

A Force-Reformer As Well As Force-Multiplier

It was said that the new information technology provided a "force-multiplier" for U.S. forces in the Gulf War.[47] Armed with more and better information, the American-led coalition swiftly defeated a large enemy field army in a very short time, and at astonishingly low cost in terms of casualties. Yet putting the emphasis on a quantitative point—the multiplier effect—overlooks a deeper qualitative point: Information is also a force-modifier, a force-reformer.

Making full use of today's information revolution implies not only adopting new technologies but also rethinking the very bases of military organization, doctrine, and strategy. All this requires reformulation in order to fulfill Clausewitz's exhortation that "knowledge must become capability"[48] in the information age. The information revolution is not simply technological in nature; it has powerful conceptual and organizational dimensions as well. The new meanings of power and information discussed earlier favor the argument that wars and other conflicts in the information age will revolve as much around organizational as technological factors.[49]

There are both entropy and complexity issues here. A doctrinal implication of the Athenan view is that "entropy" replaces Clausewitz's "friction" as a concern in warfare. The latter concept was attuned to the pre- and early industrial ages, when forces, however well organized, faced inevitable shocks and delays that caused action in war to resemble Clausewitz's notion of "moving in a resistant element."[50] Presently, a post-machine age is dawning where friction will no longer be quite the right concept. A key goal will be to minimize one's own vulnerability to disruption and disorganization—i.e., to entropy—while fostering it in an enemy's systems. The strength of a system will be a function of not only how much mass, energy and information it embodies, but also how vulnerable, or resistant, it is to "entropizing."

The U.S. military is thinking about this. One example is Horizon, an effort to ensure compatibility among all information systems in the U.S. military. According to Lt. General Carl O'Berry,

> [Horizon] brings order out of something that until now has been an atmosphere of entropy. For the first time we have taken interoperability to the domain of science instead of emotion. I'm taking the guesswork out of C4I [command, control, communications, computers and intelligence] systems architecture.[51]

As the information revolution develops further, the notion of how complex, or ecologically diverse, a system is in terms of not depending too much on any single form or principle of organization seems likely to grow in importance. A key question is whether hierarchical or networked systems are more robust in the face of disruptive campaigns. Hierarchy is the traditional form of military organization, and a hierarchical core remains *de rigeur*. Yet a body of evidence from the wars of the 20th century suggests that hierarchies, once compromised, often collapse swiftly. The fall of France in 1940 and the defeat of Iraq in 1991 offer perhaps the best examples of this phenomenon. In contrast, the networked organizational style of guerrilla fighters during the same half-century suggests the tremendous robustness of these fighters in the face of even the sternest countermeasures. The Vietnam War provides the best example of a networked insurgency withstanding everything the American hierarchy threw at it.[52]

The interplay between having complexity but not displaying it harks back to the sage doctrinal dispensations of Sun Tzu, who likens an army to flowing water, and advises that

> The ultimate in disposing one's troops is to be without ascertainable shape. Then the most penetrating spies cannot pry in nor can the wise lay plans against you.[53]

New Definitions of Weapons and Targets

Information-age warfare implies various shifts in the nature of weapons systems and their targets. One is a shift from using lethal material weaponry (e.g., tanks, planes, ships) to attack material targets, toward also using such weaponry to attack cyberspace-related targets like C3I and RISTA systems and communications networks that have no firepower but represent an enemy's electronic sensory organs, nervous system, or brain. Another aspect of the shift is the use of nonlethal electronic techniques (weapons?) to disable an enemy's lethal systems, or its cyberspace systems that store, process, and transmit information. This use of nonlethal weapons to disable lethal systems may constitute something of an historical watershed, as it allows the possibility of effectively disarming without having to kill an adversary. Previously, nonlethals have been tightly coupled with one's own lethal systems, with the former paving the way for the more efficient use of the latter.

The elucidation of these shifts is sensible but draws only lightly on the previous discussion of power and information. That discussion raises a number of speculative, challenging implications, especially if the increasing materiality of information is adopted as a framework.

This third view of information—that it is a physical property—would treat *all* military systems as being based on, if not composed of, information. This curiously implies that information may be viewed as something that, like mass and energy, can be literally hurled at an enemy. Warfare has long revolved around who can hurl the most mass—as in the aptly named *levée en masse* of the Napoleonic era, or the human wave assaults on the western front in World War I and the eastern front in World War II. In the nuclear age, the emphasis shifted to hurling energy, as exemplified by the shock waves and radiation released by the splitting or fusing of atoms in bombs. Victory depended not only on directing mass or energy to deplete an enemy's warfighting stocks, but also on keeping that enemy from hurling mass and energy at oneself, and on being able to absorb and recover from whatever mass and energy it did hurl.

If information is a veritable physical property, then in the information age winning wars may depend on being able to hurl the most information at the enemy, while safeguarding against retaliation. This notion would affect how we think about all manner of weapons systems. Compare, for example, round shot fired from an 18th century smooth-bore cannon, to a shell fired from a modern rifled artillery barrel, to a new wire-guided anti-tank missile. How do they rate, relatively, in terms of mass, energy, and information? The mass of each may be about the same, but the energy each represents differs greatly. More to the point, each consists of different materials organized in dissimilar ways. Each sums up a very different set of sciences and technologies. Thus each represents a radically different embodiment of not only mass and energy but also information to hurl at an enemy. And the one that represents the most information—the missile—is the most effective. In other words, as these systems exemplify, an historical progression has occurred in the amount of information that can be hurled by weapons.

More to the point, the Athenan view of information and power implies targeting whatever represents or embodies the most information on an enemy's side. In a war, this means ascertaining and attacking the most information-rich components of an adversary's order of battle; to do otherwise may be to court defeat. An example appears in the Falklands War, where the Argentine air force (FAA) chose to attack the British warships that were most capable of hurling mass in shore bombardments, seriously neglecting the transports that moved mass, energy and information supplies. Some observers hold that this targeting mistake cost Argentina the war.[54]

This point also applies to operations-other-than-war (OOTW). For example, an implication for counternarcotics operations is to attack traffickers' electronic funds transfers and other financial transactions, rather than trying to chase smugglers or eradicate drug crops that represent lower information content.[55]

Three decades ago Marshall McLuhan concluded, in his own way, that hurling "information" at an enemy made sense:

> Since our new electric technology is not an extension of our bodies but of our central nervous systems, we now see all technology, including language, as a means of processing experience, a means of storing and speeding information. And in such a situation all technology can plausibly be regarded as weapons. Previous wars can now be regarded as the processing of difficult and resistant materials by the latest technology, *the speedy dumping of industrial products on an enemy market to the point of social saturation.*[56]

Rising Importance of Social and Human Capital

The Athenan view implies an increased importance and capability for hurling messages and "memes" at an adversary's society through propaganda, psychological operations,[57] "public diplomacy,"[58] "knowledge strategies,"[59] and even "neo-cortical warfare."[60] As the information age advances, many if not all dimensions of international interaction may be subject to information-influence strategies. An information offensive aimed at an enemy might seek to deter and dissuade a belligerent society without having to destroy its armed forces. In this, strategic information warfare would resemble prior systems, from strategic bombing to countervalue nuclear targeting.

The oft-voiced notion that war is moving toward a largely automated and robotic future is overstated.[61] From the Athenan viewpoint, the information age will raise the value of social and human capital, as man remains the purest, richest information-hurling system. In the words of pulp cinema icon, John Rambo, "the mind is the greatest weapon." The rising importance of human capital clearly applies to the skillful training and deployment of our own and our allies' information-age warriors. At the same time, this view of capital implies that the armed forces of adversaries among less developed countries may find new ways to remain militarily viable in the information age, as the development of human capital lies well within their grasp.

The importance of human capital may be seen not only in the technical skills of warriors, but also in the continued surfacing of "true believers" ready to act indiscriminately and murderously in the name of some blind faith. To take a term from Dawkins, such fanatics and martyrs amount to "memoids"—people who are so possessed by a meme that they can justify any deed, while feeling that neither their own nor their opponents' survival matters as long as the meme goes forward.[62] In a sense, a memoid's power as capital for his or her cause, and for hurling information at an enemy, stems from total possession by a belief system and accompanying attitudes.

New Assessment Methodologies Needed

If these speculations are worth pursuing, a generation of new assessment methodologies is needed. The challenges for development may include new methods for analyzing the "information quotient"[63] of weapons and other military systems, for describing an "information order of battle," and for analyzing an enemy's intentions, capabilities, and vulnerabilities—in short, for doing a net assessment. It may turn out that a new language must be devised, lest we overburden that already overused term "information." If the concept of information continues to gain significance, a new academic discipline may be advisable.[64] New centers and schools are already being established for the U.S. military that will help address such challenges. The question might also be addressed as to what an "information war room" would look like.

As we in the United States grapple to define our own concepts, we should keep an eye on how information may be defined in other societies and cultures that are trying to gain advantages from the information revolution. To some extent, our nation should aim to identify concepts to which others can relate, and which may thus serve as bases for future alliances and other forms of cooperation, where relevant. But we should also seek knowledge of others in order to develop early warning signs of potential adversaries, including non-state adversaries, who may invent concepts that are unusually difficult for us to counter. This may be particularly the case with "neo-cortical"[65] or psychological and cultural aspects of warfare.[66]

Game Analogies: Chess/*Kriegsspiel* and *Go*

As in the past, war and other modes of conflict in the information age will continue to bear resemblances to the game of chess. But such conflicts will increasingly take on characteristics of the "double-blind" chess variant *kriegsspiel*, and of the oriental game *Go*. A refinement of chess and *kriegsspiel*, so that one's own side has sight of both his and his opponent's pieces, but the opponent can only see his own pieces, offers an analogy for military "cyberwar." A similar refinement of *Go* so that, again, one's own side sees all pieces but the opponent sees only his own pieces, is an analogy for social and other types of "netwar."[67]

In chess, each side has a king and five other types of specialized pieces. Each piece, including the king, has a different "value" and a different ability to move. Each side lines up its pieces in assigned positions on opposite sides of the game board. Thus the two sides face off across a front line. Then, each side maneuvers in ways that are generally designed to fight for control of the board's center, to shield one's valuable pieces from being taken, to use combinations of pieces selectively to threaten and capture the opponent's pieces, and ultimately to achieve checkmate (decapitation) of the one-and-only king. Warfare before World War II was often like this and, indeed, frequently continued to retain this linear flavor up through the Persian Gulf War.

For the age of cyberwar, a modified *kriegsspiel* analogy is more apt. *Kriegsspiel* is based on chess—the board, the pieces, and the rules are similar—but the game is operationally distinct. Each side has his own board and arrays his pieces as in chess. A screen to block vision stands between the two boards, manned by a monitor (referee). Thus, once the game starts, each side knows where he has moved his pieces, but cannot see where the other side moves. The monitor signals when contact has been made. Then, whoever's turn is next gets to choose whether to take the contacted piece or make another move. He does not see what piece he may take until he has taken it, and it is handed to him by the monitor. Throughout the game, each side speculates but rarely knows which of the opponent's pieces are where. The game revolves around information vacuums and uncertainties. A premium is placed on deception. Indeed, a player who opens with classic chess moves and strategies—e.g., controlling the center—is likely to lose. The edges of the board may become more important for maneuver than the center.

The aim of cyberwar is for our side (the United States) to play chess—i.e., to have full sight of our own and the opponent's pieces—while blinding him so that he has to play *kriegsspiel*, at best knowing the location only of his own pieces, and maybe not even that. In this analogy, both sides start with similar mass and energy—the same set of pieces—at their disposal. But we have an enormous informational advantage—what David Gelernter calls "topsight"[68]—and because of this, each of our pieces is well informed. This advantage means we should not require as many pieces to win; we might even be able to achieve checkmate without taking many of the opponent's pieces. The Gulf War was, in some respects, rather like this and marks a watershed in the transition from traditional attritional warfare to a new generation of information-age warfare.

The game of *Go* provides a better analogy for netwar, i.e., for networked types of conflict and crime at the opposite end of the spectrum from high-intensity conventional warfare. Whereas chess starts with all pieces on the board, this game starts with an empty board. It looks like a vast, grid-like chess board with lots of tiny squares. Each side takes turns placing pieces called "stones" anywhere on the board, one by one. But the stones are placed not in the squares as in chess, but on the points where the grid lines intersect. All stones are alike—there is no king to decapitate, and no queen or other specialization. Once placed, a piece cannot move; it can only be removed, if surrounded and captured according to the rules. But in this game, taking pieces has secondary importance. The goal is to surround and hold more territory than one's opponent. Once emplaced, a piece exerts a presence in that part of the board, making it easier for the player to place additional pieces on nearby points in the process of surrounding territory. As a result, there is almost never a front line, and the major battles are less for control of the center than for the corners and sides (since they are easier to box off). And whereas in chess no piece is ever totally secure, in *Go* a piece of territory can be made totally secure if it is surrounded in a particular way (in *Go* parlance, given two "eyes").

Thus *Go*, in contrast to chess, is more about distributing one's pieces than about massing them. It is more about proactive insertion and presence than about maneuver. It is more about deciding where to stand than whether to advance or retreat. It is more about developing web-like links among nearby stationary pieces than about moving specialized pieces in combined operations.[69] It is more about creating networks of pieces than about protecting hierarchies of pieces. It is more about fighting to create secure territories than about fighting to the death of one's pieces. It is also less linear than chess. Thus *Go* is more like social, criminal, and revolutionary forms of low-intensity conflict than like full-scale military war. It might even be said that the forces of North Vietnam and the Viet Cong played *Go* while U.S. forces tried to play chess.[70] Finally, in line with this notion of *Go's* tie with irregular warfare, the game's tactics are very unforgiving of efforts either to build fortifications or to seize unclaimed territory. Bastions or redoubts are subject to implosive attacks that bring them down from within, while "ground taking *Go*"[71] is entirely predictable, allowing a smart adversary to ambush these strung-out forces, defeating them in detail.

The metaphoric possibilities for netwar deepen if one imagines combining *Go* with the key characteristic of *kriegsspiel*: the screen that obstructs sight. Again, presume that one side has full knowledge of his own and the opponent's array, but the opponent can see only his own pieces until contact is made with an opposing piece. The dynamics of *Go* differ from those of chess/*kriegsspiel*, but the point still stands: Both sides start play with virtually equivalent mass and energy at their disposal. But the side with topsight has far more information. Thus, it should win handily over a blinded player and require (or need to risk) far fewer pieces to do so.

It might be illuminating to run experiments about this point, not only to test its validity, but also to see whether a minimum essential force size can be defined that invariably wins at chess/*kriegsspiel* or *Go* so long as its side has topsight and the other side is blinded. The experiment could vary the amount of information available to either side, in order to see what types and thresholds of information may make the most difference. To refer back to the "information pyramid," it might be found that a game will turn in favor of whoever has better knowledge and wisdom, so long as both sides have full view of the board. But the more one side is blinded, the more the game may turn simply on who has the most data and information in the narrow senses.

In addition, it might be illuminating to identify for study a series of cases where apparently small, weak military forces effectively defeated or defended against what appeared to be much larger, stronger forces. The offensive skill of the Mongol "hordes" of Genghis Khan (which were anything but hordes) comes to mind, as do the strategically defensive campaigns waged by the Royal Air Force and related elements in the Battle of Britain, and by hard-pressed U.S. Navy forces up through the Battle of Midway during the Pacific War. There are always many explanations why a smaller, weaker force wins—but a crucial constant may be superior intelligence and communications, be that because of fast scouts on horseback (the Mongol case), breakthroughs in radar and cryptography (the British and American cases), or other technological and organizational innovations. Indeed, an historical study could help illuminate not only the importance of the information factor, but also the extent to which it depends on correctly combining the technological and organizational dimensions of innovation. Such a study, along with the gaming experiment proposed above, might offer lessons for whether and how the United States could move to develop military forces that may seem lighter and leaner yet are more effective than those of any potential rival in the information age.

NOTES

[1]Sun Tzu, *The Art of War,* ed. and trans. by Samuel B. Griffith (New York: Oxford University Press, 1971), p. 129; Francis Bacon, "Of Vicissitude of Things," in M.A. Scott, ed., *The Essays of Francis Bacon* (New York: Charles Scribner's Sons, 1908), p. 270; Carl von Clausewitz, *On War,* ed. and trans. by Michael Howard and Peter Paret (Princeton: Princeton University Press, 1976), p. 147; and Michel Foucault, *Power/Knowledge,* ed. and trans. by Colin Gordon (New York: Pantheon, 1980), p. 69.

[2]A thoughtful analysis of the continuing, perhaps growing, importance of the state is by John Garnett, "Why Have States Survived for so Long?" in J. Baylis and N. Rengger,

eds., *Dilemmas of World Politics* (Oxford: Clarendon Press, 1992), particularly p. 63, where he concludes that "states enjoy decisive advantages over all other organizations in domestic and international affairs." See also Robert Jackson and Alan James, "The Character of Independent Statehood," in their edited volume, *States in a Changing World* (Oxford: Clarendon Press, 1993). Of the effects of the information revolution on states, they contend that "a major effect has been to enhance [state] significance: the State has been a major supporter and beneficiary of economic, scientific, and technological advance" (p. 6).

[3]Eugene B. Skolnikoff, *The Elusive Transformation: Science, Technology, and the Evolution of International Politics* (Princeton: Princeton University Press, 1993), especially pp. 241–246; quotes taken from p. 243 and p. 245, respectively.

[4]Criticism of empires is hardly new. The fundamental inefficiency of imperial organization is well exposed in L.H. Gann and Peter Duignan, *Burden of Empire* (Palo Alto: Hoover Institution Press, 1967), which focuses upon the failure of empires in sub-Saharan Africa. V.I. Lenin, *Imperialism: The Highest Stage of Capitalism* (New York: International Publishers, 1939) argues that empires will clash and ultimately destroy themselves in competition over ever-scarcer resources from which to extract surplus. Rupert Emerson, *From Empire to Nation* (Boston: Beacon Press, 1960) provided an argument that nationalism would triumph over great empires, whether of the more liberal (e.g., the British Empire) or totalitarian variety (e.g., the USSR). More recent studies have pointed out the inefficiencies of empire as caused by either unruly domestic political processes or hypervigilant concerns over potential external dangers. See, respectively, Jack Snyder, *Myths of Empire* (Ithaca: Cornell University Press, 1991); and Charles Kupchan, *The Vulnerability of Empire* (Ithaca: Cornell University Press, 1994).

[5]Peter F. Drucker, *Post-Capitalist Society* (New York: HarperCollins Publishers, 1993), esp. Chapter 6.

[6]For example, Kenichi Ohmae, *The End of the Nation-State: The Rise of Regional Economies* (New York, The Free Press, 1995) proposes that trans-border "region-states" are on the rise.

[7]Our threefold treatment of both information and power is deliberately sketchy, and cannot do full justice to the view of any single thinker. But that is not our intent. Rather, we seek to show that there has been an evolution in how people view these concepts. This evolution has implications that might be missed if one were to focus more on the details of specific views.

[8]A classification suggested in Robert Wright, *Three Scientists and Their Gods: Looking for Meaning in an Age of Information* (New York: Harper & Row, 1989), p. 110.

[9]Notably, Harlan Cleveland, *The Knowledge Executive: Leadership in an Information Society* (New York: E.P. Dutton, 1985); and Robert Lucky, *Silicon Dreams: Information, Man, and Machine* (New York: St. Martin's, 1989).

[10]The cognitive version is used in Jeffrey R. Cooper, *Another View of the Revolution in Military Affairs* (Carlisle, PA: Strategic Studies Institute, 1994); and John Rothrock, *Information Warfare: Time for Some Constructive Skepticism* (Stanford: Stanford Research International, 1994a, draft). A short version of Rothrock's paper was published under the same title in the *American Intelligence Journal*, Spring–Summer 1994, pp. 71–76.

[11]See, for example, Theodore Roszak, *The Cult of Information: The Folklore of Computers and the True Art of Thinking* (New York: Pantheon Books, 1986).

[12]Richard Dawkins, *The Selfish Gene* (New York: Oxford University Press, 1989), p. 94.

[13]Ibid., p. 329.

[14]Ibid., p. 192.

[15]Elaborations appear in Steve J. Heims, *The Cybernetics Group* (Cambridge: MIT Press, 1991); in Kevin Kelly, *Out of Control: The Rise of Neo-Biological Civilization* (New York: Addison-Wesley, 1994); in Lucky, *Silicon Dreams;* and in Roszak, *The Cult of Information.*

[16]See Norbert Wiener, *Cybernetics: or Control and Communication in the Animal and the Machine* (Cambridge: The MIT Press, 1948), and Wiener, *The Human Use of Human Beings* (Boston: Houghton Mifflin, 1950); and Marshall McLuhan, *Understanding Media: The Extensions of Man* (Boston: MIT Press, 1964/1994). Also see Heims, *The Cybernetics Group.* Shannon's writings are highly technical; but his basic points are presented in books cited above by Heims, Kelly, Lucky, and Wright, among others.

[17]Notably, Karl W. Deutch, *The Nerves of Government: Models of Political Communication and Control* (New York: The Free Press, 1963); and John D. Steinbruner, *The Cybernetic Theory of Decision* (Princeton: Princeton University Press, 1974).

[18]Wiener, *Cybernetics*, p. 11.

[19]Gregory Bateson, *Steps to an Ecology of Mind* (New York: Ballantine, 1972), p. 381.

[20]See especially Heims, *The Cybernetics Group*, and Wright, *Three Scientists and Their Gods.*

[21]A thoughtful exposition is by M. Mitchell Waldrop, *Complexity: The Emerging Science at the Edge of Order and Chaos* (New York: Simon & Schuster, 1992). John Horgan, "From Complexity to Perplexity," *Scientific American*, June 1995, pp. 104–109, voices the prospect that "complexity" studies may turn out to be another academic fad—as tenuous a basis for interdisciplinary theory as "cybernetics" was in earlier decades.

[22]Thus tribes, hierarchies, markets, and networks all exhibit different patterns of control and coordination.

[23]James Beniger, *The Control Revolution* (Cambridge: Harvard University Press, 1986).

[24]Wright, *Three Scientists and Their Gods*, p. 5.

[25]Tom Stonier, *Information and the Internal Structure of the Universe: An Exploration into Information Physics* (London: Springer Verlag, 1990), p. 107.

[26]Cited in Wright, *Three Scientists and Their Gods*, pp. 10–11.

[27]Ibid., p. 288.

[28]Efforts to define power remain risky, for they often verge on tautology. Herbert Simon, "Notes on the Observation and Measurement of Political Power," *Journal of Politics*, 15/4:500–516 (1953) admonishes his fellow scholars to avoid considering power tautologically, as though it simply amounted to the ability to influence others.

His admonition has been difficult to heed. For example, a classic article by Robert Dahl, "The Concept of Power," *Behavioral Science,* 2:201–215 (1957) treated power as essentially the ability to influence others. Formal quantitative studies of power sometimes reflect this emphasis. A. F. K. Organski and Jacek Kugler, *The War Ledger* (Chicago: University of Chicago Press, 1980), focus on the identification and measurement of "power transitions," and argue that national power "can be defined simply as the ability of one nation to control the behavior of another for its own ends" (p. 5).

[29]Kenneth E. Boulding, *Three Faces of Power* (London: Sage, 1989) provides one of the most systematic efforts to classify the dimensions of power. Other attempts, often resulting in fewer dimensions, include P. Bachrach and M. S. Baratz, "Two Faces of Power," *American Political Science Review,* 56:947–952 (1962). Joseph S. Nye, Jr., *Bound to Lead: The Changing Nature of American Power* (New York: Basic Books, 1990), especially pp. 173–201, relates a pertinent distinction between "hard" (tangible) and "soft" (intangible) components of power.

[30]Inis Claude, *Power and International Relations* (New York: Random House, 1962), p. 6.

[31]Bruce Bueno de Mesquita, *The War Trap* (New Haven: Yale University Press, 1981), pp. 102–109 gives an outstanding exposition of this view of power, while also noting the vitiating effects of distance on the projection of material power. He enriches the basic capabilities index by incorporating his variant of the "loss of strength gradient" introduced by Kenneth Boulding, *Conflict and Defense* (New York: Harper & Row, 1962), especially pp. 245–247. The composite capabilities index became one of the foundations of the "Correlates of War" data set maintained by the Interuniversity Consortium for Political and Social Research.

[32]Thomas Hobbes' *Leviathan* calls for using centralized organization to maximize state power. Karl Marx's *Communist Manifesto* heralds an altogether differing view of political organization, in which the greatest gains will come from the "withering" of predatory states.

[33]This is a central theme of Herbert Simon, *Administrative Behavior* (New York: The Free Press, 1957). Another example is Philip Selznick, *TVA and the Grass Roots; a Study in the Sociology of Formal Organization* (Berkeley: University of California Press, 1949). Klaus Knorr, *The War Potential of Nations* (Princeton: Princeton University Press, 1956), especially chapters 6–8, notes the overarching importance of administrative efficiency. Tibor Scitovsky, Edward Shaw and Lorie Tarshis, *Mobilizing Resources for War* (New York: McGraw-Hill, 1951) provides a policy-oriented (for its day) blueprint for developing a national-level degree of organization to maximize state power.

[34]Jack Nagel, "Some Questions About the Concept of Power," *Behavioral Science,* 13:129–137 (1968), p. 129. This view was thoroughly analyzed in Harold Lasswell and Abraham Kaplan, *Power and Society* (New Haven: Yale University Press, 1950).

[35]R. E. Smith, *The Failure of the Roman Republic* (London: Cambridge University Press, 1955), pp. 47–56, argues that Rome could not realize its power potential until it engaged in a fundamental reorganization, jettisoning its vestigial tribal structures in favor of administrative structures that could effectively command and control its ever-increasing resources and subjects. Of this period of institutional redesign, and the sometimes unpredictable behavior that accompanied it, Smith concluded that "it is a phase through which all States pass during their growth and development" (p. 53).

[36]Background appears in David Ronfeldt, *Institutions, Markets, and Networks: A Framework About the Evolution of Societies* (Santa Monica: RAND, DRU-590-FF, December 1993). Sources on the evolution from tribes to early states include Elman R. Service, *Primitive Social Organization, An Evolutionary Perspective*, Second Edition (New York: Random House, 1971); Elman R. Service, *Origins of the State and Civilization: The Process of Cultural Evolution* (New York: W.W. Norton and Company, 1975); and Joseph A. Tainter, *The Collapse of Complex Societies* (New York: Cambridge University Press, 1988).

[37]For a recent example, see David A. Lake, "Powerful Pacifists: Democratic States and War," *American Political Science Review*, 86/1:24–37 (1992), for an argument that less hierarchical systems must respond to constituent demands and thus become inherently stronger than those polities whose rulers may extract surplus from a people without their permission or support.

[38]Hans Morgenthau, *Politics Among Nations* (New York: Alfred A. Knopf, 1948), pp. 91–100. On balance, Morgenthau's view of power is dual, because he mixes intangibles like nationalism and militarism with tangible geopolitical factors (pp. 116–120).

[39]Nye, *Bound to Lead*, p. 195.

[40]See Antonio Gramsci, "Intellectuals and Hegemony," in David McLellan, *Marxism: Essential Writings* (London: Oxford University Press, 1988). It should also be noted that writers identified with the Realist approach to international relations have sometimes argued that even such matters as international trading regimes rely heavily on the "hegemonic stability" afforded by the presence and participation of a preponderant state. See Stephen D. Krasner, "State Power and the Structure of International Trade," in Jeffry A. Frieden and David A. Lake, *International Political Economy* (New York: St. Martin's Press, 1987).

[41]See Friedrich Nietzsche, *The Will to Power* (New York: Vintage Books, 1964 edn.) and *The Genealogy of Morals* (New York: Carlton House, 1887).

[42]On the importance of ideas, see G. W. F. Hegel, *Reason in History*, trans. by Robert S. Hartman (Indianapolis: Bobbs-Merrill, 1951). A modern affirmation of the Hegelian view of ideas and power appears in Francis Fukuyama, *The End of History and the Last Man* (New York: Free Press, 1992).

[43]Alvin and Heidi Toffler, *War and Anti-War: Survival at the Dawn of the 21st Century* (Boston: Little, Brown, 1993), emphasize the increasingly immaterial nature of power.

[44]Martin Van Creveld, *Technology and War: From 2000 B.C. to the Present* (New York: The Free Press, 1989).

[45]Writings in this camp include C. Kenneth Allard, "The Future of Command and Control: Toward a Paradigm of Information Warfare," in L. Benjamin Ederington and Michael J. Mazarr, eds., *Turning Point: The Gulf War and U.S. Military Strategy* (Boulder: Westview Press, 1995); Jeffrey R. Cooper, *Another View of the Revolution in Military Affairs* (Carlisle Barracks, PA: Strategic Studies Institute, 1994); Brian Nichiporuk and Carl Builder, *Information Technologies and the Future of Land Warfare* (Santa Monica: RAND, 1995); Martin C. Libicki, *The Mesh and the Net: Speculations on Armed Conflict in a Time of Free Silicon* (Washington, D.C.: Institute for National Strategic Studies, National Defense University, McNair Paper #26, 1994); George Stein, "Information Warfare," *Airpower Journal*, Spring 1995, pp. 30–39; Richard Szafranski, "Neo-Cortical Warfare? The Acme of Skill," *Military Review*,

November 1994, pp. 41–55; and Szafranski, "A Theory of Information Warfare: Preparing for 2020," *Airpower Journal,* Spring 1995, pp. 56–65. Pertinent but more reserved views are expressed by Steven Metz and James Kievit, *The Revolution in Military Affairs and Conflict Short of War* (Carlisle Barracks, PA: Strategic Studies Institute, 1994); and by John Rothrock, "Information Warfare . . ." (1994a, 1994). Three journalists have provided particularly good coverage of key ideas and issues: Peter Grier, "Information Warfare," *Air Force Magazine,* March 1995, pp. 34–37; Oliver Morton, "A Survey of Defence Technology: The Softwar Revolution," *The Economist,* Vol. 335, No. 7918, June 10th, 1995, pp. 5–20 (special insert after p. 50); and Doug Waller (*Time Magazine*). For additional discussion, see Arquilla and Ronfeldt, "Welcome to the Revolution . . . in Military Affairs," *Comparative Strategy,* Vol. 14, No. 3, Summer 1995.

[46]Rothrock, "Information Warfare . . ." (1994a), p. 7. Is there a risk of an information-age iteration of industrial-age fascism? If so, no term exists for it yet. The closest is "friendly fascism"—a term coined by socialist sociologist Bertram Gross, *Friendly Fascism: The New Face of Power in America* (Boston: South End Press, 1980), to warn that the new information technologies may be used by government and business to centralize surveillance and control over society. In some places (Singapore?), the information revolution may foster hybrid political systems and practices that purport to be democratic but are not. See also David Ronfeldt, "Cyberocracy Is Coming," *The Information Society,* 8/4: 243–296 (1992).

[47]Colin Powell, "Information-Age Warriors," *Byte* (July 1992), p. 370.

[48]Clausewitz, *On War,* p. 147.

[49]This perspective is developed at some length in John Arquilla and David Ronfeldt, "Cyberwar is Coming!" *Comparative Strategy,* 12/2:141–165 (Summer 1993).

[50]Clausewitz, *On War,* p. 120.

[51]Lt. Gen. (USAF) Carl O'Berry, as reported in *Defense News,* September 12–18, 1994, p. 54.

[52]Vietnam also provides an example of the United States playing chess against an adversary who was playing *Go.* See below for elaboration.

[53]Sun Tzu, *The Art of War,* Griffith, ed., pp. 100–101.

[54]See, for example, Jeffrey Ethell and Alfred Price, *Air War South Atlantic* (New York: Macmillan, 1983); and, from the Argentine point of view, B.H. Andrada, *Guerra Aérea en las Malvinas* (Buenos Aires: Emecé Editores, 1983), pp. 38–40. Wayne Hughes, Jr., and Jeffrey Larson, *The Falklands Wargame* (Bethesda, MD: Concepts Analysis Agency, 1986), offer an interesting official report that explores the possibilities opened up by alternative targeting. But the most severe critique of Argentine errors is rendered in Air Marshal R.G. Funnell, "It was a Bit of a Close Call: Some Thoughts on the South Atlantic War," in Alan Stephens, ed., *The War in the Air, 1914–1994* (Fairbairn, Australia: Air Power Studies Center, 1994). Funnell's conclusion is that "properly used, air power could have achieved the Argentine national aim" (p. 229).

[55]See David A. Andelman, "The Drug Money Maze," *Foreign Affairs,* July/August 1994, pp. 94–108.

[56]Marshall McLuhan, *Understanding Media: The Extensions of Man* (Cambridge: The MIT Press, 1964/1994), quote from p. 346, emphasis added.

[57]Psychological operations from an information warfare and special forces perspective is discussed by Col. Jeffrey B. Jones, "Psychological Operations in Desert Shield, Desert Storm and Urban Freedom, *Special Warfare*, July 1994, pp. 22–29.

[58]See Jarol B. Manheim, *Strategic Public Diplomacy & American Foreign Policy: The Evolution of Influence* (New York: Oxford University Press, 1994).

[59]The term "knowledge strategy" is from Toffler and Toffler, *War and Anti-War.*

[60]Szafranski, "Neo-Cortical Warfare . . . ."

[61]Statements of this notion include: Eric H. Arnett, "Welcome to Hyperwar," *The Bulletin of the Atomic Scientists*, vol. 48, no. 7 (September 1992), pp. 14–21; Manuel De Landa, *War in the Age of Intelligent Machines* (Cambridge: MIT Press, 1991); and Les Levidow and Kevin Robins (eds.), *Cyborg Worlds: The Military Information Society* (London: Free Association Books, 1989).

[62] See Dawkins, *The Selfish Gene*, pp. 330–331, where he writes: "What a weapon! Religious faith deserves a chapter to itself in the annals of war technology, on an even footing with the longbow, the warhorse, the tank, and the hydrogen bomb." Eric Hoffer, *The True Believer* (New York: Harper & Row, 1951) pointed out that an all-consuming faith need not be religious.

[63]An information quotient, once operationalized, would reflect the informational content of a weapon system relative to its mass and energy. The quotient reflects both the natural and man-made content of that system, in the context of its intended use. Many high-tech weapons systems would probably have high information quotients. However, a high-tech system (like the strategic nuclear missiles of the Soviet Union during the Cold War) might have a low information quotient even if it has very high mass or energy quotients.

[64]Ronfeldt, "Cyberocracy . . ." proposed the field of "cyberology." Thoughts of moving in this direction should be tempered by reading Heims, *The Cybernetics Group*, which recounts an unsuccessful effort in the 1940s and 1950s to create interdisciplinary studies around the concept of cybernetics.

[65]Szafranski, "Neo-Cortical Warfare . . . ."

[66]A 1962 piece by Arthur C. Clarke, "I Remember Babylon," reprinted with comment in Arthur C. Clarke, *How the World Was One: Beyond the Global Village* (New York: Bantam Books, 1992), pp. 181–193, tells of his encounter with a shady fellow who was purportedly planning to orbit satellites to broadcast television programs that would perversely charm and then undermine U.S. society.

[67]The concepts of cyberwar and netwar were fielded in Arquilla and Ronfeldt, "Cyberwar . . . ."

[68]See Gelernter, *Mirror Worlds.*

[69] However, the extension of a single piece into a line of pieces (a chain network?) might be considered a form of maneuver over time.

[70]Arthur Smith, *The Game of Go* (New York: Moffat, Yard and Company, 1908), which has gone through many reprintings, remains an unsurpassed, lucid study of the game. Sociologist Scott Boorman, *The Protracted Game: A Weich'i Interpretation of Maoist Revolutionary Strategy* (New York: Oxford University Press, 1969) assesses the Vietnam war in terms of *Go*-like principles of strategy. Deconstructionists Gilles Deleuze and Féliz Guattari, trans. by Brian Massumi, *Nomadology: The War Machine*

(New York: Semiotext[e], Foreign Agents Series, 1986), pp. 1–11, compare war to chess ("a game of State, or of the court") and to *Go* (whose pieces are "anonymous, collective").

[71]Smith, *The Game of Go,* p. 27, notes that this phrase (*Ji dori go*) is a "contemptuous epithet" for the uninspired conventionality of such strategies.

Part II

INFORMATION WARFARE

Chapter Seven

WARFARE IN THE INFORMATION AGE*

Bruce D. Berkowitz

Pentagon officials and defense analysts have a new topic to add to their list of post–Cold War concerns: information warfare, or IW, in the usual manner of military-speak. The term refers to the use of information systems—computers, communications networks, databases—for military advantage, either by the United States or by a variety of unfriendly parties.

IW is drawing increasing attention for at least two reasons. First, the United States is potentially vulnerable to IW attack. The United States, in civilian as well as military matters, is more dependent on electronic information systems than is anyone else in the world. In addition to the possibility that computer and communications systems might prove to be a vulnerable weak link for military forces, there is also a danger that hostile parties—countries, terrorist groups, religious sects multinational corporations, and so on—could attack civilian information systems directly. Attacking these systems could be easier, less expensive and certainly less risky than, say, sabotage, assassination, hijacking or hostage-taking, and a quick cost-effectiveness calculation may make IW an aggressor's strategy of choice.

The second reason why the defense community is so intrigued with IW is that it may be as much an opportunity as it is a threat. The United States may be able to develop new military strategies using

*Bruce Berkowitz, "Warfare in the Information Age," *Issues in Science and Technology,* Fall 1995, pp. 59–66. Copyright 1995. University of Texas at Dallas. Used by permission.

IW that are perfectly tailored to world conditions following the Cold War. Information technology is a U.S. strong suit, and military forces could use this know-how to improve our defense capabilities, perhaps dramatically, against hostile attack and to defeat any aggressors—and to accomplish both missions at the lowest possible cost. Indeed, U.S. military planners are already taking the first steps in this direction.

Yet, despite all of the attention the IW is receiving, several basic questions about information warfare remain to be resolved. These include:

- What is the actual IW threat, and how much should the United States worry about it? IW aficionados have suggested a number of scenarios in which IW might be used against us, but other observers think at least some of them are far-fetched.

- If the IW threat is real, what does the United States need to do in order to protect itself? Conversely, what must we do in order to make the most of the IW opportunity?

- As a practical matter, how should information warfare be integrated into overall U.S. defense planning? Will IW replace some military capabilities or merely supplement them? Should IW be considered "special," like atomic weapons or chemical weapons, and kept separate from other military forces, or should IW be part of the military's overall organization and planning process?

- What are the implications of IW for current concepts of offense, defense, coercion, and deterrence? For example, is it more difficult to deter an IW attack? Does information warfare automatically escalate to conventional warfare, or vice versa?

- What is the relationship between the military and civilian society in preparing for information warfare? Also, how can the nation protect democratic values—namely, freedom of expression and personal privacy—while taking the measures necessary to defend against an IW threat?

These are very basic issues. We have experience in dealing with similar questions in other areas of defense policy, but information warfare is in many ways quite different. So, if the world is indeed entering an Information Age and IW has the potential to improve, undermine, or just generally complicate U.S. military planning, we need to address such issues now.

ORIGINS OF THE THREAT

Military weapons and military strategy usually reflect the politics, economy, and—most especially—the technology of any given society. Even the writers of scripture understood the technological relationship between plowshares and swords, and we take for granted the two-sided nature of nuclear power, long-range jet aircraft, and rockets. Thus, today's improvements in computers, communications, and other electronic data-processing systems that are driving economic growth and changing society are also changing military thinking and planning.

Armies have always used information technology—smoke signals in ancient days, telegraphs at the turn of the century, precision-guided munitions today—but until recently information systems were second in importance to "real" weapons, such as tanks, aircraft, and missiles. Today, information systems are so critical to military operations that it is often more effective to attack an opponent's information systems than to concentrate on destroying its military forces directly.

Also, because modern societies are themselves so dependent on information systems, often the most effective way to attack an opponent is to attack its civilian information infrastructure—commercial communications and broadcasting networks, financial data systems, transportation control systems, and so on. Not only is this strategy more effective in crippling or hurting an opponent, but it often has some special advantages of its own, as will be seen.

Some recent books and films have raised the issue of information mayhem, although they may have exaggerated the dangers. High school students cannot phone into the U.S. military command-and-control system and launch a global thermonuclear strike (à la the 1984 movie *War Games*), and it would be hard for a band of international cyber-terrorists to totally eradicate a woman's identity in the nation's computer systems (as in this year's screen thriller *The Net*).

But consider some of the scenarios that the Department of Defense has studied:

- Approximately 95 percent of all military communications are routed through commercial lines. U.S. troops depend on these communications; in some cases, even highly sensitive intelligence data is transmitted in encrypted form through commercial systems. Although hostile countries may not be able to intercept and decipher the signals, they might be able to jam the civilian links, cutting off U.S. forces or rendering useless numerous intelligence systems costing hundreds of millions of dollars.

- The United States buys most of the microchips used in military systems from commercial vendors, many of which are located in foreign countries. The chips are dispersed throughout a variety of weapons and perform a range of functions. Some experts are concerned that someone might tamper with these chips, causing the weapons to fail to perform when needed.

- One lesson of Operation Desert Storm is that it is unwise to provoke a full-scale conventional military conflict with the United States and its allies. A more subtle alternative might be to send several hundred promising students to school to become computer experts and covert hackers. Such a cadre could develop the training and tactics to systematically tamper with U.S. government and civilian computer systems. But unlike pranksters, they would play for keeps, maximizing the damage they cause and maintaining a low profile so that the damage is hard to detect.

- Some strategic thinkers believe that "economic warfare" between countries is the next area of international competition. This may or may not be so, but it is possible for government experts, skilled in covert action, to assist their countries' industries by well-designed dirty tricks. For example, a bogus "beta tester" could sabotage the market for a new software product by alleging on an Internet bulletin board that the prerelease version of the program has major problems.

- Modern military aircraft, such as the B-2 bomber and F-22 fighter, are designed without a single blueprint or drawing. Rather, they use computer-assisted design/computer-assisted manufacturing (CAD/CAM), in which all records and manufacturing instructions are maintained on electronic media and shared on a closed network. This makes it possible for plants across the country to share databases and to manufacture components that fit together with incredible precision. But it also makes these programs dependent on the reliability and security of the network, which might be compromised by an insider with access.

- Like many large-scale industrial operations today, the military uses "just-in-time" methods for mobilization. That is, to cut costs and improve efficiency, the military services trim stockpiles of spare parts and reserve equipment to the minimum, and they use computers to make sure that the right part or equipment is delivered precisely when needed to the specific user. If the computers go down, everything freezes.

- There is a hidden "data component" in virtually every U.S. weapon system deployed today; this component may be in the form of targeting information that must be uploaded into a munitions guidance system or a "signature" description that tells the guidance sensor what to look for on the battlefield (for example, the distinctive infrared emission that a particular type of tank produces from its exhaust). If this information is unavailable or corrupted, even the smartest bomb regresses into stupidity.

DOD and think tanks have in recent years been actively studying the national security threats that these and other IW scenarios present to U.S. security. But it is also important to remember that, in addition to the threat to military forces, many of these same vulnerabilities apply to commercial industry and the civilian infrastructure. Virtually all communications systems are computer-controlled. Virtually all aircraft and land vehicles have computer-based components. Most transportation systems—aircraft, railroads, urban transit—are directed by remote communications and computers. Thus, virtually all of these civilian systems are also vulnerable to IW attack and could become targets to unfriendly parties.

THE CHANGING FACE OF WAR

One way to understand the impact of IW on military thinking is to recall the evolution of mechanized warfare. Beginning in the mid-1800s, the Industrial Revolution made it possible to develop new weapons that were much more capable than anything produced before: mass-produced machine guns, steam-powered armored warships, long-range artillery capable of hitting targets from several miles away, and so on. The military also benefited from technology that had been developed mainly for civilian purposes, such as railroads and telegraphs, which vastly improved the ability of military forces to mobilize and to maneuver once they arrived at the battlefield. War became faster, longer-ranged, and more deadly. Just as important, new technology also created new targets. Military forces became critically dependent on their nation's industrial base—no factories, no mass-produced weapons, and no mass-produced weapons meant no victory. So destroying a nation's industrial base became as important as destroying its army, if not more so.

The result was not just an adjustment in military thinking but a complete rethinking of how to wage war. Military planners began to understand that the faster, longer-range weapons offered the opportunity of leapfrogging the front lines on a battlefield in order to destroy an enemy's factories, railroads, and telegraph lines directly. A classic case in point is the progression from the invention of the airplane to the development of the entirely new doctrine of strategic bombing. Moreover, these military planners realized that such an expanded warfare plan was not only a possibility; in many cases, it was likely to be the dominant strategy.

Today's information revolution presents a similar situation. And just as new theories and doctrines were developed for industrial-age warfare, so have thinkers begun to develop a theory and doctrine of IW. As with mechanized warfare and strategic bombing, where it took awhile for military thinking to catch up with technology, IW concepts have required a few years to mature. In fact, just as aircraft had been in use for almost three decades before the doctrine of strategic bombing was invented, the roots of IW also go back many years. For example, most of the tactics envisioned for attacking an opponent through its information systems—destruction, denial, exploitation, and deception—can be traced to classical military and intelligence fields, such as signals intelligence and cryptography, electronic countermeasures and jamming, "black" propaganda and disinformation, and measures for concealment and camouflage.

What stands clear today is that information technology has reached critical mass. Information systems are so vital to the military and civilian society that they can be the main targets in war, and they can also serve as the main means for conducting offensive operations. In effect, IW is really the dark side of the Information Age. The vulnerability of the military and society to IW attack is a direct result of the spread of information technology. Conversely, IW's potential as a weapon is a direct result of U.S. prowess in information technology.

Indeed, many of the problems of dealing with IW are linked to the nature of information technology itself. The most important feature may simply be the falling cost of information processing; since the 1950s costs have declined at a rate of about 90 percent every five years, and most experts expect this trend to continue for the foreseeable future. One result is that information technology—and, with it, the ability to play in the IW game—is constantly becoming more available, and quite rapidly. Unlike nuclear weapons technology or aerospace weapons technology, which have been spreading steadily but slowly, the diffusion of IW technology is likely to accelerate. If a party cannot afford some form of information technology and IW capability today, it probably will be able to afford the technology tomorrow. This is evidenced in the spread of dedicated military electronic systems, but even more in the availability of commercial information technology such as computer networks, satellite and fiber-optic communications, cellular telephone systems, and so on. All of these can be used for hostile purposes, and can be attacked by a hostile power.

A second feature of information technology that affects IW is that as the technology becomes cheaper and cheaper, it becomes less and less efficient to control information from a central authority. Indeed, one reason for the current increasing pressure in society to decentralize government, corporations, and other organizations is that low-cost information technology makes it affordable and feasible to decentralize. The demand and incentives for decentralization are following the technological opportunity.

This trend runs counter to several centuries of military tradition and experience, which are based on hierarchical command structures, rank, and centralized control. The new technology does not support the traditional military model. Also, the trend toward decentralized information systems changes the government's ability to interact with the commercial sector. As result, national security officials and military planners must find new ways of issuing instructions and implementing policies.

DEALING WITH INFOWAR

With these characteristics in mind, it is possible to discuss some specific issues and problems the United States will face in dealing with information warfare.

The IW threat will grow because entry costs are low. As the cost of information technology falls, a greater number of foreign governments and non-government organizations will present a potential IW threat to the United States. Countries that could not match the United States and its Western allies in expensive modern weapons systems, such as tanks, aircraft, and warships, will be able to buy the computers and communications systems necessary to carry out IW.

One defining feature of the post–Cold War era has been that the single, large threat of the Soviet Union has been replaced by a greater number of lesser threats. The declining cost of information technology has facilitated this trend, and many of the new threats will take the form of IW. As a result, the U.S. military will need to think about IW threats coming from a number of different directions.

To complicate matters further, each threat will probably be somewhat different. One terrorist group might like to fiddle with transportation control systems; another might be dedicated to compromising DOD databases. In the past, the United States has tailored its forces and plans to deal with the single Soviet threat, and has assumed that, if it could defeat the Soviet Union militarily, it could also deal with what the Pentagon calls "lesser included threats." In the IW world, threats are likely to be as varied as tailored software, and U.S. military forces will need to deal with each on its own terms.

There will be an international learning curve. Not only will more players engage in IW, they will steadily get better at it. Because information is so easily transferred, everyone can quickly learn from the IW mistakes that others make. For example, Desert Storm was essentially a situation in which one side fought a classical 20th-century conventional war while the other side fought a classical 21st-century IW war. The Iraqi army was not out-gunned: indeed, it had a numerical edge, as well as the advantages of fighting from prepared defensive positions and its experience in battle gained during Iraq's decade-long war with Iran. The U.S. advantage was in information technology—intelligence, communications, precision-guided munitions, night vision equipment, stealth technology, and electronic countermeasures. As a result, the United States and its coalition partners were well-coordinated and could adjust their operations in real time, whereas Iraqi forces were isolated, disorganized, and blind.

It's unlikely future foes will repeat Iraq's mistakes and permit opponents such a free hand in the contest for what DOD has taken to calling "information superiority" on the battlefield. Indeed, a country or organization with even a rudimentary knowledge of IW could take countermeasures that can greatly reduce the U.S. advantage. The upshot is that the United States will have to work hard and persistently in order to maintain its present IW advantage. Also, because the U.S. advantage could potentially be tenuous and fleeting, it will be necessary to monitor the changing IW threat and develop the systems and expertise necessary to deal with it.

THE CHANGING FACE OF DETERRENCE

During the past 50 years, a well-developed body of theory about conventional and nuclear deterrence has accumulated. Although Star Wars advocates may quibble, most strategic thinkers would agree with U.S. military analyst Bernard Brodie, who noted in 1947 that it is hard to mount a foolproof defense against nuclear attack, so the more plausible strategy is to deter a nuclear attack through the threat of retaliation. Alas, the problem seems doubled for IW. So far, evidence suggests that not only will defense against IW be difficult; even an effective plan for deterrence will be hard to pull off.

One of the greatest difficulties in deterring a would-be IW threat is that an attacker may be anonymous. A country or nongovernmental group could tamper with U.S. communications and computer systems just enough to cause damage, but not enough so the perpetrator can be identified. To paraphrase a metaphor offered by Thomas Rona, a long-time IW thinker, we will be unlikely to find a smoking gun because our opponents will likely use smokeless powder. With no "attacker ID," it would be hard to determine who deserves retaliation, and without the threat of retaliation, deterrence usually fails. Indeed, a truly diabolical enemy would most likely adopt the strategy of an unseen parasite, quietly causing problems that would be attributed to normal glitches we routinely accept with software and information systems. (Have you tried installing OS-2 Warp or Windows 95 on your computer? Many people simply expect electronics to be difficult.)

Another problem for deterrence is that, even if an IW attack is identified, it may be difficult to develop an effective option for retaliation. As one DOD official has said, "What are we going to do, nuke them for turning off our TVs?" An IW attack may be just crippling and expensive, rather than lethal, so conventional retaliation (say, an airstrike) may be unpopular. On the other hand, because the United States is so dependent on information technology, we would likely come out on the losing end of a game of IW tit for tat. And mere diplomatic responses are likely to be ineffective.

Who will be responsible for IW? In the past, the usual response of the military to a new technology has been to assign responsibility for it to a new organization; for example, the Strategic Air Command (now simply Strategic Command) was created to assume responsibility for long-range bombers and missiles. Indeed, within DOD responsibility for information technologies has historically been assigned to specific organizations—the National Security Agency (NSA) in the case of signals intelligence and information systems security, the Central Intelligence Agency (CIA) in the case of covert operations such as black propaganda and covert political action, the National Reconnaissance Office (NRO) in the case of surveillance satellites, and so on.

Currently, each of the military services is developing an IW strategy to assist it in developing new weapons and doctrine, and commanders of U.S. military units deployed in the field are developing plans for IW in their theater of operation. DOD officials have mused—

briefly—whether to consolidate responsibilities for IW in a single organization. Most have quickly concluded that this would not make sense. Not only would there be turf battles among existing organizations; such an organization would be inconsistent with the trend in which information systems are, in fact, becoming more decentralized.

Indeed, the more appropriate question may be why we need large operating organizations such as NSA and NRO when information systems are becoming cheaper, networked, and decentralized. It may soon be more efficient for military units to operate their own signals intelligence and even reconnaissance systems. There already is some movement in that direction; for example, Army and Navy units operate their own reconnaissance drone aircraft.

The objective should be to permit IW technology to spread throughout the DOD organization while ensuring that IW operations are coordinated so that they are consistent with national policy and the strategy of military commanders. At the same time, DOD needs to ensure that IW systems in the military can operate with each other and with those in the civilian world, without creating an unwieldy bureaucracy or body of specifications.

PLANNING FOR IW "CIVIL DEFENSE"

Planning for IW requires cooperation between the defense sector and the commercial sector. Civilian information systems are prime candidates for attack. So just as cities are targeted in strategic bombing, in future wars we can expect civilian information systems to be hacked, tapped, penetrated, bugged, and infected with computer viruses.

Another reason for cooperation is that DOD itself depends heavily on the civilian information infrastructure. As noted earlier, not only does the military use civilian information systems for "routine" activities such as mobilization; sometimes even the transmission of sensitive intelligence data is routed through commercial links. Obviously, it would be impossibly expensive for DOD to make the entire civilian information infrastructure secure to military standards. And even if it were affordable, the passwords, encryption systems, and other security measures would make it incredibly inconvenient for public use.

Moreover, the government's ability to control or influence the civilian information industry is limited. DOD lacks the leverage it has enjoyed in other situations. For example, the Air Force can influence the design of spacecraft because it is the largest operator of space systems, but DOD's share of the total computing and communications market is quite small compared with commercial users. Also, today's commercial information industry is often ahead of the defense industry in developing new technology. So, whereas DOD once could effectively create industry standards in order to enhance security through its leading-edge role in research and development and its buying power, standards are now being set by companies in the market. Add to this the burgeoning information industry worldwide and DOD's influence is diminished further.

The upshot is that DOD cannot use traditional-style directives or specifications to improve the ability to defend the nation against the IW threat. If it tries, no matter how well-intentioned, it will likely fail. As evidence, consider the recent Clipper Chip episode, in which the federal government tried to cajole and coerce the information industry to adopt a NSA-developed encryption system. The Clipper Chip was supposedly indecipherable, but critics claimed that any system designed by the government would permit the government to read messages using the code (in cryptography parlance, this is called "back door access"). According to the critics, the government's objective was to preserve the ability of NSA and law enforcement agencies to read encrypted communications that they intercepted.

Not only did the industry reject the Clipper Chip, but the government was unable to prevent private computer programmers from developing and illegally distributing their own encryption systems that the government supposedly could not crack or systems (such as SATAN) that can detect "back doors." The lesson of the Clipper Chip is that DOD must use a more sophisticated, less heavy-handed approach to get the civilian sector to take measures to protect itself against the IW threat. Because directives and standards usually will not work, DOD officials need to learn how to use incentive systems instead.

For example, simply informing industry and individuals that they could be IW targets will often lead them to adopt "street smart" information behavior to protect themselves from both foreign and domestic attack. DOD officials themselves have suggested that the government could encourage insurance companies to charge appropriately higher rates to corporations that did not take reasonable steps to protect their data or information systems (again, on the assumption that making the insurance companies aware of the damage an IW attack could cause will generally suffice). In cases in which DOD is critically dependent on a civilian information link, it may even make sense for the government to subsidize the civilian operators so that they adopt protective measures.

In other cases, the government may need to face that some of its traditional activities will simply no longer be possible—for example, easily reading most transmissions that it intercepts. Instead, the government could concentrate on providing industry with the means to protect its information system. Indeed, in at least some cases it would seem that using the government's technical expertise to give U.S. industry an edge in the IW wars may do more for national security than collecting and decoding signals.

ENSURING DEMOCRATIC CONTROL OF IW POLICY

Reconciling information security obviously collides with allowing easy access to information systems and freedom of expression. However, IW presents another problem for American democracy.

It is possible to imagine ways in which offensive IW tactics might cost less or be more effective than conventional military options; suffice it to say that almost all the tactics ascribed to our opponents could, at least potentially, be considered for adoption by the United States. Yet the defense community rarely discusses the offensive use of information warfare. The reason for this reticence is that, like intelligence plans and systems, IW options are easily compromised once the opponent learns about them. Even in the case of defensive IW, some government officials are reluctant to discuss the threat, thinking that raising attention to U.S. vulnerabilities will encourage new groups to target the United States.

The problem is that it will be hard to integrate IW into U.S. defense planning without building public support. Citizens will need to understand why the government is undertaking IW programs and how the programs may permit other military programs to be phased out. Without public discussion and understanding of how IW capabilities might replace some conventional military systems, the nation may needlessly spend money for both conventional and IW programs. Secrecy also tends to increase costs by limiting competition and reducing the ability of DOD to draw on unclassified and commercial programs. One reason why commercial information technology is usually equal or superior to its military counterparts, and almost always less expensive, is that greater competition in the private sector forces innovation and pushes down prices.

Unless U.S. leaders deal with the problem of reconciling secrecy and democracy, IW will likely remain a marginal asset. In fact, the political system has considerable experience in dealing with such issues; nuclear weapons, intelligence operations, and covert action are all routinely reviewed by Congress and, at a more general level, are discussed in the public media. It seems reasonable that the nation can also have a public debate over the place of IW in U.S. defense policy without compromising the policy itself.

PRESCRIPTIONS FOR PREPAREDNESS

Dealing with the IW threat and especially with aggressive attackers who use IW as their main weapon against the United States will require new approaches. In most cases, it will probably be impossible to build a foolproof defense for the civilian information infrastructure. But it should be possible to prevent "cheap kills" by informing the general public and industry of the threat through formal and informal networks for government-civilian cooperation.

In the case of vital military communications links and computer systems, it may be possible to build hardened "point defenses," taking extra steps to thwart attackers. These could include, for example, building dedicated transmission lines for communications, isolating critical computers from all outside networks, and using hardware and software security systems that might be excessively expensive or inconvenient for commercial use but which are necessary for vital DOD systems. These measures would also need to be repeated in the production of hardware and software, and in some cases dedicated production lines might be necessary for the most sensitive systems.

Yet, because defense and deterrence are both so difficult to achieve in IW, the best strategy to protect the most vital information systems may be stealth—keeping the very existence of such an information system a secret so that it does not become a target. Of course, "secret information system" is the ultimate oxymoron, which is another way of saying that such systems will also likely be among the most expensive, inefficient, and difficult to use.

The most challenging measures, though, are likely to be political, economic, and cultural. IW requires new concepts within DOD because traditional approaches to military planning and military command and control will not work for it. And the same is true across society, where the measures for countering the IW threat will often collide with the essential features of the democratic, free-market system that an IW policy is intended to protect.

Chapter Eight

THE SMALL AND THE MANY[*]

Martin C. Libicki

As silicon becomes cheaper, lighter, and faster, more data is collected, processed, and transmitted, and war is altered through several stages. Pop-up warfare describes the battlefield in which the means of war are quiet or hidden until they rise and engage. The growing and (for the time being) unchallenged ability of U.S. forces to lay a Mesh over the battlefield permits the tracking and targeting of increasingly small, quick, stealthy, and transient objects. The logical consequence of this capability's spread is Fire-ant warfare, a battlefield dominated by scads of sensors, emitters, and microprojectiles.

Today, platforms rule the battlefield. In time, however, the large, the complex, and the few will have to yield to the small and the many. Systems composed of millions of sensors, emitters, microbots, and miniprojectiles, will, in concert, be able to detect, track, target, and land a weapon on any military object large enough to carry a human. The advantage of the small and the many will not occur overnight everywhere; tipping points will occur at different times in various arenas. They will be visible only in retrospect.

The triumph of the small and the many, of information technologies over industrial technologies, can be discussed in terms of its three phases. The first, Pop-up Warfare, is the expression of 1990s technology under the no-longer-valid assumption that the United States faces an enemy with comparable capabilities. The second, the Mesh,

---

[*]Martin C. Libicki, "The Small and the Many," excerpted from his *The Mesh and the Net: Speculations on Armed Conflict in a Time of Free Silicon*, Washington, D.C.: National Defense University Press, 1994, pp. 19–51. Used by permission.

describes how U.S. military power (using technologies available over the next twenty years) might work against a foe with developed industrial but underdeveloped informational capabilities. The third, Fire-ant Warfare, assumes expensive sensors will themselves be vulnerable and have to give way to networks of inexpensive information elements.

POP-UP WARFARE

A tilt toward quality in the quality-quantity equation is a good sign that a military technical revolution has occurred. During the run-up to the Gulf War, Allied and Iraqi counts—manpower, tanks and aircraft—were anxiously compared. War quickly made clear that the Iraqis could have fielded two or perhaps five times as many men, tanks, and planes without affecting the outcome much. Allied technology—both equipment and our sophistication at using it—was so superior (for the terrain) that exchange ratios were overwhelmingly in its favor. We could see and they could not. We could speak up unnoticed and catch them by surprise. Our weapons could be precisely aimed while theirs were effective only against targets several miles wide (e.g., Tel-Aviv). We were on one side of a revolution and they were on the other.

Yet consider how differently we would have had to operate if the Iraqis had had but a fraction of our capabilities (alternatively, what a conventional war against the Soviets in the 1990s would have looked like). Virtually everything we used on the battlefield would have been vulnerable had it been visible. We would have had to harden or hide our logistics dumps and command and control nodes. Our tanks, were they to survive, would have had to be hard to find except during those few moments spent scurrying or shooting. Surface ships would have been nearly useless anywhere near shore. Both sides would have been driven to pop-up warfare—a mode in which elements are hidden and quiet except during those brief and dangerous moments of engagement or movement.

Among the various elements setting the stage for pop-up warfare, the precision guided munition (PGM) has probably been the most salient. With PGMs, any locatable object can be precisely targeted and, most likely, destroyed. Any object with a fixed latitude and longitude could be targeted (with cheap, accurate aiming systems) and struck. To do this, today's PGMs use complex homing and terrain-matching devices coupled with accurate gyroscopes and accelerometers. Tomorrow's will be helped by GPS-guided seekers. External systems would relay the latitude, longitude, and altitude of the target, then the PGM would zip to that point. More sophisticated systems would use real-time updates against relatively slow-moving targets and perhaps even local (or relative) positioning systems for greater accuracy. Moreover, with new assets in space, and the increasing sophistication of airborne sensors (e.g., AWACS, JSTARS), as well as seaborne sensor packages (e.g., Aegis Cruisers), the number of objects that would fall under target scrutiny would increase as well. Thus would fixed and slow-moving targets fare poorly on a pop-up battlefield.

Pop-up warfare puts a great premium on minimizing one's own signatures (e.g., stealth) and amplifying the enemy's (e.g., the data fusion capabilities of Aegis systems). Both sides would have to stay hidden most of the time, pop up just briefly to move or shoot, and then scurry back into the background. To succeed, forces would quickly have to distinguish threats from decoys and friendlies, determine the threats' location and bearing, fire, and then disguise and eliminate their own signature.

Can large, fixed, above-the-ground targets be defended? Some targets can shoot back against incoming missiles. Capital ships, for instance, are equipped with both antimissile missiles and close-in weapons systems designed to disable incoming missiles with a hail of lead. Sufficiently valuable fixed sights might be protected by upgrades of the Patriot missile, or follow-on versions such as Erint, THAAD, or the Arrow. One proposal calls for hiding anti-SCUD missiles near potential SCUD sights to chase and overcome the latter while in boost phase.

Nevertheless, the betting has to be with the attackers rather than their targets. Targets are bigger than missiles, and missiles shoot first; they can succeed in aggregate by overwhelming the defense with numbers (many of which need only be cheap decoys). Defense against hyperkinetic projectiles could be far more challenging (the SCUD launches into Israel suggest such missiles are even more dangerous after they fall apart). A projectile that reaches Mach 10 or 20 and then releases a shower of darts clad with ceramic (to stay intact under reentry heat) can greatly damage soft targets. If the missile can elude destruction prior to decomposition, mission completion is only a matter of time.

The recent emphasis on knocking out anti-ground missiles in their boost phase suggests the realization that missiles will be very hard to hit once they stop radiating heat. As it is, today's missiles—hard enough to hit as it is—have yet to exploit a deep reservoir of stealth techniques. When they have done so, they will be far harder to hit. The logical consequence of the missile's superior penetration capability is that their targets would have to be dispersed, protected in very hard bunkers, or be moved around all the time.

Pop-up warfare will evolve as signatures can be harvested by unmanned objects: loitering missiles, unmanned drones, unattended submersibles, increasingly sophisticated mines. New techniques of data fusion can help correlate such signatures. Conversely, platforms will need more stealth to survive. The F-117A, the B-2, and submarines are already stealthy, but stealth is also mooted for missiles, surface ships, and even tanks.

The contest between stealth and anti-stealth will be long and drawnout, but again the betting has to be against stealth for any platform large enough to encompass a human. A hider must suppress a bitstream of information that constitutes its signature. A seeker tries to amplify these signals in order to read them. As information technology advances so does the ability to amplify bits. No such mechanism favors suppression. Indeed, an ecological axiom states that although removing half of a pollution stream is easy, each successive halving is harder. At very low levels, sophisticated devices to clean up one form of pollution often create another. Moreover, the cost of data collection and fusion drops with the cost of silicon. New stealth techniques, although effective, are not getting cheaper.

Thus even with stealth, everything ultimately can be found. All objects have mass and thus gravity. Every object moving in a medium creates vortices and must expend energy to do so. If nothing else, objects of a certain size have to occupy some space for some time. A set of sensors placed sufficiently close together can, in theory, eventually trap everything by getting close enough. A sufficiently fine web can intersect with any submarine. A line of sensitive receivers placed close enough together will find its line-of-sight path to a beaming object cut if a bomber—no matter how stealthy—rolls past. Neither architecture may be particularly cost-effective. Yet, both show how sensors of certain minimum discrimination placed close enough together can, at some epsilon, catch anything. Hence, the Mesh.

THE MESH

Chances are good that the United States will face a decade or probably two when it can apply military force against opponents with greatly inferior capabilities. Their strategy would not be to defeat American forces in the traditional way so much as to create as many casualties as possible in hopes that the United States would be dissuaded from further pursuit. Our strategy, in turn, is to use our longest suit to control the battlefield to the greatest possible extent so as to minimize exposure and casualties. As information gathering and processing capabilities continue to improve, our ability to see into the battlefield will increase exponentially. This advance brings with it both great opportunity and problems.

Combat requires doing two things: finding targets and hitting them (while avoiding the same fate). PGMs allow their possessors to hit most anything. Tomorrow's meshes will allow their possessors to find anything worth hitting. Every trend in information technology favors the ability to collect more and more data about a battlefield, knitting a finer and finer mesh which can catch smaller and stealthier objects.

A long period can be expected in which elements of the Mesh coexist with current platforms. The United States, for instance, will probably be able to deploy fleets of light satellites for surveillance before others can target our existing stock of heavy low-earth orbiters. During that interim the choice of using platforms or the Mesh for any particular mission would depend on which worked better or was more cost-effective. Thus, an initial architecture for the Mesh need not have all capabilities at once as long as platforms to do the same job can survive.

The Mesh, at its outset, would be one part of a cue-and-pinpoint system. Today's airborne sensor system is a multi-layer system of satellites, large aircraft, UAVs, manned aircraft, and finally, PGMs themselves. Under the sea, certain types of sonobuoys detect the presence of submarines by passive sensors, followed by active sensors which localize the submarine by pinging it, followed by torpedoes which use acoustic means to land on top of it. Similarly, the Mesh will be composed of unmanned sensors, infiltrated into existing systems composed of large and expensive platforms. ARPA's Warbreaker project is experimenting with systems that proliferate sensors in order to scan wide areas for certain types of signatures.

Challenges

Managing the enormous increases in information flow will be among the greatest challenges created by the workings of the Mesh. The technical problems—filtering, fusion, and fanning—are daunting enough, but the stickiest ones deal with the distribution of information.

Consider, for instance, a joint task force formed overnight to head off an unexpected incursion in some otherwise forgettable corner of the world. As the crisis starts, the relevant CINC will have a certain flow of information from existing sensors such as satellites, electronic listening posts, and perhaps fielded seismic and acoustic systems. Among his first acts will be to duplicate his enormous monitoring capabilities to some joint task force commander. Shortly thereafter, a new flood of information will come from various data collection platforms such as AWACS, JSTARS, Aegis, and perhaps small satellites and UAVs. Suddenly, the relative trickle of information available to the commander starts to become a current of data, far more than any human can deal with. This flow must, in turn, be apportioned to various sector commanders for their action. Atop this flow comes a new flood of information as various platforms start to deploy distributed air, water, and ground sensors in various formations. These, too, then have to be analyzed, dissected, and apportioned to the various sub-commanders each of which has a different array of capabilities. Managing such information blooming will require considerable practice.

Opportunities

The development of large effective information collection and analysis systems permits the United States to aid an ally without the commitment of military forces, and in some cases without fingerprints at all. So far, the Soviet Union has provided satellite imagery to Argentina (during the Falklands war), and we did the same for Iraq (fighting Iran) and the Angolan government (fighting UNITA). The denser the overhead information, the more help is available. Near real-time imagery of Serbian artillery, for instance, might help Bosnians more accurately target their return fire—information as a real force multiplier.

In times past, the United States has helped allies by providing equipment: examples range from the Lend-Lease program to the provision of Stingers to the Afghan rebels. If these sensors and emitters become global commodities (not necessarily a happy development), the United States could still provide the equivalent of material support. It would silently supply the pattern recognition, data fusion, and command-and-control software that makes these systems function. Bytes leave no fingerprints.

Could demonstrating a Mesh, in detail, induce surrender without the need to use much force? To do so would require persuading others that the ability to lock onto a platform's precise position is tantamount to ensuring its destruction. After all, the Gulf War allies did not have to shoot down every Iraqi plane to win air superiority. It sufficed to make a convincing demonstration of "You fly—you die." Such correlation can be delivered through open broadcast (e.g., via one of tomorrow's virtually infinite channels). The potential victim is then given opportunity to demonstrate his distance from the targeted machine. The act of seeing oneself on television futilely trying to hide may be very salutary. Thus might warfare become the child's game of hide-and-go-seek rather than the adult's game of hide-and-go-kill.

Force Sizing

The last implication of the Mesh is that it simplifies a difficult problem for the United States—sizing the forces. During the Cold War, our forces were sized against those of the Soviet Union; without so large an enemy, the task is far tougher. Force sizing based on war counting (e.g., one-and-a-half wars or win-hold-win) is likely to die a well-deserved death. The use of capabilities-based sizing cannot satisfy for long, either. The capabilities of others are a much better guide to weapons development strategies (where numbers are of limited relevance) than to weapons procurement strategies (where numbers are highly material). To say that military planners should disregard intentions and focus on the strength of others logically leads to a long-run planning goal of an armed forces capable of defeating everyone else (including our own allies) in concert.

The rising importance of the Mesh suggests a force-sizing calculus that could be made independent of the precise size of the opposing threat. One precedent is the Navy's rationale for carrier battle groups. The argument was that the Navy needed three carrier groups in every area to keep one on station at all times. Before 1980, the four areas were the Atlantic, the Mediterranean, the eastern Pacific, and the western Pacific. In 1980, adding the Indian Ocean suddenly raised requirements from twelve to fifteen. Any debate over the size of the threat (e.g., a putatively aggressive Soviet Union) could be finessed; the number of oceans rather than the size of the threat mattered. Similarly, force planners could start by estimating the establishment needed to deploy, operate, and service the targets generated by a Mesh. Such a Mesh should have minimal coverage everywhere and the ability to go to maximal useful coverage in however many trouble spots for which we have to simultaneously create targeting solutions. Done right, such calculations should be robust against wide variations in the size and intentions of likely threats.

FIRE-ANT WARFARE

At some point in the development of the Mesh, our forces will encounter the paradox that those platforms whose capabilities make other platforms vulnerable are themselves vulnerable and ultimately untenable over the battlefield. Our surveillance planes, for instance, not only come in highly non-stealthy platforms that do not move too fast, but they radiate like Christmas trees. Future engagements are likely to see even relatively backward nations target major sensor platforms. Should the platforms prove vulnerable, other ways of restoring their surveillance capabilities will have to be found, failing which, everyone returns to the days of the blind.

As argued above, an equally if not more effective way to weave a Mesh would be from millions of small objects. They are cheap, they can get closer to the target, and they are collectively most robust against deliberate attack. Because they are cheap, many can be deployed; deploy enough of them, and it becomes too expensive for the enemy to kill them.

An analogy to robots may better suggest the wisdom of distributing capabilities. People perceive robots as complex objects that, in every successive generation, come closer to resembling man. A new metaphor developed at MIT is that of robots as ants. Each one exhibits certain limited aspects of intelligence: some specialize in avoiding shadows; others, in walking without stumbling; yet others, in staying away from each other. Smart ants are less powerful than smart robots, but they are small, light, cheap, versatile, and easy to reprogram. Being cheap, they can be built in large numbers.

Battlefield meshes, as such, can be built from millions of sensors, emitters, and sub-nodes dedicated to the task of collecting every interesting signature and assessing its value and location for targeting purposes. Many of these sensors have already appeared, albeit in rudimentary form. In the future, they will be cheaper, more sensitive, and capable, collectively, of receiving signals from the various parts of the electromagnetic spectrum. Some would be optical sensors—perhaps small charge-coupled devices tied to neural net processors; they could cover not only the visible range, but also near-ultraviolet, and many shades of infrared. Others would act like small radar detectors, either singly, or in computational harmony with its like-minded neighbors. Chemical sensors could detect the passage of machines or their men. Some would sense changes in magnetism, air pressure, sounds, vibration, or even gravity, and so on.

Why this proliferation of sensor types? The easy answer is that warfighting conditions differ. Some environments (e.g., open desert) and targets (e.g., surface ships) are easy to see; other environments and targets are tougher. To detect the latter may require exploiting the inherent differences between machinery and background as they appear on several sensors. Single-sensor surveillance gives the target a single-dimension problem to solve. Tanks strive to be hard to see and thus employ camouflage and night movement. Submarines strive to stay quieter, using size, baffling, and ultra-smooth running machinery. Aircraft are stealthy by controlling their X-band reflections with special shapes and coatings. Multi-sensor surveillance, however, complicates the single-dimensional problem by obviating techniques which dampen emissions of one type at the expense of another; moreover, the multi-dimensional problem they create becomes that much more difficult to solve.

No one sensor need necessarily detect every emanation from a target. The more capabilities a sensor combines, the more expensive it gets. Thus the fewer would be used and the easier each would be to find and kill. Alternatively, specialized, perhaps even single-purpose, sensors can each collect signatures, exchange them with subnodes, and *collectively* form a picture of a target in its environment.

The Mesh would also contain cheap disposable emitters to illuminate targets with reflected radio waves, generate confusing signatures, and broadcast local positioning signals for precise targeting. Although accurate positioning systems are critical for the operation of a Mesh, full GPS capability need not be ubiquitous (GPS can also be jammed). Emitters that know where they sit and can broadcast relative distances to the other elements of the Mesh may suffice.

Some sensors may be equipped to move; they may have little cilia-like feet on land, fins in the water, and an airfoil in the air. Mobility would help right errantly laid sensors, take high ground (trees, houses, hills) in appropriate terrain, and cluster to where other cuing systems suggest the presence of target-rich environments. Moveable sensors fitted with precise chemicals or explosives (e.g., for taking out a critical piece of electronics) could be the killing mechanism in some cases.

Perhaps the prototypical sensor would be a sandwich the size of a penny. On top would sit a photovoltaic energy source or optical sensors; next would be a sliver of microprocessor, perhaps a chemical or acoustic sensor, and then a penny-sized battery, a transmitter for an antenna jutting out to the side, and finally some anchoring pod on the bottom. Another design would make the sensor look like a weed plant of a meter or two length. The shaft would be the antenna; the head a spectral sensor device would be capable of seeing as far as a human can, and the roots would be acoustic and vibration sensors, as well as anchors. To use yet another analogy, sensors might be the size of bottle caps; emitters, the size of soda straws; and miniprojectiles the size of coke bottles.

Architectures

The transition from single source sensors to distributed sensors has profound architectural implications. For instance, most radars today couple a relatively cheap emitter with a relatively expensive collector. Anti-radar missiles home in on the emitter and by so doing destroy the collector. Distributed architectures would require far more computation to translate the reflections into objects, but proliferating emitters and spreading them far from collectors complicates the targeting problem of the anti-radiation missile immensely. Emitters would survive longer and receivers would remain unscathed. When later generations of missiles learn to recognize receivers by their shape, the latter themselves could be distributed among smaller networked patches. Again, the computational requirements of putting together a big picture increase, but the costs of computation are continuing to decline.

Another advantage of distributing sensors both over space and by type is that it complicates countermeasures. An aircraft pursued by a missile knows it is being tracked, in effect, by only one sensor, and, more likely than not, in only one frequency. Thus dispersed flares, even though they travel far slower than planes, can be picked up as aircraft by IR missiles, which can recognize the bearing of a signal but not its distance (and thus speed). Tracking a plane using multiple sensors requires that the countermeasures exhibit the same three-dimensional behavior as aircraft do; using multiple sensors also requires all countermeasures to stay together rather than just appear aligned by the perspective of the missile (e.g., the flare, the jammer, and the chaff have to travel together). This is a far more complex undertaking.

The Mesh may also replace man-to-man coverage of a battlefield with zone coverage. The pursuit of a given target, which is to say, its signature, need not be performed by chasing it. Instead the overall Mesh can selectively pay attention to zones over which the target is running. It tunes into successive sub-meshes by expanding the latter's communications bandwidth and triggering external sensors to concentrate on an area. This shift has more than metaphorical significance; it also alters one of the rationales of maneuver warfare. The latter has always assumed that being there at the right part of the battlefield was paramount. But being there is not necessarily a prerequisite to seeing there, and not necessarily a prerequisite to hitting there if the range set of one's own weapons is sufficiently dense.

The last idea suggests the eventual waning of a currently popular theme in army doctrine (first the Soviet's and now ours)—the use of overwhelming force as a psychological disruption at the outset of an operation. This technique may not work as well as expected against a sufficiently well architectured Mesh. One necessary feature in a Mesh is a sufficiently high degree of disaggregation so that the difference between engaging targets all at once or one at a time is relatively minor. The second feature is at least some practiced capability for graceful degradation so that a percentage loss of capability does not mean a total loss of effectiveness. The ideal is a Mesh that has no center of gravity and thus must be defeated in detail.

Tips of the Spear

Finding targets is one thing, but ending their useful life takes more than bytes. Tomorrow's weapons would likely resemble today's PGMs. Evolutionary improvements in energy chemicals suggest that the warheads and engines could be somewhat smaller but probably not so small as to be radically different creatures.

One big change would be increased use of weapons that do not have to be borne on manned platforms; mines are a good example. Radio contact with the weapon and external cuing systems for its launch would allow the weapon to be positioned closer to its potential targets without putting platforms in harm's way. Thus a battlefield can be seeded with air-dropped munitions which can be raised, oriented, and activated on command.

A second big change would be in the logic of the seeker—or what is left of it. Today's PGMs have to find targets on their own. Sometimes they get external help (reflected laser tags or radar waves); sometimes their path is pre-programmed (e.g., cruise missiles); sometimes they have to take advantage of passive measures such as heat signatures or pattern recognition. In any case, they have a nontrivial computation to perform. Up to 90 percent of a PGM's cost is in the guidance and control, and most of that is in the guidance.

PGMs operating in a sensor mesh, however, can use the latter's intelligence. A PGM that is given a target's exact location can get there on its own in many ways. If GPS is jammed, it can use local positioning signals. If it knows where it starts from, its own gyroscopes and accelerometers will tell it where it is going. A purely ballistic flight path may work against slower targets. Others might simply home in on a sensor attached to the target. A PGM that needs less processing can use a simpler guidance system. Thus cheaper, it can be made in greater numbers and can defeat heavily defended targets by saturating them with multiple incoming warheads.

Logistics, Command and Control

The capabilities of even the most elegant military systems are useless without reasonable solutions to the problems of getting them there and talking to them when they arrive.

Getting Mesh components to where they are needed is a problem whose solution will depend on both circumstances and the architecture of the system employed. A platform to insert Mesh parts is a target no less than the platforms the Mesh was designed to fight against. Parts which are hardened can be dropped from air—even from space—or launched by artillery. Sometimes, special forces could distribute them into very small but critical areas. Micro-motors might even, at some point, allow them to walk into theater (but at no small demands on energy systems) or even drift into theater. Submarines and stealthy surface vessels may be able to lay down a naval Mesh. All these creatures can be also delivered by civilian means. A Mesh intended as a defensive field inside one's borders can be deployed as a mine field might be—except that by separating the triggers (the sensors) from the explosives (the PGMs), both are far harder to detect.

Although command-and-control functions are integral to the Mesh's operation, a Mesh sees no distinction between communications and operations; one is not overlaid atop the other.

The more information the sensors collect, the less of it they can send to a central collection point. Radio spectrum is limited (at the megahertz range; gigahertz spectrum is more available but requires more energy to tap) and battery life is precious. A high-definition video image of a scene (which is still far less than a human eye can see) requires 800 megahertz in raw form, and even 20 megahertz in compressed form. Audio input is continuous and also data-intensive. Only anomalies could be reported.

The challenge of distributed sensors is to identify an object by using disaggregated readings. Like neural nets, any such meshes would have to depend on a hierarchy of filtering and analysis. Some readings would be matched against pre-determined patterns. This matching requires that each sensor be able to make partial sense of a partial reading, and that these partial readings can be knit into an assessment.

The route between sensing and determination is bound to be complicated. Some sensors—e.g., a particularly good eye—might determine a target on their own, but that would be the exception (if nothing else, two eyes are needed to perceive depth for absolute location). Many identifications will be probabilistic based on, say, sightings, heat signatures, sounds, and perhaps chemical emanations. This faculty will be critical when the other employs decoys—not everything that appears to be a tank actually is one. Because battlefields will always feature new and different objects, sensor processors will have to be capable of some level of logic abstraction. Humans, as multi-sensor creatures, are for that reason very good at identifying objects. However, there is no inherent reason to pack two eyes, two ears, and a nose on every sensor if these functions can be distributed among many of them. (Perhaps one needs a hundred eyes as often as one needs ten ears or one nose.)

To coordinate, sensors each would have to talk to one another; their activities would have to respond to what others sense (comparable to moving eyes to follow something). Some of these sensors would have to act primarily as nodal processors, collecting information from other sensors to assess a pattern. These too would have to be proliferated to assured robustness; even higher level nodal functions would, in turn, be scattered throughout the battlefield in lesser densities, and so on down to those communicating directly to humans, off-site coordinators, and/or fire control units.

A key coordination problem among sensors is how to identify themselves upon disbursement. Each must indicate where it has landed, how well it is functioning, and who it is near (and thus will be talking to). Many sensors will die on arrival; others may be incapacitated by virtue of their poor placement. Inevitable gaps in coverage will require that sensors be added, moved around, or converted from one type to another (e.g., we have enough sensors listening to this, listen to that instead). Constant communications would then be needed to determine which sensors still work, which are silent, and which are phony (digital signature can prevent spoofing but requires that sensors know who their neighbors are). Such communications also would indicate where more coverage is needed.

Vulnerabilities

The most prominent vulnerability of a distributed Mesh is that the links among sensors, emitters, and microprojectiles are key to its operation. Unlike complex platforms which couple their various capabilities internally, capabilities of the Mesh are coupled externally; thus they may be disrupted by what the Soviets called "radio-electronic warfare."

Sensor broadcasts can, in theory, be jammed or faked, just as those from platforms can. Yet, doing so may be harder than it looks. Jamming requires knowing exactly which frequencies are being used, but more important, where signals are coming from. Today's jammers tend to disrupt a signal from one point to another operating in support of a mission (e.g., confound reflections from a large radar meant to be bounced off an incoming bomber). With proliferated sensors, the only effective jamming technique would be to overpower radio signals by jamming continuously in all directions. This technique requires considerable energy—a fact that makes a jammer a highly visible target itself. Besides taking advantage of existing techniques to avoid jamming—frequency hopping, spread spectrum, extreme directionality—the Mesh might also use laser communications, acoustic means, hopping on enemy frequencies, or just not communicating for long periods of time. Indeed, frequent among Mesh communications might be the repeated admonishment to stay quiet for a while because the enemy is trying to smoke you out. Thus, no one could be really sure that all emitting elements in would be silenced (or just waiting for the right time to turn on).

Faking the broadcast of a digital emitter is even more difficult. By broadcasting a digital signature, a sensor can simultaneously ascertain that the message is actually coming from the sensor, and that the message received was actually that which was broadcast. (Corrupted messages would be internally inconsistent.) This technique requires that each broadcasting sensor have a unique signature and that each receiving sensor memorize the signature of each broadcasting sensor—this is a memory burden, but one which becomes easier with every passing year. Moreover, techniques that allow a communicator to sign a message also permit them to send out false messages knowing that they will be ignored but hoping the enemy will, if not listen, then at least waste power jamming on a frequency not being used.

PLATFORMS AGAINST FIRE-ANTS

The fate of platforms can be illustrated by examining how they might fare against fire-ant elements.

Tanks

Consider the tank as it rolls over terrain littered with sensors and emitters backed by hidden microprojectiles. Such sensors may have arrived hours earlier or they may lie buried for years awaiting a wake-up call. Sensors to search for large ground objects need not be located on the ground. Much of the load may be carried by drones that can broadcast more information than today's models, stay aloft longer, operate more stealthily, and cost less. If costs get enough attention, the deployment of many good drones will be preferred to a few great ones.

An unfriendly tank passing through sensor fields could be brought down in several ways. The most direct solution, if available, is to broadcast the tank's location in real-time to an external missile (or some other fire-control solution). Sensors may also be rigged to take a more direct role. A sensor, for instance, that rides atop a passing tank (much as fleas on passing dogs) can serve as a homing device for an anti-tank round (before it is detected by the tank's smart skin and removed). Sensors may amble over to a tank's vulnerable parts, then kill it by eating their way through gaskets, fuzing moveable parts (e.g., a powdered aluminum-magnesium burst), befouling its air supply, jamming its electronics, smearing its optics, and so on. The latter methods may well evolve from current research on non-lethal warfare. To wit, the chemicals required to stop a tank without killing its crew may be far more compact and thus efficient than those required to blow it up.

Planes

Today's aircraft are optimized—at great expense—to win one-on-one (or one-on-not-too-many) duels against other aircraft and anti-aircraft ground units. The fate of fifty million dollars' worth of aircraft (roughly one aircraft *before* infrastructure and other tail is included) contesting fifty million dollars' worth of loitering sensors, emitters, micro-projectiles may be far less satisfying.

An air-borne sensor screen might contain thousands of nasty objects that may collectively cue firing units in real-time by announcing a target's location and bearing, illuminating it with spattered chemicals, or by bouncing radar on it. Alternatively, if such objects exploded a rain of carbon fibers or ceramic shards, they could take down the aircraft's engines on their own.

Although current technologies do not allow objects to loiter in the air very cheaply (helium balloons aside), today's drones can stay aloft for two weeks. A typical floater may, in a few decades, be the size and shape of a handkerchief, powered by a coat of photovoltaic paint, and girded by a semi-rigid skeleton acting as both antenna and airsail. Its sensors and processors, no larger than fingernails, would allow it to sense wind movements and configure itself to bob up and down accordingly. Upon detecting hostile aircraft, it so signals to fire-control units or tries to get itself and thousands of its friends to find their way softly into the aircrafts' engines. To friendly aircraft, it sends what it knows about the not-so-friendly skies and otherwise gets out of its way. These floaters need not be stealthy; when deployed in the millions, they will simply be beyond the capability of anything to shoot down.

Ships

The same problem of coping with scads of hostile objects would also bedevil ships and submarines. The elements of a Naval mesh are presaged by sonobuoys—cheap sensors routinely produced in the hundreds of thousands today. Lower power requirements, more efficient batteries, and perhaps tethered photo-voltaic collectors will give future versions longer lives. They will also be able to sense better, process more information themselves, and communicate both with their peers (vice overhead aircraft) and associated floating torpedoes. They may even be armed and could maneuver to where ships are most vulnerable. Anti-submarine aircraft squadrons will be used only for initial distribution. If sonobuoys can loiter for years until activated, a much smaller fleet of them could handle even this task.

Naval meshes might be supported by fleets of robotic submersibles—perhaps just very large torpedoes—that can chase fast or stealthy targets into heavily mined waters. To protect themselves, ships and submarines would have to physically sweep large stretches of sea before them. They may need a layered net swept fore and aft to a distance of several miles. This would slow them down considerably and reduce their efficacy in a power projection role.

Space

Tomorrow's space forces will combine very high earth orbiters with large fleets of very low earth orbiters. Their tasks will, however, be the same ones they carry out today: communications, observation, navigation.

One shift will be from strategic to tactical uses of surveillance (already being developed in the TENCAP program). To support targeting and treaty compliance, strategic surveillance needs very detailed pictures (e.g., 10-centimeter resolution) of compact spaces looking for installations that rarely move. Tactical surveillance, although it can use the detail, needs more real-time information. Coverage also needs to be wider because, in a typical tactical scenario (e.g., Bosnia) the field of action is not fixed; it can move quickly and unpredictably. Today's needs for wide-area coverage—looking for certain high-energy events like the launch of a SCUD missile, for example—are met by large satellites in geosynchronous orbit. At 40,000 kilometers up, such orbiters are usually too distant to localize such events precisely. Tactical operations need much denser coverage, and probably from much closer.

Large earth orbiters are also vulnerable to anti-satellite systems no better than those the United States demonstrated off the wings of an F-15 in the middle 1980s. Eventually, large earth orbiters will prove nearly impossible to hide because they are hard to camouflage against an earth background. Since every one must cross the equator fifteen times a day, constant searching can be confined to a small equatorial band. From a higher equatorial orbit, precise optics coupled with powerful on-board processing would make a first sighting inevitable. The movement of satellites, once spotted, can be predicted with great accuracy. Satellites that use energy to jerk into unpredictable orbits would emit characteristic energy plumes that would instantly cue seekers to the orbital path. Under such circumstances, a spacecraft would be hard put to get more than one or two passes over the battlefield before being targeted and destroyed.

Hence the watchwords will be to fly high (and thus get lost in far vaster reaches) or fly small and dense. The logic of space dominance would require getting the most capability into orbit the fastest and protecting it there against attack the longest. This capability would provide short-term tactical advantages at precisely the right moment. Satellites made small and cheap enough could proliferate and thus make their complete destruction complicated. Surveillance satellites might therefore survive better in the aggregate. Weapons satellites (if not forbidden by current treaties) might not—due to the added size and weight of a platform required to carry a minimally effective warhead.

Continuous real-time coverage from space would remain infeasible until satellites become far cheaper. The best look comes from orbiting 400 kilometers high (below which atmospheric drag pulls satellites back to earth, and above which complicates the optics problem). From there, a 30-degree field of view to each side yields a 400-kilometer swatch but requires 4,000 birds (90 birds per each of 45 orbits) to maintain continuous coverage (between the north and south 60-degree parallels). Affording this fleet within a feasible $20 billion investment budget would require that each bird and shot be less than

$5 million. Split 50:50 (assuming $6,000 per pound to low-earth or-bit) suggests that each satellite cost less than $2,500,000 and weigh less than 400 kilograms.

The data burden from such a system is big. To picture everything in the world in 1-meter resolution with 8-bit detail requires roughly 1,500 terabits. If each point is shot once a minute, a total send rate of 3,000 gigabits/second is required. Even with 10:1 image compression and 4,000 satellites, each bird must broadcast 600 megabits per second (roughly equivalent to 30 TV signals). Further reduction is possible by sending only the difference between the actual and expected image, although this requires each bird to store 18,000 gigabytes (150 terabits) of image per bird—free silicon in the extreme. If the resolution doubles, the data collected must rise fourfold. Staring satellites can cover known swathes more efficiently, but successful use of the technique assumes the area covered is significantly smaller than Bosnia. Longer revisit times return us to the current system, which is unusable for real-time operations.

Looking up rather than down, denser information technology makes it easier to construct a functioning ballistic missile defense. A dense enough sensor system should be able to track missiles, which must be large (if they are to hold nuclear weapons) and fly against a fairly clear background. Destroying the missile, once it is found, is considered the lesser half of the problem.

BROADER IMPLICATIONS

By changing the conduct of war, the Mesh changes its nature as well. It raises serious questions about human command, affects the pace of conflict, and blurs the distinction between civilian and military on the battlefield.

Human Control

Current leitmotifs of information warfare suggest that because militaries possess a command core linked to field armies by command and control networks, killing the core leads to cheap victory. Yet advances in information technologies may mean that the core need not sit in any one location. Teleconferencing, for example, permits a command center to occupy dispersed locations. The core data base can be similarly duplicated (or can be built as a distributed system to begin with).

Human command would also evolve. Information technology permits greater centralization—because better telecommunications increase the amount of data that can be sent to core. However, it also permits greater decentralization—because better computation allows units to handle more date from colleagues. Tomorrow's military systems will do both. Headquarters will be able to do more detailed unit control, but units will be able to undertake more functions in degraded communications environments.

Meshes could be engineered to take humans out of many decision loops. Complete removal from the loop is possible. Yet, a technology which *permits* less human oversight need not *compel* it. The bogeyman of an automated war machine will be no greater than it is today. As it is, many existing weapons lack call-back mechanisms. Most mines, for instance, have no man-in-the-loop between detection and explosion. Once a ship's close-in weapons system is turned on, its choice of targets is determined automatically. How different are a strategic ballistic missile that leaves human control once launched and a loitering cruise missile that searches for and destroys a target on its own?

Could fire-ant systems elude human control altogether? Hollywood likes making movies such as *Fail-Safe, Dr. Strangelove, War Games,* and *Terminator 2* that show strategic systems going autonomous. Accidental system autonomy in conventional systems is a lesser problem because they contain multiple decision points and do not have to make all decisions at once. Regardless of how complex the software, the inclusion of enough if-maybe-then-stop locks can limit the risks. An adversary may, however, establish a doomsday ant-mesh system—but these concerns have been familiar grist to nuclear theologists for decades.

On a battlefield where machines command others, foot soldiers—whose relative ranks have been dwindling for a few hundred years—may be the only humans left. Platforms already dominate low-density environments such as air, sea, plains, and deserts with their ample running room; these platforms in turn will be supplanted by the Mesh. High-density environments such as cities, jungles, and mountains remain the preserve of the foot soldier; the Mesh will take over much more slowly in such realms. Foot soldiers can still benefit from technology. Helmets, for instance, may house cellular radio receivers, IFFN transponders, video display terminals embedded in pull-down visors, and computers. The latter would coordinate sensor inputs, generate tactical assessments of battlefield conditions, and transmit maps. Passwords or biological markers could ensure that only the owner be able to use them. The individual soldier could thus be made part of the military Mesh (as well as the commercial Net).

The Pace of Conflict

The Mesh may be tomorrow's version of what the Maginot line was supposed to be, a barrier through which no platform can transit without being detected and destroyed. The Maginot line—despite its subsequent reputation—succeeded where it was placed. Unfortunately, because it cost so much to build, France was unable to finish it, and Germany ran around it to the south. Mesh warfare favors defense. However, unlike the technology of World War I, which was supposed to favor the defense, in the next century technology will permit each side to bombard the other civilian infrastructure with relative ease. Thus, it will be possible to destroy an opponent's above-the-ground civilization without being able to occupy its territory.

Conflict may then resemble siege warfare—perhaps even mutual siege warfare. The same *cordon sanitaire* technology that can protect a state against invasion can be used by invaders to blockade defenders. Offensive siege operations are a highly unsatisfactory way of going about war for all the usual reasons: they are slow, uncertain, and hurt the powerless while the powerful can claim scarce resources for their own ends. Iraq's experience after the Gulf War is a good example. Long-term maintenance is also a problem. In the 21st century, how long might technology allow a besieged party to endure a total blockade? Would modern polities have the patience or stomach to maintain sieges over years, as the besieged project pitiful images of their victims? Would technology let the besieger blockade such electronic communications or douse the besieged with messages of panic or despair? If such sieges prove impossible—societies always prove surprisingly resilient against aerial attack—what other techniques would be available to contain aggressors one could not destroy?

Mesh warfare could simultaneously be faster and slower than current conventional warfare. Compared to the several months the United States needed to deploy to the Gulf, a mesh could be laid down in several hours. A heavy lifter could transit over the affected area, dispersing large quantities of sensors, emitters, microbots, and miniprojectiles. Upon landing, they would automatically configure themselves into a coordinated network. Some countries may leave heavy lifters on runways for precisely such contingencies. Perhaps the United States could protect a future Kuwait upon first hearing that it had been invaded, although such a policy would not be an unalloyed plus. The ability to promise quick commitments may deprive decisionmakers of the time needed to contemplate the long-run consequences of such decisions. National leaders could regret not leaving presumptive allies to their own devices.

If both sides tried to set up meshes at the same time, would the race be destabilizing? Provided each mined inside its borders, the first to do so might, at worst, compel the other to follow. Often, however, such distinctions are not so pat. One party's fence may include disputed or third-party territory. Many collectors see over boundaries: airborne sensors can enjoy a 300-kilometer line of sight; sensitive seismic or acoustic sensors can monitor the entire world. Establishing the space component of the Mesh may also induce conflict particularly if the first up can prevent the second from getting up. World War I was supposedly accelerated by the competition among various countries to mobilize their troops at the border before the other side could. Once the trains, with their rigid timetables, started moving, momentum moved with them to war.

While a Mesh may be built quickly, its operation may retard war considerably. A recent RAND study argued that a squadron of B-2 bombers could destroy an invading armored column in the open. Knowing this, what country would be foolish enough to afford us such opportunity? Instead, unless an invasion could be completed in a few hours, a conventional invasion force opposing a high-information opponent would want to do so very gingerly, with methods similar to those of submarine warfare.

The Achilles heel in any information system is the extent to which it can be spoofed—a constant throughout military history. An effective strategy would have to combine false negatives (sneaking through untouched) and false positives (decoys). Some methods work better than others. To find a tank requires looking for a correlation among as many parameters as possible. Yet finders must be flexible to see that if something looks like a tank, walks like a tank, quacks like a tank, but does not smell like a tank, it may nevertheless be a tank. Conversely, a decoy does not have to simulate a tank in every respect to be classified as one—just in all features considered important by the other side. It may require many decoys to find which parameters the opposing software deems important and thus uses for target identification. All this assumes, of course, that in an attrition conflict one can trade decoys for missiles and still emerge on top. Conversely, a Mesh may let a few tanks by to hide its true parameters. For these reasons, the offense will want to move very slowly while searching for weak spots in the system.

Another technique may take advantage of the fact that the ability to transmit information among many of the nodes may be limited by the small amount of spectrum they each have. Thus a strategy of flooding certain nodes with information may degrade the system. In a poorly engineered system, relevant signature information will be randomly dropped. Even in the best engineered system, concentrating on the important data will force the less highly ranked but still threat-defining data flows to be dropped. Either way, the defense deteriorates. However, determining the information architecture of the other side's Mesh to know exactly where it is weak is anything but easy.

It is not clear how one side's Mesh would combat another side's Mesh. Most sensors and miniprojectiles would not only be small, and at least partially buried, but quiet as well; they would be listening all the time and transmitting rarely. Might hunter-killer microbots be developed to search out and destroy their opposing numbers? Both the difficulty of the likely terrain and their slow speed suggest that such an effort would be extremely drawn out. Confirming that an area is safe is even harder, particularly if the Mesh lets a few items through as a trick.

Economics may also inhibit an ant-on-ant warfare strategy. By virtue of their mobility and additional sensors, hunter-killer ants are bound to be more expensive than their more passive victims. If the hunter-killers have to get close to passive sensors to find them, then a certain percentage of the victims could be mined to blow up upon being jostled by a hunter-killer. At some percentage those employing hunter-killers must expend more resources than they disable. Killing from afar could easily require armament that is more expensive than the individual sensors themselves, and so on.

Civilian as Military

Mesh warfare not only makes it hard to keep platforms alive on the battlefield, but complicates the task of getting them anywhere near it. Logistics assets, notably airlift, sealift, and prepositioned supplies, are among the largest and slowest of military assets. The difficulty of getting there against an opposing Mesh should be of particular concern for the United States and others who help allies by projecting power over large distances.

Because, paradoxically, lift assets are among the most civilianized of military assets, the solution to the lift problem may be to consciously imitate civilian assets until very close to theater. A ship used to carry war material for West Island would be indistinguishable from one used to carry commerce to East Island. At some point its destination would be obvious, but by then, it might have already passed its load of sensors and emitters to where needed. East Island could counter this strategy by explicitly granting a digital signature to specific ships, planes, and messages it selects for its own trade. It is not clear whether other nations would cooperate in setting up an IFFN tracking system with a nation that attacks world commerce. Otherwise, East Island would have difficulty isolating West Island from military help without isolating itself from the commercial world it was increasingly networked to.

Wars are not just contests. Removing all platforms—and thus those who man them—from the field of war would not make war safe for everyone, but the opposite. If Meshes promote siege warfare or the civilianizing of military assets, then the distinction between military and civilian erodes to the great detriment of the latter—a reminder, again, that not every advance in the art of war is tantamount to an advance in civilization.

CONCLUSIONS

Regardless of how the many implications of pop-up warfare, fire-ant warfare, or the Mesh play out, one conclusion is inescapable. The days of the platform as the king of the battlefield are drawing to a close. With its eventual demise comes a similar demise of organizations built around such platforms and the systems used in acquiring them.

Chapter Nine

INFORMATION WARFARE: TIME FOR SOME CONSTRUCTIVE SKEPTICISM?*

John Rothrock

Future historians might well cite the years 1993 and 1994 as the period during which the U.S. military and associated national defense organizations identified Information Warfare as a conceptual vehicle for transitioning from the precepts of the Cold War into the new global realities of the Information Age. The concept is gaining momentum throughout the national security community at a breakneck pace.

Information Warfare's already strong institutional influence is readily evident in the spate of military and other national security organizations which have taken it on as a key element of their mission responsibilities or, as in a growing number of cases, which have been explicitly created to advance and pursue the concept. Simultaneously, millions of dollars are being programmed to provide new data bases, network architectures, advanced software, and other sophisticated capabilities all under the rubric of Information Warfare.

Also by now, most major military organizations have specially selected some of their best minds to help them define and address the new intellectual, organizational, programmatic, and technological challenges that the concept presents. Similarly, defense industry has

*This is a longer version of John Rothrock, "Information Warfare: Time for Some Constructive Skepticism?" *American Intelligence Journal*, Spring/Summer 1994, pp. 71–76. National Military Intelligence Association. Used by permission. A figure and all references to it were omitted for this version.

quickly and heavily come on board, seeing the concept to present a legitimate need and therefore also a business opportunity for bringing new, innovative mixes of its expertise to bear on post–Cold War problems. Throughout the national security community, belief in and enthusiasm for the concept seem to grow by the day as a key to coping with the ever accelerating changes that have continued to beset it since the fall of the Berlin Wall.

The following extended quote from the Secretary of Defense's 1994 report to the President and the Congress summarizes the compelling logic which undergirds this enthusiasm while also testifying to the broad acceptance which the concept seems to enjoy at the highest policy levels:

> Information Warfare is a means to not only better integrate C4I (Command, Control, Communications, Computers, and Intelligence), but also to address the comparative effectiveness of a potential adversary's C4I. It consists of the actions taken to preserve the integrity of one's own information systems from exploitation, corruption, or destruction while at the same time exploiting, corrupting, or destroying an adversary's information system and, in the process, achieving information advantage in the application of force. Thus, Information Warfare is an aggregation of and better integration of C4, C4 countermeasures, information systems security and security countermeasures, and intelligence.

> Information Warfare provides a method of better organizing and coordinating efforts to ensure an optimized information system responsive to the very demanding information requirements inherent in a smaller force structure, a rapid response capability, and advancing military technologies such as deep strike and precision guided weapons and enhanced mobility of forces. Information Warfare is an integrating strategy that makes better use of resources to provide for a better informed force—a force that can act more decisively increasing the likelihood of success while minimizing casualties and collateral effects.[1]

Certainly, if the first milestone for achieving a U.S. Information Warfare capacity suitable for the early decades of the coming century must be development of policy and resource support for the concept throughout the breadth and depth of the national security establishment, that objective now seems to be fairly well secured. The concept's impressive thrust within the national security community has accelerated to the point where most briefings and discussions of the concept now acknowledge Information Warfare to constitute a new medium of conflict even beyond the military dimension to include new modes of global economic, political, and even cultural competition.

ISSUES OF *THRUST* VERSUS *VECTOR* AND *MEANS* VERSUS *OBJECTIVES*

But, what *is* Information Warfare, beyond the nondiscriminating generalities of the DoD Annual Report and Claims that it is a new form of global competition for the Information age? The Information Warfare concept's policy and institutional *thrust* seems to be fairly well established. Now the challenge is to address the intellectually even more difficult issues of its vector.

Thus far, the specifics of the concept's achieved thrust have focused primarily upon organization, process, and resource issues—i.e., essentially the means of Information Warfare. But, beyond the generalities of the DoD Annual Report and claims of the concept's relevance as a new ubiquitous form of Information Age competition and now well established military objectives of countering enemy command and control while protecting your own, the *objectives* of Information Warfare remain relatively undefined. And, with the concept's objectives undefined, its potential implications also suffer from underdefinition and, therefore, lack of examination.

Much of this tendency to shy away from difficult definitions of conceptual objectives has to do with the traditional American intellectual style which is one of pronounced pragmatism. The American institutions generally—and the American military particularly—are decidedly more comfortable with process than with theory, with action more than reflection, with efficiencies more than effectiveness (there is often a difference), with particular performance than with general coherence, and with the particular more than with the holistic.

This inclines the U.S. military, along with many other American institutions, to reduce general propositions such as Information Warfare as quickly as possible to specific "means" issues—i.e., essentially those of resources, organization, and process—with relatively less attention paid to the more general concerns associated with objectives and the more integrated, more coherent address that such concerns demand. Traditional American resource management tools—including the DoD Planning, Programming, and Budgeting System reflect and reinforce these tendencies.

While this especially American style proves its practical mettle over and over in dealing effectively with specific problems, it has definite weaknesses in its capacity to treat several problems at once in context with each other. Unfortunately, it is exactly this sort of integrated, contextual address that an idea as complex and far-reaching as Information Warfare demands. Today, it is far from certain that the structure of institutional relationships and processes through which the U.S. Government manages the country's global security affairs—the PPBS, service department and joint service doctrinal and organizational relationships, the functional junctures of military and civil infrastructures, to name just a few—can cope with Information Warfare in all of the dimensions and manifestations that the concept's logic demands.

SOME CHALLENGING QUESTIONS

Today, when one reads about Information Warfare and hears about the concept in presentations, it remains very difficult to determine if there is anything that Information Warfare is not. A skeptical mind is soon prompted to ask, "*If Information Warfare is everything, can it be anything?*"

Several other questions might follow. For example: Is, as some of its harsher critics suspect, the concept primarily of a bureaucratic and resources thrust toward specific means with little intellectual vector toward specific objectives? Is it truly a trend or merely "trend surfing"? Might not the concept be fundamentally flawed intellectually in constituting, as it does, an attempt to *explicitly* address phenomena (those of information) which are *implicit* to all human endeavor, including warfighting? Is there a risk that Information Warfare could become a convenient lip-service repository for all of the difficult issues of post–Cold War relevance for a national security structure and military whose general forms and culture remain rooted in Cold War precepts? ("Sure, we're relevant in the new era, we subscribe to Information Warfare.")

And, more specifically: If Information Warfare holds that all or most information is valuable and targetable but that it also must be accessible and readily "fungible," what are the implications for traditional concepts of information security and classification? Can classified, heavily compartmented approaches—running as they do essentially against the grain of the Information Age's defining characteristic, that of information proliferation—be effective in pursuing a military concept supposedly suited specifically to the character of that age? Where do the military's purview and responsibilities concerning Information Warfare and information security begin? Where do they end? Are the American society and its military, as the most information-dependent society and military in the world, really wise in advocating Information Warfare as our preferred new style of conflict? If, as is increasingly espoused, Information Warfare is more than just a military proposition, must the society as a whole be capable of pursuing—and defending against—it if the military is to be able to do its part effectively? If the society has problems in meeting IW's challenges (say, for example, in mustering the national will that the concept's defensive imperatives presume), does the military have an appropriate role in helping the society deal with such non-military requirements and implications? If so, what is that role?

These are hard but fair questions which the quickly forming Information Warfare community should be prepared to answer. At a minimum, their serious consideration should provide the concept with an intellectual vector appropriate to its thrust—of course, that is *if* Information Warfare is more than the mere fashion that some skeptics suspect it to be and, also, if our national security structure is capable of recasting itself adequately to effectively implement such a comprehensive idea. If the concept is faultable on either of the latter points, the questions would of course ferret that out as well.

A SUGGESTED PRISM THROUGH WHICH TO CONSIDER INFORMATION WARFARE

But, how are such questions most effectively addressed? Is there perhaps a particularly suitable intellectual prism through which to consider Information Warfare with the necessary rigor appropriate to the importance that the concept's advocates claim for it? How best to explicitly examine a spectrum of issues as implicit to so many other considerations as those comprising Information Warfare?

THE "INFORMATION WARFARE ARROW"

The head of the "Information Warfare Arrow" is comprised of intellectual effectiveness of a highly complex sort. Probably more so than any other form of global security competition, Information Warfare will require exceptional intellectual mastery of the important but subtle hierarchical relationships between policy, strategy, operations ("campaigns"), and tactics. It will equally demand a sophisticated appreciation of the relationships of all of these perspectives to technology. Without such mastery of these relationships, Information Warfare carries with it great risks.

The best technology, even when employed with the greatest of tactical effectiveness, can be counterproductive if the technology and its employment are not orchestrated against a set of well conceived, hierarchically consistent operational, strategic, and policy objectives. While this observation is true regarding any military or quasi-military undertaking, it is especially important regarding Information Warfare which is first and foremost an intellectual rather than a technological or physical undertaking. Information Warfare carries with it especially heavy risks of "winning battles but losing wars." The best of technology and tactics cannot protect against these risks in the face of poor policy, strategy, and operational concepts and the unprecedented degree of conceptual, doctrinal, structural, procedural, and technology integration—i.e., *far beyond "jointness"*—that effective Information Warfare is certain to demand.

The arcane (and now largely irrelevant) policy and strategic machinations of the Cold War excepted, Post–World War II U.S. military thinking has been generally at its best at the levels of tactics (i.e., the specifics of "employment") and technology. True, the 1970s saw a renewed appreciation of the "operational art" perspective (also known as the "campaign level") of military employment and the Gulf War demonstrated that since then we have made great strides in organizing ourselves at that level. However, most observers agree that the operational level still does not yet constitute our military's long suit. Yet, excellence at the operational level is vital to success in Information Warfare for it is the conceptual bridge between higher-level objectives and the means for achieving them.

Beyond these concerns, our system of government necessarily places considerable ethical and political burdens upon those charged with developing policy, strategic, and higher-level operational *objectives*— burdens that are rooted in a logic borne of tradition and culture that goes far beyond the exigencies of any particular set of global security considerations. The net result is a national security and military structure that is much more comfortable in addressing the technological and resource *means* of conflict than it is in considering the higher policy and strategic objectives of conflict.

For this much greater proficiency regarding means as opposed to objectives not to constitute a potentially fatal flaw in the United States' pursuit of Information Warfare—certainly if the concept is carried to its ultimate logic—will require fundamental changes in how we understand conflict and the appropriate responses of our society to it. In fact, the changes that might be required could be so great as to raise a legitimate issue of not only whether we can but even of whether we should make them, the challenges of Information Warfare notwithstanding. Does our society *want* to be the sort that is adept at the degree and types of control of information that some of the more enthusiastic advocates of Information Warfare seem to presume?

This brings us to the concept of national will. Advocates of Information Warfare must discipline themselves to assure that the overall concept—or any particular aspects of it, even those under cover of heavy security classification—do not conflict with or exceed the imperatives of the national will and the crucial *bond of trust* between people and their government. The loss of this trust would obviously be the greatest Information Warfare disaster that can be imagined.

An Information Warfare concept that depends upon an unrealistic or warped perception of the national will, while possibly still maintaining its means thrust will certainly lack appropriate vector, possibly even to the point of coming back to victimize those employing it. In judging how and to what degree specifics of Information Warfare employment are or are not commensurate with national will, it will always be instructive to look at the factors of culture, politics, economics, and infrastructure (all as perceived by the society). If a concept runs against the reality or the societal perception of any of these guiding factors, it must be regarded as highly risky. Again, reliance upon heavy security classification to protect a concept from the extent to which it might run against the societal grain can only exacerbate the possibility and potential consequences of its failure.

INFORMATION WARFARE EMPLOYMENT AND DOCTRINE

Even if fairly conservatively applied, the Information Warfare concept will require highly integrated, *holistic* employment throughout the policy > tactics/technology spectrum of perspectives which must exceed anything our current military culture and structure has ever demonstrated to date. (If, as is implied in the narrower articulations of the concept, Information Warfare remains confined to the tactical level and middle/lower rungs of the operational perspective—such as during the Gulf War—one might ask what is to differentiate "Information Warfare" from what are now more or less conventionally held "Counter Command and Control" concepts.[2]) Without this high degree of integration, the concept is certain to founder in its practical employment for lack of coherence.

As in all military associated employment, the key to coherence in Information Warfare will be effective doctrine. In addition to the several perspectives portrayed by the "arrow," this doctrine—and the structures and procedures it implies—will have to acknowledge Information Warfare to include *three highly interdependent spheres of competition* with actual and/or potential adversaries of the United States. These are (1) the *capacity for offensive action* against the enemy's decision-making structure and processes; (2) *protection of our own capabilities* to make and effect decisions; and (3) the *capacity to create and use information for our own purposes* more effectively than adversaries can create and use information for their purposes.

Underlying all of these relationships, and adding to their maddeningly subtle complexities is a curious but unavoidable irony that is implicit to the Information Warfare concept: i.e., that the U.S. must develop very sophisticated and complex means for attacking adversaries' typically far less developed information/decision structures while still further having to protect our own highly developed infra-structure from relatively simple—but potentially grievous—threats.

The Offensive Sphere

Of the three competitive spheres, the heavy preponderance of atten-tion currently given Information Warfare seems certainly to focus on the concept's *offensive* potentials. Not only does this reflect the U.S. military's natural offensive affinity, it also probably reflects the fact that offensive concepts are less fettered by limitations of established U.S. information practice, structure, and process. An already ob-servable feature of this is the tendency for Information Warfare re-sponsibilities—even seemingly operational ones—to migrate into or-ganizations that are part of—or which are at least heavily involved with the Intelligence Community (especially its SIGINT Compo-nents). These are organizations that, at least in theory, are most suited to assessing targets for Information Warfare applications.

How these Intelligence-focused organizations will handle the inher-ent tension between the natural intelligence inclination to exploit enemy information for its intelligence potential and the operators' natural inclination to destroy or disrupt enemy information sources and flows is certain to become a major doctrinal issue. (A cynic might see something here akin to the Intelligence fox being put in charge of the Information Warfare henhouse.) Whoever is responsi-ble, the necessary doctrinal responsibility and authority to assure that offensive applications accord with all levels of conflict perspec-tive—tactical up through the policy level—are sure to be demanding ones and to require concepts of organization and process for which there is little precedent.

The Protective Sphere

The *protective* (i.e., "defensive") aspects of the Information Warfare concept are even more difficult to handle doctrinally, structurally, and procedurally. This is because convenience and operational effi-cacy in the handling of information usually imply vulnerabilities in the information and decision-making processes which can be fairly readily assessed and exploited/interfered with by an adversary.

Strong doctrinal guidance will be required to direct the IW concept through the maze of "either-or" issues that this tension between general security and immediate efficacy must inevitably raise. Whether a community which is heavily imbued with an Intelligence perspective can adequately define, let alone resolve such issues remains an important question.

The Competitive-Use-of-Information Sphere

As complex as these first two competitive spheres of the Information Warfare concept are, they pale in difficulty in comparison to the third—that of the relative effectiveness of our own information handling and decision-making structures and processes.[3]   This is where subtle asymmetries between our own objectives, capabilities, and information dependencies and those of adversaries, if not readily recognized and taken into account, can wreak disaster.

It might be useful to characterize the situation as follows: We must always be prepared to see ourselves as highly sophisticated "cyber-warriors" who might eventually need to be able to attack and defend against enemies much of our own kind. But we need more immediately the capacity to attack and defend against the equivalent of clever Information Age "neanderthals" who are less dependent upon sophisticated information means than are we but who have adequate sophistication to understand and means to exploit that fact.

Even without considering direct attacks against each other's information/decision capacities notwithstanding, the effective use of information to make timely appropriate decisions is a highly complex proposition. Again, it is a challenge primarily of intellect and only secondarily is it one of technology.

Viewed in this sense, the Command and Control process must be seen as one too profound to be left to those who are merely expert in its technical means—i.e., "communicators," computer specialists, experts in the technologies of information, and the like who in our military culture are most closely identified with the means and processes of Command and Control. To relegate the C2 information/decision-making process to the technical perspectives of these specialists would be uncomfortably analogous to having the telephone company install a telephone for you then expecting them to tell you what to say on it. The best of C2 technology and technology architectures cannot substitute for the conceptual and intellectual quality of the decisions they support.

To achieve the sophistication and doctrinal coherence and effectiveness necessary to provide that quality, especially in response to the unprecedented demands of Information Warfare, will the U.S. military culture to accept at least two conceptual distinctions with which it naturally has trouble.

First, the military must be able to better distinguish between *"efficiency" and "effectiveness"* in order to be sure that, in regard to a specific situation or objective, it is not "doing the wrong thing well." Especially in terms of Information Warfare effectiveness, the need to make such distinctions requires great effort in developing new— essentially non-attritively based measures of merit—by which to gauge the meanings of effectiveness which the concept implies.

Second, Information Warfare requires sophisticated distinctions to be made between hierarchical levels of the cognitive process by which data and information contribute to effective decisions, a process which Information Warfare wants to degrade for the enemy and to preserve and enhance for ourselves. Chief among these distinctions are those between *"awareness"* (the lowest level of cognition), *"knowledge,"* and *"understanding."* One can be "aware" of something but not know its specifics. Similarly, one can "know" something, even very well, but not "understand" its full implications, especially as they impact and are impacted by specific circumstances. (For example, the West "knew" a lot about the Soviet Union, but, as it turned out, our "knowledge" far exceeded what we actually "understood" about it.)

The two principal objectives in Information Warfare must be (1) to degrade adversaries' capacity for *understanding* their own circumstances, our circumstances, and the circumstances that affect all sides while preserving and enhancing our capacity for such understanding and (2) to degrade adversaries' capacities to make *effective use* of *whatever correct understandings* they might achieve and, again, to preserve and enhance our own capacities in this regard. (Note: As in earlier history, future conflicts could well be multilateral, with alliances brief, partial, and calculated often only for the most fleeting advantage; this is yet a further practical complication which Information Warfare advocates must directly confront.)

Achieving and preserving the advantages that will accrue in winning such a competition will be fundamental to future success in the future global security competition that is likely to evolve. As such, Information Warfare cannot be pursued as something "exotic" and separate from the mainstream of the command, control, and employment of military forces. Therefore, the ultimate Information Warfare question is this: Is the U.S. national security structure capable of the intellectual and doctrinal suppleness required to pursue an implicit set of concerns and issues using highly calculated, *specific* means, to achieve *explicit,* but *coherent* objectives?

Yet again, whether or not the limitations of our previous military experience and the resulting U.S. national security/military culture and intellectual style that it has produced will permit us to effectively meet the doctrinal demands for conceptual and employment coherence which Information Warfare poses must at this point remain an open issue.

CONCLUSION

Obviously, the post–Cold War era, most notably the aspects of it that comprise the "Information Age," requires a new approach to global security. "Information Warfare" is gaining considerable momentum as the conceptual vehicle with which the United States, especially the military, hopes to meet this challenge. However, the concept's far-reaching and complex implications dictate degrees of intellectual, structural, and procedural coherence that would exceed by far anything that the modern U.S. national security/military structures have achieved in the past.

For this reason, an objective observer must remain skeptical—if also hopeful—about Information Warfare's historical viability as a new global security concept for the United States. It seems that the only thing more difficult than readying ourselves for Information Warfare would be to conceive of an alternative to it.

NOTES

[1]Les Aspin, Secretary of Defense, *Annual Report to the President and the Congress,* Washington, D.C., January 1994, pp. 227–228.

[2]This is not to imply that we have now finally adequately developed our Counter Command and Control concepts and capabilities, even at the tactical and lower operational levels. To appreciate the full complexity and potential/implications of information conflict on those and also higher planes, see especially V.V. Druzhinin and D.s. Kontorov, "Concept, Algorithm, and Decision," Moscow, *Voinizdat,* 1972. (One of the USAF "Soviet Military Thought" translation series.) Counter C2 and information Warfare concepts that are not rooted in appreciation of issues raised by Druzhinin and Kontorov probably should be held intellectually suspect. (However, it is not necessary to agree with the authors' decidedly Soviet conclusions about many specific issues.) For a more recent, perhaps even deeper discussion of information and its use/manipulation, see also Keith Devlin, *Logic and Information,* Cambridge (UK), Cambridge University Press, 1991. For a less theoretical treatment applicable to the tactical and operational levels, see as well the current author's "Counter Command and Control in Conceptual Perspective," *Air University Review,* Jan–Feb 1980. This article, while dated in its focus on the Soviet adversary, explores several conceptual issues which probably still warrant consideration.

[3]It is in recognition of the complexities that this section addresses that the National Defense University has designated the curriculum it intends to address these issues as a curriculum in "Information-based Warfare." Others are also coming more frequently to use this term to capture the full complexity of the concept.

Chapter Ten

EMERGING CHALLENGE: SECURITY AND SAFETY IN CYBERSPACE[*]

Richard O. Hundley and Robert H. Anderson

With more and more of the activities of individuals, organizations, and nations being conducted in cyberspace,[1] the security of those activities is an emerging challenge for society. The medium has thus created new potentials for criminal or hostile actions, "bad actors" in cyberspace carrying out these hostile actions, and threats to societal interests as a result of these hostile actions.

POTENTIAL HOSTILE ACTIONS

Security holes in current computer and telecommunications systems allow these systems to be subject to a broad spectrum of adverse or hostile actions. The spectrum includes: inserting false data or harmful programs into information systems; stealing valuable data or programs from a system, or even taking over control of its operation; manipulating the performance of a system, by changing data or programs, introducing communications delays, etc.; and disrupting the performance of a system, by causing erratic behavior or destroying data or programs, or by denying access to the system. Taken together, the surreptitious and remote nature of these actions can make their detection difficult and the identification of the perpetra-

[*]Richard O. Hundley and Robert H. Anderson, "Emerging Challenge: Security and Safety in Cyberspace," *IEEE Technology and Society*, pp. 19–28 (Winter 1995/1996). Copyright 1995 IEEE. Reprinted, with permission, from *IEEE Technology and Society Magazine*. The acknowledgment section was deleted for this reprint.

tor even more difficult. Furthermore, new possibilities for hostile actions arise every day as a result of new development and applications of information technology.

The bad actors who might perpetrate these actions include: hackers, zealots or disgruntled insiders, to satisfy personal agendas; criminals, for personal financial gain, etc.; terrorists or other malevolent groups, to advance their cause; commercial organizations, for industrial espionage or to disrupt competitors; nations, for espionage or economic advantage or as a tool of warfare. Cyberspace attacks mounted by these different types of actors are indistinguishable from each other, insofar as the perceptions of the target personnel are concerned. In this cyberspace world, the distinction between "crime" and "warfare" in cyberspace also blurs the distinction between police responsibilities, to protect societal interests from criminal acts in cyberspace, and military responsibilities, to protect societal interests from acts of war in cyberspace.

We call protecting targets in cyberspace, such as government, business, individuals, and society as a whole, against these actions by bad actors in cyberspace, "cyberspace security." In addition to deliberate threats, information systems operating in cyberspace can also cause unforeseen actions or events— without the intervention of any bad actors—that create unintended (potentially or actually) dangerous situations for themselves or for the physical and human environments in which they are embedded. Such safety hazards can result from both software errors and hardware failures. We call protection against this additional set of cyberspace hazards "cyberspace safety." In the new cyberspace world, government, business, individuals, and society as a whole require a comprehensive program of cyberspace security and safety (CSS) [1]-[5].[2]

CONSEQUENCE CATEGORIES

We have used four categories to define the consequences of cyberspace attacks, categories based on the degree of economic, human, or societal damage caused. From the least to the most consequential, they are:

1) *minor annoyance or inconvenience*, which causes no important damage or loss, and is generally self-healing, with no significant recovery efforts being required;

2) *limited misfortune*, which causes limited economic or human or societal damage, relative to the resources of the individuals, organizations, or societal elements involved, and for which the recovery is straightforward, with the recovery efforts being well within the recuperative resources of those affected, organizations, or societal elements;

3) *major or widespread loss*, which causes significant economic or human or societal damage, relative to the resources of those involved, and/or which may affect, or threaten to affect, a major portion of society, and for which recovery is possible but difficult, and strains the recuperative resources of the affected individuals, organizations, or societal elements; and

4) *major disaster*, which causes great damage or loss to affected individuals or organizations, and for which recovery is extremely difficult, if not impossible, and puts an enormous, if not overwhelming, load on the recuperative resources of those affected.

We assert that it is not always possible to measure human or societal damage in purely economic terms.

PAST INCIDENTS

CSS incidents constituting a minor annoyance or inconvenience have been a frequent occurrence across the entire spectrum of target categories. For some targets (e.g., the AT&T Bell Labs computer network or the unclassified Pentagon network) such minor annoyances can occur one or more times every day. For many computer installations, such incidents have become so commonplace that they are no longer reported.

CSS incidents constituting a limited misfortune—e.g., computer installations disrupted for limited periods of time, or limited financial losses (relative to the resources of the target)—have occurred less frequently, but nevertheless numerous examples exist across the entire spectrum of targets. A number of these are reported in [1] and [4].

There have even been a few cases of incidents which many observers would class as major or widespread loss to the target(s) involved. Examples include the "AIDS Trojan" attack in December 1989, which caused (among many other things) an AIDS research center at the University of Bologna in Italy to lose 10 years of irreplaceable data [4]; the AT&T network failure on January 15, 1990, due to a software error, which disrupted and virtually shut down a major portion of the U.S. nationwide long-distance network for a period of about nine hours [1], [4]; the almost total disruption of the computers and computer networks at the Rome (NY) Air Force Base for a period of 18 days in early 1994, during which time most (if not all) of the information systems at Rome were "disconnected from the Net" [6]; and the MCI calling-card scam during 1992–1994, in which malicious software was installed on MCI switching equipment to record and steal about 100,000 calling card numbers and personal identification codes that were then sold to hackers throughout the U.S. and Europe and posted on bulletin boards, resulting in an estimated $50 million in unauthorized long-distance calls[7].

We know of no clear examples to date of a CSS incident constituting a major disaster.

POTENTIAL FUTURE INCIDENTS

Whatever may have happened in the past, we expect cyberspace security and safety incidents to become much more prevalent in the future, due to the facts that more and more people are becoming "computer smart" all over the world; bad actors of many different types are becoming more and more aware of opportunities in cyberspace; connectivity is becoming more widespread and universal; more and more systems and infrastructures are shifting from mechanical/electrical control to electronic/software control; and human activities in cyberspace are expanding much faster than security efforts.

Recent data support this expectation[8].

Accordingly, we expect that, in the future, CSS incidents constituting a minor annoyance or inconvenience will become commonplace across the entire spectrum of targets; incidents constituting a limited misfortune could also become a common occurrence; CSS incidents constituting a major or widespread loss are quite possible for all targets in cyberspace; and CSS incidents constituting a major disaster are definitely possible for some targets in special cases.

Some examples of special cases in which major disasters may be possible include the following:

- *Physical and functional infrastructures,* such as the air traffic control system, possibly leading to the crashes of one or more aircraft.

- *Military and national security.* For example, if a cyberspace-based attack were to bring down an essential military command and control system at a critical moment in a battle, it might lead to the loss of the battle. If the battle were pivotal, or the stakes otherwise high enough, this could ultimately lead to military disaster.

- *Other societal organizations and activities.* With medical care becoming increasingly dependent on information systems, many of them internetted, a perpetrator could make changes to data or software, possibly resulting in the loss of life.

Other examples of possible cases leading to major disasters may occur to the reader. Today these examples are all hypothetical. Tomorrow one or more of them could well be real. Our impression is that CSS incidents will become much more prevalent; they will impact almost every corner of society in the developed nations of the world; and the consequences could become much greater.

INFRASTRUCTURE FRAGILITY

There are many uncertainties associated with this projection of future cyberspace security and safety incidents. Attacks on vital infrastructures are one of the things most likely to cause widespread repercussions for society. Accordingly, one of the most important uncertainties has to do with the degree of robustness of current and future infrastructures: Are the key physical and functional infrastructures in various nations highly robust, due to built-in redundancies and self-healing capabilities? Or do some infrastructures have hidden fragilities that could lead to failures having important consequences?

Conventional wisdom regarding these questions is not always correct. For example, prior to 1990, the AT&T long distance network in the U.S. was usually thought to be very robust, with many alternative paths for long distance calls to take, going through different switching centers. But all of these switching centers use the same software, and when new software was introduced in 1990, every long-distance switch had the same bad line of code. So at the software level, there was no redundancy at all, but rather a fragility that brought a large part of the AT&T long-distance network down[1], [4].

The message is clear: many infrastructures may not be as robust as they seem; a detailed look at vulnerabilities of specific infrastructures is needed.

ACTORS RESPONSIBLE FOR INCIDENTS

By far the greatest portion of past cyberspace security incidents have been perpetrated by "hackers": individuals satisfying a variety of personal agendas, which in their view do not include criminal motives [9], [10]. This continues to be the case regarding current incidents.

In recent years, the role of criminals in cyberspace incidents has increased. According to law enforcement professionals consulted by the authors, this has come about not as a result of the criminal element becoming more aware of opportunities in cyberspace, but rather primarily as a result of computer hackers "growing up" and some (small) fraction of them realizing and exploiting the financial opportunities open to them via criminal acts.

There are no known cases in the open literature of cyberspace security incidents perpetrated by terrorists or other malevolent groups, commercial organizations, or nations. However, there are plenty of rumors of business organizations and intelligence agencies outside the U.S. that have mounted cyberspace-based attacks against companies in other nations as a means of industrial or economic espionage.

In addition, police authorities in Europe have recently begun to discern a number of potentially more dangerous actors manipulating and guiding some malicious hacker activity. This appears to include professional hackers, who are often the source of the penetration tools used by the "ordinary" hackers; information brokers, who frequently post notices on European hacker bulletin boards offering various forms of "payment" for specific information; private detectives, who also often use the European hacker bulletin boards as a means of obtaining information regarding targeted individuals or organizations; foreign embassies, who appear to have been behind the bulletin board activities of at least some European private detectives and information brokers; and organized crime.

Whatever may have happened in the past, in the future we expect all five of our classes of bad actors to continue participating in cyberspace security incidents.

MECHANISMS: PAST AND FUTURE

A number of mechanisms have been prevalent in past cyberspace security and safety incidents and are likely to be prevalent in future incidents as well. Many incidents involve more than one of these mechanisms, which include:

- *Operations-based attacks,* taking advantage of inadequate or lax security environments. Exploitation of deficient security environments has been a feature of many/most past successful cyberspace penetrations and is likely to continue to be prevalent in the future—as long as lax security continues to be commonplace.

- *User authentication-based attacks,* which bypass or penetrate login and password protections. Such attacks are a common feature of many/most past cyberspace security incidents and are also likely to be prevalent in the future.

- *Software-based attacks,* exploiting software features (e.g., maintenance backdoors), programmatic flaws, and logical errors or misjudgments in software implementation, as well as the insertion of malicious software.

- *Network-based attacks,* which take advantage of network design, protocol, or topology in order to gather data, gain unauthorized system access, or disrupt network connectivity. This can include alterations of routing tables, password sniffing, and the spoofing of TCP/IP packet addresses. Attacks of this type have not been common in the past. However, beginning in 1994 hackers have been detected penetrating Internet routers to install password sniffers, etc.; TCP/IP packet address spoofing was first detected in early 1995. Such attacks—including attempts to disrupt Internet connectivity—could become much more common in the future, unless Internet security is markedly improved.

- *Hardware-based attacks or failures,* exploiting programmatic or logical flaws in hardware design and implementation, or component failures. These have not been a feature of past cyberspace security incidents (i.e., deliberately perpetrated incidents), but have played a role in occasional safety hazards (i.e., accidental incidents). This is likely to continue in the future.

ADDITIONAL KEY FACTORS

There are a number of additional factors impacting on the cyberspace security problem and of necessity shaping any effective protective strategies.

Increasing Transnationalism

As is well known, cyberspace does not respect national boundaries. In recent years more and more nations throughout the world have become "connected" to the world network, and within those nations connectivity has become more and more universal.

Every year greater numbers of individuals and organizations in the U.S. are taking advantage of this increasing worldwide connectivity to become involved, via cyberspace, in economic or social activities with individuals and organizations in other nations. These transnational activities are becoming increasingly important to the U.S. individuals and organizations involved; they will not willingly give them up.

Since threats in cyberspace pay no regard to regional or national boundaries, knowledge of computer hacking techniques has spread around the globe, and the perpetrator of a security incident can just as well be on the other side of the world as across the street.

For both of these reasons—the nature of activities in cyberspace and the nature of threats—cyberspace has become effectively transnational. No nation has effective sovereignty over cyberspace. Any effective cyberspace protective strategy must take this into account.

Current Security Inadequate

The information processing systems and telecommunications systems currently in use throughout the world are full of security flaws, and new security flaws are being uncovered almost every day, usually as a result of hacker activity. As new developments and applications of information technology become available and as human activities in cyberspace continually expand, security efforts appear to be lagging behind. There is currently no effective way to police cyberspace. Considering the rapid increase in the number of reported security incidents in recent years, along with the apparent increase in the severity of these incidents, it does not appear that the "good guys" are winning; they may not even be holding their own.

Current security operations in cyberspace are inadequate. This is not the result of a lack of security technology. Rather, it reflects a very limited application of available technology; most of the available computer security technology is not used in most of the computers in the world.

Acceptance Lacking

The U.S. has had a computer security program since the 1960s. In spite of these efforts, the U.S. is full of insecure computers today. There are several reasons for this. A primary reason is that user acceptance and utilization of available computer security safeguards has been reluctant and limited. There are several causes of this lack of user acceptance.

• Typically, user interfaces accompanying security features are awkward. As a result, the secure systems are more difficult to use than the nonsecure systems. Many users are not motivated to take the extra effort.

• Users have not considered security features as adding value, and therefore are reluctant to pay extra for such features.

- Computer hardware and software manufactures have not perceived the security market as being attractive. Rather, it has usually been considered a limited, niche market. Therefore the largest commercial manufacturers (Microsoft, Apple, etc.) have not included many security features in their primary product lines.

- Many individual users do not understand the need for a communal role in cyberspace security and do not accept responsibility for such a role.

- Most users don't take computer security seriously until something bad has happened to them or to their immediate organization.

For reasons such as these, most of the computer security technology currently available is not used on most of the computers in the world. A typical computer on the Internet uses a garden variety Unix operating system with few additional security safeguards. Similarly, a typical desktop computer uses the MS-DOS, MS-DOS plus Windows, or Macintosh operating systems, once again with few additional security safeguards. The various secure operating systems, multilevel security systems, and Orange Book[3] compliant software systems that have been developed are primarily used in restricted, niche applications.

Isolation Disappearing As Option

Twenty or thirty years ago there was a simple solution to this problem: the physical isolation of computer systems, what is now called an "air gap." This is no longer a viable option. As more and more human activities move into cyberspace to take advantage of the efficiencies provided by interconnection, organizations and individuals who fail or refuse to connect will increasingly fall behind the pace of economic and social activity, will become increasingly noncompetitive in their area of activity, and will have difficulty accomplishing their missions. This idea is stated succinctly in a report of the Joint Security Commission appointed by the U.S. Secretary of Defense and the Director of Central Intelligence to develop a new approach to security to meet the challenges facing the Department of Defense and the Intelligence Community in the post–Cold War era [13]:

Those who steadfastly resist connectivity will be perceived as unresponsive and will ultimately be considered as offering little value to their customers. . . . The defense and intelligence communities share this imperative to connect.

Roles and Missions Blurred

By their nature, developments in cyberspace blur the distinction between crime and warfare, thereby also blurring the distinction between police responsibilities to protect U.S. interests from criminal acts in cyberspace, and military responsibilities to protect U.S. interests from acts of war in cyberspace.

In addition, providing protection against transnational threats in cyberspace, and apprehending their perpetrators, frequently goes well beyond the reach and resources of local and regional authorities.

These two characteristics of security in cyberspace—the blurring of the distinction between crime and warfare, and the transnational nature of many security incidents—raise new questions regarding the proper roles and missions in cyberspace security and safety. Some of the agencies, organizations, and institutions that have essential roles to play, from the viewpoint of one living in the U.S., include:

- *U.S. federal government*, including intelligence agencies, the Department of Defense, federal law enforcement agencies; civilian regulatory agencies; and other civilian agencies;

- *U.S. State and local governments*, including law enforcement agencies and regulatory agencies;

- *Nongovernmental organizations* such as CERTs, business and professional associations, vendors, industry standard-setting bodies, and private businesses;

- *Governments of other nations*, including intelligence agencies, ministries of defense, and law enforcement agencies;

- *International organizations* such as the United Nations, supranational governing bodies, Interpol, and international standards bodies.

Today this is "everybody's" problem, and therefore "nobody's" problem. It falls into all of the cracks.

USEFUL METAPHORS

These various characteristics of the current security situation in cyberspace suggest three metaphors which may stimulate thinking about protective strategies.

"Wild West" World

Cyberspace has many similarities to a Wild West world.

- In the Wild West almost anything could occur. There was no one to enforce overall law and order, only isolated packets of local law. The same is true in cyberspace.

- There were both "good guys" and "outlaws" in the Wild West, often very difficult to tell apart. "Friends" were the only ones a person could trust, even though he or she would frequently have to deal with "strangers." This is also true in cyberspace.

- Outside of the occasional local enclaves of law and order, everyone in the Wild West was primarily dependent for security on their own resources and those of their trusted friends. This is also true in cyberspace.

The message of this metaphor for cyberspace security is clear: If there is no way to enforce law and order throughout all of cyberspace, which appears to be the case, one must rely on local enclaves of law and order, and trusted friends.

Medieval World

The medieval world depended on local enclaves for security: castles and fortified cities, protected by a variety of fortifications—moats, walls, and drawbridges. Communication and commerce between these fortified enclaves was carried out and/or protected by groups of armored individuals.

This metaphor also suggests a message for cyberspace security: cyberspace fortifications (i.e., firewalls) can protect the local enclaves in cyberspace, just as moats and walls protected the castles in the medieval world.

We have found the security concepts suggested by these two metaphors—local enclaves and firewalls—to be very compelling, and usable as part of a basic paradigm for cyberspace security.

Biological Immune System

The problems faced by biological immune systems have a number of similarities to the challenges confronting cyberspace security. This suggests that the "security" solutions employed by immune systems could serve as another useful model for cyberspace security. For example:

- Higher-level biological organisms are comprised of a large number of diverse, complex, highly interdependent components. So is cyberspace.

- Biological organisms face diverse dangers (from microbes) that cannot always be described in detail before an individual attack occurs, and which evolve over time. Organisms cannot defend against these dangers by "disconnecting" from their environment. The same is true of information systems exposed to threats in cyberspace.

- Biological organisms employ a variety of complementary defense mechanisms, including both barrier defense strategies involving the skin and cell membranes, and active defense strategies that sense the presence of outsiders (i.e., antigens) and respond with circulating killers (i.e., antibodies). The cyberspace firewalls are an obvious analogue to the biological barrier defenses. But what about the active defenses? Perhaps software agents could be created providing a cyberspace active defense analogue to biological antibodies.

The biological agents providing the active defense portion of the immune system employ certain critical capabilities: the ability to distinguish "self" from "nonself"; the ability to create and transmit recognition templates and killer mechanisms throughout the organism; and the ability to evolve defenses as the "threat" changes.

Software agents providing a cyberspace active defense analogue to these biological antibodies would need the same capabilities.[4]

The message of this metaphor is clear: Cyberspace security would be enhanced by active defenses capable of evolving over time.

We find this third metaphor as compelling as the first two; however, we are not as far along in exploiting it in our analysis.

SECURITY STRATEGY

These enclaves can be of various sizes, some of them can be nested, and the firewalls can be of various permeabilities. The enclaves have protected connections to other trusted enclaves, and limited connections to the rest of cyberspace.

In this architectural concept, no attempt is made to maintain centralized law and order throughout all of cyberspace. Each authority maintains local law and order in its own enclave. Everything outside of the enclaves is left to the "wild west."

These enclaves can come in a variety of sizes, ranging from an individual computer to a complete network. The firewalls protecting these various size enclaves come in several different types, with different degrees of permeability.[5]

In the most extreme case, one can have an air gap, i.e., the absence of any electronic connection between the interior of the enclave and the outside world. Within this overall category, there can be various degrees of permeability, depending upon what software and/or data are allowed in and out, on diskettes, tapes, etc., and how rigorously this software and data are checked.

When electronic connections are allowed, a firewall computer stands between the world outside the enclave and the internal machines. Two main categories of variations are possible:

1) Different services can be allowed to come in or to go out, depending on the permeability desired of the firewall. Typical ser-

vice categories include electronic mail, file transfer (e.g., FTP), information servers (e.g., World Wide Web browsers), and remote execution (e.g., Telnet). Of these four categories, electronic mail is the safest to interchange with the outside world and remote execution is the most dangerous—in the sense of providing opportunities that hackers can exploit to penetrate the firewall barrier and gain control of internal machines. Accordingly, even the tightest firewalls usually allow the passage of electronic mail in both directions, whereas only the loosest firewalls allow the passage of remote execution services, particularly in the inward direction.

2) Some allowed services can terminate (or originate) at the firewall machine, while others can go right through the firewall to the internal machines (incoming services) or to the outside world (outgoing services). The fewer services that pass through the firewall, the tighter it is.

These variations in the permeability of electronic firewalls can be tuned to the circumstances of the particular enclave.

Protective Techniques and Procedures

In addition to firewalls, there are a number of other protective techniques and procedures which have important roles to play in our strawman protective strategy. These include:

- Improved access controls, including one-time passwords, smart cards, and shadow passwords.

- More secure software. This could include expanded use of software independent verification and validation (IV&V) techniques, to find and eliminate software bugs and security holes in widely used software, as well as more secure operating systems.

- Encrypted communications, both between and within protected enclaves.

- Encrypted files, for data that is particularly sensitive.

- Improved capabilities to detect penetrations, including user and file-access profiling.

- Active counteractions, to harass and suppress bad actors. This is something that is woefully lacking today; almost all current computer security measures are either passive or counteractive, leaving the initiative to the perpetrator.

- Software agents, perhaps acting in a manner similar to a biological immune system.

Motivating Users

The best protective strategy in the world and the best set of protective techniques and procedures will be ineffective if users do not employ them. Necessary (and hopefully sufficient) ways to motivate users include:

1) A vigorous program of education and training, of both users and managers concerned with information systems in potential target organizations—education, so that people will understand the magnitude of the risk to their interests and the importance of cyberspace security, and training, so that people will know how to protect themselves.

2) Proactive programs to demonstrate vulnerabilities—sometimes called "red teams"—and thereby to increase organizational and individual awareness of cyberspace vulnerabilities. The Vulnerability Analysis and Assistance Program (VAAP) of the U.S. Center for Information Systems Security (CISS) is a good example of such a proactive program [20].

3) Mandates, tailored to different societal elements. These can include mandatory security procedures established by an organization for all of its employees or members to follow, mandatory security standards that a computer host must meet in order to be permitted to connect to a network, security standards and procedures that organizations and individuals must adhere to in order not to incur legal liability, and even possibly laws mandating certain minimum levels of security standards for information systems engaged in certain types of public activity.

4) Sanctions, to enforce the mandates.

Complete Protective Strategy

In addition to the elements we have discussed thus far, a complete cyberspace protective strategy needs at least two additional elements.

1) A set of prescriptions governing the application of the basic security paradigm and the set of protective techniques and procedures to different security situations: for protecting different elements of society; for countering different actors; and for determining what role various agencies and organizations should play in cyberspace security, in which situations. These prescriptions—in particular those associated with the assignment of roles and missions in cyberspace security—may well differ from nation to nation.

2) A built-in mechanism or mechanisms to continually update the protective techniques and procedures, and the overall strategy, as information technology continues to evolve and its applications to expand, and as new threats emerge.

These elements remain to be developed.

OPEN QUESTIONS, KEY ISSUES

A number of open questions and key issues should be resolved in process of proceeding further. These include:

- *What specific organizations and activities comprise what we will call the "National Interest Element" in the U.S. or any other nation?* That is, what organizations, information systems, and activities play such vital roles in society that their disruption due to cyberspace attacks would have national consequences, and their protection should therefore be of national concern?

- *Which organizations (in each nation) should play what roles in the protection of the National Interest Element?*

- *How robust or fragile are essential infrastructures contained in the National Interest Element of each nation?* This is one of the key uncertainties in our current understanding of the cyberspace security situation. A detailed look at the vulnerabilities of specific infrastructures in various nations is needed to resolve this issue.

- *How does one protect against the trusted insider?* Our basic security paradigm of local enclaves protected by firewalls protects against malicious outsiders, but not necessarily against malicious insiders, individuals inside the firewall with all of the access privileges of a trusted member of the enclave. As knowledge of hacker techniques spreads throughout the population, adverse actions by malicious insiders is becoming more and more of a problem. We have not discussed this here, but it is an important threat with which any complete cyberspace security strategy should deal. It becomes particularly important for very large protected enclaves, encompassing large numbers of individuals; the more people within an enclave, the greater the probability that at least one of them might be a bad actor.

INCREASINGLY COMPLEX WORLD, EXPANDING SECURITY CONCERNS

A number of points are worth emphasizing:

Fifty years after ENIAC, the network has become the computer (paraphrasing the Sun Microsystems slogan "The Network Is the Computer").

In the future, cyberspace security and safety incidents in this networked environment will become much more prevalent; cyberspace security and safety incidents will impact almost every corner of society; and the consequences of cyberspace security and safety incidents could become much greater.

Local enclaves protected by firewalls appear promising as a basic cyberspace security paradigm, applicable to a wide range of security situations.

We're all in this together; weak links in the net created by any of us (software developers, end users, network providers, etc.) increase the problem for all of us.

Much more attention must be paid to user motivation, for all classes of users, with different approaches required for each class. Inadequate user acceptance and utilization of security techniques and procedures has been the bane of most previous attempts at cyberspace security.

No one's in charge; the problem transcends all usual categories. The question of "roles and missions" is an important one, both philosophically (e.g., do we need more centralized control, or are there decentralized effective solutions) and pragmatically (what roles do we give DoD versus FBI versus CIA; UN versus U.S.; Interpol versus whom?).

The world has become much more complex. It is useful complexity, but with this complexity has come security and safety problems that we are only beginning to understand and appreciate.

REFERENCES

1. P. Neumann, *Computer Related Risks*. Reading, MA: Addison-Wesley, 1994.

2. P.J. Denning, *Computers Under Attack: Intruders, Worms, and Viruses*. Reading, MA: Addison-Wesley, 1990.

3. K. Hafner and J. Markoff, *Cyberpunk: Outlaws and Hackers on the Computer Frontier*. New York, NY: Simon & Schuster, 1991.

4. P. Mungo and B. Clough, *Approaching Zero: The Extraordinary Underworld of Hackers, Phreakers, Virus Writers, and Keyboard Criminals*, New York, NY: Random House, 1992.

5. P. Wallach. "Wire pirates," *Sci. Amer.*, vol. 270, pp. 90–101, Mar. 1994.

6. Presentation by Air Force Computer Emergency Response Team (AFCERT), Kelly AFB, at Sixth Ann. Computer Security Incident Handling Wkshp., hosted by the Forum of Incident Response and Security Teams (FIRST), Boston, MA. July 25–29, 1994.

7. R.E. Yates, "Hackers stole phone card numbers in $50 million scam," *Chicago Trib.*, pp. 1,6. Nov. 2, 1994.

8. Data Presented by Computer Emergency Response Team (CERT), Carnegie Mellon University, at Sixth Ann. Computer Security Incident Handling Wkshp., hosted by the Forum of Incident Response and Security Teams (FIRST). Boston, MA. July 25–29, 1994—supplemented by CERT 1994 Ann. Rep. web homepage (http://www.sei.cmu.edu/SEI/ programs/cert/1994_ CERT_Summary.html).

9. S. Levy, *Hackers, Heroes of the Computer Revolution,* Anchor, 1984.

10. D.G. Johnson, *Computer Ethics,* 2nd ed. Englewood Cliffs, NJ: Prentice Hall, 1994.

11. B. Hoffman, "Responding to terrorism across the technological spectrum," RAND, Rep. P-7874, 1994.

12. *DOD Trusted Computer System Evaluation Criteria (TCSEC),* DoD 5200.28-STD. Washington, DC: U.S. Government Printing Office, Dec. 1985.

13. "Redefining security," report by the Joint Security Commission, Washington, DC 20525, Feb. 28, 1994.

14. S. Forrest, A.S. Perelson, L. Allen and R. Cherukuri, "Self-nonself discrimination in a computer," in *Proc. 1994 IEEE Symp. Res. in Security and Privacy,* 1994.

15. J.O. Kephart, "A biologically inspired immune system for computers," in *Artificial Life IV, Proc. Fourth Int. Wkshp Systhesis and Simulation of Living Systems,* R.A. Brooks and P. Maes, Eds. Cambridge, MA: M.I.T. Press, 1994, pp. 130–139.

16. W.R. Cheswick and S.M. Bellovin, *Firewalls and Internet Security: Repelling the Wily Hacker.* Reading, MA: Addison-Wesley, 1994.

17. S. Garfinkel and G. Spafford. *Practical UNIX Security,* Sebastopol, CA: O'Reilly & Associates, 1991.

18. *Proc. 17th Nat. Computer Security Conf.,* vols. 1 and 2, National Inst. of Standards and Technology/National Computer Security Center, Oct. 11–14, 1994.

19. M.R. Higgins, "Threats to DoD unclassified systems," DoD Center for Information Systems Incident Support Team (ASSIST), 1994.

20. R.L. Ayers, "Center for Information Systems Security, Functions and Services," Center for Information Systems Security, Defense Information Systems Agency, 1994.

NOTES

[1] As one consequence of the electronic digitization of information and the worldwide internetting of computer systems, more and more activities throughout the world are mediated and controlled by information systems. The global world of internetted computers and communications systems in which these activities are being carried out has come to be called "cyberspace," a term originated by William Gibson in his novel *Neuromancer*.

[2] In addressing questions of cyberspace security and safety, we have relied on a variety of anecdotal information obtained from a number of sources. The anecdotal data by no means constitute a comprehensive statistically valid sample. In principle, one could develop such a sample from databases from the various computer emergency response teams (CERTs), law enforcement databases, and private sector incident data. However, we have yet to find anyone who has done so.

There are a number of reasons for this. One is that many if not most cyberspace security incidents apparently go unreported to authorities, particularly in the financial community. It is therefore unclear if the incidents that are reported are "the tip of the iceberg," or all there is to the problem.

Lacking a comprehensive sample, the total quantitative dimensions of the cyberspace security problem are unclear. Therefore, we present here our qualitative impressions of the problem.

[3] The "Orange Book" is a common term for the DOD Trusted Computer System Evaluation Criteria (TCSEC) [12].

[4] We are not the first to be intrigued by this metaphor. Forrest *et al.* [14] and Kephart [15] discuss software implementations of certain aspects of the biological immune system metaphor.

[5] We are certainly not the first to suggest firewalls as a protective technique or as a central element of a protective strategy. See [16]–[18].

Chapter Eleven

AN EXPLORATION OF CYBERSPACE SECURITY R&D INVESTMENT STRATEGIES FOR DARPA[*]

Robert H. Anderson and Anthony C. Hearn

INTRODUCTION

"The Day After . . ." exercise methodology, developed over the past several years under the leadership of Roger Molander, has proven useful in eliciting thinking about complex strategic issues from groups of up to about 60 individuals. The exercises are also useful in "awareness building"—exposing participants to the possible ramifications of current trends, and options for altering those trends. For examples of previous uses of this methodology to explore the national security policy implications of the continued diffusion of nuclear weapons capabilities, see Millot, Molander and Wilson (1993); Mesic, Molander and Wilson (1995); Molander, Wilson, Mesic and Gardiner (1994); and Molander, Riddile and Wilson (1995). A recent application of the methodology to issues of strategic information warfare is presented in Molander, Riddile and Wilson (1996).

The U.S. Defense Advanced Research Projects Agency (DARPA) is interested in understanding strategies for the investment of research and development funds for securing the U.S. information infrastructure against "information warfare" (IW) attacks. (As Roger Molander

[*]Robert H. Anderson and Anthony C. Hearn, *An Exploration of Cyberspace Security R&D Investment Strategies for DARPA: "The Day After—in Cyberspace II,"* Santa Monica, Calif.: RAND, MR-797-DARPA, 1996. Copyright 1996 RAND. Used by permission. Some figures, tables, and text were omitted for this version.

put it, tongue in cheek, during his opening remarks at the exercise described in this report: "OK, you guys built the ARPAnet, which has become the Internet; now fix it!") A variety of recent studies (e.g., Hundley and Anderson, 1995) have documented the web of interrelated information systems comprising the national information infrastructure and its heavy dependence on the public switched telephone network. These systems are attacked every day by hackers worldwide and, less commonly but more insidiously, by trusted insiders, organized groups, commercial organizations, intelligence agencies, and other agencies of foreign governments. As our society becomes more dependent on this information infrastructure, concern rises about what strategies and technology might best be employed to substantially strengthen the infrastructure against deliberate attacks.

The Purpose of This Exercise

The purpose of this particular exercise was "to conduct an exercise informing ARPA staff and selected representatives of the user community of the principal features of (defensive) information warfare (IW) and identifying for participants the future demands that IW may place on ARPA information technology programs."[1]   Dr. Howard Frank of DARPA's Information Technology Office acted as the project monitor.

In subsequent discussions with Dr. Frank and among RAND staff, we referred to the exercise purpose as helping inform DARPA's investment strategy for research and development on the integrity and reliability of information systems on which the security and safety of the nation depend.

The Scenario and Methodology Used for This Exercise

The original "The Day After . . ." exercise methodology used a three-step process: (1) preparing a memo to a senior government executive regarding problems occurring about five years in the future, in the early stages of a crisis; (2) addressing additional problems several days to a week later, as the crisis worsens; and (3) preparation of a memo "today" (i.e., 1996) discussing measures that should be taken now to avoid problems such as those described in steps 1 and 2.[2]

In several dry runs of the DARPA exercise, conducted using RAND staff both in Santa Monica and in Washington D.C., we determined that participants became frustrated in steps 1 and 2 because there was little that could be done in the short term to ameliorate or halt the series of cyberspace-based attacks on the U.S. infrastructure. Participants also felt that there was too little time left in the exercise to discuss possible R&D programs that could be instituted today to prevent or greatly reduce such attacks in the future. For these reasons, we decided to modify the exercise so that it contained just two steps: (1) IW attacks occurring five years in the future; and (2) a discussion of what could be done beginning today to cope better with those future attacks.

A second dry run using this new methodology proved successful. Participants developed heightened awareness of the problems that could be encountered in the future in Step 1, but then had ample time left to discuss R&D measures in the new Step 2. Because the purpose of this exercise was to develop R&D strategies, this new two-step approach was clearly superior for our purposes.

We began with an existing scenario of cyberspace attacks on U.S. infrastructure used in a previous exercise[3] and tuned and expanded the cyberspace attacks for our particular purposes. We wanted to illustrate the diversity of infrastructure systems dependent on "cyberspace" that might be subject to attack, from transportation control systems to power control to key financial systems. Since the participants for this exercise were to be technologically sophisticated, we added some indications of *how* these attacks might be performed, to increase their believability and counter any possible reactions that "that couldn't possibly happen!"

The set of cyberspace incidents we evolved for the scenario used in this exercise is shown in Table 11.1.

The Conduct of the Exercise

The exercise was held on Saturday morning, March 23, 1996, in RAND's Washington, D.C. offices. After a plenary introductory

Table 11.1
Cyberspace Incidents Used in Scenario

Year 2000 background	
general	software agents roaming net and Web
1999	MEII discussed but not yet established
1998	electronic "looting" of Saudi Arabian bank ($1.2 billion)
1999	attempted placement of Trojan horse in AB-330 flight control software
1999	sniffers and logic bombs in Israeli C2 systems
general	electronic "looting" of U.S. and European banks by Russians
1998	computer virus in software causes Yen crisis in Japan
1998–99	Infonet Threat Center established in U.S.
1999	flight control software alert regarding U.S. commercial aircraft
The Crisis—Step 1	
2000 May 11	power in Cairo (90%) out for several hours — perpetrator uncertain
2000 May 11	public switched telephone network (PSTN), massive failure in Riyadh, Saudi Arabia
2000 May 11	PSTN, Ft. Lewis, WA, mass dialing attack
2000 May 11	Saudi PSTN, apparent "trap door" in switching code
2000 May 13	control malfunction, Aramco refinery, Saudi Arabia — perpetrator uncertain
2000 May 14	control malfunction, Bundesbahn train crash, Germany — perpetrator uncertain
2000 May 16	sniffers, Bank of England funds transfer system
2000 May 16	power grid for Rhein Main airbase, Germany, fails
2000 May 17	non-governmental organization "Consortium for Planetary Peace" mobilization via Internet and other media
2000 May 18	PSTN in Delaware and Maryland fails — affects air traffic control at Dover AFB
Continuing Crisis—Step 1	
2000 May 20	Automated Teller Machine networks malfunction in Georgia
2000 May 20	CNN off air for 12 minutes; issues special report
2000 May 20	worm, corrupting data in Time Phased Force Deployment List (TPFDL)
2000 May 22	flight control software malfunction; AB-340; plane crash at O'Hare
2000 May 22	recommendation that all late-model AB-340 and -330s be grounded
2000 May 22	TV signal in Saudi Arabia replaced by other broadcast
2000 May 23	PSTN, Saudi, fails; trap doors similar to earlier Saudi PSTN failure
2000 May 23	full-scale IW attack at CONUS military bases involved in deployment
2000 May 23	Chicago Commodity Exchange subjected to electronic manipulation
2000 May 23	PSTN failed, Wash./Baltimore area, similar to Saudi PSTN failure

session to review the scenario and some recent developments, approximately 60 participants were placed into five groups of about 12 persons each to discuss the Step 1 scenario.

In Step 1, participants were told to act as members of "a technical tiger team advising the Secretary of Defense and the Director of ARPA, in a time-urgent process. The group's task is to revise a draft memo to the SECDEF in preparation for the ARPA Director's meeting with the SECDEF scheduled for a few hours hence."[4]

In Step 2, participants were brought back to the "very near future— say the late spring of 1996." They were told that they were "again in the role of a top advisor to the Director of ARPA, preparing him for a meeting with the Secretary of Defense on a national R&D investment strategy for information systems security and related issues."[5]

The following section contains findings and research suggestions resulting from the groups' deliberations.

FINDINGS AND RESEARCH SUGGESTIONS

The format of the exercise, described in the previous section, lends itself naturally to two types of observations and findings: those from Step 1, involving short-term actions that can be taken to reduce or ameliorate a set of cyberspace incidents in progress; and those from Step 2 regarding longer-term research and development initiatives that might prevent or greatly reduce the likelihood of such incidents occurring in the future. We present below the key findings and recommendations from group deliberations of steps 1 and 2, concentrating on new observations arising from the discussions, rather than ideas presented in the draft memos given to the participants to stimulate their discussion. The materials presented in this section result both from the group presentations at the plenary sessions and from notes taken by RAND observers who monitored the deliberations of each individual group.

Step 1. Observations and Findings

At the conclusion of their deliberations regarding the Step 1 incidents occurring in the year 2000, the five groups presented the following observations and findings. In what follows, we have edited their remarks to omit obvious and redundant observations, concentrating on items that might affect DARPA research and development investment initiatives.

In the following discussion, we do not rigidly follow the structure of the "Memo to the SECDEF" in Step 1 of the scenario, because the issues raised there are primarily oriented toward "consciousness-raising" among the participants. Since the scenario in the year 2000 is hypothetical, so are the explicit recommendations made in response to it. We concentrate instead on broader observations about the state of U.S. information vulnerability in the year 2000 and on the tradeoffs and compromises that might be required to deal with attacks on that vulnerability.

"Safe Havens" Should Be Developed As a Fallback Means for Systems When Under Attack. The information systems supporting our nation's infrastructure have become increasingly interconnected during the past several decades. Regional power grids now exchange information and signals more substantially than before; the more than 1500 telecommunication companies providing public-switched telephone service share a common signaling system; and financial trading and exchange systems are linked worldwide with real-time networks. Because of these interdependencies, a vulnerability in one portion of a system can be used to exploit, disrupt, or deny service in other portions—at times geographically remote from the original source of entry.

A possible solution strategy to this problem is to configure these infrastructure systems so that they can quickly be isolated into self-sufficient regional systems. If, in a matter of seconds or minutes, the energy grids or telecommunication systems could be isolated into smaller units, the resulting smaller units might become safe havens protected from remote attack. At a later safe time, the units might be reassembled into an interconnected system. (See the suggestion on the use of "human firewalls" to oversee this reconnection process, under the subhead "Operational aspects of security . . ." below.)

It was also mentioned that key portions of the infrastructure should have backup repositories of software code (e.g., for telecommunication switches) positioned locally, stored in a manner in which such code can be verified as authentic and accurate. This code could be used for "rebaselining" systems that may have been corrupted. Its local storage is important in case the system in question has been disconnected from other systems, which might prevent downloading the code from a central repository.

Tactical Warning/Attack Assessment (TW/AA) Is an Important Concept for Cyberspace Security. There was considerable discussion (prompted by the draft memo to the SECDEF that was part of the Step 1 materials) regarding the concepts of tactical warning and attack assessment.[6] It was agreed that TW/AA is important, and that there is currently little infrastructure in place to perform these activities.

The main reaction was "Who's in charge?" For TW/AA to be successful, there must be a clearinghouse (a "National IW Center"?) to collect, collate, and uncover patterns in cyberspace attacks that span systems in all key infrastructures: transportation, power, finance, communication, defense, and so forth.   At present, there is no agency or entity that is mandated/empowered to collect this information, much less process it.

It was noted that, if such a center existed, it would need software tools to distinguish coordinated attacks from uncoordinated ones.

One possible activity of such a coordinating center would be to design and implement "trigger levels" of activity that would cause alerts to be broadcast to key parts of the U.S. information infrastructure. These alerts might be analogous to the DoD "DEFCON" levels used to represent the state of alert for Defense organizations.

Operational Aspects of Security (Dealing with People, Procedures, Regulations) Are Vitally Important to Any Solution. Although this exercise was focused on R&D initiatives of the type DARPA typically supports, there was considerable discussion of "operational" aspects of security that may be less amenable to R&D, but are deemed vitally important to any overall security posture. It was clear that issues related to people, procedures, regulations, training, education, and so on were a critical adjunct to any successful security technology initiative.

The following operational aspects were specifically mentioned:

The concept of "cyberspace hot pursuit" needs attention. We need software tools to aid in the backtracing of incidents, to discover the perpetrator. As such backtracing begins within the U.S. but then crosses country borders, we need clear laws and regulations stating which U.S. or international agencies are authorized to conduct such "cyberspace pursuits," what cooperation should be expected from foreign governments and organizations, and what might be done (in real time, if possible) to disable the means by which the perpetrator is instigating the incidents.

We need procedures for the prepositioning of backup systems and software. As mentioned above, the concept of "safe havens" in information systems was discussed, along with the related idea of prepositioning verifiably accurate software (and possibly hardware) for rebaselining corrupted systems. Are there standard procedures that can be developed and used for such baselining? Is each portion of the infrastructure responsible for prepositioning needed systems components, or is some more central organization and coordination desirable?

"Red teams" are needed to test system defenses. The groups tended to concur that active testing of system defenses is an important means for assessing system security. The pioneering tests by the Defense Information Systems Agency (DISA) and the Air Force Information Warfare Center (AFIWC) at Kelly Air Force Base are examples of such testing. The testing concept should be expanded to cover all key national information infrastructure systems. Among the questions needing attention are: What agencies should do the testing? Under what auspices? Would such testing be voluntary or mandatory? What safeguards are needed to protect against unintentional damage or denial of service in these infrastructures as the result of tests? What are the possible legal liabilities as a result of such tests?

Map the networks. Cyberspace is a loose concept describing interconnected information systems, with the Internet and the telephone system (PSTN) on which it depends as key—but certainly not the only—components. We need maps of the interconnections among the networks of cyberspace to resolve a number of questions, such as: How do energy grid control systems depend on the PSTN? If a perpetrator appears to be linking into the networks from Iran, or North Korea, or wherever, what are the routes that he or she may take, and can they be blocked? Some agency(ies) should be tasked with maintaining an updated map of the tens of thousands of links and interrelationships and interdependencies among key networks. A subsequent question then arises: Would that map then be widely available to inform discussions of cyberspace security, or classified so that only a select few could access it?

Personal ID verification systems should be employed. Participants felt it was important to employ such systems on all links into the infrastructure, including access through dial-in maintenance ports. In this way perpetrators may have an additional hurdle to cross, and an audit trail can be maintained to assign responsibility or blame for incidents.

The concept of "human firewalls" should be considered in an emergency. As systems are decomposed into "safe havens" (see above) when an attack is imminent, or during an attack, it might be possible to insert a human as an intelligent verification device to pass judgment before various people and systems are allowed to obtain access to critical nodes and links in the infrastructure.

A "two-person rule" might be used for critical decisions or system changes. Just as firing a nuclear missile requires the cooperation of (at least) two individuals, we should consider the advantages (weighed against additional costs and impediments) of requiring two persons to authorize and allow any key change to critical system software, or to implement a decision regarding critical links or nodes. This idea would require considerable analysis to see if it could be practical. See also the discussion of the need for research on the design of secure information systems, below. The "two-person rule" might be a part of the procedures for secure system design and implementation.

Consider better pay and status for critical system operators. Personnel might then be less vulnerable to bribes, and less likely to become disgruntled or disaffected. It is widely understood that the trusted insider poses the greatest threat to critical information systems.

Some Notable Quotations Recorded During Step 1 Deliberations. We thought the following comments added information and insight to the proceedings, and were worthy of retention.

"If the power system is at risk, everything is at risk."

Many felt that the power system was critical to literally every other component of the infrastructure.

"Corrupting compilers is a very powerful, invidious attack."

Control of compilers is a key component of an overall secure process for software development.

"There are several examples already where perpetrators have spent 18 months inserting trapdoors, etc., into financial software before beginning to steal money."

Carefully orchestrated and planned attacks are being seen, not just hackers doing their thing.

"The U.S. has two main tasks (when under cyberspace attack): (1) recover from what has occurred; and (2) prevent what has not yet occurred."

"Consider putting encryption on all critical control links (e.g., in the power system, the FAA, . . .)."

Step 2. Observations and Findings

Step 2 of the scenario involved the editing and development of a memorandum to the Secretary of Defense regarding steps that could be initiated "today" to reduce U.S. vulnerability to cyberspace-based attacks in the future. Some of the observations of Step 1, above, were reiterated. Perhaps the most interesting new observation dealt with analogies the U.S. government might consider in considering its posture and relationship with industry in working toward better cyberspace security. Three specific analogies were mentioned:

Automobile Safety Regulations. The U.S. government, in cooperation with the auto industry, created regulations that raised the safety level of automobiles. These regulations also raised awareness of safety issues within the U.S. populace in general. The safety and security of cyberspace is now in a situation analogous to that of the automobile industry many years ago. With appropriate regulations, the market could be influenced in a substantial way. This is important because market forces will ultimately have the major influence on the safety and security of U.S. information systems.

The U.S. Centers for Disease Control (CDC). The CDC acts as a worldwide clearinghouse for health and disease information; it is a central source for information when needed, from routine queries to tracking the spread of epidemics. This same clearinghouse function is needed to collect and assess information on disparate cyberspace security incidents.

Underwriters' Laboratory. It may be possible to create an institution for the testing and evaluation of the security provisions of telecommunications and other infrastructure software and systems. Perhaps, eventually, systems that don't have this "seal of approval" would not be allowed to interconnect to the infrastructure. It is an open question, however, if the safety and security of complex operating systems and application programs comprising millions of lines of source code could in fact be so tested. The evolution of software systems (multiple versions and releases, new system components, etc.) may be too rapid for this task to be accomplished in reasonable time or at reasonable expense.

R&D Investment Suggestions

We believe the following are the most important specific research and development suggestions made during the course of Step 2 deliberations.

Study "Distributable Secure Adaptable Architectures." The group that coined the phrase "distributable secure adaptable architectures" believed each word in the phrase was important. Although much research has been done on secure operating systems for individual computers or workstations, new advances are needed for systems that are inherently distributable (over telecommunication links and networks, over geographic distances, among disparate groups). These systems should be secure and adaptable, because rigid system solutions are bypassed or trashed as the environment in which they must work evolves. They must be architectural, dealing with all system levels, rather than "silver bullets" meant to solve narrow specific problems. This topic was meant as a theme for a research program, not just an individual project.

Study "Rapid Recovery" Strategies and Systems. Participants despaired of the design and implementation of verifiably secure information systems throughout the nation's infrastructure—at least in their lifetimes. But perhaps even near-absolute security would be much less necessary if systems were designed for rapid recovery. If any link or node might be disabled by a perpetrator, but could be restored in milliseconds, or at most seconds or minutes, and if the system in addition had considerable redundancy—then perhaps that would suffice for most systems and applications. What portions of the infrastructure might be amenable to such a solution? How might systems be designed with rapid recovery from malevolent (or inadvertent) acts as a design criterion?

Study "Understanding and Managing Complex Systems." The information systems controlling our national infrastructure are some of the most complex systems ever designed. They have millions of interacting components. Often, each node is controlled by millions of lines of code. We need a better science of complex systems, or at least tools for helping to understand their dynamic operation and vagaries. Among the tools that were suggested at the exercise were:

- *Data probes and selective sampling* as a means of ascertaining the health and vitality of a system during its operation;

- *Intelligent modeling tools* for representing such complexity at various levels of abstraction;

- *Tools for the visualization of information flows.* With proper visualization could abnormal patterns of activity be detected before they became destructive?

- *Interactive and multiple-scale global analysis.* How can analysis be conducted at various levels of the system, interactively during system operation?

Study the Design of Processes for Developing Secure Software Systems. Through the efforts of the Software Engineering Institute, among others, a "science" of software engineering is slowly emerging. They are developing standards for assessing the level of maturity of software development groups. We need comparable processes and an engineering discipline devoted to the design and implementation of secure information systems. Such processes must include a variety of procedures to ensure the validity of the compiler being used and protect access to it, which may require a "two-man rule" for making critical system changes (see "Operational aspects...", above), and numerous other procedural and technical safeguards. An entire science and discipline of secure system development is needed.

Study the Concept of a Minimal Essential Information Infrastructure (MEII). The scenario materials given to the participants presented for their consideration the concept of a Minimal Essential Information Infrastructure. Groups generally supported exploration of the idea, and encouraged study of

- *the essential services it must protect and carry.* How many are there? What are their information demands?

- *the functionality that must be guaranteed.* Participants stressed attention to functionality, rather than becoming absorbed in the "nuts and bolts" of specific hardware and system components.

- *the appropriate telecommunications architecture.* Do existing telecommunication systems provide the appropriate redundancy and architecture, or are alternative designs needed?

- *a global management structure.* We come back to the question: Who's in charge? Is an MEII managed in a decentralized manner, or centrally? What regulations and guidelines govern its use?

- *prototyping and exercising the system.* It was widely understood that an MEII could not be created and "put on the shelf" for use in emergencies only. The information environment is much too dynamic for such a warehoused system to remain viable. It must be used regularly to remain relevant.

Some felt that encouraging diversity in infrastructure systems (of both paths and system architecture) was more important than attempting to design or develop an MEII. Others stated that "DoD, for cost reasons, will have to fall back on a reduced functionality system like MilStar, rather than attempting to secure, or duplicate, portions of the nation's existing telecommunications system." It was unclear, however, whether such satellite links could be extended to cover the communications required by non-Defense portions of critical national infrastructures.

Study the Minimum Essential Functionality for Various Segments of Our Society. This question is related to the previous topic. Research should be undertaken to ascertain the minimum amount of information infrastructure that would sustain our society for limited periods of time. If the energy system could only provide half the normal power, would that suffice for a week? Would 2/3 of banking systems suffice; if so, for how long? If 1/4 the air traffic control systems were inoperable for 48 hours, could air transportation continue, and if so with what throughput compared to normal? Such a study would allow estimates to be generated of the minimum essential communication capacity that would be needed in an emergency, as a function of time. These estimates would in turn inform the studies of an MEII (see above).

Study the Analogy of "Biological Diversity" for Complex Information Systems. Considerable concern was expressed at the exercise about the limited diversity in our key infrastructure systems. Most telephone switches are made by one of only a few companies (e.g., Nortel, Siemens, AT&T), and these switches are almost exclusively based on the Unix or VMS operating systems. Most Internet nodes run common versions of the Unix operating system. The telephone signaling system uses the Internet's SMTP message transfer protocol. And so on. Once perpetrators discover a flaw in such systems, that flaw can be quickly exploited in thousands of copies of that system component. Biologists have long extolled the virtues of biological diversity, so that crops such as corn, wheat, etc. are not genetically identical and subject to the same diseases or infestations. In the same way, government may be called upon to mandate that sufficient dissimilarity be engineered into critical systems. Without such intervention, the market is tending toward uniformity in system components to achieve savings from mass production, replication, training, and documentation.

Consider the Biological Immune System Metaphor for Software. The Step 2 draft memo handed to group discussants mentioned as a possible research idea the concept of modeling system defenses on the tactics used by the human immune system to discover and immobilize "intruders." As described in Hundley and Anderson (1995):

> The biological agents providing the active defense portion of the immune system employ certain critical capabilities: the ability to distinguish "self" from "nonself"; the ability to create and transmit recognition templates and killer mechanisms throughout the organism; and the ability to evolve defenses as the "threat" changes.
>
> Software agents providing a cyberspace active defense analogue to these biological antibodies would need the same capabilities.
>
> The message of this metaphor is clear: Cyberspace security would be enhanced by active defenses capable of evolving over time.

Some existing research is under way based on this metaphor, for example, see Forrest et al. (1994) and Kephart (1994). Discussants at the exercise were intrigued by the concept and recommended further exploration of its possibilities.

Study "Dynamic Diversity" in Infrastructure Information Systems. A security problem with existing infrastructure systems is their stability and consistency. Once a flaw is discovered, it can be exploited for months and on multiple instances of that system throughout the country. Groups talked about the possibility of dynamic diversity, wherein software at all levels of these systems modified itself frequently in a way that didn't affect functionality, but that could foil attempts to exploit known security flaws. Perhaps if file names changed, the location of software modules moved, alternate protocols were used, and so on, it would preclude broad attacks on multiple identical system components. Is such dynamic diversity possible, while retaining the ability to perform maintenance, upgrades, training, and other activities that depend on stability in systems? The related topic of a system performing dynamic self-configuring around corrupted elements was also mentioned; this is another biologically related metaphor that recurred in group discussions.

Replace Software with Firmware? Software is modifiable. Firmware (instructions burned into read-only memory (ROM) or related memory devices) is much less so. Can software in critical systems be replaced by firmware so that it cannot be "hacked" by intruders? If so, which systems are amenable to this approach? How would the security improvements of this approach weigh against the greater difficulty of upgrading and maintaining—e.g., by the changing of ROM chips rather than remotely downloading software—the instructions controlling system behavior?

Is It Possible to "Sterilize" Data Passing Through Our Telecommunications Systems? Billions of bits of data pass through our national information infrastructure each second. Some of those bits represent information about individual citizens' login and password combinations, social security and credit card numbers, account information, health status, and innumerable other sensitive information items. Our nation has superb communications monitoring tools, housed primarily in the National Security Agency. However, the NSA is precluded by law from collecting information about U.S. citizens. When incidents of "information warfare" are being waged against U.S. systems, could key data flows be "sterilized" or "sanitized" by computer hardware and/or software in such a manner that the NSA could help monitor and track perpetrators in cyberspace without violating these laws? This topic was raised during exercise discussions. We have not studied all the relevant laws and regulations to assess whether such sterilization measures would allow the power of NSA's analyses to be brought to bear on telecommunications involving U.S. citizens, but perhaps the topic merits further investigation. If so, what kinds of pattern detection and replacement algorithms would suffice to accomplish this goal?

Study the Ability to Reengineer or Retrofit Legacy Information Systems to Enhance Their Security. There are thousands of existing information systems and components supporting the national information infrastructure, including individual PSTN switches, pipeline control systems, the air traffic control system, Internet routers, and so on. It is clearly not possible, in the next decade or two, to redesign and reprogram all these systems to enhance their security significantly. Is it possible, however, to retrofit these systems with special hardware/software devices for greater security? An analogy might be the "TCP Wrapper" technology pioneered by Wietse Venema[7] and others that is used as a software retrofit on a key Internet protocol. Are other security-enhancing "wrappers" possible in other circumstances? The entire topic of retrofitting existing systems could use substantial R&D if significant progress on infrastructure security is to be made on any reasonable time scale.

Sponsor Development of an Aircraft-Like "Black Box" Recording Device. When a cyberspace security incident happens, it is often not detected in real time, and the trail back to the perpetrator becomes lost. Could a "black box" recording device be developed, to be attached to key nodes or links of cyberspace systems, that would record every transaction passing through that node or link during the last n minutes (where n = 5 or 10, for example)? If so, that record would be invaluable in tracing the source of incidents, whether they are accidental or deliberately perpetrated. Thousands of such systems would be required to cover key links or nodes; could they be made robust, inexpensive, and ultra-reliable?

Sponsor Development of Devices That Would Record Tamper-Proof Audit Trails for Information Systems. This concept is related to the previous one. A variety of critical infrastructure systems retain some level of audit trail of system activity, to help in diagnosing problems. Many such audit trails are merely data recorded into a file for later analysis. If a perpetrator gains root access to a system, he or she can tamper with the audit trail to remove any indication of the perpetrator's presence and activities. How should systems create tamper-proof audit trails that can become accurate records of system activity? Since it is impossible for many systems to retain a record of *all* activity over lengthy periods of time, such tamper-proof audit trails may well need to be "FIFO queues" (first-in first-out), where the newest information recorded pushes out the oldest information because of limited recording space.

Develop Software That Can Perform Real-Time Pattern Detection As an Aid to Attack Assessment. Systems are currently under development, and being fielded, that monitor for suspicious or abnormal activity in real time during a system's operation. Examples include SRI's Next Generation Intrusion Detection Expert System (NIDES)[8] and work at the Air Force Information Warfare Center. Research should be conducted to evolve the capabilities of such real-time pattern detection systems, since they form a vital component of any information security program. Participants mentioned that neural nets are one appropriate technology to be considered, since they can be self-adapting as patterns of system activity change. We are aware that some existing systems already incorporate both neural-net and rule-based components. These use biological metaphors analogous to those we discussed earlier.

REFERENCES

Anderson, D., T. Fribold, and A. Valdes (1995). *Next Generation Intrusion Detection Expert System (NIDES): A Summary*, SRI-CSL-95-07. Menlo Park, CA: SRI International.

Anderson, D., T. F. Lunt, H. Javitz, A. Tamaru, and A. Valdes (1995). *Detecting Unusual Program Behavior Using the Statistical Component of the Next Generation Intrusion Detection Expert System (NIDES)*, SRI-CSL-95-06. Menlo Park, CA: SRI International.

Forrest, S., A. S. Perelson, L. Allen, and R. Cherukuri (1994). "Self-nonself discrimination in a computer," in *Proc. 1994 IEEE Symposium on Research in Security and Privacy*.

Hundley, R., and R. Anderson (1995). "Emerging Challenge: Security and Safety in Cyberspace," *IEEE Technology and Society Magazine*, Vol. 14, No. 4, Winter 1995-1996, pp. 19-28. Reprinted in RAND RP-484.

Kephart, J. O. (1994). "A Biologically Inspired Immune System for Computers," in R. A. Brooks and P. Maes (eds.), *Artificial Life IV, Proceedings of the Fourth International Workshop on Synthesis and Simulation of Living Systems.* Cambridge, MA: MIT Press, pp. 130-139.

Mesic, R., R. Molander, and P. Wilson (1995). *Strategic Futures: Evolving Missions for Traditional Strategic Delivery Vehicles,* RAND, MR-375-DAG.

Millot, D., R. Molander, and P. Wilson (1993). *The Day After... Study: Nuclear Proliferation in the Post-Cold War World,* Vols. I–III. RAND, MR-266-AF, MR-253-AF, MR-267-AF.

Molander, R., A. Riddile, and P. Wilson (1995). "Nuclear Command, Control, Communications and Intelligence Review Adjunct," RAND, internal paper.

Molander, R., A. Riddile, and P. Wilson (1996). *Strategic Information Warfare: A New Face of War*, RAND, MR-661-OSD.

Molander, R., P. Wilson, R. Mesic, and S. Gardiner (1994). *Under the Nuclear Shadow: Power Projection in the Post-Cold War World*, RAND, MR-513-AF.

Venema, W. (1992). "TCP Wrapper: Network Monitoring, Access Control, and Booby Traps," in *Proceedings of the 3rd Unix Security Symposium*, Baltimore, MD, September 1992. Also available via Web site ftp://ftp.win.tue.nl/pub/security/index.html.

NOTES

[1] From the Project Description, August 25, 1995. At the time of its writing, DARPA was referred to as ARPA. In this report, when quoting original materials we use the terminology of those materials.

[2] See the research reports cited in the first paragraph of this section for descriptions of previous exercises using this three-step exercise methodology.

[3] See Molander, Riddile and Wilson (1996).

[4] From the Step 1 scenario instructions.

[5] From the Step 2 scenario instructions.

[6] Tactical warning provides information about an attack in progress; attack assessment determines the extent and characteristics of an attack, including information on targets, consequences, and perpetrators.

[7] See Venema (1992).

[8] Anderson, Fribold and Valdes (1995); Anderson, Lunt, Javitz, Tamaru and Valdes (1995).

Part III

SOCIETAL PERSPECTIVES

Chapter Twelve

THE ADVENT OF NETWAR[*]

John Arquilla and David Ronfeldt

CONCEPTUAL OUTLINES

In our view, the information-age conflict spectrum looks like this: What we term "cyberwar" will be an ever-more-important entry at the military end, where the language is normally about high-intensity conflict (HIC) and middle-range conflict (MRC). "Netwar" will figure increasingly at the societal end, where the language is normally about low-intensity conflict (LIC) and operations other than war (OOTW—a broader concept than LIC that includes peacekeeping and humanitarian relief operations). Whereas cyberwar will usually see formal military forces pitted against each other, netwar is more likely to involve nonstate, paramilitary, and other irregular forces. Both concepts are consistent with the views of analysts like Van Creveld (1991) who believe that a transformation of war is under way, leading to increased "irregularization."

The terms above reflect two assumptions (or propositions) about the information revolution. One is that conflicts will increasingly depend on, and revolve around, information and communications—"cyber"-matters, broadly defined. Indeed, both cyberwar and netwar are modes of conflict that are largely about "knowledge"—about who knows what, when, where, and why, and about how secure a society,

[*]John Arquilla and David Ronfeldt, *The Advent of Netwar*, MR-789-OSD, 1996, pp. 3–16, 19–24, and 81–82. Copyright 1996 RAND. Used by permission. Some figures and text were omitted for this version.

military, or other actor is regarding its knowledge of itself and its adversaries.

The other assumption is that the information revolution favors and strengthens network forms of organization, while making life difficult for hierarchical forms. This implies that conflicts will increasingly be fought by "networks" more than by "hierarchies." Thus, whoever masters the network form should gain major advantages in the new era.

Both assumptions permeate this analysis and are discussed further as it proceeds. A point to emphasize here is that these assumptions affect the entire conflict spectrum. They mean that major alterations are looming in the nature of our adversaries, in the threats they pose, and for the defense measures the United States should consider. Information-age threats are likely to be more diffuse, nonlinear, and multidimensional than industrial-age threats. Cyberwars and netwars may even be mounted at the same time, in mixes that pose uncomfortable societal dilemmas. All this will place the U.S. military and society under increasing pressure to develop new concepts for organization, doctrine, strategy, tactics, and technology.

At present, the U.S. military is the world's leader with regard to thinking, planning, and preparing for cyberwar. The United States is the only country with an array of advanced technologies (e.g., for command, control, communications, and intelligence (C3I), surveillance, stealth, etc.) to make cyberwar an attractive and feasible option. But potential U.S. adversaries have the lead with regard to netwar. Here, the U.S. emphasis must be on defensive measures. This continues a long trend in which the United States has been prepared for waging major wars, while our adversaries may instead wage guerrilla warfare, terrorism, and other irregular modes of conflict. This may be partly the result of displacement—some adversaries, seeing that they should avoid or could not win at regular warfare, have opted for irregular modes, which the U.S. military may then try to treat as "lesser-included cases." Such displacement may occur again with netwar. But, hopefully, netwar will not be perceived as a "lesser-included case" of information-age conflict, for it is not.

Instead of using terms like cyberwar or netwar, many analysts have been treating such points under the rubric of the "revolution in military affairs" (RMA). Yet, this very general concept is still mainly about the information revolution and its effects and implications. It led early exponents to view technology innovation as the most important dimension of the RMA. But other, recent exponents have come to accept that the RMA is equally if not mainly about organizational and doctrinal innovation—a view we have emphasized since beginning our efforts to conceptualize cyberwar and netwar. Even so, discussions about the RMA tend to focus on HICs and MRCs that revolve around regular, albeit much-modified military forces. Exponents of the RMA have had less to say about the netwar end of the spectrum (see Arquilla and Ronfeldt, 1995).

The term "netwar" denotes an emerging mode of conflict (and crime) at societal levels, involving measures short of war, in which the protagonists use—indeed, depend on using—network forms of organization, doctrine, strategy, and communication. These protagonists generally consist of dispersed, often small groups who agree to communicate, coordinate, and act in an internetted manner, often without a precise central leadership or headquarters. Decisionmaking may be deliberately decentralized and dispersed.

Thus netwar differs from traditional modes of conflict and crime in which the protagonists prefer to use hierarchical organizations, doctrines, and strategies, as in past efforts to foster large, centralized mass movements along Leninist lines. In short, netwar is about Hamas more than the PLO, Mexico's Zapatistas more than Cuba's Fidelistas, the Christian Identity Movement more than the Ku Klux Klan, the Asian Triads more than the Sicilian Mafia, and Chicago's Gangsta Disciples more than the Al Capone Gang.

Actors across the spectrum of social conflict and crime are evolving in the direction of netwar. This includes familiar adversaries who are modifying their structures and strategies to gain advantage from the rise of network designs: e.g., transnational terrorist groups, black-market proliferators of weapons of mass destruction (WMD), drug and other criminal syndicates, fundamentalist and ethnonationalist movements, intellectual-property pirates, and immigration and refugee smugglers. Some urban gangs, rural militia organizations, and militant single-issue groups in the United States are also developing netwar-like attributes.

But that is not all: The netwar spectrum may increasingly include a new generation of revolutionaries and activists who espouse post-industrial, information-age ideologies that are just now taking shape. In some cases, identities and loyalties may shift from the nation-state to the transnational level of "global civil society." New kinds of actors—e.g., anarchistic and nihilistic leagues of computer-oriented "cyboteurs"—are also beginning to arise who may partake of netwar.

Many if not most netwar actors will be nonstate and even stateless. Some may be agents of a state, but others may turn states into their agents. Odd hybrids and symbioses are likely. Moreover, a netwar actor may be both subnational and transnational in scope.

Many netwar actors may be antagonistic to U.S. interests, such as WMD proliferators. But others, like some transnational social activists, may not. In some cases, a netwar actor may benefit U.S. interests. Many variations are possible. Thus the advent of netwar may prove mainly a bane but at times a boon for U.S. policy.

The full spectrum of netwar proponents may seem broad and odd at first glance. Some actors could be fit into standard notions of LIC, OOTW, and crime. But not all fit easily into prevailing categories. And trying to make them fit risks overlooking the underlying pattern that cuts across all these variations: the use of network forms of organization, doctrine, strategy, and communication attuned to the information age.

Despite the modernity of the concept, historical instances of netwar-like actors abound. Examples mentioned in this study include: irregular warfare in North America during the French and Indian Wars, and the American Revolution in the eighteenth century; the warfare waged by indigenous Spanish guerrillas against the Napoleonic occupation in the early nineteenth century; as well as pirates and other criminals and terrorists that have long operated on the fringes of empires and nation-states. Yet, in contrast to the currently emerging examples of netwar, these early cases were forced, largely by circumstance, into netwar-like designs; these were not designs that were determined by explicit doctrine, or that could be sustained for long, or over great distances.

We think a new term is needed to focus attention on the fact that network-based conflict and crime are increasing. No current terms about LIC and OOTW fit this purpose. Moreover, the term "information warfare" (IW) and its derivatives (e.g., "infowar," "information warriors") are both too broad and too narrow to be appropriate. On the one hand, IW is used sometimes to refer to the entire spectrum of information-age conflict; on the other hand, it is increasingly associated with narrow technical issues of cyberspace vulnerability, security, and safety.

The term "netwar" connotes that the information revolution is as much about organizational design as about technological prowess, and that this revolution favors whoever masters the network form. The term amounts, then, to both a tool and a prediction:

- *Tool*, because it illuminates—and instructs the eye to focus on—a new but elusive phenomenon requiring new concepts and methodologies to understand: the rise of network forms of organization.

- *Prediction*, because it heralds the prospect that networked adversaries will probably predominate the spectrum of conflict and crime early next century.

The term may strike some readers as fanciful, and a better term may yet be found. But meanwhile, in addition to providing a basis for this analysis, it is already being adopted by protagonists of varied political creeds who believe it resonates with their doctrines and objectives. For example, some extreme rightist militia members in the United States have been heard to declare netwar (or *netkrieg*) against the U.S. government, and have organized a virtual *netwaffe*. Also, center-left activists operating in Mexico sometimes refer to themselves now as "netwarriors."

The phenomenon of netwar is not entirely new—there are examples from decades past—but it is growing and spreading to an extent that will make it quantitatively and qualitatively different from what has gone before. It is becoming both more plentiful and more powerful, enough to compel a rethinking of the overall nature of potential threats, and of the roles and missions for responding to them.

The phenomenon of netwar is still emerging; its organizational, doctrinal, and other dimensions are yet to be fully defined and developed. But the outlines are detectable.

An archetypal netwar actor consists of a web (or network) of dispersed, interconnected "nodes" (or activity centers)—this is its key defining characteristic. It may resemble the bounded "all-channel" type of network. These nodes may be individuals, groups, formal or informal organizations, or parts of groups or organizations. The nodes may be large or small in size, tightly or loosely coupled, and inclusive or exclusive in membership. They may be segmentary or specialized; that is, they may look quite alike and engage in similar activities, or they may undertake a division of labor based on specialization. The boundaries of the network may be sharply defined or blurred in relation to the outside environment.

The organizational structure is quite flat. There is no single central leader or commander; the network as a whole (but not necessarily each node) has little to no hierarchy. There may be multiple leaders. Decisionmaking and operations are decentralized and depend on consultative consensus-building that allows for local initiative and autonomy. The design is both acephalous (headless) and polycephalous (Hydra-headed)—it has no precise heart or head, although not all nodes may be "created equal." In other words, the design is a heterarchy, but also what might be termed a "panarchy" (see below).

The structure may be cellular for purposes of secrecy or substitutability (or interoperability). But the presence of "cells" does not necessarily mean a network exists, or that it is of the "all-channel" design. A hierarchy can also be cellular, as has been the case with some subversive organizations. Or the cells may be arranged in a "chain" or "star" rather than an all-channel shape.

The capacity of this nonhierarchical design for effective performance over time may depend on a powerful doctrine or ideology, or at least a strong set of common interests and objectives, that spans all nodes, and to which the members subscribe in a deep way. Such a doctrine can enable them to be "all of one mind" even if they are dispersed and devoted to different tasks. It can provide an ideational, strategic, and operational centrality that allows for tactical decentralization. It can set boundaries and provide guidelines for decisions and actions so that they do not have to resort to a hierarchy—"they know what they have to do." That is why a nouveau term like panarchy may be more accurate than heterarchy.

The design depends on having a capacity—better yet, a well-developed infrastructure—for the dense communication of functional information. This does not mean that all nodes have to be in constant communication; that may not make sense for a secretive actor. But when communication is needed, information can be disseminated promptly and thoroughly, both within the network and to outside audiences.

In many respects, this archetypal netwar design resembles a "segmented, polycentric, ideologically integrated network" (SPIN). The SPIN concept, identified by anthropologist Luther Gerlach and sociologist Virginia Hine, stems from an analysis of U.S. social movements in the 1960s and 1970s:

> By segmentary I mean that it is cellular, composed of many different groups. . . . By polycentric I mean that it has many different leaders or centers of direction. . . . By networked I mean that the segments and the leaders are integrated into reticulated systems or networks through various structural, personal, and ideological ties. Networks are usually unbounded and expanding. . . . This acronym [SPIN] helps us picture this organization as a fluid, dynamic, expanding one, spinning out into mainstream society (Gerlach, 1987, p. 115, based on Gerlach and Hine, 1970).

The SPIN concept is a precursor of the netwar concept. Indeed, Gerlach and Hine anticipated two decades ago many points about network forms of organization that are just now coming into vogue.

This distinctive design has unique strengths for both offense and defense. On the offense, netwar is adaptable, flexible, and versatile vis-à-vis opportunities and challenges that arise. This may be particularly the case where there is functional differentiation and specialization among the network's nodes. These node-level characteristics, rather than implying a need for rigid command and control of group actions, combine with interoperability to allow for unusual operational flexibility, as well as for a rapidity of maneuver and an economy of force.

When all, or almost all, network elements can perform either specialized or general missions, the mobilization process can unfold rapidly. This capability alone should improve offensive penetration since the defense's potential warning time may be truncated. The capacity for a "stealthy approach" of the attacking force suggests the possibility that, in netwar, attacks will come in "swarms" rather than in more traditional "waves."[1]

Further, during the course of a netwar offensive, networked forces will, more than likely, be able to maneuver well within the decision-making cycle of more hierarchical opponents. This suggests that other networked formations can reinforce the original assault, swelling it; or they can launch swarm attacks upon other targets, presenting the defense with dilemmas about how best to deploy their own available forces.

In terms of their defensive potential, networks tend to be redundant and diverse, making them robust and quite resilient in the face of adversity. Because of their capacity for interoperability, and their absence of central command and control structures, such network designs can be difficult to crack and defeat as a whole. In particular, they defy counterleadership targeting (i.e., "decapitation"). This severely limits those attacking the network—generally, they can find and confront only portions of it. The rest of the network can continue offensive operations, or swarm to the aid of the threatened nodes, rather like antibodies. Finally, the deniability built into a network affords the possibility that it may simply absorb a number of attacks on distributed nodes, leading the attacker to believe the network has been harmed when, in fact, it remains operationally viable and may actually find new opportunities for tactical surprise.

The difficulty of dealing with netwar actors is deepened when the line between offense and defense is "blurred"—or "blended." When blurring is the case, it may be difficult to distinguish between attacking and defending actions; they may be observationally equivalent. Swarming, for example, may be employed to attack some adversary, or to form an antibody-like defense against incursions into an area that formed part of the network's defensive zone against a hierarchical actor. A historical example is the swarming Indian attack on General George Braddock's forces during the French and Indian Wars—an instance of a network of interconnected American Indian tribes (Gipson, 1946) triumphing over an army designed around a rigid, traditional command hierarchy. While the British saw the Indian attack as presaging a major offensive against the seaboard colonies, it was but an effort to deter incursions into the French-held

Ohio River Valley. The French and their Indian allies, outnumbered by the colonists and British imperial forces, took advantage of the disarray caused by their attack to engage in other pinprick raids. This reinforced the British view of an offensive in the making, compelling them to attend primarily to defensive preparations. This lengthened the time it took for the British to muster forces sufficient for the defense of the colonies and the taking of Canada (Parkman, 1884). Today, as discussed later, the Zapatista struggle in Mexico demonstrates anew the blurring of offense and defense.

The blending of offense and defense will often mix the strategic and tactical levels of operations. An example is the netwar-like guerrilla campaign in Spain during the Napoleonic Wars. Much of the time, the guerrillas, and the small British expeditionary force, pursued a strategic offensive aimed at throwing the French out of Iberia. However, more often than not, pitched battles were fought on the defensive, tactically. Similarly, where the guerrillas were on the defensive strategically, they generally took the tactical offensive. The war of the mujahideen in Afghanistan provides an excellent modern example.

This blurring of offense and defense reflects a broader feature of netwar: It tends to defy and cut across standard spatial boundaries, jurisdictions, and distinctions between state and society, public and private, war and crime, civilian and military, police and military, and legal and illegal. A netwar actor is likely to operate in the cracks and gray areas of a society.

A netwar actor may also confound temporal expectations by opting for an unusual duration and pace of conflict. Thus, it may not be clear when a netwar has started, or how and when it ends. A netwar actor may engage in long cycles of quietly watching and waiting, and then swell and swarm rapidly into action.

Moreover, sometimes it may not be clear who the protagonists are. Their identities may be so blurred, and so tangled with other actors' identities, that it is difficult to ascertain who, if anyone in particular, lies behind a netwar. This may be particularly the case where a network configured for netwar is transnational and able to maneuver adroitly and quietly across increasingly permeable nation-state borders.

This means, as Szafranski (1994, 1995) illuminates in discussing "neo-cortical warfare," that the challenge can be "epistemological": a netwar actor may aim to confound people's most fundamental beliefs about the nature of their society, culture, and government, partly to strike fear but perhaps mainly to disorient people so that they no longer presume to think or act in "normal" terms.

Examples can be found in the behavior of some terrorists and criminals. Terrorists, notably those using internetted, less hierarchical structures (like the "leaderless" Hamas), have been moving away from the use of violence for specific, often state-related purposes, to its use for more generalized purposes. There has been less hostage-taking accompanied by explicit demands, and more terrorist activity that begins with a destructive act aimed at having broad but vague effects. Thus, for example, Islamic fundamentalist Sheik Rahman sought to blow up the World Trade Center with the intent of changing "American foreign policy" toward the Middle East. The current rash of domestic terrorism in the United States—e.g., the bombing in Oklahoma, and the derailment in Arizona—involves violent actions and vague or no demands. This reflects a rationality that disdains pursuing a "proportionate" relationship between ends and means, seeking instead to unhinge a society's perceptions.

Criminals also use methods tantamount to epistemological warfare when they insert themselves deeply into the fabric of their societies, e.g., by wrapping themselves in nationalism, acting like local "Robin Hoods," and/or seeking to influence, if not control, their governments and their foreign and domestic policies. Examples abound, in Colombia, Italy, Mexico, and Russia, where symbiotic ties exist between criminal and governmental organizations.

The more epistemological the challenge, the more it may be confounding from an organizational standpoint. Whose responsibility is it to respond? Whose roles and missions are at stake? Is it a military, police, intelligence, or political matter? The roles and missions of defenders are not easy to define, and this may make both deterrence and defense quite problematic.

Netwar adds to the challenges facing the "nation-state." Its traditional presumptions of sovereignty and authority are linked to a bureaucratic rationality in which issues and problems are categorized so that specific offices can be charged with taking care of specific problems. In netwar, things are rarely so clear.

It is not easy to make a multiorganizational network function well—a hierarchy is easier to run. A key reason for this is that network forms of organization generally require constant dense communications. The information revolution dramatically enhances the viability of the network form (as discussed below). Thus, the new technologies strengthen the prospects and capabilities for actors to take a netwar approach to conflict and crime.

Indeed, new technologies make possible a rather "pure" variety of netwar in which all strategy and tactics—for example, disinformation campaigns and disruptive computer hacking—occur on "the Net" and in the media. But—and this should always be kept in mind— netwar is not just about the new technologies.

The latest telecommunications systems—including advanced telephone, fax, electronic mail (e-mail), and computerized billboard and conferencing systems—all contribute to netwar, and their roles in recent conflicts are often remarked about. But older technologies, like short-wave radio and cassette tape, are also important for some actors. Computerized desktop publishing, a fairly recent development, enhances the outreach of some actors, but access to traditional print and electronic media remains crucial too, depending on the actor and the audience. Meanwhile, old-style face-to-face meetings, human couriers, and regular mail have not ceased to play roles. If a terrorist or criminal sent a coded fax, this would likely be an example of netwar-related behavior, but if the same actor paid off a journalist for an article critical of some U.S. policy, this may also be an example.

Such technologies enhance the capabilities of a network's members not only to coordinate with each other, but also to collect intelligence on the external environment and on their opponents, and to broadcast or otherwise transmit messages to target audiences. The varieties of netwar actors have used all kinds of old and new, high-tech and low-tech, open and secure, and public and partisan media; indeed, many netwar actors are likely to use a layered mix. The technologies can be used to wage a very public netwar campaign (as in Mexico) or to foster a secretive "virtual conspiracy" (as may be an aim of some extreme rightists in the United States).[2]

THE RISE OF NETWORK FORMS OF ORGANIZATION

Anthropologists and sociologists have studied *social* networks for many decades. According to the most established school of thinking, basically all social organizations—families, groups, elites, institutions, markets, etc.—are embedded in networks of social relations (Granovetter, 1985; Nohria and Eccles, 1992). For this school, the network is more the "mother of all forms" than a specific type of complex organization.

Prior to the 1990s, scholarly writings occasionally appeared that treated the network as a specific, deliberate, even formal *organizational* design (e.g., Heclo, 1978; Perrow, 1979; Chisholm, 1989; also Gerlach and Hine, 1970; Gerlach, 1987). But such efforts were more the exception than the rule, and some occurred on the margins of the social sciences, including the illuminating work by Gerlach and Hine on SPINs that we quoted earlier.

Lately, and largely as a result of research by economic sociologists who study innovative corporate designs (notably Powell, 1990; and Powell and Smith-Doerr, 1994), a new school of thinking about networks is beginning to cohere. It looks beyond informal social networks to see that formal organizational networks are gaining strength as a distinct design—distinct in particular from the "hierarchies and markets" that organizational economists and economic sociologists normally emphasize:

> [T]he familiar market-hierarchy continuum does not do justice to the notion of network forms of organization. . . . [S]uch an arrangement is neither a market transaction nor a hierarchical governance structure, but a separate, different mode of exchange, one with its own logic, a network (Powell, 1990, pp. 296, 301).

This new school of analysis and the numerous examples and case studies it affords serve to validate our point that network forms of organization are on the rise and becoming more viable than ever. But the new school is mostly about economic organization. And clear, precise definitions are still lacking as to what is and is not a network.

Distinctions may be made among what are termed "chain," "star" or "hub," and "all-channel" types of networks. We focus on the all-channel type, in which all members are connected to each other and do not have to go through other members (as in a chain or hub design) to communicate and coordinate with each other.

Despite the claims of some anthropologists and sociologists about the significance of the *social* networks they study for all manner of personal and institutional behaviors, the network as a formal *organizational* design has generally had poor standing among many economists and theorists (e.g., Williamson, 1975). Networks have long been deemed inefficient and inferior as a form of organization, especially compared with hierarchies and markets. Among other things, networks were said to require too much back-and-forth, to require "high bandwidth" communication among all members, to take too long to reach decisions, and to be too vulnerable to free riders.

Indeed, all-channel networks do require rapid, dense, multidirectional communications to function well and endure—more so than do other forms of organization. The past limitations of this form of organization are closely tied to information and communications factors.

The new technologies—e.g., advanced telephone, fax, e-mail, computer billboard, and conferencing systems, supported by fiber-optic cable and satellite systems—finally provide the level of connectivity and bandwidth that favors all-channel organizational designs. Today, diverse, dispersed, autonomous actors are able to consult, coordinate, and act jointly across great distances on the basis of more, better, and faster information than ever before. The rise of the network form thus reflects, and is tied to, the information revolution.

The rise of network forms of organization is at an early stage, still gaining impetus. It may be decades before this trend reaches maturity. But it is already affecting all major realms of society. In the realm of the *state*, it is facilitating the development of interagency mechanisms for addressing complex policy issues that cut across jurisdictional boundaries. In the realm of the *market*, it has been facilitating the growth of *keiretsus* and other distributed, web-like global enterprises (and so-called "virtual corporations"). Indeed, volumes are being written about the benefits of network designs for business corporations and market operations—to the point that casual (and some not-so-casual) observers might presume that this is the realm most affected and benefited.

Yet, actors in the realm of *civil society* may be the main beneficiaries. The trend is increasingly prominent in this realm, where issue-oriented multiorganizational networks continue to multiply among activists and interest groups across the political spectrum. Over the long run, civil society is likely to be strengthened more than the other realms, in both absolute and relative terms.

What is meant by "civil society"—never a clear term—continues to evolve. Classic views, starting centuries ago, have emphasized "associations" that mediate between state and society within a nation: e.g., churches, schools, labor unions, businesses, political parties, and other voluntary groups, interest groups, professional organizations, etc. Recent views, beginning a few decades ago, do not reject the classic views but emphasize "new social movements"—such as environmental, human-rights, peace, and other movements—that are increasingly transnational in scope. Two rising indicators—listings in the *International Directory of Non-Governmental Organizations* (published since the 1970s), and subscribers to the computer networks affiliated with the Association for Progressive Communications (APC, the favored network of networks for activists since its formation in 1989)—speak to the rising importance of nongovernmental organizations (NGOs) for policy issues around the world, and the relationship between the NGOs' rise and the information revolution.

Even where civil society has been strong—as in the liberal democracies of Western Europe and North America—it has long been characterized by groups that often had to work in isolation or in fleeting coalitions and that, as a result, were weaker than state and market actors. Now, however, the new information technologies and related organizational innovations increasingly enable civil-society actors to reduce their isolation, build far-flung networks within and across national boundaries, and connect and coordinate for collective action as never before. As this trend deepens and spreads, it will strengthen the power of civil-society actors relative to state and market actors around the globe (Frederick, 1993; Ronfeldt, 1993).

For years, a cutting edge of this trend could be found among left-leaning activist NGOs concerned with human-rights, environmental, peace, and other social issues at local, national, and global levels. Many of these rely on APC affiliates for communications and aim to construct a "global civil society" strong enough to counter the roles of state and market actors. In addition, the trend is spreading across the political spectrum. Activists on the right—from moderately conservative religious groups, to militant antiabortion groups—are also building national and transnational networks based in part on the use of new communications systems.

Not only civil society but also "uncivil society" is benefiting from the rise of network forms of organization. Uncivil actors—like criminal gangs and terrorist groups—once operated pretty much in isolation from each other. Now, transnational criminal organizations (TCOs) are taking shape (Williams, 1994, 1995). What might be termed transnational revolutionary organizations (TROs) are also emerging on the political left (e.g., Hamas) and the right (e.g., among white supremacy groups). All are building global networks as "force multipliers," and using all manner of new communications technologies to do so.

This trend—the rise of network forms of organization—is still at an early stage, but it is already a very important topic for theoretical research and policy analysis. New and interesting work can be done just by focusing on this trend. At the same time, the trend is so strong that, projected into the future, it augurs transformations in how societies are organized—if not societies as a whole, then at least key parts of their governments, economies, and especially their civil societies.

The trend thus raises questions not only about the significance of the network form itself, but also relative to other forms of organization. The rise of the network form should be analyzed partly in terms of how it is interwoven with, and related to, other basic forms of societal organization.

CHALLENGES FOR U.S. POLICY AND ORGANIZATION

This research on the looming challenge of netwar continues to bear out a set of propositions that we identified some time ago about the information revolution and its likely implications (Arquilla and Ronfeldt, 1993):

The information revolution favors and strengthens networks, while it erodes hierarchies. The continued explosive growth of political, business, social, and other networks that benefit societies, as well as of criminal, terrorist, and other networks that threaten them confirm this proposition, as does the concomitant "softening" of traditional statist institutions.

Hierarchies have a difficult time fighting networks. Examples of this appear across the conflict spectrum. Some of the best may be found in the generally failing efforts of many governments to deal with TCOs. The persistence of religious revivalist movements, as in Algeria, often in the face of unremitting statist opposition, shows the robustness of the network form, on defense and offense. The Zapatista movement in Mexico, with its legions of supporters and sympathizers among local and transnational NGOs, shows that social netwar can put a democratizing autocracy on the defensive and pressure it to continue adopting reforms.

It takes networks to fight networks. The case of the Southeast Asian pirates makes this point well. The first effort to cope with the resurgence of piracy was state-centered and failed miserably. The establishment of a transnational counter-piracy network proved successful in a relatively short time. This proposition may well be analogous to others in military doctrine, particularly that "it takes a tank to fight a tank."

Whoever masters the network form first and best will gain major advantages. In these early years of the information age, those adversaries who have advanced at networking (e.g., criminals, terrorists, and activists) are enjoying a marked increase in their power relative to state agencies. While networking once allowed them simply to keep from being eradicated, it now allows them to compete on more nearly equal terms with states and with other hierarchically oriented adversaries. The history of Hamas and that of the Cali cartel illustrate this.

The information revolution is about both technology and organization. While technology innovation is revitalizing the network form, one must not ignore the importance of organizational innovation.

Indeed, every information revolution has involved an interplay between technology and organization that affects who wins and loses. For example, a millennium before the printing revolution, the early Catholic Church had a networked organization that confronted and overcame brutal opposition from one of history's most successful hierarchies, the Roman Empire. The Church later developed its own great hierarchies, ironically making it susceptible to dissent as the printing revolution emerged in the 16th century.

Today, those who want to defend against netwar will, increasingly, have to adopt weapons, strategies, and organizational designs like those of their adversaries. This does not mean mirroring the adversary, but rather learning to draw on the same design principles that he has already learned about the rise of network forms in the information age. These principles depend to some extent upon technological breakthroughs, but mainly on a willingness to innovate organizationally.

For U.S. policy, an early implication of our work is that counternetwar will require very effective interagency operations, which by their very nature involve networked structures. It should not be necessary, or desirable, to replace all hierarchies with networks. Rather, the challenge will be to blend these two forms skillfully, while retaining enough central authority to encourage and enforce adherence to truly networked processes. In this manner, states may come to be better prepared to confront the multitude of new threats emerging in this information age.

REFERENCES

Arquilla, John, and David Ronfeldt, "Cyberwar is Coming!" *Comparative Strategy*, Vol. 12, No. 2, pp. 141–165 (Summer 1993).

———, "(Book Review) Welcome to the Revolution . . . in Military Affairs," *Comparative Strategy*, Vol. 14, No. 2, pp. 331–341 (Spring 1995).

Chisholm, Donald, *Coordination Without Hierarchy: Informal Structures in Multi-organizational Systems*, Berkeley: University of California Press, 1989.

Frederick, Howard, "Computer Networks and the Emergence of Global Civil Society," Linda M. Harasim (ed.), *Global Networks: Computers and International Communication*, Cambridge, Mass.: The MIT Press, 1993, pp. 283–295.

Gerlach, Luther P., "Protest Movements and the Construction of Risk," B. B. Johnson and V. T. Covello (eds.), *The Social and Cultural Construction of Risk*, Boston: D. Reidel Pub. Co., 1987, pp. 103–145.

Gerlach, Luther P., and Virginia Hine, *People, Power, Change: Movements of Social Transformation*, New York: The Bobbs-Merrill Co., Inc., 1970.

Gipson, Lawrence H., *The Great War for Empire: The Years of Defeat*, New York: Alfred A. Knopf, 1946.

Granovetter, Mark S., "Economic Action and Social Structure: The Problem of Embeddedness," *American Journal of Sociology*, Vol. 91, No. 3, November 1985, pp. 481–510.

Heclo, Hugh, "Issue Networks and the Executive Establishment," Anthony King (ed.), *The New American Political System*, Washington, D.C.: The American Enterprise Institute, 1978, pp. 87–124.

Kelly, Kevin, *Out of Control: The Rise of Neo-Biological Civilization*, New York: Addison-Wesley Publishing Company, 1994.

Nohria, Nitin, and Robert G. Eccles (eds.), *Networks and Organizations: Structure, Form, and Action*, Boston, Mass.: Harvard Business School Press, 1992.

Parkman, Francis, *Montcalm and Wolfe: The Decline and Fall of the French Empire in North America*, New York: Collier, 1884; reprinted 1962.

Perrow, Charles, *Complex Organizations: A Critical Essay*, 2nd Edition, Glenview, Ill.: Scott, Foresman and Company, 1979.

Powell, Walter W., "Neither Market Nor Hierarchy: Network Forms of Organization," Barry M. Staw and L. L. Cummings, ed., *Research in Organizational Behavior: An Annual Series of Analytical Essays and Critical Reviews,* Vol. 12, Greenwich, Conn.: JAI Press Inc., 1990, pp. 295–336.

Powell, Walter W., and Laurel Smith-Doerr, "Networks and Economic Life," Neil J. Smelser and Richard Swedberg, eds., *The Handbook of Economic Sociology,* Princeton, N.J.: Princeton University Press & Russell Sage Foundation, 1994, pp. 368–402 (Chapter 15).

Ronfeldt, David, *Institutions, Markets, and Networks: A Framework About the Evolution of Societies,* Santa Monica, Calif.: RAND, DRU-590-FF, December 1993.

Szafranski, Colonel Richard, "Neo-Cortical Warfare? The Acme of Skill," *Military Review,* November 1994, pp. 41–55.

——, "A Theory of Information Warfare: Preparing for 2020," *Airpower Journal,* Spring 1995, pp. 56–65.

Van Creveld, Martin, *The Transformation of War,* New York: Free Press, 1991.

Williams, Phil, "Transnational Criminal Organizations and International Security," *Survival,* Vol. 36, No. 1, Spring 1994, pp. 96–113.

——, "Transnational Criminal Organizations: Strategic Alliances," *The Washington Quarterly,* Vol. 18, No. 1, Winter 1995, pp. 57–72.

Williamson, Oliver E., *Markets and Hierarchies: Analysis and Antitrust Implications,* New York: The Free Press, 1975.

NOTES

[1]Swarm networks and the capacity of networks for swarming are raised by Kelly (1994).

[2]Credit for the term "virtual conspiracy" is owed to journalist Lou Dolinar of *Newsday.*

Chapter Thirteen

SOCIETAL IMPLICATIONS*

Brian Nichiporuk and Carl H. Builder

The societal implications of the information revolution are both pervasive and profound. Prior revolutions—industrial, political, and social—may justly claim the same, but none before have conveyed power so widely or quickly downward to individuals, not just to a new set of elites. Political revolutions have sometimes diffused power more widely—as in the American Revolution—but most often they have transferred power from one elite to another. The revolutionary changes introduced through gunpowder diffused power from the castled and armored knight to a larger cadre of cannoneers and musketeers, but the transfer of power was from one very small elite to a somewhat larger elite. The information revolution is remarkable in part because it is diffusing the power of almost unlimited information to any and all who seek it. Not all may seek or elect to exploit the emerging abundance of information, but it is there for the taking, and the power it conveys depends only upon the creativity, imagination, and boldness of the individual. Never before in human history have so many had such easy access to so much potential power for so many diverse purposes.

This chapter sketches some of the major societal implications of the information revolution—changes in geopolitics and commerce that are largely due to the development of the information technologies. Not all of these implications are certain or irreversible, since they

*Brian Nichiporuk and Carl H. Builder, "Societal Implications," taken from *Information Technologies and the Future of Land Warfare*, MR-560-A, pp. 25–45. Copyright 1995 RAND. Used by permission. Some text was omitted for this version.

have not yet played out, and not all can be laid entirely at the doorstep of the revolution; but most observers do foresee major changes in social structures, commerce, and the international system.

The union of computers and telecommunications is making vast amounts of information available to large numbers of people who simply did not have such access even a decade ago. Access to overflowing information storerooms by groups, peoples, and organizations around the globe is facilitated by four characteristics of information that set it apart from physical commodities:[1]

- Information is not resource-hungry; it can often be exploited to conserve the use of physical resources.

- Information is easily transportable; it moves around the world on the wings of energy too small to be sensed without instruments.

- Information is diffusive; it leaks like a universal solvent despite great and continuing efforts to contain or restrict its spread.

- Information is shareable wealth; it seldom costs and often profits an individual to share information with one or many others.

In comparison to most industrial processes and their products, the dissemination of information requires negligible energy or other physical resources. Modern telecommunications make the transport of information a trivial matter—as we can see daily in the seamless operation of global equity and currency markets. Information, by human nature and by its own, tends to "leak" more readily than physical commodities. Monopolizing a physical resource is easier than monopolizing even a niche in the global information market; and as physical commodities find global markets—such as oil—the possession of physical resources counts for less and market information counts for more.[2]

The diffusion of power downward to individuals through the rapid spread of information on a worldwide basis is having three first-order effects. It is

- weakening traditional hierarchical structures,

- facilitating many types of transnational enterprises, and

- eroding some traditional prerogatives of national sovereignty.

Each of these first-order effects is developed further below.

A WEAKENING OF HIERARCHIES

Hierarchical organizations have been a salient characteristic of human civilization; they are the basis upon which most authority, power, and command and control have been exercised for millennia.[3] But the information revolution is weakening these structures through two different processes:

- The shift from relative poverty to abundance in information permits individuals to bypass hierarchies that have—deliberately or inadvertently—controlled or limited information.

- Alternative human organizational forms—based mainly on the network—have proved more effective and efficient for transacting information than hierarchies. In information-intensive enterprises, hierarchical organizations may not be competitive with networks.

An example of the first process, bypassing, is to be found in the breakdown of the nuclear family in the information era. Before the flood of information through television, children acquired most of their information through hierarchical structures in the family, church, and school. Their parents, clerics, and teachers could control what children saw, read, or heard. Television short-circuited those controls. If some parents were determined to control access to that attractive and compelling medium in their own homes, they could not control it in the homes of others.

Businesses, particularly those at the cutting edge of the information-intensive enterprises—computing, entertainment, and brokering—found that their networked employees could and would bypass their hierarchical business organizational structures. The tools of the trade—networked computers or other information devices, like fax machines—enabled employees to jump over divisional and echeloned barriers to get the information they needed to do their jobs, without the paper trail so characteristic of bureaucratic hierarchies.

An example of the second process, competitiveness in information-intensive enterprises, is to be found in the computer industry itself. Self-networked teams have proved superior to hierarchical business structures in developing new software and hardware.[4] The Hollywood film industry and the Nashville music industry—both quintessential information enterprises—have always been organized more as networks than as hierarchies. But the assaults upon hierarchies—whether in the form of bypassing or competitiveness—are bound up with the nature of the information revolution, which is empowering individuals with uncontrolled and uncontrollable information and increasingly shifting the content of enterprises from physical to informational commodities.

During the industrial era,[5] commercial organizations learned to adopt the hierarchical structure of the military as the most efficient way to organize individuals and allocate resources to *control* their markets.[6] With economies built mainly on the conversion of physical resources such as coal, steel, and petroleum to physical products, commercial industries dealt constantly with scarcity, bulk, limited substitutability, high transportation costs, and the risks of hoarding. Hierarchical institutions, with clear lines of authority and stark distinctions between superior and subordinate, were better suited than family or collegial relationships for ensuring economic growth and market equilibrium.[7] And since most labor during the industrial era was performed through repetitive operations—conducted according to rigid standard operating procedures—hierarchical organizations were both logical and efficient.[8] The hierarchy thus became the preferred form of organization not only for militaries, but also for businesses, civil service bureaucracies, political parties, and the media.

Today, as the wealth production in the most advanced economies is increasingly derived from information rather than physical resources, hierarchical business institutions are becoming relatively less competitive. In the United States in the year 2000, as much as 66 percent of the work force will be working in information-related areas.[9] Where they are organized according to hierarchical principles, they will find themselves and their companies less competitive than those adopting more network-like structures. Not only will hierarchically organized businesses find that their organizations no longer reflect their actual processes, they will find much of their structure to be a burden rather than an asset to productivity and competitiveness.

Throughout the developed world, many traditional hierarchies will be weakened as a result of the information revolution. Both the ability and the need to filter information before it reaches the individual are declining in most parts of the world. In addition to large corporate hierarchies, one can expect social institutions, the established media, and many parts of governments and militaries to be affected.[10] These other hierarchical institutions are not immune to the forces behind the information-driven changes now so evidently transforming commercial organizations.

There are two structural reasons why power is shifting away from traditional hierarchies and toward individuals. First, the information processing and filtering roles performed by many levels within traditional hierarchies have become obsolete. The advent of the global media and networks has greatly reduced the value added by multiple layers of information processing between the individual and the source of information.[11] Individuals can now sort through reams of unprocessed information and make their own assessments and decisions about its worth. Hierarchies need no longer serve as the exclusive conduit of information to the individual.

Second is the changing nature of the work force in advanced economies. As shown in Figure 13.1, information workers have outnumbered manual workers in the U.S. economy since the mid-1970s—the threshold of the most recent phase of the information revolution. Information workers generally do not need the structure or control provided by traditional hierarchical organizations, since their jobs require them to innovate and adapt on a daily basis.[12] Indeed, they operate most efficiently when they are given the autonomy to attack problems with their own independent approaches. Traditional hierarchies were designed to manage manual workers who mostly followed standard operating procedures each and every day. As the proportion of these workers drops in most national economies, the power and presence of traditional hierarchies will decline.

More and more human transactions in the developed world will be centered on the efficient exchange of information and commodities,

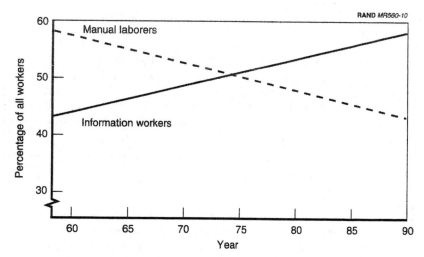

SOURCE: Theodore Modis, *Predictions*, New York: Simon & Schuster, 1992, p. 257.

**Figure 13.1—The Growing Proportion of Information Workers
in the U.S. Economy**

and those will rely more on networks and markets than on hierarchies. The preferred commercial organizations of the future are likely to be those with comparatively few management or "control" layers and in which production employees operate in autonomous multidisciplinary teams.[13] More of their workers will need to innovate on a daily basis. Managers in such organizations will manage more through motivation, exhortation, and incentive rather than solely through authority, mandates, and directives. The previous statements notwithstanding, hierarchies will not disappear, because social order will always require human transactions having to do with authority, power, and command and control. Indeed, in most fields of human endeavor, organizations will probably tend to evolve into hierarchy/network hybrids in which certain key functions will continue to be carried out in a hierarchical fashion. But in a break from the past, the network "component" of these hybrids will be significant.

The survival of hierarchical forms in many organizations will be due to the fact that management and administration are about more than just information flow. They also have to do with ensuring that budgets are adhered to, employees follow certain standards of conduct, timelines are met, clients are kept apprised of the firm's activities, the capital stock is kept up to date, and accurate market analysis occurs. At least some of these tasks will need to be carried out in a hierarchical manner.

In general, it seems plausible to make the argument that functions that are time urgent and require reactive behavior will tend to be executed by groups that are relatively hierarchical in nature, while those that are less time urgent and allow for proactive behavior will be relatively more networked. For example, in armies one would expect the fire support function to stay hierarchical. This is because its command-and-control arrangement must be capable of responding rapidly to complicated and ever-changing lists of different classes of targets. On the other hand, echelon above division (EAD) combat service support (CSS) functions may well turn out to be organized more as networks, because there is somewhat less time urgency involved and commanders can be a bit more proactive. They can decide for themselves, for example, which units ought to have priority for depot repair service before a major offensive begins. These examples are only general illustrations, but they serve to demonstrate that hierarchies will never be entirely swept away.

One final cautionary note is in order. The shift from hierarchies to hybrids (and in some cases to pure networks) will occur at an uneven rate around the world because of cultural/developmental factors. In the nations of North America, Western Europe, and Northeast Asia, the change is taking place fairly rapidly. But in areas like the former Soviet Union and the Middle East/Persian Gulf, for example, the shift may take considerably longer (and in some countries it may never occur). It is difficult to imagine the Iranian, Iraqi, Russian, or Ukrainian militaries adopting networked forms of command and control in the near future.

FACILITATING TRANSNATIONAL ENTERPRISES

Some observers proclaim that the information revolution is creating a borderless world in which transnational activities will proceed without friction.[14]   Although this assessment is probably extreme, it is true that the development of information technologies is facilitating all sorts of transnational enterprises that heretofore have been limited by communications and information.   Perhaps the starkest example is to be found in the growth in the size and power of the global foreign-exchange markets.

Before the 1970s, national central banks had substantial control over the prices of most major goods through their ability to manipulate interest rates and intervene in foreign currency markets.   By the 1990s, however, the advanced state of computing and telecommunications technology had shifted some of the power from national central banks to the global currency market, which now trades over $1 trillion worth of currency per day.[15]   The global currency market has become something of an independent actor on the world stage, sometimes forcing national governments to adjust their financial and monetary policies to prevent currency devaluation.   Transnational networks of this magnitude could not exist before the world reached the current levels of reliable, near-instant, and almost limitless informational connectivity.

The feasibility of transnational activity allows large firms to disperse their operations across the globe.   A maker of personal computers can, for example, now place its manufacturing plant in Europe, its finance division in the United States, and its marketing staff in the Far East.   Such an arrangement would put it at no disadvantage compared to a competitor with all its operations in one city.   Moreover, the dispersed enterprise can take advantage of talent, tax codes, and labor and physical resources that may vary from one part of the globe to another.   This facility for global dispersal makes it easier for large corporations to avoid tariffs, unfavorable tax laws, and excessive regulation in certain countries by simply moving facilities to more appealing business environments.   Strategic partnering between large firms, especially in high-tech industries, is yet another consequence of the increasing ease of transnational activities.[16]

Unfortunately, the increased feasibility of transnational enterprises has a dark side as well.   Transnational terrorism and organized crime are both facilitated by transnational communications networks and global markets for commodities.[17]   New kinds of illicit associations are made possible—between traditional political guerrilla or terrorist groups on the one side and religious fundamentalist groups and organized crime syndicates on the other. For example, there is evidence of at least one of the ethnic factions in the Yugoslav civil war (the Muslims) becoming involved with drug-smuggling operations. Even more disturbing are the reports that the Italian and Russian Mafias may be organizing international networks to sell weapons-grade nuclear materials from the former Soviet Union to the highest bidder.[18]

The issues of possible future transnational terrorism and organized crime point up the fact that there is indeed a "downside" to the information revolution. Along with the numerous benefits it has spawned there are substantial risks. The large, interdependent computer networks that now control many important public infra-structures (air traffic control systems, financial market records, energy grids, telecommunications networks) could be vulnerable to sudden, catastrophic failures that would not have been possible one or two decades ago. Such failures need not even be the result of foul play. While the greatest threat of "info catastrophes" will probably come from the deliberate attacks of terrorists, one must not discount the possibility that natural disasters (such as a large earthquake) or simple human error could generate such events. In today's world, there is less time available to prevent the occurrence of such disasters once an initial mistake or disruption has damaged part of an interdependent network system.

In addition to the greater opportunities created for nefarious transnational enterprises and info catastrophes, there is also the more general concern about increasing social instability in some nations as a result of the information revolution. As power diffuses downward to individuals, it is possible that the weakening of traditional lines of authority and traditional hierarchies will create systemic pressures toward a period of global instability, one in which the different types of political actors in the international system grope their way toward an understanding of their place in the coming order.

ERODING NATIONAL SOVEREIGNTY

The traditional powers of the nation-state will suffer somewhat as a result of the information revolution. It is very likely that the nation-state will remain the most powerful actor in international events for the foreseeable future. However, nation-states will increasingly find their powers curtailed by the availability of information to those who reside both within and outside their borders; and those powers that remain will increasingly have to contend with nonstate actors who are acquiring power through the availability of information. Typically, hierarchical institutions become the victims of abundant information, while networks thrive on it. Since so many of the institutions of the nation-state are hierarchical and so many of the transnational organizations are networked, the net flow of power today tends to be out of the nation-state and into nonstate actors. Nation-states still have the advantages of the disproportionate concentration of power they built up over the past three centuries, as well as the inherent "neatness" of the international political order they can produce. Only tomorrow will reveal how far this shift in power will go, who the principal challengers to the nation-state will be, and, indeed, what may be the fate of the nation-state.

The areas in which national governments now have considerably less control than they did before the information revolution include

* Currencies and their valuation

* Markets and prices

* Businesses and their regulation

* Borders and the movements of people and commodities across them

* Information available to their publics.

Currencies are now traded on global markets that can ignore what national governments may say about their value. The important commodity and product markets have gone global; they are no longer heavily subject to the policies of national governments or even cartels of national governments. Only where the sources of commodities are extremely limited in the world—such as the sources for diamonds—can national governments or cartels succeed in controlling prices. Even though much of the world's oil flows out of the Persian Gulf, there are enough other global sources at only marginally higher costs to keep Persian Gulf producers from exercising much control over prices. In a global market, other producers, standing idle, will come on line with small changes in prices.

Multinational corporations are free to move operations from one site to another, depending upon where they find favorable situations for their operations. Production plants are increasingly in excess, standing by for more favorable circumstances to reinstitute production. If Brazil, say, threatens to increase taxes on a certain production plant, the multinational corporation may remind the Brazilian government that the company has an idle plant in Spain where the production can be quickly transferred, at the invitation of the Spanish government offering favorable terms. In effect, the multinational corporations can play off national governments in seeking favorable conditions, with the governments bidding against each other in order to solve their unemployment problems and, hence, ensure their own political survival.

Borders have become porous: The Italians find themselves trying to keep the Albanians from coming across the Adriatic after watching "la dolce vita" on Italian television. The French look with concern across the Mediterranean to North Africa, where masses threaten to quietly invade their shores. The United States struggles to stem the tide of people who would leave their prospects in Mexico, Central America, and the Caribbean for the opportunities they perceive to the north. Information is driving these tides. More and more people know what is going on in the world and how the rest of the world lives, and they have decided to vote with their feet.

The rise of international television news networks (such as CNN and BBC), fax machines, and global computer networks makes governments less able to control the dissemination of information, even though many have shown that they would if they could. Regimes that depended on information control to maintain their legitimacy are being swept away by the disenchantment of newly aware and mobilized polities. The very rapid, almost catalytic collapse of the Soviet bloc in 1989–1991 is testament to the inability of most totalitarian regimes to both retain their political control and become a part of the global economy.[19] Today, the information revolution permits "information control" regimes to survive only on the sidelines of the international system. Iraq, North Korea, and Cuba still maintain national policies of information control, but these states are relegated to the margins of the current world economy and may not outlive their current leaderships.

Nonstate actors both "above" and "below" the nation-state in geographical scope are now exercising influence on national governments. Many of the world's environmental and social problems have passed beyond the scope of the nation-state. The world increasingly looks to transnational or supranational organizations[20] to solve problems that have roots in the actions or failures of national governments. At the same time, the inability of most governments to control the dissemination of information means that subnational political groupings can use information "to exert power against their governments, societies, and institutions."[21] This power is reflected in the growing numbers of ethnic conflicts around the globe—some of which are attributed to the collapse of totalitarian regimes of the Cold War,[22] which themselves were victims of the information revolution.

Although it is common to project the future enemies and threats to the nation-states as other nation-states, the future could well be one in which the principal threats to the established nation-states are subnational and transnational groups that seek nation-state status (or at least substantial autonomy) for themselves. This is certainly the pattern evident in most of the current conflicts around the world—in the persistent violence of Kurdistan, Kashmir, Chechnya, and Bosnia.

It is not yet clear whether the supranational forces tending toward a more orderly world or the subnational forces tending toward a more chaotic world will be favored in the first half of the 21st century. There is some evidence that the process of diffusing power favors the subnationals. The supranationals are acquiring power from the nation-states only to the degree it is granted by them. The reluctance of the nation-states to grant power to the supranationals is evident in the bumpy roads to the formation of the European Economic Union and the military capabilities of the United Nations. On the other hand, subnational groups tend not to wait for the granting of such powers: Quebec or the Kurds will not; they would seize power for themselves at the expense of the nation-state.

TRANSFORMATION OF COMMERCIAL ORGANIZATIONS

The business world is perhaps the most transparent laboratory of the information revolution. Driven by the imperatives of economic competitiveness rather than the preservation of political power, free from the paralysis of contending special interest groups, large corporations are reshaping themselves to take advantage of the opportunities presented by the growth in information technologies—even as those technologies threaten the power of hierarchical bureaucratic structures elsewhere.

Despite the devotion of many articles in current business journals to organizational changes attending the information revolution, change in U.S. corporate structures is not new and did not suddenly start in the 1970s. For a century, from about 1870 to 1970, U.S. business underwent a major transformation, typically from the family-owned single plant serving and dominating a local market to the stockholder-owned complex of plants and divisions serving, shaping, and competing for national markets. The constant during this century of change was the dominant corporate objective of controlling the market, first local, and later national. If markets could be controlled—created, shaped, or dominated—profits would follow. The natural organizational structure for this objective of control, proven by the military, was the hierarchy.[23]

Throughout the century of change that preceded the information revolution, the hierarchical organization in U.S. business spread and deepened. As businesses and their markets grew in size and complexity, more specialized training and more detailed standard operating procedures (SOPs) were required for increasing levels of management. Hierarchical management structures became taller and required more SOPs, and corporations trained cadres of specialized professional managers. The result was an increasing number of middle managers who mostly controlled and processed the flows of information between production workers and senior executives. The earliest information technology, electronic data processing, became available in the 1950s and 1960s and was used mostly to expand the spans of control in the traditional corporate bureaucracies.

After the mid-1970s, most major U.S. corporations (as well as some foreign firms) began to view information technologies differently. The new business environment was largely defined or characterized by four developments:

- Global markets emerged that could not be controlled by a nationally oriented business. Increased international competition (especially from Japan) forced many large U.S. companies to look for innovations as a way of insuring their survival. The margin for error in markets like automobiles and semiconductors shrank substantially as international competition increased.

- The evolving social environments in many of the advanced countries of the Northern Hemisphere, with their increased tolerance for less capable and dependable workers (evidenced in drug use, crime, and a decline in the quality of public education), required business leaders to reconsider the nature and dependability of their labor pool.

- The increased accessibility of information technology through the workstation, microcomputer, and office automation offered new opportunities for reorganizing business processes and their use of labor.

- As shown in Figure 13.2, the relative cost of labor began to rise in comparison to the cost of capital.

In response to these new realities of the 1980s, Western commercial organizations began to rethink their mode of operations more deeply than they had since the late 19th century. Large firms have become more flexible and less layered, and they rely on smaller but more sophisticated blue-collar work forces. Layers of middle management have been eliminated, making firms less vertical in nature. In many companies, process has been placed ahead of function in corporate values. The main organizational unit in a traditional corporation used to be functional departments, e.g., finance or marketing. Today, innovative firms are restructuring their organizations around process, i.e., combining all of the functions required to produce a single product—design, development, production, and marketing. The structure of these firms is centered on multidisciplinary (multifunctional) product teams that handle all aspects of a single product, from product conception to closeout. Such teams are apparently responding more rapidly to market changes than are traditional hierarchical and functional corporate structures.

Before the full flowering of the information revolution and the globalization of markets, most U.S. corporations saw diversification as a

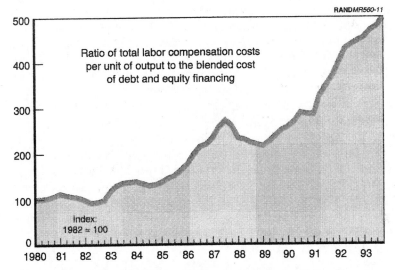

RAND*MR560-11*

Ratio of total labor compensation costs
per unit of output to the blended cost
of debt and equity financing

Index:
1982 ≈ 100

SOURCE: *Business Week*, "The Information Revolution 1994," May 18, 1994,
p. 107. Data from Regional Financial Associates.

Figure 13.2—The Rising Cost of Labor

safety net for market uncertainties and changes as they sought to control their business environments. Healthy divisions in diversified firms could "carry" divisions with weak markets; divisions could provide crossover support to their siblings for needed expertise or commodities. So long as the objective was controlling national markets under national laws, diversification was worth its costs in coordination and excess capacity.

But global markets intensified competition and removed the rules that permitted control of markets. The result is a return to focused business practices, including the concept of core competencies. The shortened design and product cycles made possible by computer-aided design and automated production make it imperative for firms to master a few key areas. Fierce competition means there is no time to diffuse energy and human capital by trying to absorb new businesses on a regular basis. Many contemporary business consultants now argue that the most important function of modern managers is to identify and cultivate a firm's core competencies.

The role of the business manager has also been transformed by the information revolution. Managers used to, almost exclusively, tell workers what to do and how to do it. Management by directive was the norm, and the directive was usually based on established standard operating procedures. But the proliferation of advanced information systems, the reduction in product cycles, and increased competition have made management by directive unsuitable in many situations in many industries. Now, as workers become fewer, more specialized, and more sophisticated, the manager's role has come to include the frequent use of facilitation instead of directive. It is now often the case that the manager's most important duty is to ensure that workers have the tools, resources, and autonomy to do their jobs properly. Managers still need to exercise their authority by directive for certain purposes, such as ensuring compliance with new regulations or guidelines, but this model of management is no longer applicable in all contexts.

With all of these changes in markets, the availability of information, and the roles of managers and workers, it is not surprising that new organizational forms have come into vogue. Much experimentation is evident. The "flattening" of hierarchical management structures is only a reactive response; the search for a replacement for the hierarchy—in theory and practice—is a hotly debated business issue. New organizational concepts have sprouted, with flamboyant names like the "pizza pie" (clusters of units like pepperoni on a pizza), "shooting stars" (new product units flying off from the parent to their own destinies), and "shamrock" (for the leaf-like arrangement of contributing elements).[24]

One of these new concepts, the shamrock organization, whatever its merits may be in practice, is worthy of further discussion here (as it was during the workshop [a two-day RAND workshop conceived and sponsored by the Army's Training and Doctrine Command to explore the potential impacts of the rapidly expanding information technologies upon the future of land warfare]) because it vividly illustrates some of the fundamental changes in business, commerce, and society described above. The shamrock organization, shown in Figure 13.3, derives its name from the arrangement of its three major components like the leaves of the shamrock.[25] The center leaf is the relatively small core of permanent professional employees who

RAND *MR560-12*

A divestiture of responsibilities for people?

Figure 13.3—The Shamrock Organization

make the company what it is and will be. The right leaf is the contingent work force, who are temporary employees hired or contracted for production or other functions of the company, only as they may be needed. The left leaf is the contractor-suppliers, who have a long-standing, symbiotic, and intimate relationship with the company.

Today's information revolution has decreased the value of many types of employees to corporate leaders. Moreover, government regulations have increased the burdens of hiring, firing, and maintaining employees on the payroll. The shamrock organization seeks to create a leaner, more efficient corporation by removing many types of nonessential, unskilled, and seasonal jobs from the permanent payroll. The permanent workers—both blue- and white-collar employees—are those the company knows it will always want and will be able to employ productively, even as products and markets change.

Temporary workers become much more numerous as positions regarded as nonessential (e.g., routine maintenance or clerical work) or subject to fluctuation (production-related) are farmed out to "temps" who must look elsewhere for their benefits and job security. If these benefits and security are not provided by other firms that supply the temporary employees, then that burden may fall upon the government. This arrangement also tends to cut the temporary employees off from access to career development and promotions within the company—the common path for many unskilled workers to the development of skills and to the achievement of middle class economic status. In this sense, the shamrock organization allows companies to shrug off the social burdens they had accepted before the information revolution and global markets—when they were controlling their national markets with the cooperation of national governments. This is a striking example of how globalization and information have broken a century-old bond between business and the state in U.S. commerce.

The wealth-generation activities of the corporation come to be performed by a small group of information managers and skilled production workers (the professional core). The contractors are those who enjoy a semipermanent relationship with the company in providing goods and services in ways that are most beneficial to the company's purposes—not necessarily at the lowest price. An example of the symbiotic relationship between company and contractors is provided by the supplier of batteries to a Japanese automobile manufacturer: The battery supplier may not supply batteries at the lowest price, but the supplier carries each battery on its own inventory costs until it is actually installed on a car on the production line—which means that batteries in the storage racks at the production plant are the property and inventory cost of the supplier. If production should halt, the inventory burden of the batteries is carried by the contractor-supplier.[26] Thus, the contractor shares in the production risks of the company and has every incentive to keep inventory costs to a minimum, while the company has an obligation to treat the contractor as a partner in the mutually beneficial sharing of information.

Although the shamrock organizational concept is only one of several ideas currently being advanced for the future of the corporation, its emphasis on reducing the permanent payroll of employees to a minimum skilled core in order to reduce fixed costs is not an anachronism. The information revolution has had the effect of enabling fewer workers to produce more and has also reduced the value of many manual-labor positions.[27] The political, economic, and social consequences of this clear trend for large sections of the U.S. labor force are likely to be enormous and mostly unhappy.

NOTES

[1]Harlan Cleveland, "The Twilight of Hierarchy: Speculations on the Global Information Society," in Guile (ed.), *Information Technologies and Social Transformation*, pp. 56–59.

[2]See Peter Schwartz, *The Art of the Long View*, New York: Doubleday/Currency, 1991, pp. 47–60, for his story of the anticipation of a global oil market by Royal Dutch Shell. Shell realized, before the event, that dealing in a global oil market through information could be more profitable than extracting the oil. When the global market emerged and eroded the power of OPEC, Shell was ready with its trading plans and arrangements.

[3]The authors are indebted to RAND colleague David Ronfeldt for his insights into the relationships between different kinds of human organizations and the transactions at which they excel. The hierarchy has proven itself throughout human history to be the superior organizational form for the transaction of authority, power, and command and control. Tribes, markets, and networks excel at distinct kinds of transactions.

[4]See, for example, Tracy Kidder, *The Soul of a New Machine*, Boston: Little, Brown, 1981.

[5]For the United States, the industrial era began in the foundries and machine shops of New England in the 1850s and lasted until the middle of the 20th century, when rampant industrialism was foreclosed by labor, tax, and antitrust laws. On the European continent, the industrial era came somewhat earlier and lasted longer.

[6][Paul J.]Bracken briefing [on the responses of commercial organizations to rapidly changing communications and computational capabilities] to the workshop [a two-day RAND workshop conceived and sponsored by the Army's Training and Doctrine Command to explore the potential impacts of the rapidly expanding information technologies upon the future of land warfare] on December 7, 1993, and Michael Hammer and James Champy, *Reengineering the Corporation: A Manifesto for Business Revolution*, New York: Harper Business, 1993.

[7]See Alfred D. Chandler, Jr., and Herman Daems, *Managerial Hierarchies: Comparative Perspectives on the Rise of the Modern Industrial Enterprise*, Cambridge, MA: Harvard University Press, 1980, and Max Weber, *The Theory of Social and Economic Organization*, Talcott Parsons (ed.), A. M. Henderson and Talcott Parsons (trans.), New York: Oxford University Press, 1947.

[8]For an organization theory perspective on this issue, see James G. March and Herbert A. Simon, *Organizations*, New York: Wiley, 1958.

[9]Cleveland, "The Twilight of Hierarchy," p. 57.

[10]Ibid., pp. 55–79.

[11]Hammer and Champy, *Reengineering the Corporation*. Also see Robert G. Eccles and Richard L. Nolan, "A Framework for the Design of the Emerging Global Organizational Structure," in Stephen P. Bradley et al. (eds.), *Globalization, Technology, and Competition: The Fusion of Computers and Telecommunications in the 1990s*, Boston: Harvard Business School Press, 1992.

[12]For a discussion of how computers are creating new organizational possibilities, see James D. Berkley and Nitin Nohria, "The Virtual Organization: Bureaucracy, Technology, and the Implosion of Control," Harvard Business School Working Paper 92-033, 1992.

[13]See *Business Week*, "The Horizontal Corporation," December 20, 1993, pp. 76–81.

[14]The best example of this school of thought is found in Kenichi Ohmae, *The Borderless World: Power and Strategy in the Interlinked Economy*, New York: Harper Business, 1990.

[15]Gregory J. Millman, *The Vandals' Crown: How Rebel Currency Traders Overthrew the World's Central Banks*, New York: Free Press, 1995, p. xi.

[16]Ohmae, *The Borderless World*, pp. 114–136.

[17]Graham H. Turbiville, Jr., "Operations Other Than War: Organized Crime Dimension," *Military Review*, January 1994, pp. 35–47.

[18]Seymour M. Hersh, "The Wild East," *The Atlantic Monthly*, June 1994, pp. 35–47.

[19]Carl H. Builder and Steven C. Bankes, "Technology Propels European Political Change," *IEEE Technology and Society Magazine*, Vol. 11, No. 3, Fall 1992, pp. 10–17.

[20]As used here, a transnational organization is one that operates across and largely independent of nations; a supranational organization is one that derives its powers through and from a group of nations. By these definitions, Amnesty International is transnational, and the United Nations is supranational.

[21]Gladys D. Ganley, "Power to the People via Personal Electronic Media," *The Washington Quarterly*, Spring 1991.

[22]William A. Stofft and Gary L. Guertner, *Ethnic Conflict: Implications for the Army of the Future*, Carlisle Barracks, PA: U.S. Army War College, March 14, 1994.

[23]Bracken briefing to the workshop on December 7, 1993.

[24]See *Business Week*, "The Horizontal Corporation."

[25]The description of the shamrock organization provided here is derived from the Bracken briefing to the workshop on December 7, 1993.

[26]Another example of this practice is provided by the wily Henry Ford, who insisted that his battery supplier provide batteries in specifically dimensioned wooden crates. The supplier subsequently learned that Ford was knocking down the boxes and using the wood, without further cutting, as floorboards for his Model T automobiles.

[27]An example of the devaluing of labor by computers is provided by the use of handheld computers by car rental firms for returning vehicles: The parking lot monitor needs only to key in the car's mileage and the contract number; the computer provides the rest of the information and prints out the billing receipt. This is a case where the computer degrades the skills required of the parking lot monitor to a few hours of instruction and eliminates the need for a counter check-in attendant.

Chapter Fourteen

TRANSNATIONAL CRIMINAL ORGANISATIONS AND INTERNATIONAL SECURITY*

Phil Williams

To understand the causes of turbulence and disorder in the post–
Cold War world it is necessary to examine sub-national and transnational forces as well as inter-state relations. The danger is that the
consideration of new security challenges will encourage the fabrication of enemies or security threats. This, however, should not inhibit
efforts to reassess the challenges to national and international security, and to identify non-traditional threats when these have a strong
empirical basis.

There are several reasons why one might object to treating transnational criminal organisations (TCOs) as an international security
problem: they are economic rather than political organisations; they
do not pose the same kinds of overt or obvious challenges to states as
do terrorist organisations; crime is a domestic problem; and law enforcement and national security are based on very different philoso-
phies, organisational structures and legal frameworks. The contention of this article, however, is that TCOs pose serious threats to
both national and international security, and are extremely resistant
to efforts to contain, disrupt or destroy them.

The first section of this article discusses the changing international
conditions that have led to the emergence of TCOs. The second sec-

---

*Phil Williams, "Transnational Criminal Organisations and International Security,"
Survival, Vol. 36, No. 1, Spring 1994, pp. 96–113. Copyright 1994 Oxford University
Press. Used by permission.

tion examines the structure and operations of these organisations, particularly in drug trafficking. The third section analyses the threats that these organisations pose to national and international security. The article concludes with an assessment of the problems faced by states in trying to control TCOs.

THE CHANGING INTERNATIONAL ENVIRONMENT

Organised crime has a long history, and has traditionally been seen as a domestic law-and-order problem. Over the past two decades, however, crime has taken on new international dimensions and criminal organisations have developed to resemble transnational corporations. Although these TCOs are usually based partly on familial ties and kinship—at least at the top level—their structures make them highly proficient, adaptable and able to "treat national borders as nothing more than minor inconveniences to their criminal enterprises."[1]

The emergence of TCOs is partly a result of underlying changes in global politics and economics, which have been conducive to the development of all transnational organisations. The emergence and development of the "global village" in the second half of the twentieth century has fundamentally changed the context in which both legitimate and illegitimate businesses operate. This has, moreover, created unprecedented opportunities for international criminal activity. Increased interdependence between nations, the case of international travel and communications, the permeability of national boundaries, and the globalisation of international financial networks have facilitated the emergence of what is, in effect, a single global market for both licit and illicit commodities. There has been a vast increase in transnational activity—the movement of information, money, physical objects, people, and other tangible or intangible items across state boundaries—in which at least one of the actors involved in the transaction is non-governmental.[2] As Edward Morse has noted, virtually all tangible items involved in such transactions are likely to have a significant economic value because they can be treated as a commodity or service to which a monetary value can be attached.[3] It is not, therefore, surprising that we have seen the development of TCOs that transport illicit commodities across national jurisdictions against the wishes of governments.[4] With the globalisation of trade and growing consumer demand for leisure products, it is only natural that criminal organisations should become increasingly transnational in character.

The scale of these activities largely reflects the opportunities resulting from changes in both international relations and within states. The second half of the twentieth century has not only witnessed a great increase in transactions across national boundaries that are neither initiated nor controlled by states, but has also seen a decline in state control over its territory. TCOs are both contributors to, and beneficiaries of, these changes.

The speed and ease of international transport has greatly increased the ability of people and products to cross national boundaries. In a 1970s discussion of the underlying conditions that had led to the emergence of multinational corporations, Raymond Vernon noted that "between 1960 and 1974 . . . passenger volume on international commercial flights rose from 26 billion passenger miles to 152 billion."[5] By 1992 the figure had increased to between 600 and 700 billion passenger miles.[6] Other statistics underline the phenomenal growth that has taken place in transnational travel and movement. In 1984, for example, 288 million people entered the United States; by 1990 the figure had increased to 422m; by 1992 it had gone up to 447m. Similar increases have occurred in the number of carriers (aircraft, ships and boats, trains, buses and cars). From 90m in 1984 the number increased to 125m in 1990 and over 131m in 1992.[7] In Western Europe not only have there been increases in the number of visitors, but, even more importantly, there has been significant immigration from Turkey, North Africa and, especially since the end of the Cold War, from Eastern Europe. In 1989 over one million people migrated into the European Community, largely as a result of the upheavals in Eastern Europe. Not all immigration has been short term however. By 1900, the number of legal immigrants from North Africa and Turkey totalled almost 1.8m in Germany and over 1.6m in France.

Closely related to the increased mobility of populations has been the growth of international trade. Facilitated by the free trade system of the post-war period, there has been a vast global increase in the import and export of goods and services. The increase in the value of global trade between 1970 and 1990 was immense. In 1970 global imports totalled $(US)331bn. By 1980 the figure had reached $2 trillion and by 1990 had increased to $3.5 trillion.[8]

The increase in transnational economic activity has made it easier to hide illicit transactions, products and movements because law enforcement agencies and customs officers are unable to inspect more than a small proportion of the cargoes and people coming into their territories. As a result, national borders have become increasingly porous.

Linked to the development of transport, communications and international trade has been the growth of global financial networks. As Laurence Krause has noted, this partly reflects the particular qualities of money:

> Money is the most fungible of all commodities. It can be transmitted instantaneously and at low cost. . . . It can change its identity easily and can be traced only with great effort if at all. These characteristics work to the disadvantages of governments in their efforts to tax, regulate and control economic activity.[9]

As a consequence of this, TCOs are able to transfer the profits from their illegal transactions with speed, ease and relative impunity. Indeed, money laundering is simply one sub-set of the much larger problem for states of maintaining even a semblance of control over global financial networks, which operate according to the logic of a global market and are not very responsive to the dictates of state economic policies or national legal requirements.

Global financial centres are associated with cities rather than countries—London, Frankfurt, New York, Tokyo and Hong Kong. Yet this is also part of a much broader phenomenon—the rise of cities that are closely linked by advanced communications and transportation systems and act as the key nodes in the global economic system. This is reflected in the cosmopolitan nature of major cities throughout the world. Cities are the repositories not only of capital and wealth, but also of technological innovation and advancement.[10] Along with corporations, they are major facilitators of transnational transactions. It is not coincidental, therefore, that cities are also now the major loci for criminal organisations. Although organised crime may have initially developed in Sicily as a rural phenomenon, ports have traditionally been favourite bases for organised crime and cities have increasingly offered even greater opportunities.[11] The cocaine trade, for example, has been dominated by cartels in two Colombian cities—Medellín and Cali. Chinese criminal organisations based in Hong Kong play a prominent role in the distribution of heroin from Southeast Asia, and Istanbul acts as a clearing house for heroin being shipped from Southwest Asia to Western Europe.

While the changing international conditions have contributed to the rise of, and continue to facilitate, these illegal activities, organisations have also taken advantage of the new markets that have resulted from the development of industrial and post-industrial "mass consumption" societies. The period since 1945 has seen unprecedented demands for goods and services, with surplus wealth creating new opportunities for recreation and leisure. While expenditure of wealth for pleasure is not new, there is an unprecedented number of people who are now able to engage in such spending.

Linked to this is the communications revolution, which has created a degree of global transparency that has both accentuated inequalities between societies and led to the emulation by developing countries of patterns of consumption in economically advanced societies. Indeed, the growing ease of travel and the expansion in international communications has led to a convergence of consumer tastes in many different countries. Although "truly universal products are few and far between," we have seen the development of a global market place in which consumers "have access to information about goods and services from around the world."[12] Entrepeneurs have recognised the opportunities this presents for global marketing and the successful corporations are those which have acknowledged the emergence of global markets and have tried to exploit them.

It is in this context that illegal drugs have emerged as a global commodity of immense significance, and TCOs have developed to meet the demands of what has become, if not a single global market, a series of regional markets. This is not new, of course, as during the nineteenth century opium was a key component of the commodity trade—albeit a trade dominated by governments. Now, however, TCOs control what has become a global industry in heroin and cocaine production and distribution. Although the type of drug differs from region to region, illicit drugs have become one of the few truly global products. Determining the scale of the drug trafficking industry has proved elusive because of its illicit nature. Some estimates, however, suggest that it is worth $500bn a year—larger than the global trade in oil.[13] Although this is one of the more generous estimates, illicit drug trafficking is clearly a major worldwide economic activity.

Moreover, it is likely that illicit drugs will become an even more significant commodity in the future. The turbulence that has arisen with the end of the Cold War, the resurgence of ethnic and regional conflicts, and the rise of sub-national groups challenging existing states has meant a growing number of groups and actors requiring armaments. Engaging in criminal activity, especially drug trafficking, is a way to obtain the funds needed to buy armaments. In the future, therefore, the development of the drug trade is likely to be increasingly influenced by political as well as economic motives.

One important implication of this is that there are likely to be new opportunities for criminal activities that are regional and global rather than local or national in scale. Furthermore, the incentives for engaging in such activities are likely to increase rather than decrease in the future. Continued inequalities, both within and between societies, combine with poverty to encourage individuals and groups to engage in illicit activities to provide a source of income. This is as true of the Peruvian and Bolivian peasants who grow coca as it is of the young Afro-Americans in US cities who sell drugs.

If opportunities and incentives are important in the globalisation of crime, so too are capabilities: the criminal groups which have developed into transnational criminal corporations have displayed both organisational skill and entrepreneurial flair. The next section of this article discusses these groups and their activities and suggests that they rival many transnational corporations in the scale and sophistication of their operations.

THE RISE OF TRANSNATIONAL CRIMINAL ORGANISATIONS

Just as the modern industrial economy and the rise of mass consumer markets encouraged the growth of organised crime in the US, so growing opportunities for transnational activities have facilitated the growth of TCOs. Not only is transnational activity as open to criminal groups as it is to legitimate multinational corporations, but the character of criminal organisations also makes them particularly suited to exploit these new opportunities. Since criminal groups are used to operating outside the rules, norms and laws of domestic jurisdictions, they have few qualms about crossing national boundaries illegally. In many respects, therefore, TCOs are transnational organisations *par excellence.* They operate outside the existing structures of authority and power in world politics and have developed sophisticated strategies for circumventing law enforcement in individual states and in the global community of states.

Samuel Huntington has argued that transnational organisations conduct centrally directed operations in the territory of two or more nation-states, mobilise resources and pursue optimising strategies across national boundaries, are functionally specific, and seek to penetrate and not acquire new territories.[14] This is also true of TCOs. Criminal enterprises, however, differ from transnational organisations that operate legally in one crucial respect: most transnational organisations seek access to territory and markets through negotiations with states[15] while TCOs obtain access not through consent, but through circumvention. They engage in systematic activities to evade government controls, which is possible because the conditions that have given rise to their emergence also make it very difficult for governments to counter them.

Transnational criminal organisations vary in size and scale. Some, such as the Colombian cartels, focus almost exclusively on drug trafficking while others, such as the Chinese triads or Japanese yakuza, engage in a wide range of criminal activities, including extortion, credit card fraud, prostitution and drug trafficking.

For most, however, drug trafficking is one of their most profitable activities. The pre-eminent TCOs in cocaine trafficking are the Colombian cartels. These organisations are not like other cartels who fix price and production levels. They are loose confederations of kinship-based organisations that both coordinate activities and engage in extensive cooperation. Brought together in 1981 partly in response to the kidnapping by the guerrilla organisation, M-19, of the sister of one of the drug kingpins of Medellín, the traffickers recognised the need for, and the advantages of, cooperation in furthering what was becoming an increasingly lucrative activity.

In some respects, the drug trafficking industry is similar to any other kind of agri-business. There is a sequence of activities beginning with the growing of coca (which is done primarily in Peru and Bolivia), the collection and transportation of either the coca leaf or coca paste, the processing of the coca into cocaine base and then cocaine hydrochloride (which in turn requires the procurement of precursor chemicals), the transportation of the finished product to the US, wholesale distribution, retail distribution and profit taking. Through vertical integration the Colombian cartels now dominate all stages of the industry, with the partial exception of the growing and retailing sectors.[16]

Although the industry is based on low technology, it has been characterised by a quest for innovation at all levels, including the development of new products and the opening of new markets. The development of crack cocaine and its marketing in the US is the best example of this entrepreneurial flair.

To circumvent law enforcement organisations the cartels use multiple transhipment points, various means of transport and concealment, and a variety of routes. In transporting cocaine into the US, for example, a Caribbean route was initially used, with the Bahamas being the transit point and Florida providing the key point of entry. As law enforcement efforts increased, however, so transportation routes shifted to the Southwest border of the US, with cocaine being flown into Mexico and then smuggled across the border to be distributed to American cities.

Interdiction efforts by the US military and law enforcement agencies have had some limited success but, for the most part, have simply forced the cartels to develop ever more ingenious evasion techniques and less obvious, if more convoluted, routes. Shipments of cocaine, for example, have been made to the US through a Brazilian electric transformer company acting as a front organization, and via Canada and Western Europe.

The Cali cartel has been particularly innovative—expanding its product range to include heroin, which has larger profit margins than cocaine, and opening an additional market in Western Europe, where the price of cocaine is generally higher than in the US. Spain and Portugal are the most important points of entry into Europe (in

1991 51% of all the cocaine seized in Europe was in these two countries), although increasing use has been made of Eastern Europe. The difficulty for law enforcement organisations is that there are many potential carriers and an even greater number of concealment techniques. In March 1992, for example, British customs officials seized 900 kilos of cocaine that had been placed inside lead ingots.

It is unlikely that government seizures account for a significant proportion of the drugs that are smuggled: 10% is the usual estimate, although even this may be too high. There has been some success against the Cali cartel but it has proved very resilient, partly because its activities have been highly compartmentalised. Moreover, some of the cartel's criminal activities, such as money laundering, have been run by support organisations. Although it has utilised support activities that operate in the grey area between illicit and licit business, the Cali cartel has generally operated as a low-profile business corporation rather than as a high-profile criminal organisation seeking confrontation with the Colombian government.

The same is not true for the Medellín cartel, which has displayed not only a willingness to use violence, but also a concern for proficiency in its use. The cartel even hired an Israeli company to provide Israeli and British mercenaries to train their private security forces. The cartel has also imported significant amounts of weapons into Colombia. In 1988, for example, an intercepted Panamanian ship destined for Colombia was discovered to be carrying enough rifles, machine guns and mortars to equip an infantry batallion.[17] Although there was some uncertainty about whether the intended recipient of the cargo was a drug trafficking organisation or one of Colombia's revolutionary groups, it is clear that some drug trafficking organisations have imported arms into Colombia, often using Antigua as the conduit.

This is not to suggest that all TCOs place the same emphasis on violence. There have been important differences between the Medellín cartel, which dominated the industry until the late 1980s, and the Cali cartel, which has since emerged as the dominant organisation within the industry. The Medellín cartel lost its pre-eminent position due to its violent confrontation with the government, the breakdown of its agreement on market shares with the Cali cartel, and the death or capture of some of its leaders, culminating in the death of Pablo

Escobar at the hands of Colombian government forces in December 1993. The Cali cartel, in contrast, has favoured cooption over confrontation. Its leaders have become part of the local and regional political and economic establishment, mixing illicit activities with legitimate businesses. The Cali cartel is a highly professional group that, although ruthless in dealing with its enemies, runs its business according to sound economic and management principles. As one observer has noted,

> The Cali cartel operates more like the senior management team at Exxon or Coca Cola. Its transportation, distribution and money laundering networks cover the globe.[18]

It is no exaggeration to say that the Cali cartel is not only the developing world's most successful TCOs, but is also its most successful transnational corporation.

Other TCOs dominate the heroin trade. Perhaps the most important of these are the Chinese triads. Based in Hong Kong and Taiwan, the triads were initially patriotic organisations which have since become involved in crime. One of the most powerful triad organisations in Hong Kong, with over 30 sub-groups and 20,000 members, is the 14K. Another triad organisation is the Chiu Chaio group, which has members in Bangkok and elsewhere in the Golden Triangle and includes the Sun Yee On, which has over 25,000 members.[19] Although individual triads are usually made up of factions and do not operate as monolithic organisations, their members engage in extensive criminal activity in both Hong Kong and the US. Chinese organisations have superseded the Mafia as the most important criminal groups in many American cities. They have long been active in smuggling illegal immigrants into the US, in money laundering, gambling, heroin smuggling and the theft of computer chips. They became the focus of considerable attention in 1986 when members of the United Bamboo Gang, a Taiwan-based triad, killed a California-based Chinese journalist who had criticised the Taiwanese government.[20] Although this act may have been politically rather than economically motivated, the gang's willingness to resort to violence was certainly not atypical. Indeed, Chinese criminal organisations are notoriously violent. According to former FBI Director, William Sessions, "violence .. . or the threat of violence is implicit in every single transaction" undertaken by Chinese criminal organisations.[21]

The Hong Kong triads have strong links with the various tongs and merchant associations located in every Chinatown in the US. While some tongs are little more than chambers of commerce, others engage in extensive criminal activity and have established very close links with Chinese youth gangs. It is tempting to conclude that this three-tier structure forms a clear hierarchy, with the Hong Kong triads providing the leadership and the commerce-based tongs and youth gangs acting as local subsidiaries. In fact, the organisational structures are fluid, allowing for initiative, enterprise and the entry of new players at both the wholesale and retail levels.[22] There have been occasions, for example, when members of Chinese youth gangs in the US have established links with Hong Kong traffickers to assist in the importation of heroin into the US. As one US intelligence assessment noted,

> ethnic Chinese criminal organisations that traffick in heroin are best viewed as syndicates or joint ventures. Participation in these organisations is based upon experience, expertise, contacts, and wealth; however, close cultural, familial or criminal affiliation (membership in a tong, triad or gang, for example) are important bona fides, which facilitate that participation.[23]

Heroin is produced in the Golden Triangle at the confluence of the borders of Laos, Thailand and Myanmar. Myanmar is the world's largest producer of raw opium and refiner of heroin. The sale and shipment of heroin to other parts of Asia is arranged by international brokers. Much heroin goes through Bangkok, but the overland route from Myanmar, through Yunnan, to Hong Kong has become increasingly important. Hong Kong is both a major transhipment point and a money-laundering centre. Unlike cocaine, which (in spite of a recent trend towards containers) is still often transported to the US in private planes, heroin smugglers favour commercial containers, although they have occasionally used Central American diplomats as couriers. Much of this heroin is sent to New York via Vancouver and Toronto, both of which have significant Chinese populations. Chinese involvement in legal businesses also provides a cover for drug trafficking and money laundering.

Chinese criminal organisations also traffick in people, including into the US through a variety of routes and carriers. Hong Kong residents, for example, have been taken through Frankfurt, London, Caracas,

Panama and Montreal before their arrival in New York, while others have used routes through Vancouver and Toronto. Unable to meet the cost of this service—which can range from $15,000 to $30,000— some illegal aliens have worked as drug couriers or become involved in other criminal activities to pay the traffickers.

The heroin entering Western Europe comes primarily from Afghanistan and Pakistan and is brought in by a variety of organisations. Although Pakistani and Iranian groups have been active in trafficking, the most significant are Turkish criminal organisations. Turkey's location between Southwest Asia and Europe has made Istanbul "the main clearing house for heroin bound for European markets," a role somewhat akin to that of Hong Kong in the trade from the Golden Triangle to the US.[24] Moreover, the extensive Turkish communities in Germany, the Netherlands and Italy provide both excellent cover and effective distribution networks. Although European law enforcement agencies have had some success in controlling this trade (in 1990 around 700 Turks were arrested for trafficking in drugs throughout Europe), the fact that organisations are largely based on familial ties reduces their vulnerability. The heroin is brought into Europe through various Balkan routes, often using the Transport International Routier lorries that are not subject to customs controls for tax purposes and are, therefore, less likely to be searched. Although the conflict in the former Yugoslavia has led to some route shifts, trafficking organisations have once again displayed considerable adaptability. The fluid nature of their networks and the absence of sunk costs in fixed installations has facilitated flexibility, making it easy both to respond to difficulties and to take advantage of new opportunities.

The most significant opportunities have emerged in Eastern Europe and the former Soviet Union. Polish amphetamine producers are one indigenous response. There is also evidence that the Colombian cartels are shipping cocaine through and to this region; that opium is being shipped into and through Central Asia from Afghanistan; and that Kazakhstan, Turkmenistan, Uzbekistan, Tajikistan and Kyrgyztan are increasingly involved in opium or hashish cultivation.

Perhaps most disquieting of all, however, has been the emergence of major criminal organisations in Russia. The pervasiveness of corruption, the loose banking regulations that provide opportunities for both fraud and money laundering, and the threat of violence could discourage Western investment in the former Soviet Union at a time when external investment is desperately needed. Of even greater concern is the growing trafficking in nuclear material. Although this has not yet involved plutonium or highly enriched uranium, the fact that some 200 smuggling operations took place in 1993 suggests that the scale and seriousness of the problem should not be underestimated.

Other key players in international drug trafficking include Nigerian criminal organisations, which deal mainly in heroin but also in cocaine, and the Japanese yakuza, which engages in a wide variety of criminal activities including shipping crystal methamphetamine, or "ice," to Hawaii and the west coast of the US. Some observers believe that the most important groups of all are still the Sicilian and Italian Mafia, which have long been economically and politically powerful in southern Italy and have been heavily involved in both cocaine and heroin smuggling.[25]

TCOs are diverse in structure, outlook and membership. What they have in common is that they are highly mobile and adaptable and are able to operate across national borders with great ease. They are able to do this partly because of the conditions identified above and partly because of their emphasis on networks rather than formal organisations. It is of interest that legitimate transnational corporations have also adopted more flexible, fluid network structures, which enable them to exploit local conditions more effectively. Perhaps not surprisingly, this is one area where TCOs have taken the lead as their illegality has compelled them to operate covertly and to de-emphasise fixed structures.

Another important trend among transnational corporations has been the growth of strategic alliances, especially between regional transnational corporations that want to develop globally. For legitimate corporations, alliances facilitate production where costs are low and allow corporations to take advantage of local knowledge and experience in marketing and distribution. TCOs pursue strategic alliances for similar reasons. Even if these organisations circumvent state structures, they may still have to negotiate with national and local criminal organisations, and strategic alliances permit them to cooperate with, rather than compete against, indigenously entrenched criminal organisations. Moreover, these alliances enhance the ability of TCOs to circumvent law enforcement agencies, facilitate risk sharing and make it possible to use existing distribution channels. Finally, strategic alliances enable drug trafficking organisations to exploit differential profit margins in different markets.

Although it is difficult to make a definitive analysis of the links between and among TCOs, there is considerable evidence that these alliances exist. Green Ice, a "sting" operation conducted over three years by the US Drug Enforcement Administration, resulted in the arrest of almost 200 people in Britain, Spain, Canada, the US and Italy in 1992. It also revealed the links between the Cali cartel and the Sicilian Mafia as the arrest included members of the Neapolitan Camorra, the Calabrian 'Ndrangheta and the Sicilians. One explanation for this was that the Sicilian Mafia was helping the Colombians break into the New York heroin market in return for franchise arrangements on cocaine in Europe.

Similar links seem to be developing between the Italian groups and some of the criminal organisations in Russia. There have been reports from the Czech police, for example, that the Mafia signed a deal with Russian gangs to traffick nuclear weapons materials and drugs.[26] Other links include ties between Pakistanis and Danish organisations, and Turkish and Dutch groups. It has also been reported that in 1992 Japanese and Italian criminal organisations held a conference in Paris to discuss their common interests in money laundering.[27]

These links between various groups, especially those engaged in drug trafficking, have made TCOs an increasingly serious problem for governments. The extent to which these activities constitute a threat to national and international security is examined next.

THE THREAT TO SECURITY

It is tempting to say that the activities of TCOs have little impact on national and international security. Unlike revolutionary or terrorist groups, TCOs have predominantly economic objectives. Moreover, it is arguable that even illicit enterprises add to national wealth, create jobs and provide a safety net against recession. TCOs also employ entrepreneurial and managerial skills that would otherwise be wasted. The profits from their activities are enormous and at least some of them are ploughed back into local and national economies, usually with some multiplier effects. In these circumstances, one might conclude that TCOs do not pose a threat to national and international security.

Such an assessment is based on a narrow military conception of security. If one defines security as not just external military threats but as a challenge to the effective functioning of society, then drug trafficking is much more serious than many issues that have traditionally been seen as a threat to security. Drug trafficking poses one of the most serious challenges to the fabric of society in the US, Western Europe and even many drug-producing countries, which have also become consumers of their product. The threats to security are more complex and subtle than more traditional military challenges. Nevertheless, drug trafficking was designated a national security threat by the Reagan Administration in 1986 and subsequent US administrations have concurred with this assessment. Taking this further, it is clear that TCOs pose threats to security at three levels: the individual, the state and the international system of states.[28]

At the individual level, security is the provision of a relatively safe environment in which citizens do not fear violence or intimidation. TCOs have had a profound geo-social impact on this security. Indeed, if individual security is inversely related to the level of violence in society—the greater the violence, the less the security enjoyed by citizens—then drug trafficking and its associated activities pose a serious security threat.

This is partly because of the close connection between drugs and violence. There are three kinds of violence usually associated with the drug industry: violence by criminal organisations to protect their "turf" and profits; crimes against people and property by drug users who need to pay for illicit drugs; and violence perpetrated by individuals under the influence of mind-altering substances.[29] It has been estimated, for example, that the average heroin user commits 200 crimes a year to feed his habit.[30]

The problems of drug-related violence have become apparent in many societies with a significant number of addicts, including those which have been used for the transhipment of drugs. It is in the US, however, that violence has become the most prevalent. The pervasiveness of gang activity and the emergence of "no go zones" for ordinary citizens and even law enforcement officers are associated, in particular, with the trafficking of "crack" cocaine. While not all violence within US society can be attributed to drug abuse or trafficking, it is clear that there are links between drugs and violence, and that the greater the level of drug abuse within society then the lower the level of security that individual citizens enjoy. Moreover, it is unlikely that these problems can be dealt with adequately as long as the flow of drugs continues unimpeded. Reducing the demand for drugs through education, treatment and rehabilitation is crucial, but unless more effective curbs are placed on drug supplies, demand reduction is unlikely to be successful. The wholesalers and retailers of the drug business, however, are experts at marketing and they have an insidious product, whose supply helps to create its own demand.

Not only does drug abuse add to the health-care burden and undermine productivity and economic competitiveness, but transnational drug trafficking also results in societies in which violence is more pervasive and individual security is, therefore, more elusive.

Transnational criminal organisations can also pose serious threats to the security of their host and home states. In some cases, their power rivals that of the state itself. Their willingness to use force against the state and its law enforcement agencies challenges the state monopoly on organised violence and can be more destabilising than the activities of revolutionary or terrorist groups. This has certainly been the case in Colombia and Italy, where TCOs have resisted state control and engaged in extensive violence and terrorism. In Colombia, the Medellín cartel posed a direct threat to the Colombian government and, despite the death of Pablo Escobar, the cost has been enormous. The Colombian judiciary has been decimated, violence has, at times, reached levels characteristic of small civil wars, and Colombian political and economic activity has been dominated by the threats posed by the *narcotraficantes*. The cartels have threatened the country's democratic values by killing journalists critical of their activities and corrupting the institutions of the state.

Similar problems have been experienced in Italy, where the Mafia has launched attacks on the judiciary and has proved to be a far more formidable opponent than terrorist organisations, such as the Red

Brigades. This is partly because the Mafia has created an illicit but effective authority structure and has its own territory, population, laws and armed forces.[31] Having gained tremendous power and wealth through its involvement in the heroin trade from Southeast Asia and the cocaine trade from Latin America, the Sicilian Mafia, in particular, has routinely used both corruption and violence to further its aims. It has had very close links with the Christian Democratic party and has infiltrated government at the local, regional and, to a degree, national levels. It has also resorted to violence to protect or advance its position: throughout the 1980s the Mafia regularly killed magistrates, policemen, politicians, civil servants and trade unionists.[32] In 1992, these killings took on a new dimension with the assassinations of Paolo Borselino, the special anti-Mafia prosecutor for Palermo, and Judge Giovanni Falcone. These killings were a similar challenge to the Italian judicial system as that posed to the Colombian judiciary by the Medellín cartel.

Although the challenge backfired and led to more strenuous efforts by the government—acting under public pressure—to confront the Mafia, the events in Italy illustrated the vulnerability of even advanced industrialised states to the challenges posed by powerful TCOs. Moreover, these challenges to state authority may be unavoidable. As one eminent criminologist has noted,

> each crime network attempts to build a coercive monopoly and to implement that system of control through at least two other criminal activities—corruption of public and private officials, and violent terrorism in order to enforce its discipline.[33]

TCOs, therefore, by their very nature undermine civil society, destabilise domestic politics and undercut the rule of law.

Transnational criminal organisations sometimes create chaos, but they also exploit the uncertainty created by other domestic and international developments. Not surprisingly, TCOs flourish in states with weak structures and dubious legitimacy, which derives from economic inequalities, the dominance of traditional oligarchies, the lack of congruence between nation and state, poor economic performance and ethnic divisions. In such circumstances, the development of parallel political and economic structures is almost inevitable. Sometimes this follows from the fact that parts of the country are outside the control of central government. In other cases, government institutions may be so corrupt that they no longer have either the incentive or the capacity to reassert control. The Cali cartel in Colombia, for example, has deliberately avoided the direct attacks on the state as perpetrated by the Medellín cartel and has instead embraced a strategy based on cooption and corruption. This is a less obvious security threat but, to the extent that it undermines the proper functioning of political and legal institutions, may be an even more insidious challenge to the integrity of the Colombian state.

It is important not to exaggerate the importance of TCOs in causing political upheaval because whenever states lose legitimacy and political authority the problems have deep and extensive roots. Nevertheless, there is an important link between the rise of TCOs, on the one hand, and the crisis of governance and decline in civil society that have become familiar features of the post–Cold War world, on the other. Whatever the underlying reason for the breakdown in authority structures, political chaos provides a congenial environment for criminal activity. One of the key features of TCOs is that they link "zones of peace" and "zones of turbulence" in the international system.[34] They take advantage of the chaos that exists, for example, in countries such as Myanmar, which lacks and effective, legitimate government, is the world's main producer of heroin, and is internationally isolated yet is penetrated transnationally. Moreover, criminal organisations have a vested interest in the continuation of weak government and the conditions which allow them to export heroin from Myanmar with impunity.

Threats to the integrity of states generate challenges to the international state system. Although the field of security studies has traditionally focused on military relations between states, in the future it will also have to consider the relationship between states and powerful non-state actors. The dominance of governments has increasingly been challenged by the emergence of such actors, operating either regionally or globally. Lacking the attributes of sovereignty is often an advantage rather than a constraint for transnational actors—they are sovereignty-free rather than sovereignty-bound and use this freedom and flexibility to engage in activities that are difficult for states to regulate.[35] The issue is control versus autonomy: states want control and transnational actors want autonomy.

Transnational criminal organisations challenge aspects of state sovereignty and security that have traditionally been taken for granted. They prove the permeability of national borders and penetrate societies that are nominally under the control of states. States formally retain sovereignty, but if they are unable to control the importation of arms, people and drugs into their territory then it loses much of its significance. Sovereignty remains a useful basis for the international society of states, but no longer reflects real control over territory. The permeability of national boundaries and the concept of sovereignty do not make easy bedfellows.

It can be argued, of course, that the activities of many transnational organisations undermine state sovereignty. Most of these groups, however, obtain access to national markets and operate on a state's territory only with the permission of the government, a process that revalidates state power and authority.[36] TCOs are different because they obtain access through clandestine methods, minimise the opportunities for state control over their activities, and prevent real sovereignty being exercised. Although the main purpose of their activities is to make a profit, an inevitable by-product is an implicit challenge to state authority and sovereignty. The threat is insidious rather than direct: it is not a threat to the military strength of the state, but is a challenge to the prerogatives that are an integral part of statehood.

This does not mean that all states oppose TCOs. Alliances of convenience between "rogue" or "pariah" states and TCOs could pose serious security threats, especially from those trafficking in nuclear material. As soon as a trafficking network is functioning effectively product diversification is easy. Organisations that deal in drugs can also traffic in technology and components for weapons of mass destruction. Whether the recipients of such transfers are terrorist organisations or "pariah" states, the link between criminal activities and security is obvious.

If non-proliferation and other regulatory regimes are to function effectively in the future, therefore, it will be necessary to curb the activities of TCOs. This will not be easy.

CONCLUSION

In a contest between governments and TCOs, the former suffer from several disadvantages. First, they have a multiplicity of purposes and constituents. Transnational crime is simply one item on a very crowded agenda—one that does not always enjoy a high priority. The short-term nature of US administrations, for example, militates against a sustained and systematic campaign against drug trafficking. Wars against drugs or crime are typically declared and then forgotten.

Governments have also found it difficult to pursue a consistent and coherent set of policies in which the activities of the different parts of the bureaucracy complement rather than undercut one another. The battle against drug-trafficking organisations is, therefore, a battle of unequals. It is a struggle between a government composed of multiple organisations and constituencies with diverse objectives and interest, and an organisation with a single purpose or goal, which is the maximisation of profits. Government agencies and departments are semi-independent fiefdoms, which do not readily collaborate with one another either through the sharing of information or through joint operations. More information is needed, for example, about the major characteristics, strengths and weaknesses of TCOs. This, in turn, requires improved intelligence and more effective bureaucratic integration. Unfortunately, intelligence about drug trafficking and TCOs is often jealously guarded, bureaucratically compartmentalised and lacking any clear sense of purpose or direction. Although these problems are particularly acute in the US, where the horizontal and vertical divisions in government enable organisations to traffick with considerable success, they are not wholly absent in other states.

Although not all are as fragmented as that of the US, most democratic governments are forced to work within a framework of rules. TCOs, by definition, work outside the rules, can be ruthless in carrying out their policies and are not democratically accountable for their behaviour. Ironically, these organisations use nationalism and the sovereignty of the home government as a defensive measure even though most of their activities undermine the sovereignty of others. The Colombian cartels, for example, tried to mobilise national support by presenting Colombia's extradition treaty with the US as a violation of Colombian sovereignty.

Another problem is a lack of experience on the part of the governments in dealing with TCOs. States are well-equipped to deal with security threats from other countries, but when they are faced with sovereignty-free actors they are unsure which instruments of influence are most appropriate and whether strategies aimed at the organisation itself or pressure on the home government are likely to be more effective.

There is a marked contrast, therefore, between the seriousness of the challenge posed to security by TCOs and the nature of the response by governments. Criminal organisations are sophisticated, adaptable and highly resilient. Governments have to acknowledge the scale and complexity of the problem, engage in more extensive functional cooperation arrangements with each other, and mobilise legitimate transnational organisations such as banks, airlines and freight transportation companies to assist them. Although progress has been made in some of these areas, especially in Western Europe, much more has to be done if one of the most insidious and long-term threats to national and international security is to be contained.

ACKNOWLEDGEMENTS

The author would like to thank Jack Karns and Paul Stares for their helpful comments on this paper, and Peter Lupsha and Carl Florez for encouraging his work in this area.

NOTES

[1] Senator Roth quoted in *The New International Criminal and Asian Organised Crime*, Report made by the Permanent Subcommittee on Investigations of the Committee on Governmental Affairs, United States Senate 102nd Congress, 2nd Session S. Print 102-129 (December 1992), p. 2.

[2] Robert Keohane and Joseph Nye, *Transnational Relations and World Politics* (Cambridge, MA: Harvard University Press, 1971), p. xii.

[3] Edward Morse, "Transnational Economic Processes," in Keohane and Nye, *Transnational Relations and World Politics*, pp. 23–47.

[4] John A. Mack and Hans-Jurgen Kerner, *The Crime Industry* (Lexington, MA: Heath, 1975), pp. 6 and 13.

[5]R. Vernon, *Storm over the Multinationals* (Cambridge, MA: Harvard University Press, 1977), p. 2.

[6]See *World Air Transport Statistics* (Switzerland: International Air Transport Association Publications), no. 37, June 1993, pp. 8–11.

[7]See *Customs USA: A Special Report on the Activities of the US Customs Service During Fiscal Year 1988* (Washington, DC: Media and Public Services Branch of the Public Information Division, Customs Service, 1988), pp. 38–40, and *US Customs Update 1992* (Washington, DC: US Customs Service, 1993), pp. 21–22.

[8]*1990 International Trade Statistics Yearbook*, vol. 1 (New York: United Nations, 1992), pp. S2–S3.

[9]L. Krause, "Private International Finance" in Keohane and Nye, *Transnational Relations and World Politics*, pp. 173–90.

[10]See Jane Jacobs, *The Economy of Cities* (New York: Random House, 1969), for a fuller discussion.

[11]The point about port cities is made in Peter Lupsha, "Organised Crime: Rational Choice not Ethnic Group Behaviour: A Macro Perspective," *The Law Enforcement Intelligence Analysis Digest*, Winter 1986, pp. 1–7.

[12]Kenichi Ohmae, *The Borderless World* (New York: Harper Business, 1990), pp. 18–26 and xiii.

[13]See Louis Kraar, "The Drug Trade," *Fortune*, 20 June 1988, pp. 27–38.

[14]See Samuel Huntington, "Transnational Organisations in World Politics," *World Politics*, vol. 25, no. 3, April 1973, pp. 333–68.

[15]Ibid, p. 355.

[16]See Rennsalaer W. Lee III, "Colombia's Cocaine Syndicates" in A. W. McCoy and A. A. Block (eds.), *War on Drugs* (Boulder, CO: Westview Press, 1992), pp. 93–124.

[17]*Connection between Arms and Narcotics Trafficking*, Hearing before the Committee on Foreign Affairs, House of Representatives, One Hundred First Congress, First Session October 31, 1989 (Washington: USGPO, 1990), p. 68.

[18]Stephen Flynn, "Worldwide Drug Scourge: The Expanding Trade in Illicit Drugs," *The Brookings Review*, Winter 1993, pp. 6–11.

[19]See *The New International Criminal and Asian Organised Crime*, 18 June and 4 August 1992 (Washington: USGPO), pp. 7–12. Also useful are Ko-lin Chin, Chinese Sub-Culture and Criminality: Non-traditional Crime Groups in America (New York: Greenwood, 1990), pp. 38–40; and *The New International Criminal and Asian Organised Crime*, December 1992.

[20]See David E. Kaplan, *Fires of the Dragon: Politics, Murder and the Kuomintang* (New York: Macmillan, 1992).

[21]Testimony in *The New International Criminal and Asian Organised Crime*, 3 October, 5–6 November 1991, p. 19.

[22]Testimony of David Cohen, Associate Deputy Director for Intelligence, Central Intelligence Agency, in *The New International Criminal and Asian Organised Crime* (Second Session 18 June and 4 August 1992), p. 70.

[23]National Narcotics Intelligence Consumers Committee (NNICC), *The NNICC Report 1992: The Supply of Illicit Drugs to the United States* (Washington, DC: Drug Enforcement Administration, September 1993), p. 22.

[24]See Patrick Cooney, Rapporteur, *Report drawn up by the Committee of Enquiry into the Spread of Organised Crime Linked to Drug Trafficking in the Member States of the European Community* (European Parliament Session Documents, 23 April 1992), p. 40.

[25]For a fuller discussion, see Claire Sterling, *The Mafia: The Long Reach of the International Sicilian Mafia* (London: Hamish Hamilton, 1990).

[26]Ray Mosely, "Cold War's end opens door for Mafia in Europe," *Chicago Tribune*, 29 December 1992.

[27]See "Global Mafia," *Newsweek*, 13 December 1993, pp. 22–28.

[28]The three levels follow Barry Buzan, *People, States and Fear* (Brighton: Wheatsheaf, 1983).

[29]P. Goldstein, H. H. Brownstein, P. Ryan and P. Belucci, "Crack and Homicide in New York City, 1988: A Conceptually Based Event Analysis," *Contemporary Drug Problems*, vol. 16, no. 4, Winter 1989, pp. 651–87.

[30]The Majority Staffs of the Senate Judiciary Committee and the International Narcotics Control Caucus, *The President's Drug Strategy: Has it Worked?*, September 1992, p. vi.

[31]"The Sicilian Mafia," *The Economist*, 24 April 1993, pp. 21–24.

[32]Ibid.

[33]R. J. Kelly, "Criminal Underworlds: Looking Down on Society from Below" in R. J. Kelly (ed.), *Organised Crime: A Global Perspective* (Totowa, NJ: Rowman and Littlefield, 1986), pp. 10–31.

[34]The concept of the two zones is developed in M. Singer and A. Wildavsky, *The Real World Order* (Chatham, NJ: Chatham House Publishers, 1993).

[35]James Rosenau, *Turbulence in World Politics* (Princeton, NJ: Princeton University Press, 1991), p. 253.

[36]See Huntington, "Transnational Organisations in World Politics," p. 363.

Chapter Fifteen

RESPONDING TO TERRORISM ACROSS THE TECHNOLOGICAL SPECTRUM*

Bruce Hoffman

The "revolution in military affairs," it is argued, heralds a new era of warfare dominated by the American military's mastery of the conventional battlefield. Just as gunpowder, the mechanization of battle, and atomic weapons previously changed the fundamental conduct and nature of warfare so will a combination of technological progress, doctrinal sophistication, and innovative force employment in turn "render . . . existing methods of conducting warfare obsolete." The assumption that the United States armed forces alone will have the capability to harness all the elements of this revolution is in large measure derived from the demonstrated superiority of American combined arms over the much larger Iraqi forces during the 1991 Persian Gulf War.[1] The effect, according to one analysis, will be profound:

> In any conventional conflict in which the United States or any of the major Western powers is pitted against a Third World adversary, the outcome is preordained. In effect, the change is so significant that we have returned to the military equation of the 19th century, when colonial wars pitted small numbers of disciplined, well-trained Western troops with rifles against hordes of tribal warriors armed only with shields and spears.[2]

*Bruce Hoffman, "Responding to Terrorism Across the Technological Spectrum." Reprinted by permission from *Terrorism and Political Violence*, Vol. 6, No. 3, Autumn 1994. Copyright @ Frank Cass and Co. Ltd.

It is equally significant, however, that the revolution in military affairs remains confined to the conventional battlefield only. Indeed, as many observers of this phenomenon themselves concede, the revolution will have little if any impact on American military capabilities so far as countering terrorism, insurgency, or guerrilla warfare are concerned.[3] Hence, while "Operation Desert Storm" may be a model for the revolution in military affairs occurring at the mid- and high-ends of the conflict spectrum, the problems that U.S. forces encountered in Somalia, for example, may be a more accurate and telling model for the types of conflict at the low end of the spectrum that U.S. military forces are more likely to find themselves involved. As our frustrating—and increasingly forgotten—experiences in Vietnam more than a quarter of a century ago demonstrate, this is by no means a new lesson. Indeed, in no realm of conflict today is the asymmetry between American capability and sophistication on the one hand and the crude, even primitive, ability of an adversary to inflict pain on the other perhaps as salient or possibly portentous as with terrorism.

TRENDS IN TERRORIST TACTICS

The contrast between the means and methods of modern warfare and the tactics and techniques of contemporary terrorism is striking. Whereas technological progress has produced successively more complex, lethally effective and destructively accurate weapons systems that are deployed from a variety of air, land, and sea platforms, terrorism has functioned largely in a technological vacuum, aloof or averse to the continual refinement and growing sophistication of modern warfare.

Terrorists continue to rely—as they have for more than a century—on the same two basic "weapons systems": the gun and the bomb. Admittedly, the guns used by terrorists today have larger ammunition capacities and more rapid rates of fire than the simple revolver the Russian revolutionary Vera Zasulich used in 1878 to assassinate the governor general of St. Petersburg.[4] Similarly, bombs today require smaller amounts of explosives that are exponentially more powerful and more easily concealed than the sticks of TNT with which the Fenian "Dynamiters" terrorized London more than a century ago.[5]

The implication of terrorist reliance on these two weapons, however, goes far beyond mere tactical convenience. It also suggests an *a priori* reluctance or aversion to killing en masse given the comparatively discrete numbers of casualties that can be inflicted with even self-loading, rapid-fire automatic weapons or powerful plastic explosives. Despite its popularity as a fictional theme, terrorists in fact have rarely attempted—much less actively contemplated—the infliction of mass, indiscriminate casualties through chemical, biological, or nuclear weapons. Indeed, of more than 8,000 incidents recorded in The RAND Chronology of International Terrorism since 1968, only 52 evidence any indication of terrorists plotting such attacks, attempting to use chemical or biological agents or to steal, or otherwise fabricate on their own, nuclear devices.[6] Thus, terrorists seem almost inherently content with the limited killing potential of their handguns and machine-guns and the slightly higher rates that their bombs have at times achieved.

This self-imposed restraint is most clearly reflected in the risk-averse tactical repertoire embraced by most terrorist groups (see Figure 15.1). Bombings, for example, account for nearly half (46 percent) of all international terrorist attacks carried out since 1968: a proportion that annually has rarely fallen below 40 percent or exceeded 50 percent.[7] The reliance on bombing by terrorists is not surprising given that bombs provide a dramatic, yet fairly easy and often risk-free, means of drawing attention to the terrorists and their causes. Few skills are required to manufacture a crude bomb, surreptitiously plant it, and then be miles away when it explodes. Bombings are also usually only one- or two- or three-person jobs and therefore do not require the same organizational expertise, logistics, and knowledge required of more complicated or sophisticated operations, such as kidnapping, barricade and hostage situations, assassination, and assaults against defended targets.

Attacks on installations (including attacks with automatic weapons as well as hand grenades, bazookas, and rocket-propelled grenades, drive-by shootings, arson, vandalism, and sabotage other than bombing) is a distant second to bombing, accounting for 22 percent of all terrorist operations since 1968.[8] Not surprisingly, perhaps, the frequency of various types of terrorist attacks tends to decrease in direct proportion to the complexity or sophistication required. Accordingly, hijackings are the third most common tactic, accounting

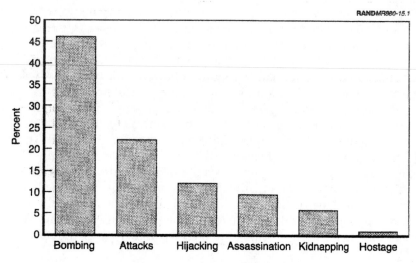

SOURCE: The RAND Chronology of International Terrorism.

Figure 15.1—Total Terrorist Tactics, 1968–1993

for only 12 percent;[9] followed by assassination (9.5 percent);[10] kidnapping 6 percent, and barricade-hostage incidents 1 percent.[11]

The fact that these percentages have remained largely unchanged for more than a quarter of a century (with one exception[12]) also provides compelling evidence that the vast majority of terrorist organizations are not tactically innovative (see Figure 15.2). Radical in their politics, these groups are equally conservative in their operations, rarely deviating from the familiar and adhering to an established *modus operandi* that, to their minds at least, minimizes failure and maximizes success. What innovation does occur is mostly in the methods used to conceal and detonate explosive devices, not in their tactics or in their use of nonconventional weapons (i.e., chemical, biological, or nuclear).

Terrorists therefore seem to prefer the assurance of modest success to more complicated and complex—but potentially higher pay-off (in terms of casualties and publicity)—operations. Indeed, this explanation possibly accounts for the overall paucity of terrorist

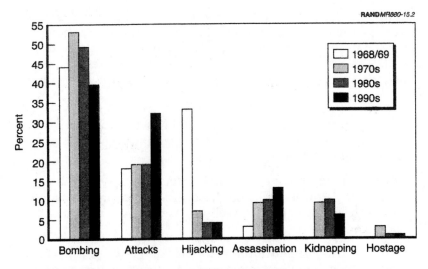

SOURCE: The RAND Chronology of International Terrorism.

Figure 15.2—Terrorist Tactics by Decade, 1968–1992

"spectaculars" and the mostly limited number of casualties histori-cally inflicted in terrorist attacks (i.e., more often in the tens and twenties if at all, rather than in the low hundreds). Indeed, since the beginning of the century fewer than a dozen terrorist incidents in fact have occurred that resulted in the deaths of more than 100 per-sons at one time.[13] The two suicide car-bombings that occurred in Israel during April 1994 by Palestinians opposed to the peace process underscores this point. Even when a terrorist deliberately sacrifices himself in the course of the attack seldom does the death toll reach double-figures: only seven persons, for example, tragically lost their lives in the first incident on 6 April; five perished in the following week's attack. The massive car-bomb that exploded in Johannes-burg, South Africa on 24 April 1994, just before that country's first open general elections, is another case in point. Despite the bombers' obvious intention to inflict mass, indiscriminate casualties, only nine persons were killed.

These proclivities, therefore, directly affect, if not limit, the weapons technology that terrorists can and will use. Accordingly, based on the historical record, future terrorist employment of either high-tech weapons systems or weapons of mass destruction (i.e., chemical, biological or nuclear) would appear unlikely. However, both the longevity of this trend and the self-imposed stasis of terrorist technology could change dramatically as a result of three emerging trends in terrorist activity:

- The resurgence of terrorism motivated by a religious imperative and the implications that it has to trigger future acts of mass, indiscriminate violence.

- The increasing "amateurization" of terrorism—a reflection, in part, of the growth of religious terrorism—which may contribute to the loosening of previous self-imposed constraints on operations and lethality.

- The increasing sophistication and evident growing tactical and technological competence of veteran terrorist organizations across the technological spectrum.

THE RESURGENCE OF RELIGIOUS TERRORISM

One of the distinguishing features of international terrorism during the past 15 years has been the resurgence and proliferation of terrorist groups motivated by a religious imperative (see Figure 15.3).[14] In 1968, for example, none of the 11 identifiable terrorist groups active throughout the world could be classified as religious—that is, having aims and motivations reflecting a salient religious character or influence.[15] Not until 1980—as a result of the repercussions from the revolution in Iran the previous year[16] do the first "modern"[17] religious terrorist groups appear. Even so, despite the large increase in the total number of identifiable international terrorist groups and concomitant increase of ethnic-separatist organizations (from three to 32), only two of the 64 groups active in 1980 were predominantly religious in character and motivation (al-Dawa and the Committee for Safeguarding the Islamic Revolution). Twelve years later, however, the number of religious terrorist groups has increased nearly six-fold while—at a time of increasingly strident assertions of ethnic, national, and cultural uniqueness throughout the world—the number of ethnic-separatist terrorist groups has declined

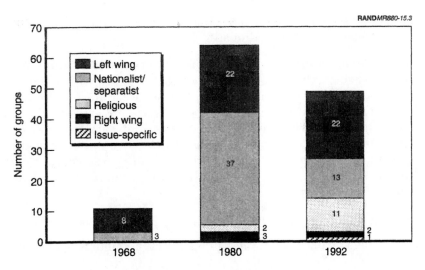

SOURCE: The RAND Chronology of International Terrorism.

Figure 15.3—Types of Terrorist Groups

and—notwithstanding the end of the Cold War—the number of Marxist-Leninist-Maoist (or some idiosyncratic interpretation of those dicta) groups has remained unchanged.

The implications of terrorism motivated by a religious imperative for higher levels of lethality is evidenced by the violent record of various Shi'a Islamic groups. Although these organizations committed only 8 percent of all international terrorist incidents since 1982, they are nonetheless responsible for 28 percent of the total number of deaths (see Figure 15.3).[18] Moreover, contrary to its depiction and discussion in Western news accounts, terrorism motivated by religion is by no means a phenomenon restricted to Islamic terrorist groups exclusively in the Middle East. Many of the characteristics of Shi'a terrorist groups—the legitimization of violence based on religious precepts, the sense of profound alienation and isolation, and the attendant preoccupation with the elimination of a broadly defined category of "enemies"—are also apparent among militant Christian white supremacists in the United States, in at least some radical

Jewish messianic terrorist movements in Israel, and among some radical Sikh movements in India.[19]

The fact that for many of these groups the elimination of whole segments of society is a major objective of their terrorist campaigns implies an almost axiomatic attempt to use weapons of mass destruction including chemical or biological warfare agents or radioactive materials. During the past decade, for example, religious terrorists or members of various religious "cults" have come closest to crossing the threshold of terrorist use of *bona fide* weapons of mass destruction. They have, for example, either attempted or at least pursued the idea of

- poisoning the water supplies of major American urban centers[20]

- dispersing toxic chemicals through internal building ventilation systems[21]

- blowing up of a religious shrine in hopes of provoking a cataclysmic "holy war"[22]

- staging indiscriminate, wanton simultaneous bombings of crowded, busy urban centers[23]

- contaminating food in public restaurants.[24]

That terrorists motivated by a religious imperative can contemplate such massive acts of death and destruction is a reflection of their belief that violence is a sacramental act or a divine duty. Terrorism thus assumes a transcendental dimension,[25] and its perpetrators are seemingly unconstrained by the political, moral, or practical constraints that affect other terrorists. Whereas secular terrorists generally consider indiscriminate violence immoral and counterproductive,[26] religious terrorists regard such violence as both morally justified and a necessary expedient for the attainment of their goals. Religious and secular terrorists also have different perceptions of themselves and their violent acts. Secular terrorists regard violence as a way of instigating the correction of a flaw in a system that is basically good or to foment the creation of a new system. Religious terrorists, on the other hand, regard themselves not as components of a system, but as "outsiders," and seek vast changes in the existing order.[27] This sense of alienation enables the religious terrorist to contemplate far more destructive and deadly types of terrorist operations than secular terrorists and indeed to embrace a far more open-ended category of "enemies" for attack: basically anyone who is not a member of their particular sect or religious movement.

Given this constellation of characteristics and convergence of motives and capabilities, religious terrorists therefore appear as the most likely terrorist entity to eventually succeed in effecting some dramatic act of violence using a weapon of mass destruction.

THE "AMATEURIZATION" OF TERRORISM

A series of terrorist incidents that occurred in the United States during 1993—the bombing of New York City's World Trade Center in February; the uncovering in June of a plot to free the terrorists arrested for the Trade Center blast by destroying two commuter tunnels and a bridge linking New Jersey to Manhattan, blowing up the United Nations building, staging a forced-entry attack on the downtown Federal building housing the FBI's New York field office, and assassinating various public officials; the unmasking the following month of a conspiracy to carry out a machine-gun and hand grenade attack against a prominent African-American church in Los Angeles as Sunday services concluded; and the chain of bombings against a variety of Asian, Jewish, and African-American targets in the Sacramento, California area last spring and summer—suggest that we may have to revise our notions of the stereotypical terrorist organization.

In the past, terrorist groups were recognizable as a group of individuals belonging to an organization with a well-defined command and control apparatus, who had been previously trained (however rudimentary) in the techniques and tactics of terrorism, were engaged in conspiracy as a full-time avocation, living underground and constantly planning and plotting terrorist attacks at times under the direct control of, or operating at the express behest of, a foreign government. The amateurish World Trade Center bombers, however, may be the model of a new kind of terrorist group: a more or less ad hoc amalgamation of like-minded individuals sharing a common religion, the same friends and frustrations, perhaps having family ties as well, who simply gravitate toward one another for specific, perhaps even one-time, operations.[28] Rather than being tightly controlled from abroad, these new part-time terrorists and independent free-lance groups are more likely to be only indirectly connected to a central command authority or a foreign government.

Moreover, since this more amorphous and perhaps even transitory type of group will lack the "footprints" or modus operandi of an actual, existing terrorist organization, it is likely to prove more difficult for law enforcement to get a firm idea or build a complete picture of the dimensions of their intentions and capabilities.[29] Indeed, as one New York City police officer only too presciently observed two months before the Trade Center attack: it wasn't the established terrorist groups—with known or suspected members and established operational patterns—that worried him, but the hitherto unknown "splinter groups," composed of new or marginal members from an older group, that suddenly surface out of nowhere to attack.[30]

Essentially, part-time terrorists, such loose groups of individuals, may be—as the World Trade Center bombers themselves appear to have been—*indirectly* influenced or remotely controlled by some foreign government or nongovernmental entity. The suspicious transfer of funds from banks in Iran and Germany to a joint account maintained by the accused bombers in New Jersey just before the Trade Center blast may be illustrative of this more indirect or circuitous foreign connection.[31] Moreover, the fact that two Iraqi nationals—Ramzi Ahmed Yousef and Abdul Rahman Yasin—implicated in the Trade Center conspiracy, fled the United States (presumably to Iraq)[32] in one instance just before the bombing and in the other shortly after the first arrests, increases suspicion that the incident may not only have been orchestrated from abroad but may in fact have been an act of state-sponsored terrorism.[33] Thus, in contrast to the Trade Center bombing's depiction in the press as a terrorist incident perpetrated by a group of "amateurs" acting either entirely on their own or, as one of the bomber's defense attorneys portrayed his client manipulated by a "devious, evil . . . genius"[34] (Yousef), the original genesis of the Trade Center attack may be far more complex.

This use of amateur terrorists as "dupes" or "cut-outs" to mask the involvement of some foreign patron or government could therefore greatly benefit terrorist state sponsors who could more effectively conceal their involvement and thus avoid potential military retaliation by the victim country and diplomatic or economic sanctions from the international community. Moreover, the prospective state-sponsors' connection could be further obscured by the fact that much of the "amateur" terrorists equipment, resources and even some funding could be self-generating. The explosive device used at the World Trade Center—constructed out of ordinary, commercially available materials, including lawn fertilizer (urea nitrate) and diesel fuel and costing less than $400 to construct—illustrates this potential.[35] Indeed, despite the Trade Center bombers' almost comical ineptitude in avoiding capture, they were still able to shake an entire city's—if not country's—complacency. Moreover, the simple bomb used by these "amateurs" proved just as deadly and destructive—killing six persons, injuring more than 1,000 others, gouging out a 180-ft wide crater six stories deep, and causing an estimated $550 million in both damages to the twin tower and in lost revenue to the business housed there[36]—as the more "high-tech" bombs constructed out of military ordnance, with timing devices powered by computer micro-chips and detonated by sophisticated timing mechanisms used by their "professional" counterparts.

In this respect, this new breed of terrorists may represent even more of a threat than their predecessors.[37] While less control from some central command authority may indeed be exerted, this may also result in fewer constraints on the terrorists' operations and targets and fewer inhibitions on their desire to inflict indiscriminate casualties.[38] It is suspected, for example, that the bombers' intent in attacking the World Trade Center was to bring down one of the twin towers.[39] It is significant too that rather than having been deterred or otherwise affected by the rapidity with which the FBI and other authorities "cracked" the Trade Center case, the 15 individuals implicated in the follow-on plot, uncovered in June 1993 to obtain the release of the Trade Center bombers, had plotted even more egregious acts of violence: including the simultaneous bombing of the Holland and Lincoln tunnels and George Washington Bridge used daily by thousands of commuters between New Jersey and Manhattan; a car-bomb attack in the United Nations building underground garage; a forced entry machine-gun and hand grenade assault on the Federal Building in lower Manhattan housing the FBI New York headquarters; and the assassination of U.N. Secretary General Boutros Boutros-Ghali, Egyptian President Hosni Mubarak, New York Senator Alfonse D'Amato, and a Brooklyn Assemblyman, Dov Hilkind.[40]

The characteristics and attendant implications of this "amateur-ization" of terrorism were further demonstrated by the rash of independent, unconnected acts of "teenage" terrorism that occurred in California and Washington State last summer. The first incident involved the 20-year-old leader of a self-styled terrorist group calling itself the "Fourth Reich Skinheads" and his 17-year-old accomplice who were arrested in Los Angeles and charged with planning a series of bombings against various Jewish targets that would culminate in a machine-gun and hand grenade assault against a South-Central Los Angeles church as its worshippers emerged from Sunday services.[41] The operation had to be postponed, however, after one of the conspirators was refused permission by his parents to borrow the family car for the attack.[42]

That same month, in an unrelated incident, a 19-year-old was arrested and charged with bombing a Tacoma, Washington National Association for the Advancement of Colored People (NAACP) meeting hall as the opening salvo in a terrorist campaign directed against rap stars, synagogues and military installations throughout the Pacific Northwest.[43] Finally, in November, the putative leader of another teen-age white supremacist group, the "Aryan Liberation Front" was arrested in Northern California and charged with fire-bombing a synagogue, the local office of the NAACP, the home of an Asian-American politician, and the state office that handles discrimination claims in Sacramento.[44] The youth—who turned 18 years of age the day after his arrest—had called a television station after one attack to announce that, "The A.L.F. takes full responsibility for the attack and promises to contribute to armed struggles whether it be by rocks, Molotov cocktails, bombs, guns, to effect the change in Jew capitalism and America politically."[45]

In the past, terrorism was not just a matter of having the will and motivation to act, but of having the capability to do so—the requisite training, access to weaponry, and operational knowledge. Today, however, it is clear that the means and methods of terrorism are readily available and accessible to anyone with a grievance, agenda or purpose or any idiosyncratic combination of the above. Whether abetted tacitly or actively by a foreign patron or facilitated by commercially obtainable published bomb-making manuals and operational guidebooks, the "amateur" terrorist can be just as deadly—and perhaps even deadlier—and destructive than his more "professional" counterpart. Given the inherent difficulty in tracking and anticipating this category of adversary—as opposed to the often more established modus operandi and patterns of existing terrorist groups—this new breed of terrorist may pose a greater future threat.[46]

IMPROVED "PROFESSIONALISM" OF TERRORISTS

Paradoxically, while on the one hand terrorism is increasingly attracting "amateurs," on the other the sophistication and operational competence of the "professional" terrorists is also increasing. They are becoming demonstrably more adept in their trade craft of death and destruction; more formidable in terms of their abilities of tactical modification, adjustment and innovation; and able to operate for sustained periods of time while avoiding detection, interception and arrest or capture. More disquieting, these "professional" terrorists are apparently becoming considerably more ruthless as well.

An almost Darwinian principle of natural selection seems to affect subsequent generations of existing terrorist groups, whereby every new terrorist generation learns from its predecessors, becoming smarter, tougher, and more difficult to capture or eliminate.[47] For terrorists, intelligence is not only an essential prerequisite for a successful operation, but a sine qua non for survival. Successor generations, therefore, routinely study the "lessons" from mistakes made by former comrades who have been either killed or apprehended. Press accounts, judicial indictments, courtroom testimony, and trial transcripts are meticulously culled for information on security force tactics and methods and are absorbed by surviving group members.

According to one German government official, terrorists belonging to the Red Army Faction (RAF), for example, "closely study every court case against them to discover their weak spots." Whereas in the past German police could usually obtain fingerprints from the bottom of toilet seats or the inside of refrigerators, RAF terrorists today apply a special ointment to their fingers that, after drying, prevents fingerprints and thus thwarts identification and incrimination.[48] As a spokesperson for the *Bundeskriminalamt* lamented, "The 'Third Generation' learnt a lot from the mistakes of its predecessors—and about how the police works . . . they now know how to operate very carefully."[49] Indeed, according to a former member of the organization, Peter-Juergen Brock, currently serving the seventh year of a life sentence for murder, the group "has reached maximum efficiency."[50]

Similar accolades have also been bestowed on the latest generation of Provisional Irish Republican Army (PIRA) fighters. The former General Officer Commanding British Forces in Northern Ireland, General Sir John Wilsey, has described the PIRA as "an absolutely formidable enemy. The essential attributes of their leaders are better than ever before. Some of their operations are brilliant in terrorist terms."[51] Even the PIRA's comparatively unsophisticated Loyalist terrorist counterparts are absorbing the lessons from past mistakes, consciously emulating the PIRA and becoming disquietingly more "professional." As one Royal Ulster Constabulary police officer observed, the Protestant groups "[m]ore and more. . . are running their operations from small cells, on a need to know basis. They have cracked down on loose talk. They have learned how to destroy forensic evidence. And if you bring them in for questioning, they say nothing."[52]

Not only are successor generations often smarter than their predecessors, but they also tend to be more sophisticated and ruthless as well as less idealistic. For some, in fact, violence becomes almost an end in itself—a cathartic release, a self-satisfying blow struck against the hated "system"—rather than being regarded as the deliberate means to a specific political end embraced by previous generations.[53] A dedicated, "hard-core" of some 20 to 30 terrorists today, for example, compose a third generation of Germany's Red Army Faction (RAF) terrorist organization. In contrast to the group's first generation, who more than twenty years ago embarked on an anti-establishment campaign of non-lethal bombings and arson attacks, the present generation has pursued a strategy of cold-blooded assassination.[54]

During the past seven years the RAF has murdered six prominent—and heavily guarded—Germans. Indeed, the group's almost relentless targeting of well-protected individuals sets it apart from the vast majority of terrorist organizations who typically aim for the "softer" (i.e., easily accessed) rather than "harder" target.[55] The RAF's last victim was Detlev Rohwedder, a wealthy industrialist and chairman of the *Treuhandanstalt,* or Public Trustee, the government agency charged with overseeing the economic transition of eastern Germany. Rohwedder was killed in April 1991 while he sat in his study with a shot fired from a high-power rifle.[56] In December 1989, financier and Deutsche Bank president Alfred Herrhausen was assassinated when a state-of-the-art remote-control bomb, concealed in a parked bicycle and triggered by a light-beam, was detonated just as Herrhausen's car passed.[57] A similar device was used the following July in an attempt to assassinate Germany's top government counterterrorist official, Hans Neusel.[58] Almost as disturbing as the assassinations themselves is the fact that, until this past Summer, the perpetrators—and their fellow conspirators—had eluded what is perhaps the most sophisticated anti-terrorist machinery in the world.[59]

The PIRA's relentless quest to pierce the armor protecting both the security forces in Northern Ireland and the most senior government officials in England illustrates the professional evolution and increasing operational sophistication of a terrorist group. The first generation of early 1970s PIRA devices were often little more than crude anti-personnel bombs, consisting of a handful of roofing nails, wrapped around a lump of plastic explosive, which were detonated simply by lighting a fuse. Time bombs from the same era were hardly more sophisticated. They typically were constructed from a few sticks of dynamite and commercial detonators stolen from construction sites or rock quarries attached to ordinary battery-powered alarm clocks. Neither device was terribly reliable and often put the bomber at considerable risk. The process of placing and actually lighting the first type of device carried with it the inherent potential to attract undesired attention while affording the bomber little time to effect the attack and make good his or her escape. Although the second type of device was designed to mitigate precisely this danger, its timing and detonation mechanism was often so crude that accidental or premature explosions were not infrequent, thus causing some terrorists inadvertently to kill themselves.[60]

In hopes of obviating, or at least reducing, these risks, the PIRA's bombmakers invented a means of detonating bombs from a safe distance using the radio controls for model aircraft purchased at hobby shops. Scientists and engineers working in the British Ministry of Defence's (MoD) scientific research and development ("R&D") division in turn developed a system of electronic countermeasures and jamming techniques for the Army that effectively thwarted this means of attack.[61]   However, rather than abandon this tactic completely, the PIRA began to search for a solution.   In contrast to the state-of-the art laboratories, huge budgets, and academic credentials of their government counterparts, PIRA's own "R&D" department toiled in cellars beneath cross-border safe houses and backrooms of urban tenements for five years before devising a network of sophisticated electronic switches for their bombs that would ignore or bypass the Army's electronic countermeasures.[62]

Once again, the MoD scientists returned to their laboratories; emerging with a new system of electronic scanners able to detect radio emissions the moment the radio is switched on—and, critically, just tens of seconds before the bomber can actually transmit the detonation signal. The almost infinitesimal window of time provided by this "early warning" of impending attack is just sufficient to allow Army technicians to activate a series of additional electronic measures to neutralize the transmission signal and render detonation impossible.

For a time, this countermeasure proved effective as well. But within the past two years the PIRA has discovered a means to outwit even this countermeasure. Utilizing radar detectors, such as those used by motorists in the United States to evade speed traps, in 1991 the group's bombmakers fabricated a detonating system that can be triggered by the same type of hand-held radar gun used by police throughout the world to catch speeding motorists. Since the radar gun can be aimed at its target before being switched on, and the signal that it transmits is nearly instantaneous, no practical means currently exists that allows the time needed either to detect or intercept the transmission signal.[63]

More recently, the PIRA's "R&D" units have developed yet another means to detonate bombs using a photo-flash "slave" unit that can be triggered from a distance of up to 800 meters by a flash of light. The device, which sells for between £60 and £70, is used by commercial photographers to produce simultaneous flashes during photo shoots. The PIRA bombers attach the unit to the detonating system on a bomb and then simply activate it with a commercially available, ordinary flashgun.[64]

As with the new "photo-flash" means of detonation, the sophistication of a device is often its very simplicity. In recent years, for example, the PIRA has mounted a highly effective campaign of "economic warfare" using simple incendiary devices left in Belfast and London department stores. Using a plastic cassette tape container, a miniature detonator, a timing device powered by a radio battery, a small amount of plastic explosive or explosive power, two or three capsules of lighter fuel and some paper to ensure combustion, the devices are small, highly portable, easily constructed and planted, and nearly risk-free to the bomber as the timer can usually be set for up to 12 hours. They cost less than £5 to produce[65] and have thus far caused more than $15 million in property damage.[66] The process of planting the devices is typically a one-person job, but allows that person potentially to operate without detection over a wide area and thus create an impression "of a concerted attack involving a large team."[67]

On a larger scale, bombs constructed out of ordinary, commercially available fertilizer (such as was used in the World Trade Center bombing) have devastated commercial districts both in Northern Ireland and on the mainland. In April 1992, in what was described "as the most powerful explosion in London since World War II," a bomb constructed with up to a ton of fertilizer exploded outside the Baltic Exchange building in the heart of the city's financial center, killing three persons, wounding 90 others, leaving a 12-foot wide crater and causing $1.25 billion in damage.[68] Exactly a year later, a similar bomb devastated the nearby Bishops Gate district, killing one person and injuring more than 40 others. Initial estimates put the damage at $1.5 billion.[69]

Long a staple of PIRA operations, fertilizer costs on average one percent of a comparable amount of plastic explosive. Although, after adulteration, fertilizer is far less powerful than plastic explosive (i.e., Semtex explodes at about 8,000 yards a second and has a high explosive rating of 1.3; improvised explosives explode at only about 3,000 yards a second and range between 0.25 and 0.8 in rating), it also tends to cause more damage than plastic explosives because the energy of the blast is sustained and less controlled.[70] Not surprisingly, therefore, the PIRA bombers have earned a reputation for their innovative expertise, adaptability, and cunning. "There are some very bright people around," the British Army's Chief Ammunitions Technical Officer (CATO) in Northern Ireland recently remarked. "I would rate them very highly for improvisation. PIRA bombs are very well made."[71] A similar accolade is offered by the staff officer of the British Army's 321 Explosives and Ordinance Disposal Company: "We are dealing with the first division," he said. "I don't think there is any organisation in the world as cunning as the IRA. They have had 20 years at it and they have learned from their experience. We have a great deal of respect for their skills . . . not as individuals, but their skills."[72] While not yet nearly as good as the PIRA, the province's Loyalist terrorist groups are themselves reportedly on a "learning curve": becoming increasingly adept in the construction, concealment and surreptitious placement of bombs.[73]

Even attacks that are not successful in conventionally understood military terms of casualties inflicted or assets destroyed, can still be a success for the terrorists provided that they are technologically daring enough to garner media and public attention. Indeed, the terrorist group's fundamental organizational imperative to act—even if their action is not completely successful, but still brings them publicity—also drives this persistent search for new ways to overcome, circumvent or defeat governmental security and countermeasures. Thus, while the PIRA failed to kill then-Prime Minister Margaret Thatcher at the Conservative Party's 1984 conference in Brighton, the technological ingenuity involving the bomb's placement at the conference site weeks before the event and its detonation timing device powered by a computer microchip nonetheless succeeded in capturing the world's headlines and providing the PIRA with a platform from which to warn Mrs. Thatcher and all other British leaders: "Today we were unlucky, but remember we only have to be lucky once—you will have to be lucky always."[74] Similarly, although the remote-control mortar attack staged by the PIRA on No. 10 Downing Street—as Prime Minister John Major and his Cabinet met at the height of the 1991 Gulf War—failed to hit its intended target, the attack nonetheless successfully elbowed the war out of the limelight and shone renewed media attention on the terrorists, their cause and their impressive ability to strike at the nerve-center of the British government even at a time of heightened security.[75]

The PIRA's impressive ability to capture headlines with daring, clever operations was most recently demonstrated by the series of remote-control mortar attacks on London's Heathrow Airport in March. Three attacks in five days nearly paralyzed air traffic[76] and provided the organization with an ideal propaganda vehicle to demonstrate terrorism's ineluctable paradox: terrorists can attack anywhere at anytime while the government's security forces are powerless and unable to protect every conceivable target all the time.[77]

CONCLUSION

What do these three salient trends in terrorism suggest for the future? First, mainstream terrorists belonging to more traditional ethnic-separatist-nationalist or ideologically motivated groups will largely continue to rely on the same two basic weapons that they have used successfully for more than a century: the gun and the bomb. What changes we see will be more in the realm of clever adaptations or modifications to existing "off-the-shelf" technology (such as the PIRA is so accomplished at adapting) or the continued utilization of readily available, commercially purchased materials that can be fabricated into crude—but lethally effective and damaging—weapons (such as the explosive device used by the World Trade Center bombers). This adherence to a circumscribed set of tactics and limited arsenal of weapons will continue to be dictated by the operational conservatism inherent in the terrorists' organizational imperative to succeed. For this reason, terrorists will always seek to remain just ahead of the counter-terrorism technology curve: sufficiently adaptive to thwart or overcome the countermeasures placed in their path but commensurately modest in their goals (i.e., amount of death and destruction inflicted) to ensure an operation's success. In this respect, rather than attacking a particularly well-protected target-set or attempting high risk/potentially high payoff operations, terrorists will merely search out and exploit hitherto unidentified vulnerabilities and simply adjust their plan of attack and tactical preferences accordingly.

Second, the sophistication of terrorist weapons, especially with bombs and explosive devices, will be in their simplicity. Unlike military ordnance, such as plastic explosive, for example, the materials used in "home-made" bombs are both readily and commercially available: thus they are perfectly legal to possess until actually concocted or assembled into a bomb. These ordinary materials are also far more difficult for authorities to trace or for experts to obtain a "signature" from. For example, the type of explosive used in the 1988 inflight bombing of Pan Am flight 103 was Semtex-H, a plastic explosive manufactured only in Czechoslovakia and sold during the Cold War primarily to other former-Warsaw Pact countries as well as to such well-known state-sponsors of terrorism as Libya, Iran, Iraq, Syria, and North Korea. In comparison, the materials used in the World Trade Center bomb, as previously noted, had no such foreign government "pedigree," were entirely legal to possess and could be traced only to an ordinary New Jersey chemical supply company. Hence, for foreign governments seeking to commission terrorist attacks or use terrorists as surrogate warriors, terrorist use—and growing expertise in the fabrication—of such "home-made" materials into devastatingly lethal explosive devices carries with it both advantage and appeal in arguably enabling the state-sponsor to avoid identification and thereby possibly escape military retaliation or international sanction.

Third, a combination of the resurgence of terrorism motivated by a religious imperative, the proliferation of "amateur" terrorist groups, and the growing sophistication of established, more "professional" groups is undeniably likely to lead to higher levels of lethality and destruction than in the past. The erosion of the self-imposed constraints that have hitherto inhibited the infliction of mass, indiscriminate casualties by terrorists is evident in each of these categories. Indeed, terrorism today increasingly reflects a deadly combination of all three types of terrorist: it is perpetrated by "amateurs," motivated by religious enmity, blind hatred or a mix of individually idiosyncratic motivations, and in some instances exploited or manipulated by terrorist "professionals" and their state-sponsors. In this respect, the availability of relatively sophisticated, off-the-shelf weaponry such as hand-held, precision-guided surface-to-air missiles, or the relative ease with which chemical or biological warfare agents can be manufactured, suggests that terrorists possessing this specific constellation of characteristics would be the most likely and have the least trouble crossing into the domain of either "high-tech" weaponry use or the employment of weapons of mass destruction.[78]

Their trajectory along this path could be facilitated further on the one hand by the diminishing control exercised in some countries of the former Soviet Union over their respective nuclear arsenals and on the other by the apparently growing interest among Russian criminal gangs (i.e., the "Mafiya") in radiological theft.[79] Indeed, the post-Cold War new world order and attendant possibilities and payoffs of independence, sovereignty, and power may entice both new and would-be nations along with the perpetually disenfranchised to embrace terrorism as a solution to, or vehicle for, the realization of their dreams. Today, when old empires and countries are crumbling and new ones are being built, the possession of a nuclear bomb or the development of a chemical or biological warfare capability may thus become increasingly attractive either to new nations seeking to preserve their sovereignty or to would-be nations seeking to attain their independence. One could envision, therefore, terrorists—acting on their own or at the behest of a foreign government—possibly attempting to acquire strategic nuclear material or even their own nuclear device either by theft or through Russian "Mafiya" middlemen.

In sum, there are both new motives and opportunities for terrorists that could portend an even bloodier and more destructive era of violence at the so-called "low end" of the conflict spectrum.

NOTES

[1] Michael J. Mazarr et al., *Military Technical Revolution: A Structural Framework* (Washington, D.C.: Center for Strategic and International Studies, March 1993), p. 15. See also, Antulioi J. Echevarria and John M. Shaw, "The New Military Revolution: Post-Industrial Change," *Parameters* (Winter 1992–93), pp. 70–79.

[2] Wayne K. Maynard, "Spears vs. Rifles: The New Equation of Military Power," *Parameters* (Spring 1993), p. 149.

[3] See, for example, Ibid., pp. 55–56; and, Mazarr et al., *Military Technical Revolution: A Structural Framework*, pp. 16–17.

[4] This act was the opening salvo in the *Narodnaya Volya's* short-lived terrorist campaign against Tsarist rule. See Walter Laqueur, *Terrorism* (London: Weidenfeld and Nicolson, 1977), pp. 11–12.

[5] Ibid., pp. 12–13; and Tom Pat Coogan, *The IRA: A History* (Niwot, CO: Roberts Rhinehart, 1993), p. 12.

[6] Among the more noteworthy exceptions are: reports that in 1979 German Red Army Faction terrorists were being trained at Palestinian camps in Lebanon in the use of bacteriological weapons; the poisoning with mercury that same year of Israeli Jaffa oranges exported to Europe by Palestinian terrorists; a police raid of an RAF safe-house in Paris that uncovered a miniature laboratory containing a culture of Clostridium botulinum, used to create a botulinum toxin, and earlier threats by the group to poison water supplies in 20 Germany towns if three radical lawyers were not permitted to defend an imprisoned RAF member; the 1984 meeting of white supremacists in Mountain Home, Arkansas who, according to a Federal grand jury indictment, plotted—and began to stockpile cyanide with which—to poison the water supplies of Chicago and Washington, D.C.; suspicions that in 1986 terrorists in India may have contemplated

poisoning drinking water tanks there; the letters sent to Western embassies by Tamil guerrillas claiming to have poisoned Sri Lankan tea with potassium cyanide; and the minute traces of cyanide discovered in Chilean grapes exported to the U.S. following threats made by a left-wing Chilean group. Source: The RAND Chronology of International Terrorism. See also, Jeffrey D. Simon, *Terrorists and the Potential Use of Biological Weapons; A Discussion of Possibilities* (Santa Monica, CA: RAND, 1989, R-3771-AFMIC), *passim*. Also, it has been reported that various terrorist groups—including the RAF, Italy's Red Brigades and some Palestinian organizations—reputedly "have recruited microbiologists, purchased bacteriological experimentation equipment and dabbled in sending toxins such as anthrax to potential victims." See "Violence: a buyer's market," *Jane's Defence Weekly*, 12 May 1990, pp. 909–911.

[7]Forty-four percent of all terrorist attacks between 1968/69 involved bombings; 53 percent in the 1970s; 49 percent in the 1980s; and 39.5 percent between 1990/93. Source: The RAND Chronology of International Terrorism.

[8]Eighteen percent both between 1968/69 and during the 1970s; 19 percent in the 1980s; and, 32 percent between 1990/93. Source: The RAND Chronology of International Terrorism.

[9]Hijackings accounted for 33 percent of all terrorist attacks between 1968/69; 7 percent in the 1970s; 4 percent of the incidents in the 1980s; and, 12 percent between 1990/93.

[10]Three percent between 1968/69; 9 percent in the 1970s; 13 percent in the 1980s; and 13 percent between 1990/93.

[11]Kidnappings accounted for just .01 percent of all terrorist attacks between 1968/69; 9 percent in the 1970s; 10 percent in the 1980s; and, 6 percent between 1990/93. There were no barricade and hostage situations recorded between 1968/69; though they accounted for 3 percent of all terrorist incidents during the 1970s; and just 1 percent in both the 1980s and between 1990/93.

[12]This is the dramatic rise between 1990/93 of attacks on installations to 32 percent from the 19 percent recorded during the 1980s.

[13]A bombing in Bessarabia in 1921; a 1925 bombing of a crowded cathedral in Sofia, Bulgaria; a largely unrecorded attempt to poison imprisoned German SS concentration camp guards shortly after World War II; the crash of a hijacked Malaysian passenger plane in 1977; the arson attack at an Abadan movie theater in 1979 that killed more than 400; the 1983 bombing of the U.S. Marine barracks in Lebanon that killed 241; the 1985 inflight bombing of an Air India passenger jet that killed all 328 persons on board; the simultaneous explosions that rocked an ammunition dump in Islamabad, Pakistan in 1988; the bombing of Pan Am flight 103 in 1988 that killed 278 persons; the 1989 inflight bombing of a French UTA flight that killed 171; and the inflight bombing, as in 1989, of a Colombian Avianca aircraft on which 107 persons perished. As terrorism expert Brian Jenkins noted in 1985 of the list upon which the preceding is an expanded version: "Lowering the criterion to 50 deaths produces a dozen or more additional incidents. To get even a meaningful sample, the criterion has to be lowered to 25. This in itself suggests that it is either very hard to kill large numbers of persons or very rarely tried." Brian M. Jenkins, *The Likelihood of Nuclear Terrorism* (Santa Monica, CA: RAND, P-7119, July 1985), p. 7.

[14]Numbers derived from the analysis of incidents recorded in The RAND Chronology of International Terrorism.

[15]Admittedly many "secular" terrorist groups have a strong religious element: the Provisional Irish Republican Army, the various Armenian groups that were active throughout the 1970s and 1980s, and perhaps the Palestine Liberation Organization as well. However, the political aspect is the predominant characteristic of these groups, as evinced by their nationalist or irredentist aims.

[16]For a detailed analysis of these repercussions and indeed Iran's sponsorship of international terrorism see Bruce Hoffman, "Recent Trends and Future Prospects of Iranian Sponsored International Terrorism," in Yonah Alexander (ed.), *Middle Eastern Terrorism: Current Threats and Future Prospects* (New York and Toronto: G.K. Hall, 1994) or the RAND Report (R-3783-USDP, March 1990) in which this analysis was first published.

[17]This form of terrorism has of course occurred throughout history, although in recent decades it has largely been overshadowed by nationalist/separatist or ideologically motivated terrorism. Indeed, as David C. Rapoport points out in his seminal study of what he terms "holy terror," the relationship between terrorism and religion is not new and until the nineteenth century "religion provided the only acceptable justifications for terror." See David C. Rapoport, "Fear and Trembling: Terrorism in Three Religious Traditions," *American Political Science Review*, Vol. 78, No. 3, September 1984, p. 659.

[18]According to The RAND Corporation Chronology of International Terrorism between 1982 and 1992 Shi'a terrorist groups committed 295 terrorist incidents but were responsible for 1134 deaths.

[19]For a more detailed analysis of the phenomena and implications of religious terrorism see Bruce Hoffman, *"Holy Terror": The Implications of Religion Motivated By A Religious Imperative* (Santa Monica, CA: The RAND Corporation, P-6450, 1993).

[20]According to a 1987 Federal grand jury indictment, 14 white supremacists met at a rural so-called "survivalist" compound in Mountain Home, Arkansas during 1984 where they plotted to poison reservoirs in Chicago, Illinois and Washington, D.C. and began stockpiling 30 gallons of cyanide.

[21]In 1987, the "Confederate Hammer Skins," a white supremacist "skinhead" group, planned to place cyanide crystals in the air conditioning unit of a Dallas Jewish synagogue.

[22]In 1984, two groups of Israeli Jewish fanatics plotted to blow up Jerusalem's Dome of the Rock, Islam's third holiest shrine, in hopes of igniting a final battle between Moslems and Jews. Information provided to the author by an American law enforcement official. See also, Thomas L. Friedman, "Jewish Terrorists Freed By Israeli," *New York Times*, December 9, 1984; Grace Halsell, "Why Bobby Brown of Brooklyn wants to blow up Al Aqsa," *Arabia*, August 1984; Martin Merzer, "Justice for all in Israel?" *Miami Herald*, May 17, 1985; and, "Jail Term of Jewish terrorist reduced," *Jerusalem Post* (International Edition), October 12, 1985. The information pertaining to the terrorists' desire to provoke a cataclysmic holy war between Moslems and Jews was verified by an American law enforcement officer, involved with the investigation of Jewish terrorist incidents in the U.S. and knowledgeable of the Jerusalem incident. For a detailed account of both the Temple Mount "plot" and Jewish terrorist attacks on Arab targets in Israel during 1983 and 1984, see Ehud Sprinzak, *The Ascendance of Israel's Radical Right* (New York & Oxford: Oxford University Press, 1991).

[23]In February and March 1993, Muslim terrorists allegedly unleashed a massive bombing campaign in downtown Bombay, India that killed more than 400 persons and injured over 1,000 others.

[24]In 1984, followers of the Bagwhan Shre Rajneesh attempted to poison with salmonella the salad bars of a small Oregon town in hopes of influencing the outcome of a local election. Secular terrorists, it should be noted, have also attempted to poison food supplies, such as the Palestinian terrorists who poisoned Israeli oranges with mercury in 1979; the Tamil guerrillas who claimed to have contaminated Sri Lankan tea shipments in 1986; and Chilean terrorists who claimed to have poisoned grapes exported from that country in 1988.

[25]See, for example, Rapoport, "Fear and Trembling: Terrorism in Three Religious Traditions," p. 674.

[26]Brian M. Jenkins, *The Likelihood Of Nuclear Terrorism* (Santa Monica, CA: RAND, July 1985, P-7119), pp. 4–5.

[27]See, for example, Amir Taheri, *Holy Terror: The Inside Story of Islamic Terrorism* (London: Sphere Books, Ltd., 1987), pp. 7–8.

[28]In the case of the World Trade Center, the four bombers appear to have joined forces based on their attendance at the same place of worship (a Jersey City, New Jersey mosque). In one case as well, family ties were involved (Ibrahim A. Elgabrowny, who—although not charged with the Trade Center bombing specifically—was nonetheless implicated in the crime and has been charged in the subsequent plot to free the bombers, is the cousin of El Sayyid A. Nosair—who was also implicated in the Trade Center bombing, is among the 15 persons indicted in the follow-on plans to obtain the bombers' release, and is already serving a prison sentence in connection with the November 1990 assassination of Rabbi Meir Kahane). See Jim Mcgee and Rachel Stassen-Berger, "5th Suspect Arrested in Bombing," *Washington Post*, 26 March 1993; and, Alison Mitchell, "Fingerprint Evidence Grows In World Trade Center Blast," *New York Times*, 20 May 1993.

[29]For example, the arrests made in connection with the World Trade Center bombing brought to light further evidence that, since 1985, at least two other worshippers of the same Jersey City mosque that two of the convicted bombers attended had been previously implicated in terrorist acts in the New York metropolitan area. The first incident involves the arrest, in December 1985, of Sultan Ibraham El Gawli, an Egyptian-born travel agent, by U.S. Customs Service officers. El Gawli was convicted of attempting to export 150 pounds of C-4 plastic explosives, 100 blasting caps, remote detonators and a 9-mm. silencer-equipped pistol to Palestinian terrorists in Israel and the Occupied Territories. He served 18 months in prison and has since been released. The second, is the assassination of Rabbi Meir Kahane by El Sayyid A. Nosair, who also was born in Egypt and like El-Gawli and the two World Trade Center bombing suspects—Mohammed Salameh, and Nidal Ayyad—worshipped at the Masjid al-Salam Mosque in Jersey City. A search of Nosair's home following his arrest uncovered bomb-making manuals, 1,440 rounds of 7.62 ammunition used in AK-47 assault rifles, manuals on the use of listening devices and explosive traps. See John Kifner, "Kahane Suspect Is a Muslim With a Series of Addresses," *New York Times*, November 7, 1990; Mary B.W. Tabor, "Kahane Suspect Remains Focal Point in Bomb Plots," *New York Times*, 23 May 1993; and John J. Goldman et al., "N.Y. Trial in Rabbi's Death Planted an Explosive Seed," *Los Angeles Times*, 4 July 1993.

[30]Interview with RAND research staff, November 1992.

[31]Federal authorities reported that they had traced nearly $100,000 in funds that had been wired to some of the suspects from abroad, including transfers made from Iran. An additional $8,000 had been transferred into a joint bank account maintained by two of the bombers from Germany. Ralph Blumenthal, "$100,000 From Abroad Is Linked to Suspects in the Trade Center Explosion," *New York Times*, 15 February 1993. According to one of the other convicted bombers, Mahmud Abouhalima, funds had also been routed through the militant Egyptian Islamic group, *Gamat al-Islamiya*, whose spiritual leader is Shiekh Omar Abdel Rahman, now awaiting trial in connection with the June 1993 plot, and by the radical transnational Muslim Brotherhood organization. Additional financing reputedly was provided by and via Iranian businesses and Islamic institutions in Saudi Arabia and Europe. Mary B.W. Tabor, "Lingering Questions on Bombing," *New York Times*, 14 September 1994.

[32]Ralph Blumenthal, "Missing Bombing Case Figure Reported to Be Staying in Iraq," *New York Times*, 10 June 1993.

[33]According to Egyptian officials who interrogated Mahmud Abouhalima, who had fled the U.S. to his native Egypt following the bombing, the plan to attack the Trade Center was conceived in Afghanistan by veterans of the "holy war" waged against Soviet occupation of that country during the 1980s. Two "self-described Iranian intelligence agents" and the two Iraqi fugitives noted above had participated in the planning as well (Mary B.W. Tabor, "Lingering Questions on Bombing," *New York Times*, 14 September 1994). Another of the convicted Trade Center bombers, Ahmad M. Ajaj, a Palestinian, had worked in a Houston pizzeria until he was arrested upon entering the U.S. from Pakistan on 1 September 1992. U.S. Customs agents found in his possession four false passports, six volumes of bomb-making manuals (that, according to prosecutors, contained formulas most likely used to construct the Trade Center bomb), as well as two videotapes demonstrating how to mix chemicals into explosives and how to stage a bombing attack against a U.S. Embassy (Richard Bernstein, "Trade Center Trial Nearing Close As Defense Team Rests Its Case," *New York Times*, 15 February 1993). See also, Mary B.W. Tabor, "Terrorism in New York: Looking for Links," *New York Times*, 27 June 1993; Richard Bernstein, "Trial Deepens the Mysteries Of the Trade Center Blast," *New York Times*, 15 November 1993; Richard Bernstein, "4 Are Convicted In Bombing At The World Trade Center That Killed 6, Stunned U.S.," *New York Times*, 5 March 1994; and, Richard Bernstein, "The Missing Piece," *New York Times*, 5 March 1994.

[34]Richard Bernstein, "Lawyer in Trade Center Blast Case Contends that Client Was a Dupe," *New York Times*, 16 February 1994. See also, Tom Morganthau, "A Terrorist Plot Without a Story," *Newsweek*, 28 February 1994.

[35]The Trade Center bomb was composed of some 1,200 lbs. of "common sulfuric and nitric acids used in dozens of household products and urea used to fertilize lawns." The detonating device was a more complex, and extremely volatile mixture of nitroglycerine enhanced by tanks of compressed hydrogen gases that were designed to increase the force of the blast. Richard Bernstein, "Lingering Questions on Bombing: Powerful Device, Simple Design," *New York Times*, 14 September 1994. See also, Richard Bernstein, "Expert Can't Be Certain of Bomb Contents at Trial," *New York Times*, 21 January 1994; Richard Bernstein, "Nitroglycerin and Shoe at Center of Blast Trial Testimony," *New York Times*, 27 January 1994; Richard Bernstein, "Witness Sums Up Bombing Evidence," *New York Times*, 7 February 1994; Edward Barnes et al., "The $400 Bomb," *Time*, 22 March 1993; and, Tom Morganthau, "A Terrorist Plot Without a Story," *Newsweek*, 28 February 1994.

Similarly, in April 1988 a Japanese Red Army terrorist, Yu Kikumura, was arrested on the New Jersey Turnpike while en route to New York City on a bombing mission. Kikumura's mission was to carry out a bombing attack against a U.S. Navy recruiting station in lower Manhattan on 15 April to commemorate the second anniversary of the 1986 U.S. airstrike against Libya. He is believed to have undertaken this operation at the behest of Libya's Colonel Qaadafi. Between his arrival in the U.S on 14 March and his arrest a month later, Kikumura traveled some 7,000 miles by car from New York to Chicago, through Kentucky, Tennessee, West Virginia, and Pennsylvania purchasing materials for his bomb along the way. Found in his possession were gunpowder, hollowed-out fire extinguishers in which to place the explosive materials and roofing nails as crude anti-personnel weapons. Kikumura was sentenced to 30 years in prison. See Robert Hanley, "Suspected Japanese Terrorist Convicted in Bomb Case in New Jersey," *New York Times*, 29 November 1988; and Business Risks International, *Risk Assessment Weekly*, Vol. 5, No. 29, 22 July 1988.

[36]N.R. Kleinfeld, "Legacy of Tower Explosion: Security Improved, and Lost," *New York Times,* 20 February 1993; and, Richard Bernstein, "Lingering Questions on Bombing: Powerful Device, Simple Design," *New York Times,* 14 September 1994.

[37]See, for example, William M. Carley and Timothy L. O'Brien, "Web of Fear: New Kind of Terrorist, Amateur and Ad Hoc, Worried Authorities," *The Wall Street Journal,* 17 March 1993; and Robin Wright, "New Breed of Terrorist Worries U.S. Officials," *Los Angeles Times,* 27 June 1993

[38]Israeli authorities have noted this same pattern has emerged among terrorists belonging to the *Hamas* organization currently active in the West Bank and Gaza Strip in contrast to the more professional, centrally controlled members of the mainstream Palestine Liberation Organization terrorist groups. As one senior Israeli security official noted of a particularly vicious band of *Hamas* terrorists: they "were a surprisingly unprofessional bunch . . . they had no preliminary training and acted without specific instructions." See Joel Greenberg, "Israel Arrests 4 In Police Death," *New York Times*, 7 June 1993; and Eric Silver, "The Shin Bet's 'Winning' Battle," *The Jewish Journal* (Los Angeles), 11–17 June 1993.

[39]Matthew L. Wald, "Figuring What It Would Take to Take Down a Tower," *New York Times,* 21 March 1993.

[40]*United States of America v Siddig Ibrahim Siddig Ali et al.,* Complaint Violation of 18 U.S.C. §§ 371, 844 (i) 23 June 1993; United States District Court, Southern District of New York, *United States of America v Omar Ahmad Ali Abdel Rahman et al.,* Indictment S3 Cr. 181, 25 August 1993. See also, Robert D. McFadden, "F.B.I. Seizes 8, Citing A Plot To Bomb New York Targets And Kill Political Figures," *New York Times*, 25 June 1993; William C. Rempel and Ronald J. Ostrow, "Bomb Plot Reportedly Hinged on U.N. Link," *Los Angeles Times,* 26 June 1993; Robert D. McFadden, "U.S. Says More Bomb-Plot Suspects Are at Large," *New York Times,* 26 June 1993; Susan Sachs, "Egypt Links Trade Center Blast to International Plot," *Los Angeles Times*, 16 July 1993; Mary B.W. Tabor, "Second Bombing Plot Casts Shadow as First Nears Trial," *New York Times,* 19 July 1993; and Mary B.W. Tabor, "U.S. Plotters Discussed Kidnapping and Hostage Taking," *New York Times,* 5 August 1993.

[41]Jim Newton, "Skinhead Leader Pleads Guilty to Violence, Plot," *Los Angeles Times,* 9 October 1993.

[42]Information provided to the author by one of the arresting police officers, August 1993.

[43]Associated Press, "Blast called part of plot," *Baltimore Sun*, 31 July 1993.

[44]Associated Press, "California Teen-Ager Is Arrested In Bombings Aimed at Minorities," *New York Times*, 8 November 1993. See also, "White Supremacists Investigated in 4 Firebombings in Sacramento," *New York Times*, 6 October 1993.

[45]Quoted in Associated Press, "California Agency Hit In Hate-Crime Attack," *New York Times*, 15 October 1993.

[46]The lethal simplicity of bomb-making was graphically demonstrated in a series of bombings carried out in upstate New York just after Christmas 1993 by an aggrieved boyfriend against his lover's family (who allegedly did not like him). Five persons were killed and two others wounded by booby-trapped plastic toolboxes manufactured by the boyfriend, a 53-year-old ex-convict, con-man and drifter, and a 56-year-old male accomplice. The bomber built prototypes of the explosive devices at his mother's house, before storing the real bombs in his accomplice's hotel room. The explosives used in the bombs had been obtained by the accomplice who was able to purchase a case of dynamite and 50 blasting caps in Kentucky using an alias. Jacques Steinberg, "Motive in Fatal Bombings Is Unclear, Authorities Say," *New York Times*, 31 December 1993; and Associated Press, "Judge Denies Bail for Two Men Suspected in Upstate Bombings," *New York Times*, 4 January 1994.

[47]See, for example, the discussion of Germany's Red Army Faction in Peter Schere, "RAF Concentrates on New Target Spectrum," *Die Welt*, December 18, 1991.

[48]See Frederick Kempe, "Deadly Survivors: The Cold War Is Over But Leftist Terrorists In Germany Fight On," *Wall Street Journal*, December 27, 1991.

[49]Quoted in Adrian Bridge, "German police search for Red Army Faction killers," *The Independent* (London), April 6, 1991.

[50]Kempe, "Deadly Survivors: The Cold War Is Over But Leftist Terrorists In Germany Fight On," *Wall Street Journal*, December 27, 1991.

[51]Quoted in Edward Gorman, "How to stop the IRA," *The Times* (London), January 11, 1992.

[52]Quoted in William E. Schmidt, "Protestant Gunmen Are Stepping Up the Violence in Northern Ireland," *New York Times*, October 29, 1991.

[53]Ibid.

[54]In April and June 1992 the RAF issued communiqués offering to suspend its terrorist campaign provided various conditions—involving mostly the release of imprisoned RAF terrorists—were met by the German government. For a detailed analysis of both the RAF and the two communiqués, see Dennis A. Pluchinsky, "Germany's Red Army Faction: An Obituary," *Studies in Conflict and Terrorism*, Vol. 16, No. 2 (forthcoming).

[55]For a detailed analysis of the Herrhausen attack and the RAF modus operandi in attacking protected persons see Dennis Pluchinsky, "RAF Assassination Herrhausen," in U.S. Department of State, Bureau of Diplomatic Security, *Terrorist Tactics and Security Practices* (Washington, D.C.: U.S. Department of State, DOS 10099, February 1994), pp. 3–12.

[56]Adrian Bridge, "German police search for Red Army Faction killers," *The Independent* (London), April 6, 1991; Stephen Kinzer, "Red Army Faction Is Suspected in German Killing," *New York Times*, April 3, 1991; and, Bernard Adamczewski, "United Germany Divided by Terror," *Conflict International*, Vol. 6, No. 3, p. 1.

[57]Pluchinsky, "RAF Assassination Herrhausen," pp. 3–12.

[58]"Bonn's top terror expert survives bomb," *The Independent* (London), July 28, 1990; and Ian Murray, "German police chief survives car bomb," *The Times* (London), July 28, 1990. As one German federal investigator observed: "When the RAF kills, it usually gets the sort of people who are impossible to replace." Quoted in Kempe, "Deadly Survivors: The Cold War Is Over But Leftist Terrorists In Germany Fight On," *Wall Street Journal*, December 27, 1991.

[59]In a July 1993 shootout at a rural railway station in the former East Germany, RAF terrorist Wolfgang Grams and a member of the crack German GSG-9 counterterrorist unit were shot dead and another RAF terrorist, Birgit Hogefeld, was captured. Until that incident, not one member of the group's "Third Generation" been either killed or apprehended. See Stephen Kinzer, "Germany's Anti-Terror Unit Buffs Its Image," *New York Times*, 18 August 1993; and Stephen Kinzer, "German Terrorist's Death Is Called a Suicide," *New York Times*, 14 January 1994.

[60]David Rose, "Devices reveal IRA know-how," *The Guardian* (London), May 18, 1990.

[61]Michael Smith, "IRA Use of Radar Guns in Bombings Described," *Daily Telegraph* (London), May 20, 1991.

[62]Ibid. See also, David Hearst, "IRA mines gap in army security," *The Guardian* (London), April 10, 1990; David Hearst, "'Human bomb' fails to explode," *The Guardian* (London), November 24, 1990; Jamie Dettmer and Edward Gorman, "Seven dead in IRA 'human' bomb attacks," *The Times* (London), October 25, 1990; Will Bennett, "Terrorists keep changing tactics to elude security forces," *Independent* (London), December 17, 1991.

[63]Ibid.

[64]Nicholas Watt, "IRA's 'Russian roulette' detonator," *The Times* (London), 16 March 1994; and "Photoflash bomb threat to the public," *The Scotsman* (Edinburgh), 16 March 1994

[65]Duncan Campbell, "Video Clue to IRA store blitz: Simplicity of incendiary device makes disruption easy," *The Guardian* (London), 24 December 1991.

[66]James F. Clarity, "On Ulster Border, Grim Days for Grenadier Guards," *New York Times*, 23 February 1994.

[67]Campbell, "Video Clue to IRA store blitz: Simplicity of incendiary device makes disruption easy," 24 December 1991.

[68]William E. Schmidt, "One Dead, 40 Hurt as Blast Rips Central London," *New York Times*, 25 April 1993. See also, William E. Schmidt, "With London Still in Bomb Shock, Major Appoints His New Cabinet," *New York Times*, 12 April 1992; "Delays Seen in London," *New York Times*, 13 April 1992; Peter Rodgers, "City bomb claims may reach £1bn," *The Independent* (London), 14 April 1992; and David Connett, "IRA City bomb was fertilizer," *The Independent* (London), 28 May 1992.

[69]William E. Schmidt, "One Dead, 40 Hurt as Blast Rips Central London," *New York Times*, 25 April 1993; and "Richard W. Stevenson, "I.R.A. Says It Placed Fatal Bomb; London Markets Rush to Reopen," *New York Times*, 26 April 1993.

[70]Roger Highfield, "Explosion could have wrecked city centre," *Daily Telegraph* (London), 13 August 1993.

[71]Ian Graham, "Official: IRA Using 'Bigger, Better' Bombs," *London Press Association*, 23 January 1992.

[72]Edward Gorman, "Bomb disposers mark 21 years in Ulster," *The Times* (London), 7 November 1992.

[73]Graham, "Official: IRA Using 'Bigger, Better' Bombs," 23 January 1992.

[74]Quoted in "Outrage not a reason for inaction," *Manchester Guardian International Edition*, October 21, 1984.

[75]Stewart Tendler, "A crude and lethal weapon to thwart the security forces," *The Times* (London), February 8, 1991; and Will Bennett "Simple bombs improved but lack accuracy," *Independent* (London), February 8, 1991.

[76]"I.R.A. Fires 5 Mortars at a London Airport," *New York Times*, 10 March 1994; John Darnton, "2d Mortar Attack on Heathrow," *New York Times*, 12 March 1994; and John Darnton, "I.R.A. Attacks and Threats Close London Airports," *New York Times*, 14 March 1994.

[77]Aphorism originally coined by Brian Jenkins.

[78]According to a 1990 report, for example, "Canberra bombers, Rapier missiles and tube artillery" can be readily obtained on the international black market. It similarly notes that while terrorist groups as diverse as Germany's Red Army Faction, Italy's Red Brigades and various Palestinian organizations reputedly "have recruited microbiologists, purchased bacteriological experimentation equipment and dabbled in sending toxins such as anthrax to potential victims" they have to date not done so. See "Violence: a buyer's market," *Jane's Defence Weekly*, 12 May 1990, pp. 909–911. See also, "Guns: Buyer's Market," *The Economist*, 16 May 1992.

[79]Michael R. Gordon, "Russian Says Gangs Try to Steal Atom Matter," *New York Times*, 26 May 1994. For detailed descriptions and analyses of the Russian "Mafiya," see Stephen Handelman, "The Russian 'Mafiya'," *Foreign Affairs*, vol. 73, no. 2, March/April 1994, pp. 83–96; and, Seymour Hersh, "The Wild East," *The Atlantic Monthly*, June 1994, pp. 61–86.

Chapter Sixteen

A COMMENT ON THE ZAPATISTA "NETWAR"[*]

David Ronfeldt and Armando Martínez

AN INSURGENCY BECOMES A NETWAR

On New Year's Day 1994, some two to four thousand insurgents of the Zapatista National Liberation Army (EZLN) occupied six towns in Chiapas, declared war on the Mexican government, proclaimed radical demands, and mounted a global media campaign for support and sympathy. Through its star-quality spokesman "Subcomandante Marcos," the EZLN broadcast its declarations through press releases, conferences, and interviews, and invited foreign observers and monitors to Chiapas.

The Mexican government's initial reaction was quite traditional. It ordered army and police forces to suppress the insurrection, and downplayed its size, scope, and sources, in keeping with official denials in 1993 that guerrillas existed in Chiapas. The rebels were characterized as "just 200 individuals with vague demands," and foreign influences from Guatemala and other parts of Central America were blamed. The government tried to project a picture of stability to the world, claiming this was an isolated, local conflict.

But during the few days that the EZLN held ground, it upstaged the government. It called a press conference and issued communiques

[*]David Ronfeldt and Armando Martínez, "Comentarios Sobre la Guerra de Red Zapatista," published in Spanish in Sergio Aguayo Quezada and John Bailey (coords.), *Las Seguridades de México y Estados Unidos en un Momento de Transición*, Mexico City: Siglo Veintiuno Editores, 1997, pp. 320–346. Used by permission. This chapter has been edited since the initial publishing.

to disavow Marxist or other standard ideological leanings. It denied all ties to Central American revolutionaries. It clarified that its roots were indigenous to Mexico, and its demands were national as well as local in scope. It appealed for nation-wide support for its agenda— which included respect for indigenous peoples; a true political democracy, to be achieved through the resignation of President Carlos Salinas de Gortari, the installation of a multi-party transition government, and legitimate and fair elections; and the enactment of social and economic reforms, including repeal of revisions in 1992 to Article 27 of the Constitution governing land tenure, and, by implication, the reversal of NAFTA. In addition, the EZLN called on civil society to engage in a nation-wide struggle for social, economic, and political reforms, but not necessarily by taking up arms. The insurgents denied that they had a utopian blueprint, or had figured out exactly how to resolve Mexico's problems. They also soon denied that the EZLN itself aimed to seize power. Finally, they called on international organizations (notably, the Red Cross) and civil-society actors (notably, human-rights groups) from around the world to come to Chiapas to monitor the conflict.

Meanwhile, the government mobilized the army and other security forces. Within days, the number of troops in Chiapas expanded from two to twelve thousand. Air and ground attacks were mounted in rebel-held areas. Reports of casualties grew into the low hundreds. Reports also grew of human-rights abuses (including by EZLN forces). As the EZLN withdrew into the jungle, army and police units retook the towns, and detained and interrogated people suspected of ties to the Zapatistas. Reports of tortures, executions, and disappearances at the hands of army and police units spread in the media. Meanwhile, government agents reportedly tried to prevent or at least delay some journalists and human-rights monitors from entering the conflict zone; some were accused of meddling in Mexico's internal affairs. This generally hard-line response reflected traditional practices, whether one refers to the suppression of the student-led protest movement in 1968, to operations against urban terrorist and rural guerrilla movements in the 1970s, or to the occasional, less severe policing of violent electoral protests in the 1980s.

The EZLN's insurrection and the government's response aroused dozens if not hundreds of representatives of numerous human-rights, indigenous-rights, and other types of activist nongovernmental organizations (NGOs) to "swarm"—electronically as well as physically—out of the United States, Canada, and elsewhere into Mexico City and Chiapas.[1] There, they linked up with Mexican NGOs to voice sympathy if not solidarity with the EZLN's demands. They began to press nonviolently for a cease-fire, military withdrawal, government negotiations with the EZLN, democratic reforms, and for access by the NGOs to monitor conditions in the affected zones.

This active response by a multitude of NGOs to a distant upheaval—the first major case anywhere—was no anomaly. It built on decades of organizational and technological groundwork, and shows how the global information revolution is affecting the nature of social conflict. The NGOs formed into vast, highly networked, transnational coalitions to wage an information-age *netwar* to constrain the Mexican government and support the EZLN's cause.

The Zapatistas are insurgents. But the widespread argument that they are the world's first post-Communist, postmodern insurgents makes a point that misses a point: Their insurgency is novel; but the dynamics that make it novel—notably, the links to transnational and local NGOs that claim to represent civil society—move the topic out of a classic "insurgency" framework and into an information-age "netwar" framework. Without the influx of NGO activists, starting hours after the insurrection began, the dynamics in Chiapas would probably have deteriorated into a conventional insurgency and counterinsurgency—and the small, poorly equipped EZLN might not have done well. Transnational NGO activism attuned to the information age, not the EZLN insurgency per se, is what changed the framework—but it took Marcos' sense of strategy to make the change work.

THE ADVENT OF NETWAR—ANALYTICAL BACKGROUND

The information revolution is strengthening network forms of organization, and this in turn is altering the nature of conflict. Here we focus on the implications for militant social conflicts that involve activist NGOs—in this case a conflict that bears directly on Mexican security and military issues. We explore the challenges that a social netwar, and its potentially liberalizing political effects, may pose for an authoritarian regime. But first, a brief overview about the nature and advent of netwar.[2]

The term *netwar* refers to conflict (and crime) at societal levels where the protagonists rely on network forms of organization, and related doctrines, strategies, and technologies. The term was coined (Arquilla & Ronfeldt 1993) to focus attention on the likelihood that network-based social conflict and crime, involving measures short of war, would increase and become a major, widespread phenomenon in the decades ahead. Thus the term is both a tool and a prediction. It reflects assessments that the information revolution is about organizational design as well as technological prowess, and that this revolution favors whoever can master the network form.

In an archetypal netwar, the protagonists may consist of diverse, dispersed, often small groups ("nodes") who share a set of ideas and interests, and agree to communicate, coordinate, and act in a highly Internetted ("all-channel") manner.[3] Ideally, this actor (or set of actors) has no single central leadership, headquarters, or command—no precise heart or head that can be targeted. The overall organizational design is flat and non-hierarchical—it is heterarchical, both polycephalous and acephalous. It functions as what might be termed a "panarchy" in that all members subscribe to a common doctrine that reflects their shared ideals and objectives, and guides their strategies. Tactical decisionmaking and operations are decentralized—they may involve mutual consultation, but they emphasize local initiative.

The result is a distinctive, flexible, adaptable design, with strengths for both offense and defense, that differs from traditional designs for conflict (or crime) in which the protagonists prefer hierarchical organizations, doctrines, and strategies, as in efforts to organize centralized mass movements, unions, and eventually parties along Leninist lines. In short, netwar is about Mexico's Zapatistas more than Cuba's Fidelistas, Hamas more than the PLO, and the Asian Triads more than the classic Sicilian Mafia.

In many respects, the archetypal netwar design resembles a "segmented, polycentric, ideologically integrated network" (SPIN). The SPIN concept was proposed by anthropologist Luther Gerlach and sociologist Virginia Hine as a result of their research on U.S. social movements in the 1960s and 1970s:

> By segmentary I mean that it is cellular, composed of many different groups. . . . By polycentric I mean that it has many different leaders or centers of direction. . . . By networked I mean that the segments and the leaders are integrated into reticulated systems or networks through various structural, personal, and ideological ties. Networks are usually unbounded and expanding. . . . This acronym [SPIN] helps us picture this organization as a fluid, dynamic, expanding one, spinning out into mainstream society (Gerlach 1987: 115, based on Gerlach & Hine 1970).

The SPIN concept is a precursor of the netwar concept. Indeed, Gerlach and Hine anticipated two decades ago many points about network forms of organization that are just now coming into vogue.[4]

Actors across the spectrums of conflict and crime around the world—including terrorists, fundamentalists, ethnonationalists, militant single-issue groups, and criminal organizations—are evolving in the direction of netwar . Some netwar proponents still fit standard notions of low-intensity conflict (LIC), operations-other-than-war (OOTW), and crime. But other actors do not fit standard notions: The spectrum increasingly includes a new transnational generation of militants who espouse information-age ideologies that are just now taking shape, and in which identities and loyalties may shift from the nation-state to the level of "global civil society." And new netwar actors—e.g., anarchistic or nihilistic leagues of computer "hackers"—are appearing.

Some actors may be inherently antagonistic to U.S. and other nations' interests (e.g., terrorist organizations), but others may not (e.g., NGO activists). Many variations are possible. In any case, the spread of netwar will add to the challenges facing the "nation-state" as its roles and structures, its sovereignty and authority, get transformed by information-age trends.

In a *social* netwar, where a network of activist NGOs may challenge a government or rival NGOs in some public issue area, the "battle" is mainly about "information"[5]—about who knows what, when, where, and why. Netwar generally involves seeking "topsight" (total intelligence) about one's own and the opponent's situation, while keeping that opponent in the dark about oneself and about its own situation. Netwar means affecting what the opponent knows, or thinks it knows, not only about its challenger but also about itself and the world around it. Among other things, this may mean trying to shape images, beliefs, and attitudes in the social milieu in which both are operating. Thus a social netwar is likely to involve battles for public opinion and for media access and coverage, at local and international levels. It may revolve around propaganda campaigns and psychological warfare, not only to inform but also to disinform, deceive, and manipulate. In other words, netwar is much more about a doctrinal leader like Subcomandante Marcos than a lone, wild computer hacker like Kevin Mitnick.

A social netwar may be progressive or regressive, violent or nonviolent, mass or sectarian, public or covert, threatening or promising for a society—it all depends. The United States is fraught with divisive social netwars. This is seen in the behavior of militant activists battling over abortion, the environment, immigration, education, gun control, and myriad other issues. The militias and related right-wing extremist groups, especially those that subscribe to a doctrine known as "leaderless resistance," seem designed for waging violent netwar (see Stern 1996).

Mexico too is being affected by netwar. The paramount example appears in the decentralized, dispersed cooperation among the numerous Mexican and transnational NGO activists who support or otherwise sympathize with the EZLN, and who aim to affect Mexico's policies on human rights, political democracy, and other major reform issues.

EMERGENCE, EVOLUTION, AND EFFECTS OF THE ZAPATISTA NETWAR

In retrospect, Mexico and Chiapas were ripe for social netwar in the early 1990s. Mexico as a whole—its society, state, and economy—was (and still is) in flux and in a deep, difficult transition. Ingrained clannish and hierarchical patterns of behavior continued to rule the Mexican system. But that system was also opening up, in part because Presidents Miguel de la Madrid and Carlos Salinas de Gortari resolved to liberalize Mexico's economy and, to a much lesser degree, its polity. Thus Mexico began adapting, with great difficulty, to modern market principles. At the same time, independent civil-society actors, including a range of Mexican NGOs, began to gain strength, and to find openings to challenge the state for lagging at democratization and neglecting social welfare issues.

Chiapas, once an isolated backwater, was becoming awash with outside forces. It was still characterized by tremendous gaps between the wealthy and the impoverished, by *caciquismo*, and by the plight of indigenous peoples who wanted their lives improved and their cultures respected. Many analysts have observed that neoliberal economic reforms, especially those instituted by the Salinas administration, made matters much worse for many *indigenas*, setting the stage for the formation and rise of the EZLN.[6]

The economics are important; but, more to our point here, Chiapas was increasingly subjected to all manner of transnational influences. During the 1980s and early 1990s, it became a crossroads for NGO activists, Catholic liberation-theology priests and Protestant evangelists, Guatemalan migrants and refugees, guerrillas coming and going from Central America, and criminals trafficking in weapons and narcotics. This exposure to transnational forces was stronger and more distinctive in Chiapas than in two other nearby states—Oaxaca and Guerrero—that were often thought to be likely locales for guerrilla insurgencies (and had been in the past). And this helps explain why Chiapas, and not another state, gave rise to an insurgency that became a netwar.

To understand fully why a social netwar emerged in Mexico, the analyst must also look outside—at trends in North and Central America. Activist NGOs are not a new phenomenon.[7] But their numbers, diversity, and strength have increased greatly around the world since the 1970s. What is new, mainly since the 1980s, is the development of organizational and technological networks for Internetting the NGOs. Their ability to mobilize in support of the Zapatistas stemmed from a confluence of infrastructure-building efforts at regional, global, and local levels.

Around Mexico, these efforts took hold in the 1970s and 1980s, when numerous, small NGOs got involved in the conflicts in Central America. Their activities varied from providing humanitarian relief and monitoring human-rights abuses, to providing alternative sources of information to the U.S. and international media and opposing U.S. policy. The key network-building organization was the innovative Committee in Solidarity with the People of El Salvador (CISPES), whose affiliates included a range of peace, human-rights, and church organizations. Activists who had access to the insurgents in El Salvador could sometimes get news of a human-rights abuse into the media faster than U.S. ambassadors or State Department officers could learn about it from their own sources. Indeed, the spread of fax machines and e-mail systems enabled the NGOs to move news items out of El Salvador and into the media, to inundate U.S. government in-boxes with protests and petitions, and to challenge what the NGOs regarded as disinformation. CISPES was a seminal effort to build a transnational network to conduct a netwar.[8]

After the conflicts in El Salvador and Nicaragua receded as front-burner issues, the proposal for NAFTA suddenly appeared. This reanimated the NGO networks that had been taking shape and provided the catalyst for a new round of infrastructure-building. In addition to holding numerous face-to-face conferences, NGOs across North America—mainly from Canada and the United States, but also with nascent Mexican participation[9]—communicated with increasing ease via faxes, e-mail, and computer conferencing systems like Peacenet. The participants included militants who had worked with CISPES, but the coalitions broadened to include center-left moderates who were concerned with North American labor and environmental issues. In the end, the diverse sets of participants coalesced around a single objective: to oppose fast-track approval of NAFTA by the U.S. Congress.

This new round of NGO activism did not prevent fast-track approval of NAFTA in 1993. Yet, the NGOs' trinational, pan-issue networks got better organized than ever before. This laid a foundation for the NGO mobilization that followed the EZLN insurrection in January 1994—just a few months after the NAFTA-related activism had subsided, and once again the infrastructure was sitting there, with more potential than ever, waiting to be reactivated.

Another current of activity involving thousands of NGOs during the early 1990s—a series of UN-sponsored conferences and parallel NGO forums on a range of global issues—also strengthened the activists' infrastructure, albeit indirectly regarding Chiapas. In particular, the UN Conference on the Environment and Development—the "Earth Summit"—held in Rio de Janeiro in 1992 put NGOs on the map as global activists and provided them with experience at formulating their own policy positions and pressuring government officials to heed them.

Meanwhile during the 1980s and early 1990s, the number and diversity of local NGOs and related movements and organizations grew rapidly inside Mexico, including with regard to issues involving Chiapas.[10] Thus, by the time of the EZLN's insurrection, the transnationally networked NGOs had many local counterparts with which to link up in Mexico City, San Cristobal de Las Casas, and other locales. And as NGO representatives rushed into Chiapas in early 1994, new organizations were established—like the Coalition of Non-Governmental Organizations for Peace (CONPAZ), which is associated with the Archdiocese of San Cristobal de las Casas—to assist with communication and coordination.

Once the netwar got under way, two types of NGOs were active in issues regarding Chiapas, and both were significant: (a) the issue-oriented NGOs and (b) the infrastructure-building and network-facilitating NGOs. The former consist of NGOs whose identities and missions revolve around a specific issue area, such as human rights, indigenous rights, peace, the environment, or trade and development. Numerous NGOs were active in each such area. To give an example, during 1994 Chiapas engaged the attention of the following NGOs concerned with the rights of indigenous peoples: transnational NGOs with no national identity—the Continental Indian Commission (CONIC), the Independent Indian Front (FIPI), and the International Indigenous Treaty Council (IITC); U.S.-based NGOs—the South and Mesoamerican Indian Information Center (SAIIC); Canadian NGOs—Okanaga Nation; and Mexican NGOs (or quasi-NGOs), such as the State Coalition of Indigenous and Campesino Organizations (CEOIC), the Coordinadora de Organizaciones en Lucha del Pueblo Maya para su Liberacion (COLPUMALI)) and the Organizacion Indigena de los Altos de Chiapas (ORIACH). Many of these have links to each other—for example, COLPUMALI and ORIACH are sister organizations within FIPI-Mexico, and FIPI is a member of CONIC. This is only a partial listing, and for only one issue area—a full listing for all issue areas would run for pages.

Acting in synergy with them are the second type of organization: the infrastructure-building NGOs. These are not defined by specific issues; rather, they assist other NGOs and activists, no matter what the issue is. They specialize in facilitating networking, notably with regard to communications services; the organization of demonstrations, caravans, and other militant events; and through education and exchange activities.

Of these organizations, one of the most important is the expanding, transnational Association for Progressive Communications (APC), a network of networks that has many affiliates, such as the U.S.-based Peacenet and Conflictnet, and the nascent LaNeta in Mexico. All are attached or have access to the Internet. The APC and its affiliates amount to a worldwide computer-conferencing and e-mail system for activist NGOs. This system enables them to consult; coordinate; disseminate news and other information; and put pressure on governments, including by mounting fax-writing campaigns.[11] The APC itself did not have activists in Mexico because of Chiapas, but other important infrastructure-building NGOs did, including: from the United States, Global Exchange; the Canadian networking NGO, Action Canada; and Mexico's CONPAZ. Again, cooperative connections exist among all these organizations.

Were Subcomandante Marcos or other EZLN leaders and sympathizers aware of this potential? Did they anticipate that activist NGOs could—and would—swarm to support them? We have no evidence of this. Nonetheless, conditions in Chiapas were already well known to many activists, despite official Mexican denials that problems were growing there. Amnesty International and Americas Watch had each published a similar report of human-rights violations in the area, the former in 1986, the latter in 1991. Minnesota Advocates for Human Rights, and the World Policy Institute, jointly published a report in August 1993 about soldiers beating and torturing a group of Mayan Indians in May 1993. The Jesuit Refugee Service, long active in the area to deal with Guatemalan refugee issues, had become increasingly alarmed about the treatment of Chiapas' Indians and issued an "Urgent Call to the International Community" in August 1993. Curiously, it made demands almost identical to those fielded a few months later by many Mexican and transnational NGOs in January 1994.

Whatever the full story, as the NGOs turned their attention to Mexico, the EZLN proved entirely receptive, and the artful Subcomandante Marcos clarified that a new model of conflict and transformation was emerging and being tested. He and his cohorts claimed to eschew Leninist, Maoist, and Fidelista models that meant an army or party must seize power as the vanguard of socialist revolution. Instead, the EZLN's agenda (e.g., political democracy, local autonomy) sounded more reformist than revolutionary (see Castañeda, 1995). Marcos denied that the EZLN wanted to occupy the seats of power (though it aimed to change the state) and proclaimed a key role for civil-society actors, like the NGOs, in the EZLN's vision of the conflict:

> We do not want state power. It is civil society that must transform Mexico—we are only a small part of that civil society, the armed part—our role is to be the guarantors of the political space that civil society needs.

In this doctrine, the mobilization of civil society—not the expansion of the insurgents' army—is the key strategic element. Indeed, once the fighting ended in January and negotiations got under way, Marcos would emphasize in March 1994 the expectation that

> war will be exorcised by the pressure put on by civil society throughout the country to fulfill the agreements. . . . The problem will arise if civil society becomes exhausted, tired, collapses; in that case every thing will be left loose and then they will jump on us through the military route.

Ever since, Marcos and other EZLN leaders have worked ceaselessly to keep foreign journalists, intellectuals, and activists focused on, and present in, the conflict zone. They have used "information operations" to deter and counteract the government's military operations. They have endeavored to dominate the "information space" (e.g., in the media, via faxes, and on the Internet) in ways that compensate for their inability to hold much physical territory.[12] International conferences that the EZLN convened in April and August 1996 to criticize the detrimental effects of neoliberalism—they were attended, or supported from a distance, by various U.S. and French luminaries of the left—are recent examples of this. Meanwhile, the activists have had many opportunities to claim that their efforts have helped prevent violence by all sides to the conflict. A symbolic highlight was their participation in one of the "Three Rings of Peace" that surrounded the initial government-EZLN negotiations in early 1994.

NGO activists sense that they are molding a new strategy of conflict based on networking (see Cleaver 1994a, 1994b). For many of them, nonviolent but compelling action is crucial; and to this end, they need rapid, far-reaching communications, as well as freedom of information and travel. Much of their netwar has been waged through the media—both traditional media like newspapers, magazines, and television, and new media like faxes, e-mail and computer billboard and conferencing systems. (Old-fashioned face-to-face and telephone communications remain important too.) Since word of the Zapatista insurrection first spread via the new media, activists have made heavy use of the Internet (and adjuncts like Peacenet and Mexico's nascent LaNeta, which came on-line in 1993) to spread information (and disinformation), mobilize their forces, and coordinate actions. Indeed, there are quite a few World Wide Web (WWW) "pages" on the Internet that convey the EZLN's views and make Marcos' statements available. Thus, in April 1995, Mexico's Foreign Minister Jose Angel Gurria was observant to comment that

> Chiapas . . . is a place where there has not been a shot fired in the last fifteen months. . . . The shots lasted ten days, and ever since the war has been a war of ink, of written word, a war on the Internet.

All sides have waged public-relations battles to affect perceptions of each other. Many NGO activists worked to ensure that the insurrection became an international media event, and that the EZLN and its ideals were portrayed favorably. NGO representatives struggled ceaselessly through fax-writing campaigns, public meetings, and other measures to make Mexican officials aware of their presence, and to put them on notice to attend to selected issues. The fax numbers of Mexican and U.S. government officials were often posted in Internet newsgroups and mailing lists—if a number became inoperable, a new one was soon discovered and posted.

This transnational social netwar has been partially effective. It helped impel two Mexican presidents to halt military operations and turn to political dialogue and negotiations: first, President Salinas in January 1994, a week after the insurrection erupted and the Mexican army took to the field in Chiapas; and next, President Zedillo in

February 1995, four days after he ordered the army to expand its presence in the conflict zone and to arrest the EZLN's leaders. Both turns of events surprised government officials, army officers, and the public at large. There are other explanations for both presidents' decisions —e.g., that worries about a backlash among foreign creditors and investors, or about damage to Mexico's image in the media, or about infighting among Mexico's leaders, led Salinas and Zedillo to halt military operations and agree to dialogue and negotiations. Our explanation, however, is that the transnational netwar was a major contributing factor, including in riling up media attention and alarming foreign investors. And this activism was made possible by networking capabilities that have emerged only recently as a result of the information revolution.

Beyond such effects on army operations, the netwar reignited public debates about Mexico's national identity and policy directions. It added to the pressures on Mexico's leaders to enact political and electoral reforms, to make the political system more transparent, accountable, and democratic, to take human rights more seriously, to accept the growth of civil society, and to heed the needs of indigenous peoples. Some analysts claim that political and electoral reforms have proceeded faster since the Zapatista movement than in years, if not decades, past. A case can also be made that the netwar contributed to the perceptions of crisis in late 1994, and then the huge peso devaluation that alarmed many foreign creditors and investors. Yet, inside Mexico, where many activists shifted their focus in mid 1994 from the conflict in Chiapas to aspire to bring about the downfall of the Institutional Revolutionary Party (PRI) in the national elections, the perceptions of crisis led Mexican citizens to vote overwhelmingly for the PRI. (The netwar may also be obliging the army to adopt institutional changes, but that remains undocumented except for the army's somewhat increased attention to public affairs, relations with NGOs, and human-rights issues).

In short, the NGOs' activism altered the dynamics of the confrontation in Chiapas and helped convert a military confrontation into a political one. It assured that what might once have remained a provincial event became a national and international event. It affected the context for decisionmaking in Mexico City; it helped impel the government to dialogue and negotiate with the EZLN; it helped keep the military at bay; and it put unusual pressures on the political system to become more democratic. In such respects, this netwar has not been bad for Mexico (nor has it jeopardized U.S. interests). However, in the short run, it has heightened uncertainty in Mexico and abroad about Mexico's stability and future prospects. At least, these are our preliminary impressions; in truth, much work remains to be done before scholars can be certain how social netwar has affected Mexico.

THE FUTURE OF NETWAR—AND COUNTERNETWAR—IN MEXICO

Mexico's transition to a new type of system that has greater evolutionary capacity is, and will continue, causing many minor and some major disturbances. At times, this may mean labor strikes; electoral protests; student demonstrations; protests by environmental, human-rights, and other activists and dissidents; and shoot-outs involving drug traffickers. At times, the scene may be a major city, but often it may be a provincial location where *caciquismo* remains entrenched. The list of possibilities is long and diverse. Presumably, most disturbances will prove manageable; they will challenge but not jeopardize the stability or the transformability of the Mexican system.

The serious risk for Mexico is not an old-fashioned civil war or another great revolution—these seem unlikely. The greater risk is a plethora of social and *criminal* netwars. Indeed, Mexico's security in the information age may turn out to be a function of netwars of all varieties. The challenge for Mexico will be to cope with these netwars in ways that ensure both the stability and transformability of the Mexican system. Both dynamics—stability and transformability—are at stake.

Here we have focused on the Zapatista social netwar. But Mexico is also the scene of criminal netwar actors, with the Internetted drug cartels being the major culprits.[13] Transnational criminal organizations (TCOs) are a growing threat around the world, largely because they are so adept at taking advantage of global and regional interconnections. As specialist Phil Williams points out:

> TCOs are diverse in structure, outlook and membership. What they have in common is that they are highly mobile and adaptable and

are able to operate across national borders with great ease. . . . They are able to do this partly because of the conditions identified above and partly because of their emphasis on networks rather than formal organizations (Williams 1994; also see Sterling 1994).

Mexico's drug-trafficking organizations have evolved aggressively in this direction since the late 1980s, in league with Colombian cartels.

Neither social nor criminal netwar actors seem likely to make Mexico ungovernable. That might occur, perhaps, if they all reinforced each other, directly or indirectly, under conditions where the country's economic recession deepened, the federal government lost credibility and legitimacy, and elite infighting threw the "revolutionary family" and its *camarillas* (political clans) into chaos. But, in many respects, Mexico seems to be in somewhat better shape now than it was in the 1980s, when some analysts (e.g., Castañeda 1986; Latell 1986) proposed that collapse seemed imminent.

To ensure that netwars do not adversely affect Mexico's stability or transformability, the government will have to improve its ability to wage *counternetwar*—not to mention its ability to maintain a credible pace of reforms. The prospects for netwar—and for counternetwar—revolve around a small string of propositions about networks versus hierarchies (Arquilla & Ronfeldt 1993, 1996b): Accordingly, the information revolution favors and strengthens actors who use network forms of organization and makes life difficult for large traditional hierarchies. In general, it can be said that hierarchies have difficulty fighting networks. It take networks to fight networks—a hierarchy may have to form its own networks to prevail against networked adversaries. Whoever masters the network form, organizationally, doctrinally, and technologically, will gain major advantages in the information age.

By implication, a government may need great agility and adaptability to cope with netwar-related threats and challenges. Waging counternetwar may require the development of highly effective interagency mechanisms and operations, since the interagency arena is where networking may best occur in the government world. Improvements at civil-military, inter-service, and intra-military networking are also implied.

How well do these propositions apply in Mexico's case? It confirms that hierarchies—such as the Mexican government, the army, and the PRI—do have difficulties fighting a networked actor (or set of actors). The case may also show that the government has had to organize its own interagency and other intergovernmental networks to prevail against the pro-Zapatista networks. While the government and the army initially responded in a traditional, heavy-handed manner to the EZLN's insurrection, they have apparently not responded idly or unthinkingly since then to this seminal case of social netwar. However, research is lacking at this time to substantiate how they have adapted, and what they have learned.

The Zapatista netwar and the government's efforts at counternetwar are far from ended. By now (May 1996), it seems clear that the EZLN's putative power and influence depend on its political support from the activist world, that the EZLN poses a symbolic more than a real threat of violence, and that its military capabilities are very limited. Meanwhile, beginning in late 1994 and extending into 1996, the army has slowly but surely reasserted a dominant presence in the conflict zone. It has gained the upper hand from a military standpoint, showing that the EZLN is a weak "paper tiger" (even though it has proven to be a successful "Internet tiger" from an information-warfare perspective).

Meanwhile, the military's image has not fared well during most of this netwar (see Wager & Schulz 1995). The army evidently resented having its field operations halted in January 1994, and again in February 1995. It also resented being blamed retrospectively for intelligence failures after the insurrection broke out, and then for human-rights abuses when it tried to restore order in a war zone. At times, the army found itself confounded, on the one hand, by NGO activists (and willing journalists) who mounted media campaigns to impugn its image, and on the other hand, by occasional indecisiveness and confusion on the part of civilian leaders. Meanwhile, the army learned in 1994 that it was not accustomed to dealing with civil-society actors clamoring for access and information in a conflict zone. Indeed, since a social netwar is not a traditional insurgency, part of the challenge is to recognize (as has probably occurred) that military roles rarely figure large in counternetwar against social actors.

Dealing with civil-society NGOs—whether as allies, as in humanitarian and disaster relief operations, or as antagonists, as in some cases of pro-democracy, human-rights, and environmental movements—is a new frontier for government officials around the world. In the period ahead in Mexico, the government may at times be tempted to repress local NGOs and restrict freedom of information, in the name of security. But that would ignore the positive roles that NGOs are generally likely to play in the information age. Will there instead be temptations to constrain just the transnational NGOs and their representatives from abroad? To some extent, Mexican agents have episodically attempted that in Chiapas.[14] However, without a transnational presence, presumably of responsible NGOs (as well as corporations), Mexico would probably not make a strong effort to evolve into a democratic, market-oriented society.

In addition, the advent of netwar may induce a rethinking of aspects of Mexico's security concept. For at least a decade, it has been defined in "integral" terms—it has emphasized a combination of political, social, economic, and military dimensions, with the military accepting, if not insisting, that the military dimensions be subordinate to the civilian ones. In 1980, Secretary of National Defense General Felix Galvan Lopez gave the concept a valuable tone when he remarked, "I understand by national security the maintenance of social, economic, and political *equilibrium*, guaranteed by the armed forces."[15] The Zapatista netwar has called critical attention to the fact that Mexico is adapting, with difficulty, to political and electoral reforms, the growth of a market system and the rise of civil society. If Mexico can continue to adapt successfully, it will establish a new "equilibrium," and this will surely prompt some reevaluation of what is meant by "national security."

There is another conceptual implication, this time for the civil-society activists. Important roles will be played—the balance between stability and instability, between advance and regression, may even be tipped—by the new generation of civil-society activists who are organized in national networks and, in some cases, have connections to transnational networks that include activists from the United States, Canada, and other countries. These activist NGO networks can have—and some are indeed having—a positive influence on Mexico's prospects for stable, democratic development. Such groups as the Civic Alliance have pressured the electoral and party systems to adopt reforms and become more open and competitive. But there is a conundrum. If the progressive left is to continue to be the cutting edge of "cybernet" activism—not only in Mexico but all across North America—it must help find a way to make peace with the market system, and to acknowledge its benefits for the evolution of complex social systems. Indeed, the success of that system is a key reason why the activist networks emerged first in North America and Western Europe, and not in another part of the world.

Meanwhile, the interests and needs continue to grow for all manner of civil-society NGOs and other nongovernmental actors to develop new ways to work with government actors all across North America. As Thorup (1995) observes, the positive result of the empowerment of civil society may be that "nations" rather than just "states" can be better represented in policymaking processes for building secure, progressive communities.

Ultimately, then, netwar and counternetwar in Mexico become a game not solely of power, but also of vision and responsibility.

IMPLICATIONS BEYOND MEXICO

This case indicates that social netwar can be waged effectively where a society is open, or slowly beginning to open up; where divisive social issues are on people's minds; and where outside activist NGOs and their networks have local counterparts with which to link. Such a society should be in a region where the activists have a well-developed communications infrastructure at their disposal for purposes of rapid consultation and mobilization. Because of such conditions, Mexico provides a much more susceptible environment for social netwar than do more closed societies (e.g., Burma, Cuba, and Iran) that are not yet fully connected to the Internet.

The Mexican case instructs that both issue-oriented and infrastructure-building NGOs are important to the development of a social netwar. It also instructs that activist swarming best occurs where the NGOs are internetted and collaborate in ways that exhibit "collective diversity" and "coordinated anarchy." The paradoxical tenor of these phrases is intentional. The NGOs often have diverse, specialized interests; thus, any issue can be rapidly singled out and attacked by at least elements of the swarm. At the same time, many NGOs can act, and see themselves acting, as part of a collectivity, because they share convergent ideological and political ideals, and similar concepts about nonviolent strategy and tactics. Although some NGOs may be more active and influential than others, the collectivity has no central leadership or command structure; it is multi-headed, impossible to decapitate. Their behavior may look uncontrolled, even anarchic at times. But in fact it is shaped by extensive consultation and coordination, made feasible by rapid communications among the parties to the swarm.[16]

Furthermore, the Mexican case hints at the kind of doctrine and strategy that can make social netwar effective for transnational NGOs. The following appear to be two important elements: (1) Make civil society the vanguard—work to build a "global civil society" and link it to local NGOs; (2) make "information" and "information operations" the decisive weapon—demand freedom of access and information, capture media attention, and use all kinds of information and communications technologies. Where this is feasible, *netwarriors* may be able to put strong pressure on state and market actors, without aspiring to seize power through violence and force of arms.

Netwar forms of organization and related doctrines, strategies, tactics, and communications infrastructures are still emerging—they are far from being fully defined and developed. Yet, it is already clear that a social netwar can disrupt a slowly liberalizing authoritarian regime, put it (and its military) on the defensive, and, to some extent, help spur new steps toward democratization. Social netwar is an agent of change that may have both positive and negative effects. Mexico is one of the first countries to experience this, but it is far from the last.

BIBLIOGRAPHY

Arquilla, John, and David Ronfeldt, "Cyberwar is Coming!" *Comparative Strategy*, 12/2: 141–165 (Summer 1993). Available as RAND reprint RP-223.

———, "Information, Power, and Grand Strategy: In Athena's Camp," in Stuart Schwartzstein (ed.), *Information and National Security*,

Washington, D.C.: Center for International and Strategic Studies, 1996a.

——, *The Advent of Netwar*, MR-678-OSD, RAND, Santa Monica, CA, 1996b.

Castañeda, Jorge G., "Mexico at the Brink," *Foreign Affairs*, Winter 1986, pp. 287–303.

——, *The Mexican Shock: Its Meaning for the United States*, New York: The New Press, 1995.

Cleaver, Harry, "The Chiapas Uprising and the Future of Class Struggle in the New World Order," for RIFF-RAFF, Padova, Italy, February 1994a (on-line at gopher://lanic.utexas.edu:70/11/la/Mexico/).

——, "Introduction," in Editorial Collective, *¡Zapatistas! Documents of the New Mexican Revolution*, Brooklyn: Autonomedia, 1994b (on-line at gopher://lanic.utexas.edu:70/11/la/Mexico/Zapatistas/).

Collier, George, with Elizabeth Lowery Quaratiello, *BASTA! Land and the Zapatista Rebellion in Chiapas*, A Food First Book, Institute for Food and Development Policy, Oakland, CA, 1994.

Frederick, Howard, "Computer Networks and the Emergence of Global Civil Society," in Linda M. Harasim (ed.), *Global Networks: Computers and International Communication*, The MIT Press, Cambridge, MA, 1993, pp. 283–295.

Gerlach, Luther P., "Protest Movements and the Construction of Risk," in B. B. Johnson and V. T. Covello (eds.), *The Social and Cultural Construction of Risk*, Boston: D. Reidel Pub. Co., 1987, pp. 103–145.

Gerlach, Luther P., and Virginia Hine, *People, Power, Change: Movements of Social Transformation*, New York: The Bobbs-Merrill Co., Inc., 1970.

Gossen, Gary H., "Comments on the Zapatista Movement," *Cultural Survival Quarterly*, Vol. 18, No. 1, Spring 1994, pp. 19–21.

Harvey, Neil, "Rebellion in Chiapas: Rural Reforms, Campesino Radicalism, and the Limits to Salinismo", *Transformation of Rural Mexico*, Number 5, Ejido Research Project, Center for U.S.-Mexican Studies, La Jolla, CA, 1994, pp. 1–43

Hernandez, Luis, "The Chiapas Uprising," *Transformation of Rural Mexico*, Number 5, Ejido Research Project, Center for U.S.-Mexican Studies, La Jolla, CA, 1994, pp. 44–56.

Kelly, Kevin, *Out of Control: The Rise of Neo-Biological Civilization*, A William Patrick Book, Addison-Wesley Publishing Company, New York 1994.

Latell, Brian, *Mexico at the Crossroads: The Many Crises of the Political System*, The Hoover Institution, Essays in Public Policy No. 6, Stanford University, Stanford, CA, June 16, 1986.

Nash, June, "The Reassertion of Indigenous Identity: Mayan Responses to State Intervention in Chiapas," *Latin American Research Review*, Vol. 30, No. 3, 1995, pp. 7–41.

Ronfeldt, David (ed.), *The Modern Mexican Military: A Reassessment*, Monograph Series, #15, Center for U.S.-Mexican Studies, University of California at San Diego, 1984.

Ronfeldt, David, "Cyberocracy Is Coming," *The Information Society*, Vol. 8, No. 4, 1992, pp. 243–296. Available as RAND reprint RP-222.

———, *Institutions, Markets, and Networks: A Framework About the Evolution of Societies*, Santa Monica: RAND, DRU-590-FF, December 1993.

———, "Batallas mexicanas en Internet, *NEXOS*, #216, Diciembre 1995, pp. 47–51.

———, *Tribes, Institutions, Markets, Networks—A Framework About Societal Evolution*, Santa Monica: RAND, P-7967, 1996.

Ronfeldt, David, and Peter Reuter, *Quest for Integrity: The Mexican-U.S. Drug Issue in the 1980s*, RAND, N-3266, 1992. Excerpts published in the *Journal of Interamerican Studies and World Affairs*, Fall 1992, pp. 89–153.

Ronfeldt, David, and Cathryn Thorup, "North America in the Era of Citizen Networks: State, Society, and Security," Santa Monica, CA: RAND, P-7945, 1995.

Ross, John, *Rebellion from the Roots: Indian Uprising in Chiapas,* Common Courage Press, Monroe, ME, 1995.

Sterling, Claire, *Thieves' World: The Threat of the New Global Network of Organized Crime,* New York: Simon & Schuster, 1994.

Stern, Kenneth, *A Force upon the Plain: The American Militia Movement and the Politics of Hate,* New York: Simon & Schuster, 1996.

Szafranski, Colonel Richard, "Neo-Cortical Warfare? The Acme of Skill," *Military Review,* November 1994, pp. 41–55.

———, "A Theory of Information Warfare: Preparing for 2020," *Airpower Journal,* Spring 1995, pp. 56–65.

Tello Díaz, Carlos, *La Rebelión de las Cañadas,* Mexico City: Cal y Arena, 1995.

Thorup, Cathryn L., "Building Community Through Participation: The Role of Non-Governmental Actors in the Summit of the Americas," in Robin Rosenberg and Steven Stein (eds.), *Advancing the Miami Process: Civil Society and the Summit of the Americas,* North-South Center Press, Coral Gables, FL, 1995, pp. xiii–xxvi.

Wager, Steven J., and Donald Schulz, "The Awakening: The Zapatista Revolt and Its Implications for Civil-Military Relations and the Future of Mexico," *Journal of Interamerican Studies and World Affairs,* Vol. 37, No. 1, Spring 1995, pp. 1–42.

Williams, Phil, "Transnational Criminal Organizations and International Security," *Survival,* Vol. 36, No. 1, Spring 1994, pp. 96–113.

NOTES

[1] Kelly (1994) provides an introduction to the concept of swarm networks and to the dynamics that may govern their behavior. We are using the term in this analytical sense.

[2] Ideas and observations about the advent of netwar stem from work done jointly by John Arquilla and David Ronfeldt. See Arquilla & Ronfeldt (1993, 1996b).

[3]In making such statements, we refer mainly to the "all-channel" multiorganizational type of network; the "chain" and "hub" (or "star") types are less pertinent to our discussion. But whatever the type of organization, the strongest will be based on distinctive doctrines, and be layered atop advanced telecommunications networks and traditional networks of personal and social ties. See Arquilla & Ronfeldt (1996b).

[4]In all fairness, it should be pointed out that Gerlach and Hine might be loath to see their concept related to netwar, since they were more concerned about global governance than conflict.

[5]For a discussion of the term *information,* see Arquilla & Ronfeldt (1996a).

[6]Sources consulted include: Collier (1994), Gossen (1994), Harvey (1994), Hernandez (1994), Nash (1995), Ross (1994), and Tello (1995).

[7]As used here, the term NGO includes many non-profit organizations (NPOs), private voluntary organizations (PVOs), and grass-roots organizations (GROs). The term does not include government-organized NGOs (GONGOs), or international governmental organizations (IGOs).

[8] Evidently in an effort to emulate this experience, a Committee in Solidarity with the People of Mexico has been recently formed.

[9]The leading example of Mexican participation was the Mexican Network Against Free Trade (Red Mexicana de Accion Frente al Libre Comercio—RMALC), a coordinating center for a number of individual Mexican NGOs.

[10]This is an important part of the story that we neglect here in order to keep the focus on the transnational actors.

[11]For background, see Frederick (1993).

[12]Colleague John Arquilla has helped generate these kinds of ideas and observations. Readers interested in them should also consult Szafranski (1994, 1995).

[13]For some discussion of how criminal elites may fit into Mexico's *camarilla* (political clan) system, see Ronfeldt & Reuter (1992).

[14]A case can be made that the Mexican government has actually been quite tolerant of this transnational activist presence. What other government would be so tolerant of such an unusual, heavy influx in response to an internal security problem?

[15]From an article in the magazine *Proceso,* September 22, 1980, p. 6 (translation; italics added).

[16]See Kelly (1994).

Part IV

EMERGING PARADIGMS

Chapter Seventeen

NEOCORTICAL WARFARE? THE ACME OF SKILL[*]

Richard Szafranski

This is the key point: the effective employment of air and space power has to do not so much with airplanes and missiles and engineering as with thinking and attitude and imagination.[1]

—General Merrill A. McPeak, Chief of Staff, United States Air Force

If General McPeak is correct, and I believe he is, the opposite proposition should also be true. That is, if our country employs air and space power thoughtlessly or unimaginatively, this power will be less effective or even disastrously impotent. To help avoid such grave risks in the future, the thesis of this article takes us at least one stop beyond. McPeak's already powerful insight. This article argues that military power resides in the domain of the mind and the will; the provinces of choice, "thinking," valuing or "attitude," and insight or "imagination." Further, it argues that, because of this, military power can increase in effectiveness even as it decreases in violence. As a consequence, the article necessarily infers that air and space operations help establish the essential preconditions for meeting national security political objectives without force, or what I call *neocortical warfare.*

Some warnings: to me, "super" power is the capability that emerges from superior minds—the mental dimension and superior values,

---

[*]Richard Szafranski, "Neocortical Warfare? The Acme of Skill," *Military Review*, November 1994, pp. 41–55. U.S. Army Command and General Staff College. Used by permission.

the moral domain. As you will see, military power, like air and space power, also takes on a different meaning. Consequently, "employment" ultimately attaches more importance to communicating with other minds than to targeting objects. Even so, I do *not* argue that we should beat our swords into fiber-optic cables or satellites. Rather, I argue that we transform our sword into a viciously sharp stiletto and that we develop, refine and continually employ other, and ultimately more useful, weapons to influence adversary choices. Last, and most important, this is a work in progress. As such, the conclusions reached are both tentative and speculative, hopefully providing some signposts to un- or under- explored areas.

WHAT WE THINK WE KNOW

In their grand synthesis, *The Lessons of History*, Will and Ariel Durant assert that "the laws of biology are the fundamental lessons of history." They describe nations or states as biological organisms, human organisms, ourselves multiplied, our good and evil natures writ large.[2] Some states have the same flaws as humans—avarice, pugnacity, pride, the selfish desire for resources and mastery—and, like humans, compete and engage in misbehavior. Historically, war has been a necessity, the biological nation's way of eating, and a recurring form of misbehavior to the Durants.[3] Analogies suggesting that states are like biological organisms are convenient, simplistic and, of course, flawed. States or nations are organized groups of people. States do not act—compete, misbehave, conduct raids, execute air strikes, wage war—it is people within the group who sanction or compel these, or who act in the name of others. Hence, to Martin van Creveld, "War . . . is a social activity resting upon some kind of organization."[4]

Society is and segmented societies are the workplace of warfare, and social change is both a cause and outcome of human conflict. People are the essential element in all of this. John G. Stoessinger's study of seven wars concludes that the "human element," including "personalities and misperceptions," constitutes the final and critical link in the chain of events that culminates in war.[5] Just as there are "disorganized personalities" among individuals, there may also be, in a lay person's terms, crazy leaders and, because of them, crazy states. War, aggressive or defensive, occurs as a consequence of human choice, of "conation," of will. Whether the people willing or choosing are sick or healthy, pugnacious or passive, war is a distinctly human activity.

Politics is also a human activity. "Politics" is the pursuit and exercise of power, and "power" is the ability to influence people who otherwise might not choose to be influenced.[6] To many, this ability to influence is seen as coercive, so much so that the "other means" Clausewitz describes as being added to the process of political dialogue in war are most often *violent* means. Consequently, among all the mammalian species on the planet, ours is the only one that engages in deliberate, intentional interspecific killing.[7] Today war is understood as violent conflict, an activity that resides at the high end of the spectrum of coercion. Warfare or war emerges when humans and human organizations choose to oppose their wills, to employ destructive means in an organized way. The object of war is, quite simply, to force or encourage the enemy to make what you assert is a better choice, or to choose what *you* desire the enemy to choose. Said another way, the object of war is to subdue the hostile will of the enemy. We cannot meet the immediate objective of war until or unless we subdue hostile will.

So far, we are on familiar ground. It is not difficult to understand "destructive means." They are the more or less brute force mechanisms and methods employed to imperil the life of biological organisms (individuals) and organic entities (states, nation-states, nations or groups of people) either directly or indirectly. We have no difficulty understanding that living organisms and organic entities are organized as systems. It also may be unremarkable to conclude that the methodical orchestration and application of destructive means against these systems are superior to disorderly or less orderly ones.[8]

It is, however, somewhat more difficult to realize that, if the object of war truly is *to subdue hostile will* or *to make the opponent comply with our will*, then we must consider enemies not just as systems, but as organisms with will. Likewise, if weapons are *means used to coerce an adversary's will*, then even our understanding of weapons must go beyond things, implements or tools. Yet, we have concentrated our attention on the *concrete* means and *material* ways used to subdue hostile will's *host*, rather than on the nature of will itself. We have been unimaginative. As a result, we have been approaching the study of the art of war from a dangerously wrongheaded perspective. This is forgivable and, until recently, a flaw we could afford. It is also a flaw we can choose, or will, to correct.

It is pardonable because the notion of will is an abstruse one. Will is as difficult to understand as concepts of mind, consciousness, cognition and creativity. Ideas of psyche, spirit, transcendence and soul are even more contentious, more difficult to comprehend. Because we believe that the entity "will" is existential and brain-centered, we concentrate our attention on the existence of brains, not on the nature of will. In so doing we may have mistakenly identified the craft of war as the *art* of war. By that I mean that our science of war is not so much the study of subduing will as it is the study of devising and applying progressively more elaborate means and methods for destroying brains. Destroy enough brains, or the correct brains, our studies seem to encourage us, and "will" necessarily dies along with the organism. Thus, we meet the *real* object of war—subduing will— if we meet it at all, indirectly by the application of physical force.

At least three shortcomings to this approach are emerging. First, killing appliances and destruction machines are usually and necessarily expensive. The more ambitious the objectives of this apparatus, the greater the expense. Every penny spent to acquire the ability to destroy is a penny that cannot be spent to build. Second, in the absence of any clear and present threat to national survival that possession of such tools can reasonably be expected to counter, our citizens and their elected representatives have advocated other plans for our pennies. Last, the intellectual energy consumed by devising newer and better ways to kill and destroy distracts us from the real object of war: subduing hostile will. Lopping the limbs off an enemy's body, or even precisely excising muscles from it, undoubtedly sends a message to the enemy's brain. Might there not be other ways to communicate with hostile brains?

The architect of the 1929 "strategy of the indirect approach," B. H. Liddell Hart, advocated a more economical approach to meeting the aim of war. Yet, even he saw the "dislocation of the enemy's psychological and physical balance" only as "the vital prelude to a successful attempt" to overthrow the enemy. Psychological dislocation occurred when one gained a favorable "strategic situation," but even then, it took a "strategic operation" to meet the military aim. Hart insisted that a strategic operation was not a "battle," but accepted that a battle might be necessary to achieve a decision.[9] If the object of war is to subdue hostile will, perhaps we would be wiser to approach the indirect approach more directly.

What if we viewed war not as the application of physical *force*, but as the quest for metaphysical *control?* What if we pursued the possibility that war might have as much or more to do with the idea of willpower and non-fighting than it does with the idea of physical power and fighting? Remember, it was Sun Tzu's assessment that "To subdue the enemy *without fighting* is the acme of skill." It follows, then, that *not* to subdue the enemy at all, or to subdue the enemy by fighting, would fall far short of the acme of skill. If, for example, Operation *Desert Storm* was a success, that is, it subdued hostile will, it is difficult to explain Saddam Hussein's continuing willful behavior. Viewed in this light, we did not even approach the acme of skill in the "last ancient war."[10]

We suspect that it might be valuable to pursue ways to subdue an enemy without fighting. It might bear fruit. After all, physical fighting is costly, with the winner and the loser both paying great expenses in blood and treasure. The hostile will attacked by physical means in one war often emerges later and with greater hostility in a new war. Moreover, the principal theorists or artists of warfare— Krishna of the *Bhagavad-Gita*, Sun Tzu, the Khan, Machiavelli, Lenin, Liddell Hart, Mao, John Boyd—and many of the masters of the craft of war—Napoleon, Clausewitz, Guderian, Patton, Slim, Magsaysay, John Warden—emphasize the importance of the moral, the mental and the will in conflicts.[11] So important are these cerebral, metaphysical things that Eliot A. Cohen and John Gooch hint that much military failure might have its genesis in the "psychological cripples" that rise to general and flag rank in the military hierarchy.[12]

To continue our inquiry we must accept that will *is* existential and brain-centered, and enter the human brain.

According to Paul McLean, the human brain is actually three brains in one, a "triune" brain. Each brain is specialized in function and interconnected with the other brains. The *reptilian* brain comprises the brain stem, the midbrain and the basal ganglia. It controls the reticular activating system, breathing and heart rate. With only the reptilian brain, we would be cold-blooded reptiles.[13]   The *limbic* brain surrounds the reptilian one. The limbic is a paleomammalian, or early mammal brain. According to Robert Ornstein and Richard F. Thompson, it is the source and regulator of the basic mammalian survival activities: feeding, fighting, fleeing and sexual reproduction. Ned Hermann describes its contributions as controlling the autonomic nervous system and its involuntary responses. The limbic registers rewards, punishments and emotions. It maintains a hierarchy of dominance and submission within the species and between the organism and the environment. The limbic drives sexual courtship, "follow-the-leader" rituals and mass migrations. The limbic also conditions behaviors such as ganging up on the weak and the new, defending territory, hunting, bonding, nesting, greeting, flocking and playing.[14]   With only the limbic and its embedded reptilian brain, we would be warm-blooded mammals.

The capstone of the brain, as we know it today, is the *neocortex* or neo-mammalian brain. The neocortex comprises 80 percent of total brain matter. It enables us to think, organize, remember, perceive, speak, choose, create, imagine and cope with or adapt to novelty. Within the neocortex 180 billion neurons or nerve cells interact without any physical connection. The possibilities for interconnections between neurons in one human brain are "greater than the number of atoms in the universe," according to Ornstein.[15]

The triune brain also appears to have specialized hemispheres. The left hemisphere of the neocortex or the left brain, is the site of cognition. It processes words and numbers and organizes data in logical and linear sequences. Unlike the left brain, the right brain is more adept at registering the images, patterns, sounds and movement discernible in phenomenological perceptions or sensory input. Using holistic processing, the right hemisphere of the brain conceptualizes, hypothesizes and maintains an intuitive sense of the whole.[16]   Because Western oral and written language and scientific notation are linear and sequential, the left brain dominates these activities. Because creation is the product of illumination or insight, pattern recognition and new or hypothetical conceptual constructs, its source may be the right brain.

If F.S.C. Northrop is correct in *The Meeting of East and West,* "culture" conditions some of the operations of the left brain. Specifically, atmospheric and linear perspective in classical Western art and the syntax of Romance languages both work together to channel cognition in ways that are different from the ways that the "undifferentiated aesthetic continuum" of Eastern art and the "syntax" of the Asian word-picture or ideogram condition the thinking of those in the East.[17] There is no "foreground, background or vanishing point" in Eastern art. There are no longer any pictographs in the Western alphabet. (Although the iconography of comic books and animated cartoons and the pixels of video are beginning to replace writing in our country. Someday these may constitute the new pictographs of an increasingly less literate United States.)

Some of these cultural variations in cognition and elucidation are clear when one compares the German version or an English translation of *On War* with any one of the many English translations of *The Art of War,* the *Canon Law* of Roman Catholicism with the "doctrines" of *The Tae Te Ching,* or the negative space in a Japanese watercolor with the meaning-filled space in Da Vinci's "Last Supper." These differences merely are interesting at first glance, but upon reflection, understanding them is important to meeting the aim of subduing hostile will without fighting.

None of this should suggest that the left brain is inferior to the right brain. Nor does it pretend to understand either how the brain functions or how or when "mind" or "will" emerged from the brain structure. Each brain and then the triune brain probably evolved, or were naturally selected, in response to some massive, catastrophic environmental change or "bifurcation point," in Ilya Prigogine's terms.[18] Perhaps the limbic evolved in response to a climatic change. The neo-mammalian might have evolved in response to competition for survival with other species.

The neocortical brain, unlike the other two brains, affords the opportunity to adapt in ways that sustain what might appear to be *un*natural selection to some—the creativity that generates genetic engineering, artificial hearts and joints, organ transplants, and so forth. Indeed, the very highly developed neocortex, the brain that elegantly integrates both neocortical hemispheres, may even exercise some control over the sympathetic and parasympathetic responses of the central nervous system.[19]   Because of the interconnections (the *corpus callosum*, the *Hippocampal commissure*, the *anterior commissure*) among all three brains and both hemispheres, the human brain structure truly makes us "the paragon of animals" on this planet.

Does it? Recall that ours is the only mammalian species that organizes for warfare and intentionally kills its own members. Do we do this because the reptilian brain forces us to kill for biological survival?

Do we kill because the limbic compels us to play, to hunt, to learn whether ours is the role of domination or submission? Perhaps we kill because our neocortex calculates that killing accrues some logical or hypothetical advantage. We kill, according to Desmond Morris, because we have artificial material weapons more potent than "tooth and nail."   According to him, we developed physical weapons "primarily as a means of defense against other species and for the killing of prey."[20]

Once we had weapons, they were readily available for uses beyond defense against other species and hunting for food. Among these other uses, weapons provide a means to express anger or serious displeasure, to coerce, to make some risks and consequences mortal. We chose, for whatever reason, to invent weapons. We *choose* to use weapons and engage in warfare. One reason is because battles and warfighting are satisfying in a paleomammalian and a neo-mammalian way. They provide what John Keegan calls "moral consolations," including "the thrill of comradeship, the excitements of the chase, the exhilarations of surprise, deception and the *ruse de guerre*, the exaltations of success, the sheer fun of prankish irresponsibility.[21] Some of these are limbic stuff; bonding, ganging up and all the chemical or hormonal effects of the massive activation of the sympathetic nervous system that occur in response to anger and fear. Others—the exhilaration of surprise and the fun of violating norms—are more neocortical. It is "war alone," writes Martin van Creveld, "that both permits and demands the commitment of *all* man's [*sic*] faculties, the highest as well as the lowest."[22]

Passion alone can sustain war, but logic alone cannot stop fighting. Little is simple for the paragon. Our left brain science, for example, is dependent on the illogic, or perhaps different logic, of the right brain.

Things essential to science cannot be proven by science: the principle of causality, theories founded on the logical error of affirming the consequent, acceptance of the principle of limited variability and the unverifiable principle of verifiability, for example.[23] That "deterrence theory," firmly grounded in the *post hoc* fallacy, survived and eventually confounded the now defunct Soviet experiment shows the value of coupling imagination, illogic and logic.

The complex interactions among brains, hemispheres and environments continue. In teaching us what we cannot know or predict, Heisenberg's uncertainty principle, Godel's proof, the Einstein-Podolsky-Rosen effect, Bell's theorem, Aspect's experiment and the recent exploratory sorties into the world of chaos and nonlinearity illuminate some of the capability of the aroused neocortex.[24] Alan Beyerchen's reframing and rendering of *On War* in defense of Clausewitz in "Clausewitz, Nonlinearity, and the Unpredictability of War" takes what appears to be a new reality—nonlinearity—and applies it to an old paradox: war.[25] Likewise, Alvin and Heidi Toffler's *Third Wave* and John Arquilla and David Ronfeldt's discussion of netwar and cyberwar are excellent works that suggest fertile new directions in war and "anti-war."[26] Many of the bits and pieces suggestive of a theory of neocortical warfare seem to be falling in place.

WHAT MAY FOLLOW FROM WHAT WE THINK WE KNOW

The triune brain suggests an analogy. Might there not also be three approaches to warfare? The reptilian approach is animalistic fighting. The socially organized paleomammalian approach relies on hunting and on ganging up to make the kill. The neo-mammalian approach requires greater organization, integration and the conceptualization of time and space. It relies on calculations, logic and sequential thinking to make the kill. This third approach also allows more discriminating application of brute force.

Even so, the neo-mammalian approach also may have within it left or right hemisphere-dominant approaches. Campaign planning, with its current emphasis on the linear processes of a system (like the military's current application of "total quality management"), predominantly is a left hemisphere-dominant approach. In this scheme, the enemy is a system, an assemblage of production nodes controlled by an organic brain. The campaign applies physical force to these nodes, as targets, using a presumed calculus that assesses effects on the whole system. A right brain-dominant approach, on the other hand, might suggest reframing conflict as warfare against minds and envisioning weapons as any means used to change the enemy's will.

As the right and left brains interact, the enemy is not seen as an inorganic system with multiple centers of gravity, but as other neocortical organisms. Neocortical warfare is warfare that strives to *control* or *shape* the behavior of enemy organisms, but without destroying the organisms. It does this by *influencing*, even to the point of regulating, the consciousness, perceptions and will of the adversary's leadership: the enemy's neocortical system. In simple ways, neocortical warfare attempts to penetrate adversaries' recurring and simultaneous cycles of "observation, orientation, decision and action."[27]

In complex ways, it strives to present the adversary's leaders—its collective brain—with perceptions, sensory and cognitive data designed to result in a narrow and controlled (or an overwhelmingly large and disorienting) range of calculations and evaluations. The product of these evaluations and calculations are adversary choices that correspond to our desired choices and the outcomes we desire. Influencing leaders to not fight is paramount. Warfare is "organized" fighting. It becomes less organized, more nonlinear, more chaotic and unpredictable once it begins. Until battle (physical fighting) begins, the leaders can stop it more easily. In very complex ways, the neocortical approach to warfare influences the adversary leaders' perceptions of patterns and images, and shapes insights, imaginings and nightmares. This is all brought about without physical violence. It is all designed to reorganize and redefine phenomenological designators to lead the enemy to choose not to fight. In neocortical warfare, enemy minds are the *Schwerpunkt* and armed military capability the *Nebenpunkte* (a term coined by John Boyd to mean "anything that is not the *Schwerpunkt*").

That nonfighting is the attribute and aim of neocortical warfare does not mean that this warfare is passive or inactive. It requires considerable effort, resources and skill—the acme of skill—to subdue an enemy without fighting. The aim is not merely to avoid battles. The aim is to *cause the enemy to choose not to fight by exercising reflexive influence*, almost parasympathetic control, over products of the adversary's neocortex. In actively enjoining the minds of adversaries to not fight, we must understand the adversary's culture, world view and the representational systems the adversary recognizes, values and uses to communicate intent. We must understand the adversary's verbal and nonverbal language. We might use tools similar to Richard Bandler and John Grinder's "neuro linguistic programming" to understand how the adversary receives, processes and organizes auditory, visual and kinesthetic perceptions.[28]

Knowing what the adversary values and using the adversary's own representational systems allows us to correlate values, to communicate with the minds of enemies in the verbal and nonverbal language of the enemy. The objective is to shape the enemy's impressions as well as the enemy's initiatives and responses, pacing the enemy through the cycle of observation, orientation, decision and action. We attain the acme of skill when we meet our objectives and the adversary chooses the nonfighting alternative voluntarily, even unaware that our decisions and our behavior led to the reframing and the redecision reached.

THE ACME OF SKILL: REINVENTING WARFARE AND WEAPONS

The single most important change that has occurred on the planet since the advent of the neocortex is crowding and overpopulation.[29] Birth control and abortion are seen by some as a biological necessity even though constituting "aggression against zygotes."[30] These measures have delayed the gloomy predictions of The Club of Rome and Donella H. and Dennis L. Meadows in *The Limits to Growth*.[31] Nonetheless, population doubling times, depletion or appropriation of the net primary product (using vegetable mass), the scarcity of nonrenewable resources and the restraints on individual freedom that lack of space and food may ultimately impose are all working together to make this *potentially* a small, dangerous planet. The collapse of the nation-state, the return to tribalism, a new Dark Age of fundamentalism or the "clash of civilizations" all loom as possibilities.[32] Even so, the global instability caused by the collapse of the Soviet empire, the proliferation of nuclear weapons and ballistic missile technologies, the rise in self-determination, or the cross-currents of persistent "waves" may pose less of a danger than our own lack of intellectual agility, our own lack of imagination, myopic vision and bad choices.

The co-evolving, co-dependent organisms on the planet, and its present nations, nation-states and groups, need to choose success strategies or failure strategies to manage conflict. In our own country, we may have reached the point where failure strategies include such concepts as armed forces sized to fight two wars, two "major regional contingencies," nearly simultaneously.[33] Whether we imagine they are "win, hold, win" or "win, win" wars, regional wars can be nothing but "lose, lose." As an alternative to unimaginatively planning to fail, perhaps we could put our imaginations and our entire neocortex to better use by pursuing neocortical warfare.

We already have awareness of neocortical warfare and some skill in waging neocortical warfare against adversaries and friends alike. Politicians necessarily are experts in this type of warfare. Hitler started one over six decades ago. Eric Voegelin observed in 1939 that, lacking "a profound and intimate knowledge of German cultural history and of the history of the German language in the last two centuries," non-Germans failed to appreciate the significance of Hitler's call for "neo-pagan" Germanic *Lebensraum.* As a consequence, non-Germans were effectively "screened" from Hitler's real expansionist motives.[34] The *Blitz* itself used nightmare and terror to achieve its general effect even while relying on arms to attain its more specific aims.

In our own country, President John F. Kennedy's decision to ignore the more hateful of Khruschev's two letters during the crisis over Soviet missiles in Cuba, for example, was critical in reframing the adversary's perceptions. Likewise, our country's large military budgets were once the product of *hypotheses* of threats and dangers, *images* of falling dominoes, *visions* of iron curtains and space shields, *theories* of nuclear deterrence, *metaphors* of escalation ladders and *nightmares* of an evil empire. Smaller budgets and smaller military forces follow in the wake of a *hypothetical* new world order, *theories* of defense conversion and *visions* of nuclear winter. These observations are small tests. What would it take to move us closer to a theory?

Analyze past and present conflicts of all kinds and in all arenas—politics, warfare, business, sports, and so forth. Look for apparently anomalous events where small, willful, fluid, fast-responding or mentally powerful forces overcame larger or more physically powerful ones. Scrutinize cases where physical attacks were unable to subdue will, such as at Stalingrad, Britain's "finest hour," Dresden, Vietnam, Afghanistan, the *intifadah*. Examine cases where nonviolence, mental attacks, nightmares, illusions, character assassinations or smear campaigns subdued hostile will, brought the mighty low or rendered the powerful impotent. Whenever the weak overcomes the strong using the power of mind or will, evidence of neocortical warfare exists.

We might then look forward and hypothesize that neocortical warfare has four characteristics. First, it recognizes that competition, conflict and conflict resolutions are permanent features of the human condition. The target of all human conflict, the battleground of all conflict resolution, is the human mind. In reframing all conflict as one form of warfare or another, neocortical warfare rejects the notion that warfare is an aberration. It accepts that conflict will never end and that we must invest resources to win its endless engagements. The Cold War may be over, but *cold* war must be the goal. Hence, military forces must envision themselves not just as "armed forces," but as elements of larger "national security forces" in neocortical warfare. Security, much to our chagrin, does not emerge from arms, but arms arise from insecurity. Conceptions of security or insecurity exist in the mind.

Second, a theory would accept that adversaries will wage—are waging even as you read this—neocortical warfare against us. (That China is quiet, for example, may not mean that we are not engaged in a conflict with China.) Neocortical warfare uses language, images and information to assault the mind, hurt morale and change the will. It is prosecuted against our weaknesses or uses our strengths to weaken us in unexpected and imaginative ways. That being the case, we have less room for the unimaginative, the mentally weak, or whatever Cohen and Gooch mean by the psychologically crippled among our leaders. Leaders are critical nodes, the targets of neocortical warfare, and they must be prepared for the adversary's assaults.

Third, we should devote the weight of effort and more resources to the deliberate and continual pursuit of nonviolent influence over the adversary. The object is to understand the enemy well enough to condition or determine the choices the adversary makes. Using the adversary's lexicon, syntax and representational systems allows the neocortical warrior to lead the adversary through the cycle of observation, orientation, decision and action. Mastery is the result.

Fourth, lean, fast-reacting, violent, almost "limbic" forces—the stiletto held in readiness to coerce with force of arms—must be created or preserved to support neocortical warfare. In some cases we may have to introduce shock, surprise and terror in the adversary's external world, through what Arquilla and Ronfeldt call "the exemplary use of our military capabilities," to fuel the nightmares and disorientation sought in the enemy's internal world.[35] We should not and cannot foreclose on the possibility that small, tremendously violent demonstrations will be necessary in the future. Even so, we also should expect that evolving constraints will cause us to characterize all future lethal military operations as "special operations" and that the principal object of these operations will be "psychological warfare."

As a consequence, all armed military forces must be or become elite forces. "Elite" means people and forces selected, organized, trained and equipped to rapidly adapt to, and even shape, changing or unforeseen circumstances. Although armed forces must operate in all media, air and space forces will occupy a critical position in the future national security force. Air and space provide speed, the medium and the means of almost instantaneously communicating images and language, the reach to quickly span the globe.

How would we "operationalize" neocortical warfare? What are the national security force structure implications? What do we need to transform the abstract into the concrete? First, acquisition of the most robust, most comprehensive intelligence-gathering and information-disseminating apparatus in the world is essential. In neocortical warfare, *understanding* is power. This apparatus would be a better integrated intelligence and information agency or a network of agencies. It would combine the best capabilities and analysts of the Central Intelligence Agency, the National Security Agency and the Defense Intelligence Agency at a level below the senior interagency group. This new network would work in partnership with our foreign service, private sector field activities and deployed training and educational entities. It is an urgent requirement to resist any attempt to reduce our global collection and analysis capability. If we are to subdue enemies without fighting, we need more field agents, more intelligence-collection capabilities and systems to support the work of intelligence analysts.

We cannot hope to influence or condition what we do not understand. What are the values of the Serbs or the Iraqis? How do the Hmong or the Kurds organize sensory data? What are the differences in the way Albanians or Macedonians approach negotiations? What is the Achilles' heel of a nation or non-state organized and operated like a business corporation? Inevitably, greater reliance on information systems equates to greater reliance on the use of space. Space systems provide a panoramic "view" of the earth across the electromagnetic spectrum. The technological exploitation of space can allow us to see, hear and sense the adversary, to recognize patterns and changes, to ask the right questions, to send the right messages quickly.

We must exploit the medium of space. Vice Admiral Jerry O. Tuttle's space and electronic warfare *Sonata* envisions one architecture that might begin to prepare us to fight prolonged neocortical warfare.[36] Other architectures aimed at providing national security in a broader sense will follow. Even so, we must appreciate that we cannot hope to control what we cannot see, hear or understand. (*Ninjitsu*, the art of invisibility, may be the best countermeasure to an adversary's space or intelligence capabilities.)

Second, neocortical warfare requires a better integrated, joint civilian and military national security control force with both armed and unarmed elements. It must be capable of sustained, cooperative and non-lethal presence in every area we have interests. Elements of it must also be capable of prompt, noncooperative and violent combined arms intervention in denied or hostile areas *vital* to our interests. The lethal elements of this force, although small by today's standards, must be morally, mentally and technologically superior to the elite guards that surround the leaders of the groups of the world. Space-based capabilities could provide these forces with information and vision. Air forces, as a category of force and not necessarily as a military department-specific force, provide the reach and a large share of the "touch" necessary for this armed portion of the force.

The non-lethal elements of our national security force deploy democratic values and behaviors within the context of local cultures; cultivate networks, markets and partnerships; teach basic skills; and penetrate the perceptions of the target country. The lethal elements would be organized as multifunctional or cross-functional teams or networks. These teams would understand the target country as a system of subsystems; know precisely when, where and how to intervene for maximum effect, and could execute overt or covert violent operations. This force will understand that, in the lexicon of the "quality" movement, the enemy is the "customer" and the enemy's segmented society is the "workplace" of neocortical warfare. Since adversaries may abound, global reach will be an important requirement in the world that is emerging.

Yet, in the future, "access" and "presence" are more likely to be the invitation to brandish our values and share our culture, than brandish our weapons and share our antiquated vision of military superpower. A revitalized and revised version of the Peace Corps and a reframing of the vision of the Army's Special Forces are required. Those who resist the assignment of nonmilitary or nonlethal missions to the uniformed men and women who serve our country should thoughtfully reconsider our country's full range of national security needs in the future.

Third, and finally, those lethal forces we possess should be small. The active, standing component should be inadequate for any great mischief not supported by our Congress and the citizens it represents. If our Congress wants us to sortie out in large numbers to "win, win" or to "win, hold, win," then our Congress must consider the wisdom of appropriating the money to raise and support such an army. Today we may be too closely wed to military hierarchies (instead of networks) and a nation of command and control (instead of guidance and monitoring in accordance with the *Abseits*) that may disencentivize authentic empowerment.[37] In the worst case, these command and control hierarchies may be sizing and shaping our huge forces as an unintended enticement to fail, making us unintentionally vulnerable to those who might lure us inadvertently into fighting the limbic warfare that willingness to become expert in neo-cortical warfare might avoid.

We should consider the possibility that today our Armed Forces may be less "armed" than they are fat with unarmed housekeepers: the administrators of contracts, records, regulations and red tape, those devoted to the maintenance of our camps, bases, factories, ware-houses and hospitals. Fat can restrict the blood going to the neocor-tex, impede thinking and blur vision. Disorientation and confusion often result. Disorientation could lead to clinging to the past in the vain hope that size alone will allow the imposition of the past's struc-tures on the present and the future.

In the view of the electorate, the idea of "forts" inside the United States, for example, perhaps is now as antiquated as the notions of "commissaries" and "military family housing." The dangers of the frontier no longer pose a threat to the homesteaders in Kansas, Ne-braska and Wyoming. Grocery stores and dwellings for military members abound in all but the most remote areas of our country.[38]

Confusion could cause us to vindicate our gross size by seeing or ex-pecting threats and dangers as the stimuli demanding our response. There are threats and dangers, but they reside more in hostile will than in hostile means. Means are impotent without the will to em-ploy them to some purpose. If we are disoriented and confused, what we may fail to see is the reality of a reflexive world wherein *we* might be the very stimulus that causes the response we subse-quently categorize as threat or danger. In any case, whatever forces emerge in the future, in this country or elsewhere, should not be de-pendent on nuclear arms. It will be increasingly difficult for our country to assert the danger of weapons of mass destruction while possessing, as we do today, great numbers of them. Would it not also be increasingly difficult for other countries to pursue or preserve theirs after we and our true friends have set most of ours aside?

The American people who sustain America's national security forces want security in return for the investment of their children and their taxes. At the acme of skill, this security arises not from subduing en-emies by fighting but subduing them without fighting. Yet, sadly, we do not appear to be pursuing the acme of skill. Physics and medicine race ahead. "Quantum connectedness" theorizes that matter and energy may be organized by instantaneous connectedness or faster-than-light communications.[39] Medicine learns that the brain intervenes to regulate the health of the body, bolster the immune system, produce endorphins to fight pain or enhance performance.[40]

Yet, the craft of war lags behind. Are we satisfied only to sift through these discoveries looking for novel, more efficient weapons and ways to kill and destroy? We choose to think and act this way, artless and unimaginative as it is. We might choose to overcome the limitations of today's weapons. Range and speed limited weapons in the past. Today space allows us to overcome the limitation of range, and cyberwar, electronic warfare and radio-electronic combat begin to change our understanding of weapons. The immediate challenge in physical weaponry, we think, is to operate at the speed of light. Yet, we already have some weapons that operate at the speed of light: images and information carried by fiber optics; the weapon of military *kanban* in the information age.[41] Warfare can evolve beyond the limitations imposed by physical weapons aimed at destruction and death.[42] Neocortical warfare could be the result.

The poet-philosopher T. E. Hulme observed at the last *fin de siècle* that the end of one *Weltanschauung* and the beginning of another always seems to spawn "the unsystematic philosopher."[43] The celebration of a new millennium and a New Age has already begun for some. We suspect or even know that the future will transform our understanding of values, conflict, warfare and technology. Neocortical warfare—subduing adversaries without violence—is not only the Warfare of the future, it is also the most demanding kind of warfare. It calls for the most imaginative and effective employment schemes. The soft *can* overcome the hard, as both Eastern wisdom and history tell us. A theory of neocortical warfare is out there somewhere, waiting for a more systematic philosopher to seize it. Perhaps that philosopher will read this.

NOTES

[1] General Merrill A. McPeak. "Flexibility and Airpower," an address presented at the Air Mobility Command Dining In. 12 June 1993, in U.S. Department of the Air Force, *Air Force Update* (June 1993), 6. Emphasis added.

[2] Will and Ariel Durant. *The Lessons of History* (New York: Simon and Schuster. 1968), 19.

[3] Ibid., 81–86.

[4]Martin van Creveld. *The Transformation of War* (New York: *The Free Press*, 1991), 157. Van Creveld had the bad luck of having this book appear at the same time the war against Iraq began. Chapters 6 and 7 of this under-appreciated book are magnificent.

[5]John G. Stoessinger. *Why Nations Go to War* (New York: St. Martin's Press, 1985), 204–19.

[6]Lee G. Boman and Terrence E. Deal, *Reframing Organizations: Artistry, Choice, and Leadership* (San Francisco: Jossey-Bass Publishers, 1991), 225–29, 237–40, and Robert L. Morlan, *American Government: Policy and Process* (Boston: Houghton Mifflin Company, 1971), 2–3.

[7]Robert L. O'Connell, *Of Arms and Men: A History of War, Weapons, and Aggression* (New York: Oxford University Press, 1989), 14–17.

[8]John A. Warden III, *The Air Campaign: Planning for Combat* (Washington DC: National Defense University Press, 1988). The challenges future campaign planners face are (1) to contrive plans that attack or engage living organisms and not just systems, and (2) to comprehend the impotence of dreadnoughts against "zodiacboats." The "non-trinitarian" wars (van Creveld's descriptive term for those conflicts that do not evidence Clausewitz's "remarkable trinity" of state, people and armed forces) or "Third Wave" wars of the future are radically different from the wars of the recent past. It may prove to be much easier to plan another violent campaign against Iraq, for example, than it is to plan one against the armed forces of a nonstate.

[9]B. H. Liddell Hart, *Strategy*, 2d ed., rev. (London: Faber & Faber, Ltd., Signet Books, 1974), x, 325–30.

[10]McPeak, *"Flexibility and Airpower."* 3. General McPeak does not assert that Desert Storm was the "last ancient war." He merely wonders whether it might have been or not. The "acme," in the opinion of some, would have been to prevent Saddam's aggression in the first place.

[11]John R. Boyd, "A Discourse on Winning and Losing." August 1987. Boyd's analysis of strategy, tactics and the operational art led him to the discovery of the now famous "OCDA loop." The loop—the cycle of observation, orientation, decision and action—led him to additional discoveries. One of the most important of these is the criticality of time in competition or conflict. Another, and equally important, analysis within the "discourse" is the nature of the fighting done by pirates, brigands, guerrilas and the essence of the counterguerrila campaign.

[12]Eliot A. Cohen and John Gooch, *Military Misfortunes: The Anatomy of Failure in War* (New York: The Free Press, 1990), 8.

[13]Paul McLean discussed by Ned Hermann, *The Creative Brain* (Lake Lure, NC: Brain Books, 1988), 31.

[14]Robert Ornstein and Richard F. Thompson, *The Amazing Brain* (Boston: Houghton Mifflin Company, 1984), 21–40, 133–71.

[15]Hermann, *Creative Brain*, 32–39 and Ornstein and Thompson, *Amazing Brain*, 24–29, 38–39.

[16]Robert E. Ornstein, *The Psychology of Consciousness*, 2d ed. (New York: Harcourt Brace Jovanovich, Inc., 1977), 20–39. See also Norman Geschwind, "Speciaizations of the Human Brain," in Rodolfo R. Linas, *The Workings of the Brain: Development, Memory, and Perception* (New York: W.H. Freeman and Company, 1990), 105–20.

[17]F.S.C. Northrop, *The Meeting of East and West* (New York: The Macmillan Company, 1946), 407.

[18]Ilya Prigogineand Isabelle Stengers, *Order Out of Chaos: Man's New Dialogue with Nature* (Boulder: New Science Library, 1984), 171–76, 297–313.

[19]Richard M. Restak. *The Mind* (New York: Bantam Books, 1988), 173–85.

[20]Desmond Morris, *The Naked Ape: A Zoologist's Study of the Human Animal* (New York: McGraw-Hill Book Company, 1967), 173–85.

[21]John Keegan, *The Illustrated Face of Battle: A Study of Agricourt, Waterloo and the Somme* (New York: Viking Penguin, Inc., 1989), 285.

[22]Van Creveld, *The Transformation of War*, 226. Let me explain the "sic." Conflict between humans may be natural, but mortal combat with weapons is not. It may be learned behavior. Some valuable martial behaviors are learned on the "playing fields" of games.

[23]Arthur Pap, "Does Science Have Metaphysical Presuppositions?" *Readings in the Philosophy of Science*, editors Herbert Feigi and Mary Brodbeck (New York: Appleton-Century-Croft, Inc., 1953), 21–53.

[24]Gary Zukav, *The Dancing Wu Li Masters: An Overview of the New Physics* (New York: William Morrow & Co., Inc., 1979; Bantam Books, 1980).

[25]Alan Beyerchen, "Clausewitz, Nonlinearity, and the Unpredictability of War," *International Security* (Winter 1992–1993), 59–90.

[26]Alvin and Heidi Toffler, *War and Anti-War: Survival at the Dawn of the Twenty-first Century* (Boston: Little, Brown and Company, 1993). Also, see John Arquilla and David Ronfeldt, "Cyberwar is Coming!" *Comparative Strategy* (April–June 1993), 141–65. Cyberwar is here. Even so, I believe there are differences between theories of cyberwar and neocortical warfare. Neocortical warfare considers conflicts involving national security as warfare, thereby eradicating the gray area between peace and war and the distinctions that could separate today's armed forces from tomorrow's national security forces. It views subduing hostile will, or control over the adversary, as the aim of conflict, including warfare. Like cyberwar, neocortical warfare suggests that there are and always have been nonviolent or less violent ways to establish control. Neocortical warfare asserts that controlling or subduing an adversary *without* fighting—because of its many advantages—ought to be the goal. In sum, cyberwar and cyberwar techniques such as propaganda, deception, illusion and concealment may be viewed as specific applications of the principles of neocortical warfare.

[27]Boyd, "A Discourse on Winning and Losing," suggests that the way to win is to operate (that is, to observe, get oriented, decide and act) more quickly than an adversary. Ways to do this include depriving the adversary of essential information, overloading the adversary with puzzling or difficult to interpret information, using the adversary's "genetic heritage" or "cultural tradition" so that the enemy is self-disconcerted or self-deceived, frustrating adversary actions, or denying the enemy feedback, or accurate feedback on the consequences of action taken. All of this is designed to "generate uncertainty, confusion, disorder, panic, chaos . . ." and shatter cohesion, produce paralysis, and bring about collapse." Because the real province of conflict is the mind, all warfare is neocortical warfare.

[28]Richard Bandler and John Grinder, *Frogs to Princes: Neuro Linguistic Programming* (Moab, Utah: Real People Press, 1979).

[29]Dr. Armin Ludwig, "Economic Growth and Resource Competition as Threats to World Stability," a lecture presented at the Air War College, 15 September 1993. Using World Bank data, Professor Ludwig forecasts that by 2020 the world population will be 8.7 billion (today it is 5.5 billion) and the world gross domestic product will be $58.5 trillion (today it is about $25 trillion). As threats to stability, population is the "weak force" and resource consumption is the "strong force." He concluded his lecture by suggesting that by 2020, "International resource conflicts will be endemic." Used with Dr. Ludwig's permission.

[30]Morris, *The Naked Ape*, 178.

[31]Donella H. and Dennis L. Meadows, *Limits to Growth: A Report for the Club of Rome's Project on the Predicament of Mankind*, 2d ed. (New York: Universe Books, Signet Books, 1974).

[32]Samuel P. Huntington, "The Clash of Civilizations?" *Foreign Affairs* (Summer 1993), 22–49. See also "Responses to Samuel P. Huntington's 'The Clash of Civilizations?'" *Foreign Affairs* (September/October 1993), 2–26.

[33]US Department of Defense. *The Bottom-Up Review: Forces for a New Era*, by Les Aspin (1 September 1993). The review postulates the need to preserve large conventional forces at least until 2000 in order to engage in two major regional contingencies "nearly simultaneously." If one accepts van Creveld's thesis, the bulk of these forces will have little military utility. If the essence of conflict resides in the "mind," then the principal purposes of such forces are as insurance against the failure of our own willpower or minds. One interpretation might be that, unwilling to shape events by a commitment to subduing enemies without fighting, we instead hope to fight them in familiar ways. See also John T. Correll, "Two at a Time," *Air Force Magazine* (September 1993), and Michael R. Gordon, "Military Plan Would Cut Forces But Have Them Ready for 2 Wars," *New York Times* (September 1993), 1.

[34]Eric Voegelin, "Extended Strategy: A New Technique for Dynamic Relations," *Journal of Politics* (1940), 189–200. Few non-Germans appreciated Hitler's *Lebensraum* as the "biopolitical" manifestation of the racist views he derived from the pseudoscience of Ernst Haeckel. This linkage is defined and explored in George J. Stein, "Biological Science and the Roots of Nazism," *American Scientist* (January–February 1988), 50–58. Stein also shows that *Mein Kampf*, in specifying the German need for *Lebensraum*, clearly forecast war in Europe as Hitler's preferred solution.

[35]Arquilla and Ronfeldt, "Cyberwar is Coming!" 160. In the future "exemplary use" will not be just selecting objects with high value—added as targets for attack or the application of physical force. More important, it will be the selection of the enemy mind—or the enemies minds—as the centers of gravity of hostile will.

[36]US Department of the Navy. *Sonata*, by Vice Admiral Jerry O. Tuttle, 1993, 1. In the "Prelude," Tuttle proclaims the arrival of a "new kind of warfare, which we call Space and Electronic Warfare."

[37]The "quality movement" can improve our ability to fight. For this to occur, we must find ways to make empowerment work within a military architecture. Leaders in the military today declare their commitment to empowerment, but many seem uncomfortable contemplating nonhierarchical organizational structures or the ways of operating that empowerment requires. In the opinion of some, such things as traditional scalar "wiring diagrams," senior officer reserved parking spaces in front of stores like the post exchange and commissary and a tendency to measure the same old

things masked in the new lexicon of quality show the difficulty of making cultural changes. Authentic empowerment requires that we adopt different views and learn different behaviors. The result, however, could be the creation of national security forces so empowered that each individual is a cooperative center of gravity, a production unit of incredible influence, force, or lethality. Such a force would be difficult to subdue.

[38]US Congress of the United States, Congressional Budget Office (CBO), *Military Family Housing in the United States*, a CBO study (September 1993). According to the "summary" accompanying the report, the CBO calculates savings of as much as $4.6 billion between 1994 and 1999 by providing less DOD housing and "relying more on cash housing allowances" that military families can use to obtain housing in the private sector. With the Census Bureau reporting that over 36 million Americans live in poverty and the electorate wanting a national health plan, like it or not, I expect our approach to military family housing will change to create more of a "peace dividend." Those changes will necessitate an evolution in our vision of bases, forts, posts and camps.

[39]Zukav. *The Dancing Wu Li Masters: An Overview of the New Physics*, 301–2. There are many physicists who believe that the quest for quantum connectedness is as chimencal as the quest for a united field theory.

[40]US Army Research Institute for the Behavioral and Social Sciences. "Training Lessons Learned from Peak Performance Episodes," Technical Report 711, by J.L. Fobes, June 1986. This Army manuscript advocates teaching soldiers the "self-regulation of endorphin levels" or using competitive sports training "for endurance management (controlling fatigue and pain for sustained performance)." Imagine an elite force of troops, trained to be, among other things, endorphin (endogenous morphine and other opiates) self-regulators. Imagine these elite troops donning their chemical defense gear to protect themselves from adversary neocortical warriors—the limbic force—armed with naloxone, an endorphin inhibitor.

[41]Taichi Ohno and Setsuo Mito, *Just-In-Time for Today and Tomorrow* (Cambridge, MA: Productivity Press, 1988). *Kanban* is "just-in-time" information derived from the workplace. It also is no more or less than the information needed. To the "risk-averse," concepts of just-in-time and more-than-enough are comforting. See also Taichi Ohno, *Toyota Production System: Beyond Large-Scale Production* (Cambridge MA: Productivity Press, 1988).

[42]Mark Tapscott and Kay Atwal, "New Weapons That Win Without Killing On DOD's Horizon," *Defense Electronics* (February 1993), 41–46. See also: David A. Fulghum, "ALCMs Given Nonlethal Role," *Aviation Week & Space Technology* (22 February 1993), 20–22; "Nonlethal Weapons Give Peacekeepers Flexibility," *Aviation Week & Space Technology* (7 December 1992), 50–51 and "Army Prepares for Non-Lethal Combat," *Aviation Week & Space Technology* (24 May 1993), 62–63.

[43]T. E. Hulme, *Speculations*, edited by Herbert Read (London: Routledge and Kegan Paul, Ltd.), 25–26.

Chapter Eighteen

INFORMATION, POWER, AND GRAND STRATEGY:
IN ATHENA'S CAMP—SECTION 2[*]

John Arquilla and David Ronfeldt

IMPLICATIONS FOR GRAND STRATEGY

According to tradition, power considerations drive strategic choices, and grand strategy consists of the "knitting-together" of a nation's political, economic and military resources and capabilities in pursuit of its overall aims.[1] Indeed, the major dimensions of grand strategy have long been the political, economic, and military ones—anything else has been deemed secondary, significant only as it affected the major dimensions. Information and related technologies and systems play a role in this tradition, but mainly a supporting one.

Yet even though information is generally deemed a subsidiary factor, it sometimes has transformative effects. Examples abound throughout history. With regard to political power, one need only look at the effect the printing press had on society. Aside from being a catalyst for the Renaissance, the printed word succeeded in empowering individuals and states in ways previously unknown. An example is provided by the Protestant Reformation in which, despite efforts to restrict the dissemination of the Bible into the various vernaculars, the word did get out. This resulted in a movement which held, first,

[*]Originally published as "Information, Power, and Grand Strategy: In Athena's Camp," in *The Information Revolution and National Security: Dimensions and Directions*, edited by Stuart J. D. Schwartzstein, Washington, D.C.: CSIS, 1996. Copyright 1996 by the Center for Strategic and International Studies. Reprinted by permission. This section and Section 1 (which appears as Chapter Six of this volume) have been copy edited since the initial publishing.

that the individual could enjoy a direct experience with God, as opposed to one filtered through a religious hierarchy. Second, the liberation of the individual from centralized control encouraged a number of emerging states to seek their own political independence from Rome. Thus, Lutheranism in Germany and Anglicanism in England were movements that fostered national political sovereignty as well as individual freedom of worship.[2]

In economic affairs, the letter of credit was well known and widely used in Roman times as an instrument for conveying information about the creditworthiness of a borrower or purchaser. It allowed for a range and velocity of commercial transactions that exceeded anything seen prior to its invention. Partly because of this instrument, the eastern Roman empire, which focused on the accumulation of wealth and the construction of extensive financial and trade networks, outlived by a thousand years its western counterpart, which denigrated commercial affairs in favor of conquest.[3]

An early example of information serving to enhance military power was the appearance of the written word, a few millennia prior to the invention of the printing press. This innovation enabled the preparation of complex orders, and the delegation of tactical, and eventually operational, command functions. As a result, larger armed forces could be mobilized and deployed effectively in combat. Extended operations by larger forces made the command and control function even more important, a trend that continued with the advent of the telegraph, telephone, and radio and remains unabated in the current revolution in military affairs, which revolves around informational factors.[4]

From its historically subsidiary position, information is now being moved into a transcendent, if not independent, role.[5] As the information revolution progresses and its conceptual and policy implications expand, information is increasingly seen to have overarching, transforming significance for all the dimensions of power and strategy. For the time being, this role is often more rhetorical than demonstrable, because it is not yet precisely clear what "information" means for grand strategy. One intent is to discern and develop a definition that improves the U.S. capacity for *combined* political, economic, and military strategies—be those, for example, to foster democracy, promote commercial openness, curtail a given conflict or generally strengthen (or retrench) U.S. power and presence abroad. Another intent is to develop information as an independent fourth dimension of national power.

Thus, the political, economic, and military building blocks of grand strategy may depend increasingly on information to realize their power potential. Once again three views emerge: The traditional one—that information is a subsidiary aspect of the three major dimensions of grand strategy—is being succeeded by the contemporary view that information has transcendent, overarching effects on them. Meanwhile, a third view—that information (and communications) should be developed independently as a fourth major dimension of grand strategy—is gaining strength.   For example, current thinking is that information has modifying effects on the traditional dimensions of strategy.   As power and information become more fused under the Athenan view, it may become a moot point as to which drives strategy. Indeed, as this fusion occurs, it may become advisable to move toward the view that information is a distinct dimension.

In our view, information should now be considered and developed as a distinct fourth dimension of national power—an element in its own right, but still one that, like the political, economic, and military dimensions, functions synergistically to improve the value and effects of the others. Table 18.1 provides a glimpse of the various ends and means of grand strategy, taking its cues on ultimate aims from President Clinton's doctrine of democratic enlargement.[6]

Given the explosive growth in the means of communication in recent years, versus the inherent constraints on either the use of force or

Table 18.1

American Grand Strategy: Ends and Means

Dimensions	Ends	Means
Political	Spread of democracy	Treaties, alliances
Economic	Growth of free markets	Sanctions, subsidies, trade, GNP increases
Military	Two-war capability	Armed services
Informational	Open access and connectivity	Telecommunications, the media, public diplomacy

economic coercion, it may well be that policymakers will increasingly want to resort to information strategies before, or instead of, more traditional approaches to state craft.[7] The preference for informational means may be even more pronounced in situations dealing with friends or allies, as opposed to adversarial crises. One can see the difference in the Persian Gulf region, where hostility to the Iraqi regime has led U.S. policy to rely on economic and limited military pressure to try to compel a democratizing change. In contrast, Saudi Arabia, a close, but non-democratic American ally, faces neither economic nor military pressure to liberalize, and political pressure is muted. Informationally, however, the United States has supported the sale, by AT&T, of a cellular communications network of enormous bandwidth. This could give Saudi citizens hitherto unknown capacities for interconnectivities, both domestically and internationally, that may unleash vibrant democratizing possibilities.

In addition, with regard to inferences to be drawn from Table 18.1, it is important to point out that, while one might pursue, say, some political ends by political means, it is not necessary to proceed in a symmetrical fashion. For example, the political goal of democratizing Haiti was pursued by means that included strong elements of economic and military coercion. Similarly, the ability to win two regional wars nearly simultaneously will rely, no doubt, upon a variety of means in addition to U.S. armed forces, including financial and manpower contributions from allies, as occurred in the recent Gulf War. Asymmetrical means may also be employed in the economic sphere, where, for example, the first American attempt to open Japanese markets in the 1850s was led by Commodore Perry's "black ships." Japan's own policies in the 1930s and early 1940s demonstrated a willingness to pursue economic ends by primarily military means. Also, American strategy has, in recent years, focused upon the use of economic leverage in pursuit of political ends. However, the limits of economic power can be glimpsed in the frequent failure of sanctions as a tool of coercive diplomacy. The stout resistance of the impoverished, from Cuba to North Korea, suggests important constraints upon this aspect of grand strategy.

Finally, we hypothesize that, in its integrative functions, information will serve more usefully, and be less attenuated, than the other dimensions of national power. Thus, when a good economy is not connected to a first-rate military, the likelihood is remote that the armed forces, endowed with dominant informational capacities, will perform poorly. Examples of the often weak connections between political, economic, and military means abound. With regard to the economic-military connection, many prosperous nations and empires have suffered military decline despite their wealth, leading to their defeat by economically backward opponents. Rome fell to barbarians whose economies might best be described as "subsistence plundering." The nomadic Mongols had only the most rudimentary notions of markets and trading, yet they conquered the leading Sinic, Muslim, and Orthodox Christian civilizations of their day. Revolutionary France arose from economic collapse to overthrow virtually all of its wealthy neighbors. Finally, Vietnam's peasant economy withstood and defeated the United States while the latter was at the height of its Cold War–era power. Thus, one can see that the connections between the three primary elements of power are often attenuated.

Information, however, has integrative effects on the political, economic, and military aspects of power that are robust and persistent. The other side of this notion is that, as beneficial as information is, the lack of it may have equally serious negative consequences for state power. With this in mind, we turn briefly to the Cold War as a period that allows for some testing of this hypothesis. Given its recent conclusion, this case certainly meets the standards of relevance to the analytic issue at hand. Also, it affords a "tough test," because the leading actors—the United States and the Soviet Union—had, throughout their rivalry, large economies and militaries, and stable political institutions. To fully understand the collapse of one and the triumph of the other, it is necessary to become aware of the deep and enduring effects that information had on the national power and grand strategies of both rivals.

The Cold War As an Information-Based Conflict

The Cold War affords a laboratory for assessing the relationship between information and national power. For over 40 years, an "open system" rich with information, the United States, strove to prevent the domination of the international community by a "closed system," whose grand strategy was often aimed at preventing the generation and dissemination of information. The protracted struggle between these contending systems resulted in triumph for the nation whose levers of power and suasion enjoyed the higher information content—politically, economically, and militarily.

At the political level, for example, the United States mobilized for the long struggle by disseminating information and debating it openly. The decision to pursue a strategy of containment occurred after extensive public discussion, including the notable exchanges between George Kennan and Walter Lippmann. Indeed, Kennan's "long telegram" became the principal instrument for mobilizing the national will and guiding overall policy.[8]

Throughout the Cold War, American political strategy held to the notion that the truth would, as the Bible suggests, "set men free." Thus were born the United States Information Agency, Radio Free Europe, Radio Liberty and Radio Martí, among others. The Soviet Union, however, adopted a contrary political strategy: It restricted access to information and to technologies such as the typewriter, both at home and abroad. If information could not be suppressed, propaganda and other dictatorial measures served to control and reshape its meaning in ways congenial to the Kremlin's interests. As the Cold War played out, openness proved a more viable instrument of political power, while efforts at suppression only postponed the eventual eruption of demand for information. The policy of openness, or *glasnost*, enacted during the tenure of Mikhail Gorbachev, came too late to prevent a political implosion, whose effects still bedevil Russia.

In the economic realm, similar forces were at work. The United States led an international coalition of states in pursuit of commercial openness, principally via the General Agreement on Tariffs and Trade (GATT). To counter this pro-market system, the Soviet Union cobbled together a competing system, the Council on Economic Cooperation (COMECON), that aimed to centrally control all economic information and transactions, including throughout the satellite states of the Soviet imperium. Since these two systems had little to do with each other, their economic competition offers a clear test of open and closed information systems in the economic sphere also. The outcome of this "test" is well known. The open, informationally driven system brought its bloc a level of economic prosperity unrivaled in history. The closed system presided over the deepening impoverishment of its denizens, fomenting their eventual revolt.

In the arena of military competition, a similar pattern emerges. The United States and its allies developed flexible doctrines, strategies, and weaponry that emphasized the importance of information. This drive reached its apotheosis with the advent of precision-guided munitions (PGMs), which were seen as a way to defend with fewer forces against a conventional Soviet attack with superior forces. Meanwhile, the Soviet Union pursued an overall strategy based on massing the greatest amount of firepower possible. This meant bigger weapons, including nuclear missiles, whose destructive power, it was hoped, would offset the vitiating factor of their relatively greater inaccuracy. In the conventional realm, the Soviet style relied, in traditional fashion, on attrition, even within the context of the adoption of many of the tenets of mechanized warfare.[9] The one protracted conflict in which the Red Army did fight during the Cold War, in Afghanistan, featured the defeat of Soviet brute force strategies by an indigenous resistance, the *mujahideen,* that turned the tide of victory with the information-laden Stinger missile.

Afghanistan aside, the Cold War nuclear rivalry provides perhaps an even better contrast of the two styles. The United States strove for highly accurate delivery systems and actually reduced megatonnage substantially (by over 40 percent) during the last two decades of the Cold War. This accuracy also allowed for the development of a "counterforce" nuclear strategy that provided, possibly, a way never to have to implement a declaratory policy that threatened to hold Soviet civilians hostage to big, inaccurate, city-busting warheads.[10] The Soviets simply couldn't match American advances in accuracy and had to maintain larger, more destructive weapons and a declaratory policy of all-out nuclear war.[11]

Finally, while we have briefly recounted the manner in which information entered into each side's political, economic, and military strategies, it is important to note that information also facilitated synergies *among* these basic dimensions of national power and grand strategy. A notable example appears in the market system's ability to foster, along with business wealth and investment capital, a multitude of innovations in defense technology. The Soviets, however, generated less capital with their suppressive central control mechanisms, and innovated little. This meant that they could sustain the competition neither quantitatively nor qualitatively.

As the information revolution gained strength in the closing decades of the Cold War, the "open" societies of the West proved better suited than the "closed" societies of the East to take advantage of the new technologies and to adapt to the challenges they posed to established concepts of sovereignty and governance. Moreover, the deliberate fostering of information and communications flows proved a powerful instrument for compelling closed societies to open up. Thus, U.S. Secretary of State George Shultz, writing in 1985, before the revolutions of 1989 proved the point in Eastern Europe, observed that

> The free flow of information is inherently compatible with our political system and values. The communist states, in contrast, fear this information revolution perhaps more than they fear Western military strength . . . . Totalitarian societies face a dilemma: either they try to stifle these technologies and thereby fall farther behind in the new industrial revolution, or else they permit these technologies and see their totalitarian control inevitably eroded . . . . The revolution in global communications thus forces all nations to reconsider traditional ways of thinking about national sovereignty.[12]

If the Soviet regime risked pursuing the new technologies, Shultz and others predicted (correctly) that its leaders would eventually have to liberalize the Soviet economic and political systems.[13]

In sum, the American triumph in the Cold War was not only a victory for our political, economic, and military systems and strategies, but also for our overall approach to information. Information variables crucially affected all the major dimensions of power—political, economic, and military. This was a key, overarching difference between the Western and Soviet systems.[14] Should one infer from this success in the Cold War that the same strategy of openness is necessarily the right one in the emerging new era?

Openness Reconsidered

Openness—the open society—is an ideal that permeates American interests and objectives, including all the political, economic, military, and informational ends and means discussed above. It is so potent an American ideal that George Soros lucidly proposes

> that we declare the creation and preservation of open societies as one of the objectives of foreign policy . . . . I propose substituting the framework of open and closed societies for the old framework of communism versus the free world.[15]

One could extrapolate from the foregoing that the decisive role of information in the Cold War, linked to a grand strategy of openness, should serve as a model for American grand strategy in the post–Cold War world. Indeed, the current doctrine of "democratic enlargement"[16] appears to grow logically from the opportunity provided by the dissolution of the Soviet Union. In terms of its power relative to others, the United States enjoys a position of preponderance unlike any in its previous experience. Also, in the ideological realm, a broad-based strategy of openness has close links with the most essential aspects of 20th century American political and philosophical thought.

However, the strategy of openness that won the Cold War may not be the same one that will best serve U.S. objectives and interests in the emerging era. First, though, it is important to recognize that the American grand strategy of openness during the Cold War had many closed aspects as well. For example, in the late 1940s and early 1950s, vigorous efforts were made in the United States to prevent the diffusion of communist ideology, much as the Soviets tried to keep liberal ideas from gaining a hearing, or a following. By the mid-1950s, though, the United States grew aware of the ethical and political bankruptcy of this policy and began to change course, fostering an open competition between the rival political ideologies. In the economic sphere, as much as the United States was open to its allies, it remained closed to its enemies, actual or potential. This policy mellowed only at the margins and persists today in such policies as the continued embargo on Cuba. Finally, with regard to military matters, advanced technologies were consistently treated in "closed" fashion. They were classified in the hope that the diffusion of knowledge could be precluded. While this effort failed in the nuclear weapons area, it succeeded, to some extent, in the realm of computerization, information systems, and, most notably, radar-evading Stealth technology.

Despite these aspects of closed approaches to information (about ideas, markets, or weapons), the overall American approach remained devoted to openness. From the increasing willingness to compare and contrast ideologies, to the creation of the greatest free-trading economic regime the world had ever seen, to the development of interoperable military systems for common use among allies, the United States fostered the free movement of information in all its incarnations. There was even a sustained effort to share information *with* the Soviet Union, to help promote stability and change. From the "hot line" that allowed for clear communication in crisis, to the transparency of information about nuclear arsenals, there was a strong belief, apparently on both sides, that openness was a condition well attuned to the needs of the bipolar international system.

In the post–Cold War era, however, the inherent stability provided by rough parity between two superpowers has given way to a period of flux and uncertainty. While the dissolution of the Soviet Union has left in its place a less powerful Russia, and the United States has seen some diminution of its own absolute military and economic power— a variety of states, great and small, are rising to recast the structure of the international system. In East Asia alone, for example, Japan and China show every sign of movement toward great power status; and even the smaller states, such as Vietnam and the Koreas, have robust capabilities.

Is the Cold War strategy of openness appropriate in such a setting? Or does the shift from a stable bipolar to a volatile polycentric world imply taking a new approach to openness? Should we be more guarded than we were, or at least become guarded in different ways than we were in the Cold War period? A key issue here may be that, in any era, the informational aspect of grand strategy may consist of a skillful blend of open and closed sectors. The challenge for the post–Cold War era will be to find the informational mix appropriate for a much "fuzzier" international environment, one in which the very meaning of openness may have to be reconsidered.

In the political realm, for example, the tenets of political liberalism once served as a rallying cry to oppose Soviet expansionism. Now these ideas, which form the core of the rhetoric of democratic enlargement, might be received as a subtle form of American ideological imperialism. To any number of state and non-state actors, this may seem quite threatening, encouraging them to balance against us.[17] Thus, one might expect, in response to current U.S. political strategy, a variety of opponents to rise. A few examples would include China, as the most likely nation-state competitor to resent pressures to democratize, and transnational Islamic revivalists, as archetypal non-state actors who will be encouraged to resist American blandishments. The implication here is not to cease efforts to spread democracy, but to recognize that Cold War–style openness may have to give way to a subtler form of spreading information about democracy throughout the world.

In terms of strategic foreign policy, a declaratory policy of openness designed to reduce uncertainty, a condition highly prized during the Cold War, might actually weaken deterrence and crisis stability in the future. The American style in international interactions remains closely tied to the Wilsonian dictum: "open agreements, openly arrived at." Most often, this means that U.S. reasoning is openly provided to opponents, allowing them to calculate their risks and opportunities quite accurately.[18]

The current Balkan imbroglio provides an example of the manner in which an adversary has been able to maximize its range of maneuver, based on information freely and regularly provided by the U.S. government about U.S. intentions and capabilities toward the Serbs. In the post–Cold War world, there may be virtue in creating, and fostering, uncertainty about possible U.S. actions. Certainly, there are times when deterrence will be enhanced, if an adversary has to worry about the possibility of an early, credible use of force by the United States, or that the chances for American intervention, at some point, might be high. Interestingly, this is something of a reversal from the Cold War, during which uncertainty about the likely U.S. response tended to encourage aggression, a point supported by attacks on South Korea in 1950, South Vietnam in 1965, and Kuwait in 1990, in the wake of ambiguous American signaling.[19]

In the economic arena, the recent creation of a World Trade Organization (WTO) devoted to the expansion of free trade and the dissemination of intellectual innovation seems a clear indicator that the market principles that served so well during the Cold War will be expanded upon, especially given the demise of the former Soviet economic bloc. Upon reflection, though, one may want to consider the need for a more nuanced economic strategy—one not as clearly demarcated between open and closed areas, as existed during the Cold War, but one flexible enough to allow for the protection of intellectual property and for the use of suasion to obtain a "fair" as well as a "free" market for international trade. The recent, and apparently successful, efforts of the Clinton Administration to obtain an agreement to grant greater access to the key automotive sector of the Japanese market are indicative of the manner in which this more nuanced approach might be applied. Indeed, the rapid follow-up of the automotive agreement with a similar U.S. claim on behalf of the photographic film industry suggests that a consistent strategy has been formulated and will be acted upon.

The key problem to address, in this regard, is that, in relative terms, the United States remains far more open than most other states, allowing them to amass wealth through trade, while U.S. debts build. This pattern began before the end of the Cold War but appears to be accelerating, as the roughly $150 billion U.S. trade deficit in 1994 indicates. It should be noted that the United States initially rose in prosperity and great power status between the end of the Civil War and the 1890s, when it had the most protected economy on earth. All this happened during a period in which the British empire, slavishly devoted to free trade, suffered decreasing market shares and increasing dependence upon foreign financial support.[20]

On this last point, one sees, even in the writings of Adam Smith, a sensitivity to the need for nuanced approaches. For example, in discussing the use of sanctions to force closed markets to open up, Smith argued that "there may be good policy in retaliations of this kind, when there is a probability that they will procure the repeal of the high duties or prohibitions complained of."[21] In the post–Cold War world, U.S. policymakers should heed Smith's admonitions, given the diminution of military threats in the wake of the Soviet dissolution, and the corresponding rise in serious economic challenges. Indeed, the information age may carry the risk of transforming the international free market system into a much more conflictual one, implying a need to develop the capability to combat neo-mercantilist networks that are designed to perform well *against* market-oriented competitors.[22]

Another questionable aspect of an economic strategy based on free flows of information concerns intellectual property. The openness that encouraged the industrial renaissance of post-war Germany and Japan, and allowed the rise of the Asian "tigers," served the purpose of helping them become viable counterweights to the Soviet threat. Today, however, the American gift of ideas may be contributing to the difficulties of many U.S. industrial sectors. As Peter Drucker has pointed out in a variety of fora for years, "knowledge workers" will predominate the future economic landscape; and their best use will require partnership with a new generation of innovative and wily captains of industry.[23] A world in which ideas may be swiftly, cheaply duplicated elsewhere is one in which the American economy will have difficulty competing on equal terms.

Regarding the implications for "open" strategies in the military realm, there is much room for reconsideration, particularly of such issues as interoperability, forward basing, and the introduction of innovations. During the Cold War, there was a distinct tilt in the direction of openness in these key areas, which tied in closely with the political demands of U.S. alliance structures. For example, NATO sought ever better levels of interoperability of weapons systems among coalition partners and required the forward presence in Europe of an entire U.S. field army (over 300,000 troops) to enhance crisis and deterrence stability. Thus a great deal of information was conveyed openly both to U.S. allies *and* adversaries. Even the advances in precision guided munitions were openly touted, both to shore up alliance cohesion and to dishearten those Soviets who might still contemplate aggression.

In the post–Cold War environment, there are good reasons to question military openness as a predominant grand strategy. Given the quantum shifts in military capabilities inherent in the advances promised by the information revolution, should one still seek to share them with allies, or inform potential adversaries of their efficacy? The risk, of course, is that these advantages are "wasting assets," susceptible to diminution as they diffuse. Thus, in a world where allies may lack the constancy they had during the Cold War, and where enemies may be both numerous and readily able to adapt to advances, once known, openness may have to give way to a certain degree of guardedness.[24]

With regard to forward basing, which sends a clear signal of commitment to potential aggressors, one must now ask whether such an approach remains optimal. The continuance of a forward defensive strategy has two problems. First, in an information age in which adversaries may all too commonly possess cruise and ballistic missiles capable of bombarding U.S. forces in place, it may become necessary, in the interest of protecting these forces against surprise attack, to keep opponents in the dark as to their whereabouts. As early as the 1960s, Field Marshal Bernard Montgomery raised this issue, arguing that "armies must go to sea." Admiral William Owens has taken up this idea with his concept of "mobile sea bases."[25]

The second problem with the amount of information conveyed by forward basing is that the emerging international system may be subject to unruliness in many regions. Potential aggressors may look at the U.S. force deployment scheme and, if their intended prey is not within some recognizable security complex, may be encouraged to try their luck. Even during the Cold War, this problem was considered a possibility and was confirmed, in the eyes of many, when North Korea invaded the South in 1950, not long after Secretary of State Dean Acheson left the latter out of the explicit American "defensive perimeter."[26] In a world with more "Koreas," continued forward basing may condemn those who lack the benefit of U.S. presence to become targets of opportunistic aggression.

Moving toward a more guarded approach could lengthen the period of U.S. military advantage and complicate the calculations of regional aggressors, particularly if American troops might be lurking over the horizon on some "floating fortress." However, new problems could emerge from this sort of shift. If we do not share information about military advances, we retain our predominance, but this might motivate allies, as well as adversaries, to enter into a new, information age arms race with the United States. In addition, a substantial shift from forward defense to a scheme more reminiscent of "depth defense" (i.e., one that rolls back aggression rather than precluding initial gains) might undermine deterrence substantially, particularly if aggressors engage in limited land grabs or *faits accomplis.*[27]

These tensions imply the need to think carefully about any move away from the form of military openness employed during the Cold

War. However, the price of failing to adjust strategically may be a quicker erosion of American advantages, undermining deterrence anyway. Perhaps the solution lies in a nuanced approach in which allies and friends are not all treated as equals. In this manner, key military information might flow to some, but not to others (e.g., Britain, but not Gulf War ally Syria); and some regions might eventually have to fend for themselves (e.g., Western Europe and South Korea).

The development of a separate informational dimension for post–Cold War grand strategy is a task that is yet to be fully addressed. Just what should the key ends or goals of this dimension be? Open access and interconnectivity, from local to global levels, look like good choices, perhaps combined with an international declaration of a "right to communicate." What should the key means or instruments be? The list should probably include the promotion of all manner of advanced telecommunications network infrastructures around the world, as well as the development of new approaches to public diplomacy and to the media. A key consideration for the American government may be learning to work with the new generation of nongovernmental organizations (NGOs), whose growth individually and in vast transnational networks is a major consequence of the information revolution.[28] Indeed, a well-developed information strategy might do more to foster the worldwide spread of democracy than do America's commercial and economic development strategies. Recent research by RAND's Chris Kedzie concludes that

> the priority of policies regarding international communication should be at least as high as the priority for foreign economic development and perhaps as high as that of some national security programs.[29]

Yet, here again, a strategy of openness involves substantial risks as well as opportunities. To begin, information, wielded as an autonomous tool of strategic statecraft, may be well-suited to the process of seeking democratic enlargement. An information strategy designed to spread democracy may even reduce the need to resort to harsh economic or veiled military pressures as part of the grand strategic mix. An informational approach may be more discriminating and less likely to generate either domestic or international political criticism of the means employed, unlike the situation faced when blunter instruments of suasion are utilized. U.S. policy toward Castro's Cuba looks like a case ripe for new thinking along these lines.[30]

A key risk inherent in fostering greater interconnectivity is that the United States may expose itself to attacks on its own information infrastructure, which could in turn lead to serious economic, and even societal, damage. How can this risk be mitigated? Should the United States try to shield its "infosphere" by strictly controlling access, internally and externally? Or can careful mapping of the information infrastructure lead to a more guarded approach that protects critical nodes while allowing the vast majority of the traffic in commerce and ideas to continue to pass uninterrupted? The latter strategy allows ample room for working to spread democracy abroad, while the former might constrain such efforts.

CONCLUSION: IN FAVOR OF GUARDED OPENNESS

While the development of information and communications as a distinct, new fourth dimension of grand strategy is a major recommendation, our concluding admonition is that U.S. strategic choices be reviewed across the spectrum of alternative approaches to openness. That spectrum might be framed by complete openness at one end and preclusive security at the other. Something that might be called "guarded openness" would define the middle range of the openness spectrum.

Guarded openness was, in many respects, the strategy that the United States pursued during the Cold War, if not before. But it is not a static strategy; moreover, it has not even been discussed much as a strategy. A review might help reveal that, for dealing with the present and future world, the overall profile of where to be open and where closed should be based on different principles from what it was during the Cold War. A review might also help ascertain what contextual factors are most important in determining the advisability of moving in open, guarded, or sometimes preclusive directions in specific issue areas.   A review could further help identify the mechanisms that should be emphasized for purposes of enhancing and protecting U.S. openness.

Given the strong commercial flavor of so much of the American infosphere, part of the answer may lie in allowing market forces to work out security arrangements. For example, with regard to telecommunications, consumers would presumably flock to companies that dealt best with security requirements, leaving the less adept competitors to founder for lack of customers. Eventually, only the informationally "fit" would survive. Could this pattern be pursued in other, or even most, sectors?

However, policies should hedge against the following kinds of problems: the potential damage that might be done in the "short run," before market forces provide a secure environment; and the possibility of "market failure," that is, the chance that the market might not be able to control risks adequately. Finally, the potential for more efficient alternatives to the market solution should be considered. These points call to mind similarities to the situation that the newly independent United States faced in the late 18th century. Many leaders thought that individual states should form their own industrial policies and take responsibility for protecting their own commerce. Alexander Hamilton, in his famous *Report on Manufactures,* took an opposing view, arguing that these separate approaches would prove both inefficient and likely to fail. His best-known illustration concerned maritime security, wherein he described the foolishness of creating 13 separate state navies, when one would be cheaper and better. We urge careful consideration of such Hamiltonian arguments, which should spark, for the emerging era, a *Report on Information.*

Overall, then, our analysis suggests that, in the political and economic spheres, it may prove useful to modify the Cold War strategy of maximizing openness, as circumstances require, or at least to develop a nuanced strategy that weaves skillfully between openness and more proprietary approaches. For the military aspects of national power, we urge the elucidation of a similarly flexible approach. The trend toward higher information-content in weapons systems and greater decentralization of military organizations should be continued, if not accelerated. At the same time, the emergence of an increasingly fluid, polycentric international system should make us wary of fostering the diffusion of military technological, organizational, and doctrinal innovations—yesterday's allies may not be tomorrow's.

Our notion here is that, while information has always "mattered," today's information revolution is creating overarching effects that raise "knowing" to a level of importance never before seen. As Richard Barnet once noted of this sea change, "[t]he world now taking shape is not only new, but new in entirely new ways."[31] Indeed, contrary to the popular view that military power may mean *less* in the information age, we think that it may become *more important,* owing to the revolutionary shifts in strategy, doctrine, and organization implied by advances in information technology. The oft-touted political and economic dimensions of national power[32] may carry less weight, or have less utility than often thought. Meanwhile, developing information as an autonomous element of national power affords the possibility of a more efficient, effective statecraft, especially with regard to the strategic aim of spreading democracy. In sum, while the political and economic tools of power may prove less widely applicable than in the past, both the military and informational aspects of grand strategy appear to be moving in the direction of relatively greater utility.

If all this is sensible and achievable, then Athena will truly have assumed the mantle of Mars. And we shall be the better for it.

NOTES

[1] Paul Kennedy, ed., *Grand Strategies in War and Peace* (New Haven: Yale University Press, 1991) adopts this definition in his volume on grand strategies from ancient Rome to the present-day United States.

[2] The classic studies are by Elizabeth L. Eisenstein, "Some Conjectures About the Impact of Printing on Western Society and Thought: A Preliminary Report," *Journal of Modern History,* March 1968, pp. 1–56, and the book version, Eisenstein, *The Printing Press As an Agent of Change,* 2 vols. (Cambridge: Cambridge University Press, 1979). While the literature on the Reformation era is mountainous, a few studies focus on the informational bases of political power. In regard to the German case, the work of German historian-strategist Leopold Ranke, *History of the Reformation in Germany* (London: Oxford University Press, 1905) stands out. Hillaire Belloc, *How the Reformation Happened* (London: Longmans, 1950) provides a similar approach, with keen insight into the reformation in England.

[3] Edward Gibbon, *The Decline and Fall of the Roman Empire,* 7 vols. (London: J.B. Bury, 1900) provides a classic analysis of this crucial difference between the eastern and western empires. He notes that the former's interest in protecting seagoing commerce remained constant, resulting in a first-rate navy that saved the eastern empire's lines of communication time and again during the hard centuries following the collapse of Rome. Joseph A. Schumpeter, *History of Economic Analysis* (New York: Oxford University Press, 1954), pp. 68–73, addresses this point in some detail, noting that the staying power of the eastern empire was directly tied to its continuing

embrace of Hellenistic notions of the power of ideas, markets, and secure lines and means of communication.

[4]On this point, Van Creveld, *Technology and War*, as well as his *Command in War* (Cambridge: Harvard University Press, 1985), takes long historical views of these issues.

[5]See Manheim, *Strategic Public Diplomacy . . .* for the view that information may be evolving toward an ever more autonomous role as a tool of state craft in many settings.

[6]See William J. Clinton, *A National Security Strategy of Engagement and Enlargement* (Washington, D.C.: Government Printing Office, 1994).

[7]The notion of information as existing autonomously has received some support. See particularly, Anthony Smith, *The Geopolitics of Information: How Western Culture Dominates the World* (New York: Oxford University Press, 1980); Hans N. Tuch, *Communicating with the World: U.S. Public Diplomacy Overseas* (New York: St. Martin's, 1990); and Howard H. Frederick, *Global Communications & International Relations* (Belmont, CA: Wadsworth Publishing, 1993). With regard to the means by which information strategies may be pursued, attention has long been given to the role of the media. Two early studies whose insights remain very useful are found in Bernard Cohen, *The Press and Foreign Policy* (Princeton: Princeton University Press, 1963); and David M. Abshire, *International Broadcasting: A New Dimension of Western Diplomacy* (Beverly Hills: Sage Publications, 1976). Chris Kedzie, "Democracy and Network Interconnectivity" (Proceeding of INET '95, Honolulu, June 1995), attends to the important implications of connectivity to the Internet for U.S. interests in fostering democracy worldwide.

[8]Kennan articulated his vision of containment in a series of lectures during 1946–1947 at the National War College, the texts of which can be found in Giles D. Harlow and George C. Maerz, *Measures Short of War* (Washington, D.C.: National Defense University Press, 1991). Walter Lippmann, *The Cold War* (Boston: Little, Brown, 1947) provides a compendium of his articles critiquing Kennan. Both were sensitive to the strategic implications of the societal structures of the adversaries, especially Kennan, who noted that "the greatest danger that can befall us in coping with this problem of Soviet Communism is that we shall allow ourselves to become like those with whom we are coping" (cited in Louis Halle, *The Cold War as History* (New York: Harper & Row, 1967), p. 106).

[9]Nathan Leites, *Soviet Style in War* (New York: Crane Russak, 1969) made this case convincingly. The most significant Soviet effort to understand and adapt to the implications of the information-driven revolution in military affairs came from Marshal N. Ogarkov, *Istoriya uchit bditel'nosti* (Moscow: Voenizdat, 1985). However, as noted in E.B. Atkeson, "Soviet Theater Forces on a Descending Path," in Derek Leebaert and Timothy Dickinson, eds., *Soviet Strategy and New Military Thinking* (Cambridge: Cambridge University Press, 1992), p. 94: "the Marshal's view of future warfare, incorporating high technology, may have carried with it the seeds of its own frustration. The devices envisioned are enormously costly and some may be beyond the capabilities of the Soviet Union to produce in the foreseeable future." Thus, a shift away from its traditional attritional approach, leavened with some elements of maneuver, may not have been possible.

[10]Though formalized in 1979 in Jimmy Carter's Presidential Directive #59, this view had been gaining currency since the 1960s.

[11]See David Holloway, *The Soviet Union and the Arms Race* (New Haven: Yale University Press, 1984), especially Chapter 3.

[12]George Shultz, "New Realities and New Ways of Thinking," *Foreign Affairs*, Spring 1985, pp. 705–721, quote from p. 716.

[13]Tom Stonier, "The Microelectronic Revolution, Soviet Political Structure, and the Future of East/West Relations," *The Political Quarterly*, April–June 1983, pp. 137–151.

[14]On this point, see Scott Shane, *Dismantling Utopia: How Information Ended the Soviet Union* (Chicago: Ivan R. Dee, 1994), which provides a journalistic *post mortem.* Readers in search of more scholarly analysis by policymakers and futurists who anticipated the effects of the information revolution on closed societies should be aware of Peter Drucker, *The New Realities: In Government and Politics, In Economics and Business, In Society and World View,* (New York: Harper and Row, 1989); George Shultz, "New Realities . . ."; and Walter B. Wriston, *The Twilight of Sovereignty: How the Information Revolution Is Transforming Our World* (New York: Charles Scribner's Sons, 1992). As Secretary of State during the Reagan Administration, George Shultz made a number of prescient speeches, notably in 1986, about the extreme difficulties that closed systems such as the Soviet Union's would have in coping with increased, freer flows of information.

[15]George Soros, "Toward Open Societies, *Foreign Policy*, #98, Spring 1995, pp. 65–75, quote from pp. 72–73. He wants U.S. policy to oppose all closed systems, including authoritarian dictatorships friendly toward the United States.

[16]President William J. Clinton, *A National Security Strategy of Engagement and Enlargement.*

[17]George Kennan, *The Cloud of Danger: Current Realities of U.S. Foreign Policy* (Boston: Atlantic Monthly Press, 1978) voiced this concern long before the current round of interest in spreading democracy. Christopher Layne, "The Unipolar Illusion," *International Security*, 17/4:5–51 (Spring 1993) picks up on this, and other points, to argue that an American drive for primacy will inevitably provoke a powerful countervailing response to curtail it.

[18]See especially Michael H. Hunt, *Ideology and U.S. Foreign Policy* (New Haven: Yale University Press, 1987) and Robert Dallek, *The American Style of Foreign Policy* (New York: Oxford University Press, 1983).

[19]The connection between ambiguous communications and conventional deterrence failure is examined in detail in John Arquilla, "Louder than Words: Tacit Communication in International Crises," *Political Communication* 9:155–172 (Winter 1992).

[20]Paul Kennedy, *The Rise and Fall of the Great Powers* (New York: Random House, 1987), p. 149, notes that, during the Victorian heyday, Britain's share of world manufacturing output fell from 23 percent to 18 percent. This drop was severe, in that global economic product grew explosively during this period (1880–1900). He also points out two dangerous long-term consequences of an economic strategy of unswerving openness: "[Britain] was contributing to the long-term expansion of other nations . . . [and] weakness lay in the increasing dependence of the British economy upon international trade and, more important, international finance" (p. 157). Aaron Friedberg, *The Weary Titan: Britain and the Experience of Relative Decline, 1895–1905* (Princeton: Princeton University Press, 1988) examines these trends, and their consequences, in detail.

[21]Adam Smith, *An Inquiry into the Nature and Causes of the Wealth of Nations* (New York: Modern Library, 1937 edition), Book 4, Chapter 2, p. 445. Edward Mead Earle, "Adam Smith, Alexander Hamilton, Friedrich List: The Economic Foundations of Military Power," in Peter Paret, ed., *Makers of Modern Strategy* (Princeton: Princeton University Press, 1986), pp. 217–261 provides a view of Smith as being far less bound by his ideas than those who succeeded him: "His followers were more doctrinaire free traders than Smith was himself" (p. 222). The key point, according to Earle, was that Smith understood that "when necessary, the economic power of the nation should be cultivated and used as an instrument of statecraft" (p. 225).

[22]The possible return of mercantilism has been a concern for some time. See especially Robert Gilpin, "Three Models of the Future," in C.F. Bergsten and L.B. Krause, eds., *World Politics and International Economics* (Washington, D.C.: The Brookings Institution, 1975), pp. 37–60. Gilpin shows particular concern about the possibility that a kind of "malignant mercantilism" will emerge.

[23]Peter F. Drucker, "The Age of Social Transformation," *The Atlantic Monthly*, 274/5:53–80 (November 1994), puts the matter starkly: "Knowledge has become the key resource, for a nation's military strength as well as for its economic strength" (p. 76).

[24]Bernard Brodie, *Sea Power in the Machine Age* (Princeton: Princeton University Press, 1944) explores in depth the dilemma of introducing innovations, in the context of 19th century British naval policy. The prevailing view at the Admiralty was of the need to monitor others' progress without revealing its own advances, thus stretching out the Royal Navy's advantages over its nearest competitors.

[25]Field Marshal Viscount Montgomery of Alamein, *A History of Warfare* (New York: World Publishing, 1969), p. 564; and Admiral W.A. Owens, *High Seas: The Naval Passage to an Uncharted World* (Annapolis: Naval Institute Press, 1995), especially pp. 162–166. The idea of garrisoning large ground forces at sea was advanced in P. Dadant, W. Mooz, and J. Walker, *A Comparison of Methods for Improving U.S. Capability to Project Ground Forces to Southwest Asia in the 1990s* (Santa Monica: RAND, 1984), which elucidated a concept of "mobile large islands" (MOLIs). See especially Appendix E.

[26]Dean Acheson, *Present at the Creation* (New York: Norton, 1969), p. 357, notes the problem and observes that only the "critical Russian error" of walking out of the Security Council, in a dispute over China, allowed the U.N. to respond at all to North Korean aggression without facing a certain Soviet veto.

[27]Alexander George and Richard Smoke, *Deterrence in American Foreign Policy* (New York: Columbia University Press, 1974) consider these forms of aggression among the most difficult to deter, as does John Mearsheimer, *Conventional Deterrence* (Ithaca: Cornell University Press, 1984), who argues for the need to be able to prevent initial overruns in order to make deterrence work. Paul Huth, *Extended Deterrence and the Prevention of War* (New Haven: Yale University Press, 1988) provides an argument that maintaining a robust local balance of forces is also a key element of a healthy environment for deterrence.

[28]On the rise of new networks of activist NGOs in civil society, see Howard Frederick, "Computer Networks and the Emergence of Global Civil Society," in Linda M. Harasim (ed.), *Global Networks: Computers and International Communication* (Cambridge: The MIT Press, 1993) pp. 283–295; James N. Rosenau, *Turbulence in World Politics: A Theory of Change and Continuity* (Princeton: Princeton University Press, 1990); Lester

M. Salamon, "The Rise of the Nonprofit Sector," *Foreign Affairs*, Vol. 73, No. 4, July/August 1994, pp. 109–122; David Ronfeldt and Cathryn Thorup, *Redefining Governance in North America: State, Society, and Security* (Santa Monica: RAND, DRU-459, August 1993); and Peter J. Spiro, "New Global Communities: Nongovernmental Organizations in International Decision-Making Institutions," The *Washington Quarterly*, Vol. 18, No. 1, Winter 1995, pp. 45–56.

[29]Chris Kedzie, "Democracy and Network Interconnectivity," finds, based on quantitative indicator analysis, that democracy correlates more strongly with Internet connectivity than with other touted social and economic factors. His research may raise interesting new questions about Seymour Martin Lipset's famous "optimistic equation"—that democracy goes hand in hand with prosperity. See Seymour Martin Lipset, *Political Man* (Baltimore: The Johns Hopkins University Press, expanded edition, 1981). Kedzie recognizes that causality may operate in more than one direction, particularly since both democracy and connectivity link to wealth. But whether the point should be about correlation or causality, Kedzie's analytic and anecdotal evidence suggest that the positive effects for U.S. interests from the prevalence of communication technologies are too strong to discount if the United States wants to advance its international influence.

However, inasmuch as connectivity is linked with wealth, it is not yet clear whether Kedzie and others have demonstrated only a correlation, or found evidence of a causal relationship.

[30]The concluding section of Edward Gonzalez and David Ronfeldt, *Cuba Adrift in a Postcommunist World* (Santa Monica: RAND, R-4231, 1992) recommends the development of a new information and communications policy to open up Cuba and strengthen civil society actors.

[31]Richard J. Barnet, "Defining the Moment," *The New Yorker*, July 16, 1990, pp. 46–60, quote from p. 48.

[32]See the discussion of "soft power" in Nye, *Bound to Lead*, especially pp. 187–195.

Chapter Nineteen

LOOKING AHEAD: PREPARING FOR INFORMATION-AGE CONFLICT

John Arquilla and David Ronfeldt

As we assembled this volume, we initially expected to conclude it in a standard manner: revisiting themes noted in the introduction, summarizing key points from the selections, and identifying issues for future research and development. This concluding chapter still has some of that flavor. But as we discussed how to write it, we realized our thoughts were cohering around four sets of ideas which, together, amount to the outlines of an integrated vision of information-age conflict—from how to think about it, to how to prepare for it and deal with it.

As a result, this chapter represents not only the conclusion of this book but also the beginning of an integrated vision of information-age conflict. This vision has four parts—conceptual, organizational, doctrinal, and strategic. Each part of this vision is tied to the others; each energizes the others.

*   Conceptual foundation: This vision entails, indeed requires, a deep, broad view of "information." This is achieved by adding to the dominant view that information is largely about "information processing" a less-developed view that is about "information structuring" or "structural information." In this latter view, information is what enables a structure to hold its form. This broad view of information refocuses thinking about the significance of information to organizations and leads to a recognition that their ideational superstructures are as important as their technological infrastructures.

- Organization: This vision emphasizes adapting to a major consequence of the information revolution—the rise of network forms of organization. The information revolution is empowering small forces and formations that can best take advantage of the network form. Some actors, such as transnational terrorists and criminals, are moving to networked designs. For governments and militaries, the challenge will be to develop *hybrids* in which "all-channel" networks are fitted to flattened hierarchies. The major benefits may accrue in the areas of interagency and interservice cooperation. Since militaries must retain hierarchical command structures at their core, their hybrids should retain— yet flatten—the residual hierarchy, while allowing dispersed maneuver "nodes" to have direct, all-channel contact with each other, and with the higher command.

- Doctrine: An integrated vision in this area should extend across the spectrum of conflict from low to high intensity, and across all services and other agencies. Our vision holds that "swarming" may be the key mode of conflict in the information age—it is more feasible than ever for offense and defense, across the entire spectrum of conflict. To develop advantages from the dynamics of networking among small, dispersed forces, a new doctrine, and related strategies and tactics, should be developed around swarming, whose full implications may mean that AirLand Battle should be superseded by a "BattleSwarm" doctrine.

- Strategy: Making this vision work depends on achieving unprecedented levels of information sharing—be that at the tactical level to enable small forces to cohere and swarm as networks in wartime, or at the level of grand strategy to advance U.S. power and influence around the world in peacetime. But U.S. interests also require that information sharing be protected. The development of a strategy of "guarded openness" is advisable at all levels, including at the level of grand strategy. We propose that a "revolution in diplomatic affairs" (RDA) be undertaken to match the revolution in military affairs (RMA) now under way.

Of course, information has always mattered; networking has long characterized some organizations; swarming has a history, especially in irregular warfare; and guarded openness is a traditional posture for democracies. What is new is the vastly increased degree to which each part of this vision matters now, and the increased degree to which the parts are interwoven.

We hope this vision proves useful for thinking about and preparing for conflicts and other interactions in the coming years. But we acknowledge that our ideas remain formative. We state them firmly, with studied conviction, but we know that more thought, research, and analysis must occur before definite answers and solutions emerge. This applies to all parts of our vision; each may develop in an uneven, perhaps ragged, fashion. Heeding the counsel of Stephen Rosen (1991, pp. 243–262), we mean to present our ideas not as though they amount to the "single best route to innovation," but rather as a road map, one of many that may merit exploration and elaboration, for helping come up with a broad, flexible "strategy for managing uncertainty" in a time of flux.

TOWARD A MORE STRUCTURAL VIEW OF INFORMATION

Lately, "information" has become an elusive concept, difficult to define. The more the information age deepens, the more this is evident. Questioning and rethinking are continually called for.

How a concept is defined affects what people think is most important. In most discourse, the term "information" is, and really can be, used without much questioning, largely because substantial traditions have grown around its usage. Thus, as an earlier study observed (see Chapter Six), information is normally regarded as being about a "message" and/or a "medium." Meanwhile, that paper noted, a speculative new idea is emerging that views some information as being "material"—as lying grandly at the core of all existence, where it may be as fundamental as matter and energy.[1] This is a heady, challenging idea that continues to gain ground; George Johnson's *Fire in the Mind* (1995) offers a good overview of the idea, much of which falls under the rubric of "information physics."

We draw on further ruminations and readings to look at information under two overarching views. One dominant overarching view is the "information processing view." We propose that it be balanced by another overarching view, a "structural information view," which has not yet received much articulation. And we identify some implications—indeed, clarifications—that this rebalancing may offer.

Information Processing and Structural Information Views

The view that "information" is mostly about signals being transmitted between senders and receivers—that is, about messages and the media through which they get communicated—is often summed up as the "information-processing view." It stems from the work of the seminal information theorists Claude Shannon, Warren Weaver, and Norbert Wiener in the 1940s; and for most contemporary theorists, it is the dominant view about information, including about its effects and implications for organizations and societies. James Beniger's *The Control Revolution* (1986, pp. 9–10) offers an exemplary picture of this view, in which "information processing is essential to all purposive activity":

> Information processing may be more difficult to appreciate than matter or energy processing because information is epiphenomenal: it derives from the *organization* of the material world on which it is wholly dependent for its existence. Despite being in this way higher order or derivative of matter and energy, information is no less critical to society. All living systems must process matter and energy to maintain themselves counter to entropy, the universal tendency of organization toward breakdown and randomization. Because control is necessary for such processing, and information, as we have seen, is essential to control, both information processing and communication, insofar as they distinguish living systems from the inorganic universe, might be said to define life itself—except for a few recent artifacts of our own species.

In recent years, expansive versions of this view have extended to claims that all physical matter (not to mention energy) as well as all biological and social systems have information at their core, and moreover that their motion, behavior, and evolution all revolve around information-processing (e.g., see Haefner, 1992; Johnson, 1995).[2] The grandest claims urge that the universe is tantamount to a giant computer or cellular automaton. In short, "everything is information."

But while much information is about processing, and while the processing view offers much that is systematic and sensible, there comes a point at which "processing" seems inadequate, inaccurate, or at least insufficient, both as a scientific concept and as a meaningful metaphor, for getting at what information is all about. One ends up with a series of processes piled on other processes. Information is not seen to have significance if it has no bearing as a message or message modifier in a process. It is seen as something that enters or exits a structure, or exists within it, primarily for the purpose of receiving, processing, and/or sending other information, matter, or energy on its way.

Yet much information may just be residing somewhere, embedded, doing little or nothing in the way of processing, while doing a lot to define a particular structure, give it shape, and hold it together—be it a physical, biological, or social structure. Such information is engaged less in "processing" than in "structuring." We do not introduce this point to deny the validity of the processing view, but rather to propose that a structural view—call it an "information structuring" or a "structural information" view—can add to our understanding of information and reorient thinking about it in useful ways.

Indeed, efforts to spell out the processing view eventually make statements about structure. According to one book, for example, information processing systems depend on the "internal information" that is a constitutive and "necessary component of every natural structure" and that allows *external* information "to be processed appropriately" (Haefner, 1992, pp. 4, 45). Moreover, "structural information" and "embodied knowledge" are essential parts of all information processing systems (Oeser, 1992, pp. 325–326). Such remarks start to elevate structure. Would it not be advisable to take steps to distinguish structure from process, and to place them on more equal analytic footings?

Structure and process are different—and in most sciences both are deemed essential for characterizing any system and its workings. Theorists in the physical and the social sciences tend to emphasize structural views—in "the structure of the atom" and "the structure of society." In contrast, "life processes" tend to get emphasized in the biological sciences. But whether structure or process is emphasized, neither is neglected—social theorists also study "the democratic process" and "the process of modernization," and biologists "the structure of the body." Indeed, theorists often bounce back and forth between issues of structure and process (sometimes by other names).

Explicit statements about the importance of including *both* structure and process are not common in the literatures of these varied sciences; theorists who study systems often use the terms without providing adequate definitions of either. But when such statements occur, the writers are often quite emphatic, as the following excerpt illustrates:

> The fact is that there are two traditions of explanation that march side by side in the ascent of man. One is the analysis of the physical structure of the world. The other is the study of the processes of life: their delicacy, their diversity, the wavering cycles from life to death in the individual and the species. And these traditions do not come together until the theory of evolution . . . . (Bronowski, 1973, p. 291).

In social and political theories, focusing on "structure" generally means focusing on actors (and "objects") and the organization of their relationships to each other (e.g., hierarchical relationships). Focusing on "process" generally means focusing on interactions and their dynamics. Structures contain the actors, processes the interactions; and both structure and process must be joined in systems theory (e.g., Bertalanffy, 1968; Waltz, 1979).[3] In many accounts, structure outweighs process—or at least it gets the dominant attention (e.g., Skocpol, 1979).[4] But in other accounts, copious processes prevail, because they may create new structures (e.g., Lenski, 1966).[5] In any case, the boundaries between structure and process are rarely sharply defined. Moreover, spirals of cause and effect involve both, inextricably. In short, both are important for understanding systems, and if one is discussed without the other, something is missing.

What does this have to do with information? Writing about information has long focused on notions about process, rarely about structure. Thinking about the concept of information, and about how a concept may have practical implications, will benefit from building up a structural view, as both a complement and a supplement to the processing view. We have not found any eminent guidance as to what a structural view of information should look like; but a working start might go like this: All structures contain embedded information. Where there is structure—or pattern or organization—there is information. Somehow, the amount of structure and the amount of information go together. Embedded information is what enables a structure—be it physical, biological, or social—to hold its form, to remain coherent, even to evolve and adapt. All forms of organization thus depend on embedded information; they do not have shape, and cannot retain their shape, without it. Indeed, the fact that incoming information may get restructured before it is absorbed, processed, and/or sent on its way may testify to the depth of the embedded information—it corresponds to a kind of cultural bias built into the structure, defining its identity and setting its predispositions. This is not to say that "everything is information" but rather that "everything *has* information" embedded in it if it has structure.

Few past efforts have gone in this direction. In one keen effort, though, Robert Wright (1989, p. 94) verges on adopting a structural view when he writes about how to define information:

> Apparently, information not only *has* structure; it is a prerequisite for the creation of structure—and for its preservation. It doesn't merely *embody* order; it advances order and maintains it. Information lies not just in form; information lies in formation. It is the stuff that leads the fight against the second law [of thermodynamics].

Unfortunately, he quickly abandons this view because it does not live up to what he thinks is needed for a definition of "real-life information," and his search for such a definition in the rest of his book is driven mainly by processing concerns.[6] But at least he illuminates a path not taken.

In this light, consider a map, any map: Does it process or structure information? Actually, it does both—and to assert that it is just one or the other is to miss half the full truth. The map serves as an information processor when the reader uses it to tell where he or she is. At the same time, the map as a whole portrays information about the structure of a territorial expanse.[7] Consider the written word: Is it for processing or structuring information? It is used for communication, which in most views is a kind of processing. Yet, a written language is based on agreements that particular assemblages of scribbled shapes have distinct meanings—what the message and the medium convey stems from deep symbolic and material structures, as well as processes, within a society. Consider a business or other organization: Is it better to view it as an information processor or structurer? Again, the best answer is "both"—although it is a more common practice these days to see an organization as a processor.

The general point, then, is not that the processing view is wrong but that, in one context after another, it is insufficient and, by itself, risks overextension if it is made the sole lens for looking at the role of information in organizations. A framework that also includes a structural view should be stronger analytically and should reveal "information" to be an even deeper, broader concept than often thought. Adding a structural view and keeping it in balance with the processing view may also have interesting, reorienting effects on the practical implications that a theoretical concept of information may lead to. Adding a structural view may help compensate for some biases that occasionally creep into the processing view (but may lead to new biases if too much weight is given to the structural view alone).

The processing view puts the spotlight on the transmission of messages, often as the inputs and outputs of a system. It lends itself to computational approaches that focus on data processing. It tends to emphasize the importance of the technological infrastructure. In so doing, it leads to thinking that organizations can be enhanced by adding new information and communications technologies, without necessarily having to change the organization's structure in order to adapt advantageously to a technology. Such biases are not always the case—the point that technology alone cannot improve an organization is well known to many expert exponents of the processing view—but they are common. Moreover, where an organization is resistant to change, an emphasis on the processing view may make it more likely that both the proponents and opponents of change shy away from posing and confronting structural questions about the nature of the organization.

In contrast, a structural view casts a spotlight on the values, goals, and principles that an organization embodies—on what matters to it and to its members, from the standpoint of its identity, meaning, and purpose as an entity, apart from whether it is doing information processing. A structural view relates to that part of the information revolution that is said to be about "knowledge"—it cannot be about "data," since data do not determine the nature of a structure. A structural view underscores how much a vibrant organization depends on deeply embedded information, and how difficult and complex it may be to change an organization. The best of the processing views may understand this as well; but it is not their normal starting point, which tends to be more about efficiency than about meaning and purpose. A structural view assumes at the start that an organization's information infrastructure is only part of the picture; more important is its ideational *superstructure* (see below). While the processing view tends to illuminate technology as a critical factor, a structural view is more likely to uphold human capital. While the processing view seems to appreciate quantitative approaches to information, a structural view is likely to be more qualitative.

We are not alone in espousing this perspective.[8] It has much in common with one espoused recently by the Japanese knowledge theorists Ikujiro Nonaka and Hirotaka Takeuchi (1995). Their criticisms of the information processing view are similar to ours. More to the point, their proposals for a broad new view that emphasizes "tacit" knowledge (which is largely qualitative and cultural, and different from "explicit" knowledge) are akin to our ideas about structural information:

> Although Western managers have been more accustomed to dealing with explicit knowledge, the recognition of tacit knowledge and its importance has a number of crucially relevant implications. First, it gives rise to a whole different view of the organization—not as a machine for processing information but as a living organism. Within this context, sharing an understanding of what the company stands for, where it is going, what kind of a world it wants to live in, and how to make that world a reality becomes much more crucial than processing objective information. Highly subjective insights, intuitions, and hunches are an integral part of knowledge. Knowledge also embraces ideals, values, and emotion as well as images and symbols. These soft and qualitative elements are crucial to an understanding of the Japanese view of knowledge (Nonaka and Takeuchi, 1995, p. 9).

It is encouraging for us to find that other thinkers are moving in this vein. Yet, while Nonaka and Takeuchi pinpoint how Western and Japanese management views may differ, the challenge for the United States will be to formulate views that have global, as well as national, appeal.

Infrastructure and Superstructure Are Both Important

Some of these points may be visualized, and summed up, by taking a new look at the "information pyramid"—the distinction between the structural and the processing views casts a new light on it. As discussed in an earlier paper (see Chapter Six), the pyramid, recast in Figure 19.1, has a wide base of raw, disorganized "data" and "facts," atop which sits a narrower stratum of organized "information." The next, still narrower stratum corresponds to information refined into "knowledge" (including "ideas"). Atop that, at the peak, sits the most distilled stratum, "wisdom"—the highest level of information. The pyramid may appear to imply that the higher levels rest on the lower, but that is true only to a degree. Each layer has some independence—more data does not necessarily mean more knowledge, and as critic Theodore Roszak (1986) objects, in a wide-ranging attack on the information processing view, "information" should not be mistaken for "ideas."[9]

The processing and structural views can be identified with different strata in this pyramid, as indicated in Figure 19.1. The processing view relates mainly to the lower two strata. Its articulators write

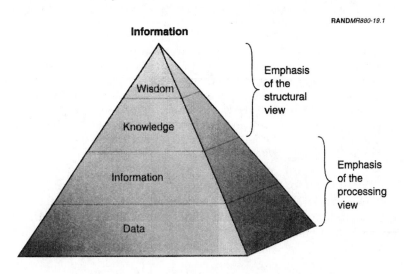

Figure 19.1—The "Information Pyramid" from Two Views

mainly about the processing of data and information; they rarely discuss knowledge processing,[10] and normally shy away from notions of wisdom processing. In contrast, the structural view shifts the focus. It is very much about the top two strata—it relates to the laws, rules, strictures, codes, goals, ideals, and values that are embedded and embodied in institutions, cultures, and other structures. The lowly data stratum may have little or no significance for a structuralist.

Can we be more specific about what a "structural information view" may look like analytically? Insofar as societal structures are the focus—and that is our key concern here, not physical and biological structures—we will borrow from the social science literature to propose that a structural view could include (or be decomposed into) the following levels or layers: an ideational superstructure, an organizational structure, a technological infrastructure, and possibly also a linguistic substructure.[11]

- The "ideational superstructure" is the level of ideas and ideologies, myths and maxims, values and norms, rites and rituals, laws[12] and rules, etc. that define, often abstractly, the nature of a culture and the structures within it. A structural view should, among other things, lead the analyst's eye to the belief systems in a society about information and communications—about what it may mean to have an "information culture," be part of the "information revolution," and develop an "information society." Debates about whether a particular government should allow people to own computers and connect to the Internet may pertain here, particularly if those debates reflect broader beliefs about the nature of a society.

- The "organizational structure" is the level of particular organizations in a society. Broadly speaking, the structural view holds that all organizations depend on information and may be analyzed as information structures. Narrowly speaking, this is the level for identifying which organizations in a society (and still more narrowly, which offices in a corporation or other entity) are concerned with information and communications matters specifically. Societies differ greatly according to the richness, or the lack, of organizations for dealing with such matters: Are they concentrated in the government sector? Or the market sector? What about civil society? As to the last, it is noteworthy that very few societies have entities like the Electronic Freedom Foundation (EFF) or Computer Professionals for Social Responsibility (CPSR).

- The level of the "technological infrastructure" refers to all the hardware and software systems, and all the connectivity, that support communications and information flows—not simply the Internet, but television, radio, telephones, etc.[13] This is, of course, the level that the information-processing view tends to focus on.[14]

- Though debatable, it may be wise to posit a "linguistic substructure" as a distinct level—this would recognize that much of what may emerge and take shape at the other levels, and especially at the ideational level, may depend on linguistics, or perhaps it would be better to say the cognitive and epistemological orientations of a society. This is the level where the most basic concepts are formed about what matters and what is possible. For example, this is the structural level where it may make a difference whether English or some other language dominates discourse on the Internet or in television satellite broadcasts.

At all these levels, information remains central to the analysis of order and change in systems, but in ways different from the case with the processing view. Ideally, there should be "coherence" within and among all levels; "information decoherence" (term from Johnson, 1995) may bring on structural instability, leading possibly to breakdown and/or radical reform. Indeed, in this view, conflicts occur because of differences in structural information (e.g., in religious beliefs at the ideational level), more so than because of differences in information processing capabilities. The structural view, like the processing view, may be used for comparing societies—but with the advantage of encouraging analysis that goes well beyond technological factors.

Figures 19.2 and 19.3 portray the two views. Figure 19.2 shows an input-output diagram of an information processing system in which a sender transmits a message to a receiver by way of a channel. The structural view requires a different diagram. Figure 19.3 depicts the information-related structures noted above—an organizational structure bound with an ideational superstructure and a technological infrastructure, and also having a cognitive/linguistic substructure at its core. This diagram is not about inputs and outputs but rather about interrelationships, as signified by the up-down arrow.

Developing a structural view to blend with the processing view could lead to the fusion of separate traditions in "communication studies" and "information theory"—and this fusion could benefit policymakers and strategists who are trying to figure out what "information strategy" America should follow today. As noted earlier, discussions based on information theory hark back to the work by Shannon and others in the 1940s and 1950s that gave rise to today's technology-oriented view of information. Indeed, Figure 19.2 modifies a diagram by Shannon, a founding father of information theory. But while "information" was receiving the kind of attention at mid-century that stressed its engineering dimensions, "communication" was receiving another kind of attention among another set of theorists who emphasized the ideational dimensions.

Everett Rogers (1994, pp. 10–16) shows that the field of communication studies developed in the 1930s and 1940s was dominated by such leading social scientists as Harold Lasswell, Paul Lazarsfeld, and Wilbur Schramm. While they were broadly interested in communications issues, World War II drove them to focus intently on understanding propaganda, measuring public opinion, analyzing the impact of the media, and using communications to influence public

RAND*MR880-19.2*

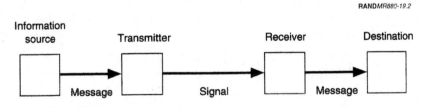

NOTE: This is a variant of a famous diagram by Claude Shannon and Warren Weaver. In particular, our variant omits the introduction of "noise" that may mean the signal sent is not the signal received. If we were to leave noise in this figure, we would have to add it to Figure 19.3—but that could raise a whole new issue for discussion that is better left to future elaborations of our present ideas.

Figure 19.2—Classic Information-Processing View

RAND*MR880-19.3*

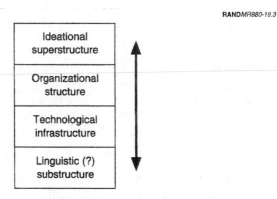

Figure 19.3

Figure 19.3—An Information Structuring View

and private behavior on behalf of the war effort (e.g., to promote the cultivation of "victory gardens"). While these social scientists gave some attention to developments abroad (e.g., to support "black propaganda"), their primary focus was defending and strengthening public morale on the home front. The guiding phrase for research came from Lasswell in 1940: "Who says what, to whom via what channels, with what effects?" But the most prescient warning for policy and strategy was sounded by Schramm shortly after Pearl Harbor: "Perhaps more than any previous war this is likely to be a war of communications."

In short, the rise of information theory depended on hard scientists, and that of communication studies on social scientists. While the work of the information theorists went into improving America's weapons systems, that of the communication experts went into protecting our value systems. While the ideas of the information theorists moved in the direction of cybernetics and general systems theory, those of the communication experts led to new schools and centers for elevating the study of public opinion, the media, and journalism.

Today, it is advisable for information strategists to develop a structural view to go with the processing view. The latter view undergirds current notions that analysts and policymakers should focus on the information technology infrastructure—and, from an information-warfare perspective, on the vulnerabilities of that infrastructure to attack. But this bias neglects the importance of the ideational super-structure—and the prospect that an information-warfare attacker may want the technology (e.g., the Net) working so that public or elite opinion can be influenced, whether by single, perhaps frightening moves, or through multiple nuanced measures that may have cumulative corrosive effects. In key respects, the history of communication studies is more about structural information, especially at the ideational level, and about protecting it from the kinds of attacks that technologists have not been attending to. This history serves to substantiate that today's information strategists should be adopting a broader view than has been purveyed by many information-warfare scenarists.[15]

Both traditions also speak to the importance of U.S. government and foundation sponsorship for innovative research. With the arrival of World War II, the fields of information theory (including cybernetics) and communication studies were given separate impetus through support provided by U.S. government (especially military) offices that not only sponsored research but also worked to create networks for sharing knowledge between government and academic researchers. For example, the Office of Facts and Figures (OFF), later the Office of War Information (OWI), and, apart from it, the Rockefeller Foundation (through the Rockefeller Communication Seminar) played key roles in the shaping of communication studies. Today, a key government role is played by a set of offices in the Pentagon, particularly in the Office of the Secretary of Defense (Command, Control, Communications, and Intelligence), which is continuing this tradition.

Building Bridges to Organization, Doctrine, and Strategy—and More

This is a preliminary basis for formulating a structural view and matching it, in a balanced way, to the processing view. Yet, working with these two overarching views seems to offer a better basis for creating a conceptual framework about information than did our earlier tripartite distinctions about the message, the medium, and the material view of information. That earlier approach is engulfed by the one presented here.

For example, a structural view appears to deepen understanding of the human and the technological factors at stake. Regarding the human factors, education and training programs obviously serve to improve the knowledge base of an organization. But the ways that information gets imparted and embedded may run deeper than explicit education. Consider the practice of daily routine marching and drilling, which was instituted by the Dutch and French armies in the 17th century (although the Roman army had set some precedents). William McNeill (1982, pp. 125–132) relates that this simple practice had unexpectedly profound psychological and cultural effects that made soldiers more efficient and effective. Through routine drill, soldiers became more prone to obey orders from their commanders, to bond socially with others in their unit, to gain a sense of *esprit de corps* even though they came from different villages and strata, and to feel separate from people in society at large. Meanwhile, they also gained knowledge about how use new weapons on the battlefield. Marching and drilling are not normally viewed as ways to embed tacit information in a fighting force—and that is why we raise it here. It materially strengthens the unit, in part by strengthening the immaterial dimensions of power: will power, discipline, and camaraderie. This is the case, as well, with later, more advanced, explicit types of training, education, exercise, and simulation.

As to technology, a structural view clarifies further what we meant earlier (see Chapter Six) by the "information package" of a weapon. That term (or alternatives, like "information quotient") refers not just to the processing systems associated with the weapon (e.g., for guidance) but to the whole set of technologies embedded structurally in it. The information revolution may make ideas more valuable than things—but a structural view implies that the distinction between "ideas" and "things" is blurring, particularly as things may be viewed as the embodiment of ideas.

The larger question for this study is: Does the addition of a structural view help with our effort to convey the organizational, doctrinal, and strategy parts of an integrated vision? We think so, and we will point out how as we discuss these parts in the pages that follow. Perhaps more than anything, the addition of a structural view illuminates how complex innovation can be, and how very difficult it can be to try to institute radical organizational, doctrinal, and strategic changes.

ADAPTATION TO NETWORKED FORMS OF ORGANIZATION

The information age is facilitating two major organizational trends: one is the rising power of small groups, the other is the rise of network forms of organization. The two trends feed on each other— networks of small actors stand to gain more power and influence than they have previously ever had.

Thus, the organizational part of our effort to posit an integrated vision of conflict in the information age reiterates a theme we have long emphasized: the rise of network forms of organization (Arquilla and Ronfeldt, 1993, 1996; Ronfeldt, 1992, 1996). The basic argument is that the information revolution favors the rise of networks, while making life difficult for hierarchies. The type of network especially favored is the "all-channel" type, in which diverse, dispersed, often small actors (or "nodes") all link together to consult, coordinate, and act jointly, preferably in a non-hierarchical manner, across greater distances and on the basis of better and faster information than ever before. Network designs have been in existence since ancient times, but new information technologies finally provide for the abundance of information connections and flows that network designs require.

The rise of network forms of organization remains at an early stage, still gaining impetus. It may be decades before this trend reaches maturity. But it is already affecting all realms of society in positive ways. For example, in the realm of the *state*, it is facilitating the formation of interagency mechanisms for addressing complex policy issues that cut across jurisdictional boundaries. In the realm of the *market*, it has been facilitating the emergence of Japanese *keiretsus* and similar distributed, web-like global enterprises (including "virtual corporations"). Indeed, volumes are being written, mostly in the United States and Japan, about the benefits of network designs for business corporations and market operations—to the point that casual observers might presume that this is the realm most affected and benefited.

However, although the evidence is still sparse, it appears that *civil society* actors are heavily favored by the effectiveness of network designs. Nongovernmental organizations (NGOs) that once had to operate largely in isolation from each other can now cluster together. The trend seems keenest among the multi-organizational networks that have been multiplying among relatively small activist NGOs (e.g., those for human rights and environmental issues) across the political spectrum—and across national boundaries. In the long run, civil society is likely to be strengthened more than the other realms. Indeed, for some NGOs the long-range aim is to construct a transnational "global civil society" powerful enough to counterbalance the roles of state and market actors.

Overall, then, the trend toward "the age of networks" is so strong that, projected into the future, it augurs transformations in how societies are organized—if not in societies as a whole, at least key parts of their governments, economies, and especially their civil societies. This all sounds positive. But, meanwhile, the rise of the network form also augurs a new epoch of conflict.

Power is migrating to small, mostly nonstate adversaries who can organize into sprawling networks more readily than can traditionally hierarchical nation-state actors. Not only civil society but also "uncivil society" is benefiting from the rise of network forms of organization. Some uncivil actors, such as terrorists and criminals, are having little difficulty forming highly networked, nonhierarchical organizations. Thus, networked adversaries may be expected to pose increasing threats to the United States and its interests around the world. Conflicts will more often be fought by "networks" than by "hierarchies."

It will not be easy for hierarchies to fight networks in the information age; to a considerable degree, it will take networks to fight networks. Yet, state actors, such as professional militaries, cannot do without their hierarchies; they must continue to uphold hierarchy at their core. At the same time, they should not forgo the advantages of using network-based designs, particularly to increase their agility and flexibility for field operations. The challenge will be to combine hierarchical and network designs. In our view, the U.S. military and other security actors should aim to adapt hierarchies to networks by synthesizing hybrids.

Networked Adversaries on the Rise

The major motivation for the U.S. government to adapt to network forms of organization comes not from alluring theories about the likely efficiency and effectiveness benefits, but rather from some distressing new realities: Many adversaries of U.S. interests are well along the path of learning to utilize networks to improve their agility and versatility. This is particularly the case with actors at the low-intensity end of the spectrum of conflict and crime.

Uncivil actors—such as terrorist groups and criminal gangs—once operated pretty much in isolation from each other. But now, hierarchical Mafia clans led by "dons" and "capos," modeled on the Roman empire, are giving way to much "flatter" transnational criminal organizations (TCOs), such as seen among the Colombian and Mexican drug cartels, the Asian triads, and even in Chicago's Gangsta Disciples. Similarly, terrorist organizations are leaving behind the era of the "great man" leader, and moving to use flexible network designs that may have multiple leaders. The PLO of Arafat is less the paradigm than the "governance of the many" seen in Hamas. Transnational terrorist organizations are emerging on the political left (e.g., Hamas) and on the right (e.g., among "white supremacy" and "skinhead" groups). All are building transnational networks as "force multipliers," and using all manner of old and new communications technologies to do so. Because of the shift from absolutist hierarchies to hydra-headed networks, none are as easy to "decapitate" as they may once have been.

Besides terrorists and criminals, the low end of the conflict spectrum is also populated by information-age revolutionaries and old-style ethnonationalists. They too seem increasingly comfortable with networked organizational structures, which are commonly enhanced by kinship ties. That these actors have gained strength and flexibility through networking is seen in two recent cases of netwar. First, as related in Chapter Sixteen, the Zapatista insurrection in Chiapas featured a small insurgent force, acting as the striking arm of a local network of Mayan peoples, that was able to build additional, transnational networks with activist NGOs from around the world in a successful effort to constrain the Mexican government from crushing the rebellion bloodily, and instead persuade it to agree to political negotiations. Second, the Chechen struggle against the Russians shows that a networked rebel force, composed of small bands of 12 to 20 fighters, can confront, and beat, a modern army. This case raises the possibility that networked forces can fight not only insurgencies, but also mid-level, and even quite high-intensity, conflicts.

The rise of a new generation of networked adversaries—terrorists, criminals, insurgents, and ethnic warriors—raises questions about whether today's professional military and police forces and intelligence agencies have the most appropriate organizational structures for an era in which new destructive and disruptive powers are migrating into the hands of small groups that are internetted with other small groups. As Van Creveld (1996, p. 58) remarks,

> In today's world, the main threat to many states, including specifically the US, no longer comes from other states. Instead, it comes from small groups and other organizations which are not states. Either we make the necessary changes and face them today, or what is commonly known as the modern world will lose all sense of security and will dwell in perpetual fear.

Endurance of Hierarchies, Advent of Networks

Can modern hierarchies do well against information-age networks? Debates about hierarchies versus networks are filling up bookshelves these days. These debates have two levels, which should not be confused. One level is deep, theoretical, and philosophical. At this level, theorists have been arguing that hierarchies or networks (or markets, for that matter) are the key form of organization, or set of dynamics, that underlies essentially all order (and maybe chaos) in the world. In the social sciences, for example, some early writings about general systems theory (e.g., Bertalanffy, 1968) and complexity (e.g., Simon, 1962) took stances lauding the roles of hierarchies. Today, arguments are coming to the fore that networks are the crucial design, such that "the web of life consists of networks within networks," not hierarchies (Capra, 1996, p. 35). This is an enlightening debate, but it is not the more practical of the two.

The second level of debate is practical and empirical; it has theoretical and philosophical dimensions as well, but they are generally tied to real-life matters in the worlds of government, military, and business affairs. In this debate, hierarchies and networks (not to mention markets) are distinct, bounded forms of organization that enable people and other societal actors to do practical things. Hierarchies, of one variety or another, are recognized as having lain at the administrative core of states, militaries, and corporations for centuries. Today, networks, especially the all-channel variety, are being touted and examined, sometimes carefully, sometimes with incautious exuberance, as the up-and-coming form of organization for gaining the agility, flexibility, and versatility that a government agency, business enterprise, or civil-society actor may desire for doing well in the information age.

This level of debate is many-faceted. However, here we focus only on two points that are consistent with our central theme for the organizational part of our vision: the advisability of moving toward networked designs. First, hierarchies are not "goners" because of the information age—but they must adapt. Second, learning to blend hierarchies and networks into workable hybrids is essential—but it will not be an easy task.

The dawning of "the age of networks" does not spell the end of hierarchy, or the nation-state, as some thinkers have speculated. Theorists should be wary of such speculations because hierarchies, of one variety and then another, have been eroding and becoming outmoded for centuries, often as a result of epochal shifts in information and communication technologies. The classic, oft-noted example is the decline in the power of that great hierarchy the Papacy, and of the Catholic Church more generally, as a result of the spread of the printing press—but this decline gave way to the rise of monarchies and then nation-states as powerful new hierarchies (Anderson, 1991; Anderson, 1974). Later, during the period from 1880 to 1918, the next generation of technological innovation, which included the telegraph, telephone, wireless radio, and the airplane, led to new shifts in peoples' perceptions of time and space, bringing a new round in "the leveling of traditional hierarchies" along with "a general cultural challenge to all outmoded hierarchies" (Kern, 1983, p. 315). But while these innovations eroded the old aristocracies and aided the rise of democracies, it was not long afterwards that new kinds of hierarchies emerged, from the awful totalitarian regimes of Adolph Hitler and Joseph Stalin, to the productive business corporations of Henry Ford, Pierre DuPont, and other capitalist innovators.

Today, the latest information revolution augurs not the end of hierarchy, but rather a new epoch of adaptation. Network designs may supplant hierarchical ones in some areas. In other areas, new kinds of hierarchies may emerge that are better suited to the information age. And in still other areas, synthetic hybrids of the two designs will be the result.

Adding a structural view to the processing view of information, as discussed earlier, clarifies that large-scale, purposeful, organizational change is a complex, dynamic, difficult undertaking. Organizations structure and process information; they are, or have at their core, systems for doing so.[16] Change the organization, and those systems change with it. Tinker with those systems, and you may be tinkering, knowingly or unknowingly, with the organization's design and performance, for better or worse. For example, there is ample evidence by now that simply "throwing computers" at an organization often proves to be a misguided way to improve its efficiency and effectiveness. What, and how much, information (from any level of the "information pyramid") an organization can process well is bound to depend partly on what, and how much, information is already structurally embedded in it. Indeed, any form of organization—a hierarchy, a network, or whatever—may not work well until it embodies the values, norms, doctrines, rituals, etc. that are appropriate to that form.

Consider the four major forms that, over the ages, appear to account for the organization and evolution of societies: tribes, institutions, markets, and networks (see Ronfeldt, 1996). Very different types of information—and different information cultures and strategies—pertain to each form. In the case of tribes (and clans), the most valued information is often about kinship ties; in the case of institutions, it is about the reasons for hierarchy; in markets, it is about opportunities for exchange; and, while it is still early to be sure about information-age networks, information about the capacity for teamwork may be highly valued.

Thus, each of these forms depends on the existence of a different information culture, and on that culture being upheld through socialization and education, as well as law and punishment. Moreover, each form requires a different complexity of information structures and processes to function well—for example, from an informational perspective, market systems are generally more complex than tribal systems. The appropriate design of technological infrastructures to support communication flows is only a part of the total picture of the ways in which information gets embedded in such systems—so deeply embedded that theorists and practitioners who are accustomed to looking more at *transmitted* than at *embedded* information may overlook how something that seems ordinary (e.g., routine marching drills, as noted earlier) may actually be a significant information agent.

Societies have spent centuries getting the hierarchical form right, all the time modifying it in accordance with new conditions. Getting the network form right in the future will be no easy task. Moreover, just as the organizational ecology of an advanced society like the United States is populated by various types of hierarchies, the future may lead to the emergence of various types of networks—and various ways of blending them with hierarchies. What emerges, and works, in one setting may not be the same in another.

At this point, a distinction should be made between the "organizational networks" and "networked organizations" that analysts have been writing about. The two are quite different. Although usage of the terms is not settled, we define an "organizational network" (or multiorganizational network) as consisting of a variety of actors who are often dispersed, who may belong to different independent organizations, and whose relationship is fundamentally nonhierarchical. A "networked organization" is a bounded organization (like a corporation) whose internal structure probably maintains a hierarchy at its core but that in other respects has evolved from a mainly hierarchical to a heavily networked design. Both types are subject to hybridization, the latter more so than the former. And both types figure in the hybrids we discuss next.

Hybrids of Hierarchies and Networks

Whoever masters the network form stands to gain major advantages in the coming epoch. For governments, this really means learning to develop hybrids.

Some hybrids already exist and are being tested. The business world is ahead of the government world in this respect. Modern corporations have spent the last few decades becoming "flatter," and more networked. Large corporations still want to retain strong central control—but their production and marketing processes may well engage widespread networks of smaller companies. In the government world, signs of hybridization appear in efforts to build interagency and interservice networks. For example, counterterrorism and counternarcotics efforts involve mechanisms, some institutionalized and some ad-hoc, that aim to combine and coordinate mixes of military, police, and intelligence components. And some parts of the U.S. armed forces are also experimenting with networked designs, as noted in the next section. But none of the endeavors in the government and military worlds have yet provided sound models for forming hybrids of hierarchies and networks. One problem that continues to bedevil effective hybridization is that of overcoming (while also safeguarding) the participants' institutional affiliations and loyalties to the hierarchies from which they come, while getting them to identify with and act in the interests of the interagency or interservice network.

While all this is being worked out, the destructive and disruptive powers of networks of small groups are gaining momentum all across the conflict spectrum. Thus, there is some urgency to learning to adapt and innovate around this factor. In the military area, for example, if the United States does not adjust to smaller units of maneuver, our large field armies, air wings, and naval battlegroups may face future difficulties grappling with nimble foes and may be quite vulnerable to their attacks. If we learn to rebuild around smaller (but stronger) military formations, the benefits may include providing for national security and military readiness at significantly reduced costs. In our view, the network, in particular the all-channel network, is the optimal form of organization for dealing with information-age conflict across the spectrum, from low to high intensity. However, this runs counter to much thinking in the defense community, where the attachment to hierarchical designs remains strong, and not without basis. Militaries, as many argue, must continue to have clear, top-down control, lest they founder under the "generalship of the many." But the choice is not between shifting entirely to networks, or remaining entirely hierarchical. Rather, the key redesign questions revolve around the manner in which networks may be skillfully blended with hierarchies, so that, in Mao's famous phrase, one may "centralize strategically, but decentralize tactically."

What might a hybrid look like in the U.S. military? The following scenario is speculative, but it is also consistent with the vision presented here: The chain of command is flattened, with many links removed that currently exist between the highest and lower levels. The highest levels of command are retained, including the regional commanders-in-chief (CINCs) and the National Command Authority (NCA). But the current structuring of forces into divisions and corps is replaced. New, small maneuver units are created as the backbone of the new structure, and their junior commanders have direct access to their CINCs (and vice versa). These units are roughly platoon-sized, and resemble the "infestation team" concept that the Marines are now experimenting with. These units are fully internetted; they are all able to communicate and coordinate with each other, independent of the higher command, although the CINC has awareness (topsight) of their communications and actions. Though headed by junior officers, the units can control and call on fire from assets "owned" by any service.

This is a radical scenario. It would surely be opposed by two- and three-star generals who currently command brigades, divisions and corps and thus stand between the CINCs and junior commanders of today's maneuver units. But there is a historical wartime precedent for the scenario: Germany's U-boat fleet during World War II. It had many of the characteristics noted above. Indeed, Admiral Dönitz, the U-boat campaign commander, made it a practice to meet as many returning U-boats as possible, often personally debriefing their junior-officer skippers (Dönitz, 1959). It is interesting to note that German submariners began to muse that they could do without the old, top-heavy hierarchy of the German military as early as World War I. But, near the end of that war, when Germany's defeat seemed inevitable, the traditional, by-now-resentful, surface-fleet commanders called for creating a U-boat "cemetery" to put an end to this threat to their authority and their control of budgetary assets (Herwig, 1981).

This scenario calls for reductions in the levels of leadership above the field grade, but below the level of regional command. This might seem analogous to the frequent calls for the downsizing of "middle management" in the business world in recent years. But this isn't quite what the scenario implies; it really targets the lower layer of upper management and views the junior commanders of the maneuver units as being more akin to middle-level managers.

The role of middle managers may turn out to be a key issue for the design of hybrid management systems. While all layers—from top to bottom—are affected by the information revolution, it is often said that middle management is the most affected—the flattening of hierarchies, in response to the information revolution, is widely supposed to spell the reduction if not elimination of many middle managers. Evidence exists for this by now, but it mainly involves middle managers who were performing information-processing and clerk-like functions. The story is not so clear where middle managers perform more innovative, operational functions. A few voices have noted this, keeping open the prospect that middle managers are far from obsolete, while more broadly defending the importance of hierarchy as an organizing principle: Layering remains entirely functional for the performance of complex tasks by large organizations, with about seven hierarchical layers being optimal (Jacques, 1990). Middle managers may be needed more than ever in the future, particularly to service and maintain links between different working groups in large organizations (Penzias, 1990). Ikujiro Nonaka and Hirotaka Takeuchi (1995) reach the farthest in not only praising middle managers for playing vital roles, but in urging that "middle up-down management" is often better than top-down or bottom-up designs for fostering knowledge creation in organizations. So, the debates about middle management's significance are far from settled (and depend partly on what layers are defined as "middle").

This aside, the foregoing scenario and the rest of our discussion indicate the likely essence of hybridization: Hierarchy is preserved, but flattening occurs, with the reductions coming from the lower-upper or the upper-middle command layers. Whether it is considered a facet of hierarchy or networking, the reformed structure allows, indeed requires, direct access and constant contact between the high-ranking commanders and the junior officers who head the maneuver units. The network design appears mainly in the all-channel links established among the maneuver units, and to the outside sources of intelligence and fire that they may call upon.

This is not a design that would work with any of today's military doctrines. It would require an entirely new doctrine.

TOWARD A DOCTRINE BASED ON SWARMING

We (not to mention our contributors) anticipate a landscape of conflict that calls not only for new organizational designs but also for related changes in doctrine. What operational behavior may be most effective for small, dispersed, mobile forces that are joined in networks? The short answer is swarming. Moving to smaller, dispersed units of maneuver may not bring advantages, and may make little sense, unless they have a deliberate, well-designed capability to swarm. If the optimal form of organization is the dispersed network, the corresponding doctrine must surely consist of the swarm.

Little analytic attention has been given to swarming (Kelly, 1994, is an exception). Yet, swarming may well become the key mode of conflict in the information age. New doctrines built around swarming are likely to emerge all across the conflict spectrum, for high- and low-intensity conflicts as well as for terrorist, criminal, and radical social conflicts. Indeed, swarming strategies are already emerging at the latter end of the spectrum.

Swarming is achieved when the dispersed nodes of a network of small (and also perhaps some large) forces can converge on an enemy from multiple directions, through either fire or maneuver. The overall aim should be *sustainable pulsing*—swarm networks must be able to coalesce rapidly and stealthily on a target, then dissever and redisperse, immediately ready to recombine for a new pulse. A swarm network should have little to no mass as a rule (except perhaps during a pulse), but it should have a high energy potential—like a swarm of bees that can fell a mighty beast, or a network of antibodies that can attack a spreading virus. The effect on an adversary is likely to be highly disruptive, and also highly destructive should the network wish to fire at will upon its disorganized foe. Today's trends toward tactical decentralization, coupled with strategic "topsight" (the term is from Gelernter, 1991), may produce war-winning advantages as long as the new organization learns to fight in a new way.

Throughout history, organizational and technological innovations have affected the balance between the offense and defense. Some innovations have initially favored the offense, others the defense. For example, the combination of tank and plane favored offensive *blitzkrieg*, whereas, a generation earlier, barbed wire and machine guns gave all the advantages to defensive trench warfare. At present, swarming is becoming more sustainable than ever for offensive operations, and more difficult to defend against. Thus, the development of a capacity for swarming, be that by a terrorist or a criminal organization, by a potential peer competitor, or by U.S. military and police forces, would probably favor whoever is determined to use swarming for offensive purposes.

Information and the Evolution of Organization and Doctrine

The correct conduct of all modes of conflict requires information—both structural information, so that people know (and are trained to know) what to do and why, in an organized manner, as well as information-processing systems, so they can spot attacks and targets, identify friend from foe, and coordinate operations. The history of warfare and other modes of conflict may be viewed, then, as a history of how organization and doctrine evolve depending on the information that can be embedded in and processed by them.

Beyond the foregoing examples, does the hypothesis about the co-evolution of information systems and battle doctrines fit the historical evidence more generally? Briefly, warfare has evolved from chaotic melees in which every man fought on his own, to the design of massed, but often rigid formations, and then to the adoption of maneuver. Each stage in this development is associated with a progression in the quantity and quality of information, from both structural and processing viewpoints. When there was little reason to train as a body, little ability to communicate during battle with one's own forces, and only notional understandings of the opponent's intentions, the free-for-all melee dominated. As means of signaling emerged (e.g., semaphores) and weaponry was introduced that benefited from coordinated fire (e.g., muskets), more controlled formations came into being (usually linear in nature). Further advances in organization and technology led to ever more supple maneuver capabilities, with mobile columns to some extent replacing linear formations (Van Creveld, 1985; Keegan, 1993). This progression in organization and doctrine—from the melee, to massing, to maneuver—appears in all the realms of war: on land, at sea, and in the air.

While examples of this progression abound in each of the spatial domains of war, our points are neatly substantiated by the most modern of the three realms—air and space. Aerial operations, which arose this century, have followed a similar pattern, in which advances in combat formations have depended on information-related advances. In World War I, battles in the air by lone fighters were expressly "dogfights," a kind of melee. Later, especially during World War II, the rise of the long-range bomber prompted the development of organized formations, with the spatial characteristics of air warfare militating against "lines" and favoring columns or "boxes" (e.g., the massed formations of B-17s). As for maneuver, air power's close ties to advanced technologies, including for communications, have led it, from World War II onward, to move toward notions that resemble swarming, far more than has been the case with ground and naval power. This is evident in the fighter-bomber campaigns in France in 1944, Korea during 1950–1953, Vietnam from 1965 to 1973, and the Persian Gulf in 1991. Each of these swarm-like campaigns depended heavily upon massive, timely information flows for air tasking and battle management, as well as for the avoidance of fratricide (i.e., the bombing or strafing of one's own troops). Indeed, without a sophisticated information-management capability, such as was afforded by JSTARS (the Joint Surveillance and Target Acquisition Radar System), the air campaign against Iraq in 1991 would have been only a fraction as effective as it proved to be (see Hallion, 1992).

The history of social conflict has been less comprehensively studied in terms of how organization and doctrine may be related to information; but it seems to contain a pattern much like that found in military history. Where groups of people are not well organized and have poor communications capabilities, riotous melees and shoving matches are often the main result. Likewise, the anarchism of violence-prone loners does not require much information from an organizational standpoint. The social equivalents of massing and maneuvering appear with the rise, in the 20th century, of Leninist parties and Maoist insurgencies. Modern-day terrorism aspires to *blitzkrieg*-like sophistication but rarely attains it.

Today, and on into the future, new information technologies enable the swarm. On the surface, it may bear some resemblance to the melee. But swarming is far more organized and requires expertly trained forces and the highest levels yet of command and control. The information revolution is the key to the development of new designs and capabilities for sustainable swarming—from the establishment of an initial posture of dispersed forces, to the coalescing of those forces for an attack, to their dissevering return to the safety of wide dispersion, and their preparation for a new pulse. Only a new generation of robust information gathering and distribution systems can support such pulsing.

History of Swarming As a Mode of Conflict

Before trying to look further into the future, we first want to clarify that swarming is not entirely new. It has occurred throughout history. Although it has not been, or been capable of becoming, a dominant approach to war and other modes of conflict until now, instructive historical examples exist of forces that maneuvered as networks and swarmed to the attack (or defense) as circumstances dictated.

A good example from medieval history is the Mongols' sweeping conquest of Asia on horseback (see Chapter Two). An excellent modern example of swarming at sea lies in the somewhat misnamed "wolf pack" tactics of the German U-boat fleet during World War II. These "wolves" did not run in a pack. Rather, they were distributed over a battlespace that, even at the tactical level (i.e., for a specific convoy battle), was spread over thousands of square kilometers. When a prime target set was located, telecommunications allowed the dispersed submarines to swarm upon the hapless convoy. This is the first case in naval history of a force whose maneuver units stayed quite far apart most of the time, then coalesced to swarm to the attack, and afterwards dissevered to return to scouting for new targets. As for swarming in the air, the Battle of Britain shows the use of radio and radar to enable the outnumbered fighters of the Royal Air Force to spot German air attacks and then swarm against them from a loose network of airfields distributed throughout central and southern England (Wood and Dempster, 1961; Deighton, 1977).

All these historical glimpses show that information is crucial to swarming, both to the coalescing of forces for the attack, and then to their dissevering return to the safety of wide dispersion. Only robust systems for gathering and distributing information can support such "pulsing" of combat forces.

This short review of doctrinal development suggests that the progression toward more complex, better organized and more effective fighting formations has gone hand in hand with advances in information management systems. In the case of air power in particular, there appears to be an emergent "swarming paradigm." Will this hold true for land and naval warfare as well? Indeed, what may such a paradigm look like on land or at sea? For land campaigns, it may be necessary to look beyond current doctrine, even though it features integral air elements already. While the war against Saddam Hussein featured swarming air support for ground operations, the tank and mechanized divisions of Desert Storm massed, maneuvered, and fought in traditional fashion—much as they had trained to fight on the plains of Europe during the Cold War. It may be necessary for the Army to look beyond its own experiences and to consider the views emerging in other strategic cultures. The Chinese view of the impact of the information revolution on land warfare, as described in the introduction to this volume, may be a fruitful area to explore. In the information age, a variation on Mao's doctrine of People's War may prove more effective than the U.S. Army's AirLand Battle doctrine. Continued American reliance upon massed, heavy mechanized forces may simply invite their destruction by precision weapons that, in the hands of skillful opponents, will themselves swarm the battlefield, as the French and Indians once did to General Braddock and his Redcoat regulars.

The Navy, whose air elements played no small part in the swarming air campaign in the Persian Gulf, has to think through a variety of issues, ranging from the future of the carrier to the potential of missile-laden "arsenal" ships. Of course, the very notion of a single ship armed with five hundred cruise missiles seems closely tied to the mentality of massing great firepower on as few platforms as possible. Other concerns relate to the ability of naval surface forces to cope with air and missile threats, and with the enduring problem of helping an amphibious force to land against a hostile shore. These are very big, complex issues, whose detailed resolution will require decades of analysis and experimentation. Fortunately, there is no serious naval rival, giving the U.S. Navy the luxury of time to think these problems through carefully. Nevertheless, the organizational impulse to keep a large amount of firepower on a few large platforms should be seen as something of a violation of the principles of swarming. Because, although the cruise missiles fired from an arsenal ship might be able to swarm an attacker, the mother ship itself is a rich, inviting target for counterstrikes—much like the Japanese carriers that had massed closely at the Battle of Midway in 1942.

While the previous discussion emphasizes military history, swarming has also long figured in social conflicts. This is often evident in precursors to protest demonstrations, violent or nonviolent, where individuals and groups rapidly assemble, in a planned or spontaneous mass, and engage in a melee or march against an authority. Early examples of swarming arose during the social revolutions in Europe beginning in 1848, when urban citizens, sometimes joined by peasants from all over the countryside (and sometimes opposed by them), came together to fight governmental authorities in chaotic street-by-street melees.[17] More recently, U.S. civil-rights and anti-Vietnam War groups in the 1960s and 1970s, some of which were linked as "segmented, polycentric, ideologically integrated networks" (SPINs),[18] often held huge protest demonstrations that were partly the result of swarming by disparate groups, although many may have thought they were pursuing mainly a massing strategy.

Many past examples of swarming in social conflicts were more happenstance than deliberate. Today, a strong trend toward swarming is emerging, coming to the fore to supplant the earlier tendencies toward either riotous melees or mass marches. Perhaps the best recent example of "social swarming" is found in the response of the dozens of U.S., Canadian, and other activist NGOs whose representatives rushed, electronically as well as physically, into Mexico to pressure the Mexican government to deal with the 1994 Zapatista uprising through political negotiations rather than armed force. The result was that fighting died out after about two weeks and was followed by two years of energetic negotiations, while the NGOs worked to make sure that "information operations" continued to predominate over military operations.

Another recent example of social swarming is seen in the activities of the Serbian radio station B-92, which opposed the overturning of legitimate election results in 1996 by Slobodan Milosevic and gave voice to a rising political opposition movement. When the Serbian regime cut off its local broadcasting, the station's personnel put their programming on the Internet (using software called "RealAudio"). There it was picked up by the international media (including the Voice of America, the BBC, and Deutche Welle), which not only proceeded to broadcast the programs back into Serbia, but also began pouring into Serbia to question the regime's behavior and cover pronouncements and demonstrations by the opposition movement. Thus, this case offers examples of both physical and virtual swarming.

Getting "BattleSwarm" Right

For swarming to be developed as a sound way to conduct conflict, new doctrines and related organizational designs, strategies, and tactics will have to be developed. Today, in the military area, advanced warfighting experiments (AWEs), such as Sea Dragon/Hunter Warrior in the Marines, and Force XXI/EXFOR in the Army, are under way that may generate innovations in this direction. None have a clear, precise focus on swarming; although the Marines' experimentation with small "infestation teams" is a significant step. More to the point, special operations forces have experimented with swarm-like tactics throughout history (Arquilla, 1996). Meanwhile, the major advances with swarming may be occurring at the other end of the conflict spectrum, among radical activists who want to use nonviolent "information operations" to put authoritarian regimes on the defensive, as in the case of the transnational activist NGOs who sided with the Zapatista movement in Mexico.

The term we would coin for referring to a well developed doctrine oriented to swarming is "BattleSwarm." By this, we mean a doctrine that could be applied across the full spectrum of conflict, from high to low intensity. At the high end, it would look beyond, and ultimately supersede, the current AirLand Battle doctrine. Just as Sun Tzu is said to be replacing Clausewitz as the key philosopher of war for the information age, so BattleSwarm may replace AirLand Battle as the optimal military doctrine. AirLand Battle refers to the close cooperation of the Army and the Air Force in a *blitzkrieg*-like maneuver campaign in a high- or middle-intensity war. Unlike AirLand Battle, a BattleSwarm doctrine would involve *all* services in pulsing, oscillating, and, frequently, joint operations. BattleSwarm would also apply to conflicts at the low end of the spectrum, where it would guide nonmilitary as well as military operations against terrorist, guerrilla, and transnational criminal organizations.[19]

Achieving BattleSwarm would require the development of numerous new, relatively small, decentralized, team-like units of maneuver that are networked not only organizationally but also in terms of their access to command, control, communications, computers, and intelligence surveillance and reconnaissance (C4ISR) systems that enable the distribution of topsight. As noted earlier, the basic strategic, operational, and tactical aim would be to have a capability for *sustainable pulsing*, whereby the units can coalesce against a target, then dissever, redisperse, and be ready to recombine repeatedly until an adversary is defeated by disruption or destruction. In some situations, the dispersed units may join rapidly in a mass against a target; in other situations, they may remain dispersed while massing their fire in battle. Some situations may require high-precision stand-off strikes; others, close-in combat capabilities. Developing a BattleSwarm Doctrine and a set of forces to go with it would require unprecedented advances in information structuring and processing, not only so the maneuver teams could do what they are supposed to do under good circumstances, but also to ensure that they have robustness against electronic disruption.[20]

AirLand Battle has strong proponents who would surely dispute our ideas about moving toward BattleSwarm. For example, Harry Summers (1995) argues that the "revolution in military affairs" has little substance, and that the old ways of AirLand Battle are tried and true. He believes that the United States actually needs a much bigger military to pursue the strategy of being able to win two major regional conflicts in close succession. From a similar perspective, Caspar Weinberger and Peter Schweizer (1997) maintain that, since winning the Cold War, the United States has gone back to having "hollow" armed forces that risk being caught short by the conflict scenarios that the two envision. They, like Summers, recommend increases in military spending and prefer to expand on the ideals of AirLand Battle rather than to entertain radical doctrinal and organizational change.

Nonetheless, discussions about doctrinal change are well under way in the U.S. Army, where the leading views combine visions of dispersed deployment with notions of "convergent assault" (see Sullivan and Dubik, 1993; Coroalles, 1991; and Rothmann, 1991). While a step in the right direction, these views emphasize technology and, so far, have not extended to organizational redesign—they retain both the existing divisional structures, and the distinction between "heavy" (i.e., armored) and "light" divisions. Moreover, despite some interest in nonlinear operations, the main means of maneuver being envisioned is heliborne mobility. This does allow flexibility in unit movement; but helicopters are vulnerable to ground fire and are likely to remain so.

Heliborne mobility is likely to be an important aspect of deployment under a BattleSwarm doctrine—but not in the context of division-sized units of maneuver. Alexander (1995) sensibly urges a shift toward the adoption of much smaller, nimbler units of maneuver—a view that is in keeping with the emergence of BattleSwarm.

Another radical view is offered by the Friedmans (1997), who urge an equivalent of swarming in terms of the convergence of distant missile fires. Their approach would reduce the need for large field forces—but it does not seem suited to forcing a decision against an opponent that has dispersed his own forces, or deployed them in civilian population centers. A small, nimble opponent will be very hard to hit with distant missile fires from the United States or from American orbital platforms.

A BattleSwarm Scenario

One way to envision the likely contours of a BattleSwarm doctrine— in this case, one that may supersede AirLand Battle—is to sketch a scenario of a future conflict in which traditional approaches seem too costly, untimely, or uncertain as to the ultimate outcome. The Persian Gulf region continues to provide a good place for such a scenario since vital U.S. interests are unquestionably involved there, U.S. friends and allies are weak, the United States has few forces stationed in the region, and the strongest regional states (Iran and Iraq) are unfriendly. Indeed, the region continues to be a subject of study, even as a likely catalyst for the outbreak of "strategic information warfare" (Molander, Riddile, and Wilson, 1996).

In the scenario we envision, assume that, ten years from now, the American policy of "dual containment" of Iran and Iraq has led to an *entente* between the two, aimed at diminishing U.S. influence in the region. Assume also that democratizing forces in Saudi Arabia are undermining the ruling regime, through a mix of violent acts as well as nonviolent "information operations" designed to uncover the foibles and misdeeds of King Fahd—a continuation and expansion of the current real-life campaign being waged by Mohammed al Masari against the Riyadh government. Finally, assume that some spark (e.g., a succession crisis after the passing of the king) ignites an internal conflict in Saudi Arabia in which the insurgents are supported by Iran, Iraq, and Yemen (the last of which also has very frosty relations with, and deep resentments against, the Saudi regime).

The externally supported rebels in Saudi Arabia quickly seize control of cities and ports, swarming over them in a few days and presenting the United States with a *fait accompli*. A provisional government of the new "Islamic Democratic Republic of Arabia" (IDRA) is swiftly recognized by Iran, Iraq, and Yemen (and by many other Islamic governments, notably Oman), who pledge military support. Many Islamic NGOs also declare their support for the new regime. Defensive preparations against an American counterintervention begin, with small detachments of Saudi rebels, Iranians, Iraqis, and Yemenis being stationed throughout the country. Further, the Iranians announce that they will close the Straits of Hormuz to any warships; the Yemenis make a similar pledge regarding passage to and through the southern approaches to the Red Sea. The field armies of the "big three" supporters of the revolution, which together total 100 divisions, are placed on alert, with roughly 12 divisions moved into the IDRA.

To cope with this catastrophe, let us assume that the United States strives first to cobble together an international consensus opposed to the new regime—but that it finds only lukewarm support in the U.N. and from its NATO allies. Russia and China threaten to use their vetoes to block U.N. authorization for use of force. At the same time, the small U.S. military contingents already in Saudi Arabia are expelled to Kuwait, which itself is now surrounded by hostile forces and isolated. Finally, American public opinion is confused, because the IDRA seems democratic and is offering continued oil sales at reduced prices. The Joint Chiefs tell the president that a U.S. intervention will require 750,000 troops, and casualties will be high. There is no friendly forward basing area, as the Omanis have not only refused permission for U.S. forces to deploy there, but, when asked to be accommodating, mobilize their own armed forces and call for help from the new IDRA government!

In short, the United States faces an apparently insuperable obstacle to restoring the Saudi *ancien regime* by forceful means. That is, it looks impossible to duplicate Desert Storm (or any other example of AirLand Battle). However, the president is persuaded that the U.S. military has been preparing itself for just such an impossible task. After convincing the American public that the "sovereignty" (and oil) of Saudi Arabia must be rescued, he (or she?) authorizes the Pentagon to unleash Operation "Desert Swarm."

What follows is a campaign like none other in history. Two Marine divisions and the two Army divisions of the XVIII Airborne Corps (the 82nd and the 101st) redistribute their combat troops into roughly 100 company-sized (250 men) "task groups." They are augmented by a similar number of small (6–8 man) Special Forces teams. All are linked electronically by a "SwarmNet," allowing communications with each other and with the sea-based air and missile forces that will give them fire support. The Air Force is set to deliver strategic bombardment, with smart bombs and cruise missiles, as well as close air support for the ground maneuver units. Once lodgements on the Arabian peninsula are gained, forward air bases will be established for even more timely air support. A key element of the campaign is gaining the support of the heir apparent to King Fahd, who rallies his loyalists and calls for U.S. intervention.

The campaign that follows begins with many landings by U.S. forces on the long Red Sea coast of Saudi Arabia, after the Navy and Air Force quickly neutralize Yemeni patrol craft and missile bases at the southern approaches to the Red Sea, allowing fast landing and attack ships to transit this chokepoint. The Suez Canal is not used for initial landings but is employed for the movement of follow-on forces and supplies, since Israel and Egypt have declared their neutrality in the conflict. Along with the heir apparent and his loyalists, U.S. forces help to liberate the holy places of Mecca and Medinah and engage Yemeni forces at numerous places in the south and Iraqis in several areas across the north. They have no idea how to grapple with the small American task groups, who are highly dispersed, able to maneuver, coalesce against a target, concentrate fire upon their opponents at will, and then dissever faster than the Yemenis (or any other forces) can respond. Since they cannot succeed on the offensive, they hole up in fortified areas. But these defenses are soon overcome by concentrated smart bombs and cruise missiles.

The Iranians, seeing that the Americans are not attempting to intervene via the Persian Gulf or Oman, attempt to send their four divisions to the western battle zone. But there is no fixed zone, no front, for their forces to focus on; and they are cut up by aerial bombing and special forces as they search for an enemy to engage. In a week, Desert Swarm's troops defeat the Islamic Alliance's regular forces, inspiring Saudis sympathetic to the heir apparent to rise up against IDRA and their foreign occupiers. The Alliance attempts to retreat, and is routed. Two weeks after the initial landings, the legitimate Saudi government is restored. American losses amount to 100 killed and 600 wounded. Twelve enemy divisions have been destroyed, and many others seriously damaged as they tried to engage the liberators. Thus, with fewer casualties, and by far fewer troops, Desert Swarm resulted in an even greater victory than the original Desert Storm.

After-action assessments conclude that the Saudi regime might well have been more permanently supplanted by IDRA if its leaders had waged a primarily nonviolent social netwar, attracting huge support from Islamic and Western activists, without involving Iranian or other outside military forces. Some U.S. intelligence analysts had warned of this possibility for several years, but they had been dismissed by their Saudi counterparts. Fortunately for U.S. interests, the radical Jihadist leadership behind IDRA had hubristic pretensions—while it presumed, correctly, that the United States would be unable to muster allies to replicate a Desert Storm, it took the further step of believing it could achieve a quicker, surer, and much sweeter seizure of power if it brandished arms and invited outside military support partly just to create an impossible, embarrassing situation for the United States. IDRA's leadership had no inkling (for that matter, hardly anybody did) that the United States was capable of a Desert Swarm.

This scenario about the prospects for a BattleSwarm doctrine highlights the manner in which small, nimble, internetted forces might achieve great results against far more numerous opponents who subscribe to traditional doctrines. However, it is important to be mindful of the vulnerabilities of such a way of war before making any decisions to reshape U.S. forces radically. First, and foremost, all elements of a swarm must have robust communications capabilities; if the enemy can delink the task groups, which may be operating scores of miles apart, they might be attacked and defeated in detail. A swarm is made possible by information flows and is thus held at risk by their disruption. This means that the task groups must have "hardened" communications—and have plenty of spare radios—to cope with electromagnetic pulse as well as high-powered microwave weapons that might appear on the scene.

The foregoing suggests two necessary ingredients for moving toward a new doctrine with which to wage war in the information age: innovative organizational designs and a full appreciation that information flows are the ultimate *logistical* support required for combat operations.[21] The military must network itself if it is to effect BattleSwarm. It must cut across service differences and distinctions, for a true swarm cannot exist where organizational loyalty to a service, branch, or combat specialty comes first. This organizational internetting must be held together, at the same time, by communications links never before approached in timeliness and comprehensiveness. Thus, even as organizational power diffuses down to quite small units, their ability to centralize fire upon targets may reach unparalleled heights of military effectiveness. This may be the essence of information-age military operations.

TOWARD A STRATEGY OF GUARDED OPENNESS

To function optimally, the organizational and doctrinal changes that we propose require unprecedented levels of information sharing. Such sharing is essential for the fulfillment of our vision. At the same time, this sharing must be protected, or secured, to prevent interference, surveillance, or predation by outsiders. For these reasons, this strategic part of our vision revolves around the concept of "guarded openness," a theme we raised in the preceding chapter.

In our view, guarded openness should be the guiding strategic principle that extends from the battlefield, to enable small units to network and swarm; through the level of grand strategy, where information is emerging as a distinct dimension, if not a new domain, of power. It should already be apparent from the organizational and doctrinal parts discussed above that swarm networks require robust systems for communications and information sharing. So, rather than amplify further on field-level concerns, we focus in this part on the grand strategic level.

We make three major points: First, "information" is reshaping the traditional political, economic, and military domains of grand strategy. Second, a distinct new domain of information strategy is emerging; and it may have its own dynamics, including its own subset of political, economic, and military concerns. Third, pursuing a strategy of guarded openness—a deliberately ambivalent pairing of words—will entail a constant balancing act, in which competing goals and concerns may be at stake, involving tensions and trade-offs between whether to stress openness or guardedness.

Basic Dynamics and Dimensions of Information Strategy

Information and communications have always been important to strategy. But now they are moving from being subsidiary concerns to becoming overarching ones. This is happening for reasons that did not exist even 20 years ago. One reason is the growth of a vast information infrastructure—notably the Internet, but also cable, direct broadcast satellites, cellular phones, etc.—in which the balance is shifting from one-to-many media (e.g., traditional radio and television broadcasting) to many-to-many media (e.g., the Internet and interactive Websites). A second reason, largely but not entirely a function of the first, is the huge increase in global interconnectivity, which is brought about by the ease of entry/access that exists in many nations, as well as by the growing, though varied, interests of so many parties in using the new infrastructure for commercial, social, diplomatic, military, and other interactions. A third reason is organizational: Vast arrays of nonstate interest groups are emerging that are explicitly concerned with information and communications issues, such as the Electronic Freedom Foundation, and the Computer Professionals for Social Responsibility. These groups span the political spectrum and have diverse objectives that range from simply helping people get connected to the Net, to influencing government policies and laws, and advancing particular social causes at home or abroad.

Yet a fourth, mostly ideational, reason is a spreading recognition that information and power are increasingly linked. Across all political, economic, and military areas, we see the rise to primacy of informational "soft power" (see Nye and Owens, 1996), as opposed to the more traditional, material measures of power. This trend will require many years, probably a few decades, to unfold; and, in the interim, many traditional methods of exercising power may remain squarely at the center of conflict. But ultimately, the advent of "soft power" implies giving, sooner rather than later, a lot of innovative attention to the formulation of information strategy, since "power," "security," and "strategy " are increasingly up for redefinition.

In these and other respects, the advance of the information revolution over the last two decades has created a new strategic landscape that is replete with paradoxes and ambivalences. For example, war will likely be less bloody—but possibly much more disruptive to societies. The more advanced states may have greater technological capabilities—but also a richer set of targets for their "inferiors" to aim at. New nation-states are forming in many parts of the world—at the same time, power is diffusing rapidly to nonstate actors, often of an unruly variety. The rise of the network form heralds a new efficiency and effectiveness for all sorts of actors—but also poses the possibility that malefactors can start netwars (see Chapter Twelve) with low "entry costs" and sustain their efforts over long periods of time.

Some of these ambivalent and paradoxical dynamics go to a core concern for U.S. information strategy: Will the information revolution truly favor openness, or lead to new modes of political control? There is evidence that the new information technologies—especially the increased interconnectivity that comes with them—serve to open up closed systems. However, in some countries, the new technologies are creating incentives to reassert centralized control. For some government and corporate actors, the aim is to ensure social control over people. But even where that is not the case, such actors may believe that they will not be able to maximize the benefits promised by interconnectivity unless they exert control over it.

The standard presumption is that power, particularly state power, goes hand in hand with control—in short, maximizing power means maximizing control. But this standard presumption is only partly correct. Power is sometimes optimized through harmonious decontrol. This may be the case, particularly over long time spans, when a major new system emerges that can best serve the overall functioning of a society if the system is left to operate according to its own rules and dynamics. A good example of this is the gradual rise of the market system in Europe during the 16th–18th centuries. The absolutist states of the times were accustomed to controlling commercial and other economic activities, and their inclinations to continue doing so, despite mounting control problems, gave rise to a period of mercantilism, before states realized that market systems would work better, and more to the benefit of home governments (including through the generation of tax revenues), if markets and business enterprises were left to their own dynamics. The growth of markets, and of the businesses that invigorated them, was greatly enabled by the electrical information revolution of the 19th and early 20th centuries (e.g., the telegraph, telephone, and wireless radio). Meanwhile, the domain of "economic strategy" came into being and developed separately from the domains of political and military strategy. More to the point, societies where state actors have learned to coexist and work with market actors—that is, where power extends as much from decontrol as from control—are today generally stronger and more influential than societies where states continue to dominate nascent market actors.

Today, the world appears to be on the threshold of another long-term systemic change, this time owing to the rise of the network form of organization, the attendant strengthening of civil-society and other nonstate actors, and the enabling effects of the digital information revolution. This systemic change, as much as anything, may turn out to be the catalyst for the emergence of information strategy as a distinct domain of grand strategy. But meanwhile, most (if not all) states are behaving as though the way to protect their power vis-à-vis this new generation of nonstate actors is to control them. In that sense, the dawning of the "age of networks" on the eve of the

21st century is mirroring a phenomenon that characterized the dawning of the "age of markets" in the 18th century: There is an increasing outcry for "freedom of information," as there once was (and generally still is) for "freedom of trade." But many states may prefer to try to prolong a period of strong control, a period of "information mercantilism" (not unlike the earlier period of economic mercantilism). Once again today, state power is being identified with control, even though the real, long-term benefits to the leading-edge states may ultimately accrue from letting a new network-based system "go" and learning to work with the civil-society actors who seem likely to form its core (Ronfeldt, 1996). In this interim period, some proclivities toward info-mercantilism may be unavoidable, and the development of information strategy will probably involve a curious interplay between the dynamics of control and decontrol.

How should the United States approach such an era? What might a strategy of "guarded openness" look like? If there is a single, overarching principle that should define the goals and principles of American information strategy, it should be a drive to foster openness. Politically, economically, and socially, the aim should be to encourage the creation and expansion of open, interconnected information systems. With regard to openness at the political and economic levels, we would urge a public diplomacy that serves to expand global interconnectivity, since this should not only help to foster the spread of free markets and open civil societies, but also pose political control problems for authoritarian regimes. The commendability of openness also applies in the military sphere; in the future, there will be a critical need for open lines of communications of all sorts—to one's dispersed forces as well as to one's allies. Indeed, the "freedom of the airwaves" may come, eventually, to replace the older strategic notion of the importance of the "freedom of the seas."

But while openness should be the watchword of U.S. information strategy, there exist, on the guarded side of considerations, some serious risks to pursuing a uniform, across-the-board approach to openness. For example, in some international situations, it may be questionable to encourage political movements espousing free speech where they might spark the downfall of a friendly regime, such as the Fahd government in Saudi Arabia. Also, should diplomacy always strive for "open agreements, openly arrived at," to use

Woodrow Wilson's phrase?   Such openness characterized U.S. diplomacy during the early years of the recent Balkan War; but this gave Serb leaders the information that they needed—about the risk of U.S. intervention—to continue to pursue their expansionist, genocidal aims. Only when American policy turned a little more wily and unpredictable and began to include credible forceful options short of war, did the Serbs accept incentives to pursue a peaceful resolution to the conflict.

Furthermore, there are areas of great importance to national security where guardedness equates to protection, and openness may, in some situations, lead to unacceptable risks. In the military area, for example, governments and their militaries now depend on commercial off-the-shelf (COTS) products to enable and maintain their essential information infrastructures, in a world where there is little separation between national and global connectivity, and where COTS products are seldom under the control of single states. This reliance on COTS for military telecommunications, while providing a continuing means for obtaining the most advanced equipment at the lowest possible costs, may nevertheless engender risks of disruption, as potential adversaries will have an intimate understanding of their COTS-armed opponents' communications capabilities and vulnerabilities.

These examples highlight the point that democratic systems have generally aimed to strike a balance that promotes openness in principle, yet allows for guardedness in areas crucial to national security. But finding the right balance often proves elusive—and these few examples indicate that achieving the right mix between openness and guardedness will remain a nettlesome challenge.

Clearly, we believe that information strategy is emerging as a distinct domain, becoming more than just a modifier of the other elements of grand strategy. Similarly Alvin and Heidi Toffler (1993) discuss the rise of "knowledge strategy" as a new domain for "knowledge warriors." In their view (1993, p. 230), which we share,

> Peace can sometimes be promoted by economic measures or imposed by force. But these are not the only available tools. Peace at the dawn of the twenty-first century requires the surgical application of a less tangible but frequently more potent weapon: knowledge.

However, neither we nor anyone else yet has a clear sense of what the boundaries of information strategy are, nor of precisely how information strategy differs from and compares in performance to the classic political, economic, and military domains of strategy. Can information strategies really help the United States to deal more effectively with its adversaries, open up closed societies, foster better relations with friends and allies, deter and manage conflicts abroad, and repel attacks on U.S. information assets?

To foster further thinking about this, we illuminate below one challenge likely to characterize the future—that of designing strategies to open up closed societies.[22] We inquire as to how an informational approach may compare with, and improve upon, traditional approaches for dealing with a particular problem: Castro's Cuba.

An Illustrative Case: Opening a Closed Society

As a leading democracy, the United States has long made efforts to open up closed societies. It has generally done so by creating international political coalitions to upbraid dictatorships and by applying economic sanctions to pressure regimes to allow an opening of these societies. Military coercion has also been employed, both in the form of threats and actual interventions.

A prime example of the use of these traditional approaches is Cuba. Fidel Castro's regime has been the object of American political, economic, and military coercion for over 35 years, initially with the intent of isolating and toppling the regime, more recently with an emphasis on compelling the regime to liberalize. The United States has tried mightily to limit Cuba's diplomatic links, has maintained an economic embargo (recently trying to tighten it through the Helms-Burton legislation), and has even used military power to try to coerce changes in, or simply punish, the regime (e.g., the invasion of Cuban territory at the Bay of Pigs in 1961; the assault upon the Cuban detachment in Grenada in 1983; and other "strategic special operations").[23]

None of these efforts has succeeded in toppling Castro's regime or compelling the liberalization of Cuba. Cuba has maintained extensive diplomatic relations with a multitude of countries throughout the period of U.S. efforts to achieve its political isolation. Economic coercion efforts have been parried, first, by Cuba's having a "special" economic relationship with the Soviet Union, more recently by its cultivation of foreign investment, which has encouraged some countries to defy American policy. Furthermore, the Castro regime has retained the ability to convince the Cuban people to suffer hardships in response to American coercion. Finally, in the military realm, Cuban forces defeated the Bay of Pigs invasion; extracted a non-intervention pledge from the United States as part of the settlement of the 1962 Missile Crisis; and, from the mid-1970s through the early 1980s, engaged in a series of defiant military interventions in Africa.

The Cuban case does not represent a failure for U.S. strategy—in many ways, U.S. strategy has succeeded at containing and limiting the Castro regime. But U.S. strategy has not worked well in opening up this closed system. Does the case call out for the application of information strategy? Proposals have been fielded to that effect:

> U.S. policies to isolate the Castro regime are well developed in the traditional areas of politics and economics. Meanwhile, technology advances are giving rise to a new area: information and communications policy. A lesson from the recent democratic revolutions in the East is that increased information and communications flows from the West, along with the adoption of related confidence-building measures in security areas, can penetrate and open up closed systems. Cuba may be ripe for application of this lesson. A comprehensive policy to open Cuba up could involve a range of steps, some of which may require modifying the embargo or other U.S. laws and restrictions (Gonzalez and Ronfeldt, 1992, p. 70).

What would an information strategy toward Cuba look like? Basically, it would aim at improving information flows into and out of the country, for reasons that include fostering the rise of civil society actors who would work to liberalize the country from within—in contrast to the traditional U.S. approach that emphasizes exerting pressures from the outside. For years, the United States waged an incipient information campaign built around Radio and TV Martí. But this is not enough. Among other initiatives, a broad-based information-age strategy might, for example, seek to provide Cubans with better connections to the Internet and better access to computer and network technologies. Such a strategy might also encourage Cubans to create NGOs concerned with information issues and communications rights.

In other contexts, such an informational approach has been treated as a possible general tool of U.S. foreign policy. The State Department has taken the position that "[t]he ability of people to communicate freely has long been recognized as a basic check on despotism" (United States Department of State, 1991, p. 2). In the 1980s, the Reagan Administration incorporated substantial informational elements into its foreign policy, as evinced by its support for the Solidarity movement in Poland and its direct pressure on the Soviet Union to open itself up. Indeed, the favorable Russian response, openness in the form of *glasnost,* unleashed social and political forces that the Kremlin simply could not control.

Could information strategy succeed in liberalizing Cuba where other elements of grand strategy have failed? Information strategy toward Cuba could hardly do worse than earlier approaches—and it may cost less and engender fewer political and military risks. Moreover, an American information strategy, depending on how it is shaped, might be viewed positively by the international community, a striking difference from the lack of international cooperation with current U.S. policy.

However, an information strategy toward Cuba may also face inherent, major limitations: the absence of independent NGOs and other elements of a full-fledged civil society; the presence of a strong state apparatus with many controls (including over the media); and the currently poor distribution of and limited access to communications technology, including Internet connections. For all these reasons, an information strategy toward Cuba may have to be treated as a long-term campaign, beginning with steps to improve Cuban information infrastructure, as well as to foster the rise of civil society. It might be best if the pursuit of these first, enabling steps of an information strategy could be led by transnational NGOs rather than by explicit U.S. government initiatives. But there again a limitation exists. Many NGOs are more sympathetic to Cuba's plight than with U.S. policy.

As to the utility of information strategy, the Cuban case highlights the possibility that informational approaches may sometimes be competitive with more coercive measures. For example, an effort to open Cuba up to the world might be contradicted by a continuing effort to strive for its political isolation, or to keep the economic embargo. To be sure, the information strategy against the old Soviet Union was coupled with continued political, economic, and military coercion (e.g., the American plan for a "Strategic Defense Initiative" posed a military threat that forced the Russians to spend more on defense at a time when their own economy was worsening). But the USSR was, in its time, a global power that jeopardized U.S. interests on every level for nearly half a century. This made it relatively easy to keep military pressure on the Soviet Union with one hand, while trying to open it up informationally with the other. Any notional Cuban "threat" pales by comparison. This implies that the United States can afford selectively easing military, economic, and diplomatic pressures against the Castro regime if that would help with the process of putting an effective information strategy in place. But any initiatives of these sorts should be considered warily. There is little reason to believe that easing up on such pressures would directly benefit either the few reformers inside the regime or the few dissidents who are pressing it from outside (Gonzalez, 1996). Moreover, we must recognize that Fidel Castro has long proven his own mastery of information strategy in his extended confrontation with the United States.

Broader Concerns About Opening up Closed Societies

Suppose we are not talking about just a single case, such as Cuba; but rather a range of cases around the world where informational approaches are attractive for inducing political, economic, and social liberalization. Then, we would be talking about engaging in a broad grand strategy of opening up closed societies—as is called for by the grand strategy known as "democratic enlargement." And, whether information strategy is pursued in conjunction with political, economic, and military initiatives, or on its own, it faces three general concerns that will inevitably arise: Is the strategy consistent, controllable, and ethical?

First, can one conceive of a *consistent* information strategy toward fostering open societies? If the hypothesis that increasing interconnectivity raises the price of repression is true, as seems the case, then liberalizing effects should be generalized when such an approach is employed. But can information strategy be used so generally? Here it is important to consider the nature of the path to liberalization, which may include the serious social disruption of an authoritarian state. While this may seem desirable in the case of Cuba, it may pose unacceptably high risks in the case, say, of Saudi Arabia. Information might be used to bring down the regime of King Fahd; but this could also cause serious disruption in Saudi society, affecting vital oil flows, and possibly even aiding a successor government that is unfriendly toward the United States. Thus, pursuing a general information strategy of opening up closed societies must be viewed with caution—that is, "guardedly."

A second concern relates to controllability—states are not able to control nonstate actors. The information revolution is empowering individuals and NGOs in ways that enable them to pursue their own strategies independent of state preferences. Some NGOs, notably ones that include expatriate dissidents, may even base themselves in an open society that is likely to defend their right to destabilize an authoritarian regime, even though it may be an ally of the state providing the launching point for the NGOs. Because information, and cyberspace, are transnational, or even supranational, the possibility exists that dissidents, physically located in one country, may exploit the Internet (or faxes, etc.) to undermine the political or social order in another country. In a recent example of this, the Britain-based Saudi Arabian expatriate, Mohammed al-Masari, mounted an Internet and fax campaign against the Fahd regime that led to strained Saudi-British relations.

A third concern is an ethical one. It flows from the paradox that supporting the desirable goal of opening up closed systems may entail fostering the outbreak of a great deal of social—and sometimes militarized—violence, with all the attendant consequences. In an ideal future, free speech should be protected as a public good and a personal right. However, the protection of all forms of free speech may create permissive conditions, notably for the waging of social netwars designed to disrupt state stability and control. It is possible to argue that such disruption, if of a democratizing nature, is ultimately beneficial. However, there are difficulties and dilemmas, possibly moral as well as practical, that may be posed by the near-term disruption of friendly, even if authoritarian, states.

While this may be an inevitable cost of supporting freedom of speech, it may be prudent to search out ways to mitigate these societal costs. For example, a way to discourage the use of one state as a sanctuary for cyberspace political attacks upon another might exist if the "attacker" were an expatriate. Without undermining the principle of freedom of speech, the host government might communicate to the expatriate that the government could choose not to allow the expatriate to remain within its borders permanently. This control strategy might be attractive to states facing similar "hosting" dilemmas and might serve as a basis for an informal international cooperative regime. No doubt such a course of action would be fraught with legal complexity, highlighting just how difficult it will be to "secure" friends and allies from cyberspace activism, and how ripe the international system is for "social netwar" by nonstate actors in the information age.

These are but a few of the issues raised by the idea of developing information strategies to open up countries like Cuba, and to cope with the complications that may arise from seeing such strategies used to open up countries like Saudi Arabia. But the complications do not override a deeper point: Information strategy is likely to become a major domain and tool of statecraft in the decades ahead. It may well be that informational measures will eventually replace economic sanctions as the key tool of suasion in the information age, for two reasons. First, economic sanctions have just about run their course as an effective (some would say, ineffective) tool—it rarely works well. Second, information strategy should entail fewer costs, both to the innocent mass publics of the states being pressured, and to those countries who currently forgo trade with a target state as part of the economic war against it. If properly developed, information strategy may prove ethically, as well as practically, superior to the strategy of economic coercion.

Needed: An "RDA" to Match the RMA[24]

Developing information strategy as a distinct domain will take a while. In the meantime, a host of information-age conflicts will likely arise, and means must be found to deter and prevent them when possible, and if not, then to manage them and achieve their termination. Conflict prevention, management, and resolution are principal tasks of diplomacy. Diplomacy, though it has received little attention in this volume, normally plays crucial roles in the dramas of conflict prevention, management, and resolution. The challenges may be all the more complicated as information-age capabilities get mixed with the war-like, atavistic intentions that still haunt much of the world (Huntington, 1996; Kaplan, 1994). Diplomacy must not, therefore, be left out of any broad vision of information strategy.

It may be time to rethink diplomacy in terms of the themes elucidated in this volume—notably, the growing relationship between power and information, the rising utility of networked organizational designs, and the emergence of swarming capabilities. The United States has been undergoing a revolution in business affairs since the 1960s, and an RMA that began in the 1980s. Is it now time for a counterpart "revolution in diplomatic affairs" (an RDA)? A few voices have hinted at this (Cambone, 1996; Solomon, 1997; Nye and Owens, 1996; the U.S. Advisory Commission on Public Diplomacy, 1997). But for the most part, they have not yet been heard and heeded.

There are good reasons why the business and military worlds are in the throes of information-driven revolutions, and the diplomatic world is not. A key reason is that those worlds are driven by competition, in the first case between corporations, in the second between services. In addition, the business and military worlds are eager for technological enhancements. Also, the military suffered a major "defeat" in Vietnam that opened it up to innovative rethinking and redesign. None of this has been the case with the diplomatic world. The State Department has not been subject to much organizational competition. It has had little interest in technology and, like much of the government, has lagged in adopting it. Moreover, it has not suffered a defeat like Vietnam that would prompt radical innovation.

However, the diplomatic world is feeling some heat of competition now, especially from agile nonstate actors—both from those with which the State Department would like to cooperate, such as disaster-relief NGOs, and those that spell conflict, such as transnational terrorist and criminal organizations. Also, the State Department may be feeling a bit of competition vis-à-vis the military. The military and diplomatic communities have yet to master real-time, close-in cooperation (except in the case of the recent Dayton Accords)—and there is a growing need for such cooperation. As the information age leads to new modes of conflict, there will be an increasing need to overcome compartmentalization and increase interagency, politicomilitary coordination. (Note the interplay between competition and cooperation here: The urge to compete is motivating—and it helps explain why and when a business, military, or diplomatic actor opts for innovation. But gaining a competitive edge depends not only on strengthening one's ability to compete against rivals and adversaries, but also on one's ability to cooperate with partners. One way to outcompete is to out-cooperate, a dynamic that is likely to be more important in the information age than in the industrial age as a result of the rise of the network form of organization.)

In another significant change for the diplomatic world, technologists are on the verge of producing tools that are as relevant for this world as they have been for the commercial and military worlds. Digital technology is now gaining momentum in such areas as: ubiquitous computing (with wireless, crypto, and handheld, low-cost devices everywhere); digital object infrastructures; intelligent agents; and tools for information visualization, including global networks of geographic information systems. Before long, video cameras will easily upload to the Internet; and satellite and other surveillance systems with high resolution will be widely available. At present, few diplomatic offices even have connectivity to the Internet; and few officers are even aware of technology developments that may prove useful to them. But interest is starting to grow in some diplomatic circles.

As the heat of competition and the allure of technology motivate diplomats to consider creating something like an RDA, they are becoming more aware that the information revolution is unsettling their world, often with the same ambivalent and paradoxical forces that the business and military worlds long ago recognized. Radical changes are now being recognized in the diplomatic world that mirror the changes that long ago aroused the business and military worlds. For example, there are rising tensions between the twin trends of, on one hand, an increasing *centralization* of control over diplomacy (within governments), and on the other hand, an increasing *decentralization* of control (due to the emergence of so many new nonstate actors). Moreover, like leaders in the business and military worlds, diplomats now increasingly complain that advanced telecommunications and other aspects of the information revolution are altering the nature of diplomatic time and space: The information revolution is quickening the tempo of diplomacy, and forcing open its once-staid, largely closed processes. Ambassadors are finding that ever more actors involve themselves in a variety of issues—often in a public fashion—making it difficult for the ambassadors to speak as the sole authority. They have to engage more, and more diverse, actors early on. Their once orderly world is being roiled by the very same, deep dynamic that we have repeatedly called attention to: the dual shift in power (a) from large, hidebound actors to smaller, more agile ones, like NGOs; and (b) to actors, big or small, that can move away from stand-alone to networked forms of organization and behavior.

In short, there is now enough impetus in the world of diplomacy to propose that an RDA is plausible. Suppose it is: What would it look like? How might it unfold? First, it would have to heed a broad theme of this volume: Engaging in an information-based revolution is no simple matter; it is as much an organizational as a technological challenge and involves a broad rethinking of concepts, missions, doctrines, and strategies. Just hooking diplomats to the Internet and giving them cellular telephones might be small steps in the right direction; but this would not, in the overall scheme of things, do much to realize an RDA.

More to the point, an RDA would be well advised to heed a second, related theme of this volume: Whoever masters the network form stands to gain major advantages; for governments, this means coming up with hybrids of hierarchies and networks. One implication for the diplomatic world is to build networks to achieve a "deep coordination" between political and military officials, and between state and civil society actors. Building a range of collaborative networks between the public and private sectors, and between state and civil-society actors, would improve their mutual abilities to assess and address conflict-related issues. Both horizontal (e.g. interagency, and interstate) and vertical (e.g., state to nonstate) communications and coordination would have to be strengthened in the process, in efforts to resolve the tensions between centralization and decentralization.

In addition, an RDA should emphasize the establishment of numerous dispersed "nodes" that belong to the State Department. If so, it should cease its recent focus on closing consulates and refocus on working to create more small consulates around the world.[25] This could help give the United States better knowledge for dealing with local conflicts. Despite all the talk that the information revolution spells "the end of territory" (because actors anywhere can now join together despite distance), local knowledge still matters greatly to diplomacy. Indeed, the next generation of technological tools, like geographic information systems, may well provide greater capabilities than ever for sharing local knowledge. As the "rise of geography" displaces the "end of territory" as a consequence of the information revolution, diplomats and other officials will surely see the importance of having small nodes dispersed worldwide as part of a vast array of "sensory organizations" made possible, perhaps imperative, by the information revolution (Ronfeldt, 1996).

Thus, for an RDA, like the RMA, the key challenge would be organizational. It has been said that the United States has developed a "works with" economy. An RDA implies developing a "works with" government—particularly one in which government actors increasingly engage nonstate actors in partnerships, including by building hybrid, just-in-time, virtual teams that can move quickly to address conflicts.[26] This poses the prospect that "information dominance" (Arquilla, 1994) may become as much a watchword for an RDA as for the RMA, and that information-sharing becomes the key to creating and exercising "soft power" (see Nye and Owens, 1996).

Who should take the initiative to foment an RDA? It should be the State Department. But if the State Department is not yet a ready environment for this, then institutions on its periphery may be better suited to providing the initiative—such institutions as the United States Information Agency, the Agency for International Development, and the United States Institute for Peace (which is sponsored by Congress).

* * * * *

It seems fitting to conclude this volume about how to prepare for conflict in the information age by emphasizing three insights that may help further the process of conflict limitation. First, while there will be much conflict in the future, it may well be more disruptive than destructive—making for far less bloodletting. This points to a hope that the 21st century will see the numbers of casualties drop to a minuscule fraction of the 20th century's 100 million war dead. A second insight is that the era of massive armed forces is coming to an end—and with it the need for massive military expenditures. Perhaps we can all look forward to an "information dividend" that will prove far more real than the chimerical post–Cold War "peace dividend." Finally, we see a possibility that informational resources and capabilities, judiciously employed, may actually prevent the outbreak of conflict. Our vision of a "revolution in diplomatic affairs" might thus be seen as a call for the rise of a global civil society devoted to "peace through wisdom"—an endeavor that would surely attract Athena's full support.

REFERENCES

Alexander, Bevin, *The Future of Warfare,* New York: W. W. Norton, 1995.

Allard, C. Kenneth, *Command, Control, and the Common Defense,* 2d edition, Washington, D.C.: National Defense University Press, 1997.

Anderson, Benedict, *Imagined Communities: Reflections on the Origin and Spread of Nationalism,* Revised Edition, New York: Verso, 1991.

Anderson, Perry, *Lineages of the Absolutist State,* London: Verso, 1974.

Arquilla, John, "The Strategic Implications of Information Dominance," *Strategic Review,* Summer 1994, pp. 24–30.

——, *From Troy to Entebbe: Special Operations in Ancient and Modern Times,* Lanham, Md.: University Press of America, 1996.

Arquilla, John, and David Ronfeldt, "Cyberwar Is Coming!" *Comparative Strategy,* Vol. 12, No. 2, Summer 1993, pp. 141–165.

——, *The Advent of Netwar,* Santa Monica, Calif.: RAND, MR-789-OSD, 1996.

Beniger, James R., *The Control Revolution: Technological and Economic Origins of the Information Society,* Cambridge, Mass.: Harvard University Press, 1986.

Bertalanffy, Ludwig von, *General System Theory: Foundations, Development, Applications,* Revised Edition, New York: George Braziller, 1968.

Bowker, Geoffrey, "Information Mythology: The World of/as Information," in Lisa Bud-Frierman, ed., *Information Acumen: The Understanding and Use of Knowledge in Modern Business,* New York: Routledge, 1994, pp. 231–247.

Bronowski, Jacob, *The Ascent of Man,* Boston, Mass.: Little, Brown and Co., 1973.

Cambone, Stephen A., *Kodak Moments, Inescapable Momentum, and the World Wide Web: Has the Infocomm Revolution Transformed Diplomacy?* McLean Va.: The Center for Information Strategy and Policy, Science Applications International Corporation, September 1996.

Capra, Fritjof, *The Web of Life: A New Scientific Understanding of Living Systems,* New York: Anchor Books, 1996.

Chalmers, David J., *The Conscious Mind: In Search of a Fundamental Theory,* New York: Oxford University Press, 1996.

Coroalles, Anthony M., "The Master Weapon: The Tactical Thought of J.F.C. Fuller Applied to Future War," *Military Review,* Vol. 71, January 1991, pp. 62–72.

Deighton, Len, *Fighter: The True Story of the Battle of Britain,* London: Jonathan Cape, 1977.

Dönitz, Karl von, *Memoirs: Ten Years and Twenty Days,* Cleveland: World Publishing Co., 1959 (reissued, Westport, Conn.: Greenwood Press, 1976).

Friedman, George and Meredith, *The Future of War,* New York: Crown, 1997.

Gelernter, David, *Mirror Worlds, or the Day Software Puts the Universe in a Shoebox . . . How It Will Happen and What It Will Mean,* New York: Oxford University Press, 1991.

Gerlach, Luther P., "Protest Movements and the Construction of Risk," in B. B. Johnson and V. T. Covello (eds.), *The Social and Cul-*

tural Construction of Risk, Boston: D. Reidel Pub. Co., 1987, pp. 103–145.

Gerlach, Luther P., and Virginia Hine, *People, Power, Change: Movements of Social Transformation*, New York: The Bobbs-Merrill Co., Inc., 1970.

Gonzalez, Edward, *Cuba, Clearing Perilous Waters?* Santa Monica, Calif.: RAND, MR-673-OSD, 1996.

Gonzalez, Edward, and David Ronfeldt, *Cuba Adrift in a Postcommunist World*, Santa Monica, Calif.: RAND, R-4231-USDP, 1992.

Haefner, Klaus, ed., *Evolution of Information Processing Systems: An Interdisciplinary Approach to the Understanding of Nature and Society*, New York: Springer-Verlag, 1992.

Haefner, Klaus, "Evolution of Information Processing—Basic Concept," in Haefner, ed., 1992, pp. 1–46.

Hallion, David, *Storm over Iraq: Air Power and the Gulf War*, Washington, D.C.: Smithsonian Press, 1992.

Harris, Marvin, *Cultural Materialism: The Struggle for a Science of Culture*, New York: Random House, 1979.

Herwig, Holger, *Luxury Fleet*, Boston: Allen and Unwin, 1981.

Hobsbawm, E. J., *The Age of Revolution: 1789–1848*, New York: New American Library, 1962.

Huntington, Samuel P., *The Clash of Civilizations and the Remaking of World Order*, New York: Simon & Schuster, 1996.

Jacques, Elliot, "In Praise of Hierarchy," *Harvard Business Review*, January–February 1990, pp. 127–133.

Johnson, George, *Fire in the Mind: Science, Faith, and the Search for Order*, New York: Alfred A. Knopf, 1995.

Kaplan, Robert, "The Coming Anarchy," *Atlantic Monthly*, February 1994, pp. 44–76.

Keegan, John, *A History of Warfare*, New York: Vintage, 1993.

Kelly, Kevin, *Out of Control: The Rise of Neo-Biological Civilization,* New York: Addison-Wesley Publishing Company, 1994.

Kern, Stephen, *The Culture of Time and Space: 1880–1918,* Cambridge: Harvard University Press, 1983.

Lenski, Gerhard, *Power and Privilege: A Theory of Social Stratification,* Chapel Hill: The University of North Carolina Press, 1966/1984.

Marx, Karl, "The Defeat of June 1848," in Lewis S. Feuer, ed., *Marx and Engels: Basic Writings on Politics and Philosophy,* New York: Doubleday, [1850]1959, pp. 281–307.

McNeill, William H., *The Pursuit of Power: Technology, Armed Force, and Society Since A.D. 1000,* Chicago: The University of Chicago Press, 1982.

Melody, William, "Electronic Networks, Social Relations, and the Changing Structure of Knowledge," in David Crowley and David Mitchell, eds., *Communication Theory Today,* Stanford: Stanford University Press, 1994, pp. 254–273.

Molander, Roger C., Andrew S. Riddile, and Peter A. Wilson, *Strategic Information Warfare: A New Face of War,* Santa Monica, Calif.: RAND, MR-661-OSD, 1996.

Nonaka, Ikujiro, and Hirotaka Takeuchi, *The Knowledge-Creating Company: How Japanese Companies Create the Dynamics of Innovation,* New York: Oxford University Press, 1995.

Nye, Joseph S., and William A. Owens, "America's Information Edge," *Foreign Affairs,* March/April 1996, pp. 20–36.

Oeser, Erhard, "From Neural Information Processing to Knowledge Technology," in Haefner, ed., 1992, pp. 320–340.

Penzias, Arno, *Information and Ideas: Managing in a High-Tech World,* New York: Simon & Schuster Inc., 1990.

Rogers, Everett M., *A History of Communications Studies: A Biographical Approach,* New York: The Free Press, 1994.

Ronfeldt, David, "Cyberocracy Is Coming," *The Information Society*, Vol. 8, No. 4, 1992, pp. 243–296.

———, *Tribes, Institutions, Markets, Networks: A Framework About Societal Evolution*, Santa Monica, Calif.: RAND, P-7967, 1996.

Rosen, Stephen Peter, *Winning the Next War: Innovation and the Modern Military*, Ithaca: Cornell University Press, 1991.

Roszak, Theodore, *The Cult of Information: The Folklore of Computers and the True Art of Thinking*, New York: Pantheon Books, 1986.

Rothmann, Harry E., "The U.S. Army, Strategic Formulation, and Force Planning," Newport, R.I.: Naval War College, 1991.

Simon, Herbert A., "The Architecture of Complexity," *Proceedings of the American Philosophical Society*, No. 106, December 1962, pp. 467–482 (reprinted in Herbert A. Simon, *The Sciences of the Artificial*, Second Edition, Cambridge: The MIT Press, 1981, pp. 193–229).

Skocpol, Theda, *States and Social Revolutions: A Comparative Analysis of France, Russia, and China*, New York: Cambridge University Press, 1979.

Solomon, Richard H., *The Global Information Revolution and International Conflict Management*, Address to the conference on "Virtual Diplomacy," Washington, D.C.: United States Institute for Peace, April 1997.

Sullivan, General Gordon L., and James Dubik, *Land Warfare in the 21st Century*, Carlisle, Pa.: Army War College, 1993.

Summers, Harry, *The New World Strategy*, New York: Simon and Schuster, 1995.

Toffler, Alvin, and Heidi Toffler, *War and Anti-War: Survival at the Dawn of the Twenty-first Century*, Boston: Little, Brown and Company, 1993.

Tufte, Edward R., *The Visual Display of Quantitative Information*, Cheshire, Conn.: Graphics Press, 1983.

————, *Envisioning Information,* Cheshire, Conn.: Graphics Press, 1990.

United States Advisory Commission on Public Diplomacy, *A New Diplomacy for the Information Age,* Washington, D.C.: United States Advisory Commission on Public Diplomacy, 1997.

United States Department of State, *Bureau of International Communications and Information Policy,* Washington, D.C.: U.S. Department of State, Publication 9860, 1991.

Van Creveld, Martin, *Command in War,* Cambridge: Harvard, 1985.

————, "In Wake of Terrorism, Modern Armies Prove to Be Dinosaurs of Defense," *New Perspectives Quarterly,* Vol. 13, No. 4, Fall 1996, pp. 57–58.

Vandenbroucke, Lucien S., *Perilous Options: Special Operations As an Instrument of U.S. Foreign Policy,* London: Oxford University Press, 1993.

Waltz, Kenneth, *Theory of International Politics,* New York: McGraw-Hill, 1979.

Weinberger, Caspar, and Peter Schweizer, *The Next War,* Chicago: Regnery, 1997.

Wood, Derek, and Derek Dempster, *The Narrow Margin: The Battle of Britain and the Rise of Air Power,* London: Hutchinson, 1961.

Wright, Robert, *Three Scientists and Their Gods: Looking for Meaning in an Age of Information,* New York: Harper & Row, 1989.

NOTES

[1]In a somewhat wry paper, historian Geoffrey Bowker (1994) observes that, over the ages, the more information has seemed central to the world's economic processes, the more it has affected peoples' views of time and space, and the more it has come to be viewed as a key organizing principle of the universe, finally giving rise to expansive philosophical and scientific claims that "everything is information."

[2]Johnson (1995, pp. 110–111) writes: "Most of us are used to thinking of information as secondary, not fundamental, something that is made from matter and energy. Whether we are thinking of petroglyphs carved in a cliff or the electromagnetic waves beaming from transmitters on Sandia Crest, information seems like an artifact, a human invention. We impose pattern on matter and energy and use it to signal our

fellow humans. Though information is used to describe the universe, it is not commonly thought of as being part of the universe itself. But to many of those at the Santa Fe conference, the world just didn't make sense unless information was admitted into the pantheon, on an equal footing with mass and energy. A few went so far as to argue that information may be the most fundamental of all; that mass and energy could somehow be derived from information."

[3]For example, Bertalanffy (1968, p. 27), using the term "function" to cover process, writes, "In the last resort, structure (i.e., order of parts) and function (order of processes) may be the very same thing: in the physical world, matter dissolves into a play of energies, and in the biological world structures are the expression of a flow of processes." Waltz (1979, p. 40), using the term "interaction" instead of process, writes, "A system is then defined as a set of interacting units. At one level, a system consists of a structure, and the structure is the systems-level component that makes it possible to think of the units as forming a set instead of a mere collection. At another level, the system consists of interacting units. . . . Any approach or theory, if it is rightly termed 'systemic,' must show how the system's level, or structure, is distinct from the level of interacting units."

[4]For example, according to Skocpol (1979, p. 4), "Social revolutions are rapid, basic transformations of a society's state and class structures . . . . Social revolutions are set apart from other sorts of conflicts and transformative processes above all by the combinations of two coincidences: the coincidence of societal structural change with class upheaval; and the coincidence of political with social transformation. . . . Political revolutions transform state structures but not social structures, and they are not necessarily accomplished through class conflict. And processes such as industrialization can transform social structures without necessarily bringing about, or resulting from, sudden political upheavals or basic political-structural changes."

[5]For example, according to Lenski, (1966, p. 43), "In analyses of social stratification, it is a temptation to turn immediately to the interesting and much debated structural problems, such as those concerning the nature, number, and composition of classes. While such questions must inevitably be a part of any adequate treatment of the subject, they are secondary in importance to questions about the processes which give rise to the structures. Moreover, to attempt to deal with the structural problems without prior attention to these processes, as is sometimes done, is to put the cart before the horse and create confusion."

[6]Cognitive scientist David Chalmers (1996) makes an intriguing attempt to treat information as the link between the physical and phenomenal worlds that may be required to arrive at a theory of consciousness. He relies on the "it from bit" kind of theoretical physics (e.g., by Edward Fredkin) that figures in Wright's book.

[7]Much the same may occur with visual displays—graphics—of quantitative information. As Tufte (1983, p. 191) writes, "What is to be sought in designs for the display of information is the clear portrayal of complexity. Not the complication of the simple; rather the task of the designer is to give visual access to the subtle and the difficult—that is, the revelation of the complex." Tufte (1990, p. 51) adds, "What about confusing clutter? Information overload? Doesn't data have to be 'boiled down' and 'simplified'? These common questions miss the point, for the quantity of data is an issue completely separate from the difficulty of reading. *Clutter and confusion are failures of design, not attributes of information.*"

[8]Actually, we still have a lot of literature to consult, including by philosophers who talk about "practices" and "disclosive spaces" and "clearings" (our thanks to Peter Denning for pointing this out).

[9]Roszak (1986, p. 90) defines "ideas" as "integrating patterns" and associates them with knowledge. Building up a structural view to balance the processing view may provide a way to ease the concerns of harsh critics, like Roszak.

[10]Recognizing this, Xerox has announced a research effort, supported by its Palo Alto Research Center (PARC), to design computerized tools and methods to discriminate "tacit knowledge" from run-of-the-mill information in corporate settings. The success of this effort could spell a major advance toward establishing a knowledge processing capability.

[11]The terms "structure" and "infrastructure" are quite common. The term "superstructure" and its identification with ideational structures comes from Karl Marx, in connection with his argument that the nature of a society's "base"—its mode of production—determines the nature of its superstructure. Building on Marx, Harris's (1979) anthropological theory of cultural materialism re-terms this base as the infrastructure and distinguishes it from a society's structure and superstructure. His use of terms is the closest we have found to our own. However, our use of the term infrastructure is more technological than his, in keeping with the term's usage today to refer to local, national, and global information infrastructures. We do not subscribe to the proposition that the infrastructure largely determines the superstructure. Laws and related rules and regulations are sometimes treated as an infrastructure.

[12]Studies about business and market systems often view laws and regulations as belonging to the "legal infrastructure" of those systems. In noting this, we recognize that there are other approaches than the one we pose here for us to consider as we seek to further develop and refine our framework. In the present framework, we are viewing law in a very broad sense. We would include, by the way, laws about freedom of assembly and association and about rights to communication and information— these may have particular bearing on a people's ability to establish local NGOs and connect to the Internet.

[13]Libraries and the print media might be included here as well.

[14]We may find, in future efforts to confirm and elaborate on this framework, that the information-processing view has its own ideational, organizational, technological, and even linguistic layers. If so, this could help with building a framework that bridges the structural and processing views.

[15]These points are consistent with another point: Around the world, in places as diverse as Canada, China, Iran, and France, people knowledgeable about the information revolution evince some concerns about the vulnerabilities of their information and communications infrastructures to destructive attacks, but they are equally, if not considerably more, concerned about how the presence of the Internet and other advanced telecommunications infrastructures may expose their cultures to erosion. They may worry about a particular process (Americanization), but their ultimate fear is more structural (the risks to their identity and sovereignty).

[16]Much the same may be said for societies as a whole. Melody (1994) provides a structure-oriented statement about this, and Beniger (1986) a process-oriented statement.

[17]The causes and patterns of defeat of these violent social swarms are analyzed by Marx ([1850]1959, pp. 281–307). Hobsbawm (1962, p. 361) observes that there was, nevertheless, a sense of promise in 1848: "An entire continent waited, ready by now to pass the news of revolution *almost instantly* from city to city by means of the electric telegraph" (emphasis added).

[18]We discuss SPINs in Arquilla and Ronfeldt (1996). The SPIN concept, first identified by anthropologist Luther Gerlach and sociologist Virginia Hine (Gerlach, 1987; Gerlach & Hine, 1970), refers to the following characteristics that they found in U.S. social movements in the 1960s and 1970s: "By segmentary I mean that it is cellular, composed of many different groups . . . . By polycentric I mean that it has many different leaders or centers of direction . . . . By networked I mean that the segments and the leaders are integrated into reticulated systems or networks through various structural, personal, and ideological ties. Networks are usually unbounded and expanding . . . . This acronym [SPIN] helps us picture this organization as a fluid, dynamic, expanding one, spinning out into mainstream society" (Gerlach, 1987, p. 115).

[19]More to the point, the doctrine we elucidate here might just as easily be redrawn and developed from the viewpoints of a terrorist, criminal, or other adversarial organization at the low end of the conflict spectrum. Some U.S. militia groups have already moved in this direction, notably those that subscribe to the doctrine known as "leaderless resistance" espoused by Aryan nationalist Louis Beam (see Arquilla and Ronfeldt, 1996).

[20]Allard (1997) provides solid, practical advice about how to restructure information flows to optimize military performance.

[21]As for regular logistics, a suggestion has cropped up in one briefing we have seen that it should move toward a concept of "swarm logistics" in the future.

[22]This is but one type of scenario that may be used to illuminate information strategy. We hope to explore others in future writings. These scenarios might reflect challenges such as working with allies, defending the United States from a broad-based information attack (one that is perceptual as well as technological), and enhancing our ability to cope with a burgeoning politico-military crisis.

[23]Vandenbroucke (1993) details the many coercive military efforts mounted against the Castro regime, focusing principally on the Bay of Pigs invasion.

[24]The ideas in this section are based largely on the attendance by one of the authors at the conference on "Virtual Diplomacy: The Global Communications Revolution and International Conflict Management," organized by the U.S. Institute for Peace, Washington, D.C., April 1–2, 1997.

[25]This point about consulates was made by former Secretary of State George Shultz at the conference on "Virtual Diplomacy" in April 1997 (see footnote immediately above).

[26]Canada's Foreign Ministry has reportedly moved much farther in this direction than has the U.S. State Department.

CONTRIBUTORS

Robert H. Anderson, Senior Information Scientist, RAND.

John Arquilla, Professor, Defense Analysis, Naval Postgraduate School.

Bruce Berkowitz, National Security Policy Analyst, Adjunct Professor, Carnegie Mellon University.

Stephen J. Blank, Douglas MacArthur Professor of Research, Strategic Studies Institute, U.S. Army War College.

Carl H. Builder, Senior Policy Analyst, RAND.

Jeffrey R. Cooper, Director, Center for Information Strategy & Policy, Science Applications International Corporation.

Norman C. Davis, National Security Agency, Information Warfare Support Center.

Anthony C. Hearn, Senior Information Scientist, RAND.

Bruce Hoffman, Professor and Chair, Political Science Department, St. Andrew's University.

Richard O. Hundley, Director, Information Studies Group, RAND.

Martin C. Libicki, Professor, Information Warfare and Strategy, National Defense University.

Armando Martinez, Senior Fellow, World Policy Insitute, New York.

Brian Nichiporuk, National Security Policy Analyst, RAND.

David Ronfeldt, Senior Social Scientist, RAND.

John Rothrock, Director, Center for Global Strategic Planning, Stanford Research Institute International.

Richard Szafranski, Principal, Toffler Associates.

Phil Williams, Professor of Public and International Affairs, Director, Ridgway Center for International Security Studies, University of Pittsburgh.